3ds Max Design 2014 Fundamentals

ASCENT – Center for Technical Knowledge®

autodesk®
authorized author

ISBN: 978-1-58503-797-1

AF864800

SDC Publications

SDC Publications
P.O. Box 1334
Mission KS 66222
(913) 262-2664
www.**SDCpublications**.com

Publisher: Stephen Schroff

Printed in the United States of America

Table of Contents Part 1

Preface

The *Autodesk® 3ds Max® Design 2014 Fundamentals* training guide provides a thorough introduction to Autodesk 3ds Max Design 2014 software that will help new users make the most of this sophisticated application as well as broaden the horizon of existing self-taught users.

The practices in this training guide are geared towards real- world tasks encountered by the primary users of Autodesk 3ds Max Design: professionals in Architecture, Interior Design, Civil Engineering, and Product Design industries.

Topics include:

- Introduction to Autodesk 3ds Max Design 2014
- Autodesk 3ds Max Design Interface and Workflow
- Project Configuration
- Assembling Files
- 3D Modeling with Primitives and 2D Objects
- Materials
- Autodesk 3ds Max Design Lighting
- Lighting with Autodesk 3ds Max Design mental ray
- Camera and Rendering
- Animation for Visualization

Icon Reference Chart

The following icons are used throughout this training guide to help you to quickly and easily find helpful information.

	Indicates the Learning Objectives that are covered in the current chapter or section of the training guide.
	Indicates items that have been enhanced in the Autodesk 3ds Max 2014 software.
	Indicates items that are new in the Autodesk 3ds Max 2014 software.

Appendix C includes a list of the Autodesk Certification topics and objectives for the AutoCAD software. References to content in this training guide have been included to assist you in preparing for the certification exam.

Free Autodesk Software for Students and Educators

Free products are subject to the terms and conditions of the end-user license and services agreement that accompanies the software. The software is for personal use for education purposes only and is not intended for classroom or lab use.

The Autodesk Education Community is an online resource with more than five million members that enables educators and students to download for free the same software used by professionals worldwide (see website for terms and conditions). You can also access additional tools and materials to help you design, visualize, and simulate ideas. Connect with other learners to stay current with the latest industry trends and get the most out of your designs.

Get started today. Register at the Autodesk Education Community (www.autodesk.com/joinedu) and download one of the many available Autodesk software applications.

Class Files

To download the Class Files that are required for this training guide, type or click the following in the address bar of your web browser:

www.sdcpublications.com/downloads/978-1-58503-797-1/

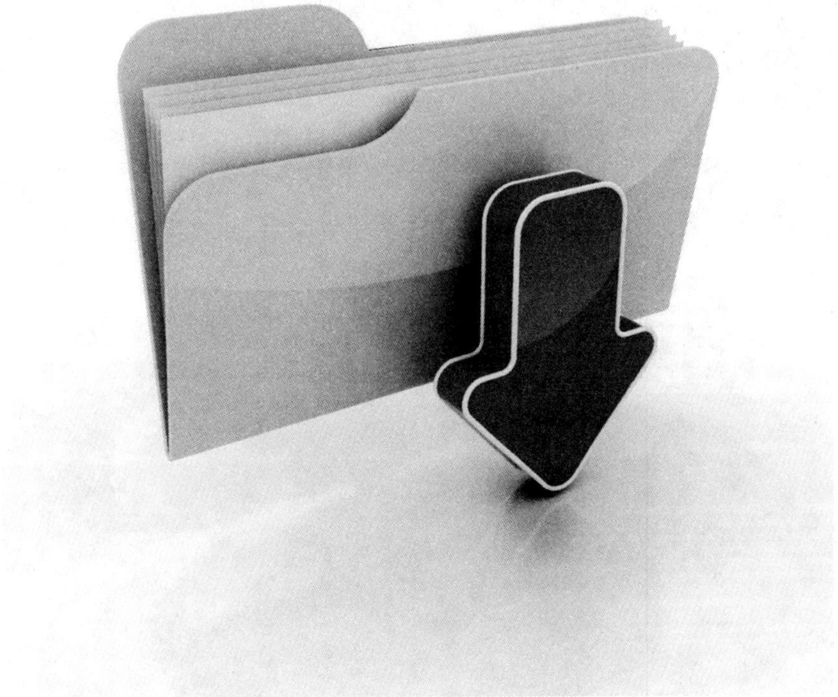

Chapter 1

Introduction to Autodesk 3ds Max Design

In this chapter you learn how to plan your visualization projects and launch the Autodesk® 3ds Max® Design software, and become familiar with the basic layout of the Autodesk 3ds Max Design interface. You also learn how to set the project folder, configure the paths for using external files, use the various display drivers available with the software, and use the default viewport display and labels.

This chapter contains the following topics:

- ✓**Overview**
- ✓**Visualization Workflow**
- ✓**The Autodesk 3ds Max Design Interface**
- ✓**Preferences**
- ✓**Setting the Project Folder**
- ✓**Configure Paths**
- ✓**Display Drivers**
- ✓**Viewport Display and Labels**

1.1 Overview

Learning Objectives

- Identify the various data sources that can be imported into the Autodesk 3ds Max Design software.
- Understand the difference between vector data files and raster images, and identify the output data created by the software.

The Autodesk® 3ds Max® Design software is the premier modeling, rendering, and animation package used for design visualization. It can be used to create high-quality 3D models, single-frame still renderings of virtually any size (including large-format presentation graphics), and desktop animations. The software has all of the functionality of the Autodesk 3ds Max software (the entertainment version of the software), for creating Hollywood style special effects and adding ultra-photorealism to renderings and animations.

Difference Between Autodesk 3ds Max and Autodesk 3ds Max Design

The Autodesk 3ds Max software is the world's most popular 3d modeling and animation package, which is used in a wide variety of industries to create 3D content and imagery. The Autodesk 3ds Max Design software is the same software, which has been customized for the design visualization and CAD community. It contains tutorials that follow the workflow and typical projects that a design visualizer is going to encounter. Additionally, the default settings of the tools are intended for the architectural, mechanical, or civil visualization industries.

Starting with the 2010 release, you can now install both products on a single machine simultaneously, because they are separate executables.

This training guide is designed for the Autodesk 3ds Max Design software. If you are using the Autodesk 3ds Max software, the Lighting Analysis and the Civil View functionality are not available.

Feature-wise, the two products are nearly identical. Each product comes with one bonus feature. The Autodesk 3ds Max Design software has a tool that is specific for Lighting Analysis and Civil View. The Autodesk 3ds Max software (the classic version) ships with the Software Developers Kit (SDK) as a bonus feature. High-end design visualization specialists who want to write custom plug-ins can join the Autodesk Developers Network (ADN) and obtain the SDK through ADN.

File Compatibility

An Autodesk 3ds Max Design .MAX file is called a *scene* file. The Autodesk 3ds Max Design 2014 software is parallel in version and file format to the Autodesk 3ds Max 2014 software, as well as all other Autodesk 2014 CAD products. You can load an Autodesk 3ds Max Design file in the Autodesk 3ds Max software, and vice-versa. After creating a scene in the Autodesk 3ds Max Design 2014 software, you can save the file as the default .MAX file, which is the 2014 version of the software, or save it in the 2013, 2012, or 2011 versions of the software. You can also save a character assembly as a 3ds Max Character file (.CHR).

Input Into Autodesk 3ds Max Design

Both 2D and 3D data can be created in the Autodesk 3ds Max Design software. Data can also be imported into the Autodesk 3ds Max Design software from multiple data sources, including the following:

- **AutoCAD® drawing files (.DWG, .DXF):** Including objects created in vertical applications, such as the AutoCAD® Architecture and AutoCAD® Civil 3D® software.
- **Autodesk® Revit® Architecture designs:** Imported into the Autodesk 3ds Max Design software using .RVT files or exported .FBX or .DWG files. The Autodesk® Revit® Structure and Autodesk® Revit® MEP software can also be imported using .DWG.
- **Autodesk® Inventor® files (.IPT, .IAM):** The Autodesk Inventor software must be installed on the same machine as the Autodesk 3ds Max Design software to import these files.
- **3D Studio Mesh format (.3DS):** A common data format used when transferring between 3D applications.
- Autodesk® Alias® .Wire files and the Autodesk® Showcase® .APF (Autodesk Packet File).
- LandXML and DEM data files.
- **Adobe Illustrator (.AI):** The Autodesk 3ds Max Design software only supports the Adobe Illustrator 88 software.
- Several other file types.

- **Only in the Autodesk 3ds Max Design software:** Using Autodesk Civil View, you can import files from various civil design programs, including the .VSP3D file from the AutoCAD Civil 3D software.

All of these data formats are considered to be vector data.

- Graphics displayed from vector data formats are based on individual objects that are defined by point locations and mathematical formulas.
- Vector geometry is referenced to one or more coordinate systems.
- Since their data is defined mathematically, vector graphics can be redrawn or regenerated as needed at different scales or from different 3D viewpoints.
- The Autodesk 3ds Max Design software native data file format (.MAX file) is also a vector data file.

It is important to understand the difference between vector data and raster data, because the Autodesk 3ds Max Design software is typically used to create raster images or raster-based animations. The Autodesk 3ds Max Design software can also be used to create vector data for real-time virtual characters and environments.

Output from Autodesk 3ds Max Design

Although the Autodesk 3ds Max Design software stores its data in vector-based .MAX files, it is most often used to generate raster images as final products.

- These images, called *renderings*, can be configured as simple illustrations, fully realized photorealistic images, or anything in-between.
- The most common Autodesk 3ds Max Design animations are created by combining a series of individually-rendered raster images into a desktop animation file (such as Windows .AVI or QuickTime .MOV).

Computer graphics stored in raster formats are different from those in vector formats in many of the following ways:

- Raster graphics consist of a grid of colored points (called *pixels*) instead of the geometrically defined objects that are used in vector data files. Figure 1–1 shows a raster image that has been enlarged so that the individual pixels become visible.

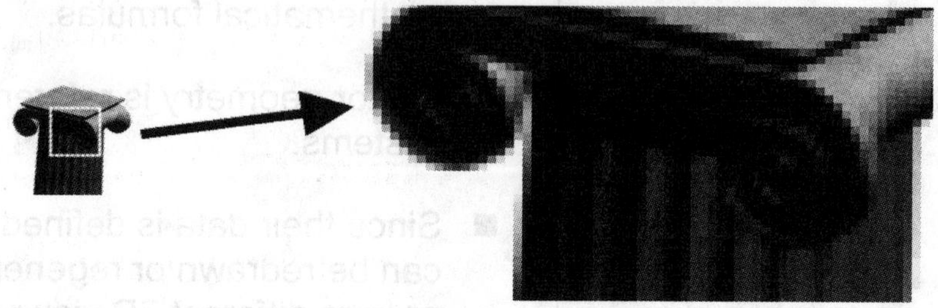

Figure 1–1

- Ideally these pixels are viewed at a resolution at which they cannot be identified individually, and instead are permitted to present a unified image (such as the original image shown on the left in Figure 1–1).
- Visualization software, such as the Autodesk 3ds Max Design software, is primarily used to create raster output. Raster formats display the subtle shadow and color depth necessary for photo-realism more efficiently.
- Raster image renderings must be recreated (re-rendered) if the point-of-view is animated or otherwise changed.
- Autodesk 3ds Max Design renderings, digital, and scanned photographs, are examples of raster graphic files. Common raster file formats include .JPEG, Windows bitmap (.BMP), and .TIFF files.

Most of the static graphics found on the Internet are raster images, as are desktop backgrounds and logos inserted into Microsoft Word files or other types of documents. Raster images can also be used as input into the Autodesk 3ds Max Design software to supplement the vector geometry as follows:

- Scanned or digital photographs of a proposed construction site that are used as a background image.
- Images that illustrate material texture, such as wall coverings, wood grain, or a scratched metal surface.
- Image files created in other computer graphic applications can be used as signs, posters, or company logos.

1.2 Visualization Workflow

Learning Objective

- Understand the common workflow process to help plan your visualization projects.

Each visualization project can be very different from the next, but most follow a common general workflow. A suggested approach to help you begin to plan out your first visualization projects is as follows.

1. Setting Goals and Expectations

Every project should start with a clear understanding of the deliverables. When visualization projects start it is tempting to start modeling right away, but you should work out exactly what the expectations are first.

- Save time and effort by agreeing on viewpoints, animation paths, lighting conditions, and other essentials whenever possible before starting the modeling. Otherwise, fully realizing a large project from every possible camera angle under multiple lighting conditions might take much longer than required.
- Sketching a mock-up storyboard might be useful so that everyone can agree on the content and scope of a complex animation before starting the modeling.
- Note that there are almost always time delays when visualizing. Simple oversights (and even some major design problems) are often found during the visualization process. Add problem resolution time whenever possible.
- Once you have a schedule, do your best to follow it. It can be tempting to keep working on a minor detail until it is perfect, but doing so can quickly overrun the budget. Your models might not be perfect, but create them as well as you can within the time available.
- Keep a detailed journal recording the amount of time you spend on specific tasks in the visualization process to help guide the budget in your next project.

2. Scene Creation and Modeling

The next step is to gather data together into scenes (.MAX files).

- Create a project folder to store all of your data. Gather the source material, such as site photos, textures, drawings, scans, or anything else available. Store the files in the appropriate locations.
- When 2D or 3D data is available from other design applications, the next step is to link or import it into one or more scene files.
- When a project requires multiple scene files, they can be merged together or externally referenced, as needed.
- Any modeled geometry is typically added now. The **Graphite Modeling** tools have many new features for creating new geometry on the surfaces of imported files.

3. Material Design

Often the next step is to configure the surface characteristics using the Material Editor. It is recommended that you consider the lighting and rendering. Materials might need to be coordinated with renderers and lights.

- Materials define how surfaces display and how light interacts with them.
- Materials can be detailed to help simplify the geometry. For example, you do not need to model the grout along a brick wall. Material definitions, such as bump mapping, can add the appearance of depth.
- Materials can be as simply defined or realistic as needed. Often the best results require time to be spent fine-tuning the material properties.
- Lighting and materials often need to be adjusted together, but it can be useful to have a first draft of your materials completed before adding lights.

4. Lighting Design

For realistic results, the 3D models need light sources to illuminate the objects.

- There are different approaches to lighting scenes in the Autodesk 3ds Max Design software, some are more straightforward and some are more technical.
- Most projects are never as simple as adding lights and rendering. Almost all of the scenes require lighting adjustments. This can take a significant amount of time, possibly as much or more than one quarter of the project.

5. Configuring Rendered Views and Animations

Once your model, materials, and lights have been initially configured, you can focus on the final output.

- The length of any animations, their frame rate, and the required time display should be assigned first.
- Autodesk 3ds Max Design camera objects can then be positioned to set up both single-frame still renderings and animations.
- Objects are then animated. In the case of walkthrough or flyby animations, the camera is animated to move through the scene. Animated details can be added, such as clouds blowing through the sky, pedestrians on the sidewalks, and cars driving by.
- The rendering options should also be configured now.

6. Testing and Final Adjustments

Next you need to test the rendering and adjust the model, materials, and lights to achieve the required results.

- This phase can often take up the bulk of the time available for a project.
- When estimating the project schedule, note that computer processing of the renderings can be very time-consuming, especially for long animations or large still renderings.

7. Post Production

You can add details to your final renderings outside the Autodesk 3ds Max Design software.

- You might need to add title blocks or logos, remove elements from background images, or make other image adjustments to raster-file renderings. This can be done using third-party image editing programs, such as Adobe Photoshop or Adobe AfterEffects. The Autodesk 3ds Max Design software comes with **Composite**, a compositing tool based on Autodesk Toxic technology.
- Some special effects require other applications, such as combining two separate animations with a cross-fade. These are often done in video post-production software, such as Autodesk Combustion, Adobe Premiere, or in the Composite module.
- Usually, the finished animation segments are mixed with actual video footage, voice-over narration, background sound effects, and music in a different software (such as Apple's Final Cut Pro, AVID Composer, or another video editing and assembly tool). Most mixing can be done in the Autodesk 3ds Max Design software. This is not usually the preferred workflow.

1.3 The Autodesk 3ds Max Design Interface

Certification

Topic:

✓*UI/Object Management*

Objectives:

✓*Describe View configuration and ViewCube navigation*

Learning Objective

Understand the various components in the Autodesk 3ds Max Design interface.

To launch the Autodesk 3ds Max Design software, use one of the following methods:

- Double-click on (3ds Max Design) on your desktop.
- Click the **Start** button in the Windows Task Bar and select **All Programs>Autodesk>Autodesk 3ds Max Design 2014> 3ds Max Design 2014**.

If you are opening the software for the first time, a Welcome Screen displays. In it you can play the Essential Skill Movies, connect to online help about what is new in 2014, access learning movies on the 3ds Max YouTube Channel, or access additional resources on the web. The Welcome Screen also provides options for creating a new empty scene or opening a .MAX file. A list of recently opened files is also provided.

You can clear the **Show this Welcome Screen at startup** option to prevent the Welcome Screen from displaying when you launch the Autodesk 3ds Max software. If you leave this option selected, the Welcome Screen displays each time you launch the software.

The Autodesk 3ds Max Design software consists of the main modeling window, called the *viewport*, which is surrounded by interface tools and panels. In the example shown in Figure 1–2, a model of a box has been created, using the **Edit Poly** modifier to display the different interface features. Initially, the scene is set as four equal viewports that display the model at different viewing angles.

You can toggle between the four viewport displays or maximize any of the viewports (as shown in Figure 1–2), by clicking  (Maximize Viewport) or pressing <Alt>+<W>. When multiple viewports are displayed, the active viewport displays a yellow border. Clicking in empty space in a viewport makes it active.

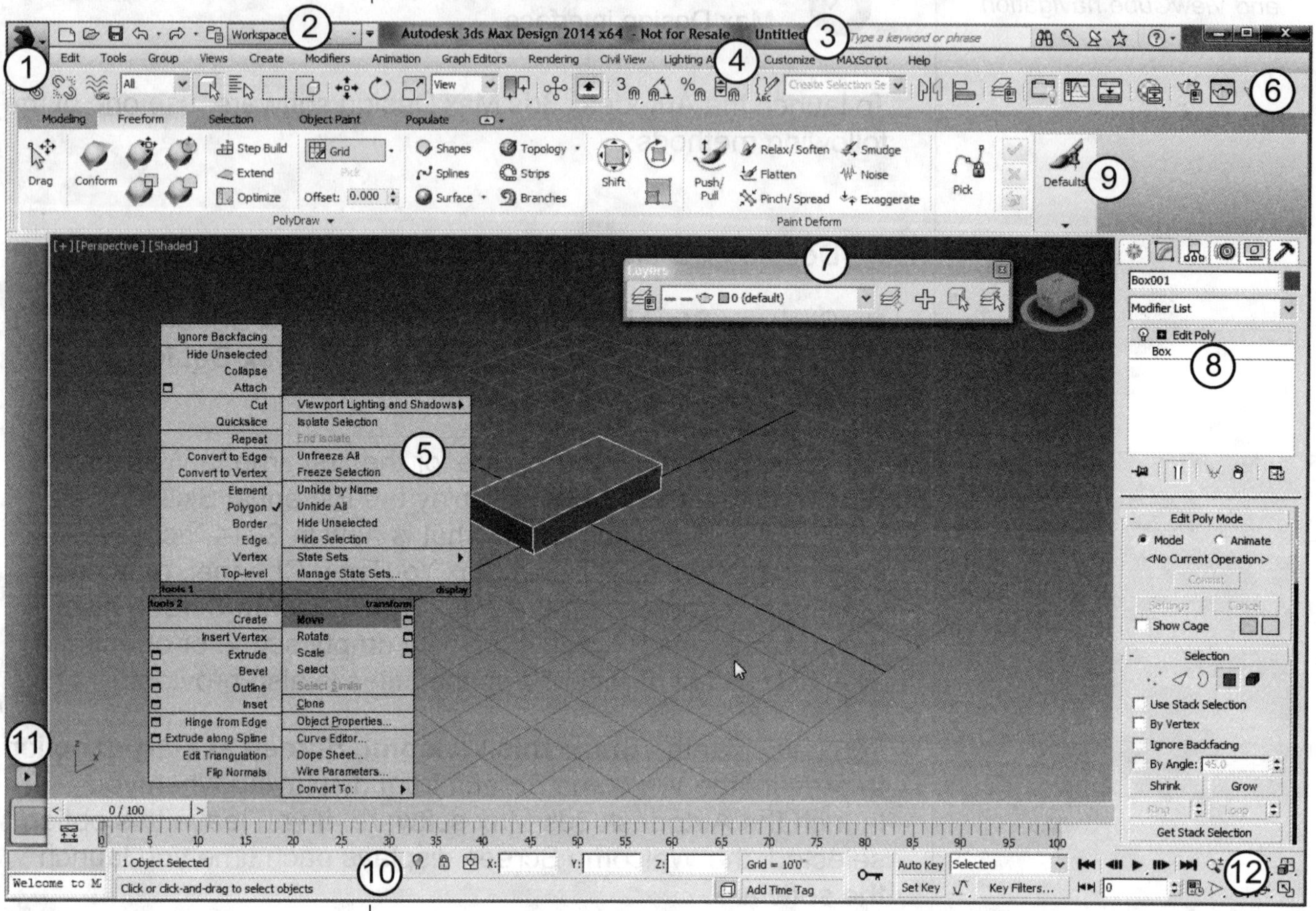

Figure 1–2

1. Application Menu

 (Application Menu) provides access to the file commands, settings, and recently opened files, as shown in Figure 1–3. The Recent Documents can be sorted by date and pinned in the stack to prevent them from scrolling. The icon display can be customized to display them as icons or viewport thumbnails. The icon display can be controlled by expanding  and selecting an option, as shown in Figure 1–3.

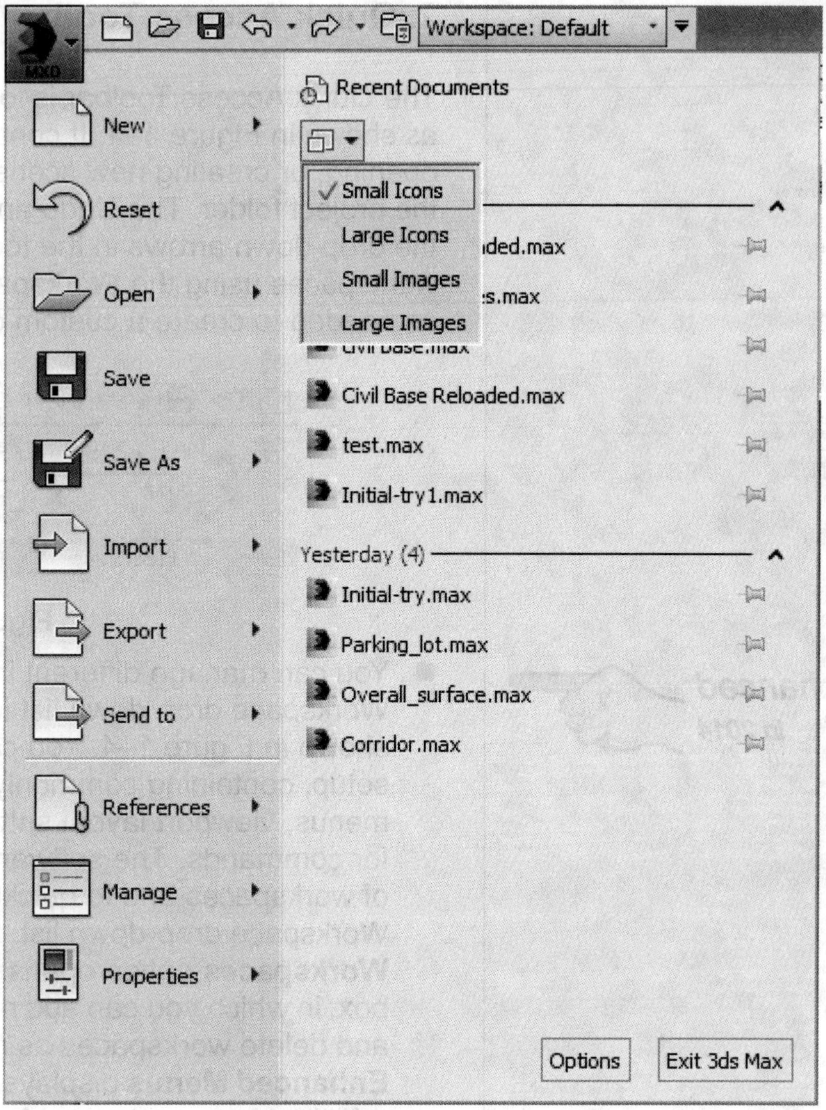
Workspace: Default
Recent Documents
Small Icons
Large Icons
Small Images
Large Images
New
Reset
Open
Save
Save As
Import
Export
Send to
References
Manage
Properties
Civil Base Reloaded.max
test.max
Initial-try1.max
Yesterday (4)
Initial-try.max
Parking_lot.max
Overall_surface.max
Corridor.max
Options
Exit 3ds Max

Figure 1–3

2. Quick Access Toolbar

The Quick Access Toolbar is located at the top of the interface, as shown in Figure 1–4. It contains one-click tools for saving, opening, or creating new scenes, using undo/redo and setting the project folder. The Undo and Redo stack is accessed using the drop-down arrows in the toolbar. You can manage your workspaces using the Workspace drop-down list and add tools as needed to create a custom quick access toolkit.

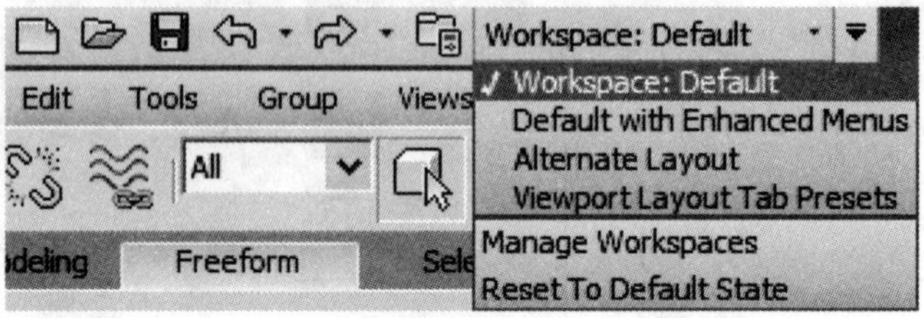

Figure 1–4

Enhanced in 2014

- You can manage different interface setups using the Workspace drop-down list in the Quick Access Toolbar, as shown in Figure 1–4. You can create a custom interface setup, containing commonly used toolbars, menus, quad menus, viewport layout settings, Ribbon tools, and hotkeys for commands. The software enables you to save a number of workspaces and to quickly switch between them using the Workspace drop-down list. Selecting the **Manage Workspaces** option opens the Manage Workspaces dialog box, in which you can add new workspaces, edit workspaces, and delete workspaces as needed. Selecting **Default with Enhanced Menus** displays an enhanced interface containing additional menus in the Menu Bar, tooltips linking to relevant help topics, a display that is highly configurable, and a keyboard search for menu commands.

3. InfoCenter

The InfoCenter is located at the top right of the interface, as shown in Figure 1–5. It enables you to quickly search for help on the web, access the subscription services and communication center, save and access topics as favorites, and access the Autodesk 3ds Max Design help.

Figure 1–5

4. Menu Bar

The display of the Menu Bar can be controlled using the Quick Access Toolbar by clicking  *and selecting* ***Hide/Show Menu Bar*** *in the drop-down list.*

The Menu Bar containing the pull-down menus displays under the Quick Access Toolbar. Working commands are grouped together in each of the pull-down menu titles. The **Lighting Analysis** and **Civil View** menu options are only available in the Autodesk 3ds Max Design software and not in the Autodesk 3ds Max classic software. The 2014 version comes with two different Menu Bars: Standard and Enhanced. The pull-down menus in the Standard Menu Bar are as follows:

Edit	Contains undo and redo functions, object selection options, copying (cloning), and delete functions.
Tools	Contains the **Mirror**, **Array**, **Align**, and **Measure Distance** options.
Group	Contains tools to create and edit Autodesk 3ds Max Design group objects. Groups function similar to AutoCAD groups.
Views	Contains features, such as preset viewport views, viewport display options, and ViewCube and SteeringWheel options.
Create	Contains options that enable you to create objects, such as 3D geometry, 2D shapes, cameras, and lights.
Modifiers	Contains sub-menus categorized by the available modifiers.
Animation	Contains common features used when creating animations.
Graph Editors	Contains several Track View features. Track View offers advanced controls for animations.
Rendering	Contains functions for rendering, such as setting up the scene environment, advanced lighting controls, and output image resolution.
Lighting Analysis	Contains features for Lighting Analysis, including the ability to create a daylight system, assign general materials, create and calculate light meters, and image overlay render effects.
Civil View	Contains features that can be used for displaying the contents of a scene created in a civil design program and to create visualizations of civil engineering projects. It offers support for various civil design programs, including the AutoCAD® Civil 3D® software. If you are opening Civil View for the first time, you need to initialize it and set the system units, country resource kit, and start mode.
Customize	Contains features for customizing the user interface, setting up the drawing units, and setting the overall Autodesk 3ds Max default options.
MAXScript	Contains tools for working with the MAXScript programming language used by the Autodesk 3ds Max Design software.

Help	The **Help** menu connects you directly to the Autodesk 3ds Max Help documentation on the autodesk.com website. It contains features, such as Online Reference manuals, Tutorials, and Network-version license borrowing and return options.

New in 2014

Enhanced Menu Bar

The Enhanced Menu Bar is part of the enhanced interface option in the Autodesk 3ds Max Design 2014 software. It can be displayed by selecting **Default with Enhanced Menus** in the Workspaces drop-down list in the Quick Access Toolbar. The menus included in the Enhanced Menu Bar are: **Objects**, **Edit**, **Modifiers**, **Animation**, **Simulate**, **Materials**, **Lighting/ Cameras**, **Rendering**, **Scene**, **Civil View**, **Customize**, **MAXScript**, and **Help**. The commands and functions are organized as menu items, with submenus containing the relevant commands. Hovering the cursor over an item displays an information tooltip (as shown in Figure 1–6), and provides a link to the relevant help topic.

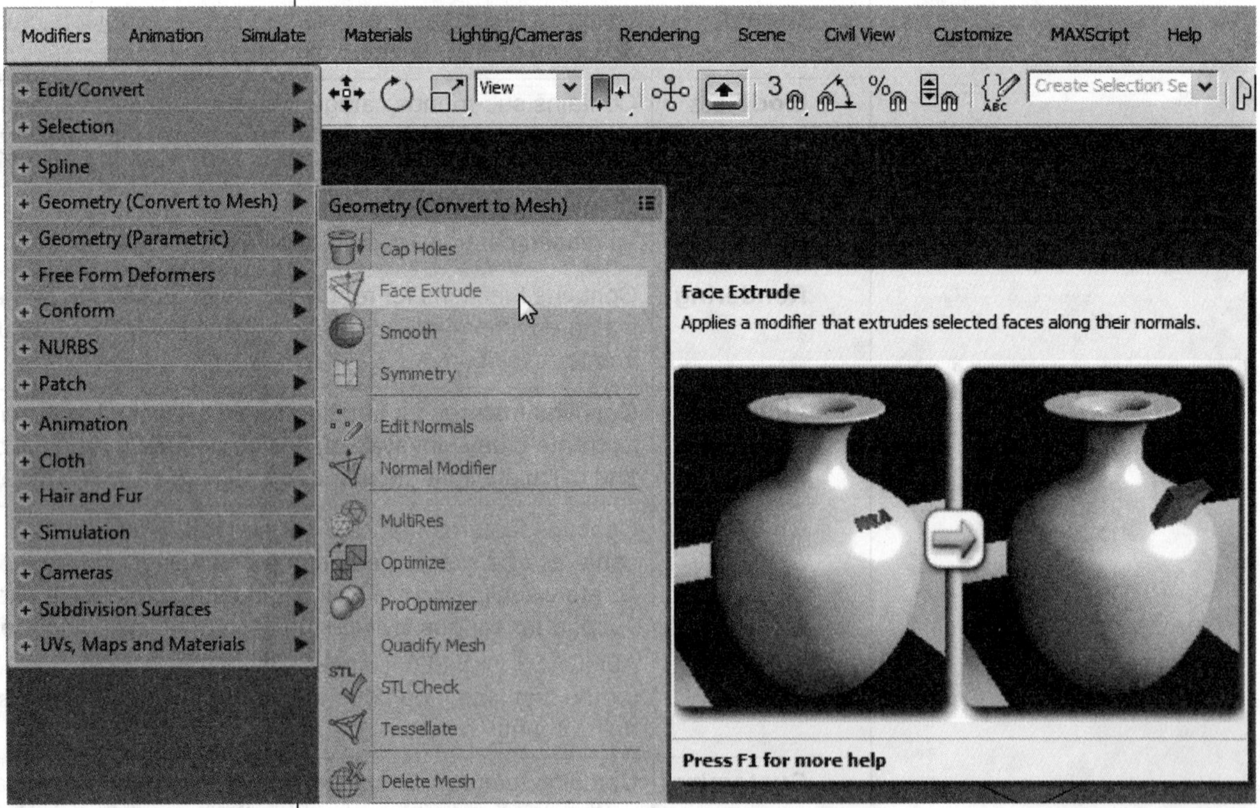

Figure 1–6

Hint: Global Menu Search

In the Autodesk 3ds Max Design 2014 software, you can search for any menu command or action using the global menu search method. Press <X> to open the Search actions edit box at the cursor location. In the Search edit box, enter the name of the command or action that you want to use. As you enter the first letter of the command, a list of matching actions displays below the Search edit box, as shown in Figure 1–7. Select an option in the list or enter another letter to display a more specific list of actions. To clear the search action, click the red **X** icon in the upper right corner of the Search edit box. Click in empty space or press <Esc> to exit the search feature.

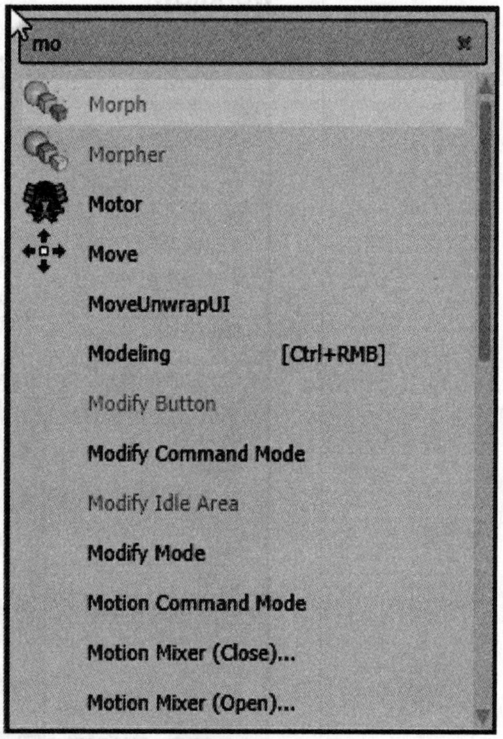

Figure 1–7

5. Quad Menu

Selecting and right-clicking on one or more objects in the Autodesk 3ds Max Design software opens context-sensitive menus called the *Quad menu*, as shown in Figure 1–8. The Quad menu is a convenient way of launching commonly used options that specifically apply to the current selection. The commands are displayed in different quadrant areas and each Quad menu can have a maximum of four quadrant areas, as shown in the bottom left of Figure 1–8. Quad menus also display when nothing is selected. Different quad menus display when <Ctrl>, <Alt>, or <Shift> are combined with right-clicking. Quad menus can be customized for fast access to tools in a specific workflow.

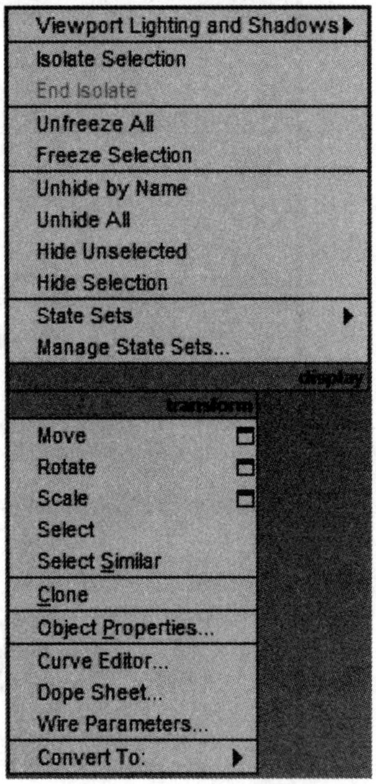

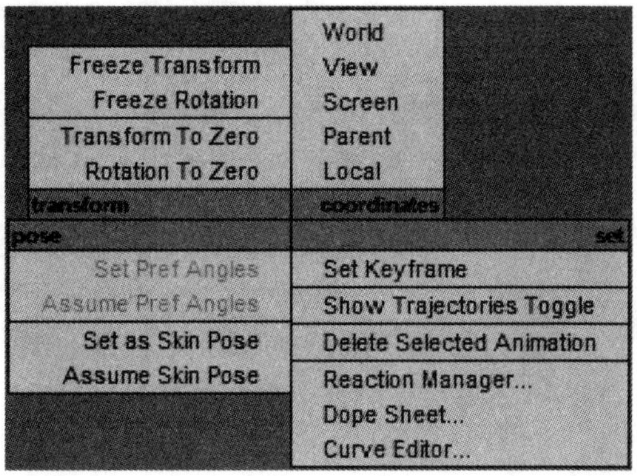

Figure 1–8

6. Main Toolbar

The Main toolbar (shown in Figure 1–9), contains some of the most important options in the Autodesk 3ds Max Design software, including the **Selection**, **Transforms**, and **Rendering** tools.

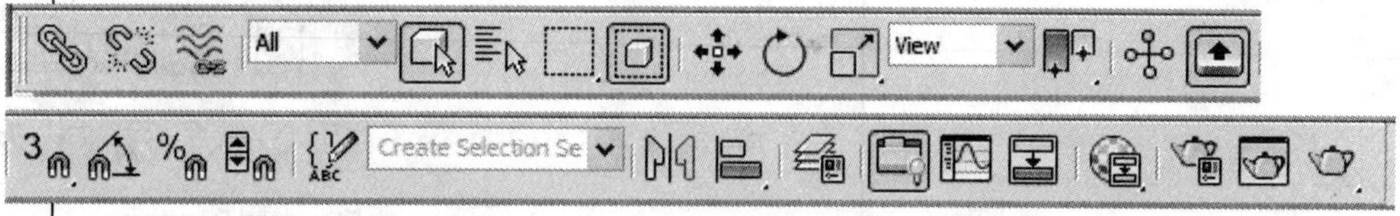

Figure 1–9

The Main toolbar is long and might extend beyond the interface. To slide the buttons left or right, float the cursor over the gray open area, hold down the left mouse button and drag. The cursor displays as the Pan cursor.

7. Toolbars

By default, the toolbars (except the Main toolbar) are not displayed. If you want to use them, they can be added to the interface. As with other interface components, you can float or dock the toolbars. Right-click on the title bar of an open toolbar or on the gray empty space of a docked toolbar to open the **Customize Display** menu, as shown in Figure 1–10. All of the available toolbars are listed. Selecting the required toolbar name displays it on the screen.

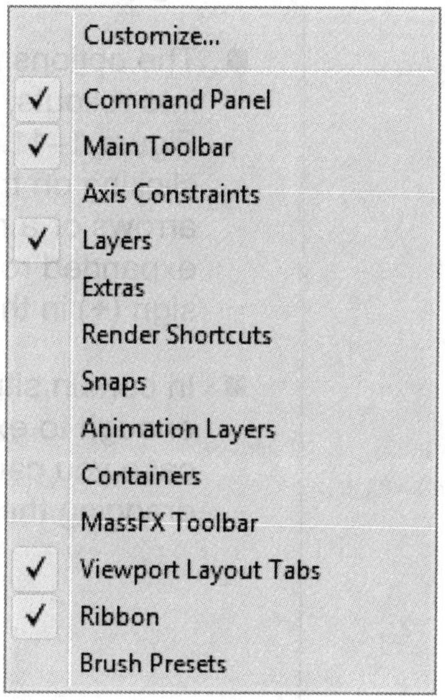

Figure 1–10

8. Command Panel

The Command Panel (shown in Figure 1–11), is a unique interface feature in the Autodesk 3ds Max Design software that enables you to efficiently create, edit, and manage the settings of 3D objects.

Figure 1–11

- The Command Panel contains six different panels or tabs, each with a different appearance and function. In Figure 1–11, the *Create* panel ( ), is active.
- The options in the lower portion of each panel are grouped into rollouts, such as the Object Type rollout shown in Figure 1–11. You can expand and collapse the rollouts by clicking on the title bar of the rollout. Upward facing double arrows or a minus sign (**-**) in the title bar area indicate an expanded rollout. Downward facing double arrows or a plus sign (**+**) in the title bar area indicate a collapsed rollout.
- In certain situations the list of rollouts can be extensive enough to extend beyond the bottom of the interface. In this case you can pan the list up and down by holding and dragging the mouse button in the Command Panel.

- By default, the Command Panel is docked along the right side of the viewport window. You can minimize the Command Panel to help simplify the interface. Right-click on the upper left edge of the Command Panel, next to the *Create* panel, and select **Minimize**. To display the Command Panel, when in minimized condition, hover the cursor over the Command Panel title bar on the right side of the interface. To return it to the interface display, hover the cursor over the Command Panel title bar and then right-click on the upper left edge and select **Dock>Right/Left** or **Float**.

Create Panel

The *Create* panel enables you to interactively create objects in the Autodesk 3ds Max Design software. It contains seven categories of object types, as shown in Figure 1–12.

Figure 1–12

Some categories have a sub-category drop-down list (e.g., the Standard Primitives drop-down list in the *Geometry* category).

	*Geometry* is 3D objects.
	*Shapes* are 2D objects.
	*Lights*
	*Cameras*
	*Helpers* are non-rendering tools that help with layout or work with other objects, such as a distance measuring tape object.
	*Space warps* are non-renderable objects that deform or otherwise influence the geometry of other objects. They are used to create ripples and waves, using forces such as wind and gravity.
	*Systems* contains the Sunlight and Daylight Systems, Biped, and the controls for some 3rd party plug-ins.

Modify Panel

The *Modify* panel shows the selected object's parameter values, a list of modifiers added to an object, and the parameters that apply to them.

- Modifiers are geometric modifications and additional property controls that can be added to objects, as needed.
- Object and modifier parameters can be changed at any time after the object's creation, if the Modifier stack remains intact.
- The **Modifier List** drop-down menu contains all of the modifiers that can be applied to the currently selected object(s).
- The area below the Modifier List displays the Modifier Stack, which lists the modifiers that have been applied to an object. For example, Figure 1–13 shows the Modifier Stack of a circle that was edited, extruded, and tapered into a 3D column shaft.

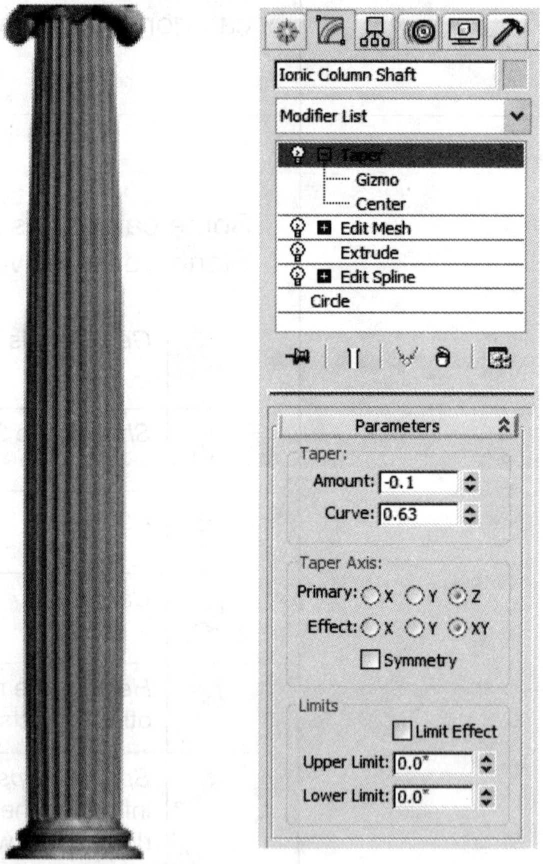

Figure 1–13

- The *Modify* panel is blank if no object is selected or if more than one object is selected.

Hierarchy Panel

Contains controls for objects that are linked together into hierarchies, such as for mechanical equipment with interconnected parts.

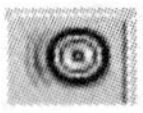

Motion Panel

Contains sophisticated motion controls for animating.

Display Panel

Contains object-level visibility controls, to hide or unhide objects individually or by category, independent of the layer settings.

Utilities Panel

Contains a number of miscellaneous utilities as follows:

- **Asset Browser:** Enables you to review and select content such as 3D objects or 2D bitmaps from your local drive or across the web.

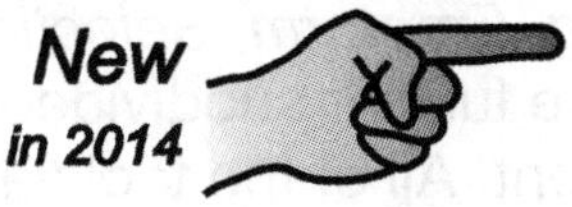

- **Perspective Match Utility:** Helps match the position and field of view of the camera in your 3D scene to the perspective photographic background image.
- **Collapse Utility:** Removes the modifiers from an object's stack, turning the object into an editable mesh or poly.
- **Color Clipboard Utility:** Stores color swatches for copying from one map or material to another.
- **Measure Utility:** Lists the surface area and volume of objects.
- **Motion Capture Utility:** Enables you to animate virtual objects with the real-time movement of the mouse or other input device.
- **Reset XForm Utility:** Removes rotation and scale values of an object, applying them to the XForm modifier gizmo.
- **MAXScript:** Accesses a scripting language that can be used to automate repetitive functions or build new tools and interfaces.

- **Flight Studio Utility:** Enables you to open and manage the open Flight models.

- [More...]: Provides access to a complete list of Utilities, including the controls for many 3rd party plug-in applications.

9. Modeling Ribbon

Enhanced in 2014

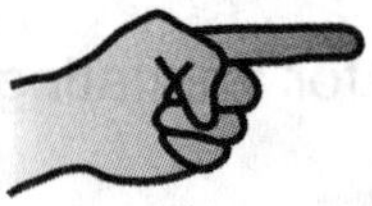

The Modeling Ribbon (shown in Figure 1–14), is located below the Main toolbar and provides easy access to polygon modeling tools, including the editing and modification tools used at sub-object level. The Ribbon contains most of the commonly used tools in the *Modify* panel (at the Edit Poly sub-object level) in the Command Panel.

If the Ribbon is not displayed, in the Menu Bar, select ***Customize>Show UI>Show Ribbon****. Alternatively, you can click*  *(Toggle Ribbon) in the Main toolbar or select* ***Ribbon*** *in the Customize Display right-click menu.*

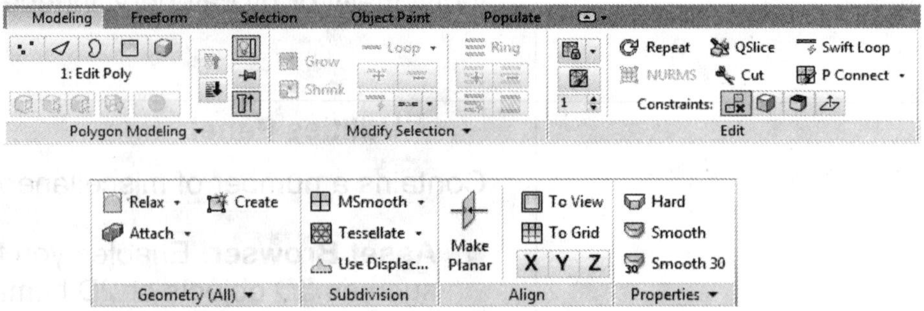

Figure 1–14

The Ribbon contains five tabs: *Modeling*, *Freeform*, *Selection*, *Object Paint*, and *Populate*. The tabs are further subdivided into various panels that are context dependent. All of the tools are grouped based on context and are placed in separate panels. For example, the *Modeling* tab contains the tools used for modeling and are grouped in the *Polygon Modeling* panel, *Modify Selection* panel, *Edit* panel, etc. Each of the panels has a set of related tools and commands present for easy access. For example, the *Polygon Modeling* panel contains tools used for **Edit Poly** modifier, as shown in Figure 1–15.

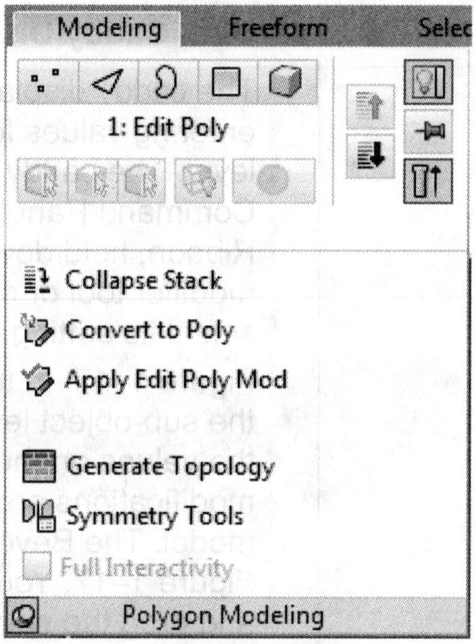

Figure 1–15

- The Ribbon might be minimized to the panel tiles, and is docked under the Main toolbar. Click to maximize the Ribbon.

- The display of the tabs and panels can be controlled by right-clicking on the Ribbon and select the options in the menu, as shown in Figure 1–16.

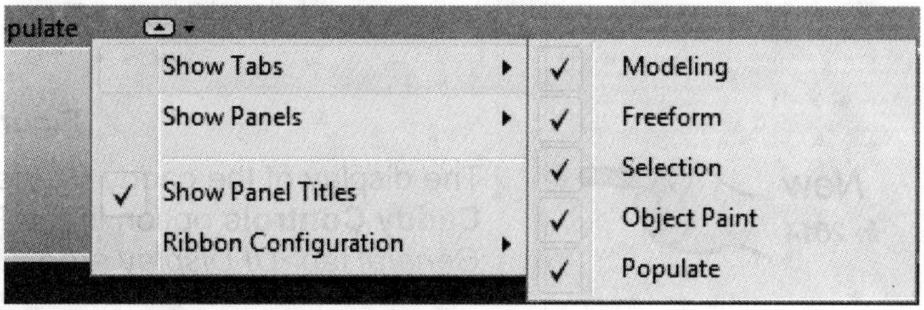

Figure 1–16

- If you are continuously using the options from a panel, you can click located at the beginning of the panel title, once you have expanded it. This locks the expanded panel onto the screen.

Hint: Caddy Display for Edit Poly Modifier

The caddy display is an easy and convenient method of entering values for various modifiers at the Edit Poly sub-object level. The caddy interface can be accessed through the Command Panel and Modeling Ribbon. In the Modeling Ribbon, hold down <Shift> and select the sub-object level modifier tool or click the down arrow next to the modifier and select its setting, as shown for the Bevel modifier in Figure 1–17. In the Command Panel, click  (Settings) next to the sub-object level modifier option. This enables you to enter the values on the screen while performing the operation. The modifications are dynamically updated and reflected in the model. The Bevel Caddy display is shown on the right in Figure 1–17. You can enter the values in the edit boxes or hold and drag the spinner arrows for dynamical viewing and updating of the changes. Click  to accept the change or click  to accept the change and continue in the same modifier.

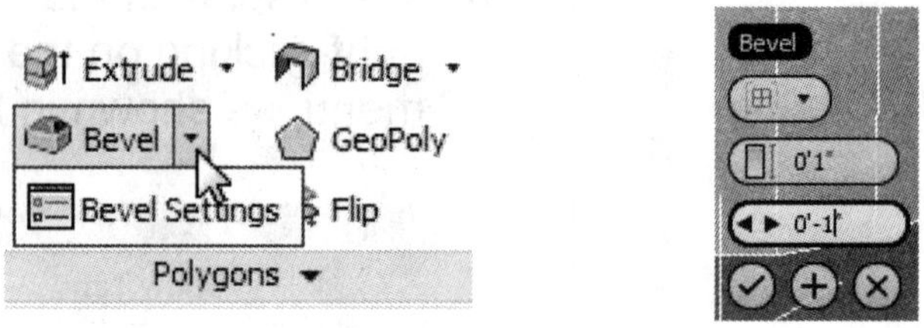

Figure 1–17

New in 2014

The display of the caddy interface is controlled by the **Enable Caddy Controls** option in the Preference Settings dialog box> *General* tab>*UI Display* area. By default, the option is selected.

10. Status Bar

Along the bottom left and center of the interface is the Status Bar, as shown in Figure 1–18. The Status Bar contains features to keep track of what is currently selected, show the position of a selected object, and other functions.

Figure 1–18

From left to right these elements are:

- **MAXScript Mini-Listener:** Enables you to enter commands and receive feedback (**MaxScript** commands).
- **Status Line:** Identifies the number of objects selected.
- **Prompt Line:** Prompts for the next action or input that is required.
-  **(Isolate Selection Toggle):** Zooms the current selection in the active viewport while temporarily hiding unselected objects in all viewports (except the Camera viewport). This enables you to work on the required object without the other objects getting in your way and also to avoid visual distraction. It also enhances performance when you are working on larger models with multiple objects. You can also access this command by selecting **Tools>Isolate Selection** or pressing <Alt>+<Q>.
-  **(Selection Lock Toggle):** Toggles a lock to prevent you from changing your current selection between options. When ready to make a different selection, press this toggle to unlock your current selection. Pressing the spacebar toggles this on or off.
- 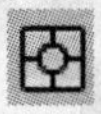 **or**  **(Relative/Absolute Transform Mode Toggle):** Enables you to toggle between absolute and relative transform modes.
- **Transform Type In:** Enables you to review and adjust transform values for the X, Y, and Z coordinates.
- **Grid Setting Display:** Controls the distance between grid lines. Select **Tools>Grids and Snaps>Grid and Snap Settings** to open the dialog box. Use the *Home Grid* tab to adjust the spacing. To toggle the Grid on or off, press <G>.
-  **(Adaptive DegradationToggle):** Enables you to toggle adaptive degradation on or off. Right-click to open the Viewport Configuration dialog box in the *Display Performance* tab (the *Adaptive Degradation* tab is for legacy drivers). You can improve the viewport quality progressively and set the resolution for the texture display (for nitrous drivers). It also contains options for controlling adaptive degradation.

- **Time Tag:** Enables you to add or edit time tags, which are labels describing specific points of an animation. You can use these to quickly navigate to a predefined point in time in your animation.

11. Viewport Layouts tab bar

The Viewport Layouts tab bar is available on the left side of the interface screen, as shown in Figure 1–19.

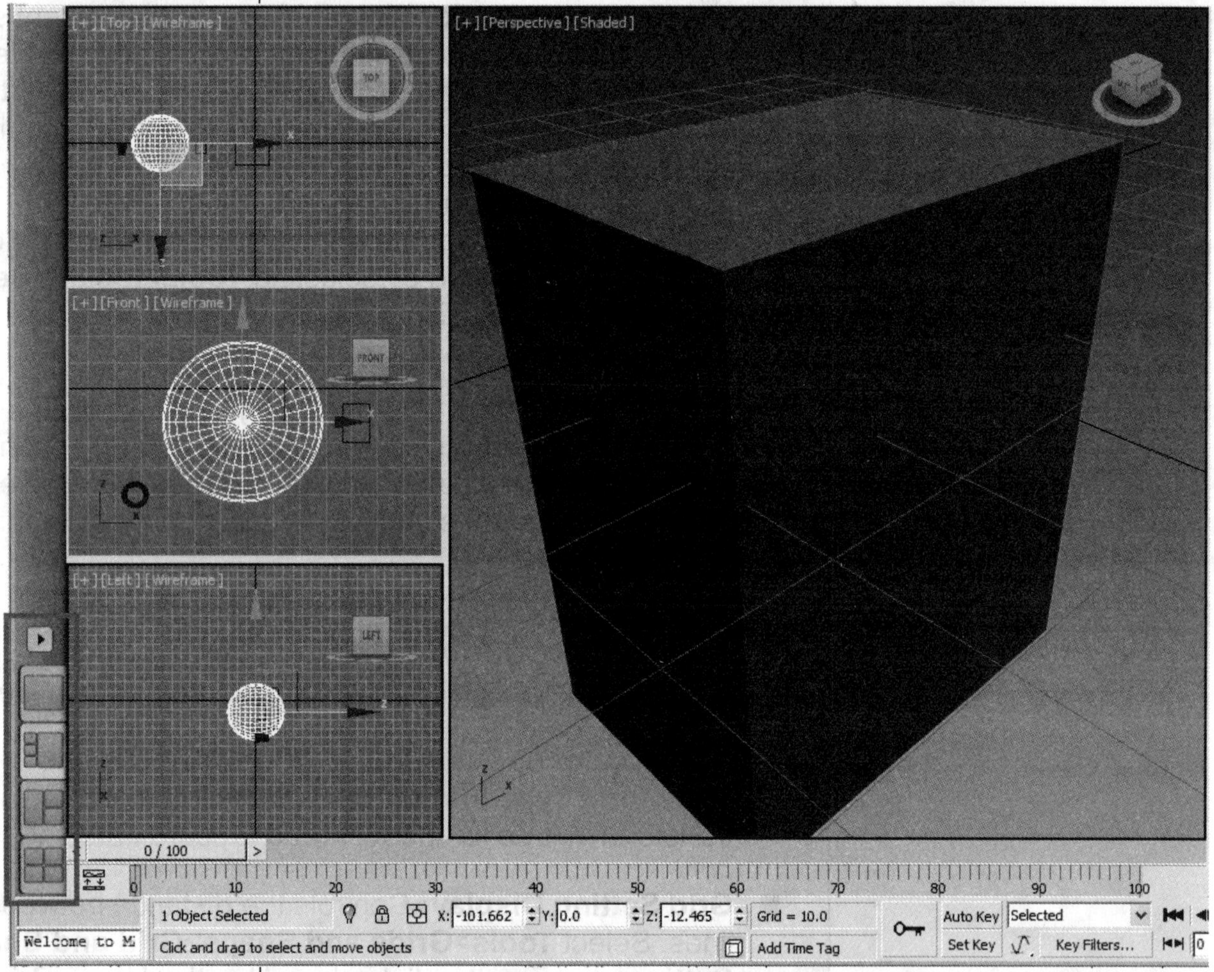

Figure 1–19

This vertically, expandable bar provides you with a list of viewport layouts that can be selected to quickly change the layout of the viewports. For a new scene, a single layout tab is available. Once you have customized and saved additional viewport layouts, they are listed along with the default one. The Viewport Layouts tab bar in Figure 1–19 displays the default layout and three additional viewport layouts that were saved.

Twelve standard viewport layouts (as shown in Figure 1–20), are available for selection and customization in the default list. They are accessed by clicking [icon] at the top of the layout tabs, as shown in Figure 1–20. Once you have selected a layout, it is listed in the tab bar with any previously saved layouts and the viewports are displayed as the new layout.

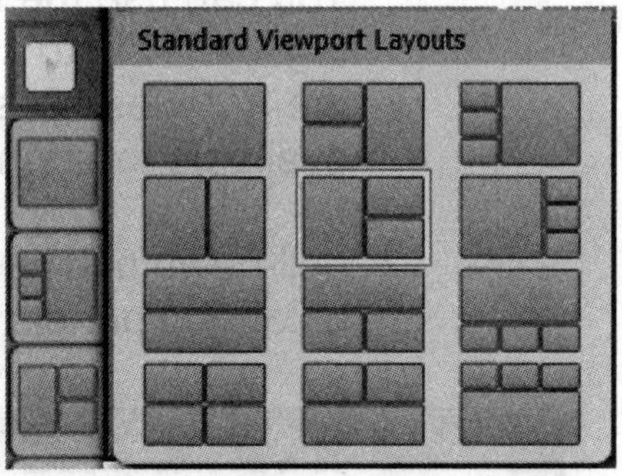

Figure 1–20

To customize the shape of a preset layout, select it from the preset layouts. Once active, you can move the boundaries by clicking and dragging them to new positions. You can also set the required Point of View and Shading modes. Once customized, save your viewport layout by right-clicking on the tab in the tab bar and selecting **Save Configuration as Preset**. You can set its name by entering a new name in the edit box. The newly saved viewport configuration is saved in the Viewport Layouts tab bar when the scene is saved so that it can be quickly recalled in a later session.

12. Viewport Navigation Tools

The navigation tools are discussed in detail later in the training guide.

The navigation tools (shown in Figure 1–21), are located in the lower right corner of the interface and contain tools for navigating and displaying objects in the viewports. The tools are dependent on the active viewport.

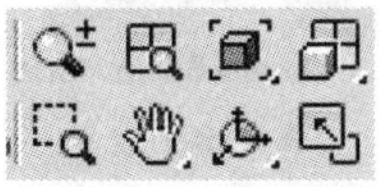

Figure 1–21

1.4 Preferences

Learning Objective

- Understand the working of different tabs in the Preference Settings dialog box.

You can use the Preference Settings dialog box, as shown in Figure 1–22, to control many important operational settings for the Autodesk 3ds Max Design software. The dialog box is available through the Application Menu or in the **Customize** pull-down menu. Expand  and click 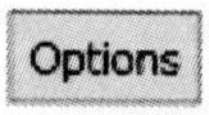

in any of the extended panels or select **Customize>Preferences**.

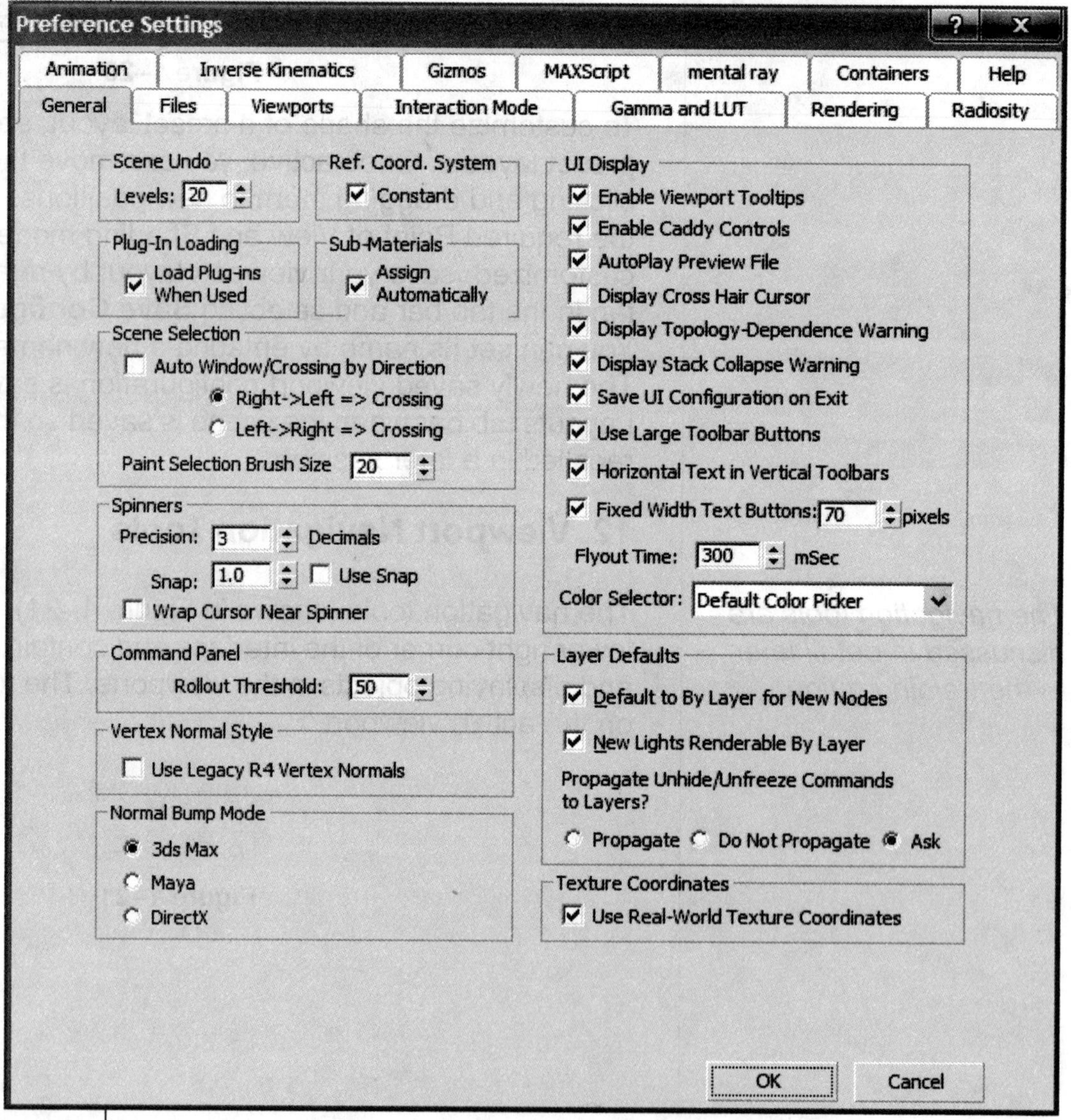

Figure 1–22

The Preference Settings dialog box has tabs that control the display and operational settings at the program level.

The various tabs are:

- ***General* tab:** Controls the interface settings, such as Number of Scene Undo steps (levels) that are saved, settings for the transform center, user interface display options, etc.
- ***Files* tab:** Contains options for file handling, such as Automatic backup save settings.
- ***Viewports* tab:** Contains options for viewport settings and mouse controls defining button behavior.
- ***Interaction Mode* tab:** Sets how the mouse and keyboard shortcuts are going to behave. You can set the mouse shortcut behavior to match **3ds Max** or **Maya**.
- ***Gamma and LUT* tab:** Sets the compatibility options with respect to other Autodesk programs for a consistent display of colors among various programs.
- ***Rendering* tab:** Controls the rendering settings, such as the ambient light default color settings.
- ***Animation* tab:** Controls the various animation settings. You can assign the sound plug-ins and controller defaults.
- ***Inverse kinematics* tab:** Sets the Applied IK (for accuracy) and Interactive IK (for real-time response) settings.
- ***Gizmos* tab:** Sets the display and behavior of the Transform gizmos.
- ***MAXScript* tab:** Sets the various features used for the MAXScript editor, such as what font and font size to use.
- ***Radiosity* tab:** Controls the radiosity settings in viewports and if the light levels with radiosity are saved with a file or not.
- ***mental ray* tab:** Controls the settings for the mental ray renderer such as how to show the progress of Final Gather visually in the renderer.
- ***Containers* tab:** Controls the Status and Update settings in viewports.

Enhanced in 2014

- ***Help* tab:** Controls where help documentation is accessed from. By default, help is accessed through the Autodesk.com website. Alternatively, you can download the documentation locally and then specify its installation path in the *Help* tab.

Hint: Gamma and LUT Settings Mismatch

Gamma and LUT Settings are saved with the defaults for the current file based on the current UI. Opening or merging a scene, whose file gamma or LUT settings are different from the gamma and LUT settings of the system in which it is being opened, causes the Mismatch dialog box to open, as shown in Figure 1–23. It provides you with options to use the current settings or adopt the file settings.

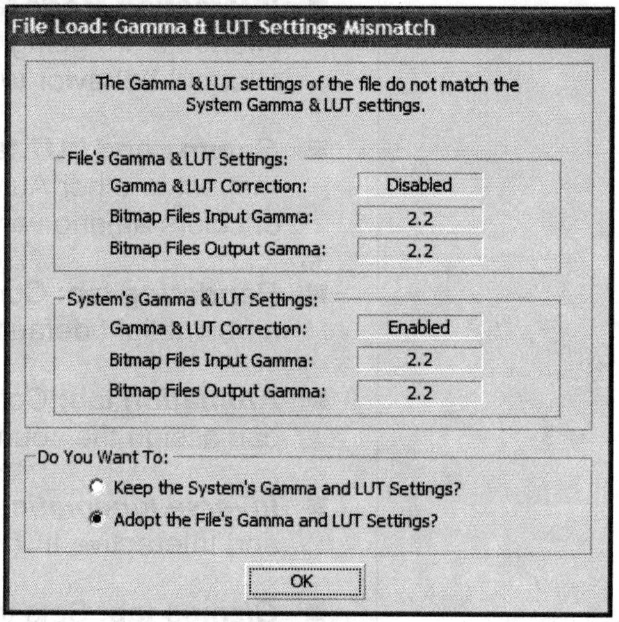

Figure 1–23

1.5 Setting the Project Folder

Learning Objective

- Set the project folder to organize all of the files in the project.

When working with the Autodesk 3ds Max Design software, you should first set a project folder. Doing so enables you to better organize all of the files for a project. By default, the project folder creates a new folder in *\My Documents\3dsmaxDesign*. Once the project folder is created, a series of subfolders (e.g., scenes, renderoutput) are generated. The project folder is maintained when the Autodesk 3ds Max Design software is restarted. However, you can reset the project folder at any time. In the Quick Access Toolbar, click (Project Folder) to open the Browse For Folder dialog box. Select a folder to be set as your project folder or create a new folder to be used as your project folder and click OK. In the Quick Access Toolbar, hover the cursor over (Project Folder) to display its name, as shown in Figure 1–24.

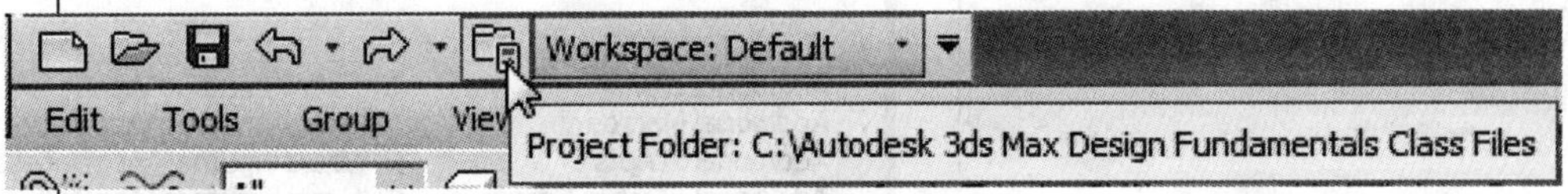

Figure 1–24

You can also set your project folder in the Application Menu. Expand , expand Manage, and select **Set Project Folder**. In the Browse For Folder dialog box, browse and select the folder, and click OK.

1.6 Configure Paths

Learning Objective

- Identify and set the path locations of reusable data files and reconfigurable items.

Most projects make use of external files such as fonts, image maps for materials, IES (Illuminating Engineering Society) data files for lights, etc. The locations of these and other necessary data files are identified in the two Configure Paths dialog boxes. Selecting **Customize>Configure System Paths** opens the Configure System Paths dialog box and **Customize>Configure User Paths** opens the Configure User Paths dialog box.

Configure System Paths

The Configure System Paths dialog box, as shown in Figure 1–25, stores paths to data files and these files are generally the same for all users on a workstation (fonts, startup MAXScript files, etc.).

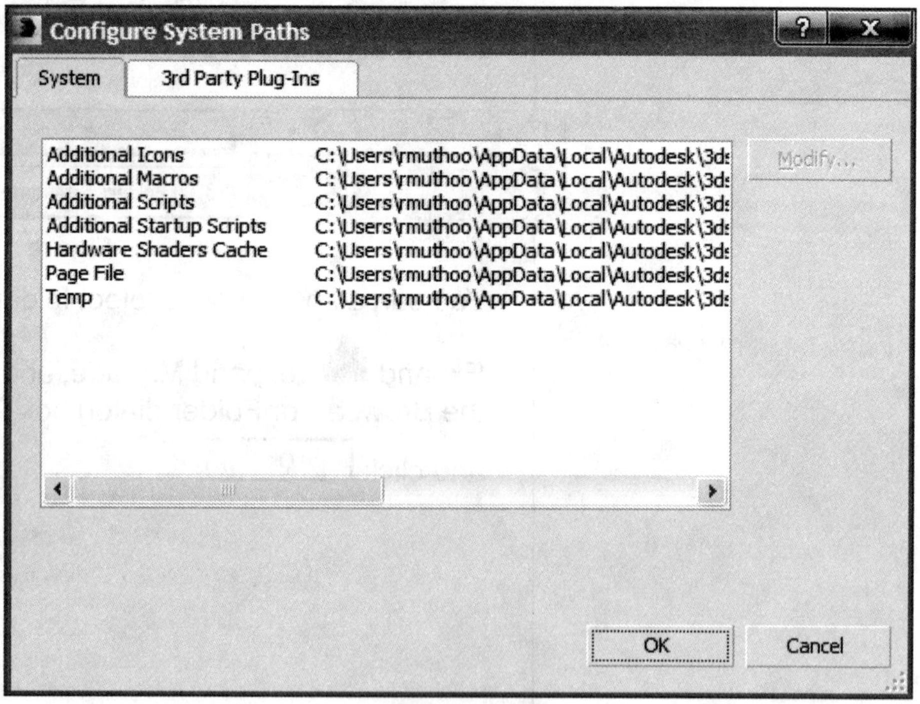

Figure 1–25

The Configure System Paths dialog box has two tabs:

System	Paths used for additional buttons, macros, scripts and startup scripts, and temp files.
3rd Party Plug-Ins	Default paths to search for add-on application data (some standard functions and 3rd party products).

Configure User Paths

The Configure User Paths dialog box, as shown in Figure 1–26, stores items that might be reconfigured for different users or for different projects. The User path settings can be saved as a path configuration (.MXP) file and later re-loaded as required.

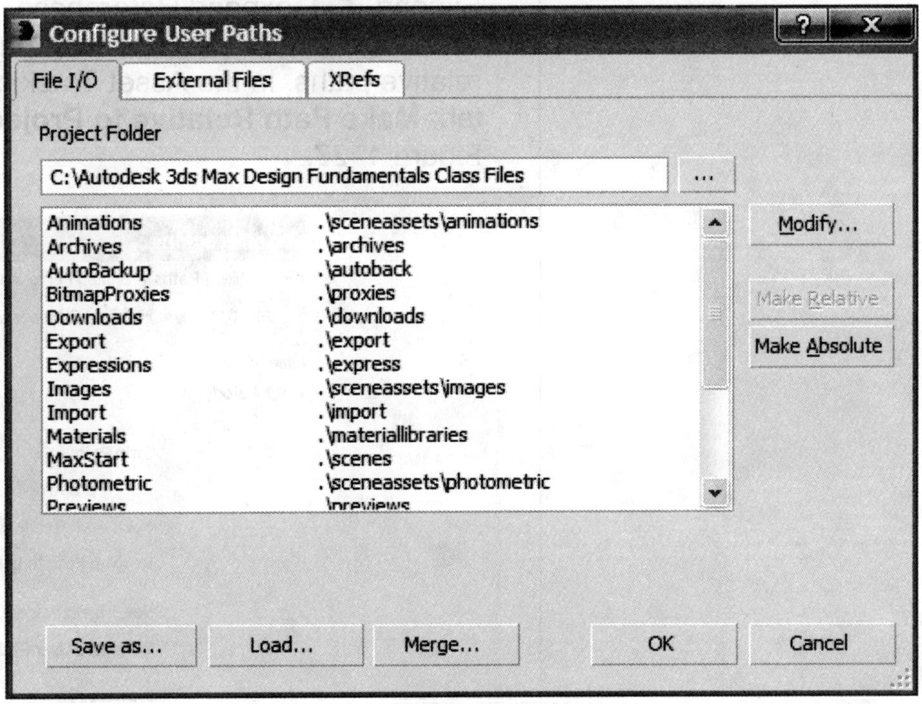

Figure 1–26

The Configure User Paths dialog box has three tabs:

File I/O	Paths used to locate files for options such as open, save, export, etc.
External Files	Paths to external data files such as image maps, IES files, etc.
XRefs	Paths that are searched to find externally referenced objects and scene files.

- Since multiple workstations often make use of the same data files, it is often helpful to create shared network locations for these files (especially when network rendering).

- Relative paths are used to help prevent *missing external files* problems when sharing or moving files from one location to another. In the Configure User Paths, all of the paths are preceded with a dot and backslash (.\). The dot and backslash indicate a relative path.

- You can use the Configure User Paths dialog box to change hard-coded absolute paths from earlier versions to Relative paths. In the Configure User Paths dialog box, select the path and click Make Relative.

Hint: Asset Tracking

Expand the application menu, expand References, and select **Asset Tracking** to change hard-coded absolute paths from earlier versions to relative paths. In the Asset Tracking dialog box, select *Paths* tab>**Make Path Relative to Project Folder**, as shown in Figure 1–27.

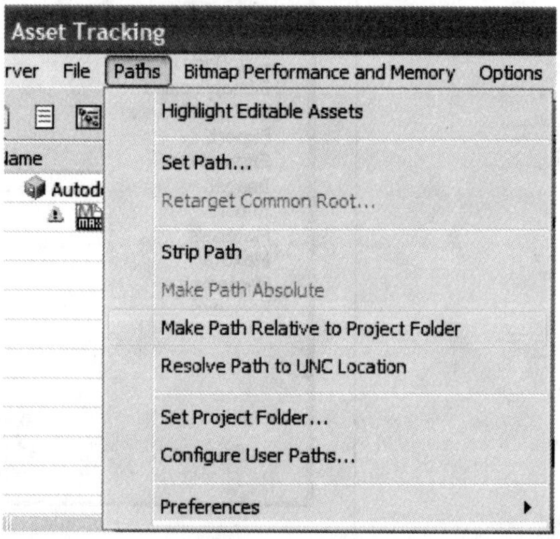

Figure 1–27

1.7 Display Drivers

Enhanced in 2014

Learning Objective

- Identify the display drivers available with the Autodesk 3ds Max Design software.

The Nitrous Direct3D 11 driver is the default and recommended display driver, but you can change to the other Nitrous drivers or legacy drivers using the Preference Settings dialog box. To access this dialog box, select **Customize>Preferences**. In the *Viewports* tab, in the *Display Drivers* area, click Choose Driver... . The Display Driver Selection dialog box opens, as shown in Figure 1–28. If you change the display driver, you need to close and reopen the software for the changes to take affect.

You can also change the graphics driver outside the software using the Windows Start menu. Select Windows ***Start>All Programs> Autodesk>Autodesk 3ds Max Design 2014> Change Graphics Mode****. This launches the software and provides the option of selecting the display driver.*

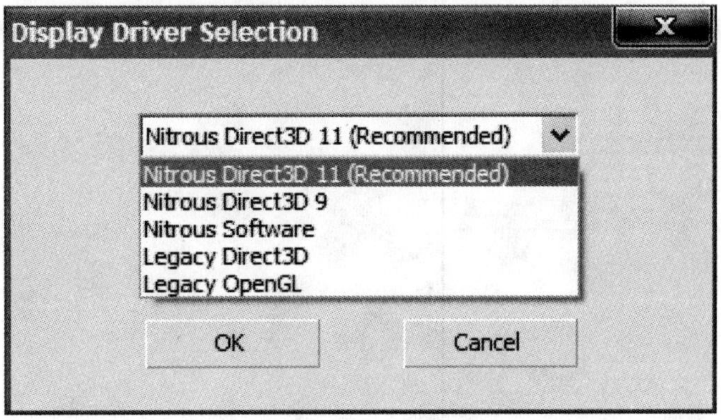

Figure 1–28

The following display drivers are available:

New in 2014

- **Nitrous Direct3D 11:** The Nitrous Direct 3D 11 driver requires Direct 3D 11.0. This driver takes advantage of video card features (when available), and provides high quality realistic viewport display options and faster rendering times. The visual display is render quality and supports unlimited lights, shadows, tone mapping, etc. The Nitrous driver also enables you to display your scenes in stylized images (pencil, acrylic, ink, etc.) in the viewports. Windows XP does not support Direct3D 11.
- **Nitrous Direct3D 9:** The Nitrous Direct 3D 9 driver requires Direct3D 9.0. It works in the same way as the Direct3D 11 driver. Both Windows XP and Windows 7 support Direct3D 9.0. This driver becomes the default if your system has Windows XP or the graphics card does not support Direct3D 11.

New in 2014

- **Nitrous Software:** The Nitrous Software driver has similar capabilities to the other nitrous drivers, but the hardware support is not required and it might be slower during rendering. Windows XP does not support this driver.

*The **OpenGL** and **Direct3D** options are useful if your system supports those forms of hardware acceleration. You might need to experiment to determine the best option for your workstation.*

- **Legacy Direct3D:** The Direct3D driver supports data culling and works well for the high-color displays. This driver was recommended for use before the release of the Autodesk 3ds Max Design 2012 software when the Nitrous driver was incorporated in the software.
- **Legacy OpenGL:** The OpenGL driver works well for hardware acceleration, including geometry acceleration and rasterization acceleration. You cannot display shadows or ambient occlusion in viewports while using this driver.

1.8 Viewport Display and Labels

Learning Objective

Understand the viewport display labels and the various options available within them.

Geometry opens in the Autodesk 3ds Max Design software through one or more viewports, which can be configured to show objects from different viewing angles and with different viewport shading modes.

Three Viewport label menus display in the upper left corner of each viewport [+] [Perspective] [Realistic]: a **General** Viewport label menu marked with a plus sign [+], a **Point of View (POV)** Viewport label menu, and a **Shading** Viewport label menu. Clicking on a label opens its corresponding label menu.

General Viewport

The **General** Viewport label menu, as shown in Figure 1–29, provides options for viewport activation, configuration, and general display. It includes the ability to display grids, the ViewCube, and the SteeringWheels. You can also open the Viewport Configuration dialog box. It contains tools for the **xView** functionality, which enables you to show statistics and diagnose problems in polygonal geometry such as overlapping faces, unwelded vertices, or face normal orientation issues.

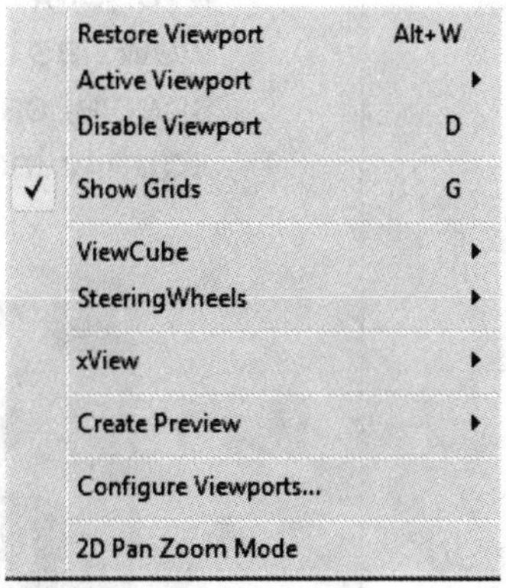

Figure 1–29

Point Of View

The **Point of View** label menu displays the name of the view projection, such as Perspective, Orthographic, etc., that is being shown in the viewport. Clicking on this Viewport label enables you to change the view type. You can also change from one view to another using the shortcut keys that are listed next to the type in the label menu. For example, press <T> for Top and <B> for Bottom.

The three most common view types are:

- **Perspective View:** This view uses vanishing points to make distant objects appear to recede from view. Perspective view displays what is seen with human vision. Most output from the Autodesk 3ds Max Design software is shown through perspective views or the camera objects assigned to display them. Figure 1–30 shows the Camera view of a scene.

Figure 1–30

- **Orthographic (Axonometric Rotated) View:** Orthographic views, as shown in Figure 1–31, do not use vanishing points or convergence; therefore objects do not seem to recede over distance. It might be helpful to think of Orthographic views as being similar to Isometric views (Isometric views are special cases of Axonometric views where the axes are equally inclined to the screen.).

You might find Orthographic views easier to navigate (especially when zooming with a mouse wheel), but the rendered output often does not display as realistic as from a perspective view.

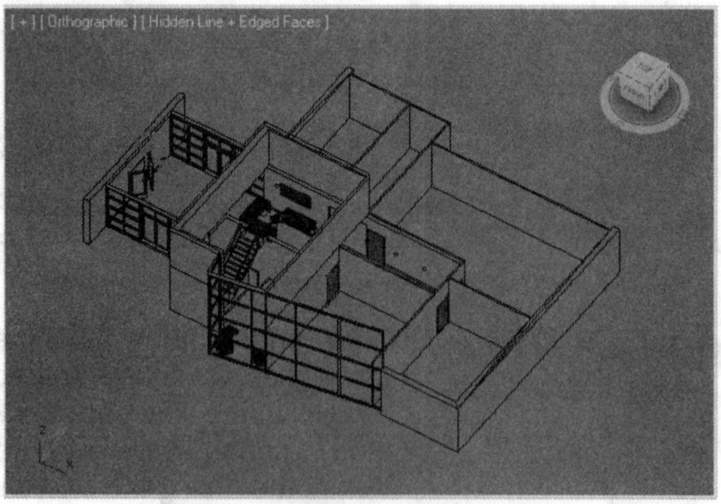

Figure 1–31

- **Other Views:** The Left, Right, Top, Bottom, Front, and Back views are all other types of pre-defined views, which show a 2D projection of the model. The Top view is most like an AutoCAD top (plan view).

Visual Style

The Visual Style label displays the shading method used, such as Realistic, Consistent Colors, Shaded etc. Clicking on the label opens the **Visual Style** label menu, as shown in Figure 1–32. The options in this menu enable you to change the shading method in the viewport. You can select between modes that show edges or surfaces or both. In addition to shading, this menu contains tools for the new **Stylized** options, **Lighting and Shadows**, and **Viewport Background**. You can use the **Display Selected** options to control the display of selected geometry in shaded viewports.

Enhanced in 2014

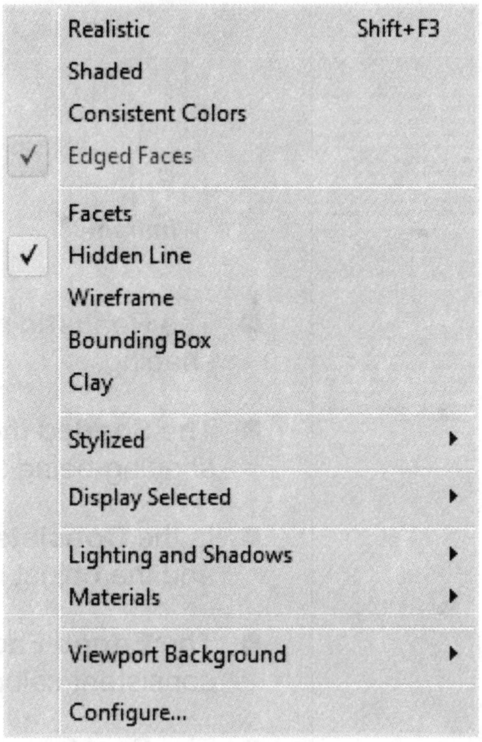

Figure 1–32

For the Nitrous display driver, the viewport display options have been enhanced. If you are using a legacy display driver, the viewport display options vary.

Some of the viewport shading modes are shown in Figure 1–33. A Visual Style can be assigned by clicking on the label and selecting the required option from the label menu.

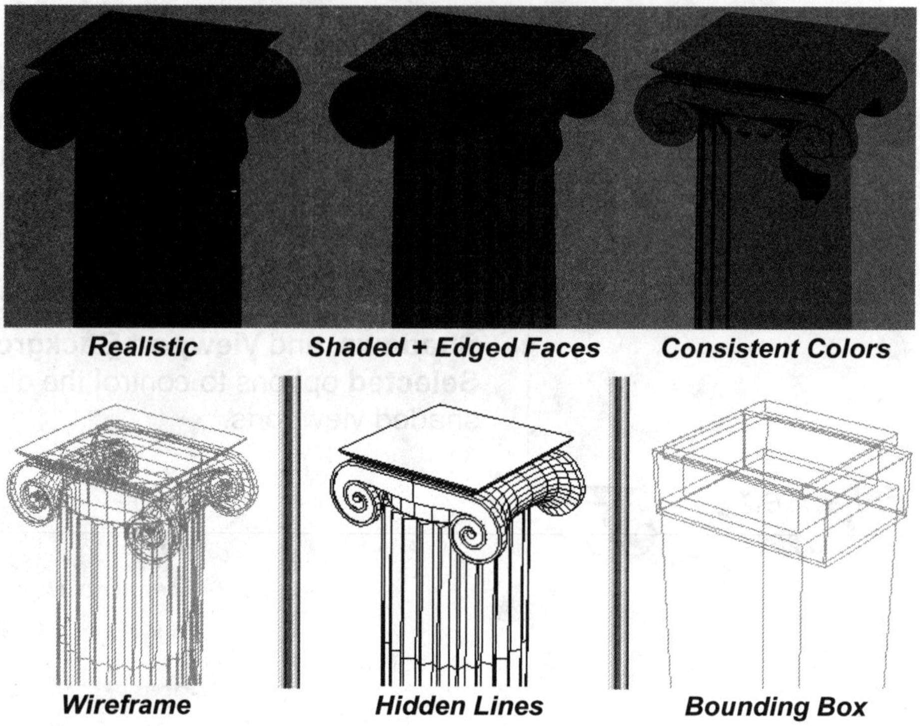

Figure 1–33

- The **Realistic** mode displays objects with high quality shading.
- The **Shaded** mode displays the object as smooth with Phong shading being applied to it.
- In the **Consistent Colors** mode, lighting effects are disabled and the object is displayed with just the color.
- The **Edged Faces** option overlays a realistic, shaded, or consistent color view with wireframe.
- The **Facets** option always displays the geometry as faceted even if the Smooth modifier or Smoothing have been applied to the object. This enables you to precisely locate the edges in the model and makes it easier to work with the geometry.
- The **Hidden Line** option improves the Wireframe display by hiding the lines that are on the backside of the objects. This option mode enables you to see the wireframe, but not see through the objects.

- The **Bounding Box** option is useful when scenes are extremely complex and software performance is an issue. Alternatively, in this situation individual objects can be set to view as bounding boxes through Object Properties.
- The **Clay** option displays the geometry in a terracotta color without any material or texture color that might have been applied to the model.
- The **Stylized** menu options enables you to display objects with a variety of effects that are non-photorealistic. Figure 1–34 displays the object in the Graphite, Color Pencil, and Pastel stylized options.

Figure 1–34

Practice 1a Organizing Folders and Working with the Interface

Learning Objectives

- Set the project folder to organize all of the files in the project.
- Configure User Paths to set the *Materials*, *Maps*, and *Scene* folders.
- Create different Viewport Layouts by changing the viewing angles and using different viewport shading modes.
- Navigate the graphic user interface and modify an object using the Command Panel.

Estimated time for completion: 20 minutes

In this practice you will work with the Autodesk 3ds Max Design software by setting the project folder, as well as configuring the user paths. To complete the practice you will open a file and begin to investigate the interface.

Task 1 - Set the Project Folder.

1. Download the practice files from the link provided on the Class Files page. Install the practice files to a folder on your local hard drive by double-clicking on the self-extracting .EXE file. The install directory is *C:\Autodesk 3ds Max Design Fundamentals Class Files*.

If you are opening the software for the first time, a Welcome Screen is displayed. Close the Welcome Screen.

2. Launch the Autodesk 3ds Max Design 2014 software if it is not already running. If it is already running, reset the program by expanding  and selecting **Reset**. This closes the current file and opens a new blank file. If an unsaved scene is open, you might be required to save or discard the changes to the scene. Click  to not save changes to the current file. Click  to reset the file.
3. In the Quick Access Toolbar, click  (Project Folder) to set a project folder.
4. In the Browse For Folder dialog box, navigate to C:\ and select the *Autodesk 3ds Max Design Fundamentals Class Files* folder.

If an Invalid Path dialog box opens, click OK.

5. Click OK. You only have to set the project folder once.

Task 2 - Setting Preferences.

1. In the pull-down menu, select **Customize>Preferences**. The Preference Settings dialog box opens.
2. In the *General* tab, in the *Ref. Coord. System* area, select **Constant** (if not already selected), as shown in Figure 1–35. This enables the Transform types to use the same Reference Coordinate System, rather than remembering the last one used for each.

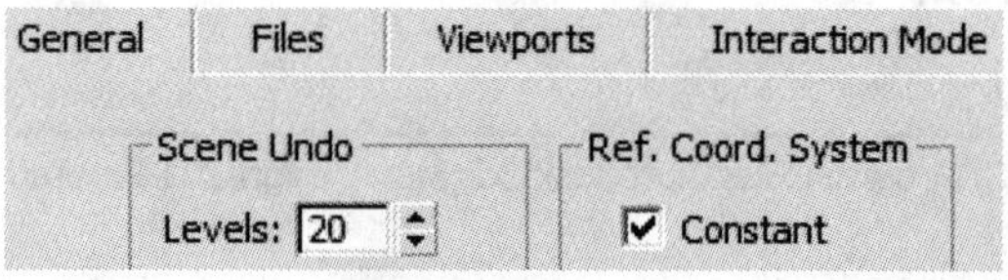

Figure 1–35

3. In the *Layer Defaults* area, clear **Default to By Layer for New Nodes**, as shown in Figure 1–36. This enables you to define the individual display of objects and to determine that the objects are not affected by the layer properties on which they are created. Click OK.

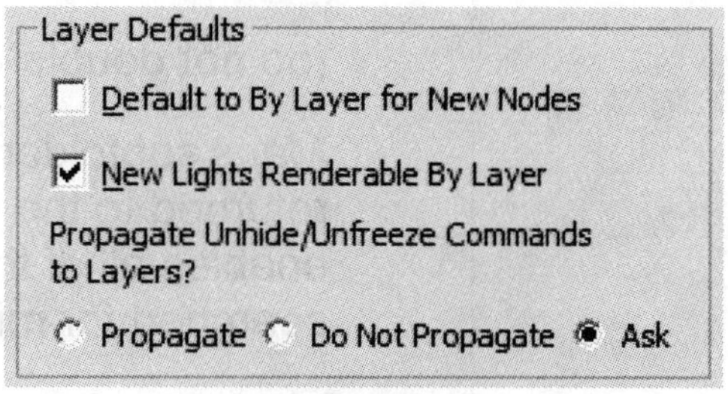

Figure 1–36

Task 3 - Configure the User Paths.

1. Select **Customize>Configure User Paths** to open the Configure User Paths dialog box.

If a folder contains a subfolder and you select it (rather than double-clicking), you might need to click Use Path *twice to return to the Configure User Paths dialog box.*

2. Verify that the *File I/O* tab is selected. Select **Materials** and click Modify... . In the Choose Directory for Materials dialog box, browse to the material libraries folder in the root installation (usually *C:\Program Files\Autodesk\3ds Max Design 2014\materiallibraries*). At the bottom of the dialog box, the path should display as shown in Figure 1–37. Click Use Path .

Figure 1–37

3. In the Configure User Paths dialog box, select the *External Files* tab and click Add... .

4. In the Choose New External Files Path dialog box, navigate to *C:\Autodesk 3ds Max Design Fundamentals Class Files* (do not double-click). Click Use Path . Double-click on the *Maps* subfolder and click Use Path . Verify that you have returned to the Configure User Paths dialog box. This enables all of the folders under the main folder to be searched for missing external files.

5. In the Configure User Paths dialog box, verify that the Maps new path is still selected and click Move Up . Continue clicking Move Up until the new path is first in the list, as shown in Figure 1–38. Verify that Move Up is grayed out, which indicates that the folder is at the top of the list. (The paths are searched in order from top to bottom, so moving a custom path to the top saves time when searching for files.)

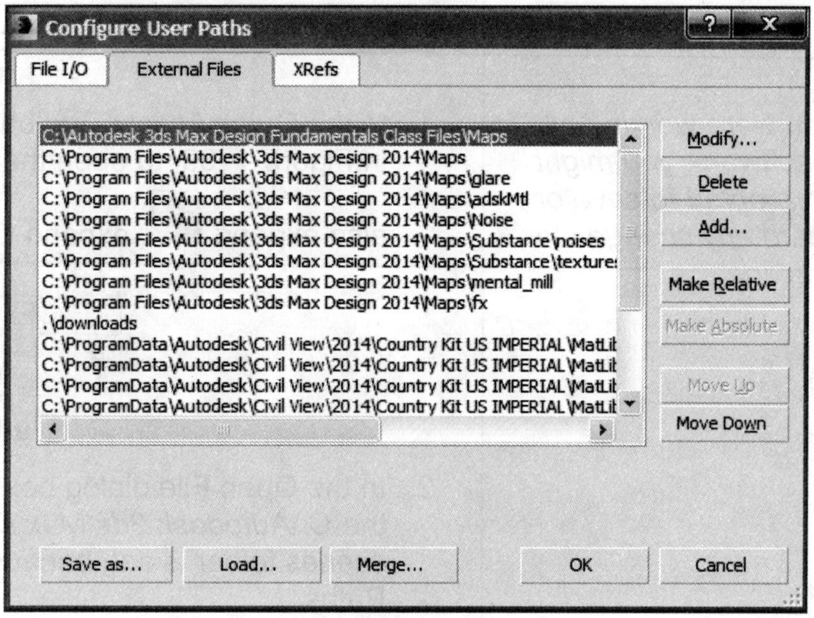

Figure 1–38

6. Select the *XRefs* tab, click Add... . In the Choose New XRef Path dialog box, navigate to C:*Autodesk 3ds Max Design Fundamentals Class Files* (do not double-click). Click Use Path . Double-click on the *scenes* subfolder and click Use Path . Click OK to exit the Configure User Paths dialog box.

These settings are not specific to the scene file, so there is no need to save the file at this point.

Hint: Using maxstart.max

You can configure a scene that includes default objects, materials, and other scene-specific data to be used as a basis for new scene files (similar to how other applications use template files). To do so, save your customized scene with the name **maxstart.max** and place it in the MaxStart support path, which can be found by selecting **Customize>Configure User Paths**. New scene files are created as a copy of your **maxstart.max** file.

The Autodesk 3ds Max Design software also has the ability to save these settings as a Scene State. This feature provides the means to save different conditions with camera lighting, environment, material, and object properties that can be quickly recalled. Scene states are similar to using a **maxstart.max** file, but they can be restored using any scene file. You can access scene states through the right-click quad menu.

Task 4 - Setting a Viewport Layout.

If you were working in the software, you might be prompted to save or discard any changes to the scene.

1. In the Quick Access Toolbar, click (Open File), as shown in Figure 1–39, to open the Open File dialog box. You can also expand , expand Open, and select **Open**.

Figure 1–39

2. In the Open File dialog box (shown in Figure 1–40), note that the *C:\Autodesk 3ds Max Design Fundamentals Class Files\scenes* folder is set, because you have already set the User Paths.

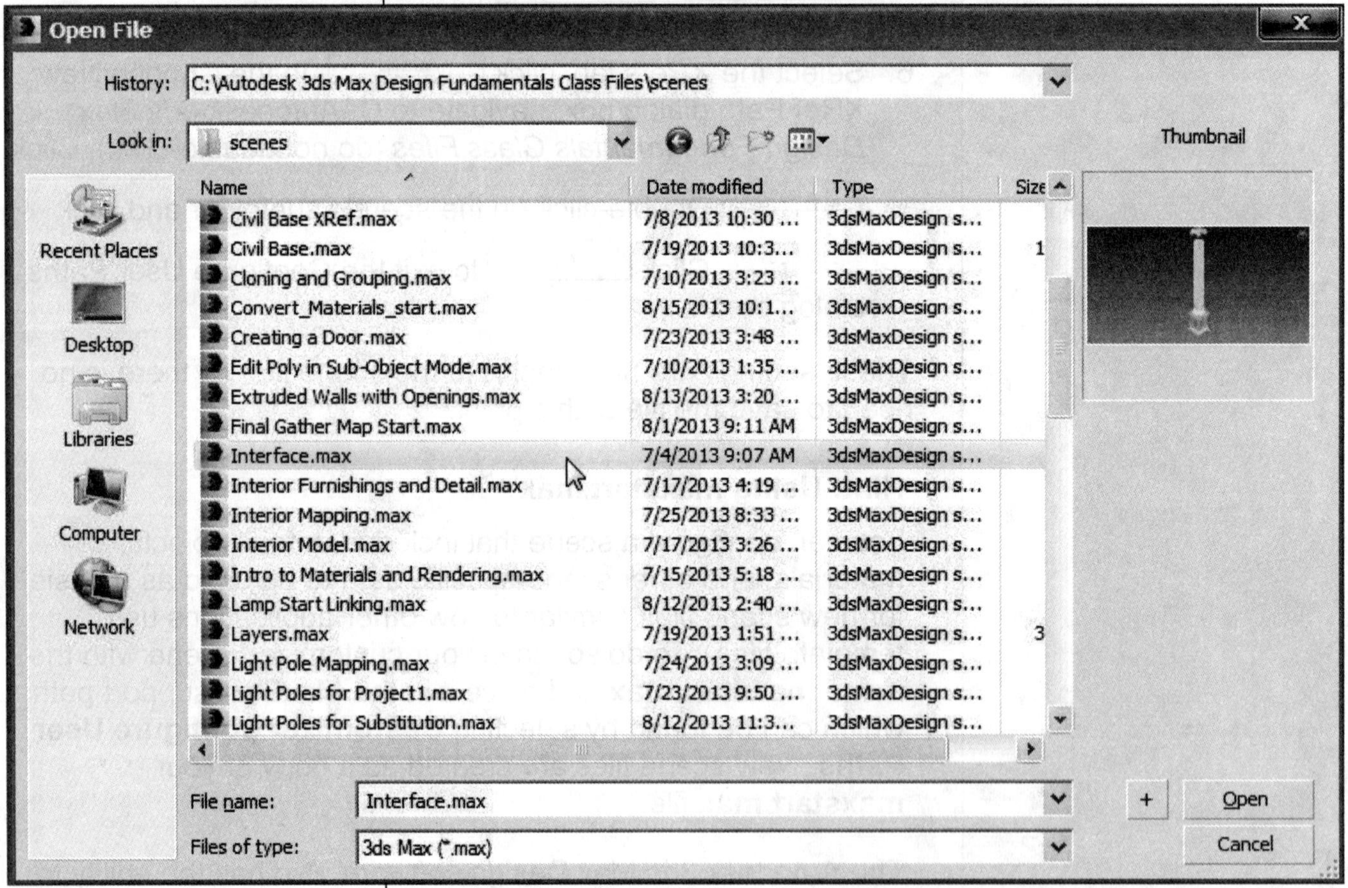

Figure 1–40

If a dialog box opens prompting you about a File Load: Mismatch for Gamma & LUT settings, click OK *to accept the default values.*

3. Select the file **Interface.max** and click Open.

If the Ribbon is covering the top portion of your model, minimize it by clicking ▭.

4. The model should display similar to that shown in Figure 1–41. Note that it opens in one maximized viewport layout, which was previously saved with the scene.

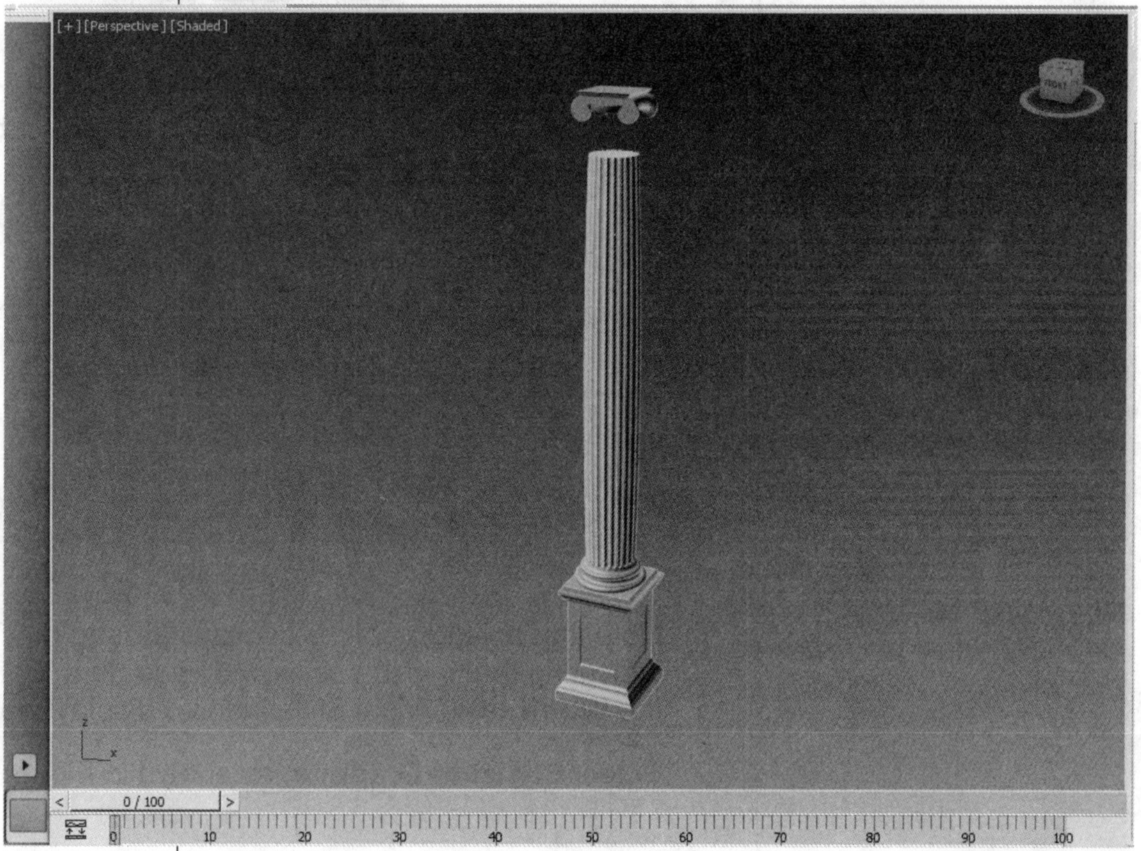

Figure 1–41

- The file has been zoomed out by rolling the middle mouse button to display the complete model in the viewport.

5. Along the left side of the viewport, in the Viewport Layouts tab bar, click  (as shown in Figure 1–41) to expand the *Standard Viewport Layouts* panel. Select the layout as shown in Figure 1–42 (second row, second column).

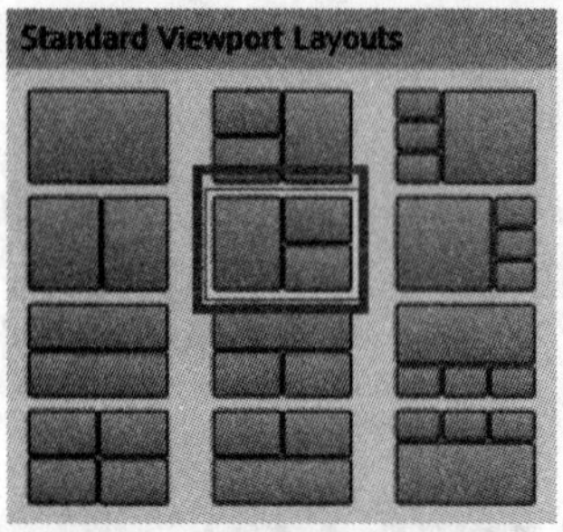

Figure 1–42

- Note that the model displays in three viewport layouts and that the newly selected layout is added to the tabs list, as shown in Figure 1–43.

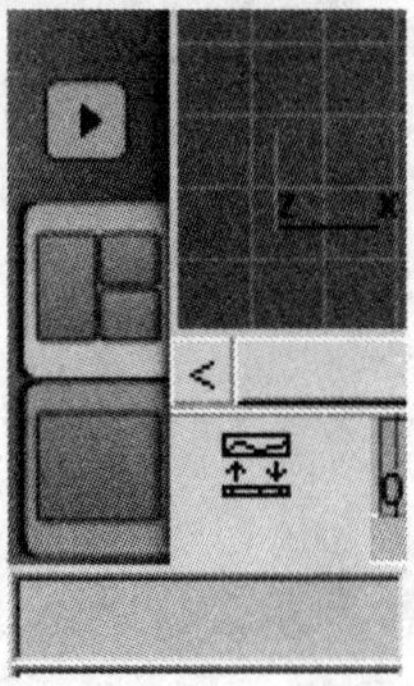

Figure 1–43

6. Note that a yellow border displays around the Top viewport, indicating that it is the active viewport. In this viewport, select the **Wireframe** Visual Style label to display the menu.

7. Select **Stylized>Graphite**, as shown in Figure 1–44.

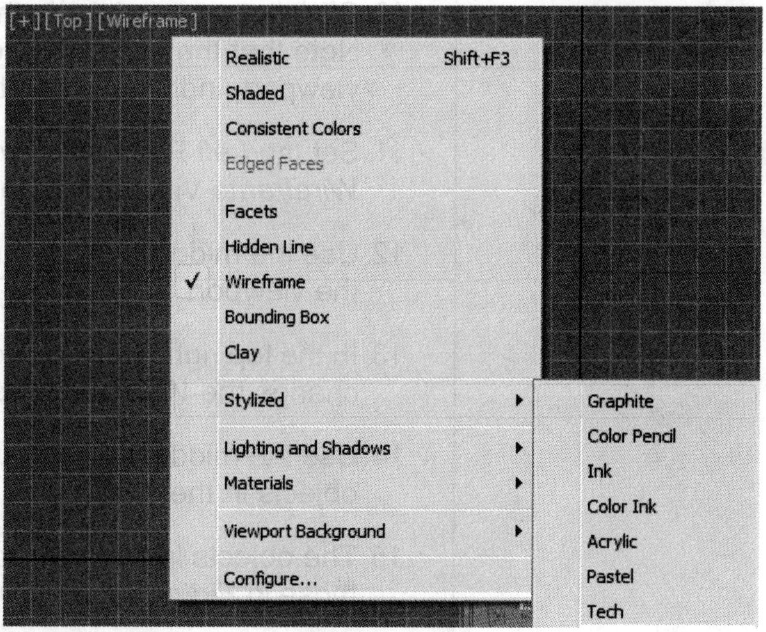

Figure 1–44

- Note the change in the display of objects in this viewport.

8. Select the **Top** Point of View label to open the menu. Select **Right**, as shown in Figure 1–45. Alternatively, you can press <R> to display the right view of the object.

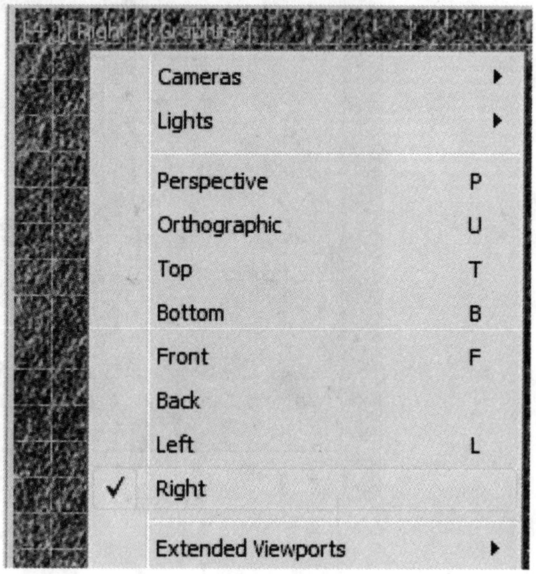

Figure 1–45

9. Use the mouse wheel to zoom out so that the complete model is displayed in the viewport. While holding down the middle mouse button, drag the cursor to pan the objects so that they are centrally located in the viewport.

10. Click in empty space in the lower right viewport (Left view). Note that the yellow border now displays around this viewport, indicating that it is the active viewport.
11. Set the *Left* Point of View label to **Perspective** and the *Wireframe* Visual Style to **Shaded**.
12. Use the middle mouse button to zoom and pan the objects in the viewport.
13. In the top right viewport, leave the Point of View as **Front** and change the *Wireframe* Visual Style to **Clay**.
14. Use the middle mouse button to pan and zoom to display the objects in the viewport.
15. The objects in this viewport layout should look similar to those in Figure 1–46.

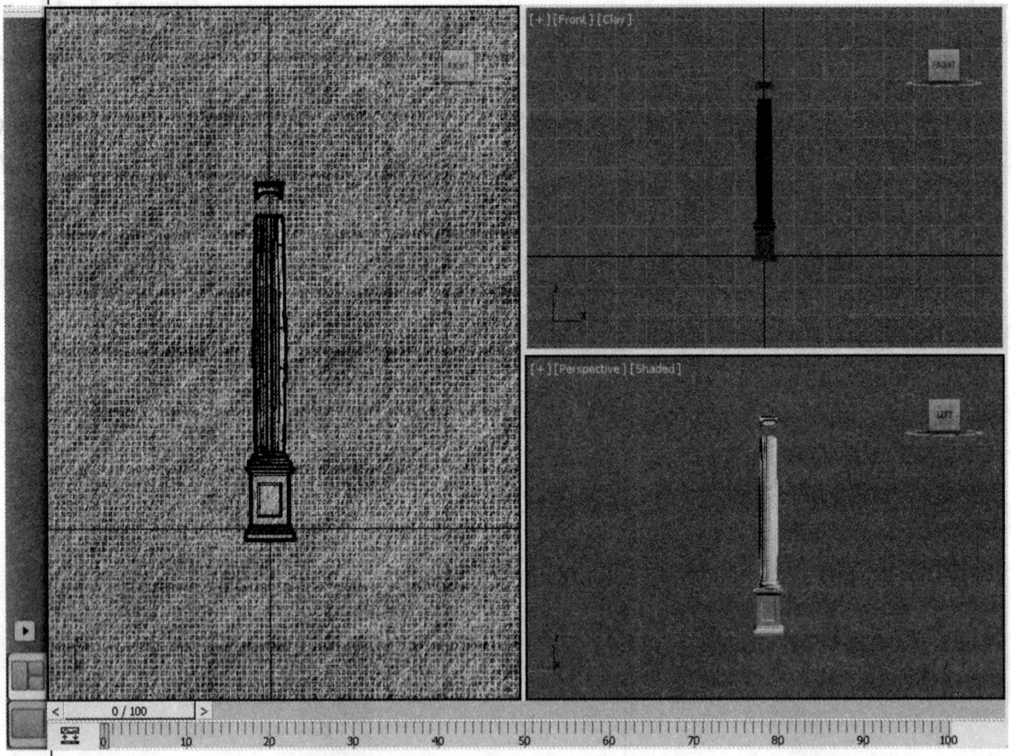

Figure 1–46

Task 5 - Modifying the objects using the Command Panel.

1. In the Viewport Layout tab bar, select the initial layout that existed with the scene. It is listed at the bottom of the list in the Viewport Layouts tab bar, as shown in Figure 1–47.

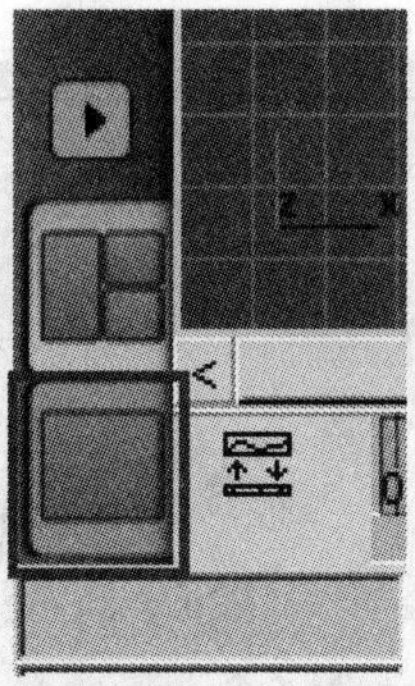

Figure 1–47

- The objects display in a single viewport in the **Perspective** view with the **Shaded** Visual Style.

2. In the Command Panel, select the *Create* panel ( ), as shown in Figure 1–48, if required (active by default).

Figure 1–48

3. Select the *Geometry* category by clicking (Geometry), if required (active by default). The different types of geometry that you can create are listed here.

4. In the Command Panel, select the *Modify* panel ( ). The panel is empty as no objects are currently selected.

Names only display when the cursor is hovered over an unselected object. Once the object has been selected, its name is displayed in the Modifier Stack.

5. In the Main toolbar, click (Select Object), if required (active by default).

6. Hover the cursor over the cyan (blue) object to display its name, **Ionic Column Shaft**. Click the object to select it. The name and modifiers that have been applied are displayed in the Command Panel. The Status Line at the bottom of the viewport, displays **1 Object Selected**, as shown in Figure 1–49.

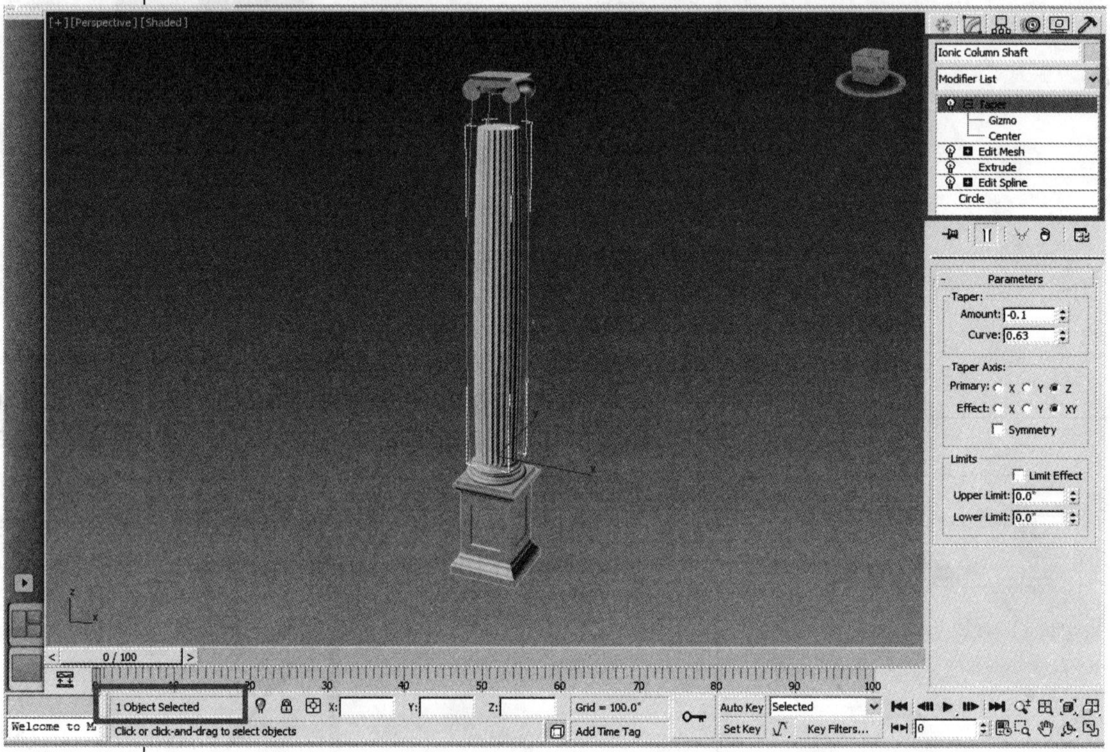

Figure 1–49

7. In the Command Panel, next to the object name **Ionic Column Shaft**, select the color swatch. Select a different color and click OK to change the color of the column shaft.

8. In the Modifier Stack, the list of modifiers that have been used on the column shaft are displayed, as shown in Figure 1–50.

   Click (Light Bulb) next to the **Taper** modifier to toggle the taper off and then on again and note the effect on the object. Leave it on.

Figure 1–50

9. In the Modifier Stack, select the **Extrude** modifier. In the Warning dialog box, click Hold/Yes to continue.

You can adjust parameters at any level of the Modifier Stack. To change the parameter, enter the value in the Amount edit box or use the spinners.

10. The **Extrude** parameters are displayed in the rollouts. Note that the *Amount* displays the height of the shaft. Change it to **440.0** (as shown in Figure 1–51), and press <Enter>. The column shaft is extended and touches the top. The modifiers above the extrude are automatically reapplied to the object with its new height.

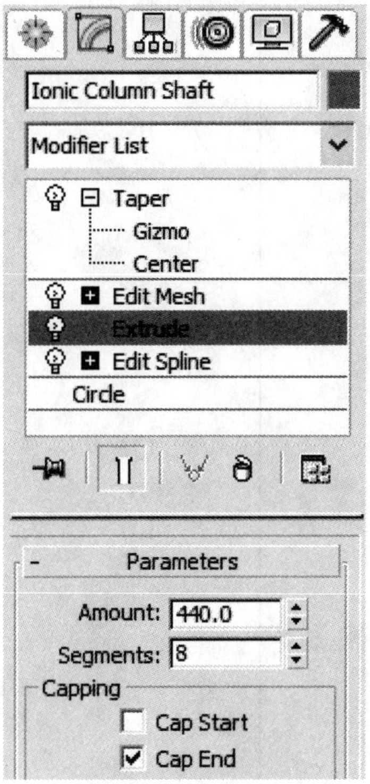

Figure 1–51

*Click (Save File) in the Quick Access Toolbar or expand and select **Save**, to save the file by overwriting the existing file. If you are saving an unnamed file for the first time, these options work as **Save As**.*

11. Expand and select **Save As** and save your work as **MyInterface.max**.
    - When you save a file, verify that it is being saved to your *Class Files* folder, in the *scenes* subfolder.

Practice 1b Autodesk 3ds Max Design Quickstart

Learning Objectives

- Create primitive objects using tools in the Command Panel.
- Apply basic animation to a primitive object.

Estimated time for completion: 15 minutes

In this practice, you will model and animate a teapot driving through a city made up of pyramids. This practice will introduce you to the Autodesk 3ds Max Design interface and workflow fundamentals. Many of the commands used in this practice have been discussed later in the training guide.

Many of you will probably never need to animate a teapot driving through a city of pyramids. This practice is designed to introduce you to interactive 3D modeling and animation as well as working with the interface.

Task 1 - Create Primitive Objects and Use Basic Animation.

If an unsaved scene is open, you might be required to save or discard any changes to the scene.

1. Expand  and select **Reset**. This closes the current file and starts a new file in one step. Click 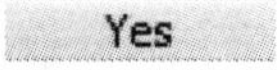 in the confirmation dialog box.
2. In the Command Panel, verify that the *Create* panel (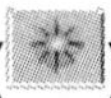) and  (Geometry) are selected (active by default).
3. Ensure that the *Standard Primitives* sub-category is displayed. This category has the 3D primitive objects, such as Box, Sphere, Cone, etc.

4. In the Object Type rollout, click Pyramid to activate it, as shown in Figure 1–52.

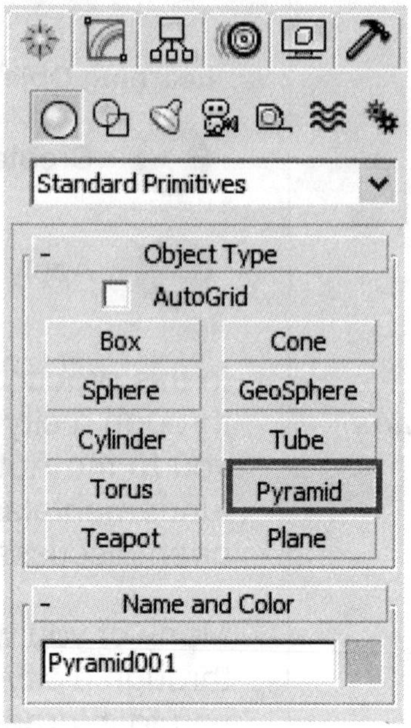

Figure 1–52

5. In the Perspective viewport (which is maximized), near the center of the grid, click and drag to create the base for a pyramid. Release the mouse button and continue to move the cursor up to set the height of the pyramid. Click to end the creation process, when your pyramid is displayed correctly, similar to that shown in Figure 1–53.

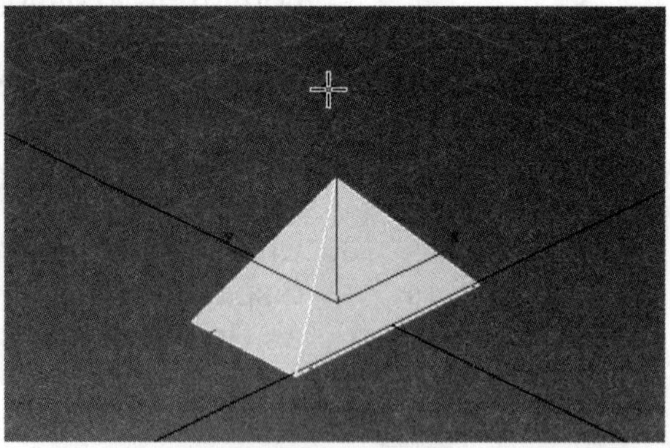

Figure 1–53

6. You can assign a color to the pyramid as needed, using the Name and Color rollout. Click the **Color** button to the right of the pyramid name and select a color in the Object Color dialog box. Verify that **Assign Random Colors** is selected in the dialog box. This enables you to create objects with different colors automatically. You do not need to change the color for the subsequent objects. Click OK.

7. In the Navigation toolbar in the lower right corner of the interface, click (Maximize Viewport). Note that the pyramid is displayed in four equal viewports with different viewing angles.

The transform tools are discussed in detail, later in the training guide.

8. You might need to move the pyramid to the upper left quadrant of the home grid. In the Main toolbar, click (Select and Move). In the Top view (upper left viewport), right-click to make it active with the object still selected.

   - Clicking in a viewport makes it active, but loses the selection of objects. To maintain the selection of objects, right-click to activate the viewport.

9. Click and hold the yellow square of the Transform gizmo, as shown in Figure 1–54. While holding the object, drag it to the new location. Leave the gizmo once the object is at the correct location.

   - The Transform gizmo is a tripod with three arrows. These arrows enable you to move the object in a constrained axis or plane of movement.

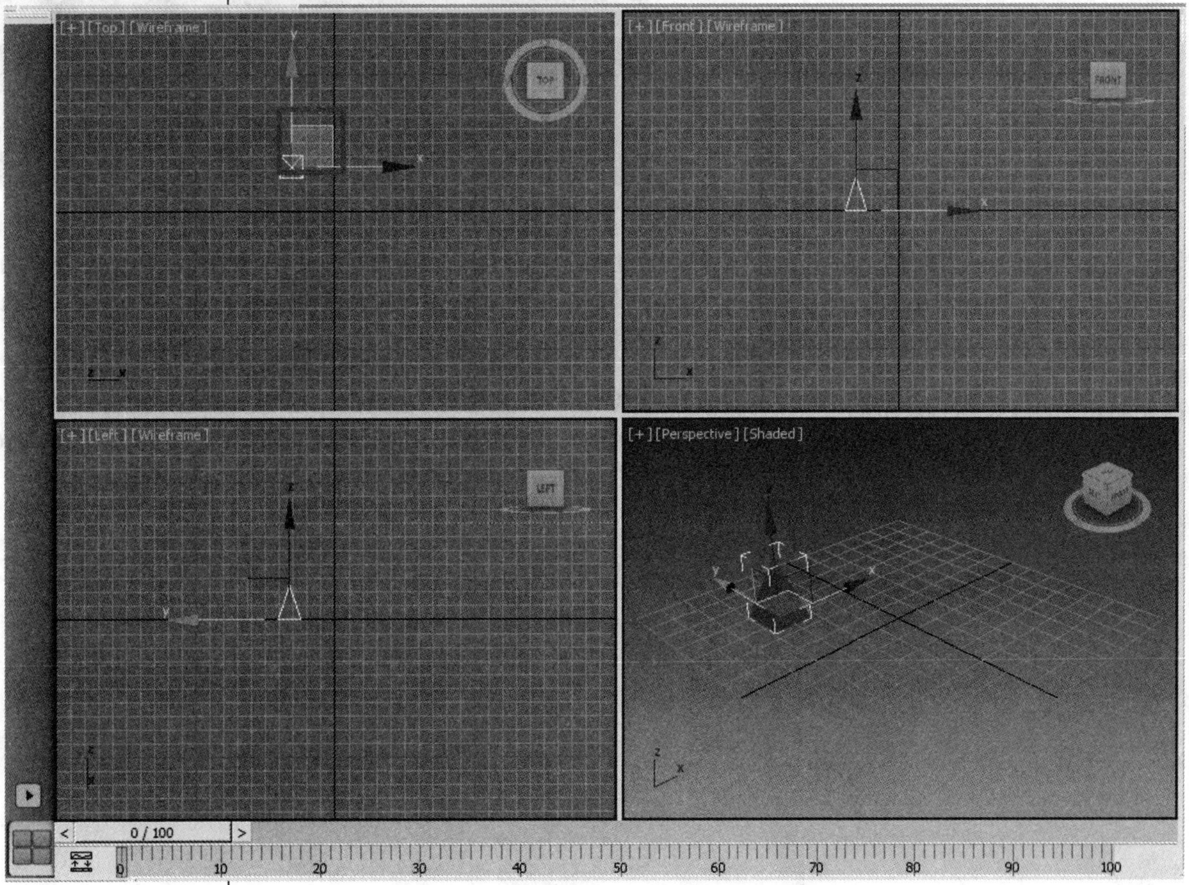

Figure 1–54

10. In the Object Type rollout, click Pyramid again. In the Top viewport (upper left quadrant), click and drag to create the base for another pyramid next to the first one. Release the mouse button and continue to move the cursor up to set the height of the pyramid. Because you are in the Top viewport, the height of the pyramid is not displayed. Note the other three viewports in which the height is displayed. Once the pyramid displays as required, click to complete the command.

You can create objects in any viewport, but the orientation of the objects depends on the viewport created. Note that their creation is also displayed interactively in other viewports.

11. Similarly, create a number of pyramids on the home grid. Create a row of pyramids in one direction and a few others to create a street corner in the pyramid city, as shown in Figure 1–55. Try to keep all of the pyramids in the grid visible in the Perspective viewport.

Figure 1–55

To display all of the pyramids in a viewport, use the middle mouse wheel to zoom in and out and press, hold, and drag it to pan.

12. Once the required number of pyramids have been created, right-click in empty space or press <Esc> to exit the **Pyramid** command.

13. Make the Perspective viewport active. You can click anywhere in empty space to clear a selected object and activate the viewport.

14. In the *Create* panel ( )> (Geometry), in the Object Type rollout, click Teapot to activate it.

15. In the lower left area of the Perspective viewport, click and drag to create a teapot, as shown in Figure 1–56.

Figure 1–56

Animation controls are discussed in detail later in the training guide.

16. The Animation controls are next to the Status Bar at the bottom of the screen. Click 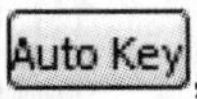

, as shown in Figure 1–57. The **AutoKey** button, time slider bar, and border around the active viewport (Perspective viewport) are highlighted in red.

Figure 1–57

17. Drag the time slider in the red slider bar until the frame indicator displays 30/100 (

), as shown in Figure 1–58.

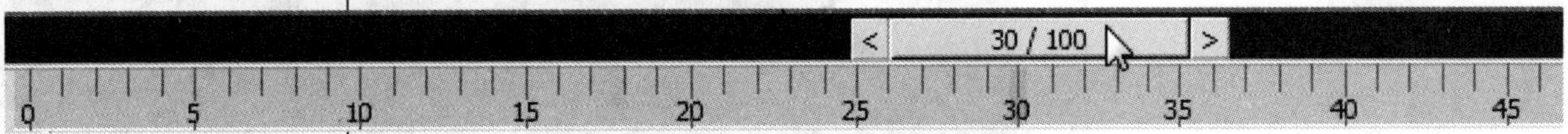

Figure 1–58

18. Click on the teapot, right-click and select **Move** in the transform **Quad** menu, as shown in Figure 1–59.

Alternatively, in the Main toolbar, click (Select and Move) after selecting your teapot.

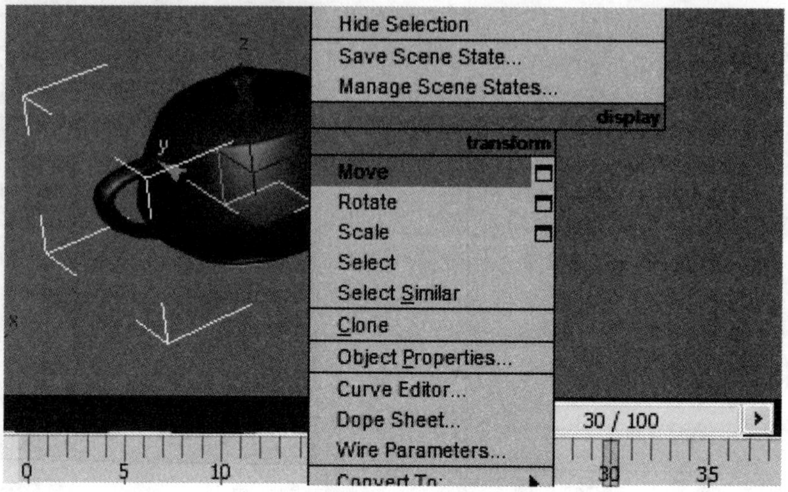

Figure 1–59

19. Move your cursor over the X axis of the teapot Move gizmo so that it displays in yellow. Hold and drag to move the teapot in the X direction, as shown in Figure 1–60. Move it to midway between the original position and the intersection of the home grid.

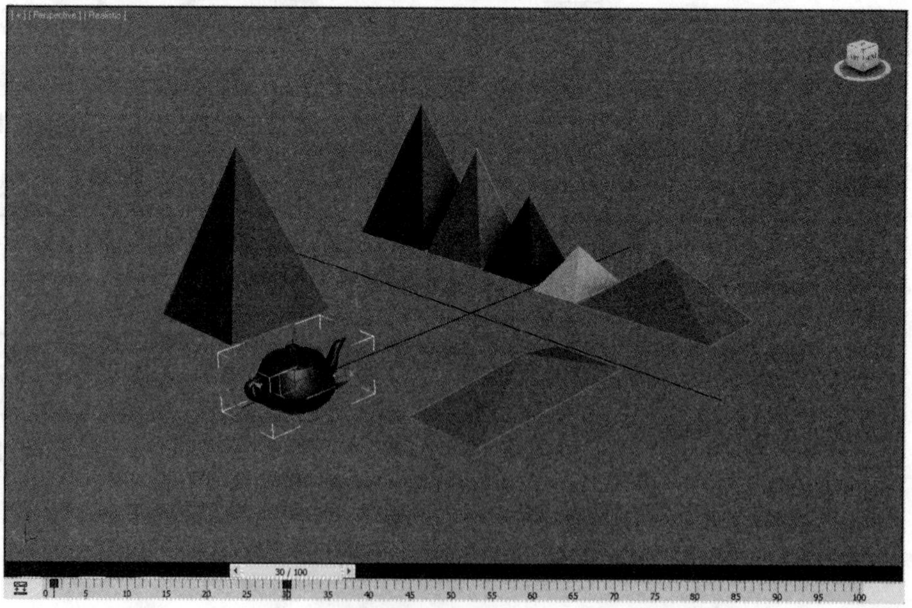

Figure 1–60

20. Move and drag the time slider again to read **60/100**.

21. Move the teapot in the X direction till it reaches the intersection of the horizontal street, as shown in Figure 1–61.

Figure 1–61

22. Move and drag the time slider to read **90/100**. Move the teapot in the Y direction (left) till it reaches the end of the horizontal street, as shown in Figure 1–62.

Figure 1–62

- The track bar below the time slider now has four red boxes indicating that the keyframes have been set at frames 0, 30, 60, and 90.

23. In the Animation Controls ( ) located near the bottom right of the screen, click (Play). The teapot is now animated in the viewport, moving through the pyramid city. Click (Stop Animation) to stop the animation.

24. You can add a rotation to the teapot. Drag the time slider to frame **60**. In all of the viewports, note that the teapot also moves to the grid intersection position. Right-click on the teapot and select **Rotate**. You can also click (Select and Rotate) in the Main toolbar.

25. The Rotation Transform gizmo is displayed on the teapot. Move your cursor over the horizontal axis; when it displays in yellow, rotate the teapot counter-clockwise. You see the rotation angle displayed in the viewport, as shown in Figure 1–63. The rotation angle is also displayed in the *Transform Type-in* fields in the Status Bar.

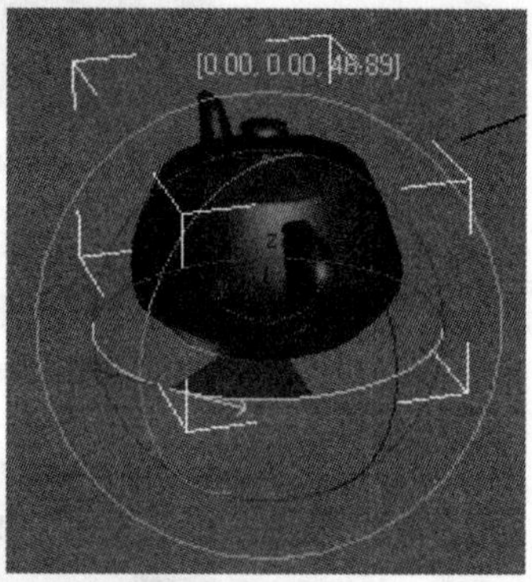

Figure 1–63

- At frame 60, the time slider now displays a red and green box indicating both rotation and position keys

26. Play the animation using (Play). Click (Stop) to stop the animation. You can also view the animation by dragging the time slider back and forth. This is called *scrubbing* the time slider.

27. To only rotate the teapot after frame 45, add a keyframe rotation of **0** between frames 45 and 60. Play the animation to view the changes.

28. Toggle off **Auto Key** mode by clicking the red Auto Key.

29. Click in empty space to clear the object selection.

30. Expand and select **Save As**.

31. Save your work as **MyPyramidCity.max**. Verify that it is being saved in your Class Files folder in the *scenes* folder.

- You can also open **Pyramidcity.max** from your Class Files folder to compare with a similar type file.

Chapter Review Questions

1. Which of the Autodesk 3ds Max Design interface components contains  (Selection Lock)?
   a. Modeling Ribbon
   b. Status Bar
   c. InfoCenter
   d. Quick Access Toolbar
2. Which of the following tabs are part of the Modeling Ribbon? (Select all that apply.)
   a. Freeform
   b. Display
   c. Utilities
   d. Modeling
3. In the Configure User Paths dialog box, which tab stores the location of the files for open, save, export, etc.?
   a. *XRefs* tab
   b. *System* tab
   c. *External Files* tab
   d. *File I/O* tab
4. Which display driver is supported by Windows XP?
   a. Nitrous **Direct3D 11**
   b. Nitrous **Direct3D 9**
   c. Nitrous Software
5. Which of the following is not a **Stylized** menu option?
   a. **Color Pencil**
   b. **Graphite**
   c. **Shaded**
   d. **Pastel**

Command Summary

Button	Command	Location
	**Create panel**	■ **Command Panel**
	**Open**	■ **Quick Access Toolbar** ■ **Application Menu:** Open>Open
	**Project Folder**	■ **Quick Access Toolbar** ■ **Application Menu:** Manage
	Save As	■ **Application Menu:** Save As
	**Save File**	■ **Quick Access Toolbar** ■ **Application Menu:** Save

Chapter 2

Autodesk 3ds Max Design Configuration

In this chapter you learn to use the viewport navigation tools and set the layout and display settings of your viewports in the Viewport Configuration dialog box. You learn about the different object selections methods available in the software. You also learn to setup the units for a scene and how to set the layer and object properties.

This chapter contains the following topics:

- ✓**Viewport Navigation**
- ✓**Viewport Configuration**
- ✓**Object Selection Methods**
- ✓**Units Setup**
- ✓**Layer and Object Properties**

Certification

Topic:
✓UI/Object Management
Objectives:
✓Describe View configuration and ViewCube navigation

2.1 Viewport Navigation

Learning Objective

Understand the different navigation tools and how to use them to move around in a scene.

Navigation tools are used to change the point of view in viewports. Perspective, User, and Orthographic views (non-camera views such as Top, Front, etc.) share common viewport controls. These controls are available in the lower right corner of the interface. Many of the buttons are organized into flyouts, indicated by the arrow symbol in the lower right corner. To expand the flyout, hold down the required button. The navigation tools are different in the non-camera and camera views.

Viewport Navigation Toolbar

The navigation tools are shown in Figure 2–1.

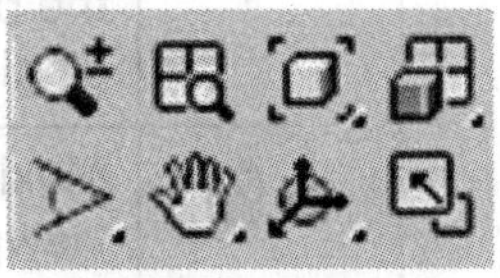

Figure 2–1

Zooming with the mouse wheel in a perspective view might not work in some scenes, due to roundoff issues. If you are unable to zoom in or out, click  *(Zoom Extents) and click*  *(Zoom) instead of the mouse wheel.*

	When this tool is active, click, hold, and drag the cursor to zoom in or out of the active viewport.
	Activate and then click and drag to zoom in or out simultaneously in all viewports.
	Zooms to the extents of all visible objects in the active viewport.
	Zoom to the extents of selected objects only in the active viewport.
	Zoom to the extents of all visible objects in all viewports.
	Zoom to the extents of selected objects only in all viewports.
	Zoom Region (zoom window) in the active viewport.
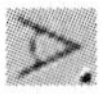	Change the Field of View of the active viewport. This is a flyout option in Zoom Region, available only in Perspective or camera view. It adjusts the perspective of the view, similar to changing the focal length of a camera. Even small changes to the Field of View setting can cause large distortions. To reset, enter a default field of view value of **45 degrees** in the Viewport Configuration dialog box.

New in 2014

	Pan View. Hold down in a viewport and drag to pan your objects. You can also hold and drag the middle mouse wheel to pan.
	2D Pan Zoom mode. A flyout option in Pan View, available in Perspective and Camera views only. It enables you to zoom/pan on objects in a viewport that are not located in the rendering frame. Therefore, in the camera view, the camera remains unchanged when you are panning and zooming in the Camera viewport. It is not available for Orthographic viewport.
	Change to Walkthrough mode. A flyout option in Pan View, available in Perspective and Camera views only. Click and hold while moving the cursor to change where you are looking. Use the arrow keys to walk forward, back, and to the side. Move up or down by pressing <Shift>+<Up> or <Down>. To speed up a movement hold down <]> (right bracket) while moving, and slow down movement by pressing <[> (left bracket).
	Orbit around a view. **Orbit Selected** and **Orbit SubObject** options are available in the flyout. Enables you to rotate the view by clicking and dragging inside or outside a trackball. Dragging inside the trackball causes the view to rotate around the scene, while dragging outside causes the view to twist in place. Clicking and dragging on the boxes that display along the trackball constrains the rotation to a single axis.
	Maximize Viewport toggles between the display of multiple viewports and the display of a single maximized viewport. You can also toggle between the multiple viewport display and a single maximized viewport by pressing <Alt>+<W>.

New in 2014

Hint: Switching Maximized Viewports

When you maximize a single viewport from a multi-viewport layout, you can switch to other viewports while in the current maximized viewport display. In the maximized viewport display, hold down <Win> (the Windows logo key, which might also be <Start>) and then press <Shift> (do not hold down <Shift>). An overlay opens displaying all of the available viewports in the layout, as shown in Figure 2–2. Holding down <Win>, press <Shift> again. The next viewport option highlights. Press <Shift> repeatedly, to highlight the next viewport. Release <Win> to maximizes the highlighted viewport.

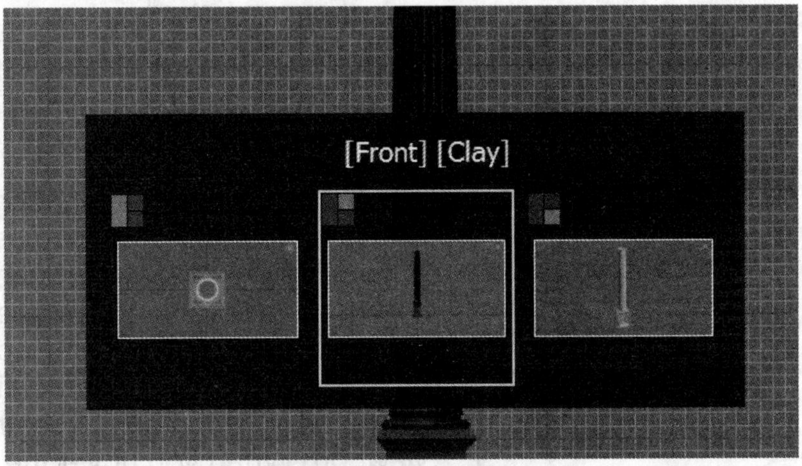

Figure 2–2

Camera objects are used to set up and/or animate a view for rendering. Normally cameras show a perspective view, but they can be set to show a User or Orthographic view if needed.

Viewport Navigation Toolbar (Camera Viewport)

Camera viewports show what is visible to the camera object based on its Field of View. Similar to other viewports, camera viewports can be directly navigated, but some of the controls are slightly different. The navigation tools in Camera view are shown in Figure 2–3.

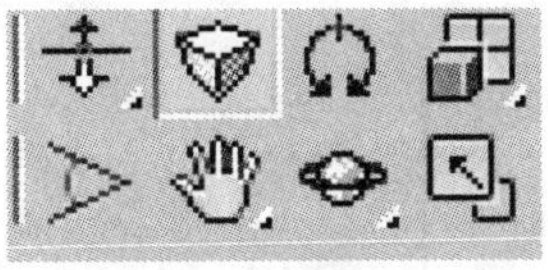

Figure 2–3

Note: Most of these controls actually move the camera or target object.

Navigation Buttons Unique to Camera Views

	**Dolly Camera** is similar to the **Zoom** button. The flyout contains options to dolly (move) the camera, the target, or both along the camera's directional axis.
	**Perspective** is a combination of **Field of View** and **Dolly** that attempts to maintain the same scene composition while changing the camera's Field of View.
	**Roll Camera** rotates a camera along the axis of its view.
	**Orbit Camera** rotates a camera around the target position similar to **Orbit**. The flyout option (**Pan Camera**) rotates the target around the camera instead.
	**Truck Camera** is similar to Pan when used in a Camera view.

Viewport Navigation using ViewCube

The ViewCube navigation technology is standard to many Autodesk products. You can use ViewCube functionality to orient a model face in a viewport parallel to the screen. By default, the ViewCube, as shown in Figure 2–4, displays in the top right corner of each viewport. Selecting any of the ViewCube faces, causes the viewport to immediately swing around to that view. Click and drag the compass ring at the bottom to rotate the viewport. When you hover the cursor over the ViewCube, the **Home** icon becomes visible near the top left corner. Clicking the **Home** icon resets the viewport. You can also select the ViewCube and drag the mouse to quickly rotate the Viewport.

Figure 2–4

Right-clicking on the ViewCube provides additional options that enable you to set the current view as Home, Orthographic, Configure etc. Selecting the **Configure** option, opens the Viewport Configuration dialog box in the *ViewCube* tab. Alternatively, use the **Configure** option in the Viewport label and then select the *ViewCube* tab. The *ViewCube* tab includes options to show or hide the ViewCube, control its size and display, and control what happens when dragging on the ViewCube. You can also customize your Quad menu by adding Toggle ViewCube Visibility for quick access to hide this navigation device. ViewCube is a navigation tool that is used in most other Autodesk programs including the Autodesk Revit software.

Viewport Navigation using SteeringWheel

A second tool for navigation is the SteeringWheel, as shown in Figure 2–5. It is attached to your cursor and provides instant access to zoom/pan, orbit, etc. The **Rewind** feature is unique to this tool and provides a thumbnail of all of your previous views. It also enables you to visually select any of them to return to that view. Press <Shift>+<W> to toggle the SteeringWheel on and off. You can also press <Esc> to hide its display.

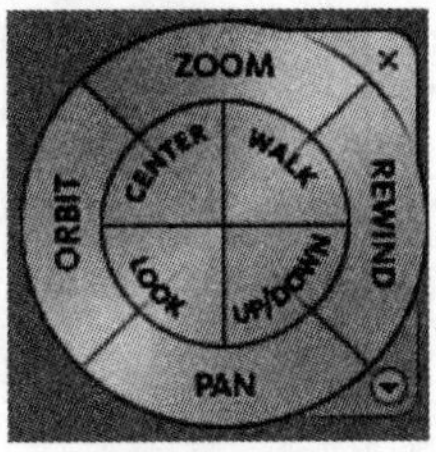

Figure 2–5

Both the SteeringWheel and ViewCube tools can be controlled with options in the **Views** pull-down menu.

2.2 Viewport Configuration

Certification

Topic:

✓UI/Object Management

Objectives:

✓Describe View configuration and ViewCube navigation

Learning Objective

- Understand the use of various tabs in the Viewport Configuration dialog box.

The layout and display settings of your viewports can be set through the Viewport Configuration dialog box. In the Viewport label, click [+] (General label) to display the label menu and select **Configure Viewports**, as shown in Figure 2–6, or select the **Visual Style** label and select **Configure**. Alternatively, select **Views>Viewport Configuration**.

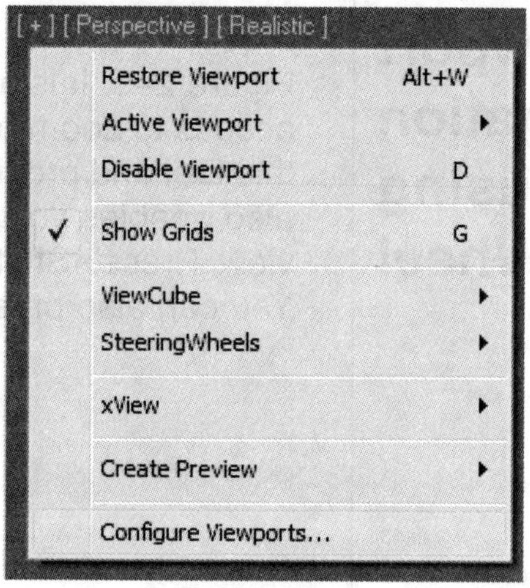

Figure 2–6

The Viewport Configuration dialog box (*Visual Style & Appearance* tab) opens.

If you have selected one of the legacy display drivers (Direct 3D or OpenGL), the Rendering Method tab is displayed instead of the Visual Style & Appearance tab.

Some of the tabs in the Viewport Configuration dialog box are as follows:

- The remaining tabs are discussed throughout the training guide when required.

Visual Style & Appearance tab

This tab (shown in Figure 2–7), contains the viewport's Visual Style options, Lighting and Shadows options, including the intensity of shadows and Ambient Occlusion, Field of View angle for the perspective user view, and the selection groups. This dialog box also enables you to set the rendering method for the viewports. This tab is only available when one of the Nitrous viewport drivers is selected.

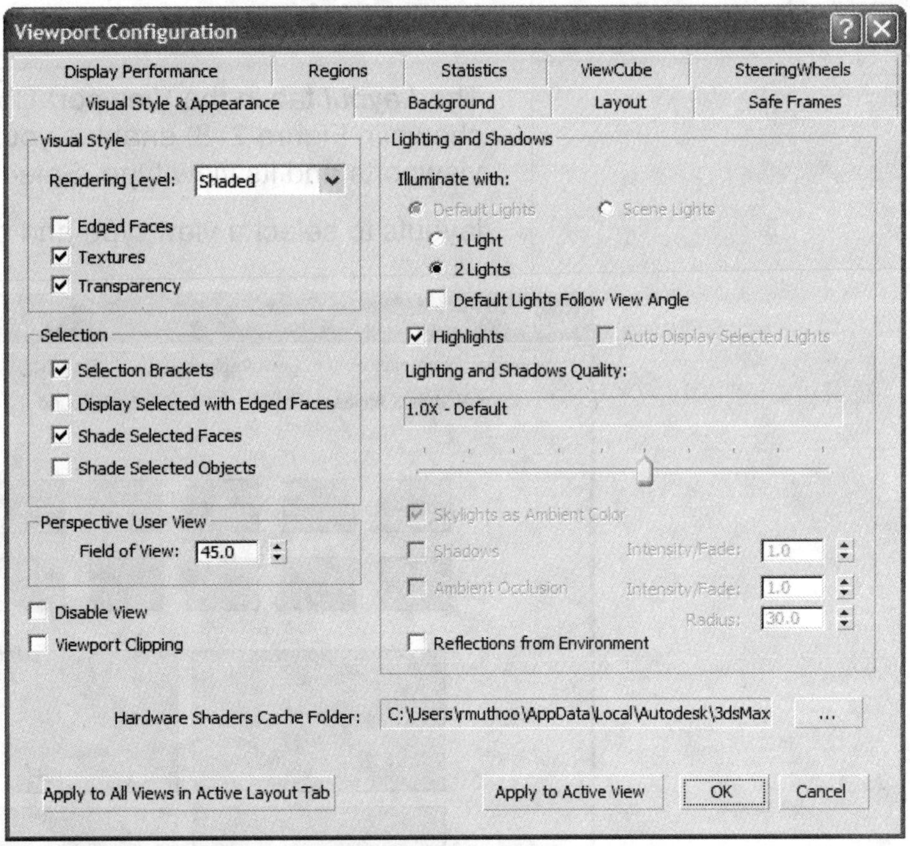

Figure 2–7

- In the *Lighting and Shadow* area, the default lights are used to illuminate the scene. The default lighting provides even illumination and you can select **1 Light** (default) or **2 Lights**.
- In the *Lighting and Shadow* area, the **Default Lights Follow View Angle** option tracks changes to the position of the viewport using two default lights.
- The **Skylights as Ambient Color** option is available when your Visual Style is set to **Realistic**. This option causes the skylights to emit ambient color and not cast shadows. This option helps improve the interior scenes display.
- The **Shadows** options renders the scene with shadows and the **Ambient Occlusion** helps improve the display of shadows.

Layout tab

The *Layout* tab in the Viewport Configuration dialog box, as shown in Figure 2–8, enables you to set the size and shape of viewports and its view type. Select one of the preset viewport layouts to select a view type and click OK.

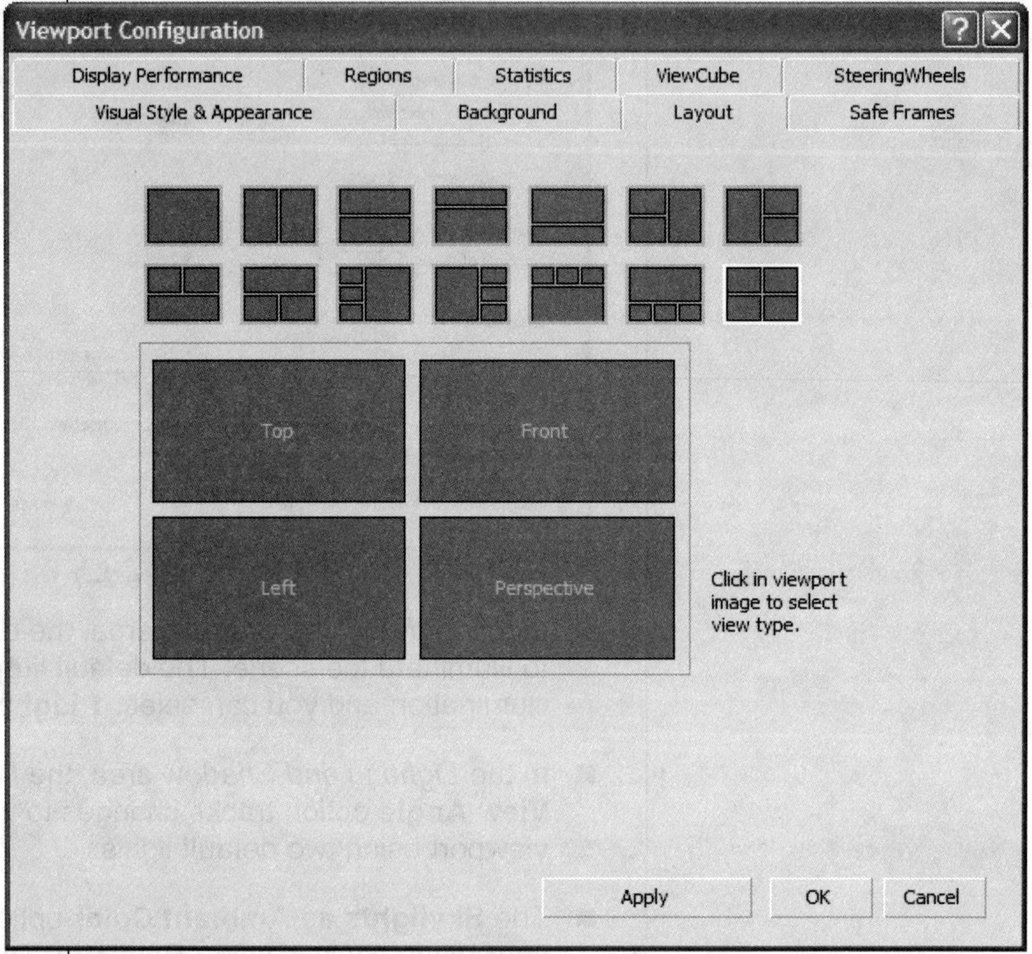

Figure 2–8

A Viewport Layouts tab bar is located on the left side of the interface display. This enables you to set up multiple viewport layouts and switch between them by selecting the saved tab. This is an easy and efficient method of setting up multiple viewports and then displaying the one with which you want to work. All of the added viewports are saved with the scene file.

SteeringWheels tab

The *SteeringWheels* tab (as shown in Figure 2–9 enables you control the properties of the Steering Wheel. The Steering wheels can be displayed as Big or Mini Wheels and you can set their respective sizes and opacity. You can control whether you want to display the tool tips and tool messages. You can also set the options for tools, such as the **Zoom** tool and the **Orbit** tool.

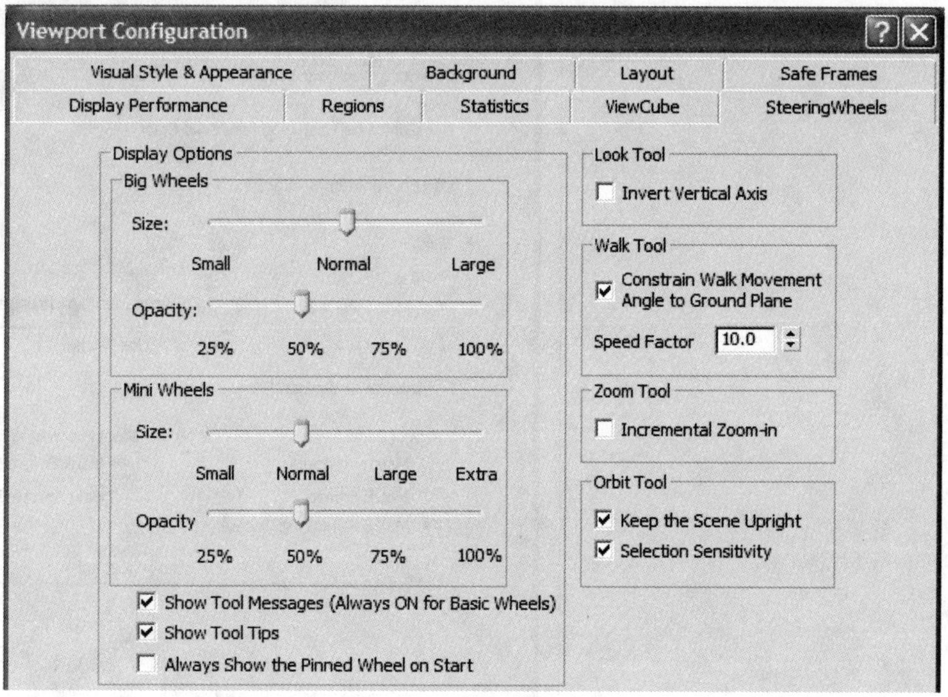

Figure 2–9

ViewCube tab

Similar to the *SteeringWheels* tab, the *ViewCube* tab has options for controlling the display of the ViewCube. You can control the size of the ViewCube, what the ViewCube displays when selected, and the position of the compass.

Statistics tab

The *Statistics* tab enables you to customize the display of various statistics for the selected geometry or the complete scene. You can display the number of polygons in a scene, number of triangular faces, number of edges, number of vertices, etc., in the viewports The statistics can be displayed by selecting the **General Viewport label menu>xView>Show Statistics** or pressing <7>.

Background tab

The *Background* tab (as shown in Figure 2–10), enables you to set an image, environment map, or animation as the background of your active viewport or all viewports.

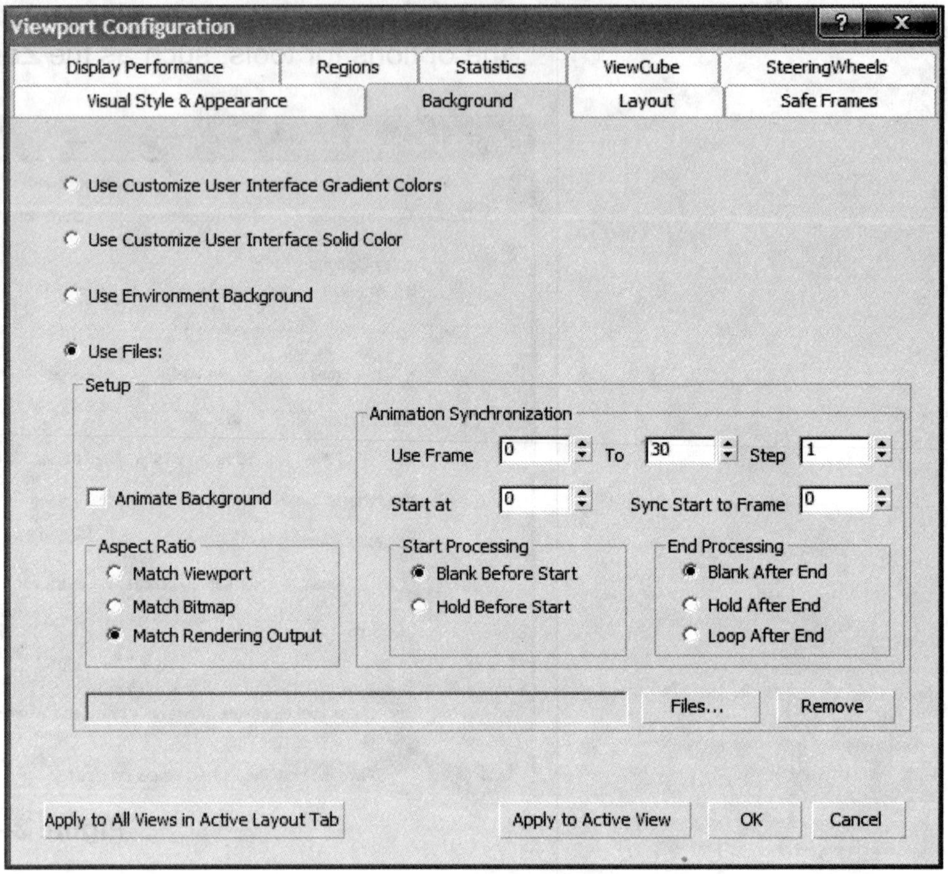

Figure 2–10

Practice 2a Viewport Configuration and Navigation

Learning Objectives

- Change the configuration of the viewport.
- Move around a scene using different navigation tools.

Estimated time for completion: 5 minutes

1. In the Quick Access Toolbar, click (Open File) or click >**Open**>**Open**, to open the Open File dialog box. If you were working in the software, you might be prompted to save or discard any changes to the scene.
   - In the Open file dialog box, note that the *C:\Autodesk 3ds Max Design Fundamentals Class Files\scenes* folder is set, because you have already set the Project Folder. If you did not set the path to your *Class Files* folder, return to the **Introduction to Autodesk 3ds Max Design** chapter and complete Task 1 to Task 3 of the **Organizing Folders and Working with the Interface** practice. In it you can also set your *Class Files\Maps* and xref as your User Path.

If a dialog box opens prompting you about a Mismatch, click OK to accept the default values.

2. In the Open File dialog box, select **Navigation.max** and click Open.
   - The file opens the objects in four equal sized viewports. Along the left side of the viewports, in the Viewport Layouts tab bar, note that the file has been saved with two viewport layouts.

Alternatively, select the required viewport layout in the Viewport Configuration dialog box>Layout tab.

3. To create another layout, in the Viewport Layouts tab bar, click [icon] to expand the *Standard Viewport Layouts* panel. Select the layout shown in Figure 2–11.

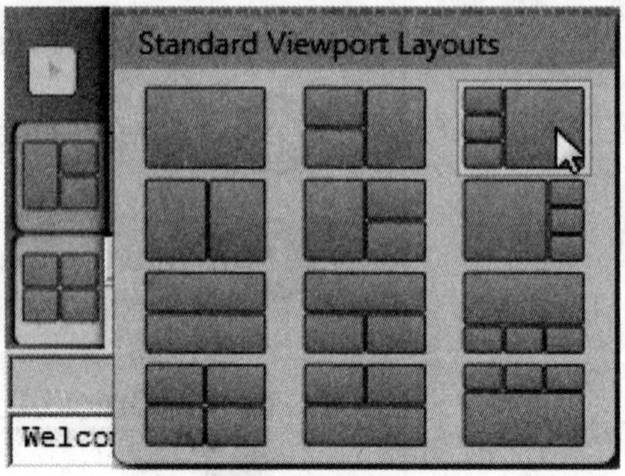

Figure 2–11

- The pillar objects display in the 3 X 1 viewport layout and another layout tab is added to the Layouts tab bar.

4. Note that the Top viewport is the active viewport (it displays a yellow border). In the Navigation toolbar, note the available navigation tools for the Orthographic view, as shown in Figure 2–12.

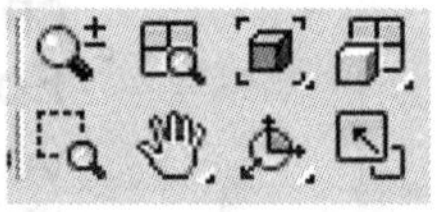

Figure 2–12

5. The complete objects are not displayed in the viewports. Click [icon] (Zoom Extents All) to zoom to the extents of all of the objects in all of the viewports.

6. In the Front viewport, select the base object, expand the Zoom Extents flyout, and click [icon] (Zoom Extents All Selected). You have zoomed to the extents of that object rather than the extents of the entire scene. This also works when multiple objects are selected.

7. With the object selected, click [icon] (Zoom Extents All). It zooms to the extents of all of the objects in all of the viewports.

8. Right-click in empty space in the Left viewport. Note that the Left viewport becomes active and the base object remains selected.

9. Click in empty space in the Top viewport to make it active and clear the selection.

10. Hover the cursor over the left edge of the Perspective viewport. The cursor displays as a two-sided arrow. Click and drag the arrow to resize the viewports, as shown in Figure 2–13.

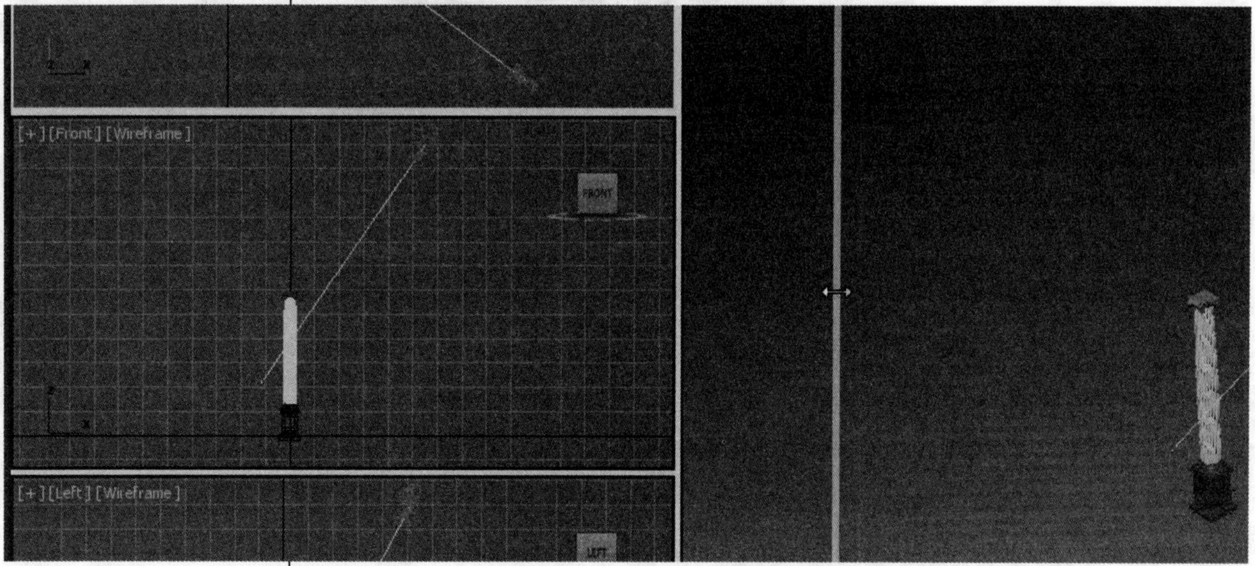

Figure 2–13

11. Click in the Perspective view to make it active. In the navigation tools, note that (Field-of-View) has been added.

12. With the Perspective view still active, in the Viewport navigation tools, click (Maximize Viewport Toggle) to maximize the viewport. Select the toggle again to return to the four viewport arrangement. Alternatively, press <Alt>+<W> to toggle between the maximized single viewport and multiple viewports. Leave the Perspective viewport maximized.

13. Hold down <Win> and press <Shift>. An overlay displays all of the available viewports in the layout, as shown in Figure 2–14. Hold down <Win> and press <Shift> repeatedly to cycle through all of the viewports. When [Left] [Wireframe] is highlighted (as shown in Figure 2–14), release <Win> to maximize the viewport.

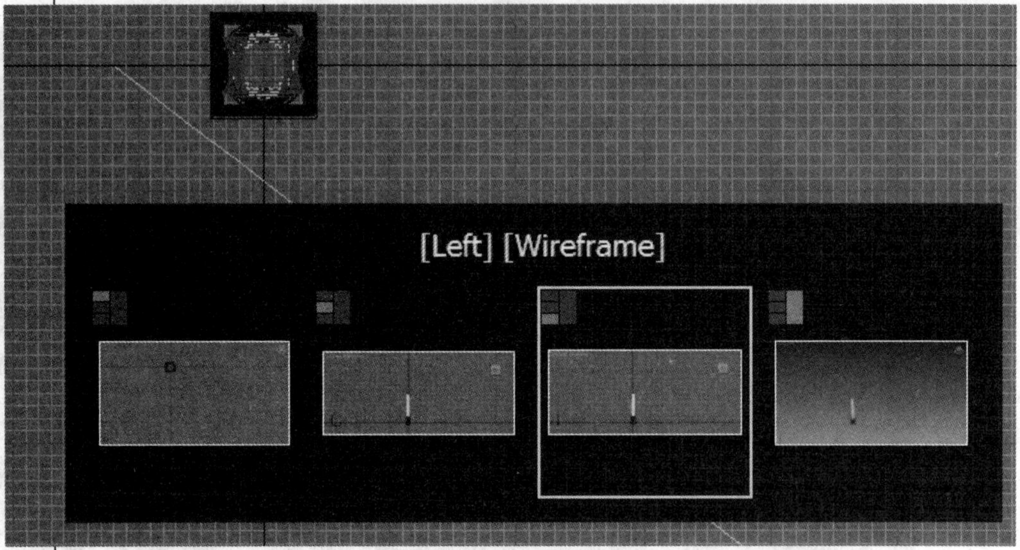

Figure 2–14

14. Select the **[Left]** Point of View label. In the label menu, select **Cameras>SE Camera**, as shown in Figure 2–15, to display the camera view.

Figure 2–15

15. Note that the navigation tools are different in a camera viewport, as shown in Figure 2–16.

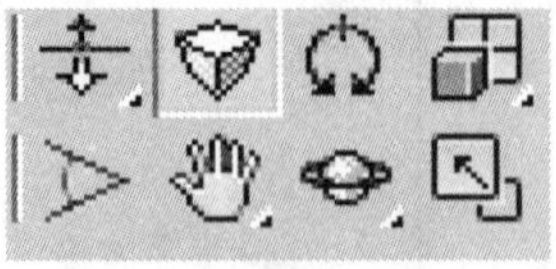

Figure 2–16

16. Click  (Maximize Viewport Toggle) to toggle to the four viewport display.

17. Click (Zoom Extents All). Note that the SE Camera (lower left viewport) does not change because the non-camera navigation tools do not affect the camera views.

18. Click in the Perspective view to make it active and note how the navigation tools change.

19. Click in the SE Camera viewport to make it active.

20. Click (Orbit Camera) and use it in the SE Camera viewport to orbit the camera. In the other viewports, note that the camera object is moving simultaneously as the pillar object moves in the camera viewport.

21. Experiment with changing the camera position using (Roll Camera) and (Dolly Camera).

You can use the mouse wheel to zoom in and out in a viewport and hold down and drag the middle mouse button to pan.

22. In the Perspective viewport, practice navigating with the **Zoom**, **Zoom Selected**, **Orbit**, and **Pan View** options.

23. Close the file without saving.

Certification

Topic:

✓*UI/Object Management*

Objectives:

✓*Identify Selection Regions and methods*

2.3 Object Selection Methods

Learning Objective

Understand how to select objects using the object selection tools.

Working with modifiers and other functions requires you to be able to select objects accurately. Below is a list of some of the more common ways to make selections. All of these tools are located in the Main toolbar as shown in Figure 2–17.

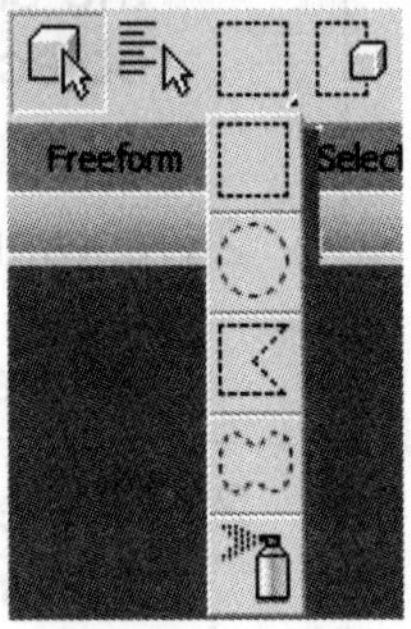

Figure 2–17

(Select Object) enables you to select objects and enables you to drag selection regions inside your viewports depending on the selected Region selection type.

- You can add to your current selection if you select or drag a region while holding down <Ctrl>. You can remove items from the selection with <Alt>.
- You can also select with the **Move**, **Rotate**, and **Scale** tools.

  It is recommended that new users work with (Select Object) as much as possible, to avoid accidentally moving, rotating, or scaling objects.
- You can also access **Select** in the **Quad** menu.
- If one of the **Transform** tools is active, you can click (Select Object) by pressing <Q>. If (Select Object) is already active, press <Q> repeatedly to cycle through the various Region selection types.

(Select by Name) provides access to the Select From Scene dialog box to enable you to select one or more objects. This is often helpful in complex scenes where it might be difficult to select a particular object from the screen. This feature supports Autodesk® Revit® Families as a category in the tool, enabling you to easily sort and select by Autodesk Revit category, Autodesk Revit Family, and Autodesk Revit Type as shown in Figure 2–18.

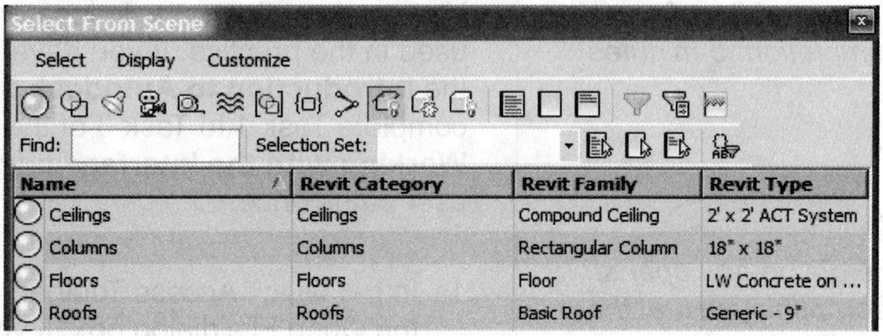

Figure 2–18

Edit Menu: The **Edit** pull-down menu also has a number of important selection options including **Select All**, **Select None**, **Select Invert**, **Select Similar**, **Select Instances**, and **Select By** (e.g., **Color**). These options also work in Sub-object mode.

(Rectangular Selection Region) (in the Main toolbar) enables you to draw the shape of your selection region. The default is a rectangular region. There are also flyout options for **Lasso**, **Paint**, **Circular**, and **Fence** selections, as shown in Figure 2–17. Paint selection is particularly useful when you have thousands of objects or vertices that need selecting. Instead of repetitive clicking, you can sweep the cursor over a large quantity of them.

/ (Window/Crossing) enables you to define either the *Window Selection Region* (only objects completely within the region are selected), or *Crossing Region* (objects within or crossing the boundary are selected) as the selection toggle.

(Layer Manager) (in the Main toolbar) lists and select objects directly from the Layer Manager.

(Edit Named Selection Sets) (in the Main toolbar) enables you to create and edit named selection sets. Named Selection Sets are different than layers, in that an object can be in many different named selections. An object can only be on one layer, making Named Selection Sets more flexible.

Practice 2b Selection Methods

Learning Objectives

- Select objects using the **Window** and **Crossing** selection tools.
- Select objects using the **Select by Name** selection tool.

Estimated time for completion: 5 minutes

You must set the paths to locate the External files and Xrefs used in the practice. If you have not done this already, return to the **Introduction to Autodesk 3ds Max Design** chapter and complete Task 1 to Task 3 of the **Organizing Folders and Working with the Interface** practice. You only have to set the user paths once.

If a dialog box opens, prompting you that there is a File Load: Mismatch, click OK *to accept the default values.*

1. In the Quick Access Toolbar, click (Open File) to open the Open File dialog box. If you were working in the software, you might be prompted to save or discard any changes to the scene. Open **Selection Methods.max** from your *Class Files* folder.
2. Click in the Perspective viewport to make it active.
3. Maximize the Perspective viewport to fill your screen by clicking (Maximize Viewport Toggle) or by pressing <Alt>+<W>.

*Depending on how you rotate the viewing angle, it might be difficult to select a specific object. Setting the viewport shading to **Wireframe** can make it easier to select.*

4. Select one of the parking lot light poles in the viewport.
5. Expand Edit and select **Select None** or click in empty space to clear your selection.
6. In the Main toolbar, verify that the Window/Crossing toggle is set to (Crossing) and the Selection Region is set to (Rectangular). Starting in a blank area, click and drag the cursor to create a rectangular crossing region around the light pole. The scene is complex and might need to select several other objects as well. (The Status Line at the bottom left of the screen displays the number of objects selected.)
7. Click in empty space to clear the selection.

8. Toggle the Selection/Crossing toggle from (Crossing) to (Window). Drag the selection region around light pole.

9. In the Status Line, verify that you have fewer objects selected.

10. Click (Select by Name) to open the Select From Scene dialog box.

11. The objects listed depend on the selection tools that are toggled on in the toolbar in the dialog box. In the toolbar, click (Display None) to clear any selection group, as shown in Figure 2–19.

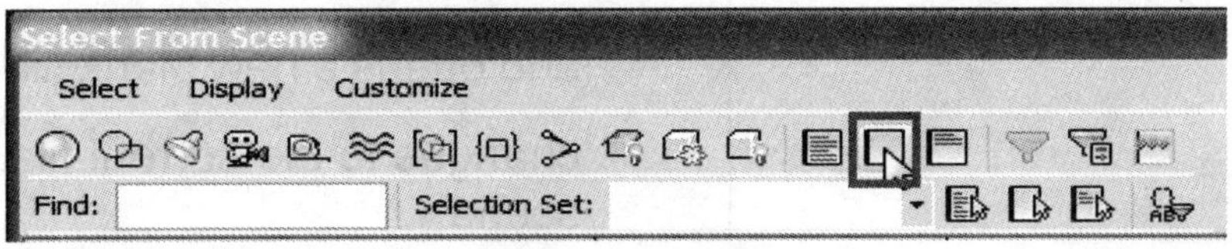

Figure 2–19

12. In the toolbar, click (Display Geometry) to display all of the geometry objects in the scene. Note that some objects are highlighted with a dark gray band, indicating that they are selected in the viewport.

13. In the Select From Scene dialog box, click (Select None), as shown in Figure 2–20, to clear any previous selection.

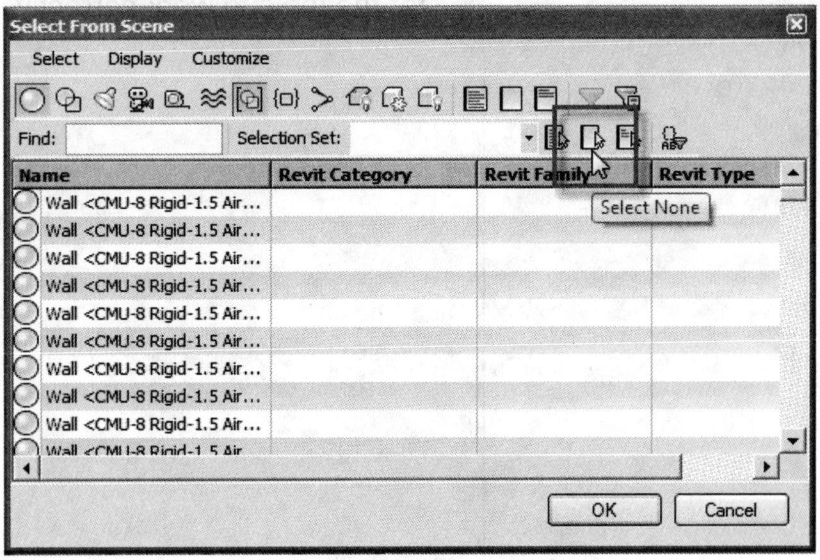

Figure 2–20

14. In the Select From Scene dialog box, click (Display None) and click (Display Shapes) as shown in Figure 2–21. This enables you to filter the number of items listed in the dialog box so that you can easily select the required items.

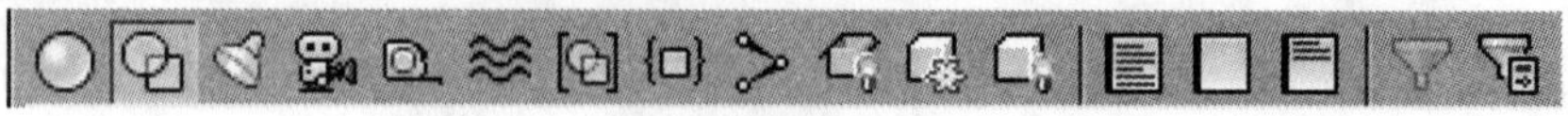

Figure 2–21

15. Select all of the **Layer:LIGHTPOLE_SINGLE** shapes. Click OK to close the dialog box. All of the Single light poles are selected.

16. Expand MXD and select **Reset**. This closes the current file and opens a new blank file. Click Don't Save for not saving changes to the current file. Click Yes to reset the scene.

Hint: Using the Select From Scene dialog box

In addition to clearing the display of various items to easily find and select an item, you can use the *Find* field in the Select From Scene dialog box. Enter the initial letters to automatically select objects.

In the Select From Scene dialog box, in the **Display** pull-down menu, verify that the Display options (**Display Children**, **Display Influences**, and **Display Dependants**) are all cleared for the tools to work correctly.

2.4 Units Setup

Learning Objective

Understand how to assign and change units in a scene.

Each scene file is based on a unit of measurement called the System Unit Scale. You can change and assign the units settings using the Units Setup dialog box. Select **Customize> Units Setup** to open the Units Setup dialog box, as shown in Figure 2–22. In the dialog box, click 

to open the System Unit Setup dialog box, as shown in Figure 2–22.

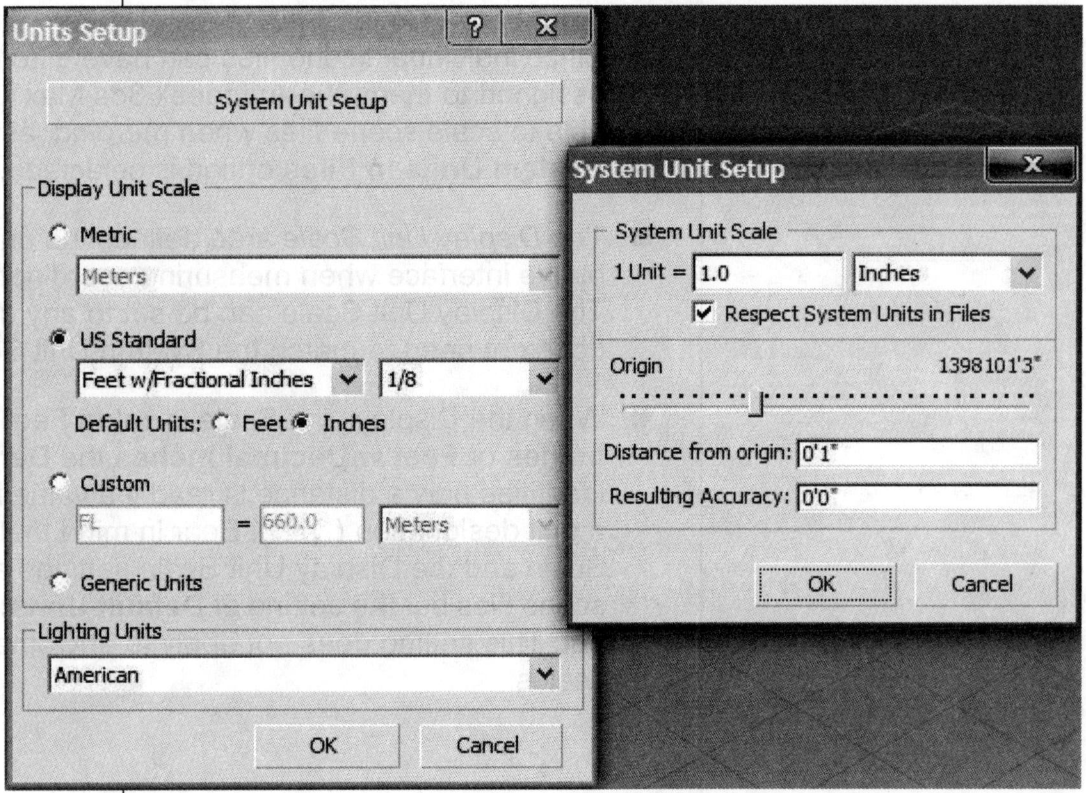

Figure 2–22

- For efficient viewport rendering, the Autodesk 3ds Max Design software does not make calculations to the same level of accuracy as many CAD programs. As a result, very large and very small numerical values might incur round off errors, as displayed by the slider bar in the System Unit Setup dialog box. These round off errors could result in display and navigational issues. These become problematic when the geometry is located further away from the center of the virtual universe.

- The Autodesk 3ds Max Design Help recommends that you center scene geometry close to the origin and not have any significant details smaller than one system unit. (As an example, a unit scale of meters might not be appropriate for architectural work. Instead you might consider using a **System Unit Scale** of inches, millimeters, or centimeters.) Generally do not make changes to the System Unit Scale unless there is a viewport problem due to very small or large models.

- You should assign the unit scale before adding any geometry to the scene. Changing the System Unit Scale later does not rescale the objects already present. (To rescale objects, use the **Rescale World Units** utility in the *Utilities* panel () in the Command Panel.)

- Since individual scene files can have different Unit Scales assigned to them, the Autodesk 3ds Max Design software is able to scale scene files when merging, as long the **Respect System Units in Files** option is selected.

- The *Display Unit Scale* area defines the units to be displayed by the interface when measuring coordinates and distances. The Display Unit Scale can be set to any unit you need and does not need to match the System Unit Scale.

- When the Display Unit Scale is set to **Feet w/Fractional Inches** or **Feet w/Decimal Inches** the **Default Units** option identifies how a distance is read if a value is entered without a unit designation (' or "). Bear in mind that the System Unit Scale and the Display Unit Scale settings are retained with scene files but the setting of **Default Units: Feet or Inches** is not. This setting does not apply to any other display unit scales.

- If the current System Unit Scale does not match the System Unit Scale of a file that is opened, you are warned with the Units Mismatch dialog box, as shown in Figure 2–23. It is recommended to select **Adopt the File's Unit Scale**, unless you specifically want to change the Unit Scale of the file being opened. When Adopt the File's Unit Scale is selected, your System Unit Scale is changed to match the incoming files definition. This remains changed until you manually switch it back to its default. A **Reset** does not affect this.

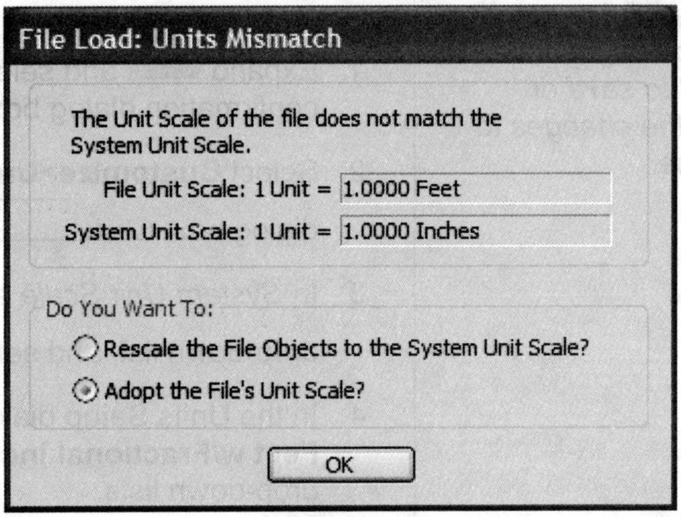

Figure 2–23

Practice 2c Working with Units Setup

Learning Objective

- Assign and set up units in a scene.

Estimated time for completion: 5 minutes

If an unsaved scene is open, you might be required to save or discard the changes to the scene.

In this practice you will setup units for the projects.

1. Expand and select **Reset**. Click Yes in the confirmation dialog box.
2. Select **Customize>Units Setup** to open the Units Setup dialog box. Click System Unit Setup.
3. In *System Unit Scale* area, set *1 Unit* = to **1.0**, expand the drop-down list, and select **Inches**. Click OK.
4. In the Units Setup dialog box, select **US Standard**. Select **Feet w/Fractional Inches** and **1/8** in the respective drop-down lists.
5. Set the *Default Units* to **Inches**, as shown in Figure 2–24.

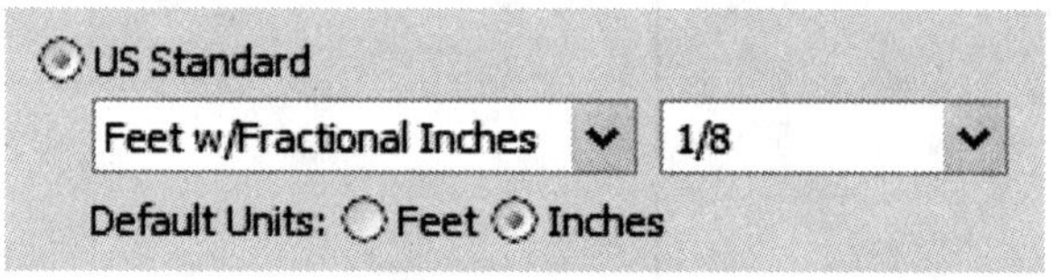

Figure 2–24

- Note that the **Display Unit Scale** and **System Unit Scale** can be different. For example, the Autodesk 3ds Max Design software can report distances as one unit (Display Unit) while the file geometry is stored in another unit (System Unit).

6. Set the *Lighting Units* to **American**.
7. Click OK to close the Units Setup dialog box.
8. Expand and select **Save As** to save your work as **MyUnits Setup.max**. Verify that it is being saved in your *Class Files*, in the *scenes* subfolder.

2.5 Layer and Object Properties

Learning Objectives

- Group similar objects together in a layer using the tools in the Layers toolbar.
- View and adjust layer properties using the Layer Manager.
- Modify the display settings of layers using the Layer Properties dialog box.
- Modify the properties of an object using the Object Properties dialog box.

Objects in the Autodesk 3ds Max Design software have a large number of properties. It can be convenient to group similar objects into layers to modify these objects' properties and control their visibility together.

- Autodesk 3ds Max Design layers function is similar to AutoCAD layers and have similar controls.
- Also when importing data from AutoCAD you have the option of maintaining original layer system from AutoCAD.

Layers Toolbar

By default, the Layers toolbar is not displayed in the Autodesk 3ds Max Design software. To display the Layers toolbar, right-click anywhere on the blank space in the Main toolbar, and select **Layers**. The Layers toolbar is displayed, as shown in Figure 2–25.

Figure 2–25

- In the Layers toolbar, you can set a layer current by selecting it from the drop-down list.
- The layer drop-down list displays the current layer and not the layer of the currently selected object (unlike the AutoCAD Layers list).

- The various tools in the toolbar are:

	Opens the Layer Manager.
	Creates a new layer.
	Adds selected objects to the current layer.
	Selects all objects in the current layer.
	Sets the current layer to the layer of a selected object.

Layer Manager

In the Main toolbar, click (Manage Layers) to open the Layer Manager, as shown in Figure 2–26. Alternatively, click (Manage Layers) in the Layers toolbar or select **Tools> Manage Layers**. It is a modeless dialog box that can remain open while you work in the Autodesk 3ds Max Design software.

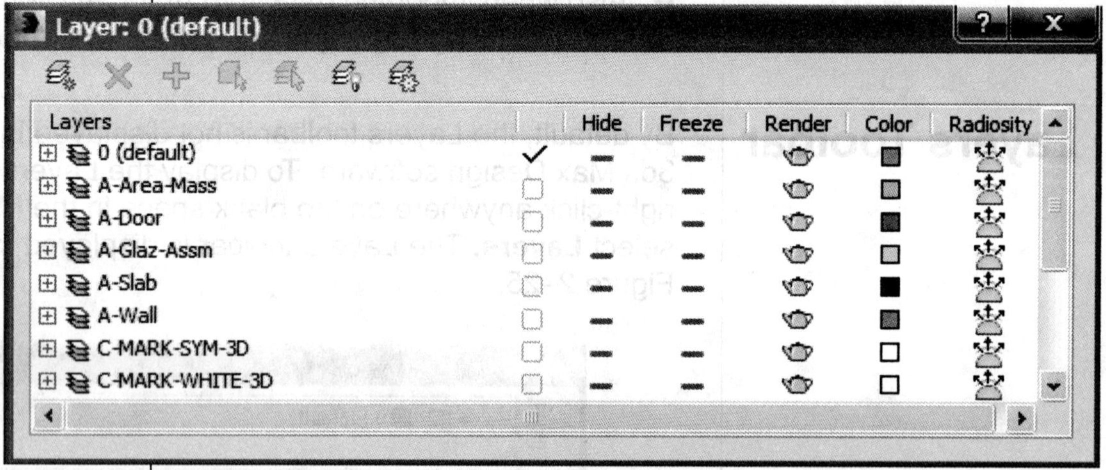

Figure 2–26

- In addition to the five column settings shown (*Hide*, *Freeze*, *Render*, *Color*, and *Radiosity*), a large number of other layer properties can be viewed and adjusted by right-clicking on the name of the layer and selecting **Layer Properties** or by clicking before each layer. Layer properties apply to all objects on that layer that do not have overrides set in their Object Properties.

- You can expand a layer by clicking ⊞ to view all of the objects on that layer, as shown in Figure 2–27. Right-clicking on an object in the list enables you to select and/or change its **Object Properties**.

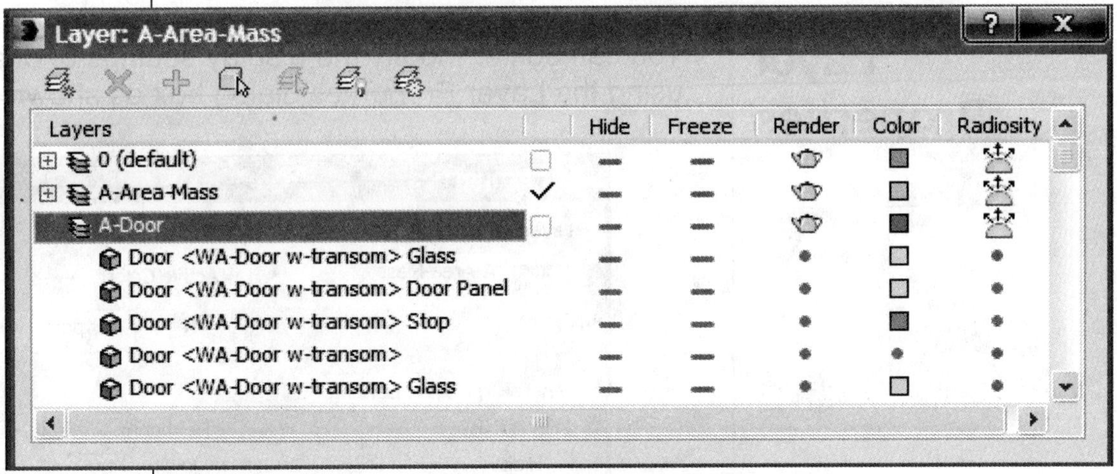

Figure 2–27

- Hiding a layer (or individual object) makes those objects invisible in the viewports and in renderings.
- Freezing a layer (or individual object) leaves those objects visible but makes them not selectable. Frozen objects display gray in the viewports but render normally.
- If a layer (or individual object) has a horizontal bar (—) in the *Render* column, the layer is not displayed in rendered output.
- If a layer (or individual object) has a horizontal bar (—) in the *Radiosity* column, the layer is ignored in radiosity calculations.

Additional Tools in the Layer Manager

	Creates a new layer. Using this button in the Layer Manager automatically moves highlighted objects to a new layer.
	Deletes a highlighted layer (the layer must be empty and not current).
	Adds objects selected in the viewport to the highlighted layer.
	Selects objects in the scene that you have highlighted in the Layer Manager.
	Highlights layers of objects you have selected in the scene.

	Hides or Unhides all layers.
	Freezes or Thaws all layers.

Layer Properties

You can edit or modify the display settings of one or more layers using the Layer Properties dialog box as shown in Figure 2–28.

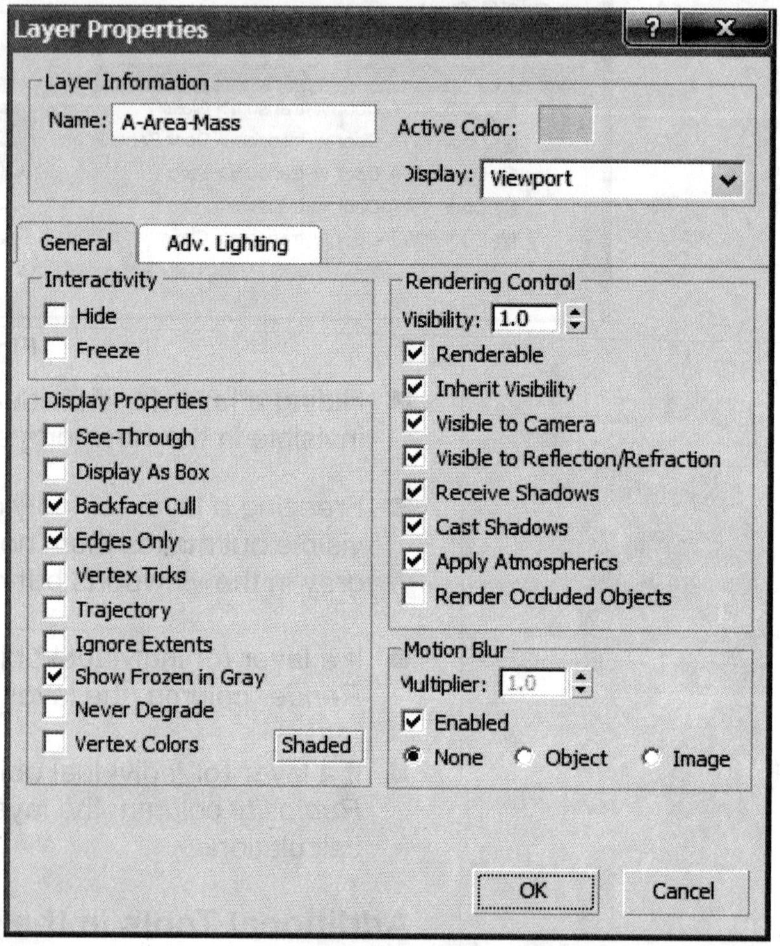

Figure 2–28

In the Layer Manager dialog box, right-click on a Layer name or click  before each layer, to open the Layer Properties dialog box. The dialog box has two tabs, *General* and *Adv. Lighting*. Use the *General* tab to set the display properties, hide and freeze options, or the rendering options of the layer. In the *Adv. Lighting* tab, you can set the Radiosity properties such as whether the layer objects can cast shadows and receive illumination.

Object Properties

You can edit or modify the properties of an object by using the Object Properties dialog box, as shown in Figure 2–29. Right-clicking on the object in a viewport (or right-clicking on its name in the Layer Manager) and selecting **Object Properties** opens the Object Properties dialog box. The Object Properties dialog box lists important information about an object, such as the name of the object, how many faces it consists of, the material assigned to it, whether its properties are controlled by layer or by object, etc. Changes made in the Object Properties dialog box override any layer settings for that object.

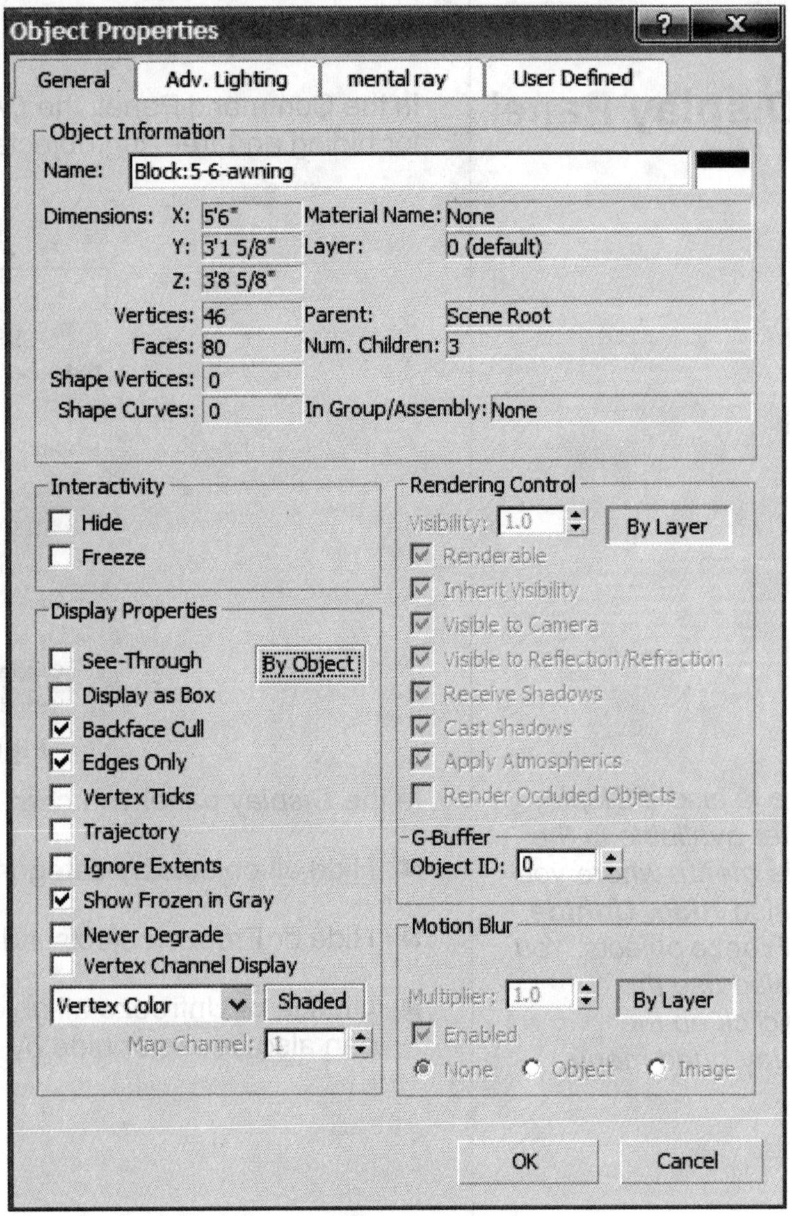

Figure 2–29

For example, you might have an object that you do not want to cast shadows, but all of the other objects on its layer should. This setting can be changed for that one object in the *Rendering Control* area of the Object Properties dialog box. Another example is if an object is blocking your view in the scene from a top or left viewport (such as a hemispherical dome displaying a sky background), by setting that object to **see-through**, it becomes transparent in your viewports (but not renderings).

To override the layer properties for an object, click the appropriate By Layer so that it changes to By Object.

Display Panel

In the Command Panel, the *Display* panel ( ) also has controls for hiding and freezing objects, as shown in Figure 2–30.

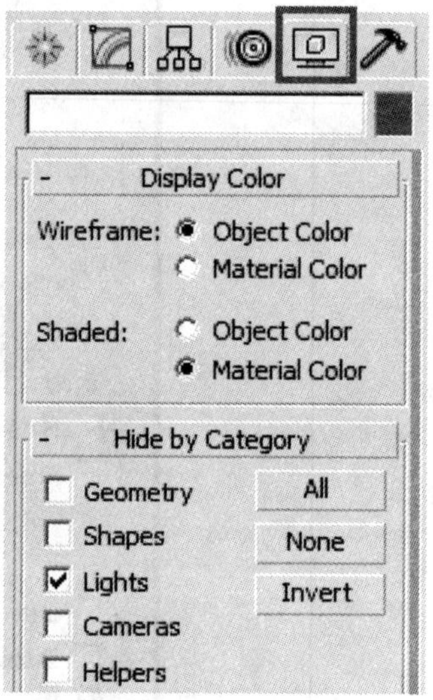

Figure 2–30

*There is also a Display Floater available in the **Tools** menu, where you can also **Hide**, **Unhide**, and **Freeze** objects. You can also use the right-click on the **Display** quad menu.*

In the *Display* panel you can:

- Hide all objects by category (all lights, all geometry, etc.).
- Hide or Freeze objects individually or by selecting them first.
- Unhide or Unfreeze all objects, or do so by object name. You can also freeze or hide by hit.

Practice 2d Layer and Object Properties

Learning Objectives

- Create a new layer and move similar objects in this new layer.
- Set properties of all of the objects in this layer using Layer Properties.
- Modify the properties of only one object on this layer using Object Properties.

Estimated time for completion: 10 minutes

In this practice you will move several objects to a new layer and adjust the properties of the layer and of an individual object.

You must set the paths to locate the External files and Xrefs used in the practice. If you have not done this already, return to the **Introduction to Autodesk 3ds Max Design** chapter and complete Task 1 to Task 3 of the **Organizing Folders and Working with the Interface** practice. You only have to set the user paths once.

Task 1 - Practice Layer Management.

*Use (Open File) in the Quick Access Toolbar or click > **Open>Open**.*

If a dialog box opens prompting you about a File Load: Mismatch, click OK to accept the default values.

1. Open **Layers.max** from your *Class Files\scenes* folder.
2. In the Main toolbar, right-click anywhere on the blank space and select **Layers** to display the Layers toolbar. In the Layers toolbar, click (Manage Layers) to open the Layer dialog box (Layer Manager). (Manage Layers) is also located in the Main toolbar.
3. Click ⊞, next to layer **0 (default)** to expand it and list all of the objects on this layer.

   Some of these objects are ground surfaces (**Parking Lot Surface**, **Outside Grading**, **Outside Curbing**, **Inside Grading**, **Inside Curbing**, and **Building Pad**), and it might be helpful to move those to their own layer. These objects are a part of a group called **Site XREF**

   - You can verify by selecting any of the layers and, in the dialog box toolbar, clicking (Select Highlighted Objects and Layers). In the Command Panel, note that the name is displayed as **Site XREF**.

4. To remove them from the **Site XREF** group, in layer **0 (default)**, select **Site XREF**, and click (Select Highlighted Objects and Layers) as shown in Figure 2–31. This selects the group with the name **Site XREF**.

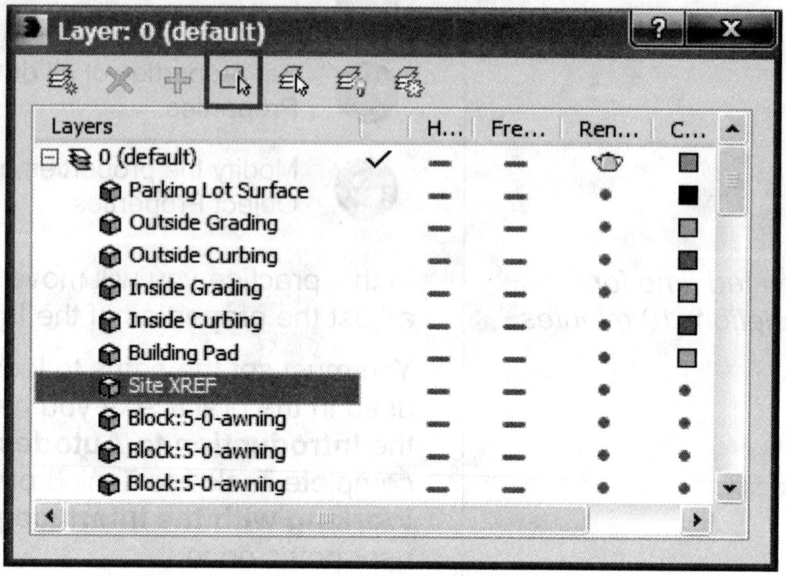

Figure 2–31

5. In the Menu bar, select **Group>Open**. The Site XREF group is now open.

   - Select any of the layers and click (Select Highlighted Objects and Layers). In the Command Panel, note that the name displays its own name.

6. In the Layer dialog box, select the six ground surfaces by selecting **Parking Lot Surface** and then <Shift> and select **Building Pad** as shown in Figure 2–32. Click (Select Highlighted Objects and Layers). In the viewport, all of these objects are now selected.

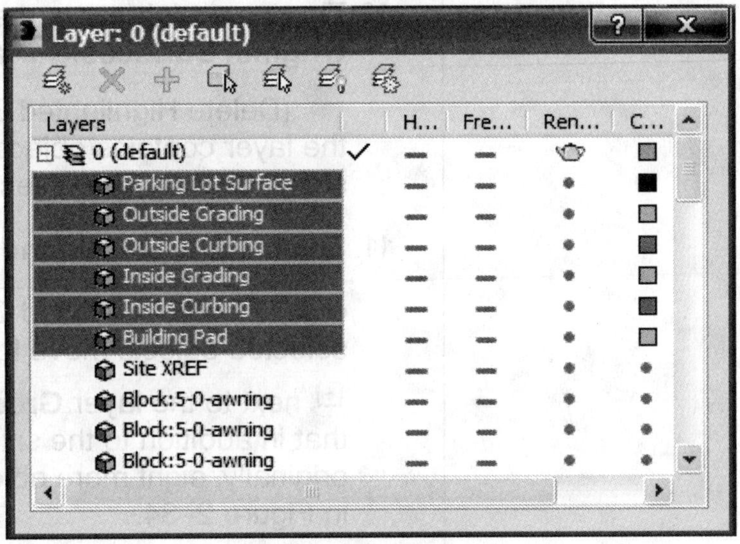

Figure 2–32

7. In the Menu bar, select **Group>Detach**.

*You can also use (Create New Layer) in the Layer toolbar, which opens a dialog box. Verify that **Move Selection to New Layer** is selected and then click the **OK** button.*

8. In the Layer dialog box with the six ground surfaces selected, click (Create New Layer). The Autodesk 3ds Max Design software automatically creates a new layer called **Layer001** and places these objects on it.

9. Right-click on the layer **Layer001** and select **Rename**. Rename the layer as **Ground Surfaces**. Expand this layer by clicking ⊞ next to it and verify that the six ground surfaces are listed in the layer. Note that the Autodesk 3ds Max Design software automatically set this layer to be the current layer, which is indicated by ✓ (checkmark) as shown in Figure 2–33.

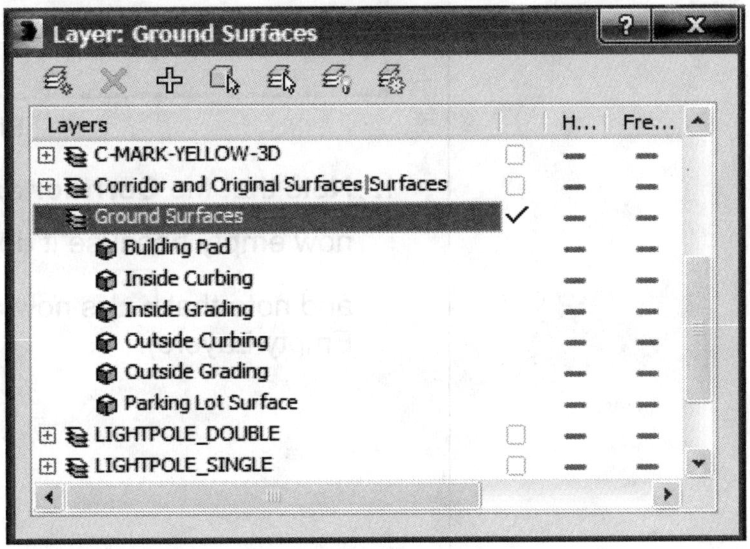

Figure 2–33

10. There are eight ground surfaces on the layer **Corridor and Original Surfaces|Surfaces**. Select this layer and note that (Delete Highlighted Empty Layers) is grayed out because the layer contains objects. Right-click on the layer name and select **Select**. The objects on that layer are now selected.

11. Select the layer **Ground Surfaces**. In the Layers toolbar, click (Add Selected Objects to Current Layer). The selected objects move to the layer **Ground Surfaces**. Click ⊞ next to the layer **Ground Surfaces t**o open it and verify that in addition to the six ground surfaces that were placed originally, eight more objects are listed in this layer, as shown in Figure 2–34.

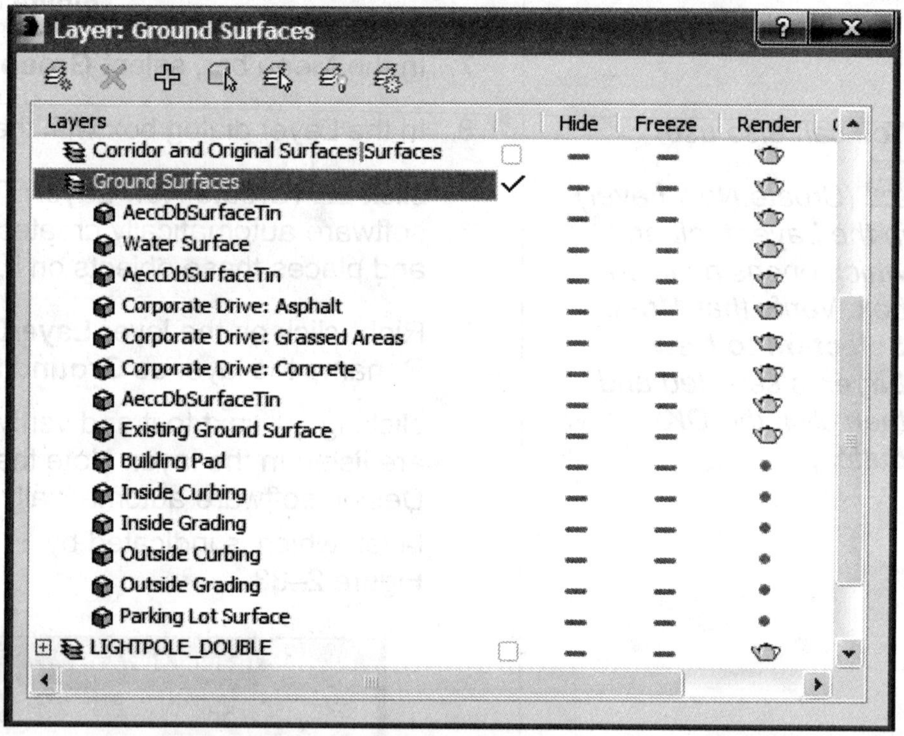

Figure 2–34

12. Note that the **Corridor and Original Surfaces|Surfaces is** now empty because it does not display ⊞. Select the layer and note that is now active. Click (Delete Highlighted Empty Layers).

13. Select the empty box next to layer **0 (default)**, as shown in Figure 2–35, to make it the current layer.

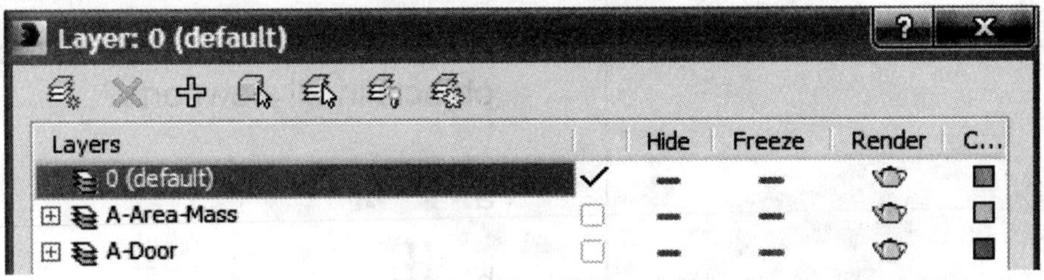

Figure 2–35

Task 2 - Set Layer and Object Properties.

To speed up future renderings, set the ground surfaces such that it does not cast shadows. These objects will still receive shadows, but they themselves will not create any. This simplification can save rendering time without significantly affecting the final output when using relatively flat ground surfaces. If retaining walls or hills are involved, some of those surfaces might still need to cast shadows for best results.

1. Right-click on the layer **Ground Surfaces** and select **Layer Properties**. In the *Rendering Control* area, toggle off **Cast Shadows** and click OK.
2. You can override this setting for one of the ground surfaces. In the Layer Manager, expand the layer **Ground Surfaces**. Right-click on Outside Grading and select **Object Properties**.
3. In the Object Properties dialog box, in the *Rendering Control* area, click By Layer so that it changes to By Object. Verify that **Cast Shadows** for this object is enabled and click OK.
4. Close the Layer dialog box.
5. Expand , select **Save As**, and save your work as **MyLayers.max**.

Chapter Review Questions

1. Which tool can be used to zoom to the extents of all visible objects in all viewports?

   a. 

   b. 

   c. 

   d. 

2. In the *Visual Style & Appearance* tab in the Viewport Configuration dialog box, the **Skylights as Ambient Color** option is available when your Visual Style is set to:

   a. **Shaded**

   b. **Realistic**

   c. **Consistent Color**

   d. **Facets**

3. After selecting a number of objects, which key do you press to remove items from the selection?

   a. <Shift>

   b. <Ctrl>

   c. <Alt>

   d. <Esc>

4. In the maximized viewport display, along with holding down <Win>, which key do you need to press to open the viewport layout for switching to a different view?

   a. <Shift>

   b. <Ctrl>

   c. <Alt>

   d. <Tab>

5. You should assign the unit scale before adding any geometry to the scene. Changing the **System Unit Scale** later does not rescale objects that are already present.

   a. True

   b. False

6. In the Layer Manager, which option makes objects unselectable, but leaves them visible in the viewport and renders them normally?
   a. **Hide**
   b. **Freeze**
   c. **Render**
   d. **Radiosity**

Command Summary

Button	Command	Location
Layers:		
	**Add Selection to Current Layer**	■ **Layers Toolbar**
	**Create New Layers**	■ **Layers Toolbar**
	**Manage Layers**	■ **Main Toolbar** ■ **Layers Toolbar**
	**Select Objects in Current Layer**	■ **Layers Toolbar**
	**Set Current Layer to Selection's Layer**	■ **Layers Toolbar**
Object Selection:		
	**Crossing**	■ **Main Toolbar:** Window/Crossing Toggle
	**Rectangular Selection Region**	■ **Main Toolbar**
	**Select Object**	■ **Main Toolbar**
	**Select by Name**	■ **Main Toolbar**
	**Window**	■ **Main Toolbar:** Window/Crossing Toggle
Viewport Navigation:		
	**Dolly Camera**	■ **Viewport Navigation Toolbar (Camera Views):** Dolly Camera flyout
	**Dolly Camera + Target**	■ **Viewport Navigation Toolbar (Camera Views):** Dolly Camera flyout
	**Dolly Target**	■ **Viewport Navigation Toolbar (Camera Views):** Dolly Camera flyout
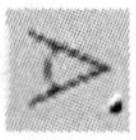	**Field-of-View**	■ **Viewport Navigation Toolbar:** Zoom Region flyout in Perspective and Camera views
	**Maximize Viewport Toggle**	■ **Viewport Navigation Toolbar**

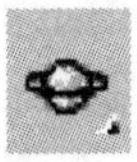	**Orbit Camera**	■ **Viewport Navigation Toolbar (Camera Views)**
	**Orbit**	■ **Viewport Navigation Toolbar (Non-Camera Views):** Orbit flyout
	**Orbit Selected**	■ **Viewport Navigation Toolbar (Non-Camera Views):** Orbit flyout
	**Orbit Sub-Object**	■ **Viewport Navigation Toolbar (Non-Camera Views):** Orbit flyout
	**Pan View**	■ **Viewport Navigation Toolbar**
	**Perspective**	■ **Viewport Navigation Toolbar (Camera Views)**
	**Roll Camera**	■ **Viewport Navigation Toolbar (Camera Views)**
	**Walk Through**	■ **Viewport Navigation Toolbar:** Pan View flyout in Perspective and Camera views
	**Zoom**	■ **Viewport Navigation Toolbar (Non-Camera Views)**
	**Zoom All**	■ **Viewport Navigation Toolbar (Non-Camera Views)**
	**Zoom Extents**	■ **Viewport Navigation Toolbar (Non-Camera Views):** Zoom Extents flyout
	**Zoom Extents Selected**	■ **Viewport Navigation Toolbar (Non-Camera Views):** Zoom Extents flyout
	**Zoom Extents All**	■ **Viewport Navigation Toolbar:** Zoom Extents All flyout
	**Zoom Extents All Selected**	■ **Viewport Navigation Toolbar:** Zoom Extents All flyout
	**Zoom Region**	■ **Viewport Navigation Toolbar (Non-Camera Views)**

Chapter 3

Assembling Project Files

In this chapter you learn about file linking and importing. You learn how to create new presets and to modify them as required. You also learn to incorporate objects or other scene files into the current scene by externally referencing them.

This chapter contains the following topics:

- ✓**Data Linking and Importing**
- ✓**Linking Files**
- ✓**References**

Certification

Topic:
- ✓*Data Management/ Interoperability*

Objectives:
- ✓*Differentiate common file types and usages*
- ✓*Use the import feature to import model data*

3.1 Data Linking and Importing

Learning Objectives

- Understand the difference between File Linking and File Importing in the Autodesk 3ds Max Design software.
- Understand how to edit the linked data files.

While the Autodesk® 3ds Max® Design software has a robust 2D and 3D modeling system, many users find it most efficient to link or import some or all of their design data from other applications. This is especially the case if the bulk of the design work is completed in other Autodesk software, such as AutoCAD®, Autodesk® Revit® Architecture, AutoCAD® Architecture, or Autodesk® Inventor®. Sometimes this linked or imported data is complete before it is brought into the Autodesk 3ds Max Design software, while in other cases simplified data is brought in as a starting point and additional modeling is required.

Linking vs. Importing

In the Autodesk 3ds Max Design 2014 software, files can be either linked or imported using the **File Link** and **Import** tools. The files that can be linked are: .DWG, .DXF, .FBX, and .RVT. A large variety of file types can be imported into the Autodesk 3ds Max 2014 software including Autodesk® Inventor® files (.IPT, .IAM), Autodesk® Alias® .Wire files and the Autodesk® Showcase® .APF (Autodesk Packet File), LandXML and DEM data files, and Adobe Illustrator (.AI) files.

The difference between linked and imported geometry is that linked geometry remains connected to the source file. If the source file is edited, the Autodesk 3ds Max Design Scene can be updated to show those changes, similar to how changes to an AutoCAD XREF can be reloaded. Imported geometry maintains no connection to the source file.

- If a source .DWG, .DXF, .FBX, or .RVT file is likely to change (or you would prefer to make changes in the .DWG, .DXF, .FBX, or .RVT directly), then **File Linking** might be the best way to incorporate this data into the Autodesk 3ds Max Design software.

- **Importing** might be faster than linking when bringing a lot of data into the Autodesk 3ds Max Design software. Complex geometry, such as 3D faces from large Land Desktop terrain models, might be faster to re-import (especially through LandXML) than to update through a file link.
- File links and imports are launched by clicking (as shown in Figure 3–1): expand , expand Import, and select **Link Revit/Link FBX/Link AutoCAD** or expand , expand Import, and select **Import**.

Figure 3–1

Editing Linked Data

- Linked geometry can be edited but not directly deleted from a scene file. Alternatively, the layer on which the objects are placed might be ignored during a reload or set to **Hide** in the Layer dialog box.
- Edits applied to linked geometry (such as through modifiers) are automatically re-applied after a link is updated. Some complex modifications might not apply as expected, however, if the source geometry is changed dramatically be sure to verify. You should always review your geometry carefully after a link is updated.
- Links to drawing files are not bi-directional, so that changes you might make to the data in the Autodesk 3ds Max Design software do not update the original .DWG, .FBX, .DXF, or .RVT file.
- Linked files can also be bound, where the geometry stays in the scene file as-is but the connection to the source file is dropped.

Importing

- To import a .DWG from the Autodesk Revit software, it is recommended to export from the Autodesk Revit software using the **Export as ACIS solids** option. This will also create a better geometry than the other option (polymesh). Also it's not obvious, but you must have a 3D View active to export to DWG.
- The FBX importer is an independent plug-in that is frequently updated. There is a **Web Update** button in the FBX Import dialog box. Using this button, you can check for web updates, download the latest updates, and install those. Close 3ds Max when you do the install.

Merging Autodesk 3ds Max Design Scene Files

Objects already saved in Autodesk 3ds Max Design scenes (.MAX files) are imported into the current scene using the **Merge** option (**>Import>Merge**) and not the **Import** option. Merging files is a one-directional transfer that does not maintain any connection between the two files. Using the **Merge** option, you can either load only a few objects from a scene or you can load a complete scene into the current one.

Practice 3a Ground Surfaces using Civil View

Learning Objective

- Open a Civil3D data file in a scene file using Civil View.

Estimated time for completion: 20 minutes

In this practice you will open a .VSP3D file for importing ground surfaces. Civil View is available only in the Autodesk 3ds Max Design software. If you are using the Autodesk 3ds Max software skip this practice.

You must set the paths to locate the External files and Xrefs used in the practice. If you have not done this already, return to the **Introduction to Autodesk 3ds Max Design** chapter and complete Task 1 to Task 3 of the **Organizing Folders and Working with the Interface** practice. You only have to set the user paths once.

Task 1 - Initialize Civil View.

It is recommended that you import 3D ground surfaces from Civil/Survey products, such as AutoCAD Civil 3D or Land Desktop using the vsp3d data format. The import process involves using Civil View in Autodesk 3ds Max Design.

You only have to initialize Civil View once.

1. In the Menu bar, select **Civil View>Initialize Civil View** to initialize Civil View.
2. In the Initialize Autodesk Civil View dialog box, set the *System Unit* to **Feet** because the civil project that you will be opening uses Feet as its unit of measurement. Verify that **Don't warn me about System Units again** is selected.
3. In the *Select a Country Resource Kit* area, select **US IMPERIAL** and verify that *Start Mode for Civil View* is set to **Manual**. Click OK.
4. Restart the Autodesk 3ds Max Design software.

Hint: Starting Civil View

Once you have initialized Civil View, the next time you launch the Autodesk 3ds Max Design software, you need to start Civil View because *Start Mode for Civil View* is set as **Manual**. You can change this setting later and set it so that Civil View starts when you launch the Autodesk 3ds Max Design software. In the Civil View Preferences dialog box, in the *General* tab, select **Automatically start Civil View?** as shown in Figure 3–2.

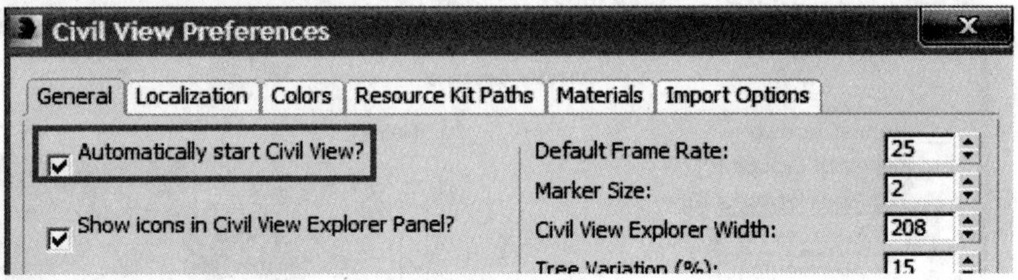

Figure 3–2

5. Open **Civil Base XRef.max** from your *Class Files\scenes* folder. If a dialog box opens prompting you that there is a Mismatch, click OK to accept the default values. If prompted, click OK to accept the file's **Unit Scale**. This is an empty max file in which the System Unit Scale has been set to **1 Unit=1.0 Feet**.

6. If required, start Civil View by selecting **Civil View>Start Civil View**.

7. In the Menu bar, select **Civil View>Geometry Import>Civil 3D (VSP 3D) File**, as shown in Figure 3–3.

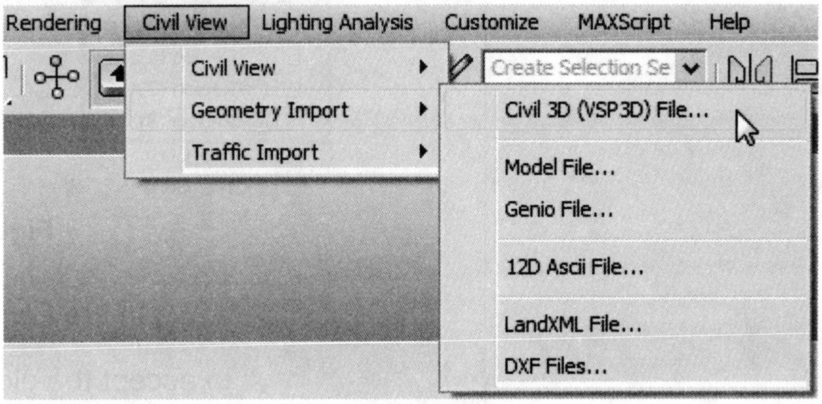

Figure 3–3

8. In the *Civil 3D Import* panel, click Open. In the Select a VSP3D File dialog box, browse to your *Class files\Import* folder and open **Civil surfaces.vsp3d** file.

The objects listed include surfaces, site/ grading featurelines, corridor (surfaces, baselines, featurelines etc.),and point groups, etc.

9. In the *Civil 3D Import* panel, a list of objects contained in the AutoCAD Civil 3D .DWG file are listed. In the left pane, select **Surfaces [9]** to display all of the surfaces in the right pane. Select **Building Pad**, hold down <Shift>, and select **Parking Lot Surface** to highlight the first seven surfaces. Select the checkbox for Building Pad to select all seven highlighted surfaces, as shown in Figure 3–4. You can select them individually as well.

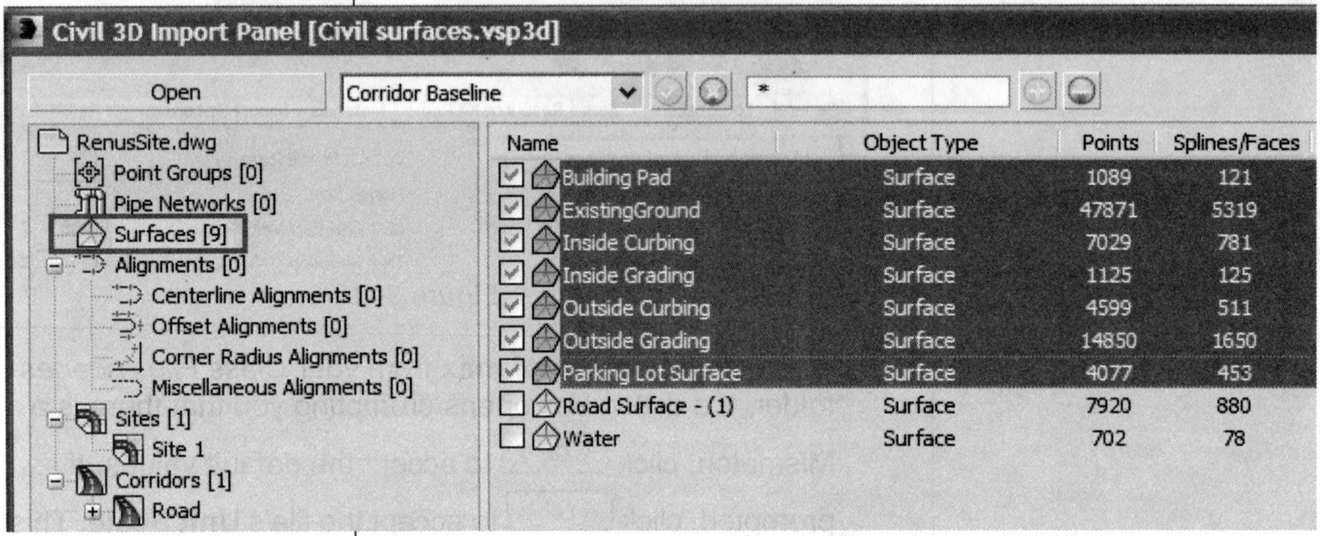

Figure 3–4

10. You will select the corridor surfaces and the baseline. In the left pane, select **Corridors [1]** and in the right pane, select **PrimaryAccess**, **Region(1)**, **Region(2)**, and **Region(3)**, as shown in Figure 3–5.

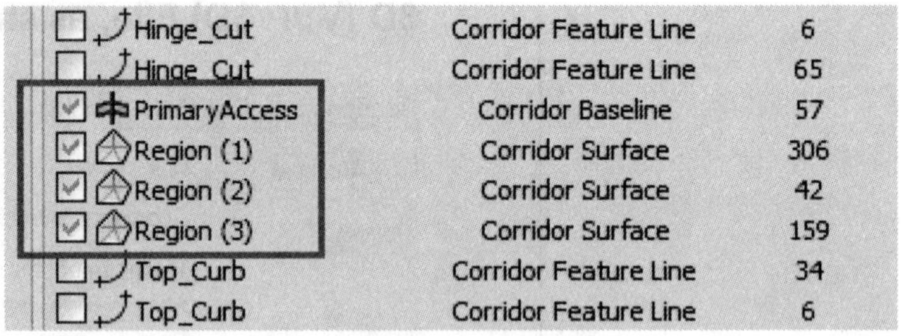

Figure 3–5

11. Click 

. In the Civil View Information, click 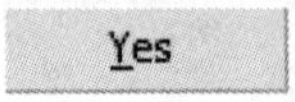

to accept the global shift values.

12. You did not select any feature interpretation. Click 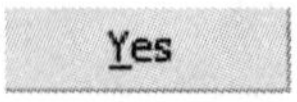

to proceed without a feature interpretation style.

It takes a few minutes to load the file.

13. The ground surfaces, building pad, corridor, and parking lot are displayed in all of the viewports. If not, click (Zoom Extents All). Note that only the corridor displays the surface material and that the rest of the surfaces display a checkerboard material.

14. In the Menu bar, select **Civil View>Civil View>Civil View Explorer** to open the Civil & View Explorer. Dock it along the left side of the screen.

15. Verify that the *Civil Explorer* tab is open. Expand **Civil View Objects>Imported Objects**, if not already expanded. Select **Surfaces** and in the Object List rollout, note that all of the surfaces are listed, as shown in Figure 3–6.

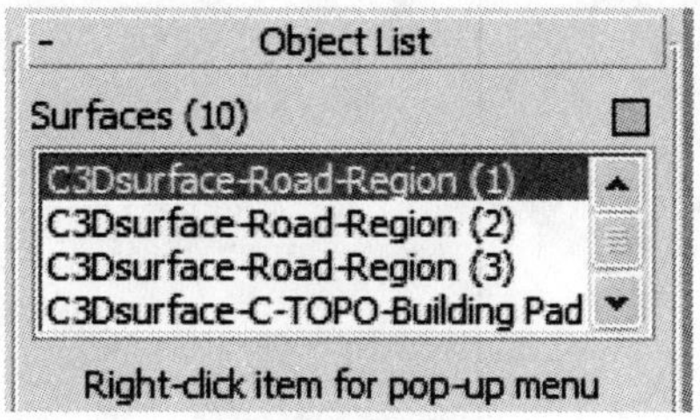

Figure 3–6

A material is not required for the first three corridor regions.

16. In the Object List rollout, select **C3Dsurface-C-TOPO-Building Pad**. In the Surface Parameters rollout, select the *Statistics* tab and note that in the *Face Selection Sets*, in *By Material ID*, **[31] Ground Type 4** has been assigned, as shown on the left in Figure 3–7.

The complete list might not be visible in the Explorer. Hover the cursor in empty space in the information area until it displays as a hand cursor. Grab and slide the Explorer panel up or down to display all of the information.

17. Right-click on [31] Ground Type 4 and select **Modify Material ID Assignment**, as shown on the right in Figure 3–7.

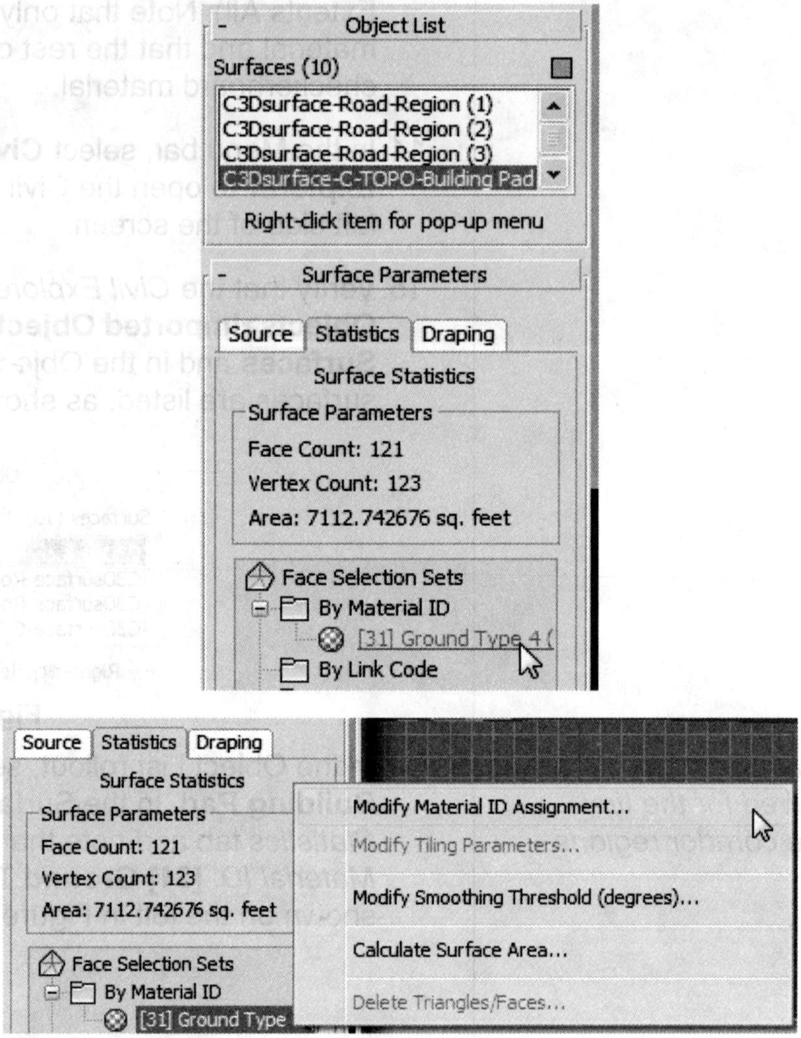

Figure 3–7

18. Click Yes in the Warning dialog box.

19. In the Modify material channel dialog box, select **[22] Concrete Type 1** as shown in Figure 3–8. Click OK.

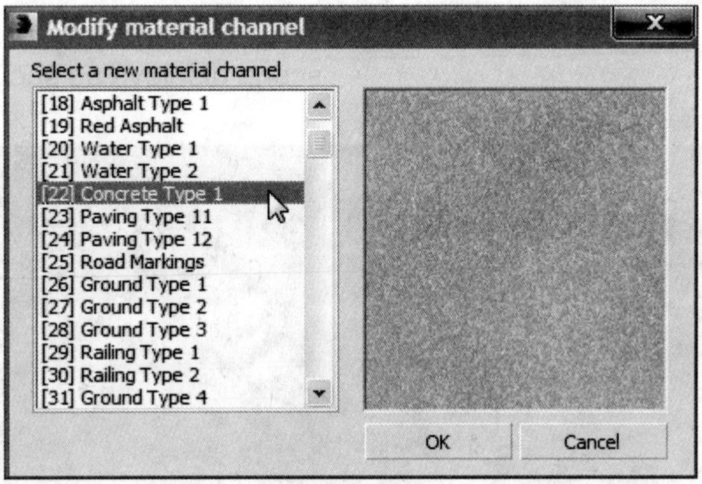

Figure 3–8

20. In the Perspective viewport, use **Zoom** and **Pan** to zoom into the building pad. Note how the new material is applied.

21. If required, select **Surfaces** again and in the Object List rollout, select **C3Dsurface-C-TOPO-Existing Ground**. Select the *Statistics* tab, right-click on [31] Ground Type 4, and select **Modify Material ID Assignment**. In the Warning dialog box, click Yes.

22. In the Modify material channel dialog box, select **[28] Ground Type 3** and click OK. In the Perspective viewport, note that the new ground type material is applied to the ground surface.

23. Similarly, for the other surfaces, apply the material types as follows. A material is not required for the first three corridor regions.

    - C3Dsurface-C-TOPO-Inside Curbing: **[38] Concrete Type 3**
    - C3Dsurface-C-TOPO-Inside Grading: **[28] Ground Type 3**
    - C3Dsurface-C-TOPO-Outside Curbing: **[38] Concrete Type 3**
    - C3Dsurface-C-TOPO-Outside Grading: **[28] Ground Type 3**
    - C3Dsurface-C-TOPO-Parking Lot Surface:**[39] Asphalt Type 4**

24. Close the Civil View Explorer.

25. Click (Zoom Extents All). In the Perspective view, the scene displays as shown in Figure 3–9.

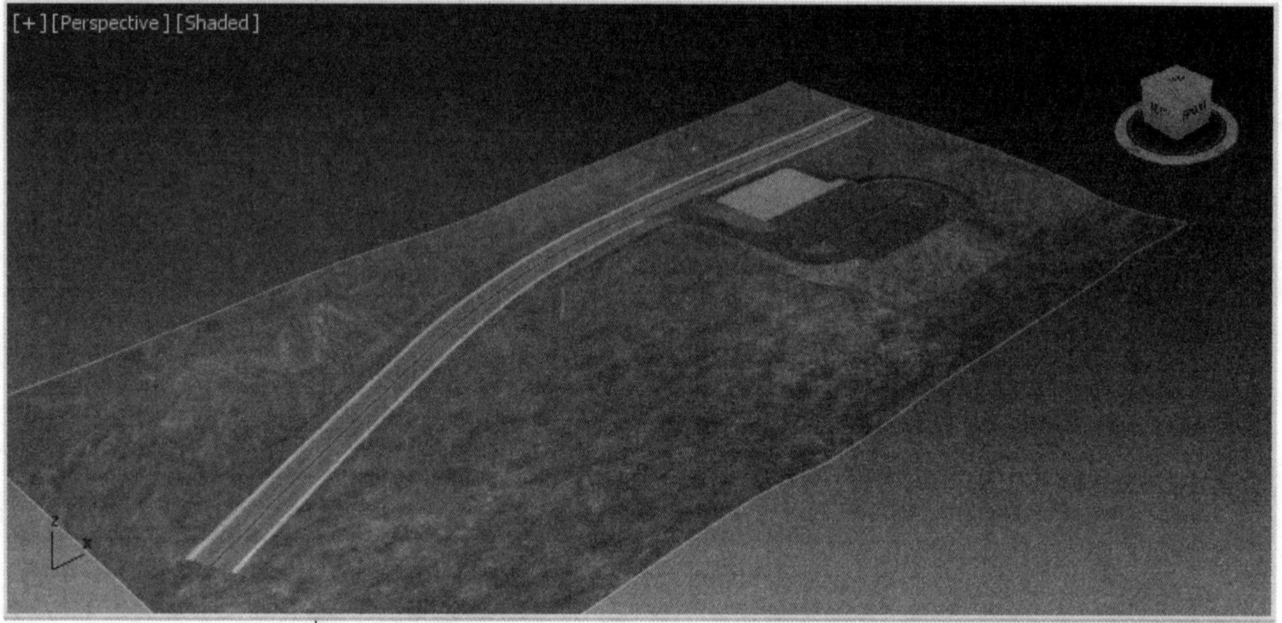

Figure 3–9

26. Save your work as **MyCivil Base XRef.max**.

Certification

Topic:

- *Data Management/ Interoperability*

Objectives:

- *Differentiate common file types and usages*
- *Use the import feature to import model data*

3.2 Linking Files

Learning Objectives

- Combine entities from .DWG, .DXF, .FBX, and .RVT files into the current Autodesk 3ds Max Design scene.
- Understand how to link AutoCAD DWG/DXF files and understand the working of the provided options.
- Understand how to link Generic FBX files and the Autodesk Revit RVT/FBX files and understand the working of the provided options.
- Create and modify the presets using the respective File Link Settings dialog box.

File linking is useful when you are working on a visualization project and know that all design decisions have not been made. If a source file is likely to change (or you want to make changes in the .DWG, .DXF, .FBX, or RVT directly), **File Linking** might be the best way to incorporate this data into the Autodesk 3ds Max Design software as the scene can be updated to display those changes. You can link files using the Manage Links dialog box that can be opened as follows:

- **>Import>Link Revit:** Links the .RVT files from the Autodesk Revit Architecture software.
- **>Import>Link FBX:** Links the .FBX files that can be created in the Autodesk Revit, Autodesk MotionBuilder, Autodesk Maya, and Autodesk Mudbox software.
- **>Import>Link AutoCAD:** Links the .DWG and .DXF files from the AutoCAD software.

You need to open the file to link and the Manage Links dialog box opens in which you can select the settings. You can also open the Manage Links dialog box by expanding , expanding References, and selecting **Manage Links**.

Linking DWG Files

When linking or importing AutoCAD .DWG or .DXF files, it is efficient to combine multiple, related objects together into a single Autodesk 3ds Max Design object to control their display and visibility.

- In CAD data files it is common to have large numbers of objects since most of these objects can be effectively managed by a handful of layer settings and object properties.

- The detail involved when creating a 3D visualization usually requires a lot more information, often applied through object properties and modifiers. This can make dealing with thousands of similar, related entities in the Autodesk 3ds Max Design software very cumbersome. For example, a 2D architectural AutoCAD floor plan made up of individual line segments might be much easier to work with as a single, combined spline object. If you are planning to create 3D objects from these splines it is necessary to combine them into a single line.

When multiple entities are combined into compound Autodesk 3ds Max Design shapes (2D objects) and meshes (3D objects), you can still access and adjust the original geometry in the Sub-object level of Modifiers, such as **Edit Spline**, **Edit Mesh**, and **Edit Poly**.

Therefore combining individual entities does not mean giving up editing control of the original geometry.

Objects or portions of objects can even be detached to form new objects, if necessary.

- Modifiers like **Edit Spline**, **Edit Mesh**, and **Edit Poly** can be used to edit the imported and linked geometry in addition to regularly created splines and primitives in the Autodesk 3ds Max Design software.

Linking FBX and RVT Files

Autodesk has put a lot of work recently into making the Autodesk Revit and Autodesk 3ds Max Design software work better together. The Autodesk Revit and Autodesk 3ds Max software share mental ray renderer and both the products use the Autodesk Material Library materials.

The .RVT and .FBX file format supports the Autodesk Material Library and also supports the import of photometric lights, both interior artificial lights and exterior daylight systems. The disadvantage is that sometimes the file size can become very large and it is impossible to import a project in a single file. You can use a section box in the **3D View** in the Autodesk Revit software to limit the amount of the scene you are exporting at a specific time.

Manage Links Options

The Manage Links dialog box (shown in Figure 3–10) contains the following tabs:

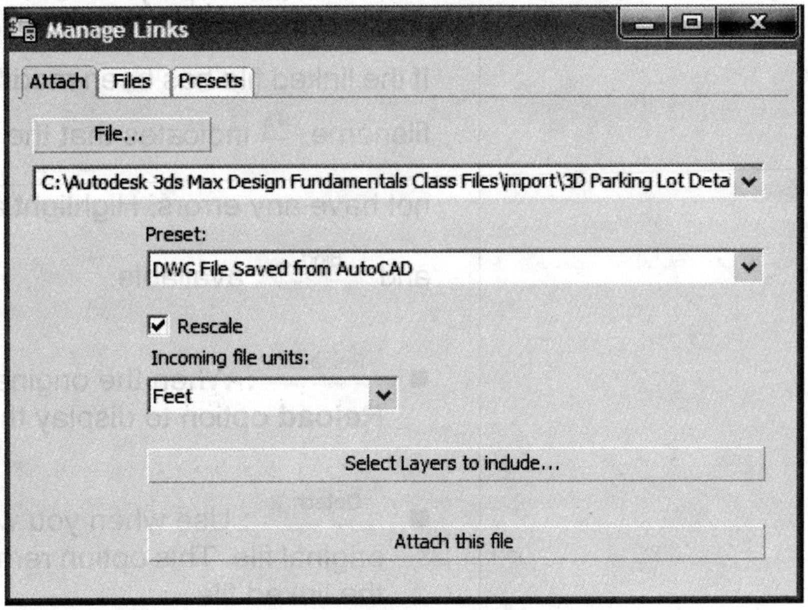

Figure 3–10

Attach Tab

You can open a file (.DWG, .DXF, .FBX, or .RVT) for linking using 

which opens the Open dialog box. The selected filename and its path display in the File drop-down list. If the file that you selected is a .RVT file with more than one camera view, you are prompted to select a camera view. You can select the preset settings in the Preset drop-down list. The Presets listed here can be created or modified using the *Presets* tab. You can set the units by selecting them in the Incoming file units drop-down list. 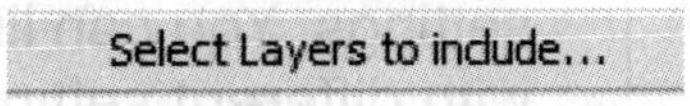

is only available with .DWG and .DXF file types and enables you to select the layers that you want to be included with the drawing file. 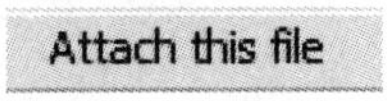

links the selected file with the specified preset settings to the current Autodesk 3ds Max Design scene.

Files Tab

The *Files* tab displays a list of files that are linked to the current scene. An icon in front of the filename indicates its current status. If the linked file has been modified,  is displayed with the linked filename.  indicates that the linked file is unchanged and does not have any errors. Highlight a file to make Reload..., Detach..., and Bind... available.

- Reload...: When the original file has been changed, use the **Reload** option to display the changes in the current scene.
- Detach...: Use when you want to remove the link with the original file. This option removes all geometry associated with the linked file.
- Bind...: Removes the link with the original file, but the geometry stays in the current scene, although the link between the original file is broken. Changes made to the original linked file cannot be reloaded.

Presets Tab

Many options are available before files are linked to your current scene. These options are configured and saved as **Presets** and can be used when linking files at a later stage. Many of these options require trial and error to find the most appropriate settings. You can link a file and then reload (or detach and relink) with different settings until you achieve the required results. If you are linking a file for the first time, you should create a new preset.

The *Presets* tab lists all existing presets and contains options for creating new presets, modifying existing presets, copying existing presets, renaming and deleting them. You need to select a preset for the **Modify**, **Copy**, **Rename**, and **Delete** options to be available, as shown in Figure 3–11. If no preset is selected, **Copy** is replaced by **New** and is the only available option.

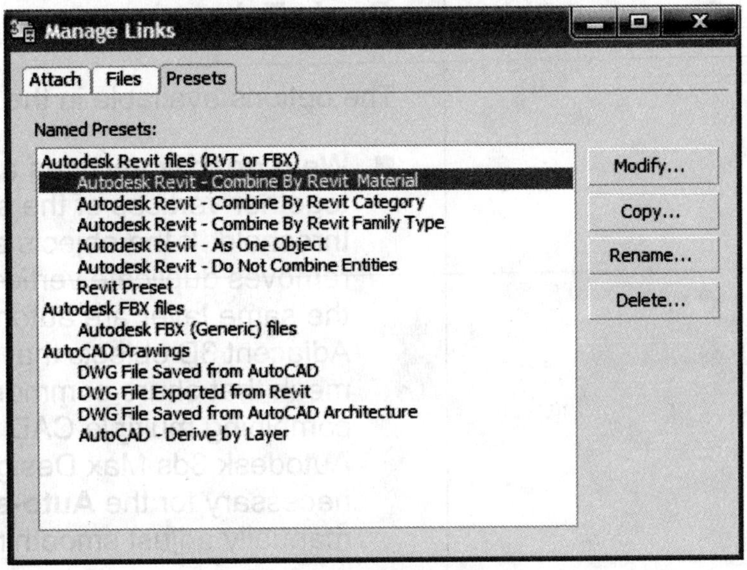

Figure 3–11

Depending on the type of preset selected (.RVT, .FBX, or .DWG), clicking Modify... opens a specific File Link Settings dialog box. This dialog box enables you to define the way you want the geometry to be linked, what portions of the file are to be modified on **Reload**, and how the geometry is combined.

File Link Settings: DWG Files

In the Manage Links dialog box, in the *Presets* tab, selecting an AutoCAD DWG file preset and clicking Modify... opens the File Link Settings: DWG Files dialog box, as shown in Figure 3–12.

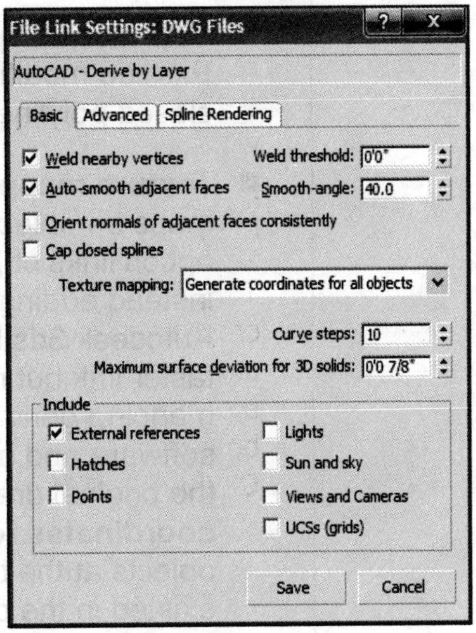

Figure 3–12

Basic Tab

The options available in the *Basic* tab are:

- **Weld nearby vertices** and **Weld threshold:** Welding joins together vertices of the same object that fall within the weld threshold. If the objects are joined by layer, this option removes duplicate vertices so that the adjacent 2D objects on the same layer are automatically combined into splines. Adjacent 3D objects that are welded become faces in a single mesh that share common vertices. Welding is essential for combining multiple CAD entities into a smaller number of Autodesk 3ds Max Design objects. Welding is often necessary for the **Auto-smooth** option to be effective and manually adjust smoothing through smoothing groups.
- **Auto-smooth adjacent face** and **Smooth-angle:** Auto-smooth enables adjacent faces in the same 3D mesh to display smooth if the angles of separation between their face normals (a directional vector perpendicular to the face) is equal to or less than the Smooth-angle. Otherwise the adjacent faces have a faceted edge between them. This is the same smoothing process used in the Edit Mesh and Edit Poly modifiers. You can adjust smoothing later if you still encounter smoothing issues after import.
- **Orient normals of adjacent faces consistently:** This option attempts to coordinate the face normals of linked objects. This option should be left off by default unless some faces of your 3D objects are missing after the link.
- **Cap closed splines:** This option automatically assigns an Extrude modifier to all closed 2D geometry (e.g., circles and closed polylines).
- **Texture mapping:** Texture mapping is used to locate texture maps on objects. The **Generate coordinates on-demand** option links objects without adding any texture mapping at all, instead adding the mapping when it is first called for by the Autodesk 3ds Max Design software. This option enables a faster link but might cause some discrepancies between the mapping generated in the Autodesk 3ds Max Design software and any mapping that might have been present in the original drawing file. The other option, **Generate coordinates for all objects**, adds texture mapping to all objects at the time of the link, matching any that might have existed in the original drawing file.

- **Curve steps:** This setting defines the number of segments to subdivide each 2D curve segment into if they are later extruded in the Autodesk 3ds Max Design software. This setting applies to circles, arcs, polyline curves, spines, and similar curved objects.

- **Maximum surface deviation for 3D solids:** This setting defines the allowed deviation distance from a parametric AutoCAD 3D curve (such as a curved AutoCAD extrusion) and the resulting Autodesk 3ds Max Design mesh. The lower the value, the more a 3D curve is subdivided. This option is necessary because although the AutoCAD software and some vertical applications support true 3D curves, the Autodesk 3ds Max Design software does not. In the Autodesk 3ds Max Design software all 3D curves must be segmented, though geometry can appear perfectly smooth if it is assigned to appropriate smoothing groups. It is common practice to set this value very low, (0.01) when importing work with smooth curves.

- **Include area options:** These options enable you to select the type of objects to be brought into the Autodesk 3ds Max Design software. Cleared (not selected) object types are ignored during the link. Note that the **Lights** option only brings in Lights from AutoCAD drawings pre-2007. If you are trying to bring in Lights from the 2009 line of CAD products, the Lights do not come in, even if the **Lights** option is on. The exception to this is if you have Sun and Sky checked, a daylight system is created based on the information in the incoming DWG file from the Autodesk Revit 2009 software.

Advanced Tab

The *Advanced* tab (shown in Figure 3–13), controls the import of AutoCAD primitives and the effect of scene materials while importing.

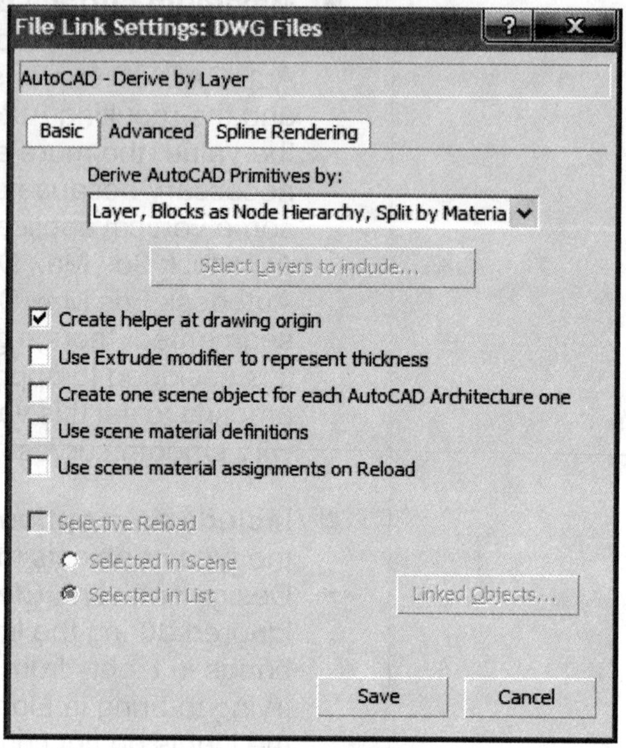

Figure 3–13

The options available in the *Advanced* tab are:

- **Derive AutoCAD Primitives by:** This option controls how AutoCAD objects are combined when linked. This setting does not apply to some vertical application objects such as those in AutoCAD Architecture.

Layer	Creates one object for each AutoCAD layer. Each AutoCAD block links as a single object called a VIZBlock. The Autodesk 3ds Max Design software might not translate AutoCAD block materials correctly if a block contains objects with different materials applied.
Layer, Blocks as Node Hierarchy	This option is similar to **Layer**, but it preserves material assignments in linked AutoCAD blocks. It structures each as a hierarchy of objects rather than single objects.

Layer, Blocks as Node Hierarchy, Split by Material	This option works similarly to the one above but takes into account drawings that have more than one material applied to objects on the same layer. With this option separate hierarchies are created for each material type on each layer, to better preserve the AutoCAD material assignments. New users should consider using this as their default link option.
Color	Combines AutoCAD objects by color. All objects of one color are joined in as a single object, regardless of layer.
Entity	This option does not combine AutoCAD objects at all. Instead, each AutoCAD object becomes an individual object. The use of this option is discouraged except for simple drawing files.
Entity, Blocks as Node Hierarchy	This option includes all non-blocks as separate, individual objects. Blocks are preserved as hierarchies, however, organized by layer.
One Object	This option combines all AutoCAD objects into a single Autodesk 3ds Max Design object. For example, this is useful when linking a drawing file that contains many thousand AutoCAD 3D faces on different layers that you intend to use in the Autodesk 3ds Max Design software.

- **Create helper at drawing origin:** This option adds an origin point helper at the origin of the current coordinate system. All of the linked geometry is part of a hierarchy parented by this helper, so all of the linked objects can be repositioned as one by transforming the helper.
- **Use Extrude modifier to represent thickness:** When linking 2D AutoCAD objects with a non-zero thickness value, these objects translate into the Autodesk 3ds Max Design software as a 3D mesh when this option is disabled. When enabled, objects translate as 2D objects with a parametric extrude modifier. The resulting geometry is the same but when this option is enabled the extrusion properties (such as height) can be modified after the link or import using the modifier stack.
- **Create one scene object for each AutoCAD Architecture one:** With this option off, AutoCAD Architecture (formerly ADT) and AutoCAD MEP objects are subdivided into separate objects by material. It is recommended to leave this option as cleared, since AutoCAD Architecture objects often contain more than one material. Linking each AutoCAD Architecture object as a single Autodesk 3ds Max Design object would require you to configure Multi/Sub-Object materials to show different materials on different parts of the same object.

- **Use scene material definitions:** When left as cleared, the Autodesk 3ds Max Design software includes the current state of any material applied to the linked objects in the AutoCAD software. When selected, if the current scene has a material with the same exact name as the AutoCAD material, then the scene material is used instead.

- **Use scene material assignments on Reload:** When left as cleared, the Autodesk 3ds Max Design software re-loads the current state of any AutoCAD materials present in the drawing file when the link is updated. When enabled, the Autodesk 3ds Max Design software maintains the current state of any materials in the scene file after a link is updated. If you intend to adjust linked materials in the Autodesk 3ds Max Design software then you should enable this option. If you intend to perform your material adjustments in the AutoCAD software you should not.

- **Selective Reload:** Enables you to reload a subset of the original file. If you select this option, you can select objects to reload by selecting them in the scene or by selecting them from a list. If you select **Selected in List**, and click Linked Objects... a list is displayed.

Spline Rendering Tab

The options present in the *Spline Rendering* tab (shown in Figure 3–14), enable linear objects (2D and 3D lines, polylines, etc.) to display as extruded 3D objects in the viewports or rendering. Normally splines cannot be rendered because they do not have surface area to interact with scene lighting. These options enable splines to link into the Autodesk 3ds Max Design software as 3D linear objects with a cross-sectional radius or a rectangular length and width. This provides the surface area for rendering.

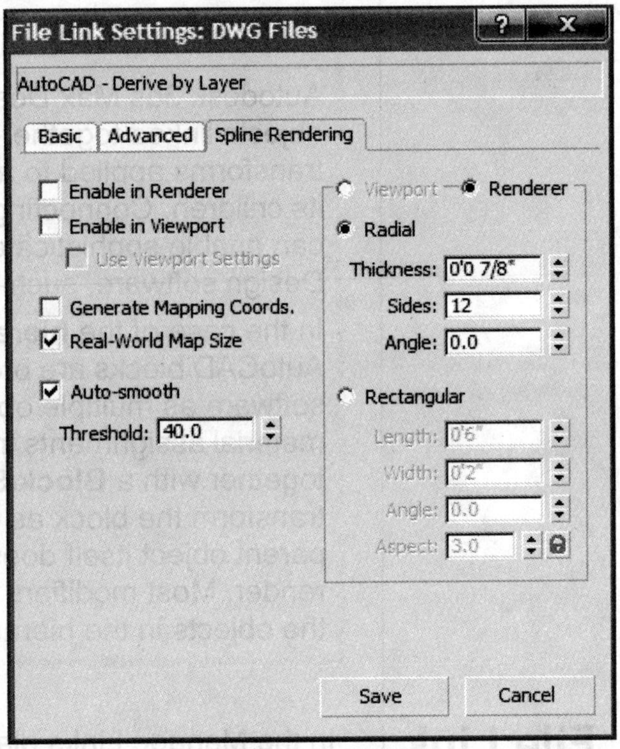

Figure 3–14

- If splines are to be rendered with materials then smoothing, mapping coordinates, and/or real-world map size are often important.
- When enabled, all of the splines linked with this setting are renderable, and all have the same cross-section geometry.
- If you want to make only certain 2D objects renderable (or want some to render differently than others) you could alternately apply a Renderable Spline modifier directly to those objects after linking, as shown on the right in Figure 3–15.

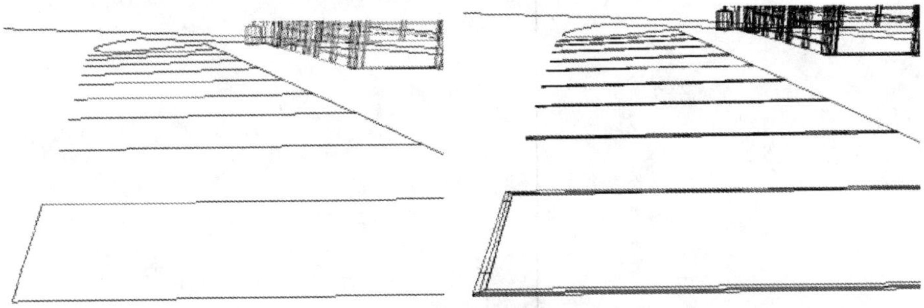

Figure 3–15

> **Hint: Hierarchies and File Linking**
>
> Autodesk 3ds Max Design Hierarchies are collections of objects linked together into parent/child relationships where transforms applied to a parent are automatically passed on to its children. Connecting multiple objects in a hierarchical chain can enable sophisticated animations in the Autodesk 3ds Max Design software, such as the motion of jointed robotic arms.
>
> In the case of the **hierarchy** file link options, incoming AutoCAD blocks are brought into the Autodesk 3ds Max Design software as multiple objects so that they can maintain multiple material assignments from the AutoCAD software. They display together with a **Block/Style Parent** object, enabling you to transform the block as a unit by selecting the parent. The parent object itself does not have any geometry and does not render. Most modifiers (such as Substitute) must be applied to the objects in the hierarchy rather than the parent.

File Link Settings: Revit Files (RVT or FBX)

In the Manage Links dialog box, in the *Presets* tab, selecting an Autodesk Revit file and clicking Modify... opens the File Link Settings: Revit Files (RVT or FBX) dialog box, as shown in Figure 3–16.

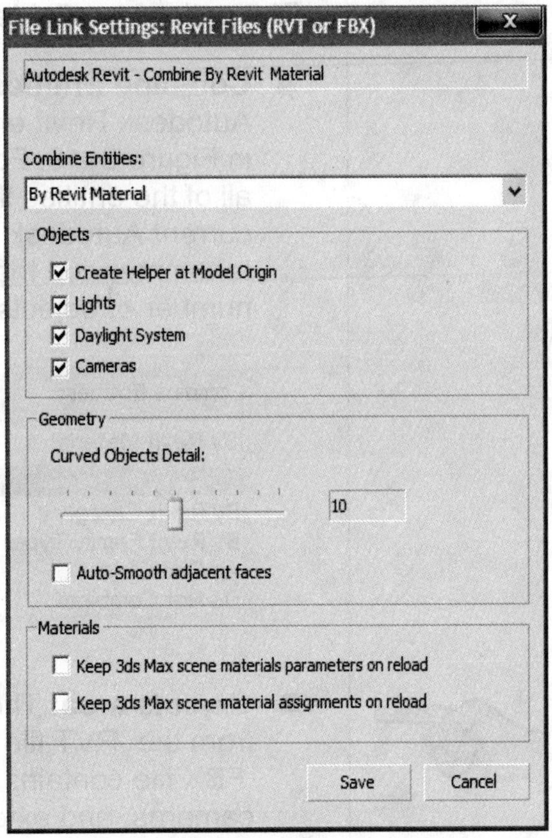

Figure 3–16

In the Manage Links dialog box, in the *Presets* tab, you can also select Autodesk FBX (Generic) file preset and click Modify... . This opens the File Link Settings: FBX Files dialog box, as shown in Figure 3–17. This dialog box is similar to the Autodesk Revit Files (.RVT and .FBX) without a *Geometry* area for controlling the segments and smoothing the linked geometry.

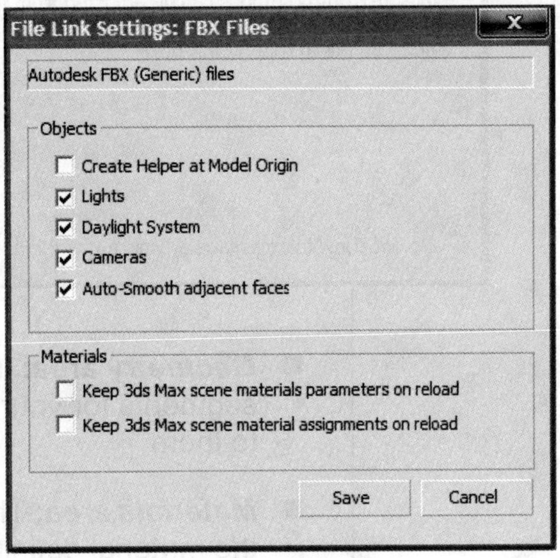

Figure 3–17

The options available are:

- **Combine Entities list:** This option enables you to select the Autodesk Revit entities that you want to combine, as shown in Figure 3–18. For example, if you select **By Revit Material**, all of the entities that have the same material are linked in the current Autodesk 3ds Max scene as a single object. It is recommended that you combine entities as it reduces the number of objects.

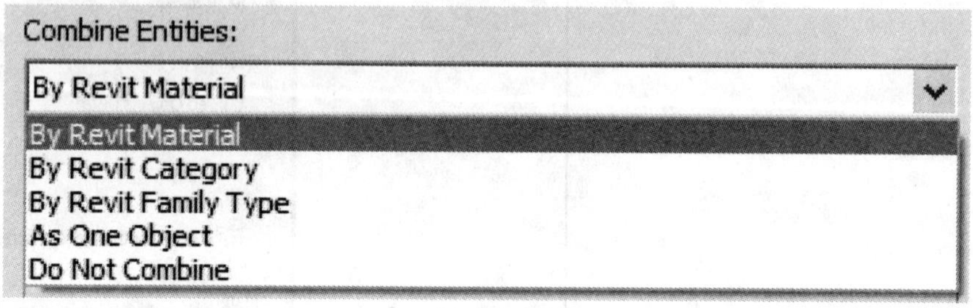

Figure 3–18

Enhanced in 2014

- ***Objects* area:** The selected options in this area are linked from the .RVT file to your current scene. If the .RVT file or .FBX file contains photometric lights, interior artificial lights, cameras, and exterior daylight systems, you can select the associated options in the File Link Settings dialog box. While linking the daylight system from the .RVT/.FBX file, the Autodesk 3ds Max Design software recommends that you toggle on the exposure control, as shown in Figure 3–19.

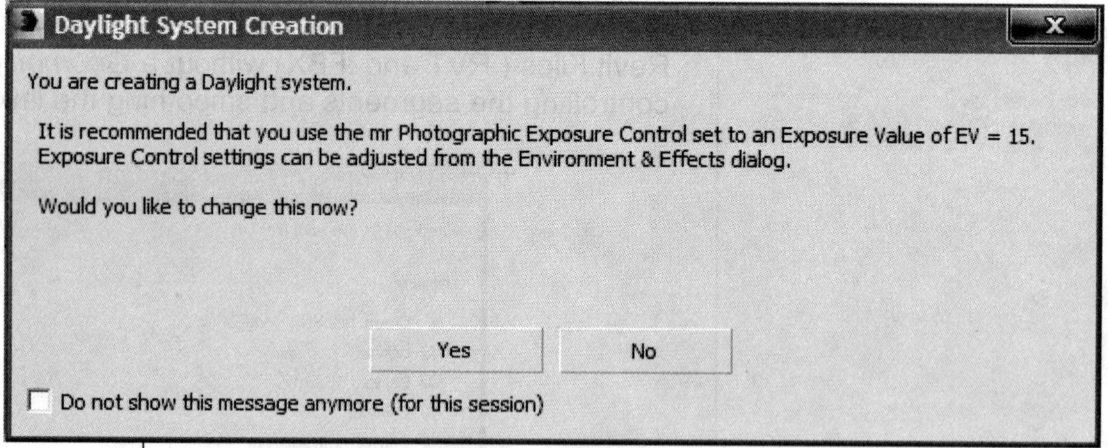

Figure 3–19

- ***Geometry* area:** In this area, you can set the number of segments for your curved entities and apply auto-smoothing to them.

- ***Materials* area:** The options in this area enable you to control the material definitions and assignment settings.

Practice 3b Linking an AutoCAD DWG

Learning Objectives

- Create a preset to link an AutoCAD .DWG file and reposition the file using the Helper object.
- Revise the link settings and reload the linked file.

Estimated time for completion: 20 minutes

In this practice you will link AutoCAD geometry to represent the parking lot details, such as pavement markings and other details. The 3D markings were created by projecting 2D lines to the elevation of a terrain model.

You must set the paths to locate the External files and Xrefs used in the practice. If you have not done this already, return to the **Introduction to Autodesk 3ds Max Design** chapter and complete Task 1 to Task 3 of the **Organizing Folders and Working with the Interface** practice. You only have to set the user paths once.

Task 1 - Link an AutoCAD .DWG File.

If a dialog box opens prompting you about a File Load: Mismatch, click OK to accept the default values.

1. Continue working in the file **MyCivil Base Xref.max** or open **Civil Base.max** from your *Class Files* folder.
2. Expand (application menu), expand Import, and select **Link AutoCAD**. In the Open dialog box, browse and open the *import* subfolder in your *Class Files* folder. Select **3D Parking Lot Detail.dwg** and click Open.

3. The Manage Links dialog box opens with the path and the filename displayed, as shown Figure 3–20.

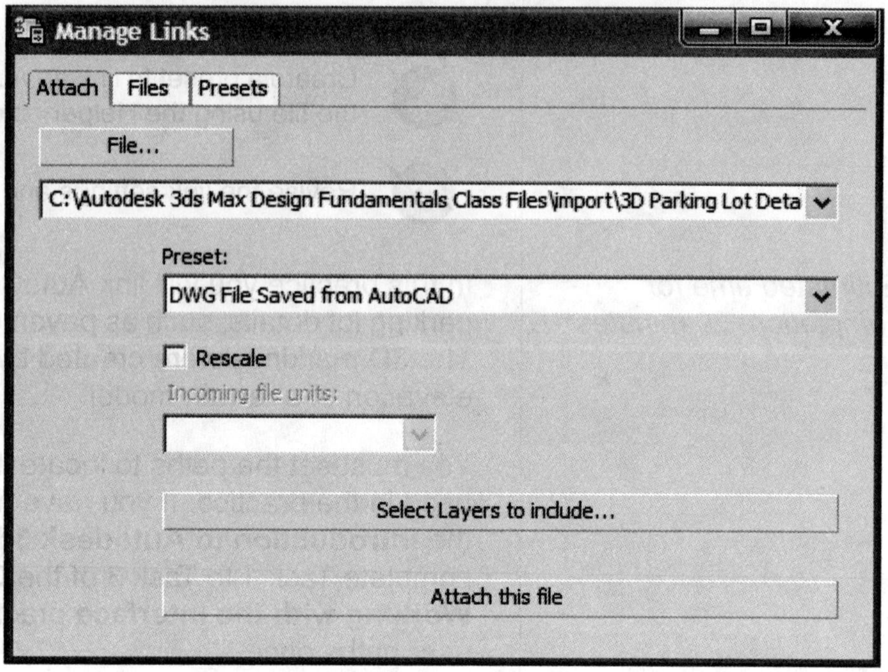

Figure 3–20

If no preset is selected, only New... *is available.*

4. You will configure and save a link preset before linking the drawing file. Select the *Presets* tab and click New... to create a new preset.
5. In the New Settings Preset dialog box, set *New Name* as **AutoCAD – Derive by Layer**. Note that the *Format* is selected as **AutoCAD Drawings**. Click OK.
6. Now you will modify the preset settings. In the Manage Links dialog box, select the newly created preset, **AutoCAD – Derive by Layer**, as shown in Figure 3–21. Note that the **Modify**, **Copy**, **Rename**, and **Delete** options are now available. Click Modify....

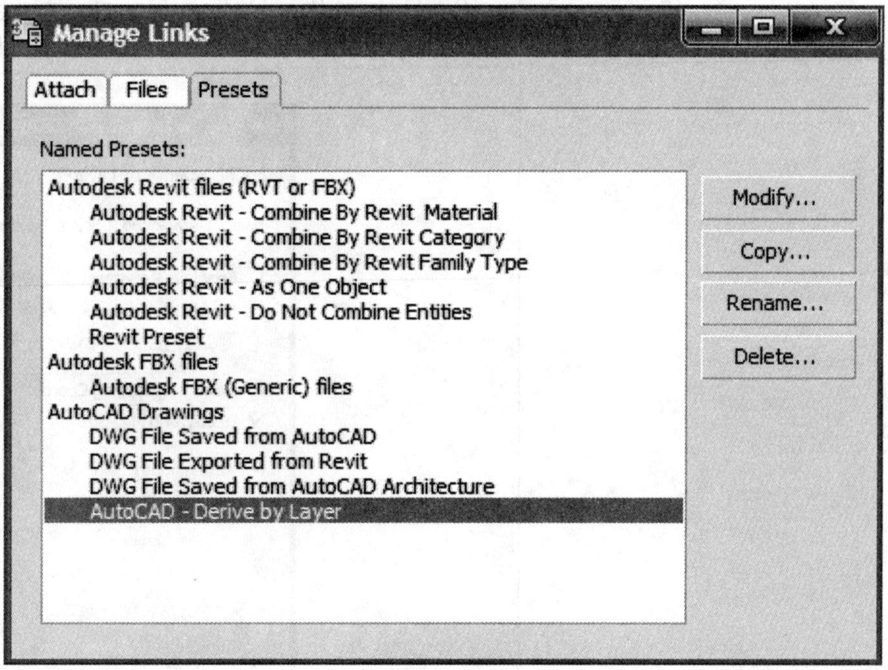

Figure 3–21

*The **Create Helper at drawing origin** option adds a helper object at the origin of the linked file.*

7. In the File Link Settings dialog box, in the *Basic* tab, set the link options, as shown on the left in Figure 3–22. Select the *Advanced* tab. Select **Create helper at drawing origin** and leave all of the other options as their defaults, as shown on the right in Figure 3–22.

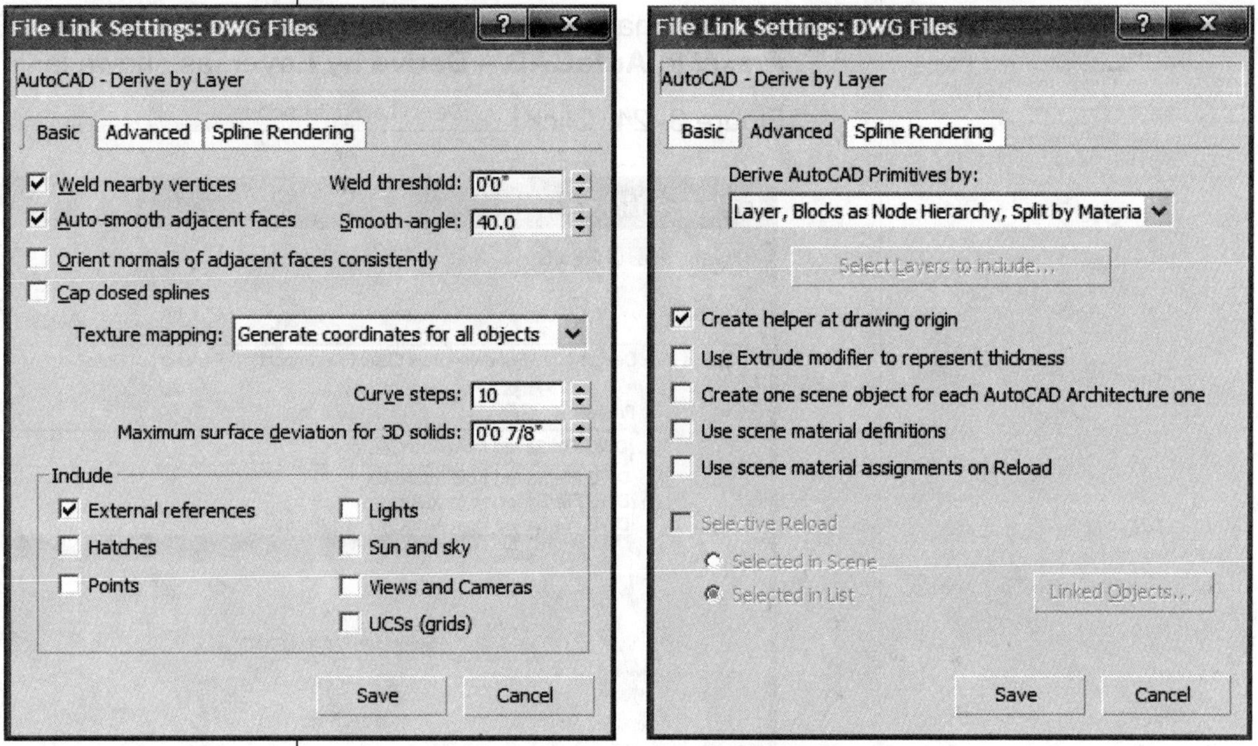

Figure 3–22

8. Select the *Spline Rendering* tab and verify that the link options are set as shown in Figure 3–23.

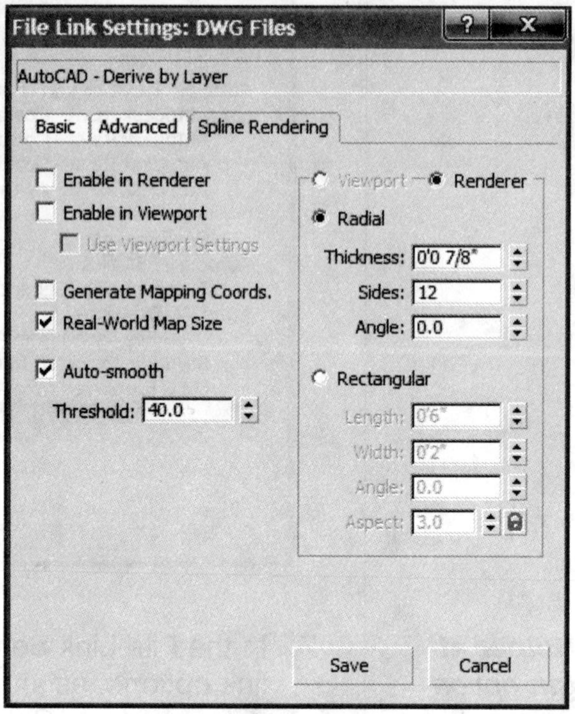

Figure 3–23

9. Click Save.

10. In the Manage Links dialog box, select the *Attach* tab. Set *Preset* to **AutoCAD – Derive by Layer**, as shown in Figure 3–24. Click Select Layers to include....

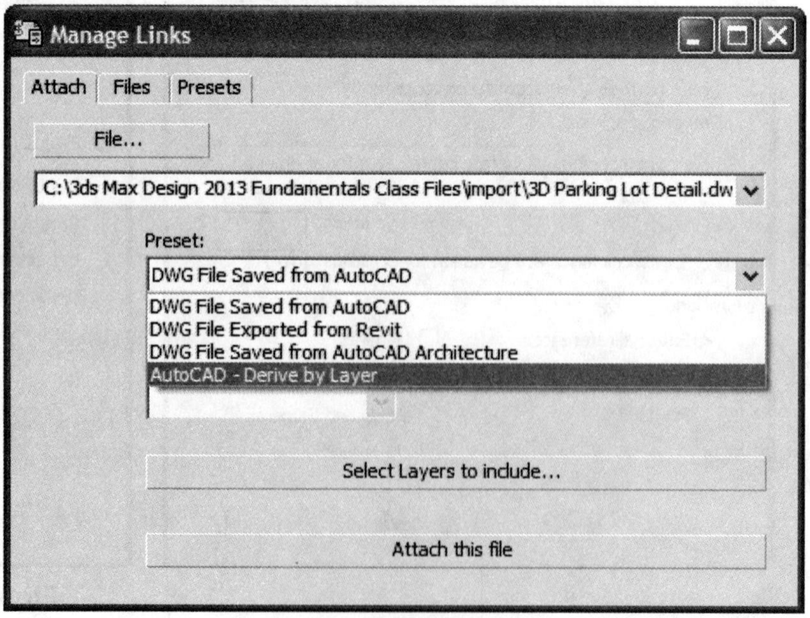

Figure 3–24

11. In the Select Layers dialog box, select **Select from list**. Select **0** and **DEFPOINTS** to clear them, leaving rest of the layers selected, as shown in Figure 3–25. Click OK.

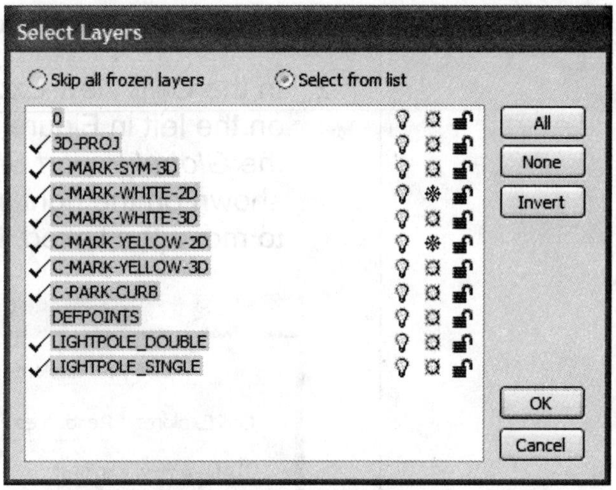

Figure 3–25

12. In the Manage Links dialog box, click Attach this file. Note that the parking lot details have been added to the scene, but are located far away from the origin, as shown in the Top viewport in Figure 3–26. Close the Manage Links dialog box.

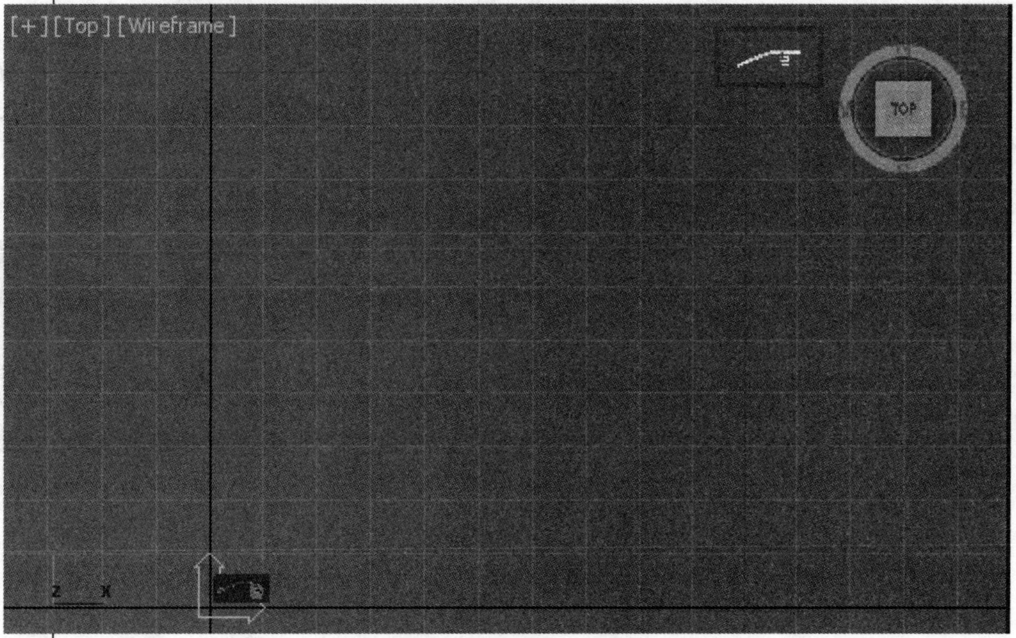

Figure 3–26

Task 2 - Relocate the Linked Geometry.

You might need to start Civil View, if it is not set to open automatically.

1. You need to move the parking lot details by the global shift values in Civil View. In the Menu Bar, select **Civil View>Civil View>Civil View Explorer**.

2. In the Civil View Explorer, select Scene Settings, as shown on the left in Figure 3–27. In the Scene Settings rollout, note the *Global Import Shift* values for *X Shift* and *Y Shift*, as shown on the right in Figure 3–27. You will use these values to move the linked .DWG file.

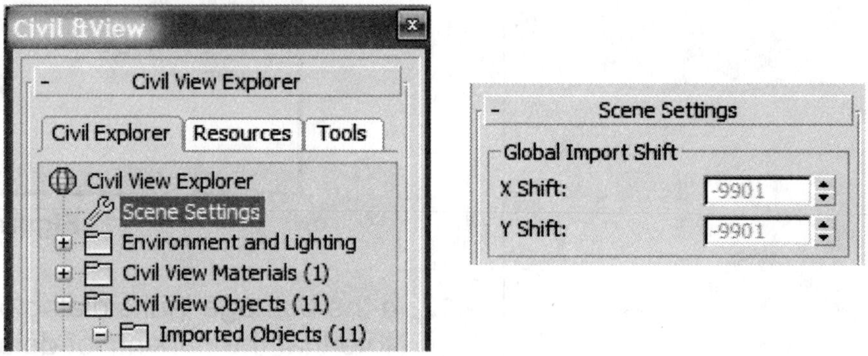

Figure 3–27

3. In the Main toolbar, click  (Select and Move).

4. In the Top viewport, select the helper object (the **User Coordinate System** icon) for the linked .DWG file, which is located at the origin, as shown in Figure 3–28. Selecting the helper objects selects all of the objects in the linked file and enables you to modify them together.

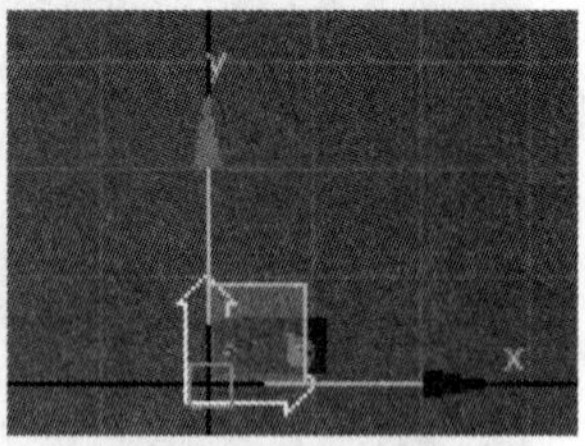

Figure 3–28

5. In the Status Bar, verify that (Absolute Mode Transform) is displayed. In the *X* edit box, enter **-9901'0".** Click in the *Y* edit box, enter **-9901'0"**, and press <Enter>, as shown in Figure 3–29.

Figure 3–29

6. Click (Zoom Extents All). Note how the parking lot details are placed exactly on the parking lot surface.

7. In the Perspective viewport, use (Zoom) and (Orbit) to zoom into the Parking lot area and tilt the view so display the area below the surfaces, as shown in Figure 3–30. Note that in addition to the 3D pavement markings, 2D line markings are imported through the link. A reload of this file would enable you to revise the link settings and/or to update the scene if the drawing is modified.

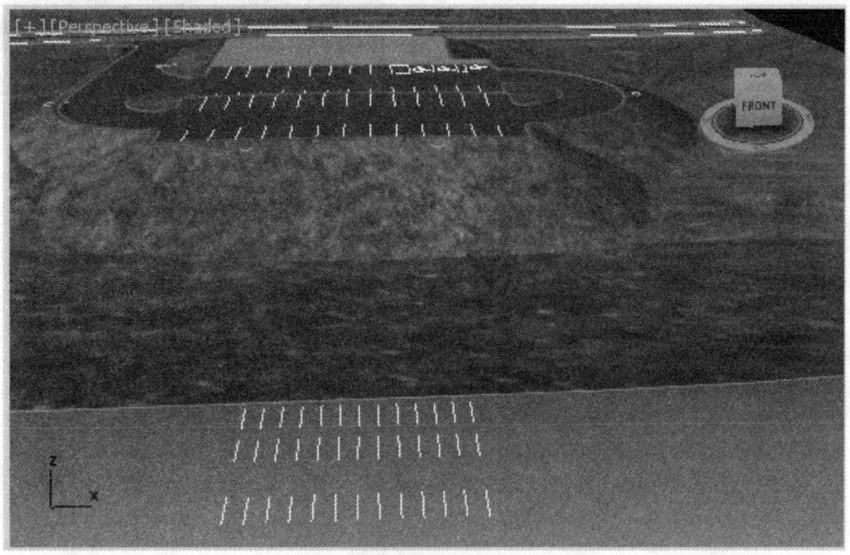

Figure 3–30

In the Files tab, if the linked file has been modified, and the linked filename are displayed. You can use Reload... *to update the file in the scene. indicates that the linked file has not changed and does not have any errors. In this case, use* Reload... *to revise the link settings.*

Task 3 - Revise the Link Settings.

1. Click **>References>Manage Links** to open the Manage Links dialog box.

2. In the Manage Links dialog box, select the *Files* tab and note that the linked file displays , indicating that the file has not changed. Verify that **Show Reload options** is selected, and click Reload.... (Detach... removes a linked drawing from the scene. Bind... inserts the drawing as is and removes the connection.)

3. The File Link Settings dialog box opens. In the *Advanced* tab, click Select Layers to include.... Select all of the 2D layers, (**C-MARK-WHITE-2D**, **C-MARK-YELLOW-2D**, and the two **LIGHTPOLE** layers) to clear their selection, as shown in Figure 3–31.

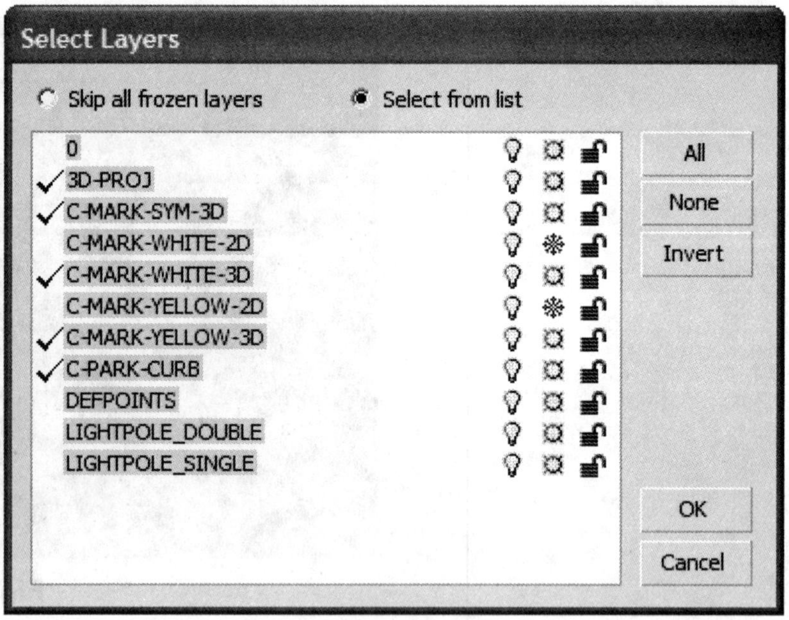

Figure 3–31

4. Click OK twice to close both dialog boxes. The 2D linework should no longer display, keeping the scene smaller.

   Close the Manage Links dialog box by clicking X.

5. Save your work as **MyCivil Base.max**.

Practice 3c Linking and Reloading Autodesk Revit File

Learning Objectives

- Link an Autodesk Revit file to the current scene.
- Reposition the Autodesk Revit file using the Helper object.
- Incorporate the changes made to the original Autodesk Revit file into the current scene using **Reload**.

Estimated time for completion: 20 minutes

In this practice you will link a .RVT file and reload a modified version of the file.

You must set the paths to locate the External files and Xrefs used in the practice. If you have not done this already, return to the **Introduction to Autodesk 3ds Max Design** chapter and complete Task 1 to Task 3 of the **Organizing Folders and Working with the Interface** practice. You only have to set the user paths once.

Task 1 - Link an Autodesk Revit (.RVT) file.

If a dialog box opens prompting you about a File Load: Mismatch, click OK *to accept the default values.*

1. Continue working in the file **MyCivil Base.max** or open **Civil Base Link.max** from your *Class Files* folder.
2. Expand , expand Import, and select **Link Revit**.
3. In the Open dialog box, in the *import* subfolder of your *Class Files* folder, select **Revit Building-1.rvt** and click Open.

If there are multiple cameras in the .RVT file, the Select Revit View dialog box opens.

4. The Link Revit View dialog box opens indicating the progress of the file as it is loading. Once loaded, the Select Revit View dialog box opens as shown in Figure 3–32.

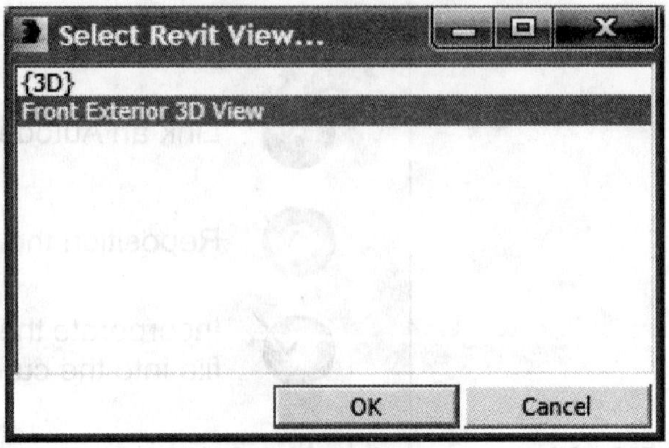

Figure 3–32

5. You need to select one camera view. Select **Front Exterior 3D View** and click OK.
6. In the Manage Links dialog box, select the *Presets* tab.
7. Click New... to create a new preset. In the New Settings Preset dialog box, set *New Name* to **Revit Preset** and *Format* to **Autodesk Revit (*.rvt,*.fbx)**. Click OK.
8. Select **Revit Preset** to highlight it and click Modify....

*The **Create Helper at Model Origin** option adds a helper object at the origin of the linked file. Selecting and applying transforms (move, rotate, or scale) to the helper object applies the transform to the linked geometry together.*

9. In the File Link Settings dialog box, expand the Combine Entities drop-down list and select **By Revit Category**. In the *Objects* area, clear **Lights** and **Daylight System**. Select **Create Helper at Model Origin** and **Cameras**. In the *Geometry* area, set *Curved Objects Detail* to **6**. Verify that both **Keep 3ds Max scene materials parameters on reload** and **Keep 3ds Max scene material assignments on reload** are cleared, as shown in Figure 3–33. Click Save.

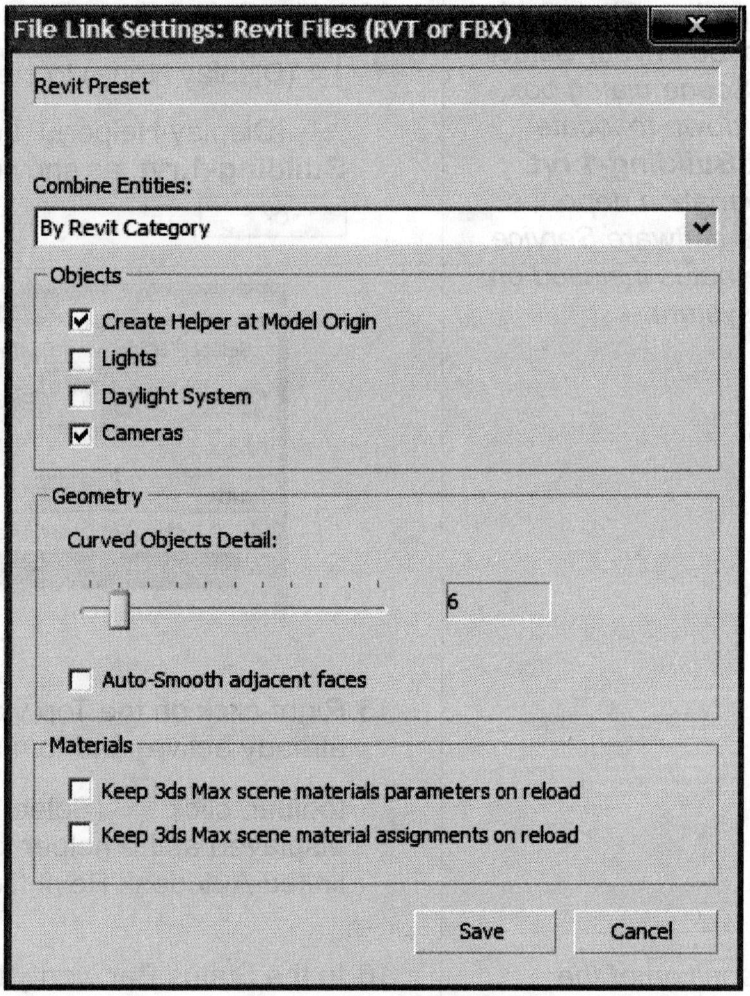

Figure 3–33

10. Select the *Attach* tab. Expand the Preset drop-down list and select **Revit Preset**.

11. Click Attach this file. (It might take a few minutes to load the file). Note that the Autodesk Revit building and camera are loaded at the 0,0,0 location in the viewports.

12. Close the Manage Links dialog box by clicking .

13. In the Main toolbar, click (Select by Name).

If a long list of helpers is displayed in your Select from Scene dialog box, scroll down to locate ***Revit Building-1.rvt****. The variation depends on the software Service Pack that is installed on your system.*

14. In the Select From Scene dialog box toolbar, click (Display None) to clear any selection group and click (Display Helpers). Locate and select **Revit Building-1.rvt**, as shown in Figure 3–34, and click OK.

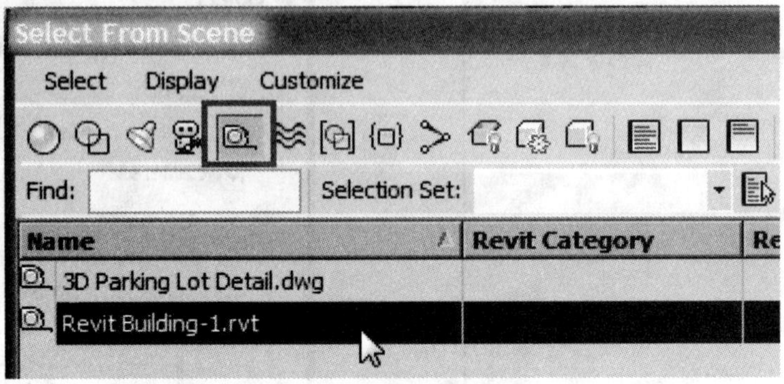

Figure 3–34

15. Right-click on the Top viewport to make it active (if not already active) and to maintain the selection. In the Main toolbar, click (Select and Move). The Transform gizmo is displayed at the helper location, which is the origin of the linked Autodesk Revit file.

The position of the building pad from the origin has been calculated.

16. In the Status Bar, verify that (Absolute Mode Transform) is displayed. In the *X* edit box, enter **800'0"**. Click in the *Y* edit box and enter **382'0"**. Click in the *Z* edit box, enter **154'6"**, and press <Enter>, as shown in Figure 3–35.

Figure 3–35

17. Click (Zoom Extents All). Note how the building is placed on the building pad.

Grid has been hidden for clarity. Press <G>.

18. In the Front viewport, use (Zoom Region) and create a rectangular window around the building to only zoom into the building. Select the **Wireframe** Visual Style label and select **Realistic**. The building displays as shown in Figure 3–36

Figure 3–36

19. In the Perspective viewport, use (Zoom) and (Orbit) to zoom into the building and parking lot area, as shown in Figure 3–38.

20. In the Left viewport, select the **Wireframe** Visual Style label and select **Shaded**. Select the **Left** Point of View label, and select **Camera>3D View: Front Exterior 3D View**. The camera view that was selected when the Autodesk Revit file was linked displays.

Figure 3–37

21. Use **Pan** to display the complete building in the viewport, as shown in Figure 3–38.

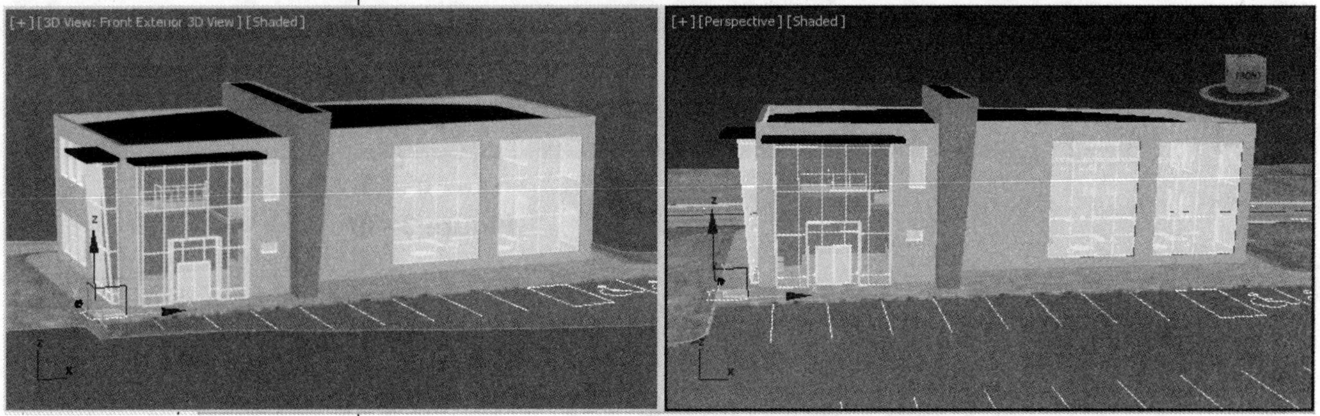

Figure 3–38

Task 2 - Reload the variation of the .RVT file.

Changes can be made in the source file and reloaded directly into the linked file in the Autodesk 3ds Max software. A variation to the .RVT linked file (windows have been added) has been included in your *Class Files\import* folder.

1. In Windows Explorer, open the *import* folder of your *Class Files* folder (*C:\3ds Max Design Fundamentals Class Files\import*).
2. Select **Revit Building-1.rvt**, right-click and select **Rename**.
3. Rename the file as **Revit Building-1_ORIGINAL.rvt**.
4. Select **Revit Building-2.rvt**, right-click and select **Copy**. Paste a copy of this file into the same directory. Right-click on the copied file, select **Rename**, and rename the file as **Revit Building-1.rvt**. This must be the same name as the original file that was linked to indicate that the original linked file has changed.
5. Return to the Autodesk 3ds Max Design software. Click **>References>Manage Links** to open the Manage Links dialog box.
6. In the Manage Links dialog box, select the *Files* tab. Note that is displayed in front of the .RVT filename (as shown in Figure 3–39), indicating that changes have been made to the original linked file.

indicates that the linked file has not changed and does not have any errors. indicates that the linked file has been modified.

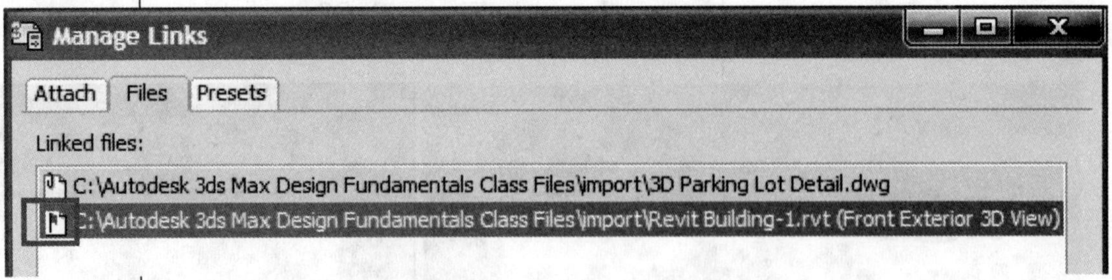

Figure 3–39

7. Verify that the filename is still selected and click Reload....

8. In the File Link Settings dialog box, in the *Materials* area, select **Keep 3ds Max scene material assignments on reload** to keep the materials that have been applied in the Autodesk 3ds Max software. Click OK. The scene is refreshed with the new changes.

9. In the Manage Links dialog box, in the *Files* tab, the icon has changed to the icon shown in Figure 3–40. This indicates that there are no differences between the original file and the linked file.

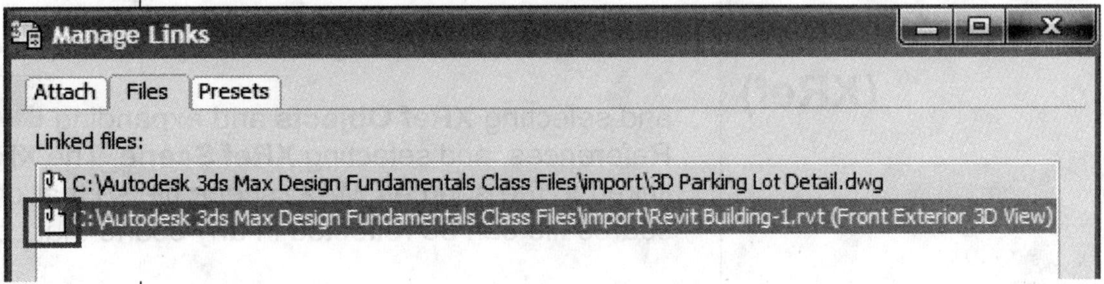

Figure 3–40

10. Close the Manage Links dialog box.

11. In the viewports, the modified building is displayed. Note that more windows have been added to the building, as shown in Figure 3–41.

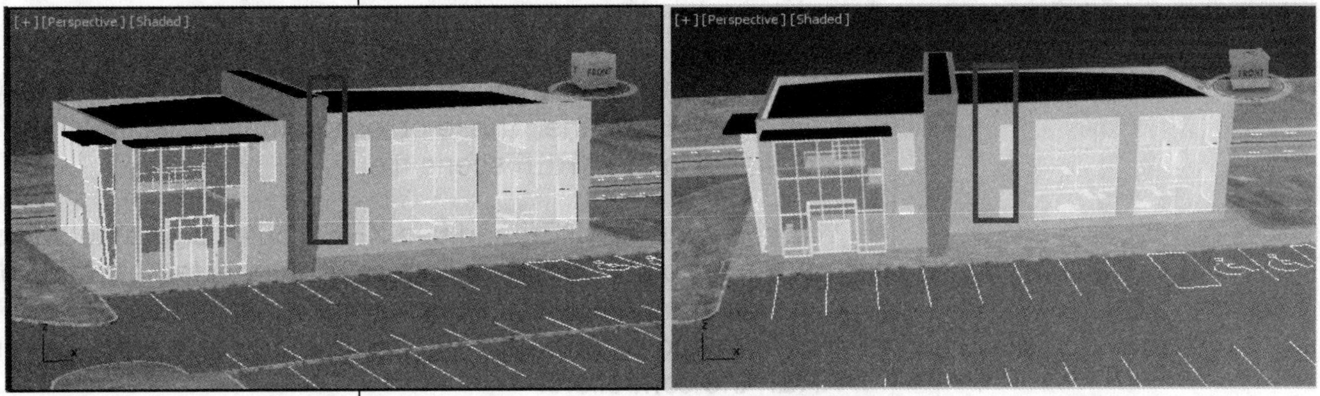

Figure 3–41

12. Save the file as **MyCivil Base Link.max**.

3.3 References

Learning Objectives

- Incorporate objects or other scene files into the current scene by externally referencing them.
- Manage data using the asset tracking systems.

External References (XRef)

Autodesk 3ds Max Design Scene files can also reference data from other scene files by expanding , expanding References, and selecting **XRef Objects** and expanding , expanding References, and selecting **XRef Scene**. The XREF data remains linked to the source (.MAX) scene file so that changes in the source file can be reflected in any scene that contains the XREF.

- External References are useful to break up large projects into more manageable pieces, permit more than one person to work on the same project at the same time in separate files, and to enable the same core scene geometry to be used in multiple files with different lighting conditions and/or animations.
- **XRef Scenes** bring in the entire scene. All of the XREF objects are non-selectable and cannot be modified.
- **XRef Objects** enable you to select individual objects (or all) from an XREF scene. These objects remain selectable and modifiable in the XREF scene file.
- You can snap to XREF and use XREF objects with AutoGrid. You can also use XREF objects as alignment targets and you can select an XREF object's coordinate system for object transformation. XREF support parameter wiring and you can XREF the controllers.
- In the Autodesk 3ds Max Design software, a referenced .DWG, .FBX, .DXF, or .RVT file is a linked file and not an XREF. An Autodesk 3ds Max Design XREF is a reference to the data in another .MAX scene file. Objects in scenes (.MAX) are imported into other . MAX scenes using the **Merge** option.

Data Management and Asset Tracking

In addition to merging and externally referencing other scene file geometry, the Autodesk 3ds Max Design software also enables you to manage your data through Data Management (DM) solutions, which are also referred to as Asset Tracking Systems (ATSs).

- DM solutions such as the Autodesk® Vault software enables you to store scene files and any supporting data (like material maps) in a single database repository.
- These systems can be accessed simultaneously by multiple users who might be assigned different rights based on their project responsibilities. Data can be checked out for editing by one individual at a time while still being referenced by other users. Users can see who is editing which portion of the project at any time.
- By centralizing the files in a DM system it is much easier to adjust paths for external files like image maps.
- Data files can be versioned through DM solutions, so that the older versions of files can be readily accessed, if needed.
- Asset Tracking is an important application for users working on complex projects in a multi-user environment. Working with these sophisticated solutions places their use outside the scope of an introductory-level course. For more information see *Asset Tracking* in the Autodesk 3ds Max Design Help files. Asset Tracking is available by expanding , expanding References, and selecting **Asset Tracking**.

Practice 3d XRef and Merge Objects

Learning Objectives

- Link an AutoCAD .DWG file to the current scene.
- Incorporate objects from another scene file into the current scene using **XREF**.
- Merge objects into the current scene file.

Estimated time for completion: 15 minutes

In this practice create a new scene file that will contain linked AutoCAD objects and XRef objects from the Civil Base scene.

You must set the paths to locate the External files and Xrefs used in the practice. If you have not done this already, return to the **Introduction to Autodesk 3ds Max Design** chapter and complete Task 1 to Task 3 of the **Organizing Folders and Working with the Interface** practice. You only have to set the user paths once.

Task 1 - Assemble the Data.

If an unsaved scene is open, you need to save or discard the changes to the scene.

1. Expand and select **Reset**. Click Yes to reset the scene.
2. The Architectural scene should have the System Unit Scale For the Civil 3D surfaces, the system units scale was set to **Feet**. To change it back to **Inches**, select **Customize>Units Setup**. In the dialog box, verify that *Display Unit Scale* is set to **US Standard**, **Feet w/Fractional Inches**, *Default Units* is set to **Inches**, and *Lighting Units* to **American**. Click System Unit Setup. In the System Unit Setup dialog box, set *System Unit Scale* to **Inches**. Click OK in both the dialog boxes.
3. Expand , expand References, and select **Manage Links**. In the *Attach* tab, click File.... In your *Class Files* folder> *import* subfolder, select **Exterior AutoCAD Architectural Model.dwg**. Click Open.

4. In the *Preset* drop-down list, select **AutoCAD – Derive by Layer** and click Attach this file. Once the file has been loaded, close the dialog box by clicking X.

   - The AutoCAD Architectural objects were not joined together by layer. Each was subdivided by material type into different objects. Materials previously assigned in AutoCAD Architecture were preserved on these separate objects.

5. Click (Maximize Viewport Toggle) or use <Alt>+<W> to display the four viewport view.

6. Click (Zoom Extents All) to display all of the objects in all of the viewports.

7. In the Front viewport, select all of the objects by creating a window around the objects. In the Main toolbar, in the *Named Selection Sets* field, enter **exterior AutoCAD Architectural building**, as shown in Figure 3–42 and press <Enter>.

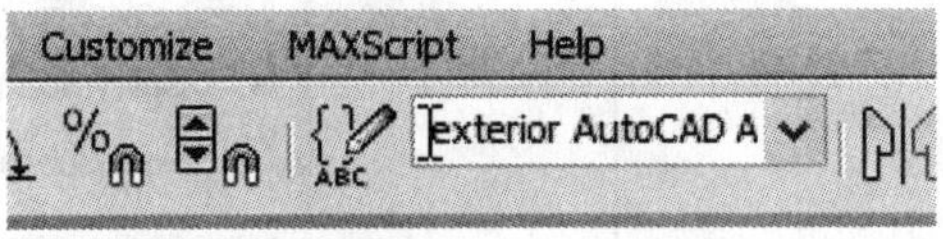

Figure 3–42

You select objects to XREF rather than the entire scene because XREF scene objects cannot be selected or modified.

8. Expand , expand References, and select **XRef Objects**. In the XRef Objects dialog box, click (Create XRef Record from File) as shown in Figure 3–43.

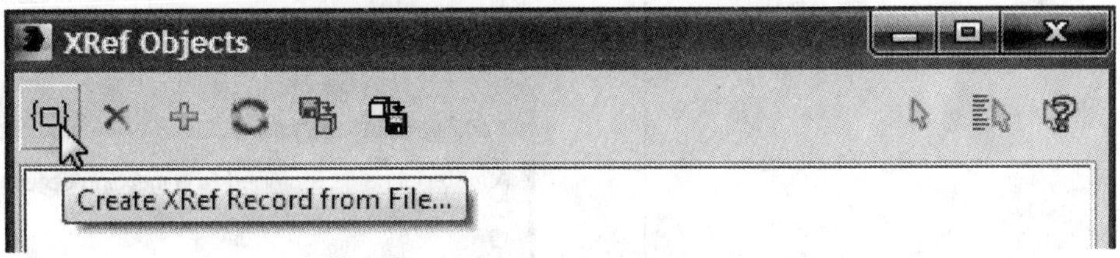

Figure 3–43

9. In the Open File dialog box, select **Parking Lot Detail.max** (*Class Files* folder>*import* subfolder) and click Open.

10. In the XRef Merge dialog box, click All (at the bottom of the dialog box) to select all of the objects, as shown in Figure 3–44. Click OK.

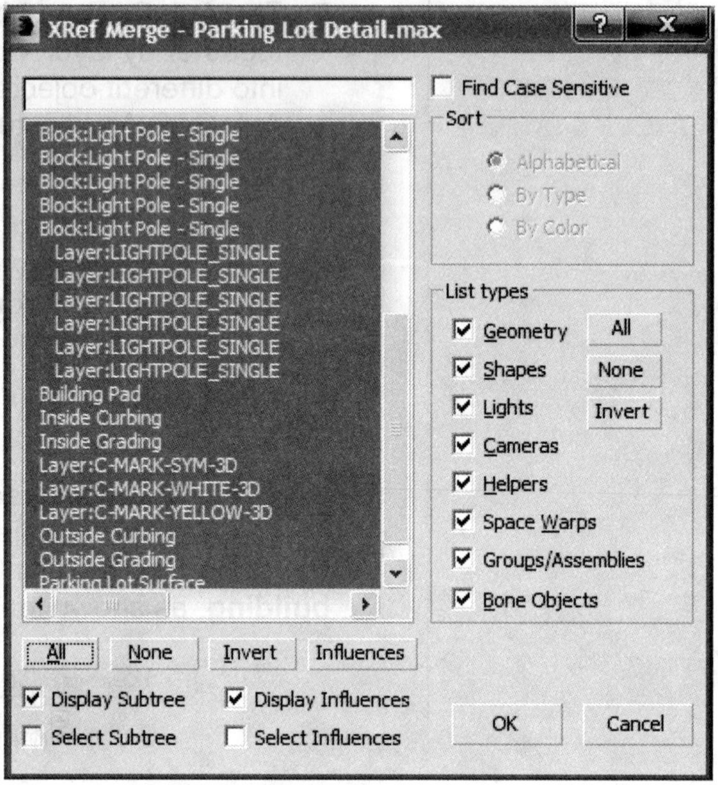

Figure 3–44

11. The Duplicate Material Name dialog box opens prompting you that there is an incoming material with the same name as an existing scene material. Select **Apply to All Duplicates**, as shown in Figure 3–45, to keep both materials and click Auto-Rename Merged Material.

Figure 3–45

12. In the XRef Objects dialog box, note that the .MAX filename is displayed. Close the dialog box by clicking .

13. Click (Zoom Extents All). Note that the Civil Base objects are located far from the origin. This is a coordinate system discrepancy and not a scale issue. It is common for Architectural drawings to be based in a different coordinate system and scale than the accompanying Civil/Survey drawings.

Task 2 - Coordinate the Data.

In this task you will relocate the Civil Base in the Architectural Data. To line up the data accurately you will need the exact coordinate translation and rotation. You can measure ahead of time in programs, such as AutoCAD by comparing the coordinates of points common to both files.

Alternatively, you can press <Ctrl>+<A> or select all of the objects using the cursor.

1. In the Main toolbar, click (Select by Name). In the Select From Scene dialog box, click (Display None) and click (Display Object XRefs). Click (Select All) to select all of the XRef objects in the list and click OK.
2. With only the XRef objects selected, select **Group>Group**.
3. In the Group dialog box, set the *Group name* to be **Site XRef** and click OK.
4. In the Main toolbar, click (Select and Move). In the Reference Coordinate System, select **World**, as shown in Figure 3–46 and click (Use Transform Coordinate Center).

Figure 3–46

5. In the Status Bar, verify that (Absolute Mode) is displayed (which means it is enabled).

6. In the *Transform Type-in* area, set *X:* to **-197'4"**, *Y:* to **-30'0"**, and *Z:* to **-4'11"**, as shown in Figure 3–47, and press <Enter>. (The translation coordinates have already been measured in AutoCAD.)

Figure 3–47

7. In the Main toolbar, click (Select Object) to exit the **Move** transform operation.

8. Click (Zoom Extents All). In the Perspective viewport, use (Zoom), (Orbit), and **Pan** to zoom into the parking lot and building area (as shown in Figure 3–48), and verify the building is located on the building pad. Even though the XREF had a different Unit Scale (feet), it scaled correctly to the current scene (in inches).

Figure 3–48

9. Save your work as **MyArchitectural Scene.max**.

Task 3 - Merging Objects.

In this task you will merge the light poles.

1. Expand , expand Import, and select **Merge**. In the Merge File dialog box, select **Light Poles for Project1.max** from your *Class Files\scenes* folder. Click Open. In the Merge dialog box, click All (bottom of the dialog box) to select all of the objects and click OK.

Merge enables both objects to have the same name, Skip ignores the incoming object, and Delete Old removes the original object.

2. The Duplicate Name dialog box opens, prompting you that an object with the same name already exists in the scene. Select **Apply to all Duplicates** and click Auto-Rename.
3. The light poles are displayed in the viewport, as shown in Figure 3–49.

Figure 3–49

4. Save your work.

Chapter Review Questions

1. The following file types can be linked to the current Autodesk 3ds Max Design scene:
   a. .DWG, .OBJ, .APF, .FBX
   b. .DWG, .DXF, .FBX, .RVT
   c. .DWG, .DXF, .MAX, .RVT
   d. .DWG, .OBJ, .FBX, .RVT
2. In the Manage Links dialog box, in the *Files* tab, which of the following options do you use to remove the link with the original linked file but maintain its geometry in the current scene?
   a. Reload...
   b. Detach...
   c. Bind...
3. Which command do you use to combine objects from a saved Autodesk 3ds Max Design scene (.MAX file) into your current .MAX scene?
   a. **Import**
   b. **Link**
   c. **Open**
   d. **Merge**
4. While linking Autodesk Revit files in the current Autodesk 3ds Max scene, which of the following options are provided in the Combine Entities List? (Select all that apply.)
   a. By Revit Material
   b. By Revit Layer
   c. As One Object
   d. By Revit Camera
5. When an entire .MAX scene is brought into the current scene using **XREF Scenes**, the XREF objects are selectable but cannot be modified.
   a. True
   b. False

Command Summary

Button	Command	Location
	**Absolute Mode**	■ **Status Bar**
	Asset Tracking	■ **Application Menu:** References
	Import	■ **Application Menu:** Import
	Link AutoCAD	■ **Application Menu:** Import
	Link FBX	■ **Application Menu:** Import
	Link Revit	■ **Application Menu:** Import
	Manage Links	■ **Application Menu:** References
	Merge	■ **Application Menu:** Import
	**Select by Name**	■ **Main toolbar**
	**Select Object**	■ **Main toolbar**
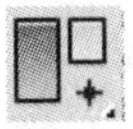	**Use Transform Coordinate Center**	■ **Main toolbar**
	XRef Objects	■ **Application Menu:** References
	XRef Scene	■ **Application Menu:** References

Chapter 4

Basic Modeling Techniques

In this chapter you learn to model using primitive objects and to apply transforms to move, rotate, and scale them. You learn about Sub-object modes and how to use them to modify the objects at sub-object levels. You also learn to clone and group objects and to model objects using the Graphite Modeling tools located in the Ribbon.

This chapter contains the following topics:

- ✓**Model with Primitives**
- ✓**Modifiers and Transforms**
- ✓**Sub-Object Mode**
- ✓**Reference Coordinate Systems and Transform Centers**
- ✓**Cloning and Grouping**
- ✓**Polygon Modeling Tools in the Ribbon**
- ✓**Statistics in Viewport**

4.1 Model with Primitives

Learning Objective

- Understand the different kinds of primitive objects provided with the software.

The Autodesk® 3ds Max® Design software enables you to create and adjust 3D geometry by creating a complex model from simple 3D objects called primitives, as shown in Figure 4–1.

Figure 4–1

- Different kinds of already built objects, such as Standard Primitives, Extended Primitives, Compound Objects, etc., are listed in the **Create>Geometry** Command Panel, as shown in Figure 4–2. Each of these categories consists of a group of objects that can easily be modeled by selecting an object type and drawing the model in the viewport. You can use the mouse to drag to the locations (length, height, etc.) or enter the precise values in the Parameters rollout in the Command Panel. These primitives can be used to create simple or complex objects by modifying them.

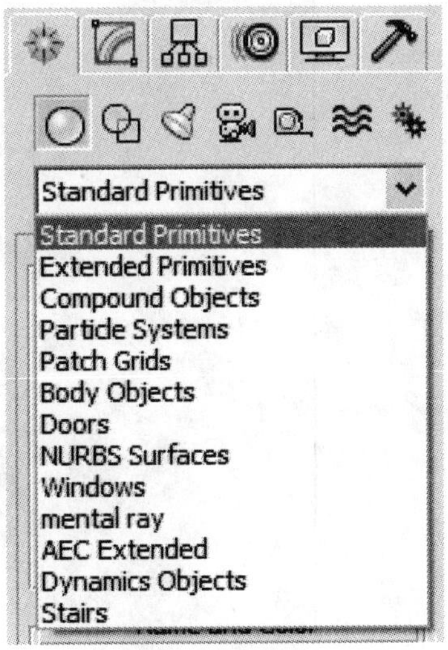

Figure 4–2

- Not everyone works with the Autodesk 3ds Max Design software as their primary modeling tool. However, even for those who do not, modeling with Autodesk 3ds Max Design primitives might still be useful for additional dressing or background objects to add to your imported scenes.
- Modeling with primitives is only one approach to creating geometry in the Autodesk 3ds Max Design software. Other processes, such as modeling with modifiers, creating loft compound objects, or creating a 3D terrain from 2D contour objects, can also be done.

Practice 4a Modeling with Primitives

Learning Objectives

- Create primitive objects by using standard primitives and entering their parameters in the Command Panel.
- Modify the object using the *Modify* panel in the Command Panel.

Estimated time for completion: 10 minutes

In this practice you will model the base for the parking lot light fixtures.

You must set the paths to locate the External files and Xrefs used in the practice. If you have not done this already, return to the **Introduction to Autodesk 3ds Max Design** chapter and complete Task 1 to Task 3 of the **Organizing Folders and Working with the Interface** practice. You only have to set the user paths once.

If a dialog box opens prompting you about a File Load: Mismatch, click OK *to accept the default values.*

1. Open **Modeling with Primitives.max** from your *Class Files* folder. It is an empty base scene file.
2. Click in the Top viewport to make it active. The orientation of the object being created depends on the active viewport. For this practice, you will create the cylinder with its height in the Z-axis direction.
3. In the Command Panel, verify that the *Create* panel ( ) is selected. Verify that (Geometry) is selected as well and that **Standard Primitives** is displayed in the drop-down list. In the Object Type rollout, click Cylinder.

The 0,0,0 location corresponds to the default axes (center of the active grid) of the construction plane. Any value entered for X,Y, and Z, offsets the object by that number in the specified direction.

You can enter the values directly in their respective fields or use the spinner arrows to increase or decrease the values. After entering a value in a field, click in another edit field or press <Enter> to assign the values to the object.

4. If the Keyboard Entry rollout is collapsed, click the plus (+) sign to expand it. In the Keyboard Entry rollout, leave the X, Y, Z coordinates at **0'0"**. The software places the base center of the cylinder at 0,0,0, location. Set the *Radius* to **1'0"** and the *Height* to **3'0"** and press <Enter>, as shown in Figure 4–3. Click Create.

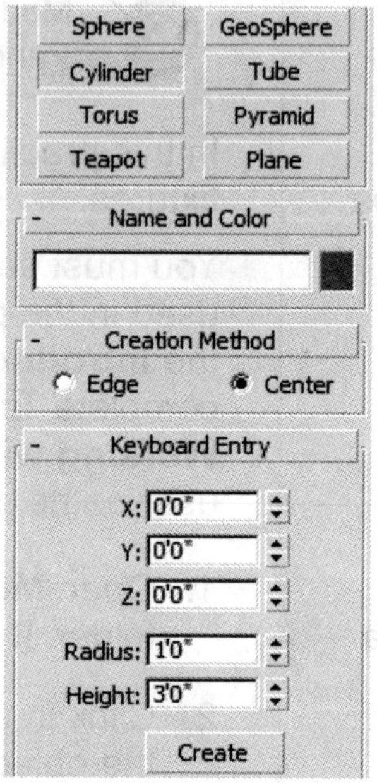

Figure 4–3

> **Hint: Creating Objects**
>
> After creating an object, you cannot change the parameters in the Keyboard Entry rollout. Changing the parameters in the Keyboard Entry rollout and clicking Create adds a second object. If you created another object, in the Quick Access Toolbar, click (Undo) once to undo the creation of second object.
>
> After creating an object, use the *Modify* panel ( ) to change the parameters. Select the object if necessary and select the *Modify* panel.

5. Click (Zoom Extents All) display the base more clearly. Note that it zooms into the cylinder in all of the viewports.
6. With the cylinder still selected, in the Command Panel, select the *Modify* panel ( ). At the top of the modifier list, in the *Name* field, rename the object from Cylinder001 to **LP Base**.

7. In the Parameters rollout, set *Radius* to **1'6"**. You can also set the number of segments and sides for the object. Try changing these values to see what effect they have on the geometry. Set both *Height Segments* and *Cap Segments* to **1** (default) and *Sides* to **20**, as shown Figure 4–4.

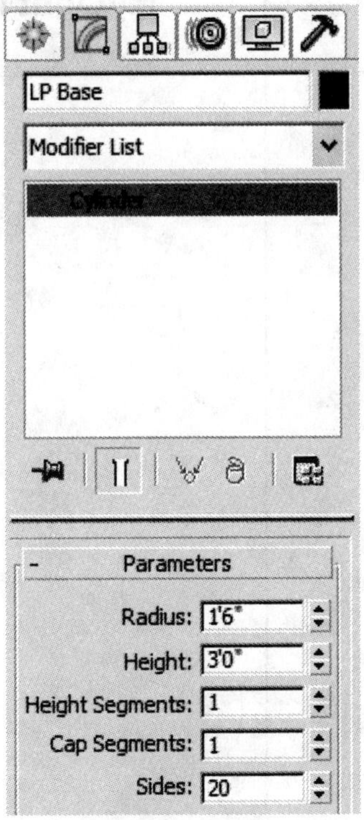

Figure 4–4

8. Select the *Create* panel ( ) and in the Object Type rollout, click Box to create the anchor base plate. In the Keyboard Entry rollout set *X, Y, Z* coordinates to **0'0"**, **0'0"**, **3'0"**. This will create the center of the base of the box at the 0,0,3 location, which is the top of the cylinder (the height of the cylinder is 3'-0"). Set the *Length* and *Width* to **1'4"** and the *Height* to **0'2"**. Click Create. A box is created on top of the Base cylinder, as shown in Figure 4–5.

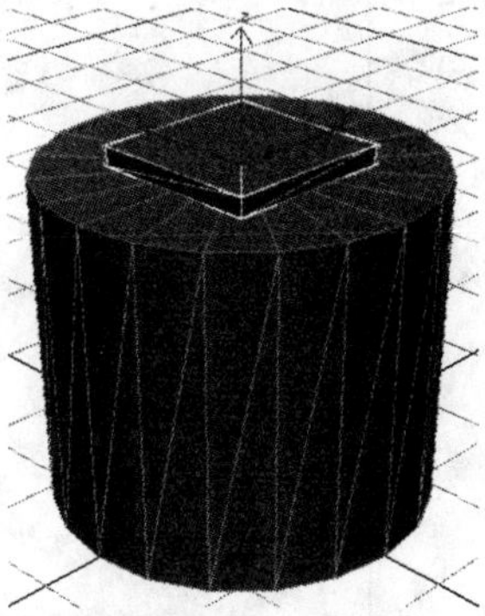

Figure 4–5

9. With the box still selected, select the *Modify* panel () and rename the object as **LP Anchor Base**.

10. Expand and select **Save As** and save your work as **MyLight Pole.max**.

Certification

Topic:

✓UI/Object Management

Objectives:

✓Describe and use object transformations

4.2 Modifiers and Transforms

Learning Objectives

- Apply changes to the model geometry using the modifiers provided with the software.
- Move, rotate, and scale objects using the **Transform** tools.
- Understand how to constrain the movement of the **Transform** tools using the toolbar and the gizmo.

Many CAD and 3D graphic programs consider **Move**, **Rotate**, and **Scale** as modify options similar to **Stretch**, **Break**, and **Trim**. However, in the Autodesk 3ds Max Design software there is a significant distinction between modifiers and transforms.

- **Modifiers** add geometric and property alterations to objects. They are listed in the Modifier Stack and their parameter values are available for adjustment afterwards.
- **Transforms** are used to translate (move) and scale objects in the scene. The three Autodesk 3ds Max Design transforms are **Move**, **Rotate**, and **Scale**. Transforms are conducted by accessing a transform mode and entering new values or graphically transforming objects on the screen.
- Transforms are applied to objects after basic parameters and modifiers have been taken into account (except world-space modifiers). For example, if you scale a box, the **Length** parameter shown in the Modifier Stack does not take into account the effects of the scale transform.
- An object can have any number of modifiers, but only has a single set of transform values at any time.
- Transforms and almost all object and modifier parameters can be animated in the Autodesk 3ds Max Design software. For example, a walkthrough animation can be created using Move Transform to move the camera or its target or both.
- Transform modes are initiated by selecting the required buttons in the Main toolbar or by using the Transform modes in the right-click quad menu.

Modifier List

Any object that you create can be modified using the modifiers in the Modifier List, as shown in Figure 4–6. This list is located in the *Modify* panel () on top of the Modifier Stack. Click the down arrow to display the list. Modifiers are placed in groups and then listed alphabetically. The list of modifiers is long and the complete list does not display on the screen. Click and drag the scroll bar on the right of the Modifier drop-down list to display the modifiers at the bottom of the list. If you know the name of the modifier, you can enter the first letter to jump to that part of the selection list.

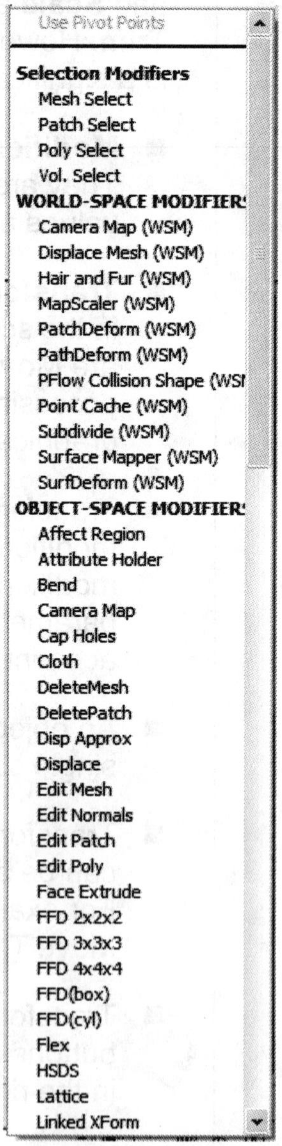

Figure 4–6

Transform Tools

The available Transform tools are:

	Select and Move
	Select and Rotate
	Select and Scale: Scaling has three flyout options: (Uniform), (Non-uniform), and (Squash). **Non-uniform** enables you to scale one or two axes independently. **Squash** enables you to do the same, but scaling one or two axes applies a simultaneous opposite scaling to the other(s). The Scale Transform gizmo also has the tools for Non-uniform scaling.

Hint: XForm Modifier with Scale

It is recommended that you do not to use the Scale transform directly on objects. Instead, apply an XForm modifier to the objects and then **Scale** the XForm gizmo. This avoids many problems in animation, because you can define when the scale is taking place at the sub-object level.

To display a toolbar, right-click anywhere on an empty space in the Main toolbar and select the required toolbar.

Transforms can be constrained to one or two axes by selecting one of the buttons in the Axis Constraints toolbar, as shown in Figure 4–7. However, it is more common to use the gizmos or the keyboard shortcuts to constrain the transforms. This toolbar is hidden by default.

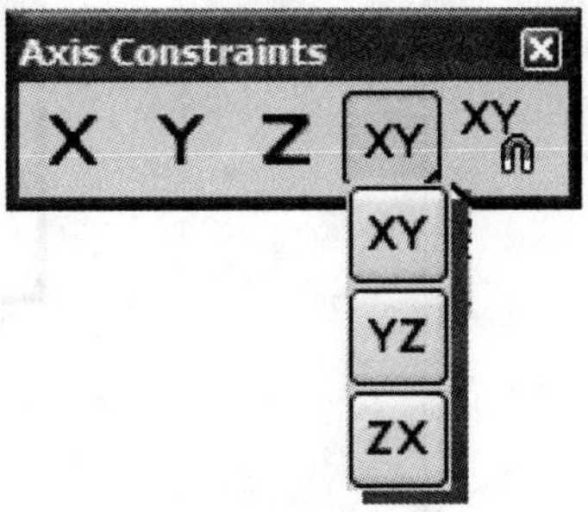

Figure 4–7

When a transform mode is active, a Transform gizmo displays, as shown in Figure 4–8, on the selected object on the screen.

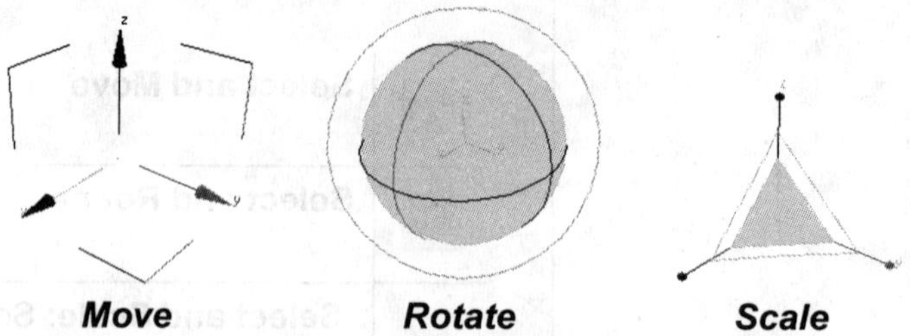

Figure 4–8

Clicking and dragging over the gizmo enables you to perform the transform interactively on the screen. You can also constrain the transform by highlighting an axis handle on the gizmo before clicking and dragging.

You can apply a transform accurately by entering the required transform values in the *Transform Type-In* area in the Status Bar, as shown in Figure 4–9. You can also use the spinners next to each constraint to change the values.

Figure 4–9

In the Main toolbar, right-click on the **Transform** button to open its Transform Type-In dialog box, as shown in Figure 4–10 for the Move transform.

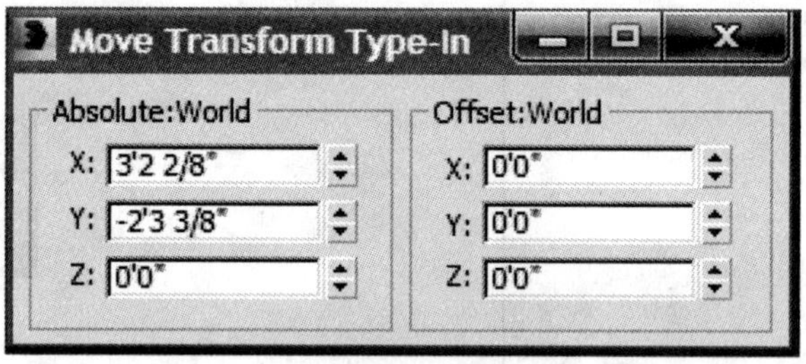

Figure 4–10

The Transform Type-In dialog box can also be accessed by right-clicking on the object and clicking (Settings) to the right of **Move**, **Rotate**, or **Scale**, as shown in Figure 4–11.

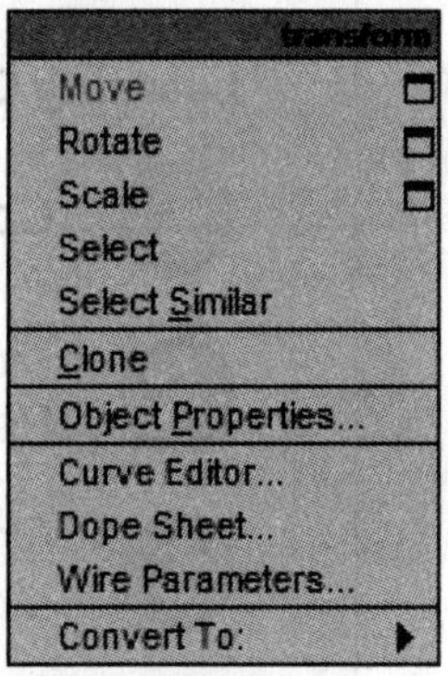

Figure 4–11

Transform modes remain active until they are canceled. One way to cancel a transform mode is by clicking (Select Object) in the Main toolbar or pressing <Q>. You can click (Select Object) after you have finished a transform to avoid accidentally moving, rotating, or scaling objects while making selections.

Practice 4b Modeling with Modifiers and Transforms

Learning Objectives

- Create a 2D shape and then extrude it into a 3D object.
- Modify objects using the *Modify* panel in the Command Panel.
- Create primitive solids dynamically in the viewport using the mouse to define the various parameters.
- Move and rotate objects to place them at the right location using the **Transform** tools.

Estimated time for completion: 20-30 minutes

In this practice you will refine the parking lot lighting fixture with Modifiers, then use Transforms to locate objects in the correct scene positions.

You must set the paths to locate the External files and Xrefs used in the practice. If you have not done this already, return to the **Introduction to Autodesk 3ds Max Design** chapter and complete Task 1 to Task 3 of the **Organizing Folders and Working with the Interface** practice. You only have to set the user paths once.

Task 1 - Extrude and Adjust the Light Pole.

Modeling 3D geometry from 2D shapes is discussed in detail later in the Training Guide.

To create the rectangular light pole, create a 2D cross-section shape and then extrude it into a 3D object. This approach is another way to create 3D geometry.

1. Continue working with the file created in the previous practice, **MyLightPole.max**. If you did not complete it, open **Modeling with Modifiers and Transforms.max** from your *Class Files* folder.
2. Verify that the Top viewport is active.
3. In the *Create* panel ( ), click (Shapes) to create 2D objects. Verify that the *Splines* sub-category is displayed in the drop-down list and click Rectangle, as shown in Figure 4–12.

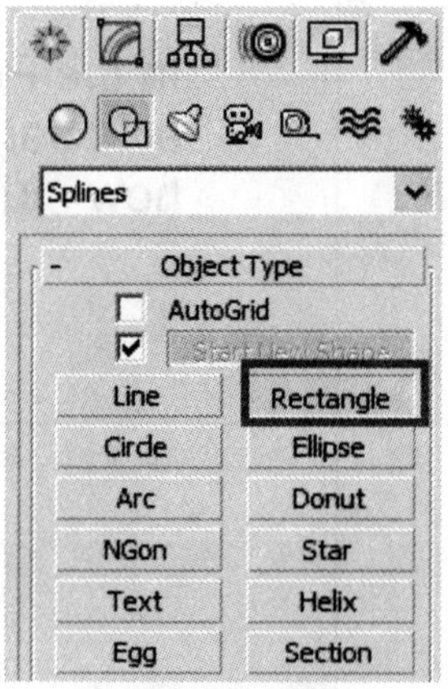

Figure 4–12

4. In the Command Panel, expand the Keyboard Entry rollout and set *X, Y, and Z* to **0'0", 0'0"**, and **3'2"**. Set *Length* and *Width* to **0'6"** each and set *Corner Radius* to **0'1"**. Click Create.

The modifiers in the Modifier drop-down list are placed in groups and then listed alphabetically. Click and drag the scroll bar to the right of the Modifier drop-down list to display the modifiers at the bottom of the list.

5. A 2D rectangle is created on top of the base plate. With the rectangle still selected, select the *Modify* panel ( ). Expand the Modifier List by clicking the down arrow. In the drop-down list, select **Extrude** in the *OBJECT SPACE MODIFIERS* category. Note that Extrude is listed in the Modifier Stack above the Rectangle entry, as shown in Figure 4–13.

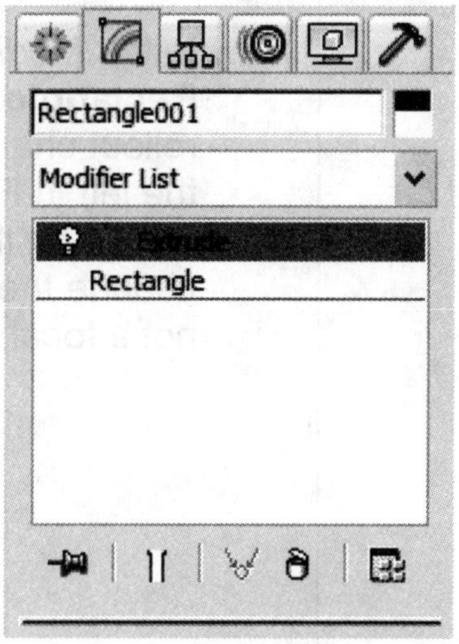

Figure 4–13

6. In the Parameters rollout, set *Amount* to **15'0"** and leave the other parameters at their default settings.

7. Rename the object *Rectangle001* as **LP Pole**.

8. In the Perspective viewport, use (Zoom) and **Pan** to get a closer look at the light pole, as shown in Figure 4–14. Note how much detail the light pole's fillet adds to the model.

Figure 4–14

- The Extrude modifier is listed directly above the Rectangle object in the Modifier Stack. The rectangle's parameters are still accessible and can be changed after the extrude is added.

> **Hint: Simple Models**
>
> You should remove any unnecessary detail if the object is meant to be a background item and not the main focus of the visualization. Keeping models simple reduces the file size and speeds up software performance and rendering times.

9. In the *Modify* panel ( ), in the Modifier Stack, select **Rectangle**. It is highlighted as dark gray. In the Interpolation rollout change *Steps* to **2** and press <Enter>, as shown on the left in Figure 4–15. The fillet divisions are reduced, as shown on the right in Figure 4–15. (In your projects you might change the *Steps* to **0** or not use fillets at all, if the object is not a focal point of the visualization.)

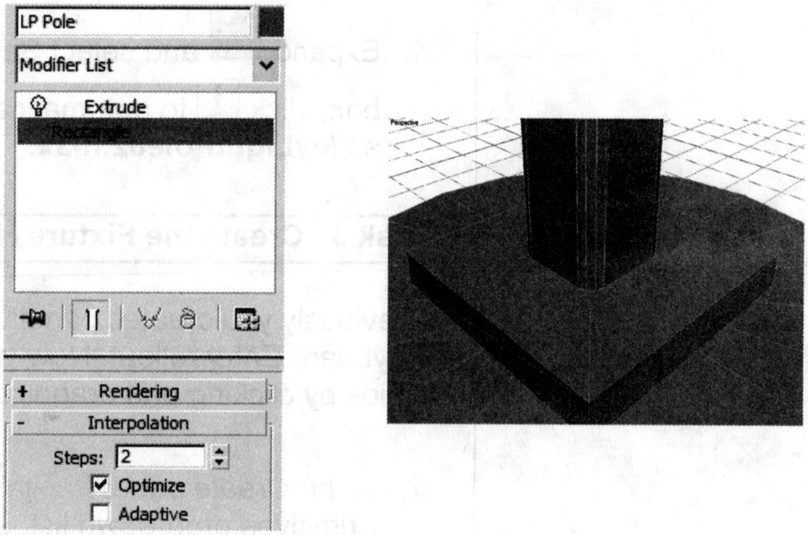

Figure 4–15

10. Expand [icon] and select **Save As** and save your work as **MyLightPole01.max**.

Task 2 - Taper the Light Pole.

Click and drag the scroll bar in the Modifier List drop-down because Taper is located near the bottom of the list and is not displayed on the screen.

1. In the Modifier Stack, select **Extrude** (so that the next modifier Taper is applied after the Extrude). In the Modifier List, select **Taper**, located at the bottom of this list. Note that the Taper displays above the Extrude in the Modifier Stack, as shown in Figure 4–16. The Modifier Stack lists modifiers in reverse historical order.

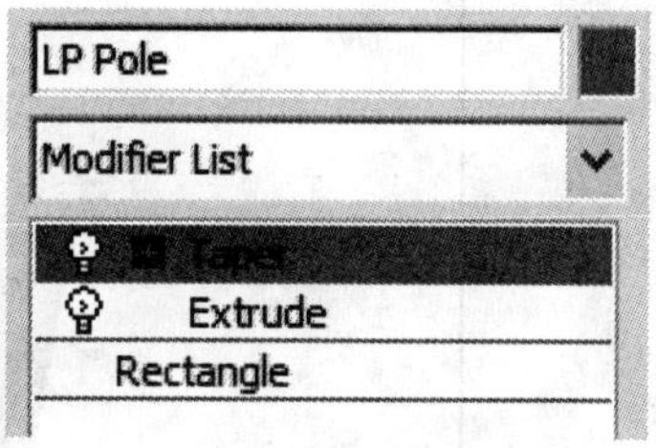

Figure 4–16

2. In the *Taper* area of the Parameters rollout, set *Amount* to **-0.5**, which relates to approximately a 50% size reduction over the height of the object. Press <Enter>. You can still adjust the original **Rectangle** and **Extrude** parameters by selecting them in the Modifier Stack.

3. Click [icon] (Zoom Extents All) to see all of the objects in the viewports. Note the taper on the pole towards the top.

4. Expand and select **Save As**. In the Save File As dialog box, click + to automatically save your work incrementally as **MyLightPole02.max**.

Task 3 - Create the Fixture Housing and Globe.

Previously you created primitives by keying in exact values in the Keyboard Entry rollout. Now you will roughly size the primitive solids by clicking and dragging with the mouse in the viewport.

1. In the *Create* panel ( )> (Geometry), in the Standard Primitives drop-down list, select **Extended Primitives** as a sub-category. In the Object Type rollout, click ChamferCyl.
2. In the Perspective viewport, next to the base (LP Base), click and drag the left mouse button to size the radius to roughly **2'0"** (note the Parameters rollout in the Command Panel where the Radius changes interactively as you move the cursor). You do not have to be accurate because you will modify the dimensions later. After releasing the mouse button, move the cursor up the screen slightly to give the cylinder a height of approximately **1'0"**. Click a second time to set the cylinder height. Then move the cursor up and down the screen until you can roughly define a **0'2"** fillet. Complete the object creation process with a third click. The object should display as shown in Figure 4–17.

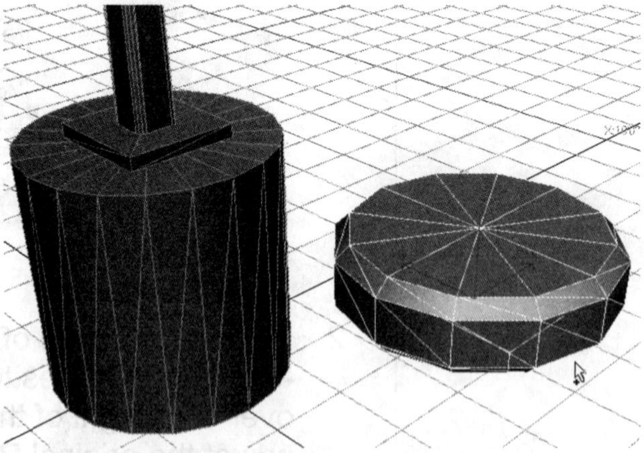

Figure 4–17

- All primitives can be sized by clicks and drags as you did here. You can enter the parameters of the object before creating it or you can sketch in an object this way and fix its dimensions and position after creating it.

3. With the ChamferCyl object still selected, in the Command Panel, select the *Modify* panel ( ) and modify the parameters, as shown in Figure 4–18.

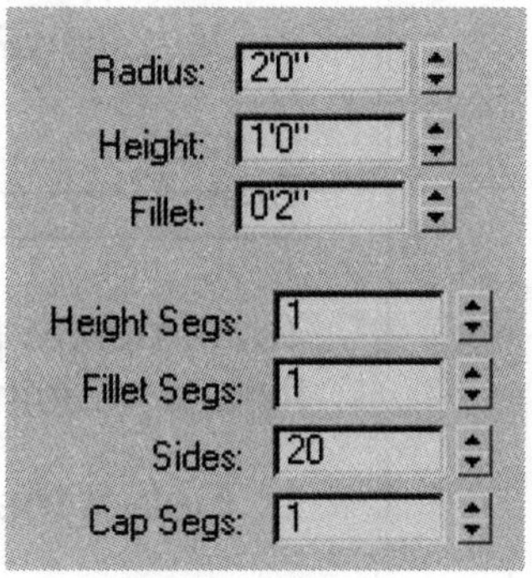

Figure 4–18

4. Name the object **LP Fixture Housing**.

5. In the *Create* panel ( ), verify that (Geometry) is selected. In the drop-down list, select **Standard Primitives** as a sub-category. In the Object Type rollout, click Sphere to create the fixture's globe. Click and drag anywhere on the screen to size a sphere of approximately **1'0"** in radius.

   Select the *Modify* panel ( ) and assign the parameters, as shown in Figure 4–19. Note the effects that each of them has on the model, specifically the **Hemisphere** and **Smooth** values. A value of **0.5** for the hemisphere creates half a sphere.

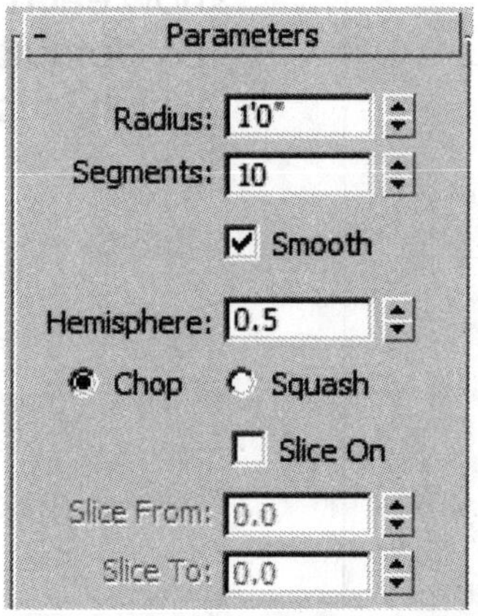

Figure 4–19

6. Select the **Squash** option in the rollout. This option generates more faces and creates a smoother appearance. Since the globe is often where the viewer's attention will be focused when looking at the light pole, you should make it look as good as possible while keeping the polygon count low.

7. Rename the hemisphere **LP Fixture Globe**.

8. Expand [icon] and select **Save As** and click [icon] to automatically save your work incrementally as **MyLightPole03.max**.

Task 4 - Use Transforms to Position Objects.

To complete this practice you will rotate and move the light pole fixture housing and globe into position.

1. Select the **LP Fixture Housing** (the chamfered cylinder) and in the Main toolbar, click [icon] (Select and Move).

2. In the Main toolbar, set the *Reference Coordinate System* to **World** by selecting it from the drop-down list and click [icon] (Use Pivot Point Center), as shown in Figure 4–20.

Figure 4–20

3. The Move gizmo displays over the object, as shown in Figure 4–21. Move the fixture housing by clicking and dragging the gizmo's axis handles and plane handles, noting how each constrains the movement to a certain axis or plane. By default, the gizmo displays at the object's pivot point, which is located at the bottom center for this object.

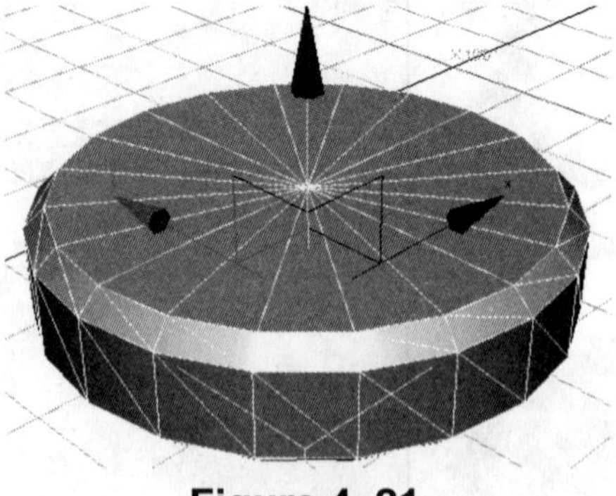

Figure 4–21

4. To position the object precisely, use the Transform Type-In controls located in the Status Bar at the bottom of your screen. Verify that (Absolute Mode Transform Type-In) is displayed in the Status Bar. The **Absolute Mode** button toggles with (Offset Mode). (Absolute Mode Transform Type-In) should display.

   - If the values are entered in **Offset Mode**, they are added to the current coordinates. **Offset Mode** is useful if you want to move an object a certain distance but are not sure what the resulting coordinates will be.

5. Set *X* to **0'0"**, *Y* to **-6'0"**, and *Z* to **19'0"**, as shown in Figure 4–22, and press <Enter>.

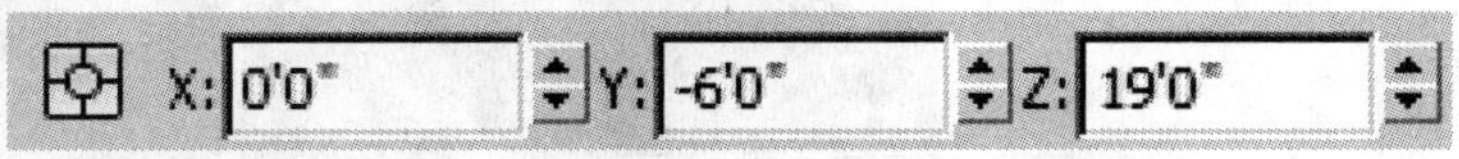

Figure 4–22

6. Click (Zoom Extents All) to display all of the objects in the viewports. In the Left viewport, note that the **LP Fixture Housing** (the chamfered cylinder) has now moved to the top right side of the light pole assembly.

7. As the **Move** transform and **Absolute Mode** are already active, select **LP Fixture Globe** (hemisphere) and enter the same X, Y, Z coordinates. The half globe moves inside the fixture housing.

8. Click (Zoom Extents All) to display all of the objects in the viewport.

9. With the half globe still selected, in the Main toolbar, click (Select and Rotate).

10. In the Status Bar, the *X, Y, Z Transform Type-In* fields display the current rotations which are **0**. Set *X* to **180** and note the position of the globe is inverted. The object should display as shown in Figure 4–23 for the Left viewport.

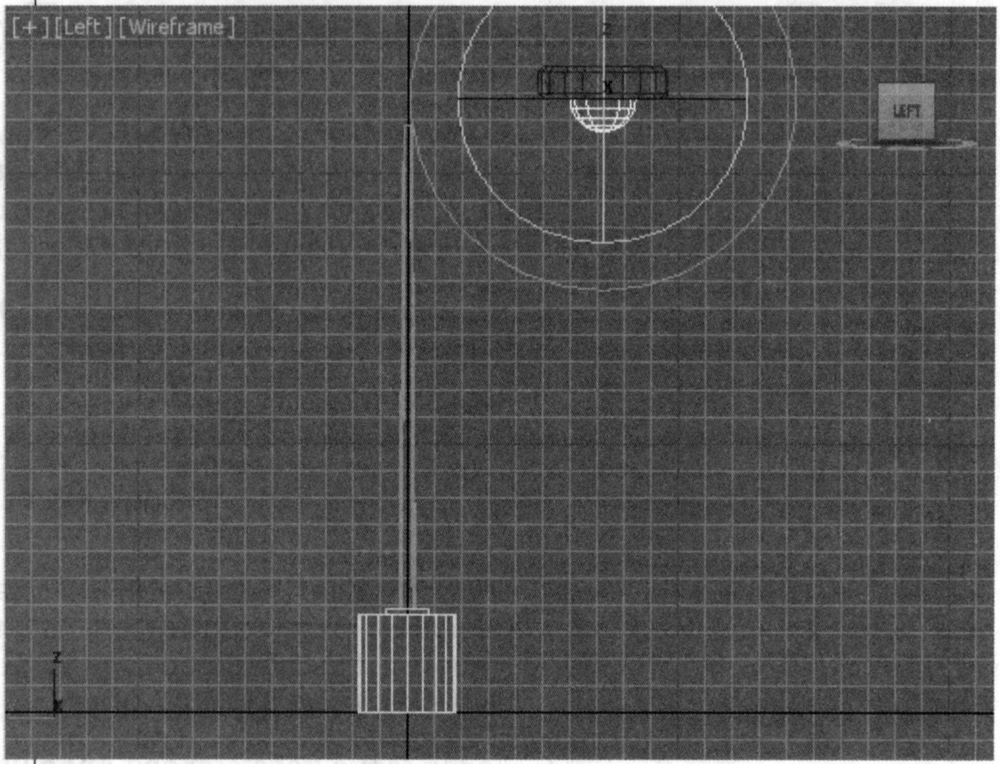

Figure 4–23

11. Click  (Select Object) or press <Q> to end the **Rotate** transform as a precaution to avoid rotating objects accidentally.

12. Expand  and select **Save As** and click  to automatically save your work incrementally as **MyLightPole04.max**.

Certification

Topic:

✓*Modeling*

Objectives:

✓*Use polygon modeling tools*

4.3 Sub-Object Mode

Learning Objective

Modify objects at a sub-object level using the Sub-object modes.

Many of the objects and modifiers in the Autodesk 3ds Max Design software contain sub-objects that can be independently adjusted through transforms and special modifier controls.

These sub-objects are adjusted through a special Autodesk 3ds Max Design state called Sub-object mode. For example, the **Taper** modifier in the column has Gizmo and Center sub-objects, as shown in Figure 4–24, that can be adjusted to position the Taper.

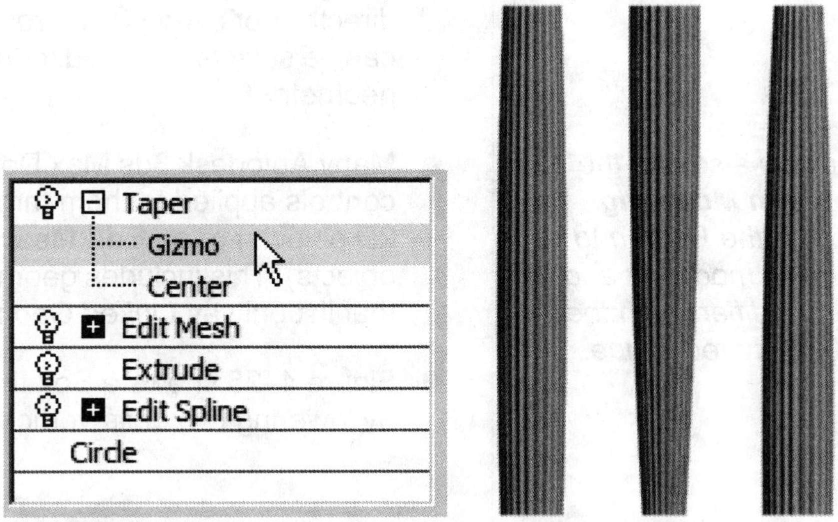

Figure 4–24

Working in Sub-Object Mode

Sub-object mode is activated through the Modifier Stack. You can expand the modifier by clicking next to the name of an object or modifier that has sub-objects, then clicking sub-object level to be adjusted.

- You normally can have only a single object selected to enter the Sub-object mode.
- When Sub-object mode is active, the sub-object level (or the modifier name if the sub-object list has not been expanded) is highlighted in yellow (with the default user interface settings).

- Normally you cannot clear the currently selected object while in Sub-object mode. Therefore, to edit another object you must first exit Sub-object mode. To do so, select the level of the Modifier Stack presently highlighted in yellow, or select the name of the modifier where you are in Sub-object mode.
- If you see your Modifier Stack highlighted in yellow accidentally, (where you did not intend to be in Sub-object mode) simply select the yellow highlighted item to exit the mode.

Geometric Edits through Sub-objects

A whole range of explicit geometric changes can be made through Sub-object mode.

- Objects imported into the Autodesk 3ds Max Design software often take the shape of **Editable Splines** or **Editable Meshes**. These have sub-object controls that can be edited directly. For example, a group of vertices in an Editable Mesh can be selected, moved, or deleted separate to the rest of the geometry.

*You can also use the **Polygon Modeling** tools in the Ribbon to perform modeling and use modifiers with the **Edit Poly** technique.*

- Many Autodesk 3ds Max Design objects can also have these controls applied to them through an **Edit Spline** modifier (for 2D objects) or an **Edit Mesh** or **Edit Poly** modifier (for 3D objects). This includes geometry linked to AutoCAD drawings that list only as *Linked Geometry* in the *Modify* panel.
- Figure 4–25 shows a Box that is being edited geometrically by lowering two of its vertices with the **Move** transform.

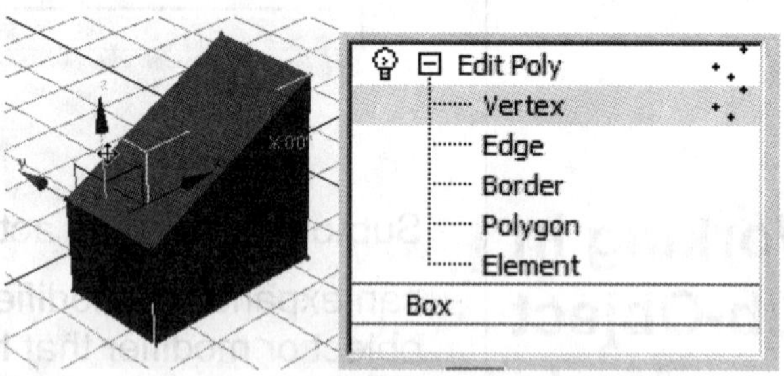

Figure 4–25

- The **Edit Mesh** modifier is best for objects based on a triangular mesh, such as triangulated terrain models. The **Edit Poly** modifier is best for objects with faces of more than three vertices, such as rectangular objects.

- In general it is best to adjust objects through their core parameters (such as the length, width, and height of a Box primitive) and standard modifiers whenever possible. This makes it easier to review the changes and adjust them. For cases where this is not possible, Spline, Mesh, and Poly editing can be an effective alternative.

Geometric Sub-Objects

The Editable Spline, Editable Mesh, and Editable Poly objects (as well as any other object with an Edit Spline, Edit Mesh, or Edit Poly Modifier applied to it) share a number of common Sub-object modes. These are:

	Vertex: The individual 3D points that define an object (Edit Spline, Edit Mesh, or Edit Poly).
	Segment: A single line or curve segment of an Editable Spline.
	Spline: A series of one or more connected Editable Spline segments. Segments are considered connected if they share a common vertex.
	Edge: The linear segments connecting vertices with Edit Mesh or Edit Poly. Three edges are shown in the button.
	Face: The triangular surface area defined by three edges (Edit Mesh only).
	Border: A series of edges that define an opening in an Editable Poly (only).
	Polygon: Enables you to work with coplanar faces (Edit Mesh) or a defined polygon (Edit Poly).
	Element: Enables you to work with all of the faces or polygons that form a contiguous whole (Edit Mesh or Edit Poly).

Smoothing

One of the most important properties controlled at the face or polygon sub-object level is smoothing. Figure 4–26 shows the same geometry with and without smoothing applied.

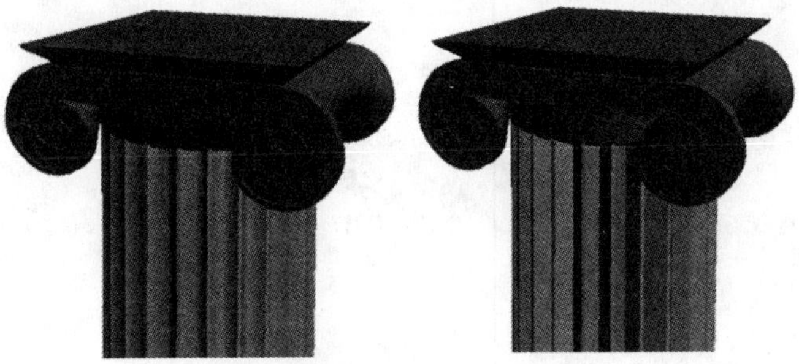

Figure 4–26

- The Autodesk 3ds Max Design software can have two adjacent faces appear to be smooth or faceted. This distinction becomes very important when dealing with curved or gently undulating objects. When smoothed, faces appear smooth but the Autodesk 3ds Max Design software does not adjust the actual geometry.

- Smoothing is controlled by smoothing groups. Each face or polygon can be a member of up to 32 smoothing groups. If two adjacent faces share a common smoothing group, the Autodesk 3ds Max Design software attempts to blend the surfaces together to disguise the edge that separates them.

- As an example of the controls for polygon smoothing groups (in Edit Mesh and Edit Poly), Figure 4–27 indicates the smoothing groups for the selected faces. When some but not all selected faces fall into a particular smoothing group, that group's box is shown without a number.

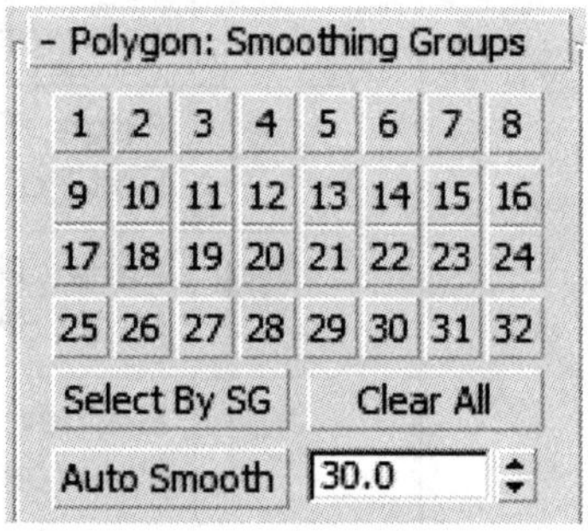

Figure 4–27

As an alternative to manually assigning smoothing groups there is an Auto Smooth feature. This feature automatically places adjacent selected faces into smoothing groups if their normal vectors have an angle of separation equal to or less than the Auto Smooth angle. (Normals are formally described in the rendering material).

Practice 4c Modeling with Edit Poly in Sub-Object Mode

Learning Objective

- Modify objects at a sub-object level using the Sub-object modes.

Estimated time for completion: 15 minutes

In this practice you will add some detail to the concrete base of the light pole by chamfering (beveling) the outside top of the cylinder.

You must set the paths to locate the External files and Xrefs used in the practice. If you have not done this already, return to the **Introduction to Autodesk 3ds Max Design** chapter and complete Task 1 to Task 3 of the **Organizing Folders and Working with the Interface** practice. You only have to set the user paths once.

1. Continue with the file created in the previous practice **MyLightPole04.max**. If you did not complete it, open **Edit Poly in Sub-Object Mode.max** from your *Class Files* folder.

2. In the Perspective viewport, select **LP Base** and click (Zoom Extents Selected). Use (Zoom) and (Orbit) to display a base similar to that shown in Figure 4–28.

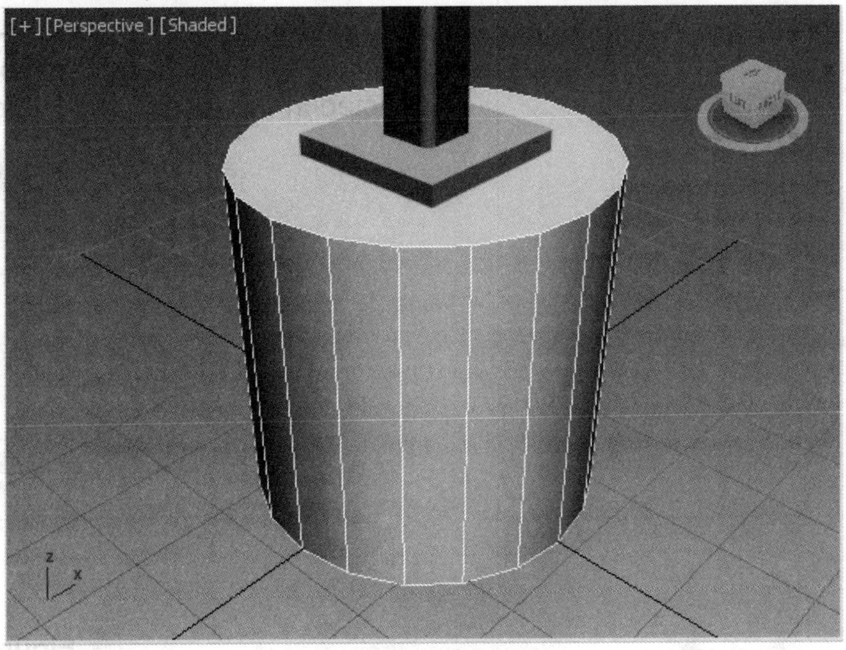

Figure 4–28

3. In the *Modify* panel ( ), select **Edit Poly** from the Modifier List. Click **+** (plus sign) for Edit Poly to display its Sub-object modes. Select **Polygon** to activate the Sub-object mode at the Polygon level. The yellow highlighting in the Modifier Stack indicates that you are in the Polygon Sub-object mode, as shown in Figure 4–29.

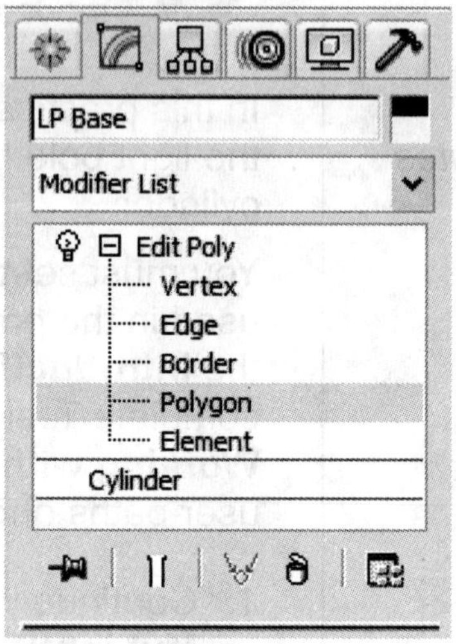

Figure 4–29

Hint: Using Modeling Tools in the Ribbon

You can also perform all of the commands using the **Polygon Modeling** tools in the Modeling Ribbon. With the object selected, select *Polygon Modeling* tab in the *Modeling* tab in the Ribbon. In the drop-down list, select **Apply Edit Poly Mod**, as shown in Figure 4–30. Click for Polygon sub-object level. Note that the selections that you make in the Ribbon are reflected in the Command Panel and vice-versa.

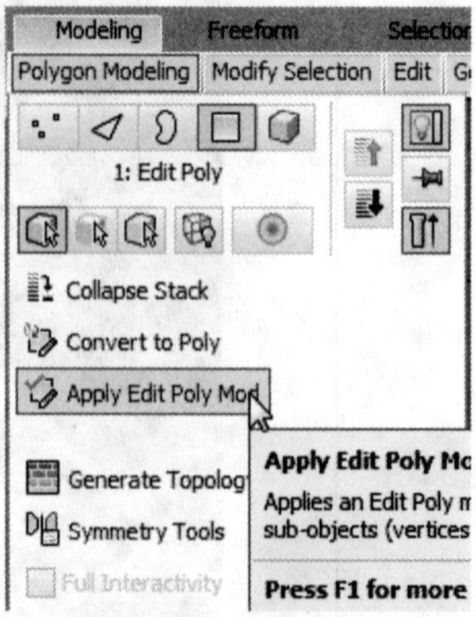

Figure 4–30

4. Select the polygon at the top of the cylinder, as shown in Figure 4–31. The selected polygon tuns red.

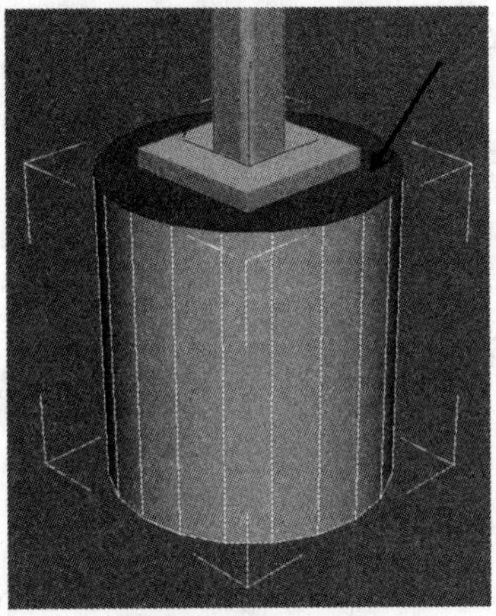

Figure 4–31

5. Creating a 1” bevel will raise the cylinder top by 1”. In preparation, you will first lower the top of the cylinder by that same 1”. In the Main toolbar, click (Select and Move). Note that the Move gizmo is only displayed for the selected polygon.

6. In the Status Bar, click (Absolute Mode Transform) to change it to (Offset Mode Transform) and set *Z* to **-0’1”** and press <Enter>. The cylinder geometry is adjusted by moving the polygon down.

7. Right-click to activate the Left viewport (keeping the polygon selected) and zoom into the base area. Note that the base is not touching the base plate anymore.

*The rollouts in the Command Panel might extend below the display window. To scroll, hover the cursor over an empty gray area until is displays as a **Hand** icon, then hold and drag the cursor up or down to locate the required rollout.*

8. In the Command Panel, locate the Edit Polygons rollout. You might need to scroll down to locate this rollout. Expand the Edit Polygons rollout, next to Bevel, click (Settings), as shown in Figure 4–32.

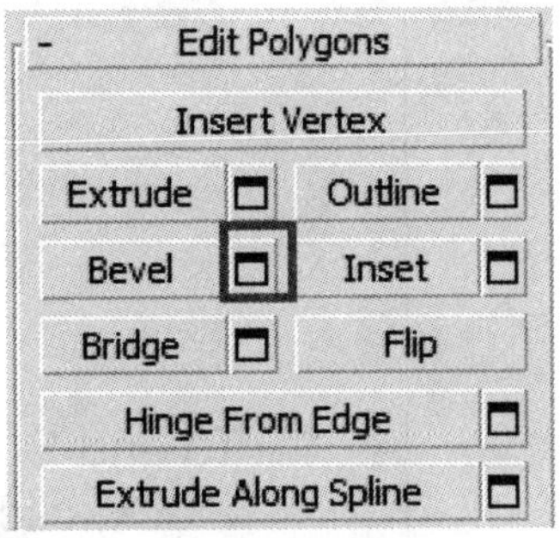

Figure 4–32

In the caddy display, when you select the edit box, its icon displays as a spinner and the edit name (Height or Outline) is displayed in addition to the modifier name (Bevel) at the top. You can enter new values in the edit box or use the spinner to change the values.

9. The caddy display opens on the screen. Hover the cursor over the *Height* edit box and set its value to **0'1"** and an *Outline* of **-0'1"**, as shown in Figure 4–33. Click .

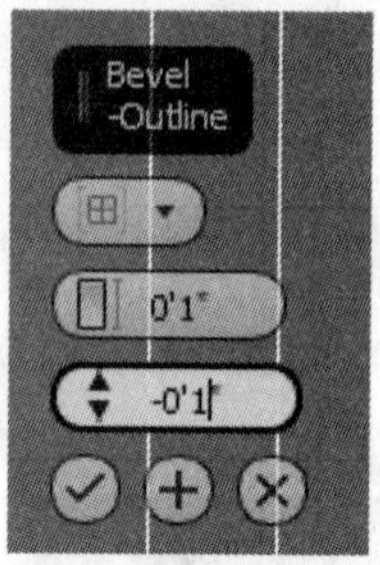

Figure 4–33

- The base is beveled as shown in Figure 4–34.

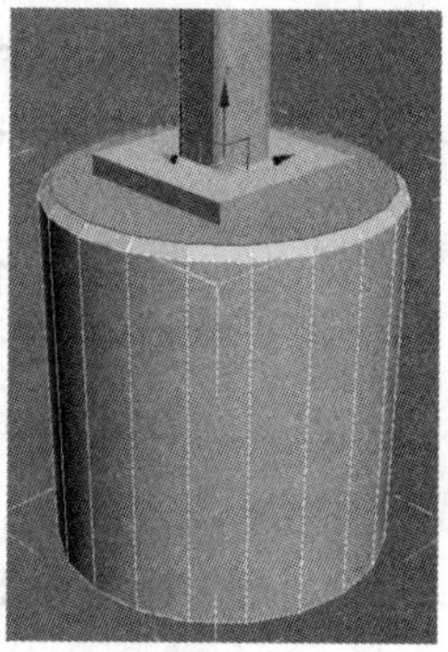

Figure 4–34

10. To make the newly created faces smooth you will adjust the smoothing groups. While still in Polygon Sub-object mode, in the pull-down menu, expand Edit and select **Select All** to select all of the polygons in the base object. In the Command Panel, locate the Polygon: Smoothing Groups rollout by scrolling down. Click Clear All to remove the existing smoothing. Set the *AutoSmooth angle* to **30**, as shown in Figure 4–35, and click Auto Smooth.

Figure 4–35

11. To end Sub-object mode, in the Command Panel Modifier Stack, click the Polygon that is highlighted in yellow to clear the selection.

*To display the smoothing effect, toggled off **Edged Faces** in the Viewport Shading label, if it is enabled.*

12. To display the effect of the smoothing change, in the Perspective viewport, clear the object selection by clicking anywhere in empty space. The angle of 30 degrees enabled the newly created faces to smooth across each other, but the faces are not smoothed with the top of the cylinder, as shown in Figure 4–36. This is the chamfered appearance that was originally intended. A larger smoothing angle enables the chamfered faces between the top and sides to smooth out.

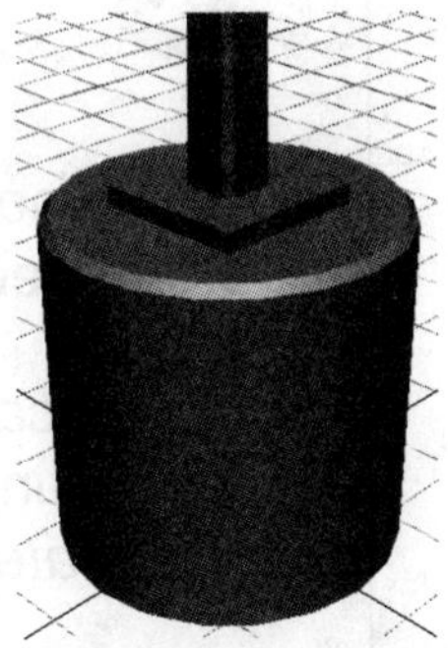

Figure 4–36

13. In the Main toolbar, click (Select Object) to end the Move Transform mode as a precaution to avoid moving objects accidentally while making further selections.

14. Save your work as **MyLightPole05.max** or use + in the Save As dialog box if using the **MyLightPole04.max** file.

Certification

Topic:
✓*Modeling*
Objectives:
✓*Differentiate reference coordinate systems*

4.4 Reference Coordinate Systems and Transform Centers

Learning Objective

Understand the various coordinate systems and transform systems that can be used during modeling.

All geometry in the Autodesk 3ds Max Design software is referenced to a base coordinate system called the Home Grid.

- You can create your own coordinate systems by creating and locating grid objects, available in the Helpers Category in the *Create* panel.
- User Coordinate Systems created in AutoCAD® can automatically be brought into the Autodesk 3ds Max Design software as grid objects.
- You can also create objects in AutoGrid mode, which creates a temporary Grid aligned in 3D to the object directly under the crosshairs. The option to enable **AutoGrid** is located in the *Create* panel, in the Object Type rollout, as shown Figure 4–37 (AutoGrid is similar to the Dynamic UCS feature introduced in AutoCAD 2007). If you hold down <Alt>, the AutoGrid remains available for future use. If you use AutoGrid without any key pressed, the grid disappears after object creation.

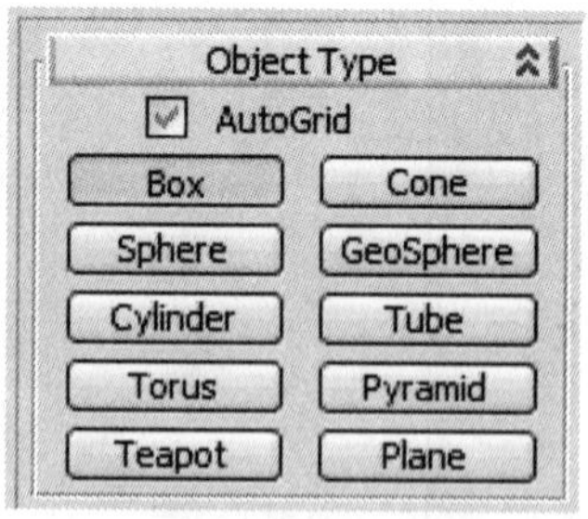

Figure 4–37

Reference Coordinate Systems

Although a single grid is active at any one time, the current Reference Coordinate System might differ depending on which view you are in and which transform is active. It is recommended that new users stay in the **World** system as much as possible to avoid confusion from changing axis labels. By default, the Reference Coordinate system is set to **View**.

- In the Main toolbar, the options listed in the Reference Coordinate System drop-down list, as shown Figure 4–38, control how transform values are read.

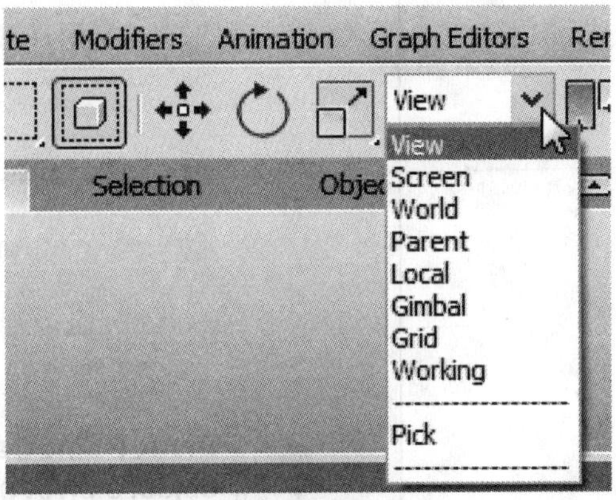

Figure 4–38

- In the **World** coordinate system the X, Y, and Z axes are interpreted based on the Home Grid, even if a user-defined grid is active. To use the coordinates of the active user-defined grid instead, select the **Grid** option.
- In the **Screen** coordinate system the X-axis is always measured along the bottom of the viewport, the Y-axis is always measured along the side, and the Z-axis is measured perpendicularly out of the screen. For example, in a front view using the Screen reference system the Y-axis is measured up the screen. That same view in the World system would measure Z-axis up the screen instead.
- The **View** system is a combination of World and Screen. In an orthographic view the Screen system is used, while other views use the World system.
- The **Pick** option enables you to pick any object in the viewport or from a list and use the reference coordinate system of that object as the reference for transforms. You can use XRef objects with the **Pick** option.
- The **Working** option enables you to use the Working Pivot. It is a temporary modeling pivot tool you create from the *Hierarchy* panel's *Pivot* tab. Generally you need to assign a hotkey to **Use Working Pivot** and **Edit Working Pivot** to make them functional tools.

Transform Centers

Transforms are applied through a Transform Center point indicated by the Transform gizmo. There are three options for the Transform Center and can be accessed in the Main toolbar, in the Transform Center flyout, as shown Figure 4–39.

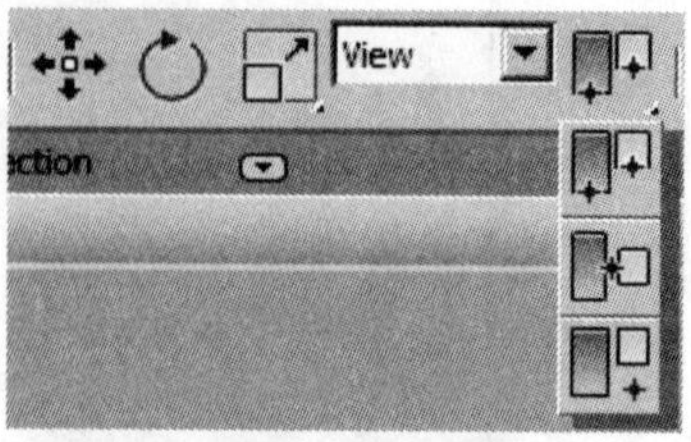

Figure 4–39

Pivot Point Center: Transforms are applied through each selected object's pivot point. Pivots often default to the bottom center or geometric center of objects. Pivot points can be adjusted through controls in the *Hierarchy* panel. Select this option if you want to rotate many objects, each around its own center.

Selection Center: Transforms are applied through the geometric center of all selected objects.

Transform Coordinate Center: Transforms are applied through the origin point of the current Reference Coordinate System. For example, if you wanted to rotate objects around their individual pivot points about the World Z-axis, you would select the World Coordinate System and Pivot Point Transform Center. Alternatively, to rotate all of the objects around the origin, you would do the same with the Transform Coordinate Center.

- The Transform Center might automatically change depending on whether one or multiple objects are selected, and on the active transform.
- The Reference Coordinate System and Transform Center can be held using **Constant** in **Customize>Preferences>** *General* tab, as shown in Figure 4–40.

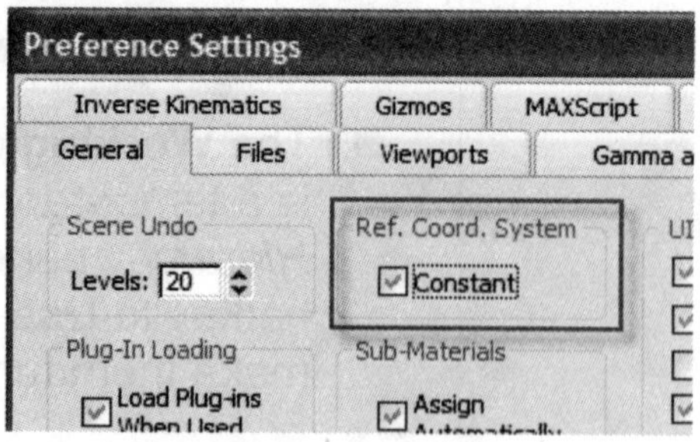

Figure 4–40

Practice 4d Modeling with Coordinate Systems

Learning Objective

- Create an object using the coordinate system and then modify the parameters.

Estimated time for completion: 10 minutes

For the next step in the Light Pole model you will add the Light Pole Mounting Arm.

You must set the paths to locate the External files and Xrefs used in the practice. If you have not done this already, return to the **Introduction to Autodesk 3ds Max Design** chapter and complete Task 1 to Task 3 of the **Organizing Folders and Working with the Interface** practice. You only have to set the user paths once.

1. Continue with the file **MyLightPole05.max** created in the previous practice. If you did not complete it, open **Modeling with Coordinate Systems.max** from your *Class Files* folder.
2. Activate the Front viewport, if required.
3. Use a combination of **Zoom** and **Pan** to zoom into the top portion, as shown in Figure 4–41. If the Grid is showing in the Front view, in the Viewport label, click [+] and select **Show Grids** to clear it. Alternatively, you can press <G> to toggle the grid on or off.

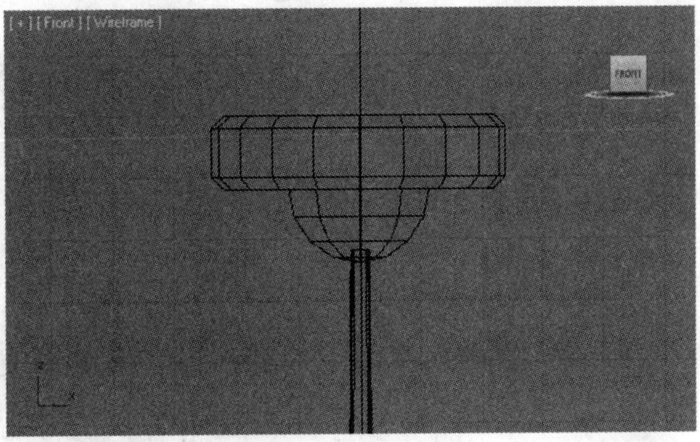

Figure 4–41

4. In the *Create* panel ( )> (Geometry), click Box. Use the cursor to approximate dimensions for *Length*, *Width*, and *Height*, create a small box, and center it on the top of the light pole, as shown in Figure 4–42.

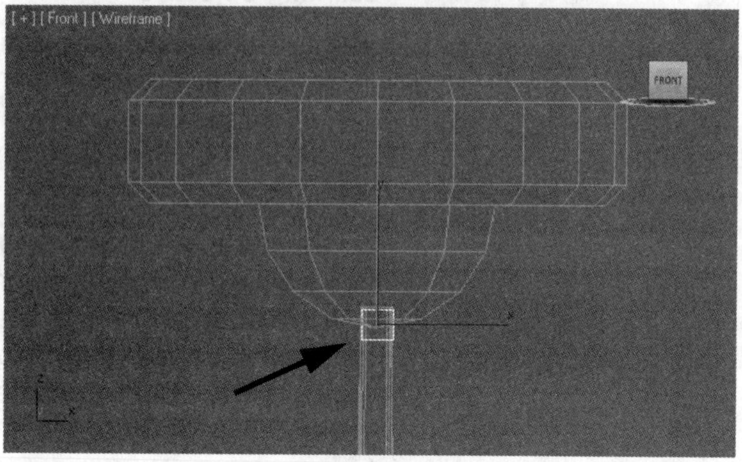

Figure 4–42

The object creation orientation depends on the viewport in which it is being created.

5. With this box still selected, in the *Modify* panel ( ), in the Parameters rollout, set *Length* and *Width* to **0'3"** and *Height* to **4'6"**. Set the *Height Segs* to **6** and rename it to **LP Mounting Arm**.
6. Since you created the box in the **Front** viewport (rather than the Perspective viewport) the height of the box is measured perpendicular to the view, in this case along the world Y-axis. This is displayed in the Perspective view, as shown in Figure 4–43.

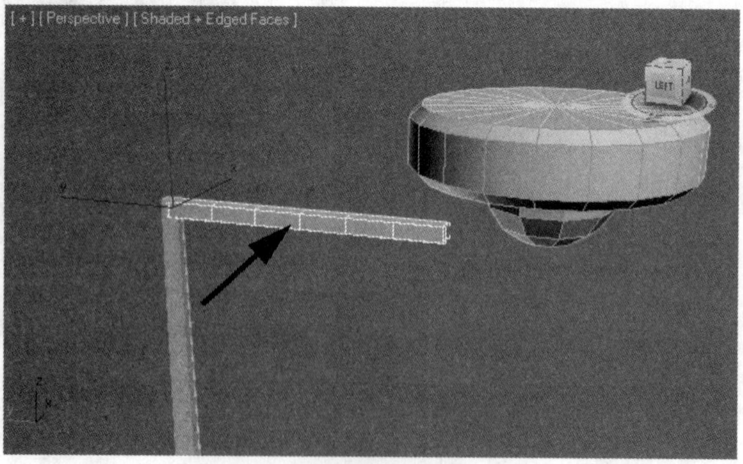

Figure 4–43

7. With the LP Mounting arm selected, click (Select and Move). In the Status Bar, set transform mode to (Absolute mode) and set the location of the mounting arm with *X* as **0'0"**, *Y* as **0'0"**, and *Z* as **18'0"**, as shown in Figure 4–44.

Figure 4–44

8. In the Modifier List, select **Bend** to curve the arm to the housing. Set *Bend Angle* to **30** and *Direction* to **-90** degrees, and note the effect of each change. The arm is bent as shown in Figure 4–45.

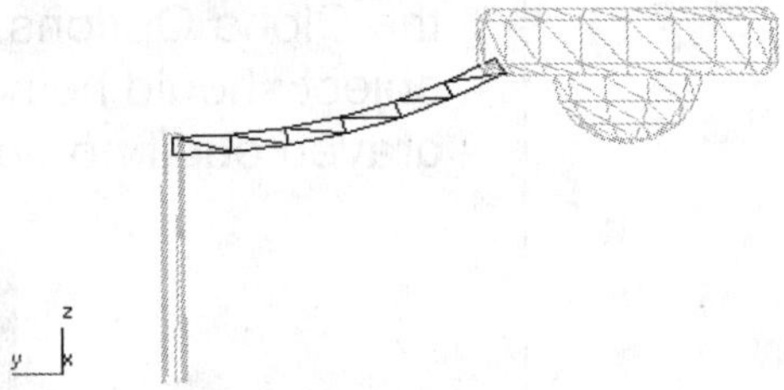

Figure 4–45

9. Save your work as **MyLightPole06.max** or use in the Save As dialog box if using the **MyLightPole05.max** file.

Certification

Topic:

✓*Modeling*

Objectives:

✓*Identify Clone types*

4.5 Cloning and Grouping

Learning Objectives

- Understand how the different options of the **Clone** command can be used to create copies of the same object.
- Understand how the different **Group** options can be used to treat multiple objects as a single unit.

Cloning

In the Autodesk 3ds Max Design software, objects can be duplicated with the **Clone** option (**Edit>Clone**). When cloning you have the option of enabling the duplicate object to maintain a dynamic link to the source object. Selecting **Edit>Clone** opens the Clone Options dialog box, as shown in Figure 4–46. An object should be selected to access the **Clone** option. It remains grayed out if no object is selected.

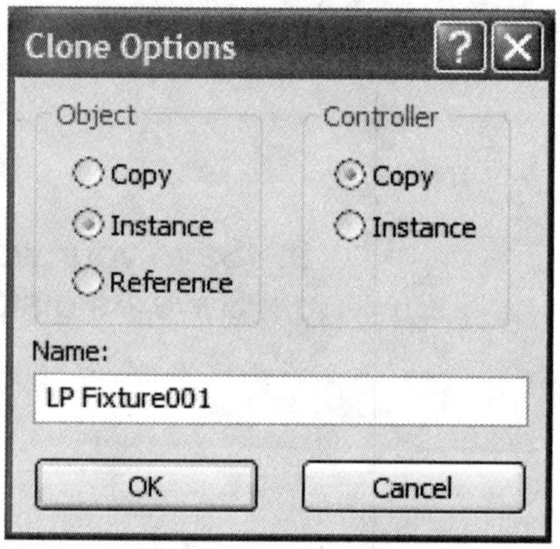

Figure 4–46

Copy	Makes an independent copy without a dynamic link to the source object.
Instance	Makes the duplicate and original Instances of each other. Changes made to any Instance automatically update all Instances, including changes to Modifiers, property changes, and material assignments (but not Transforms).
Reference	A one-directional link where changes made to the original object affect the duplicate, but you can apply Modifiers to the Reference without affecting the Source object.

- You can also clone an object by holding down <Shift> while transforming through a click and drag on the Transform gizmo. In this procedure you also have the option of specifying the number of copies you want to make, which are arrayed at the same Transform value.

- The *Controller* area in the Clone Options dialog box applies to objects in a group or hierarchy and refers to transform controllers.
- Objects that are instanced or referenced display with the Modifier Stack text in bold type. Instancing or referencing can be disabled by right-clicking on the item in the Modifier Stack and selecting **Make Unique**.

Grouping

Grouping enables multiple objects to be treated as a single unit for selection and transforms. The **Group** options are available in the **Group** pull-down menu, as shown in Figure 4–47.

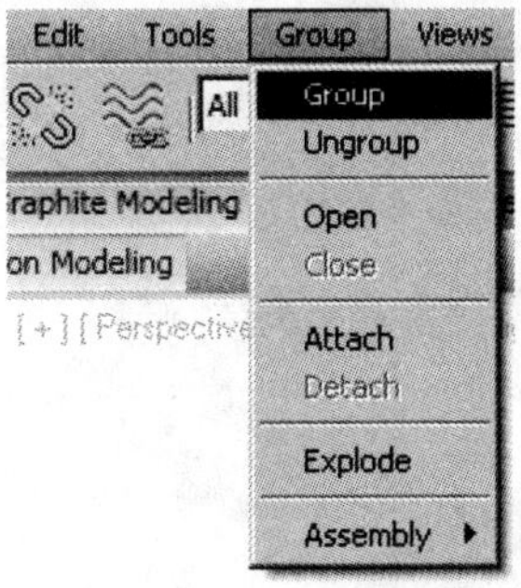

Figure 4–47

Group	Creates a group out of all of the currently selected objects. Groups can have other groups inside them (nested groups).
Ungroup	Dissolves any selected groups back into their constituent objects. Explode dissolves the selected groups and any groups nested inside.
Open/Close	Enables you to select, modify, and transform individual group members as if they were not in a group. The group is still defined; however, it can be Closed to treat the objects as a single unit again.
Attach	Enables you to add another object to a group. First select the objects to be attached then select the **Attach** option in the **Group** menu. When prompted select a closed group to which to add the objects.
Detach	Enables you to remove selected objects from a group. You must first open the group to select the objects to be detached.
Explode	Dissolves the selected groups and any groups nested inside them.
Assembly	Special case object grouping that are intended for creation of lighting assemblies called luminaires, and for character assemblies. Assemblies have a special helper object called a head that helps build groups that will be animated.

- Groups are located in the Command Panel, in the *Modify* panel, with group name in bold type, and a blank Modifier Stack. The Modifier Stack of individual group members is displayed if it is opened.
- Groups can be copied, instanced, and referenced. AutoCAD blocks imported into the Autodesk 3ds Max Design software can be brought in as instanced versions of the same group.
- Avoid the use of Grouping on objects that are linked into a hierarchy and then animated.

Practice 4e Cloning and Grouping

Learning Objectives

- Create a single unit of multiple objects using the **Group** command.
- Clone an instance of the group and modify a component so that the original object is modified as well.

Estimated time for completion: 10 minutes

In this practice you will complete the model of the light pole using Cloning and Groups.

You must set the paths to locate the External files and Xrefs used in the practice. If you have not done this already, return to the **Introduction to Autodesk 3ds Max Design** chapter and complete Task 1 to Task 3 of the **Organizing Folders and Working with the Interface** practice. You only have to set the user paths once.

1. Continue with the file **MyLightPole06.max** created in the previous practice. If you did not complete it, open **Cloning and Grouping.max** from your *Class Files* folder.

2. Click (Select by Name) or press <H> to open the Select From Scene dialog box. In the dialog box toolbar, click (Display None) and then click (Display Geometry). Select **LP Fixture Housing**, **LP Fixture Globe**, and **LP Mounting Arm** (hold down <Ctrl> to select multiple items). Click OK to close the dialog box. The three items are now selected in the scene.

3. In the Menu bar, select **Group>Group** to combine the three objects together into a single, selectable unit. In the Group dialog box, name the group **LP Fixture**, as shown in Figure 4–48 and click OK.

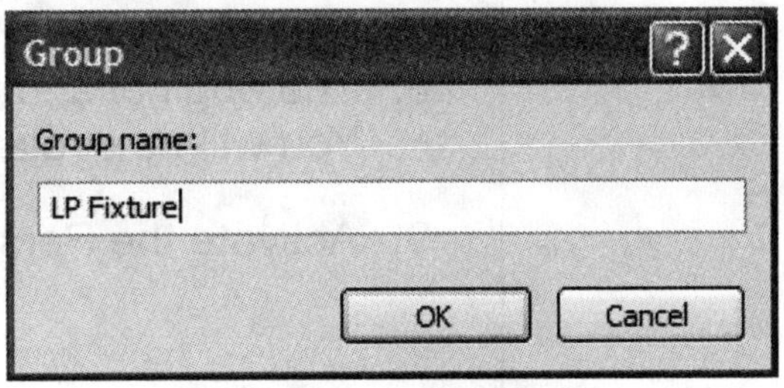

Figure 4–48

4. Click (Select by Name) or press <H> to open the Select From Scene dialog box again. Click (Display Groups) and review the new **LP Fixture** group. The group name is identified with the symbol. Select the group and click OK to close the dialog box.

5. In the Menu bar, select **Group>Open**. The group remains intact as indicated by the pink bounding box. Once opened you can select, manipulate, and transform the three component objects separately, but the group remains intact.

6. With one or more of the group components selected, in the Menu bar, select **Group>Close**. The pink bounding box is cleared with all of the group objects selected, indicating that it is treated as a single object and that the individual components cannot be modified separately.

7. With the **LP Fixture** group selected, in the Menu bar, select **Edit>Clone** to create a second fixture. In the Clone Options dialog box (shown in Figure 4–49), select **Instance**, if not already selected. This enables the original group and the copy to share identical geometries. Leave the other options at their default values. Click OK.

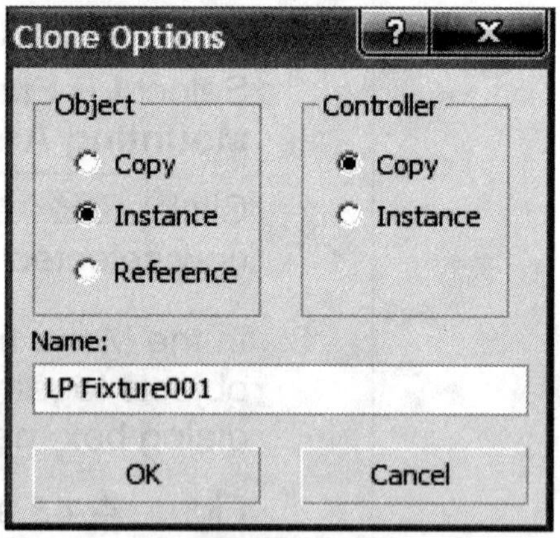

Figure 4–49

8. The original and the copy now directly overlay each other. You will now rotate the (second) light fixture.

9. Activate the Perspective viewport.

10. Click  (Select by Name) or press <H> and in the Select From Scene dialog box, select **LP Fixture001**. Click OK close the dialog box.

11. In the Main toolbar, click  (Select and Rotate).

12. The position of the Transform gizmo is dependent on the active **Use Transform**. If you use  (Use Pivot Point Center) or  (Use Selection Center), the position of the Transform gizmo is at the center of your current selection, but the rotation does not place **LP Fixture001** in the correct position. In the flyout, click  (Use Transform Coordinate Center), as shown in Figure 4–50, to use the coordinate system origin as the center of rotation. Note that the Rotation gizmo moves to the base of the light base, which is the coordinate system origin.

Figure 4–50

13. In the Status Bar, in the *Transform Type-In* area, set *Z* to **180.0**, as shown in Figure 4–51, to rotate **LP Fixture001** by **180°** about the Z axis. Press <Enter>. The round off error might result in a -180° value. This is a common occurrence and is not necessarily indicative of a problem.

Figure 4–51

14. The cloned group is moved opposite to the original group, as shown in Figure 4–52.

Figure 4–52

15. Click  (Select Object) to end the Rotate transform mode.

16. To verify that the groups are instanced, with **LP Fixture001** selected, select **Group>Open**. A pink bounding box displays around the group. Select **LP Fixture Housing001** (chamfered cylinder). In the *Modify* panel, reduce the *Height* from a **1'0"** to **0' 8"**. Both Fixture Housings update and have reduced height as shown in Figure 4–53.

Figure 4–53

17. Select **Group>Close** to close **LP Fixture001**.

18. Save your work as **MyLightPole07.max** or use  in the Save As dialog box if using the **MyLightPole06.max** file.

Certification

Topic:
✓Modeling
Objectives:
✓Use polygon modeling tools

4.6 Polygon Modeling Tools in the Ribbon

Learning Objective

- Modeling using the **Polygon Modeling** tools in the Ribbon.

The Autodesk 3ds Max Design software is a powerful environment for creating 3D models of virtually anything you can imagine. The box modeling technique is probably the most popular method of construction. It is also called polygon modeling or mesh modeling. Essentially it is the interactive creation of vertices, edges, faces, and surfaces in a free and artistic way. The term box modeling comes from the common practice of starting by building a box. The original components of the box are manipulated to create the entire model. You could as easily start with a plane, or any other 3D primitive, or a 2D Shape object.

Box modeling can be performed using either the **Edit Mesh** or **Edit Poly** modifiers, or be converted to an **Editable Mesh** or **Editable Poly** object. Any of these methods give you the access to the sub-object levels needed to do this type of modeling. The **Edit Poly** modifier is the most recent modeling technology added to the Autodesk 3ds Max Design software, so it should be the preferred choice in many cases. However, if you find unexpected results using Edit Poly, you can always convert the object to an editable mesh or editable poly object and discard the modifier. You can also use the Edit Mesh modifier which is the older technology and should be the most stable.

***Enhanced** in 2014*

The Modeling Ribbon (*Modeling* tab) provides easy access to polygon modeling tools, including the editing and modification tools used at sub-object level. The Ribbon contains most of the commonly used tools that are present in the *Modify* panel in the Command Panel at the Edit Poly sub-object level. In the *Modeling* tab, the polygon modeling and modifying tools are organized into panels. It provides a convenient way of accessing the most commonly used tools while polygon modeling. The Ribbon can be minimized to the panel tiles, and is docked under the Main toolbar. Click [icon] to maximize the Ribbon. If the Ribbon is not displayed, in the Menu Bar, select **Customize>Show UI>Show Ribbon** or click [icon] (Toggle Ribbon) in the Main toolbar.

Practice 4f Poly Modeling using the Ribbon

Learning Objectives

- Create an organic model using the box modeling technique.
- Edit and modify the geometry in an Edit Poly mode using the **Modeling** tools in the Ribbon.

Estimated time for completion: 40 minutes

In this practice you will learn some of the tools and techniques of box modeling using the Edit Poly modifier and the modifier tools located in the Ribbon.

Task 1 - Model the Armchair.

1. Expand and select **Reset** to reset the scene.
2. In the *Create* panel ( )> (Geometry), click Box in the Object Type rollout to activate the **Box** tool.
3. In the Perspective viewport, click and drag to define the length and width of the rectangle. Click and continue moving the mouse upwards to define the height.
4. Initially you can use the Parameters rollout in the *Create* panel to edit the values. After completing a command, you will use the *Modify* panel ( ) to edit the values. Set the *Length* to **4'2"**, *Width* to **2'9"**, and *Height* to **0'10"** and press <Enter>. In the Perspective viewport, the box should look similar to that shown in Figure 4–54.

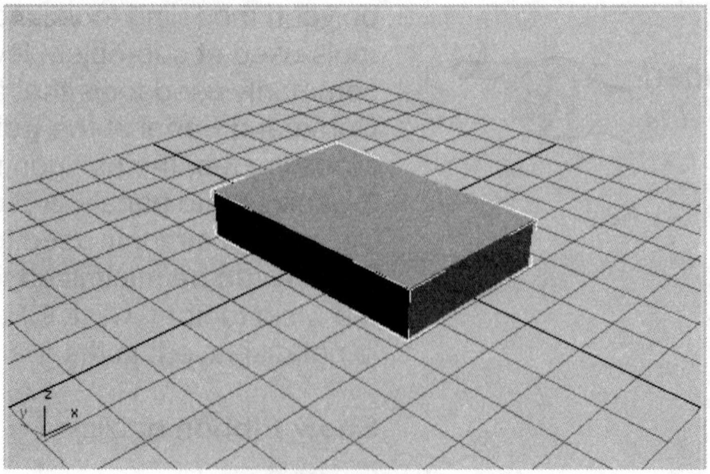

Figure 4–54

5. In the *Name and Color* field, name the object **armchair**.

6. To display the edges more clearly, change the display mode to wireframe by selecting the **Visual Style** label and selecting **Wireframe**.

7. Press <G> to hide the grid.

8. If the Modeling Ribbon is only displaying tabs, click (Show Full Ribbon) to display the tools and the panels.

9. Verify that the *Modeling* tab is active. Expand the *Polygon Modeling* panel and select **Apply Edit Poly Mod**, as shown on the left in Figure 4–55. This adds an Edit Poly modifier to the Box object. This is also displayed in the Command Panel.

   Note that the *Modify* panel ( ) is already open and that the Modifier Stack displays the **Edit Poly** modifier as shown on the right in Figure 4–55.

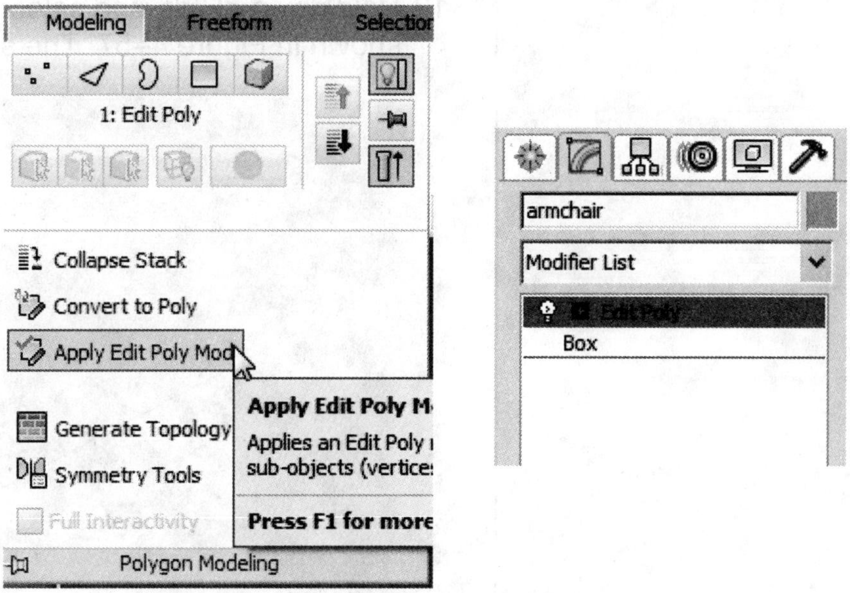

Figure 4–55

10. In the *Modeling* panel of the Ribbon, click (Edge) as shown in Figure 4–56, to activate Edge Selection. Alternatively, you can press <2> to select it. Expand the Edit Poly modifier in the Modifier Stack and note that **Edge** is already selected (highlighted in yellow).

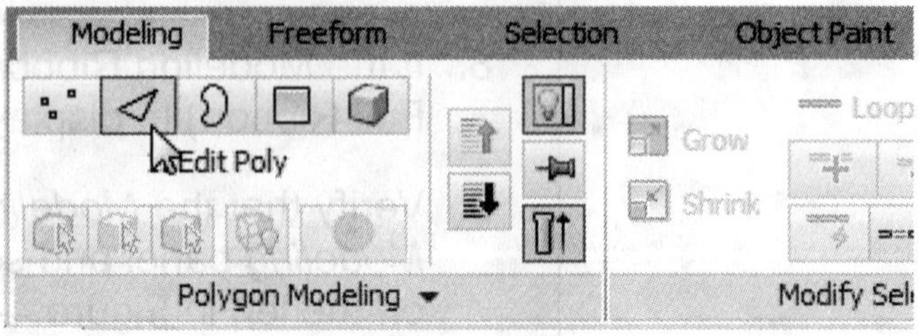

Figure 4–56

11. In the Navigation toolbar, click (Zoom Extents All Selected).

12. Hold down <Ctrl> and select the upper two long edges, as shown in Figure 4–57. The selected edges display in red.

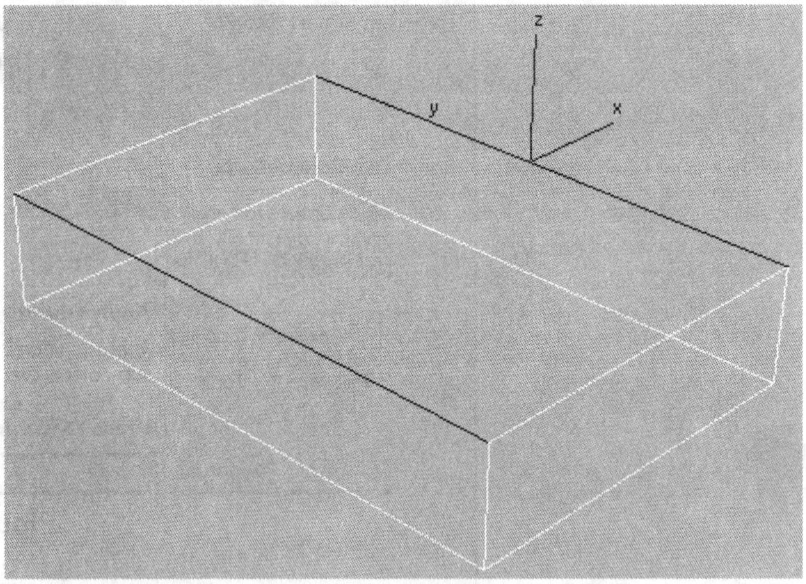

Figure 4–57

13. Hold down <Shift>, and in the Ribbon, in the *Loops* panel, click (Connect) to open the **Connect Edges** caddy display.

14. In the Connect Edges caddy display, set *Segments* to **2** and *Pinch* to **70** and press <Enter> (leaving *Slide* as **0**). Note that two edges are placed along the two short edges, as shown in Figure 4–58.

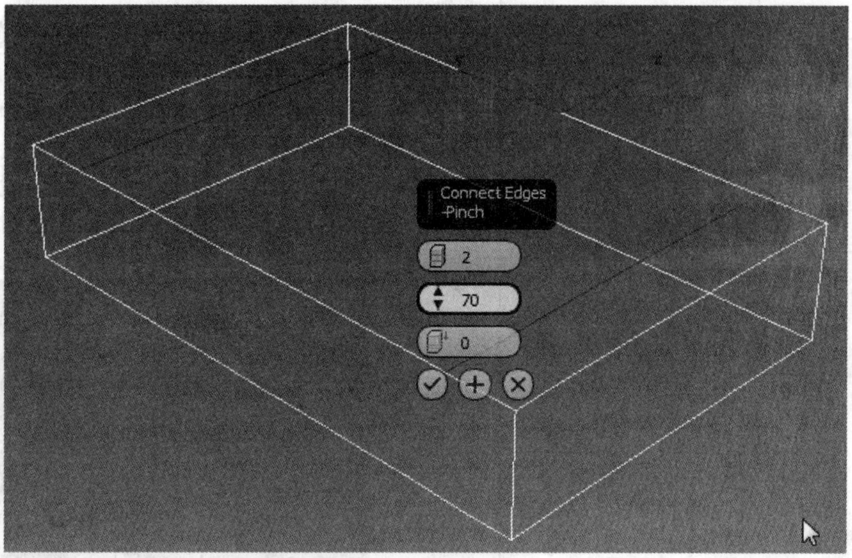

Figure 4–58

Use (Apply and continue) when you need to continue in the same tool. If you want to use another tool, use (OK) to exit the caddy display

15. Click to place a new set of segments along the long edge of the box.

16. Leave the *Segments* at **2**. Using the spinner arrows to change the *Pinch* and *Slide* values (*Pinch* brings the lines closer to one another and *Slide* moves both of them in the X-direction) to create a rectangle towards the back of the armchair, as shown in Figure 4–59. You can drag their slider arrows in either direction viewing the changes dynamically. The values of *Pinch* and *Slide* are approximately **-30** and **-180** respectively. Press <Enter> each time if you enter a new value in the edit box, to see how it affects the lines. Click (OK).

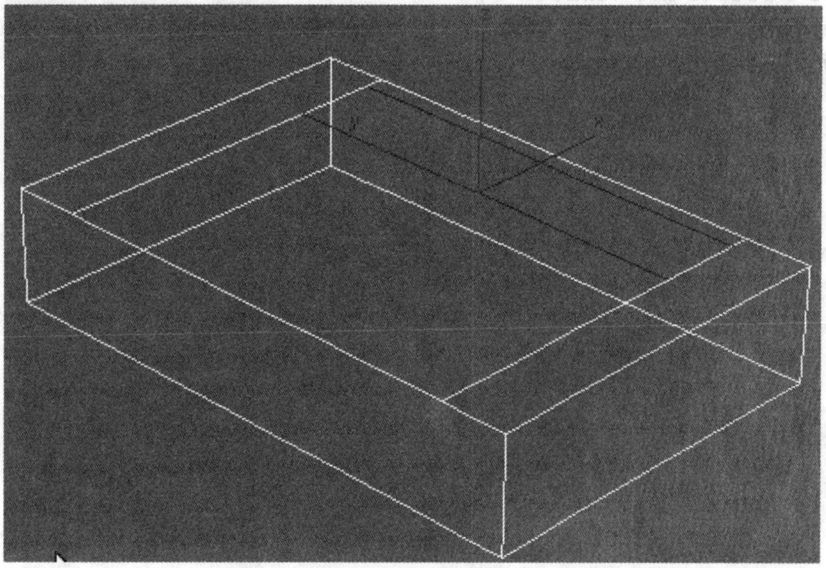

Figure 4–59

17. In the *Modeling* panel, click (Polygon), or press <4> to change the sub-object selection level from *Edge* to **Polygon**. Alternatively, select **Polygon** in the Edit Poly modifier in the Modifier Stack. In the viewport, right-click and select **Select**. Hold down <Ctrl> and select the two polygons along the shorter side of the box, as shown in Figure 4–60.

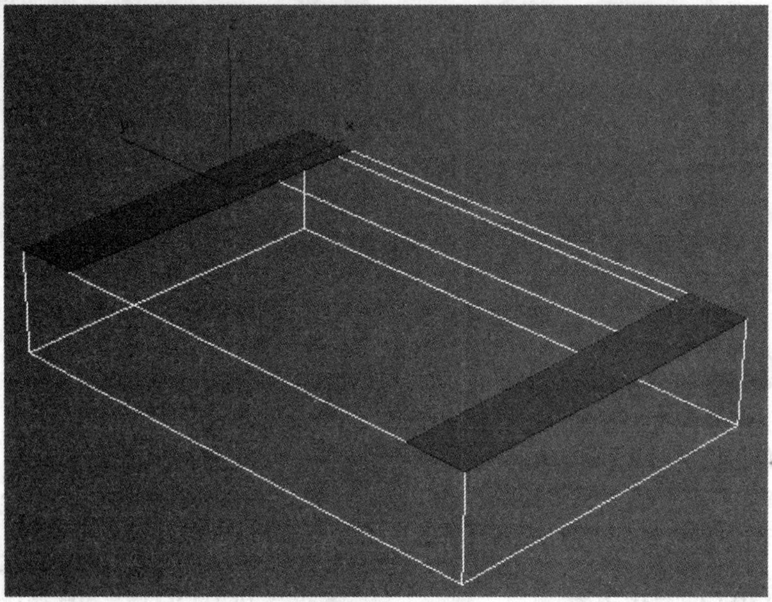

Figure 4–60

Remember to press <Enter> after entering your values. If you do not do so, you need to click twice. The first time accepts the values and the second time exits the caddy display.

18. In the Modeling Ribbon, in the *Polygons* panel, hold down <Shift> and click (Extrude) to open the **Extrude Polygons** caddy display. Set *Height* to **0'2"** and click , as shown in Figure 4–61. Click again to exit the caddy display if you did not press <Enter> after entering the *Height*.

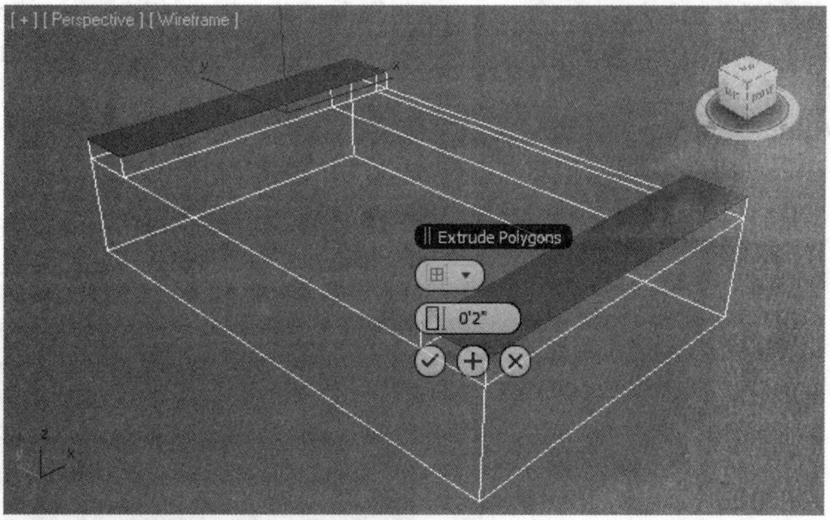

Figure 4–61

19. In the *Polygons* panel, hold down <Shift> and click  (Bevel) to open the **Bevel** caddy display. Set *Height* to **0'1"** and *Outline* to **-0'1"**, and click , as shown in Figure 4–62. Click  again to exit the caddy display.

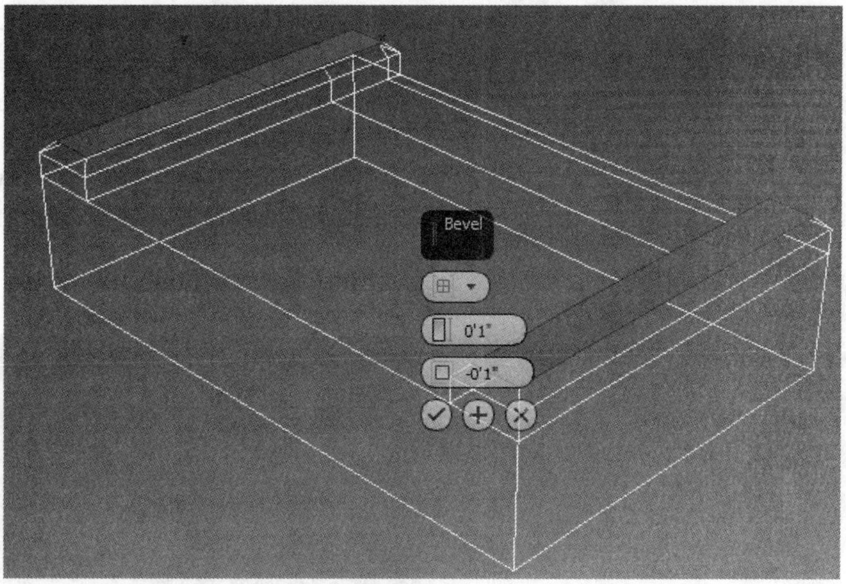

Figure 4–62

20. In the Navigation toolbar, click  (Orbit) to orbit in the Perspective viewport so that you can see the back of the armchair. The shortcut for Orbit is <Alt> + middle mouse button.

You might need to right-click in empty space to exit the ***Orbit*** *command first and then select the polygon.*

21. Select the long, thin rectangle at the top (along the longer end) for the back of the chair. In the *Polygons* panel, hold down <Shift> and click (Extrude) to open the **Extrude Polygons** caddy display. Extrude the back of the armchair to **0'5"** as shown in Figure 4–63. Press <Enter> and click .

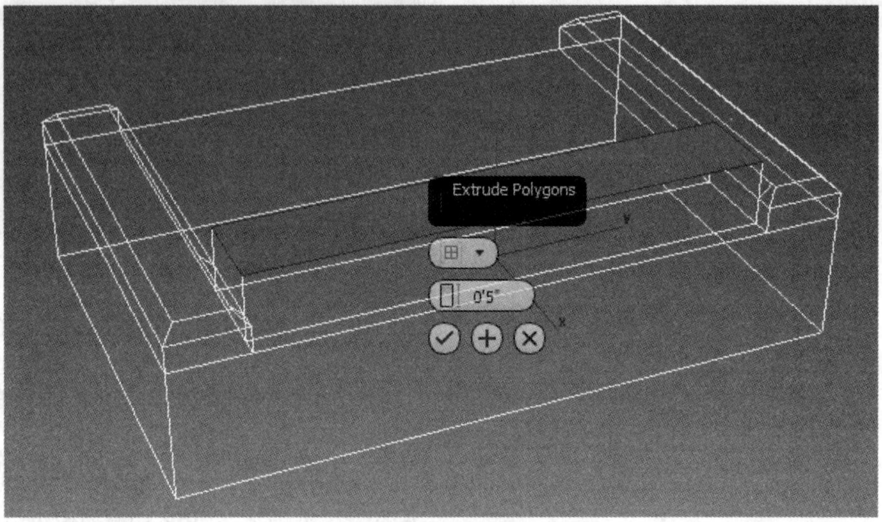

Figure 4–63

22. In the *Polygons* panel, hold down <Shift> and click (Bevel) to access the Bevel caddy display. Bevel up the back of the chair, as shown in Figure 4–64. Do not to bevel too much or the edges will overlap. The values are approximately **0'7"** for *Height* and **-0'2"** for *Outline*. Press <Enter> and click .

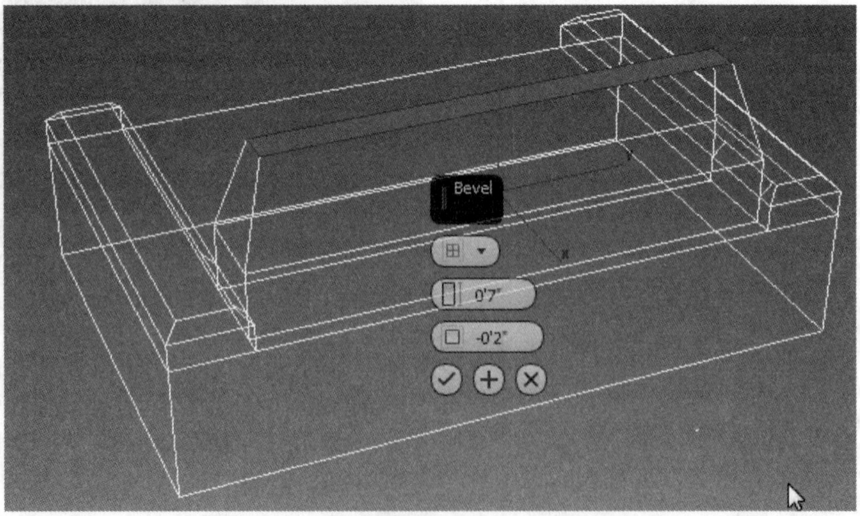

Figure 4–64

Use (Orbit) or <Alt> + middle mouse button to orbit in the Perspective viewport for a better view around the object.

23. In the Main toolbar, click (Select and Move) and move the selected polygons backwards along the X-axis, as shown in Figure 4–65. Orbit the viewport to view the design.

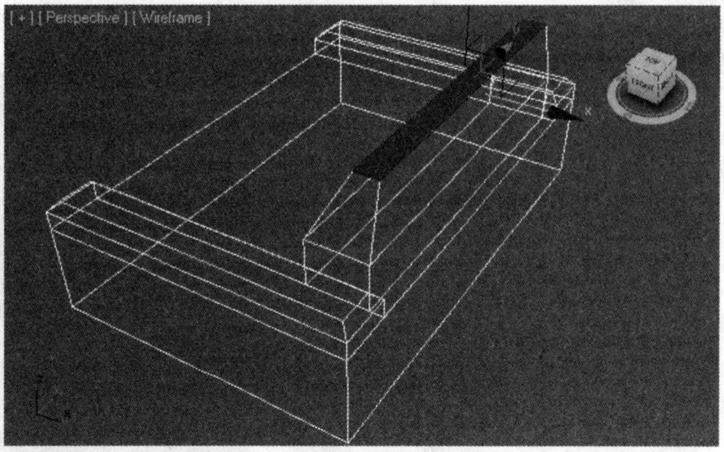

Figure 4–65

24. Press <2> to change to the **Edge** selection level.

    Alternatively, click (Edge) in the *Modeling* panel or select **Edge** in the Modifier Stack. If some edge(s) have already been selected, click in an empty area in the viewport to clear the selection.

25. In the *Modify Selection* panel, click (Ring Mode). This enables to select a ring of edges when a single edge is selected.

26. Select one of the long edges at the top of the chair back. Because **As Ring Mode** is toggled on, all of the other edges along the first edge are selected and display in red.

27. In the *Modify Selection* panel, click (Ring Mode) again to toggle it off.

Use (Orbit) or <Alt> + middle mouse button to orbit in the Perspective viewport for easy access for clicking the edges at the back side.

28. In the *Modify Selection* panel, click (Shrink Ring) to clear one edge on either side of the ring. Alternatively, you can hold down <Alt> and select one edge in front and one edge in the back to remove them from the selection. Only six edges should be selected, as shown in Figure 4–66.

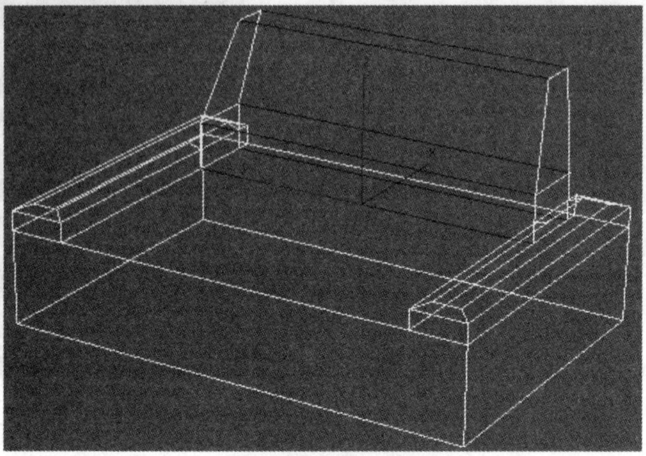

Figure 4–66

29. In the *Loops* panel, hold down <Shift> and click (Connect). In the **Connect Edges** caddy display, reset the Pinch and Slide to 0, and set the segments to **21** and press <Enter>. This adds 21 vertical segments, as shown in Figure 4–67. Click (OK).

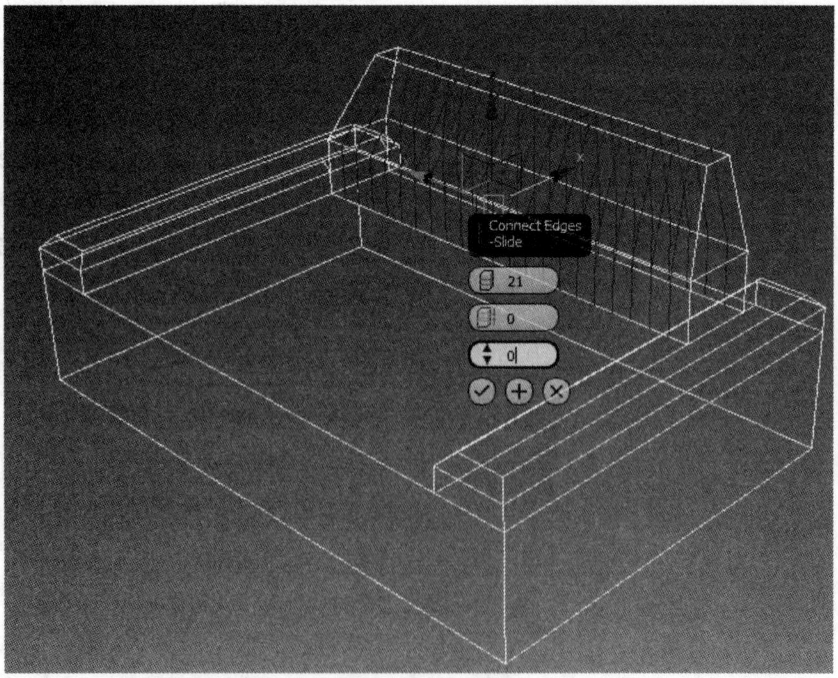

Figure 4–67

Sometimes clicking (+) does not work correctly when you need to continue in the same modifier. You can use (✓) and then reopen the modifier.

30. Hold down <Shift> and click (Connect) to open the **Connect Edges** caddy display. Change the *Segments* to **3** and click (+). If you pressed <Enter> after entering **3**, you do not need to click (+). This adds three rows of horizontal segments between two horizontal edges along the armchair back. Click (✓) to exit the caddy display.
31. Click (Maximize Viewport) to display all four viewports.
32. Click in the **Left** viewport to make it active (and clear the selection as well) and maximize it by clicking (Maximize Viewport). Use the **Zoom** and **Pan** tools to display the complete model in the viewport.
33. In the Modeling Ribbon, in the *Polygon Modeling* panel, click (Vertex) or press <1> to switch to Vertex selection mode.
34. In the Main toolbar, click (Select and Move). Drag a selection rectangle around the top row of vertices, selecting only the middle vertices and leaving four vertices on each side unselected, as shown in Figure 4–68.

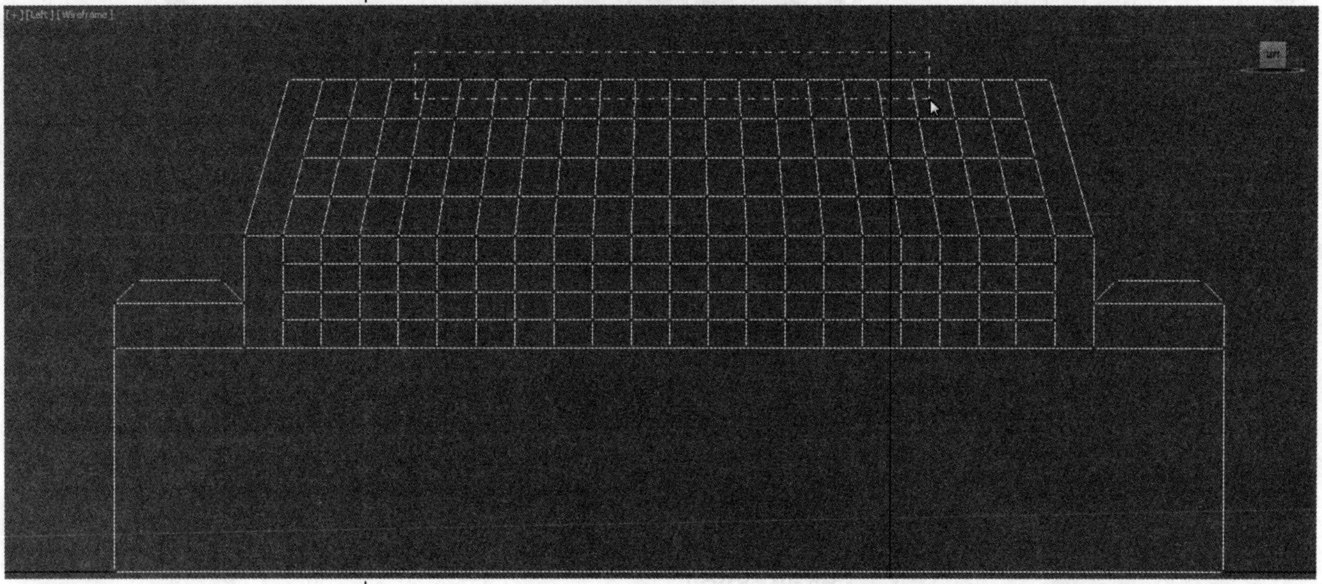

Figure 4–68

35. The row of vertices selected display in red.

36. Click (Maximize Viewport) again to display all of the four viewports. In the Perspective view, use (Orbit) and verify that you have selected the correct row (only the top most row) of vertices.

37. In the Command Panel, note that you are in the *Modify* panel with the Modifier Stack indicating that you are in the **Edit Poly>Vertex** level. Expand the Soft Selection rollout. Select **Use Soft Selection** and adjust the *Falloff* as shown on the left in Figure 4–69. A rainbow color is displayed. The Red/Yellow/Orange/Green vertices will be affected by the selected transform (e.g., **Move**), while the Blue vertices remain unaffected. Using soft selection, you can verify the vertices that will be affected. You can change the Falloff values to add or remove vertices from the affected/unaffected group. The resulting model might differ from that shown in Figure 4–69, based on the values and vertices that you selected.

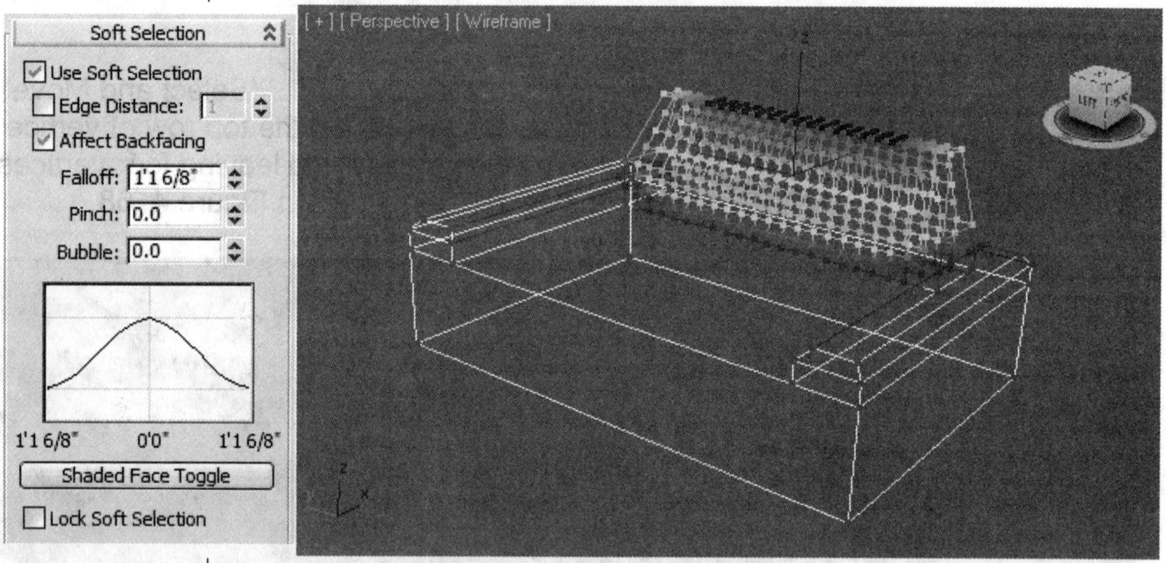

Figure 4–69

You can change the size of the Transform gizmo using the <->(hyphen) and <=> (equal sign).

38. Verify that (Select and Move) is still selected. Move the vertices up by moving the gizmo along the Z-axis, to create the curved chair back, as shown in Figure 4–70. Note that while moving the vertices, the dark blue vertices remain unaffected.

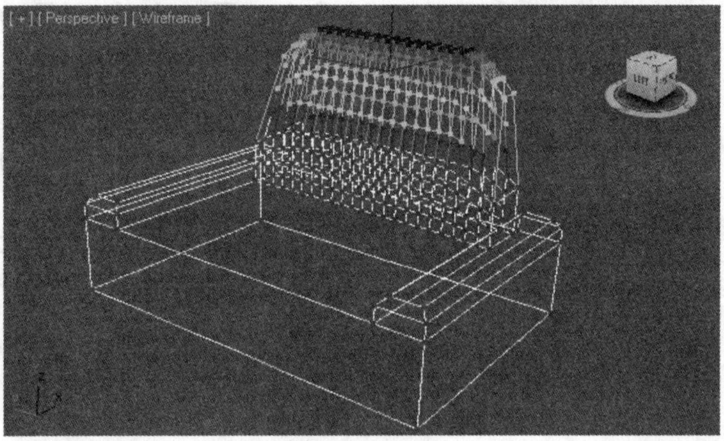

Figure 4–70

Hint: Assign Hotkey

You can assign a hotkey to interactively adjust the Soft selection falloff and pinch in the viewport. To do this, assign a hotkey to **Edit Soft Selection Mode**. For the exact procedure see: To edit a soft selection in the Viewport in the Autodesk 3ds Max Help.

39. In the Modifier Stack, select **Edit Poly** to toggle off the sub-object selection. The Edit Poly modifier should be highlighted in gray.

40. Click anywhere in empty space in the Perspective viewport to clear the selection. Press <F3> to toggle from *Wireframe* to **Realistic** mode and press <F4> to toggle on **Edged Faces** mode. Alternatively, you can click the **Viewport Shading** menu and select **Realistic** and **Edged Faces**. The model displays as shown in Figure 4–71.

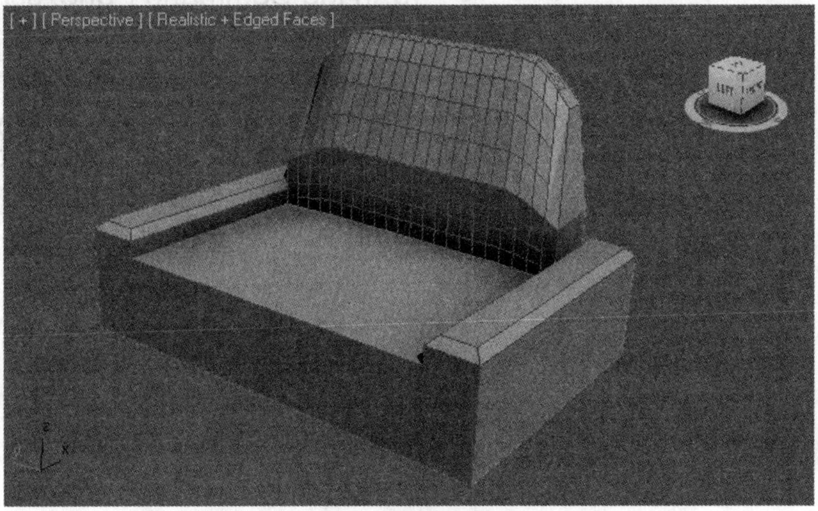

Figure 4–71

41. Select **Rendering>Environment** to open the Environment and Effects dialog box. In the *Background* area, select the *Color* swatch and select **White** in the Color Selector dialog box. (Move the Whiteness slider all the way down.) Close both dialog boxes. Verify that the Perspective viewport is active. In the Main toolbar, click  (Render Production). The rendering should display as shown in Figure 4–72.

Figure 4–72

42. Note that there are some problems with smoothing and that the chair looks extremely faceted. Select the chair and in the Modifier Stack or Ribbon, select **Polygon** or press<4> to access the Polygon sub-object level.

43. In the Command Pane, scroll down and expand the Polygon: Smoothing Groups rollout. Press <Ctrl>+<A> to select all of the polygons, and click Auto Smooth in the rollout, as shown in Figure 4–73. Click in empty space in the viewport to clear all of the selections. Note that there is a subtle change in the viewport display and that the edge is softened in the upright chair back.

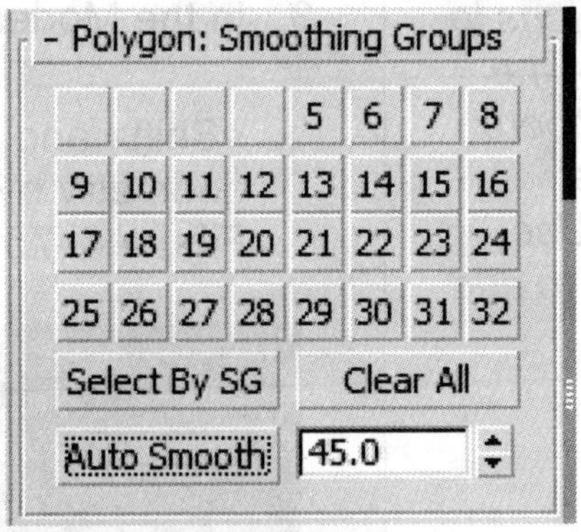

Figure 4–73

44. Select **Edit Poly** to toggle off Sub-object mode. Render the scene by clicking (Render Production) or pressing <F9>. The rendering indicates that the smoothing problem has been fixed, as shown in Figure 4–74.

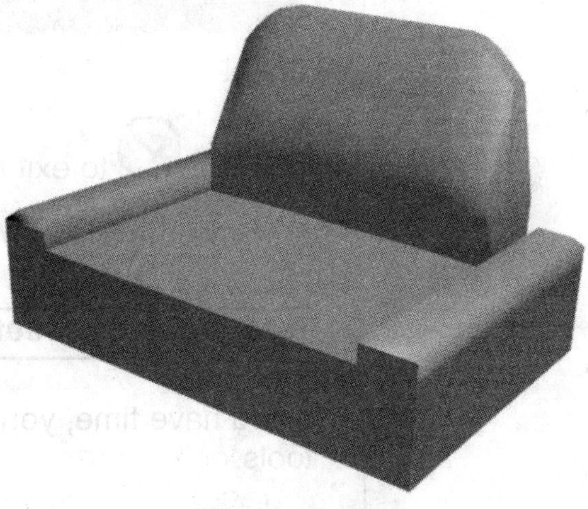

Figure 4–74

Task 2 - Apply Geometric Smoothing.

In this task you will add Geometry Smoothing using the **MSmooth** operation.

1. In the Perspective view, select the chair. In the Modeling Ribbon, in the *Polygon Modeling* panel, click (Polygon), or press <4>.
2. Press <Ctrl>+<A> to select all of the polygons. If they are completely displayed in red, press <F2> to only display the faces in a red outline (edges).

You can add divisions to the seat portion of the chair for the MSmooth modifier to have a smoother effect. Use the Slice modifier to add divisions.

3. In the Modeling Ribbon, in the *Subdivision* panel, hold down <Shift> and click (MSmooth). **Msmooth** changes the geometry by adding density to the mesh, as shown in Figure 4–75.

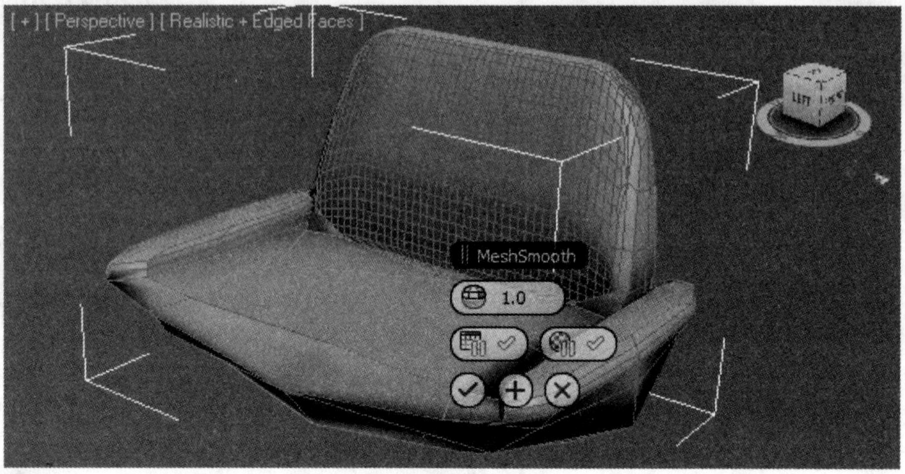

Figure 4–75

4. Click to exit the caddy display.
5. Save the file as **My Armchair.max**.

Task 3 - Using Freeform tools.

If you have time, you can soften the model using the **Freeform** tools.

1. Continue creating the armchair.
2. In the *Polygon Modeling* tab, click (Polygon), if it is not selected. You can also select **Edit Poly** in the Command Panel Modifier List. Press <Ctrl>+<A> to select all of the polygons.
3. Select the *Freeform* tab, as shown in Figure 4–76.

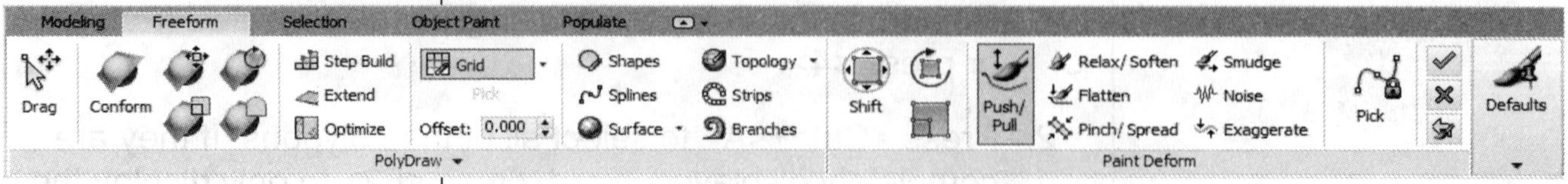

Figure 4–76

4. In the *Paint Deform* panel, click (Shift).

5. When you start this command, a *Shift Options* panel displays on the screen, in which you can change the brush size and brush strength. Set *Full Strength* to **100** and *Falloff* to **300**, as shown in Figure 4–77. In the Quick Access Toolbar, click  (Undo) if you moved the wrong vertices.

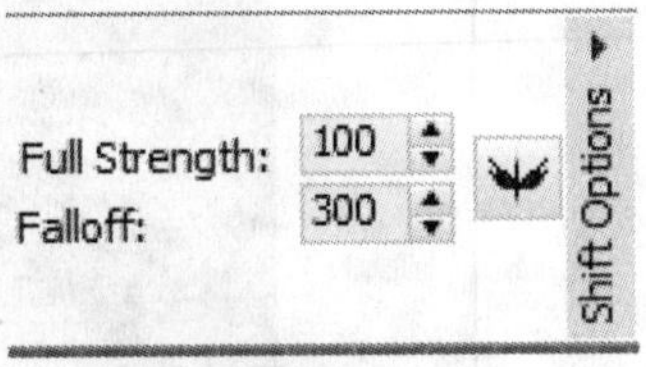

Figure 4–77

6. Right-click to activate the Left viewport (with the selection on) and hover the cursor, which displays as two circles over the top of the back. Stretch the back upward as shown in Figure 4–78.

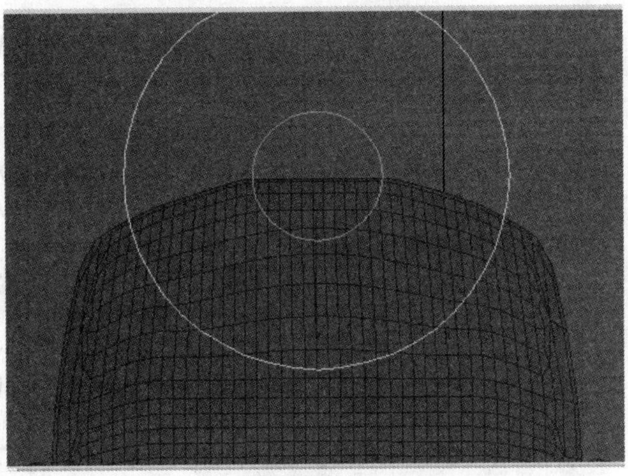

Figure 4–78

7. Reduce the brush size and strength in the *Shift Options* panel (30 and 50). In the Front viewport, use the **Shift** tool to stretch and deform the chair back, as shown in Figure 4–79.

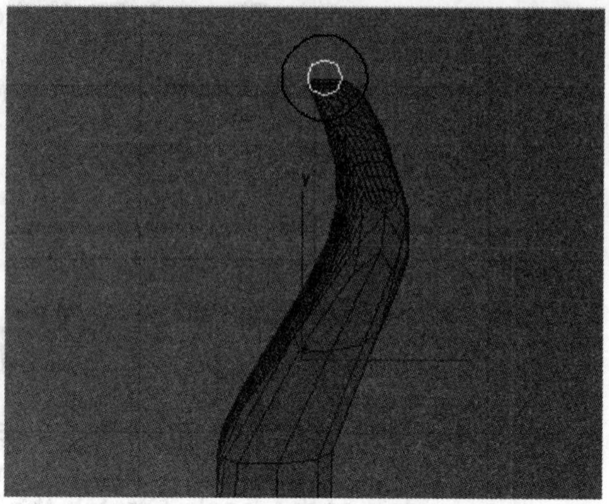

Figure 4–79

Task 4 - Optimize the Mesh.

The shape of the chair has been softened. Now you need to reduce the polycount so the file can be used efficiently. The ProOptimizer modifier will achieve this.

1. Select the **Edit Poly** modifier in the stack to disable Sub-object mode. In the Modifier drop-down list, select **ProOptimizer**. It will be displays in the Modifier Stack, as shown in Figure 4–80.

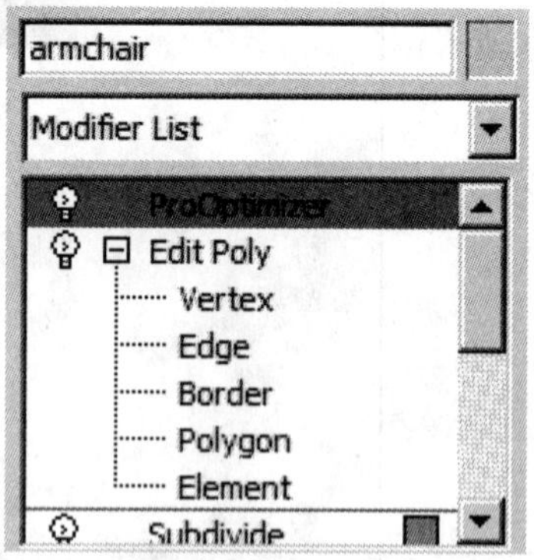

Figure 4–80

2. In the *Modify* panel, in the Optimization Levels rollout, click [Calculate]. Change the *Vertex %* to **22**. Use the spinner to move it up or down as shown in Figure 4–81. Keep watching the viewport and also the statistics are displayed in the rollout.

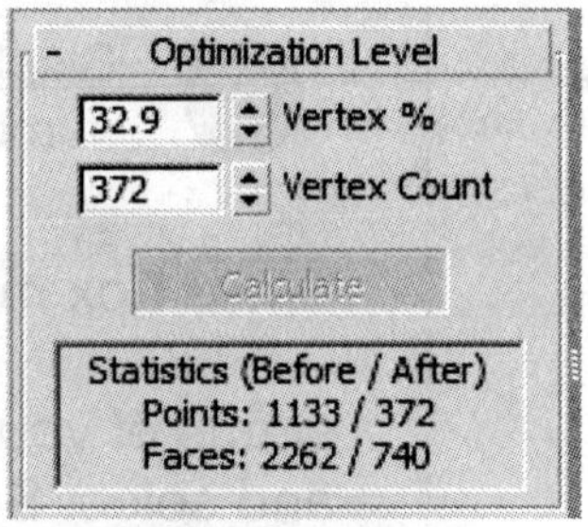

Figure 4–81

Save your work as **Myarmchair_softened.max**.

Hint: Using Optimize and MultiRes Modifiers

The **Optimize** and **MultiRes** modifiers are both accessed in the Modifier List. They can be used to reduce the number of vertices and polygons. The **Optimize** modifier reduces the model geometry, but does not critically change the appearance of the model. **MultiRes** reduces the model geometry and you can specify the exact vertex count to be used for reduction. **MutiRes** should be used if you have to export the models to other 3D applications because it maintains the map channels.

4.7 Statistics in Viewport

Learning Objectives

- Review the status of the model using the **Summary Info** command.
- Display information about the scene, such as polygon count, number of vertices, etc., in the viewport.

While Box modeling it is a good idea to frequently review the status of your model. You can expand , expand Properties and select **Summary Info** to find out a lot of information about the file. You can also **Show Statistics** directly in the viewport. To launch statistics, in the Viewport label, click [+], select **xView**, and select **Show Statistics**. The total number of polygons, vertices, and Frames Per Second are displayed in the viewport, as shown in Figure 4–82, and are dependent on the options selected in the Viewport Configuration dialog box. Alternatively, press <7> to toggle the statistics display in the viewport on and off in the active viewport.

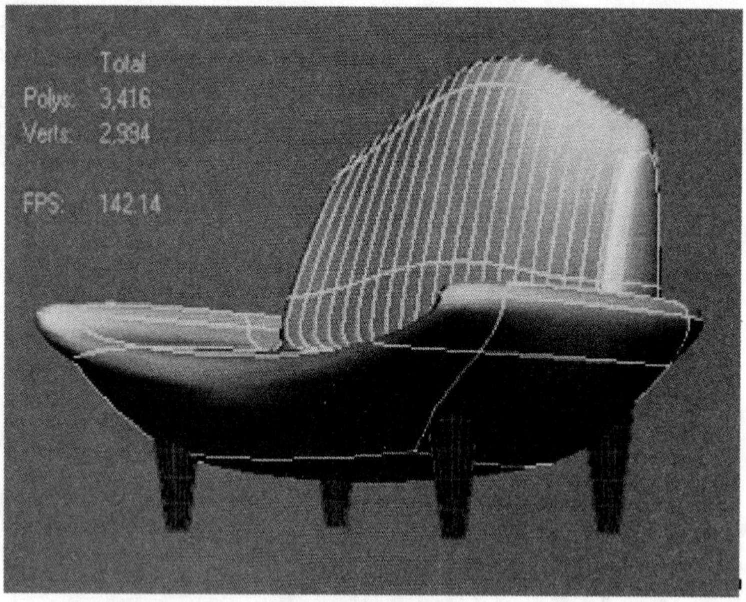

Figure 4–82

The statistics options can be controlled by selecting **Views> Viewport Configuration** and in the *Statistics* tab of the Viewport configuration dialog box, as shown in Figure 4–83. Alternatively, in the Viewport label, click [+] and select **Configure Viewports** to open the Viewport Configuration dialog box. In the Viewport Configuration dialog box, in the *Statistics* tab customize the display (e.g., **Polygon Count**, **Triangle Count**, **Edge Count**, **Vertex Count**, etc.).

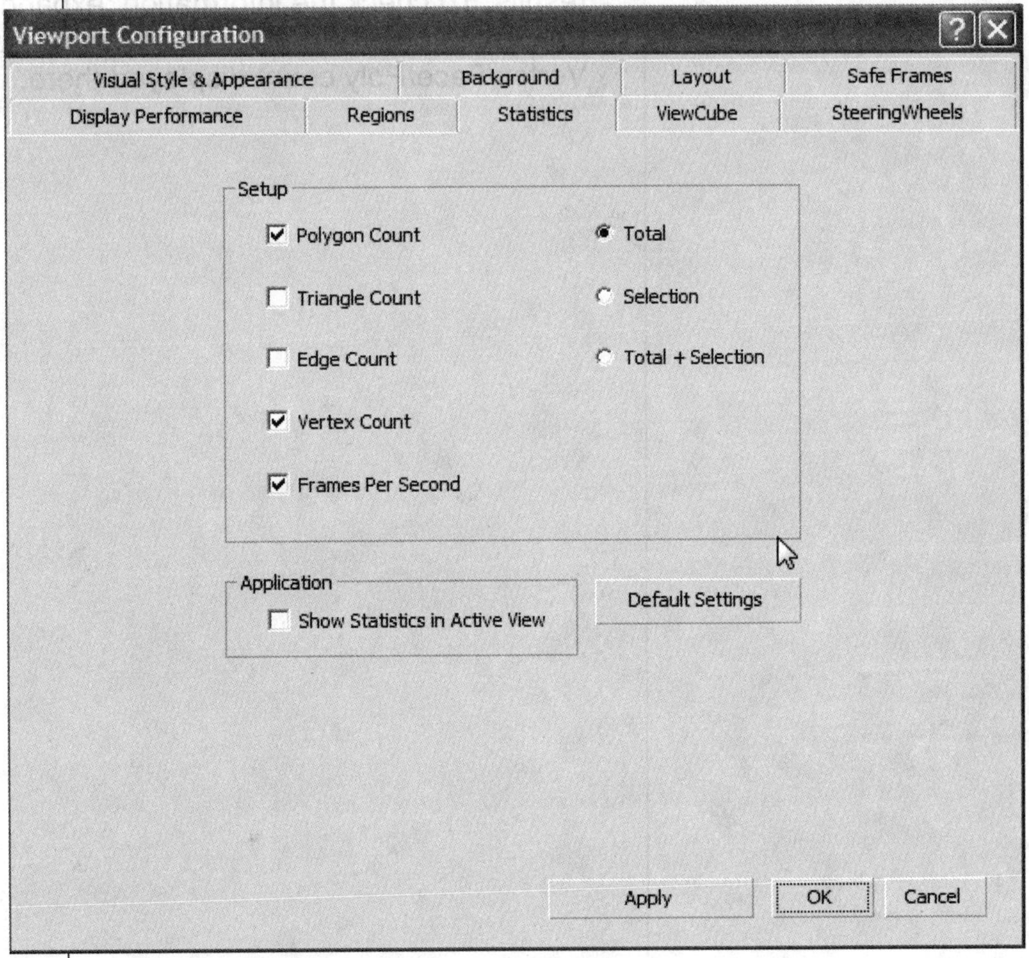

Figure 4–83

Hint: Low Polygon Count

When designing, it is a good idea to keep your **Polygon Count** or **Triangle Count** as low as possible to speed up rendering and viewport performance. If you are creating real time models, this impacts the interactive viewport navigation and playback speed.

- When working in the Autodesk 3ds Max Design software, you can toggle the view of the statistics on and off when you need to see it. Performance might be improved if you keep this off when not in use.

> **Hint: Use Summary Info**
>
> Sometimes **Show Statistics** does not seem to give correct results. To check the information, expand , expand Properties, and select **Summary Info** and then compare the Vertex/Face/Poly count displayed there.

Chapter Review Questions

1. Which of the following are the **Transform** tools in the Autodesk 3ds Max Design software? (Select all that apply.)
   a. **Move**
   b. **Stretch**
   c. **Trim**
   d. **Scale**
2. Which of the following do you press to change the size (shrink and enlarge) of the Transform gizmo?
   a. <-> and <+>
   b. <+> and <=>
   c. <-> and <=>
   d. </> and <+>
3. Which **Transform center** option do you select if you want to rotate many objects, each around its own center?
   a. 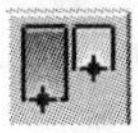 (Pivot Point Center)
   b.  (Selection Center)
   c.  (Transform Coordinate Center)
4. Which clone option creates a one-directional link in which changes made to the original object affect the duplicate, but the modifiers applied to the duplicate do not affect the source object?
   a. **Copy**
   b. **Instance**
   c. **Reference**

5. In addition to the **Polygon Modeling** tools, the *Modeling* tab in the Ribbon contains the commonly used tools from which panel of the Command Panel?

   a. *Modify* panel ()

   b. *Hierarchy* panel ()

   c. *Display* panel ()

   d. *Utilities* panel ()

6. Which key on the keyboard can be used as a shortcut to toggle the statistics display in the viewport on and off?

   a. <1>

   b. <3>

   c. <5>

   d. <7>

Command Summary

Button	Command	Location
	**Ribbon (Graphite Modeling Tools)**	■ **Main Toolbar** ■ **Customize:** Show UI>Show Ribbon
	**Select and Move**	■ **Main Toolbar** ■ **Edit:** Move
	**Select and Rotate**	■ **Main Toolbar** ■ **Edit:** Rotate
	**Select and Uniform Scale**	■ **Main Toolbar:** Scale flyout ■ **Edit:** Scale
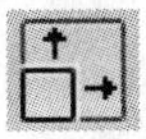	**Select and Non-uniform Scale**	■ **Main Toolbar:** Scale flyout
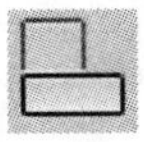	**Select and Squash**	■ **Main Toolbar:** Scale flyout
	**Use Pivot Point Center**	■ **Main Toolbar:** Transform Center flyout
	**Use Selection Center**	■ **Main Toolbar:** Transform Center flyout
	**Use Transform Coordinate Center**	■ **Main Toolbar:** Transform Center flyout

Chapter 5

Modeling From 2D Objects

In this chapter you learn to create 2D shapes and then use the Lathe, Extrude, and Sweep modifiers to create 3D geometry. You learn to modify the 2D shapes by adding and subtracting them using the 2D Boolean operations. You also learn about the 3D Boolean operations and how to use the ProBoolean compound object.

This chapter contains the following topics:

Certification

Topic:

✓Modeling

Objectives:

✓Identify and use line tool creation methods

✓Identify Vertex types

5.1 3D Modeling from 2D Objects

Learning Objective

- Create 3D models from 2D shapes, such as lines and closed shape objects (rectangle, ellipse etc.).

2D shapes can be created from scratch in the Autodesk® 3ds Max® Design software using  (Shapes) in the *Create* panel () in the Command Panel. You can create the shapes in the form of splines and NURBS. The splines that you can create consist of the basic shapes, such as **Line**, **Rectangle**, **Ellipse**, etc., as shown in Figure 5–1. You can also create some extended shapes, such as **WRectangle**, **Channel**, **Angle**, etc. You can use modifiers such as Edit Spline to apply edits like trim, extend, fillet, and chamfer to 2D objects. Although the Autodesk 3ds Max Design software does include these 2D tools, it is not a drafting application. Most users prefer to create 2D design geometry in CAD packages and link or import that data into the Autodesk 3ds Max Design software. There are many times however, where it is more practical to work directly using the 2D tools within the Autodesk 3ds Max Design software, especially when modeling organic smooth curved surfaces.

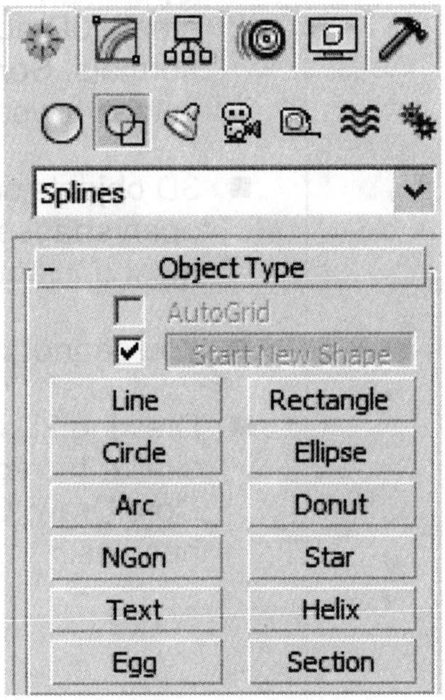

Figure 5–1

Drawing 2D Shapes

The Autodesk 3ds Max Design software is intended to give you lots of freedom in drawing lines and curves, and also enables you to have control and precision.

Drawing lines is done in a freeform interactive manner, rather than in a typical CAD workflow. While you can use the keyboard entry method, it is much easier to click in the viewport and start drawing. Precision can be accomplished using snaps and vertices can be shifted after placement. Precise manipulation of vertices can be accomplished using the Transform Type-In functionality.

The important things to understand about lines and shapes in the Autodesk 3ds Max Design software are:

- Lines can be drawn to create three kinds of shapes: open, closed, and self-intersecting.
- Closed shapes can also be created using other shape object types, such as Rectangle, Ellipse, Ngon, or Text.
- 3D objects can be created by extruding closed shapes using the **Extrude** modifier. The outside of these objects is visible and renderable from all sides. All face normals point away from the center of the object.
- Open shapes and self-intersecting shapes can be extruded to create 3D objects, but these objects have mixed face normals. Some faces do not render and might not be visible in the viewport.
- 3D objects can be created by using the **Lathe** modifier on open shapes. Revolving a profile is one of the simplest and most ancient methods of modeling.
- You cannot draw a 2D line that forks or branches.
- Drawing 2D lines in the Autodesk 3ds Max Design software is similar to vector illustration packages like Adobe Illustrator or CorelDraw. Curves can be manipulated using **Bezier** vertex handles.

The **Line** tool has two basic drawing techniques:

Method 1: You can draw straight line segments by clicking and moving the cursor repeatedly. This method does not create any curves at first. All of the vertices created are Corner type. After clicking to set the vertices, you select the line vertices individually or in sets and then change their type from *Corner* to **Bezier** or **Smooth** to create curves.

Hint: Preventing Self-intersecting Shapes

When drawing using Method 1, if you draw quickly, the program might translate your motions into press and drag, and self-intersecting shapes can be inadvertently drawn. In the *Create* panel's Creation Method rollout, change the drag type to **Corner** to prevent this. In doing so, you are not able to drag curves interactively.

*You cannot create Bezier vertices by clicking, holding, and dragging if both the Initial Type and Drag Type have been set to **Corner** in the Creation Method rollout in the **Line** tool.*

Method 2: Draw curves directly by clicking, holding, and dragging to create **Bezier** vertices rather than **Corner** vertices. This is a faster method but is hard to control, since you are defining the curve on both sides of the vertex in a single move. Holding down <Alt> while dragging enables you to define the curve on the leading side of the vertex, introducing an angle between the vertex handles.

Using either method, these curved segments are created out of smaller straight line segments. Increasing the segments makes the curve smoother. The *Steps* value in the Interpolation rollout sets the number of segments.

- Drawing while holding down <Shift> also draws straight lines and perpendicular lines.
- Press <Backspace> to undo the last drawn vertex in a line.

Practice 5a Drawing Lines

Learning Objectives

- Create an open and closed 2D shape using the **Line** command.
- Move the location of the vertex and change the shape of the curve using the Bezier handles.

Estimated time for completion: 20 minutes

You must set the paths to locate the External files and Xrefs used in the practice. If you have not done this already, return to the **Introduction to Autodesk 3ds Max Design** chapter and complete Task 1 to Task 3 of the **Organizing Folders and Working with the Interface** practice. You only have to set the user paths once.

Task 1 - Drawing 2D lines.

If a dialog box opens prompting you about a File Load: Mismatch, click OK to accept the default values.

1. Expand and select **Reset** to reset the screen.
2. Click (Maximize Viewport) or press <Alt>+<W> to open the four viewport display.
3. Click in the Front viewport to make it active. Click (Maximize Viewport) to maximize the Front viewport.
4. Press <G> to hide the grid. In the Command Panel, in the *Create* panel ( ), click (Shapes), as shown in Figure 5–2.

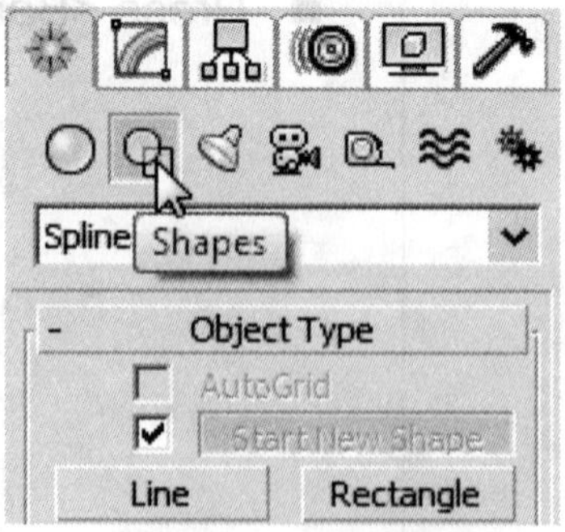

Figure 5–2

5. In the Object Type rollout, click Line.

6. In the Front viewport, draw a saw-tooth pattern line as shown in Figure 5–3. Click to set the first point, move your cursor to the next location for placing the point and click to place the second point. The first line displays. Continue the pattern. Right-click to end, once you have placed the last line. An open shape is created.

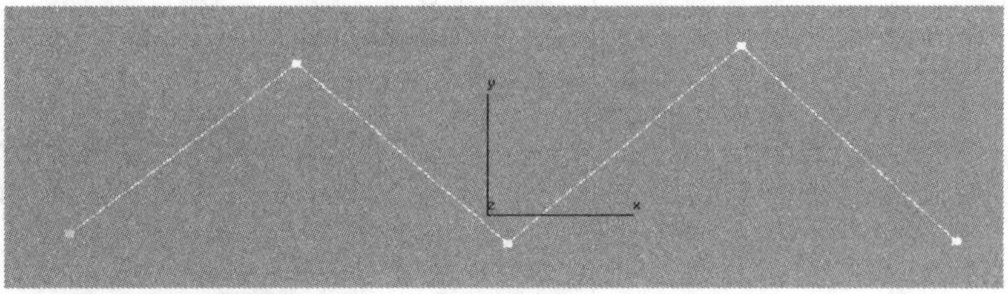

Figure 5–3

7. Delete the lines by pressing <Delete>.

Closed shapes and open shapes are both used in creating 3D objects. Modifiers, such as Extrude, Lathe, and Surface modifiers, can all be used to build 3D surfaces based on 2D shapes.

8. You are still in the **Line** command. Repeat the drawing process, to create a closed shape as shown in Figure 5–4. Click to set each point and select the starting point (yellow vertex) to complete the shape. In the Spline dialog box, click Yes to close the shape. Right-click in the empty space to come out of the command. Do not delete this shape.

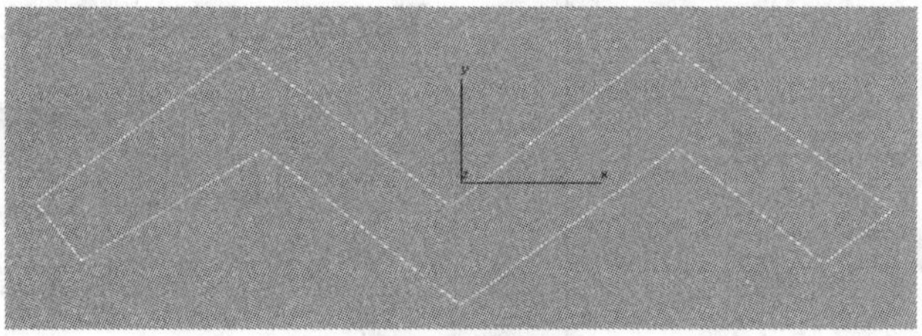

Figure 5–4

9. You can also draw curved lines. Click Line and in the Creation Method rollout, change the *Drag Type* to **Bezier**, as shown in Figure 5–5.

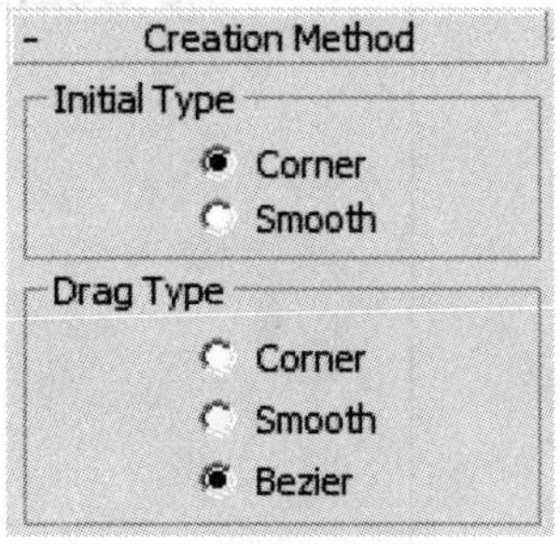

Figure 5–5

10. Click to set the first point, move your cursor, click and drag to create a Bezier curve running through the second point. Each time you click and drag, the curve extends through the new point. This draws a nice curve, but it is difficult to control, since dragging affects the curve on both sides of the point at the same time. Draw a curved line similar to shown in Figure 5–6. Right-click to end and press <Delete> to delete to this curved line.

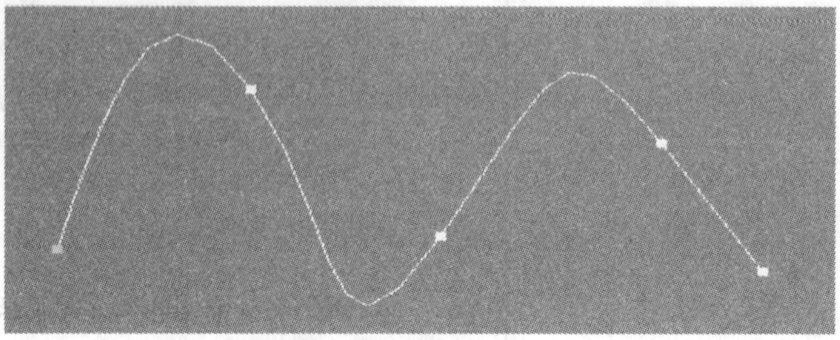

Figure 5–6

11. The most controllable way to create curves is to edit the vertices after you have drawn the lines. Right-click to exit the **Line** command. Select the closed shape that was previously created. In the Command Panel, select the *Modify* panel ( ). Click in the Modifier Stack to expand **Line**. Select **Vertex** at the sub-object level, as shown in Figure 5–7.

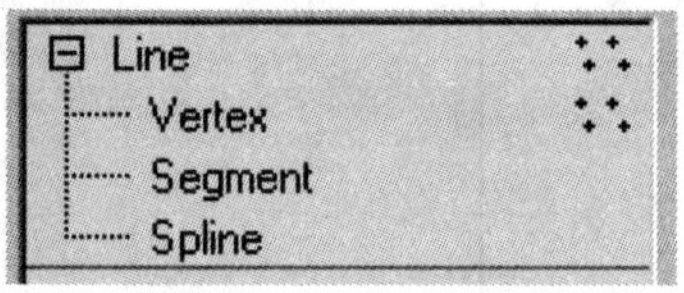

Figure 5–7

12. In the viewport, select one vertex at the top of the saw tooth pattern. The selected vertex displays in red. Right-click and select **Bezier** in the tools 1 quadrant of the quad menu. Note that the vertex corner is replaced by a Bezier curve and that the Bezier handles are displayed.

13. In the Main toolbar, click  (Select and Move). The Transform gizmo is displayed with the bezier handles. Click the yellow plane at the interior of the gizmo and move the vertex from its initial position, as shown in Figure 5–8. You can move the vertex or either handle separately. The handle movement is constrained by the Transform gizmo usage. If you click the yellow plane at the center of the Transform gizmo, you can move the location of the vertex. Click and drag either handle end (green square) to move the handles and not the vertex. Moving the handle, changes the shape of the curve. Note that both the handles move together.

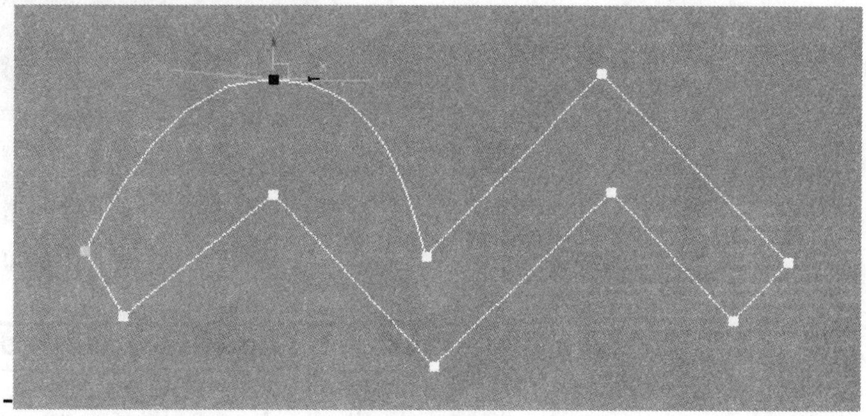

Figure 5–8

Hint: Transform Gizmo Size

<-> (hyphen) and <=> (equal sign) can be used to decrease or increase the size of the Transform gizmo. If the Transform gizmo handles extend beyond the vertex handles, you might have trouble moving the vertex handles.

If you move the Transform gizmo in one axis, the movement of the bezier handles is constrained to that axis. To have the handles move freely, select the yellow square of the gizmo to have movement in the XY-axes. This can also be controlled using the Axis Constraints toolbar.

14. Hold down <Shift> and move one of the handles. This changes the command to **Bezier Corner**. This enables you to break the continuity of the curve to manipulate the handles on one side of the curve separately from the other, as shown in Figure 5–9. Right-click on the vertex and select **Reset Tangents** to return the original curve shape. To return to Bezier, right-click and select it again in the quad menu.

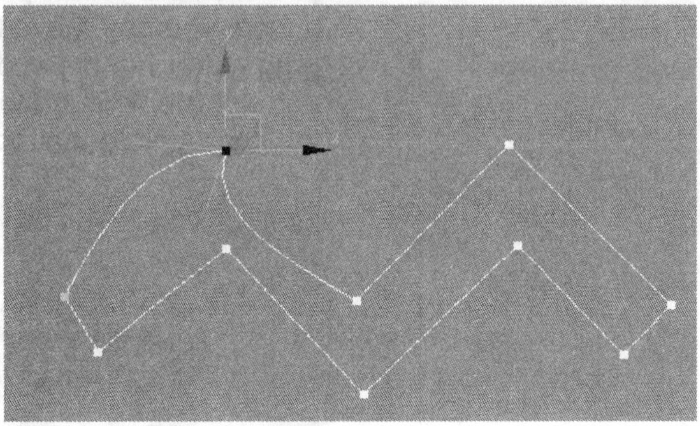

Figure 5–9

Task 2 - Using 2D Shapes to draw a candlestick model.

In this task you will draw a model of a candlestick to practice these tools. A reference photo of an actual candlestick is shown on the left in Figure 5–10. The reference photo is located in your Class Files>*Maps* folder with the filename **Candlestick_pewter.jpg**.

1. In the Modifier Stack, select **Line** to exit sub-object selection mode. If required, select all of the lines that you have drawn and delete them using <Delete>.

2. In the *Create* panel, click (Shapes) and click Line. In the Creation Method rollout, in the *Drag Type* area, select **Corner**, if required.

Holding down <Shift> creates straight lines at a 90 degree angle (vertical direction) and 180 degree angle (horizontal direction).

3. Start at the bottom right (the yellow vertex indicates the start point) and click to place the first line vertex as shown on the right in Figure 5–10. Hold down <Shift>, move the cursor to the left, and click to draw the base of the candlestick. Still holding down <Shift>, move the cursor up in the viewport to draw the long straight vertical line segment, and then click to place the vertex. Release <Shift> and continue clicking and drawing in a clockwise direction. Press <Backspace> to undo the points if you make a mistake.

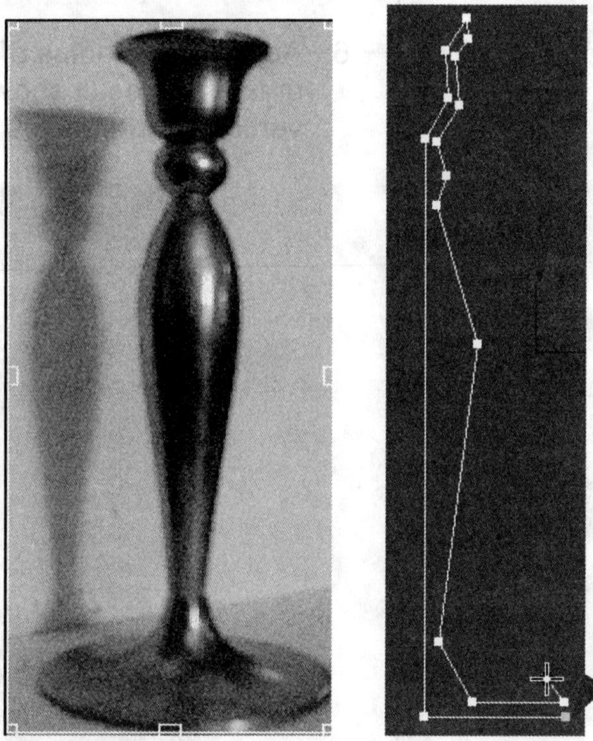

Figure 5–10

4. Altogether, place approximately 17 points. Close the shape by clicking over the first point and click Yes. Right-click to exit the **Line** command.

5. In the *Modify* panel ( ), in the Modifier Stack, expand Line and select the **Vertex** sub-object level. Holding down <Ctrl>, select the four vertices, as shown on the left in Figure 5–11. Right-click and select **Bezier** in the quad menu. This changes these to Bezier vertices with the handles. Click in empty space to clear the selection so that you can modify each vertex separately.

6. Adjust the handles of each using  (Select and Move) to obtain the result shown on the right in Figure 5–11. Move the vertices and handles as required.

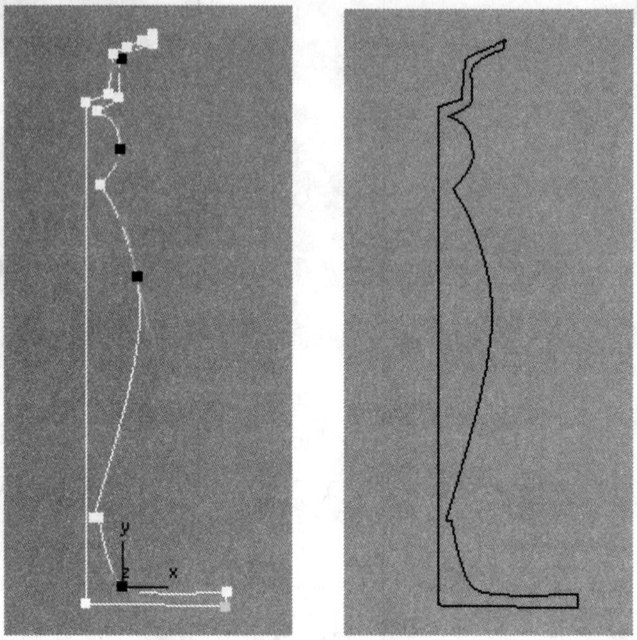

Figure 5–11

7. Save your work as **MyCandlestickProfile.max**. For comparison, you can open the file **Candlestick_Profile.max** from your *Class Files* folder.

Certification

Topic:

✓Modeling

Objectives:

✓Use object creation and modification workflows

5.2 The Lathe Modifier

Learning Objective

- Revolve a profile around an axis using the Lathe modifier.

A common way to create a 3D object is to revolve a profile around an axis. In AutoCAD®, the **Surfrev** tool creates a surface in this way. In the Autodesk 3ds Max Design software, you can use the **Lathe** modifier to revolve a profile around an axis. The Lathe modifier is available in the Modifier List in the *Modify* panel ( ) in the Command Panel.

To create a 3D object using the Lathe modifier, use the following steps:

1. Select a profile (usually a line object).
2. Apply a **Lathe** Modifier.
3. Adjust the axis of revolution.
4. Adjust the alignment of the axis with the profile.

Practice 5b Creating a Candlestick

Learning Objective

- Revolve a 2D shape around its axis using the Lathe modifier to create 3D geometry.

Estimated time for completion: 5 minutes

In this practice, you use the **Lathe** modifier to create the solid geometry for the candlestick.

You must set the paths to locate the External files and Xrefs used in the practice. If you have not done this already, return to the **Introduction to Autodesk 3ds Max Design** chapter and complete Task 1 to Task 3 of the **Organizing Folders and Working with the Interface** practice. You only have to set the user paths once.

If a dialog box opens prompting you about a File Load: Mismatch, click OK *to accept the default values.*

1. Continue working with the file created in the previous practice, **MyCandlestickProfile.max**. If you did not complete it, open **Candlestick_Profile.max** from your *Class Files* folder.

2. If you opened the file from your *Class Files* folder, maximize the Front viewport. Verify that the profile is selected. In the Command Panel, select the *Modify* panel ( ), if required. In the Modifier Stack, select **Line** to exit sub-object level, if necessary. Verify that the **Line** is highlighted in gray and that no sub-object level is highlighted in yellow.

3. In the Modifier List, select **Lathe**. The profile revolves around a center point, but the alignment is off, as shown on the left in Figure 5–12.

*Sometimes, lathed objects display inside-out. If something looks wrong with your candlestick, use the **Flip Normals** option in the Parameters rollout.*

4. In the Parameters rollout, in the *Align* area, click Min. The candlestick should now display as shown on the right in Figure 5–12.

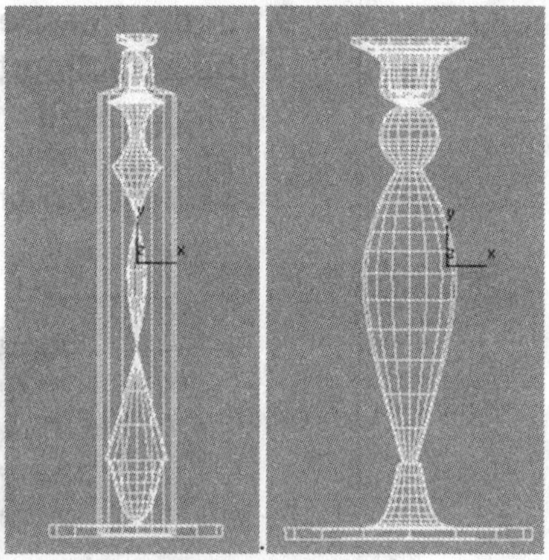

Figure 5–12

5. In the Modifier Stack, expand Lathe and select **Axis**. Move the X-axis in the viewport to show you that you are not locked into the three Alignment options of **Min**, **Center**, and **Max**.

6. In the Quick Access Toolbar, click (Undo) or press <Ctrl>+<Z> to undo the axis moves.

7. Select **Lathe** (highlighted in gray) to exit the Sub-object mode. Press <Alt>+<W> or in the Viewport Navigation toolbar, click (Maximize Viewport) to display the four viewports.

8. Assign a color to the geometry by selecting the candlestick first, selecting the color swatch next to the Line name, and selecting a color in the Object Color dialog box.

9. In the Perspective viewport, switch to **Realistic** display option by selecting the **Shaded** label and selecting **Realistic** in the label menu. In the Viewport Navigation toolbar, click  (Orbit) and examine the geometry as shown in Figure 5–13.

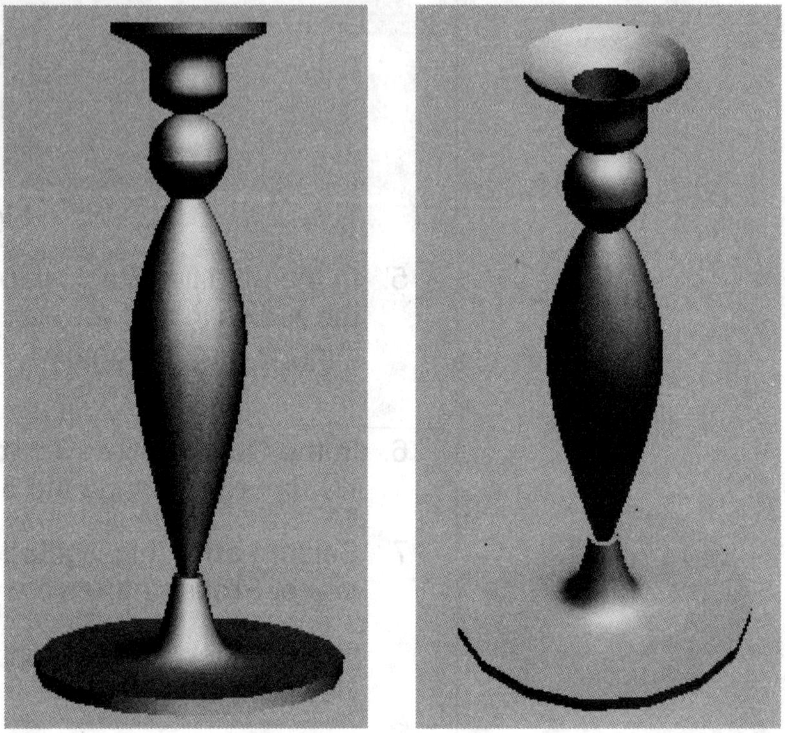

Figure 5–13

10. Save your work as **MyCandlestick.max**.

Certification

Topic:
✓Modeling
Objectives:
✓Use object creation and modification workflows

5.3 2D Booleans

Learning Objective

Add and subtract shapes at a sub-object level using the 2D Boolean operations.

When doing any kind of real world work, you will require to create shapes by combining drawn lines and shapes, such as ellipses and rectangles. 2D Boolean operations enable you to build up shapes by adding or subtracting at the Spline sub-object level while using the **Edit Spline** modifier.

All shapes that are to be combined using 2D Boolean operations must be part of a single shape. You can use the **Attach** command to join multiple shapes into a single shape. Use the **Edit Spline** modifier to convert a shape to an editable spline and then use the **Attach** command to combine multiple shapes into a single shape. The 2D Boolean operations are available in the Spline sub-object level, in the **Geometry** parameters, as shown in Figure 5–14.

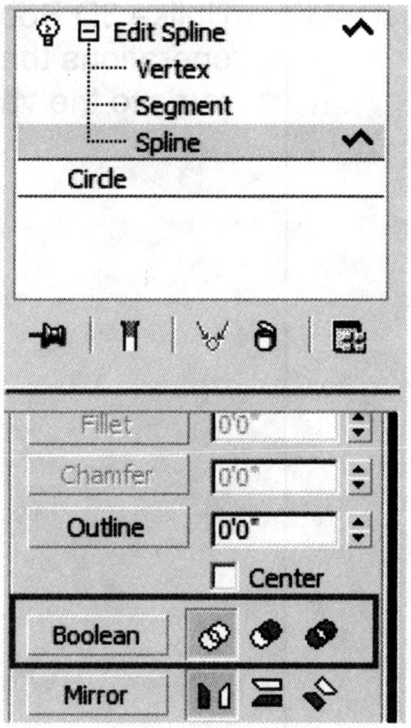

Figure 5–14

When drawing shapes, in the Object Type rollout, if you clear the **Start New Shape** option (as shown in Figure 5–15), all of the subsequent shapes that you create are joined into one single shape. If you have a shape already selected, anything you draw becomes part of that shape. You do not need to attach the shapes before using the 2D boolean operations. The **Start New Shape** option is selected as the default before you start drawing any shapes.

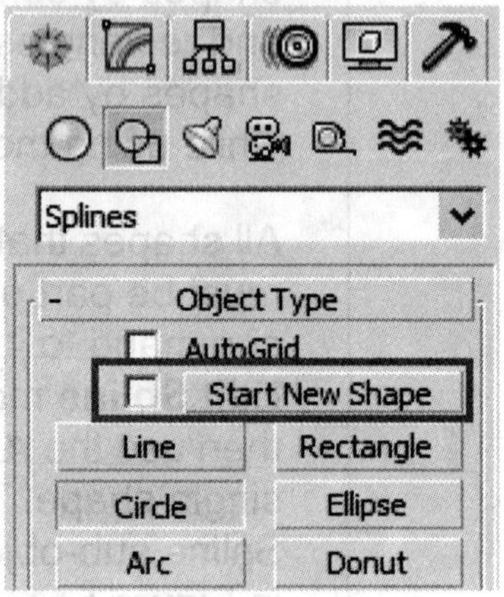

Figure 5–15

Unlike 3D Booleans, no history is associated with 2D Boolean operations that are saved with the file. You are not able to retrieve the various Boolean components after saving.

Practice 5c 2D Booleans

Learning Objective

- Modify the shape of the candlestick by adding and subtracting rectangles using 2D Boolean operations.

Estimated time for completion: 5 minutes

In this practice, you will use 2D Booleans to change the shape of the profile for the candlestick.

You must set the paths to locate the External files and Xrefs used in the practice. If you have not done this already, return to the **Introduction to Autodesk 3ds Max Design** chapter and complete Task 1 to Task 3 of the **Organizing Folders and Working with the Interface** practice. You only have to set the user paths once.

If a dialog box opens prompting you about a File Load: Mismatch, click OK to accept the default values.

1. Continue working with the file created in the previous practice, **MyCandlestick.max**. If you did not complete it, open **Candlestick.max** from your *Class Files* folder.
2. Activate the Front viewport and click (Maximize Viewport) to maximize it.
3. Select the candlestick and select the *Modify* panel ( ).
4. In the Modifier Stack, click (Lightbulb) next to the **Lathe**. This toggles the Lathe modifier off in the viewport. The line profile and the Lathe axis is visible.
5. In the *Create* panel ( ), click (Shapes).

6. Click Rectangle. Draw four rectangles intersecting the right edge of the profile, as shown in Figure 5–16.

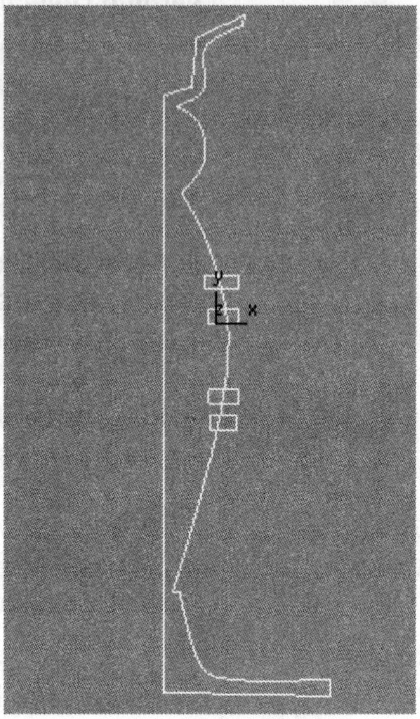

Figure 5–16

7. Right-click to cancel the command. Select the candlestick profile.

8. In the *Modify* panel ( ), in the Modifier Stack, select **Line**. Scroll down in the Geometry rollout and note that the Boolean is not available (it is grayed out). Click Attach Mult..

9. In the Attach Multiple dialog box, click (Display Shapes) to make it active, if it is not active (A yellow background in the button means it is active). Select all of the Rectangles (Highlighted in blue) and click Attach. All of the rectangles become part of the candlestick profile spline object.

10. In the Modifier Stack, select the **Spline** sub-object in the Line object and select the candlestick profile in the viewport. The original profile display in red and the rectangles remain white (unselected).

11. In the Geometry rollout, scroll down to display Boolean and note that it is now available.

12. Click Boolean (Boolean) and verify that (Union) is selected (it displays a yellow background). When you move the cursor over one of the rectangles, it displays as a Union cursor. Select the topmost rectangle. Select the second rectangle. Observe that in each case, the profile is extended to the right to include part of the rectangle, and the inner part of the rectangle is discarded.

13. Click Boolean (Subtraction). Select the next rectangle. Repeat for the last rectangle. For these shapes, the rectangle is subtracted from the candlestick. The first two rectangles create a rim, and the last two create an inscribed groove, as shown in Figure 5–17.

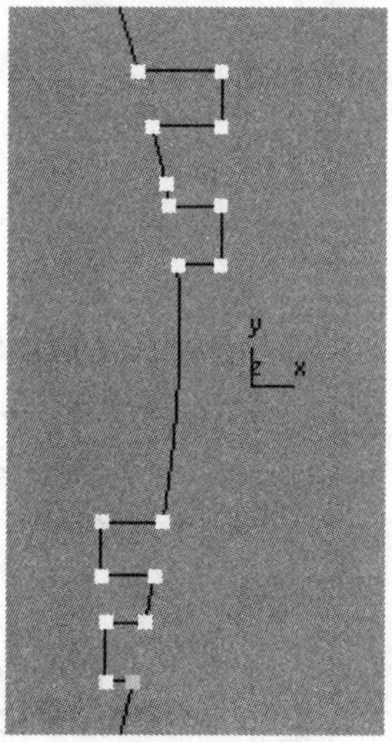

Figure 5–17

14. In the Modifier Stack, click (Lightbulb) next to the **Lathe** to toggle it on. Select **Lathe** to highlight it.

15. Press <Alt>+<W> to return to four viewports. Activate the Perspective viewport and review the results in **Realistic** display mode. The two rims and two grooves are created in the candle stick, as shown in Figure 5–18.

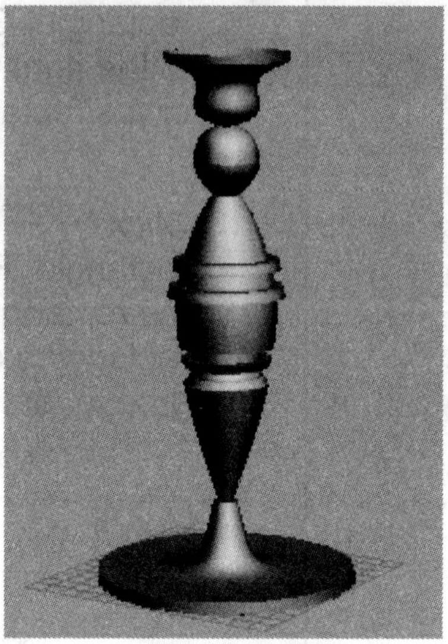

Figure 5–18

16. (Optional) Modify some of the vertices. In the *Modify* panel, select **Line** and **Vertex** sub-objects as shown in Figure 5–19. Select one of the vertices in the first ridge that you just created.

17. (Optional) In the Modifier Stack, click  (Show end result on/off toggle) as shown in Figure 5–19. This tool enables you to see the object as an end product.

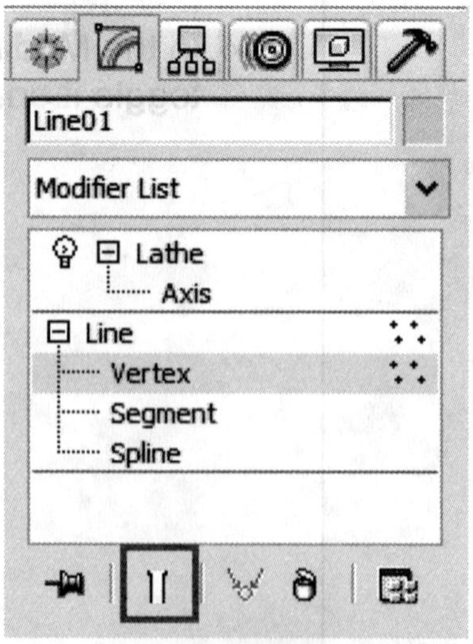

Figure 5–19

18. (Optional) Move the selected vertices in the viewport. You are now sculpting the candlestick in real time, as shown in Figure 5–20.

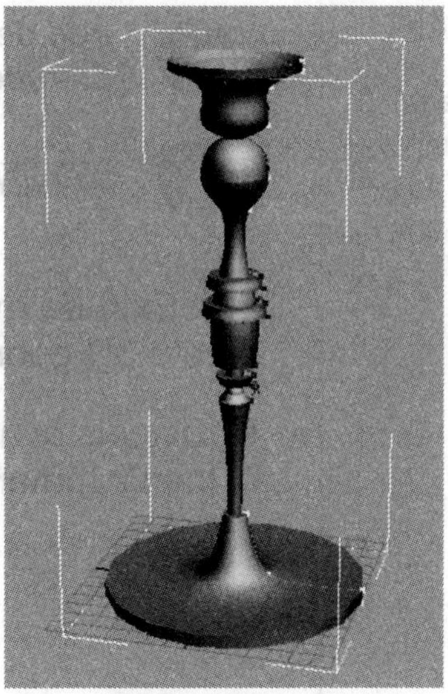

Figure 5–20

19. Save your work as **MyCandlestick01.max**.

20. (Optional) Consider using the Lathe modifier to create the legs for the armchair you designed earlier.

Certification

Topic:

✓*Modeling*

Objectives:

✓*Use object creation and modification workflows*

5.4 The Extrude Modifier

Learning Objectives

- Add depth to a 2D shape to create 3D geometry using the Extrude modifier.
- Identify and understand the different Extrude options.

The Extrude modifier is a method to add depth to a 2D shape to create 3D geometry. As with other modifiers, the Extrude modifier is available in the Modifier List in the *Modify* panel ( ) in the Command Panel, as shown in Figure 5–21.

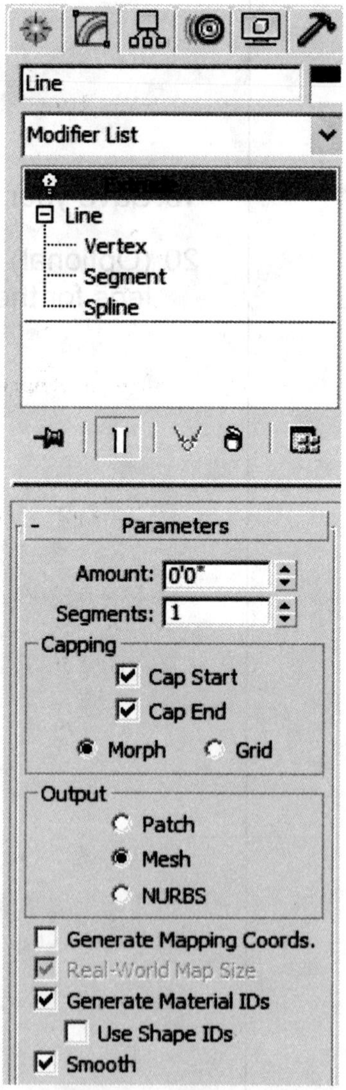

Figure 5–21

Capping Start and End

In the Parameters rollout, the **Cap Start** and **Cap End** options enable you to control whether the object displays open or closed.

- Capping only applies when extruding closed shapes. Open shapes can be extruded but they cannot have a top or bottom.
- Closed shapes often do not cap if they double-back or cross themselves, or if they include more than one vertex at the same location.
- You can also extrude with a height of 0 to create a flat surface. In this situation, only the start or end cap is necessary.
- An extruded shape with No Capping, Cap Start, and Cap End options are shown in Figure 5–22.

Original Shape ***No Capping*** ***Cap Start*** ***Cap End***

Figure 5–22

Capping Type

There are two types of capping: Morph and Grid, which can be selected in the *Capping* area in the Parameters rollout, as shown in Figure 5–23.

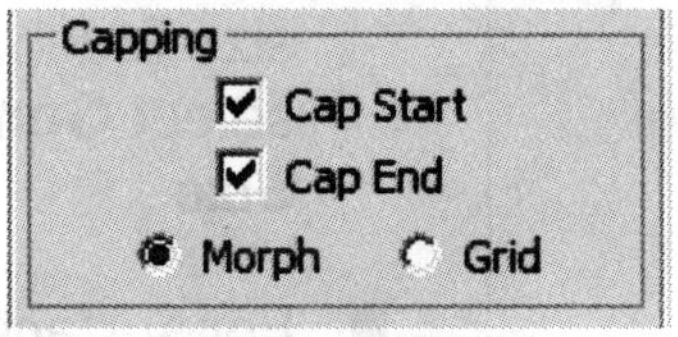

Figure 5–23

- **Morph** linearly interpolates across the vertices to create the cap, as shown on the left in Figure 5–24. This option creates less geometry and is the default setting.
- **Grid** breaks down the cap into a repeating grid of vertices, in square shapes, as shown on the right in Figure 5–24. The grid method enables more complex modeling on the surface of the cap, but adds a great deal of geometry.

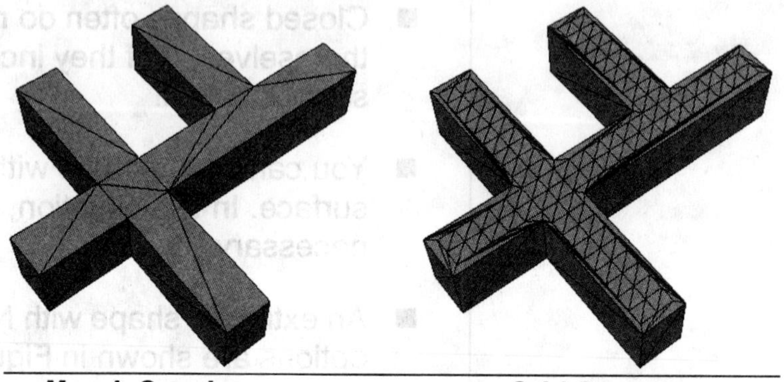

Morph Capping ***Grid Capping***

Figure 5–24

Output

The *Output* area options controls the kind of object that is derived if you simplify (collapse) this object. For most geometry you want to select the default option of **Mesh**. **Patch** and **NURBS** options are used to create complex curved geometry.

Mapping Coordinates

The options for mapping coordinates and real-world map sizing are described with materials.

- For surfaces that have tiled, repeating textures of a specific size (such as carpeting, wall surfaces, grass, and metal) select **Generate Mapping Coords** and **Real-World Map Size**.
- For surfaces meant to show textures that are scaled explicitly (signs, labels, company logos, paintings, computer screens, etc.) you might still benefit from using the **Generate Mapping Coords** option but the **Real-World Map Size** option can be left cleared.
- Select **Generate Material IDs** to apply a different material to the sides, start, and end cap through a Multi/Sub-object material.

- Selecting the **Use Shape IDs** option assigns the material IDs that have been applied to the segments of the spline that you extruded.

Hint: Adjust Tiling Values

Note that sometimes problems can occur when you open files from earlier versions. For example, you might find the textures are tiled in a very peculiar way in the Material Editor. You might have to toggle off Real-World Map Size and then adjust Tiling values of U=1, V=1 before you can see the bitmap properly.

Extruding Nested Splines

When linked or imported geometry is merged together (such as by layer with the weld option) or when 2D objects become attached to form complex splines, these combined 2D objects are sometimes called **nested splines**. When extruding a nested spline, as shown in Figure 5–25, the enclosed areas form solid masses. This can be extremely useful for modeling wall systems and similar geometry.

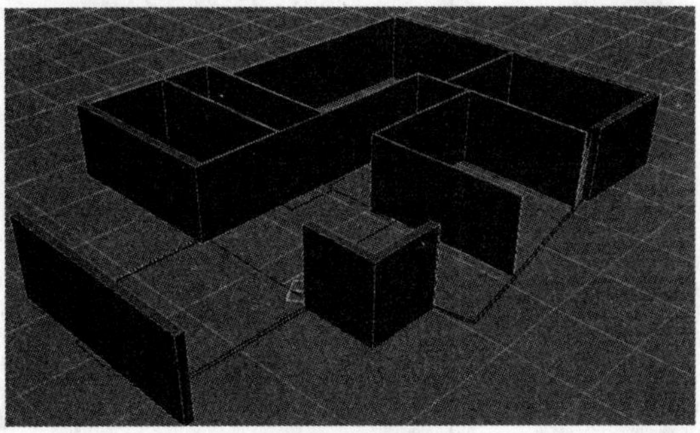

Figure 5–25

Certification

Topic:

✓*Modeling*

Objectives:

✓*Use ProBoolean*

5.5 Boolean Operations

Learning Objectives

- Combine two or more 3D objects to generate a third 3D object by performing Boolean operations on their geometry.
- Understand the best practices that should be followed while using the Boolean operations.

Named after the algebra-based logic of nineteenth-century mathematician George Boole, Boolean operations enable you to graphically bring together two 3D objects to generate a third 3D object. With practice, this offers an intuitive way to create complex geometry from simple 3D primitives and extruded 2D shapes.

The Boolean objects are available in the *Create* panel ( ), by clicking (Geometry) and selecting **Compound Objects** in the drop-down list. You can select the required Boolean object in the Object Type rollout, as shown in Figure 5–26.

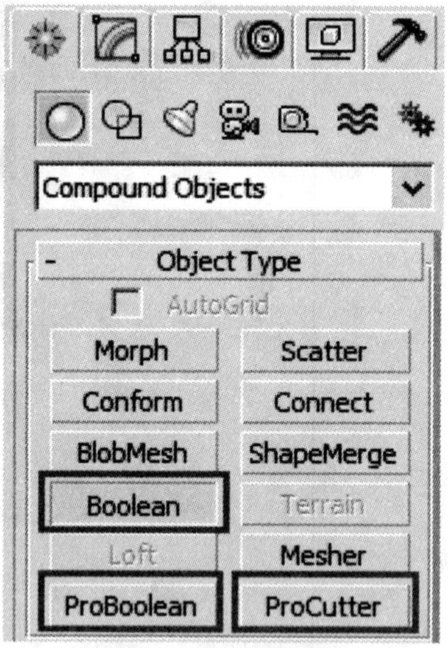

Figure 5–26

The Autodesk 3ds Max Design software creates three types of Boolean objects:

- **Boolean compound object:** Combines two 3D objects to generate a third 3D object by applying a logical operation.

- **ProBoolean compound object:** Similar to the Boolean compound object, except that it uses a different algorithm that permits more advanced functionality and improved stability. At the same time, it achieves more usable geometric results. In general, ProBoolean is the recommended tool for combining the 3D objects.

- **ProCutter compound object:** Enables you to separate objects into pieces so that you can use them in dynamic simulations.

Boolean Operations

- The original objects are referred to as **Operands** and the final result is a **Boolean** object.

- The Autodesk 3ds Max Design software enables you to combine the operands in three ways: by subtraction of one from the other, by finding the intersection where their geometries overlap, or by the union of the two together, as shown in Figure 5–27.

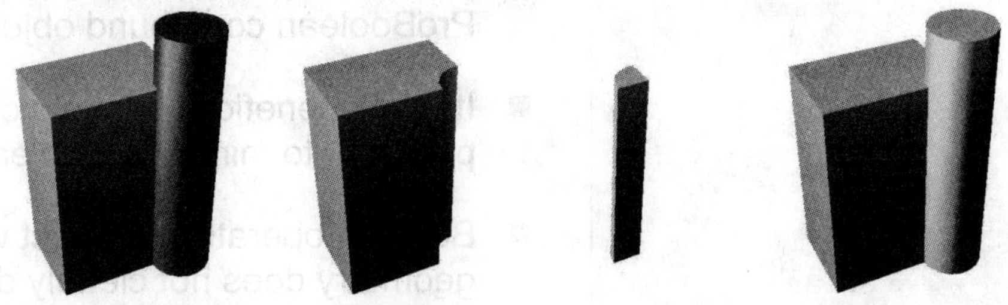

Original Operands ***Subtraction*** ***Intersection*** ***Union***

Figure 5–27

- Boolean operations can be nested where the results of one operation can be used as input to the next. **ProBooleans** offer superior methodology when creating objects with multiple operands. It enables you to reorder and change the operations interactively.

- Boolean operations can be animated, this is often a technique used to reveal or hide geometry in a presentation.

Adjusting Boolean Results

- The results of a Boolean operation can be adjusted dynamically by making changes to the operands' parameters or modifier stack.

- This dynamic update requires that operands be identified as a reference or instance on creation (or an extracted operand is selected to be an instance).
- The original operands can be maintained for editing after the fact or they can be reconstituted (extracted) from the Boolean result later on.
- The practical application of adjusting Boolean results is best left for Intermediate course material.

Best Practices

- In the past, Boolean operations would not produce expected results if operand geometries contained gaps, had irregular face normals, did not overlap each other, shared coplanar faces (some faces of both lie in the same plane), or had other related layout issues. All of these issues have been addressed to some degree. The Boolean system is much more robust than in previous releases, but you should still avoid these issues whenever possible. It was the general problems with Booleans that led to the inclusion of the ProBoolean compound object.
- It is still beneficial to avoid coplanar operands, whenever possible, to minimize Boolean complexity.
- Boolean operations expect water-tight geometry. If the geometry does not cleanly define a volume, the Boolean might not work, as shown in Figure 5–28.

Figure 5–28

Collapsing Booleans

When an object has been sufficiently modeled with Boolean operations you can leave the result as a Boolean object or simplify (collapse) it to a mesh.

- To collapse a Boolean object to an editable mesh, in the modifier stack, right-click on the Boolean and select **Convert to: Editable Mesh** or **Convert to: Editable Poly**.

- If you are using a Boolean result as an operand for another Boolean operation and are not getting the expected results, it might help to convert the original Boolean object to an editable mesh before the second operation. Using ProBooleans is a good idea if you have multiple operands.
- Boolean objects that originate from linked AutoCAD geometry might react unpredictably after an updated DWG link. (If you select a selective reload and avoided the layers used to create your Booleans, any connected Boolean objects would simply be removed from the scene).
- Many other kinds of 3D objects besides Booleans can be collapsed to a mesh to simplify them.
- Once any object is converted to a mesh it loses all of its parametric controls. Therefore converted Boolean objects cannot be updated by editing instanced operands or a file link update.

Practice 5d Extrude Walls and Create Wall Openings

Learning Objectives

- Add depth to a 2D spline to create 3D walls using the **Extrude** modifier.
- Create openings from doors in the walls by subtracting objects using the ProBoolean compound object.

Estimated time for completion: 20 minutes

You will extrude walls from a spline and then refine the walls by creating openings for a corridor and the doors. You will use ProBoolean objects to graphically subtract two objects from the walls.

You must set the paths to locate the External files and Xrefs used in the practice. If you have not done this already, return to the **Introduction to Autodesk 3ds Max Design** chapter and complete Task 1 to Task 3 of the **Organizing Folders and Working with the Interface** practice. You only have to set the user paths once.

Task 1 - Extrude the Walls.

If a dialog box opens prompting you about a File Load: Mismatch, click OK to accept the default values.

1. Open **Spline Walls Bound.max** from your *Class Files* folder.
2. In the Main toolbar, click (Select by Name). In the Select from Scene dialog box, click (Display None) and click (Display Shapes). Select **Layer:VIZ-1-Walls** and click OK. Alternatively, you can select the layer **VIZ-1-Walls** in the Layer Manager and click (Select Highlighted Objects and Layers). The shapes in this layer are selected in the viewport.
3. In the Command Panel, select the *Modify* panel ( ). The name **Layer:VIZ-1-Walls** displays in the Command Panel and is an Editable Spline in the Modifier Stack.

4. In the Modifier List, select **Extrude** (not a Face Extrude). In the Parameters rollout, set *Amount* to **11'0"** (the height of the first floor walls), as shown in Figure 5–29. Press <Enter> after entering a value.

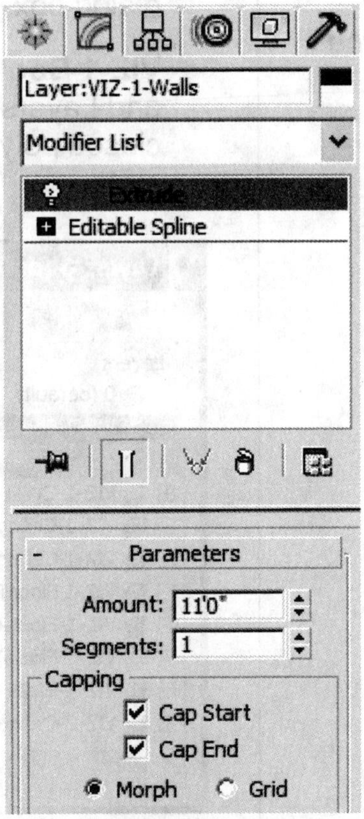

Figure 5–29

5. Click (Zoom Extents All). Only the areas enclosed by the wall linework are extruded, as shown in Figure 5–30. (The missing wall sections eventually contain curtain walls.)

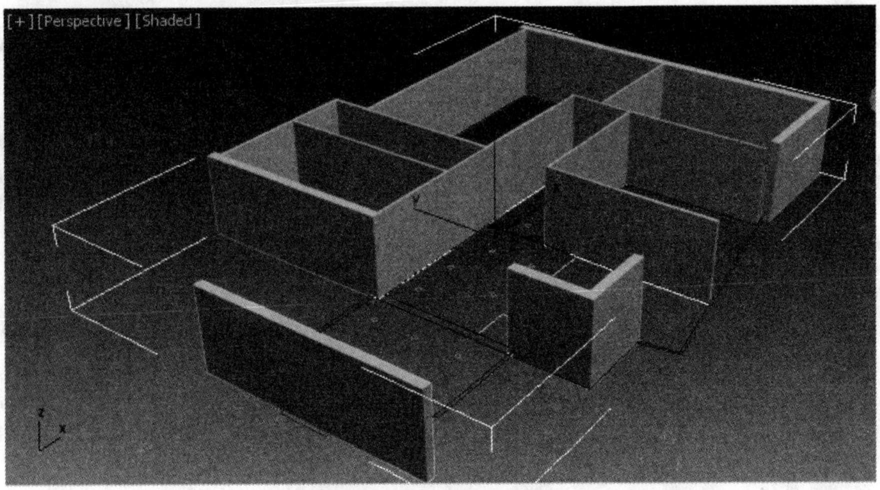

Figure 5–30

Task 2 - Creating the Subtraction Operands.

The Layer dialog box is a modeless dialog box. It remains open while you are working in the viewport.

1. In the Main toolbar, click (Manage Layers). In the Layer dialog box, select the two layers **VIZ-1-Boolean-Soffit** and **VIZ-1-Boolean-Doors**, click (Select Highlighted Objects and Layers), as shown in Figure 5–31. These layers contain closed polylines that define the openings you are about to make.

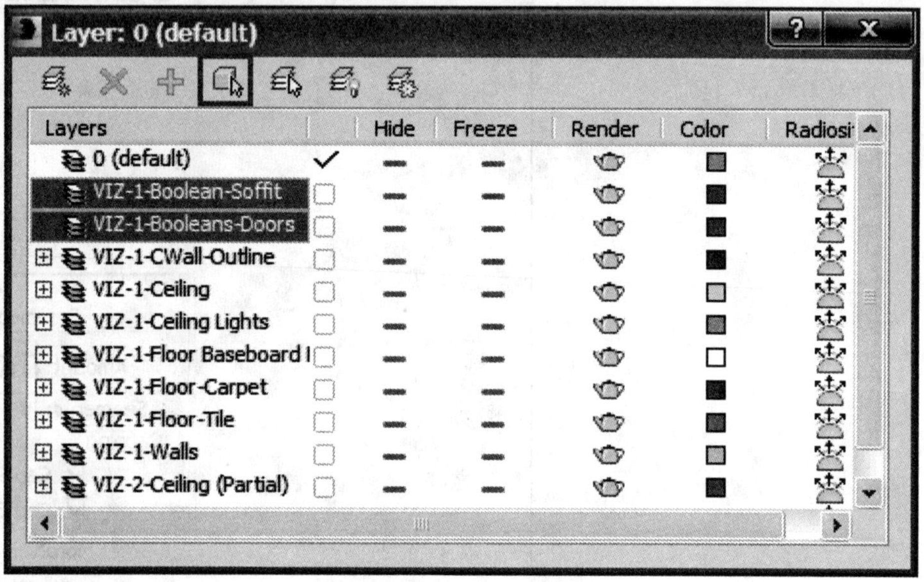

Figure 5–31

2. To avoid a coplanar face along the floor, first move these objects below the floor level. In the Main toolbar, click (Select and Move). Set coordinate system to **World** and click (Use Transform Coordinate Center), as shown in Figure 5–32.

Figure 5–32

3. In the Status Bar, in the *Transform Type-In* area activate (Offset Mode Transform), enter **-1'0"** in the *Z* field, and press <Enter>, as shown in Figure 5–33.

Figure 5–33

4. In the Main toolbar, click  (Select object) as a precaution against accidentally moving other objects.

5. In Layer dialog box, highlight only the layer **VIZ-1-Boolean-Soffit** and click  (Select Highlighted Objects and Layers). This layer contains a single polyline defining an opening in one of the walls.

6. In the Command Panel, select the *Modify* panel (), if not already open. The name **Layer:VIZ-1-Boolean-Soffit** displays in the panel.

7. In the Modifier List, select **Extrude**. In the Parameters rollout, set *Amount* to **9'0"** and press <Enter> (this is **8'** + the **1'** that was just used to lower the object). Leave all of the settings as is. The first subtraction operand (8'0") is created as shown in Figure 5–34. It is required to create the opening.

8. Repeat Steps 6 to 8 for **VIZ-1-Booleans-Doors**. Select the layer **VIZ-1-Booleans-Doors** and extrude it with an *Amount* of **8'0"**. The 7'0" subtraction operands are created, as shown in Figure 5–34.

Figure 5–34

Task 3 - Creating the Wall Openings.

1. In the Layer dialog box (if you closed it, open it again), select **VIZ-1-Walls** and click (Select Highlighted Objects and Layers).

2. In the *Create* panel ( )> (Geometry), select **Compound Objects** in the drop-down list, as shown in Figure 5–35. Click ProBoolean to convert the wall system into a Boolean object. The walls are now your Operand A.

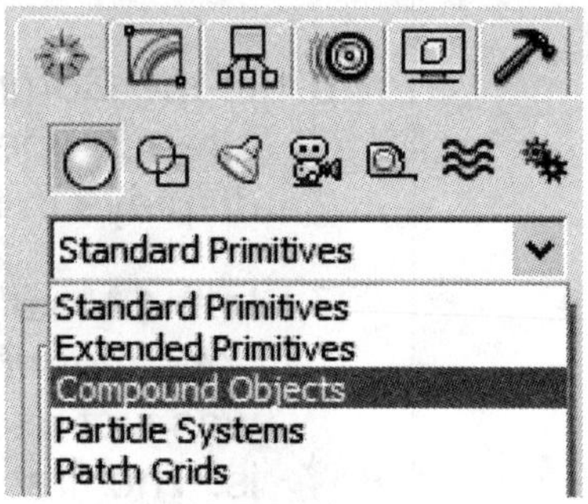

Figure 5–35

3. In the Pick Boolean rollout, verify that **Move** is selected. This will remove the subtraction object after the operation.

4. In the Parameters rollout, in the *Operation* area verify that **Subtraction** is selected. This subtracts **Operand B** (the soffit opening) from **Operand A** (the walls). In the Pick Boolean rollout, click Start Picking, as shown in Figure 5–36.

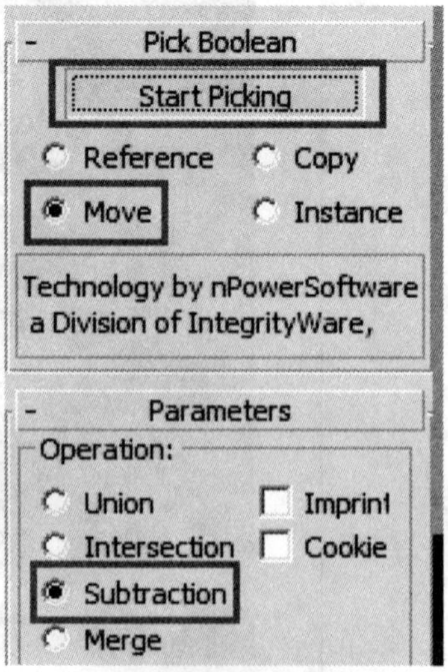

Figure 5–36

5. In the viewport, select the Boolean Soffit extrusion (**VIZ -1-Boolean Soffit**, the 9'0" operand that was created first). The volume contained by the Soffit object is removed from the walls, as shown in Figure 5–37.

6. Click any of the **VIZ-1-Boolean-Doors** objects to complete the second ProBoolean subtraction operation. The volume contained by the Doors object is removed from the walls, as shown in Figure 5–37.

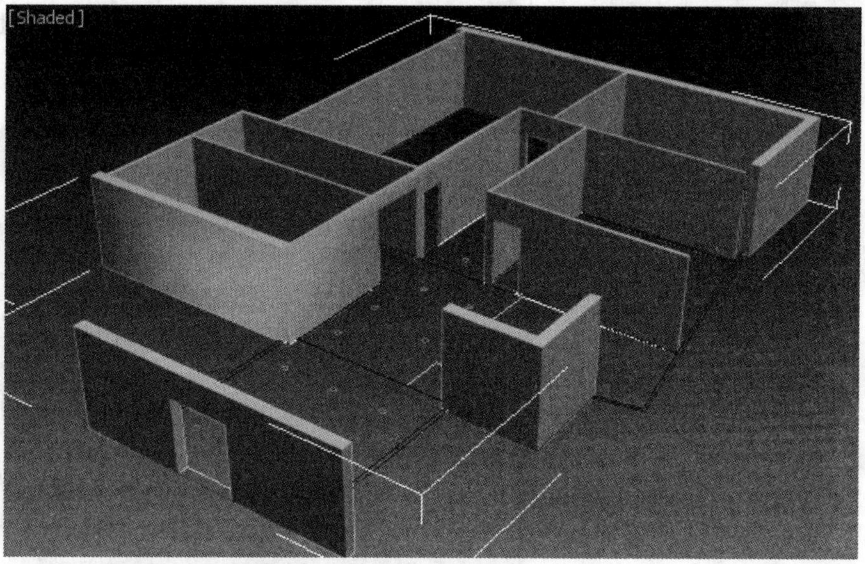

Figure 5–37

7. Click [Start Picking] again to end the ProBoolean operation.

> **Hint: Boolean and ProBoolean objects**
>
> This is a much easier workflow than the one required if you use the regular Boolean compound object. The ProBoolean compound object enables you to pick multiple objects one after the other. Using the standard Boolean object, you can only subtract one object, then you have to create a new nested Boolean to subtract again.
>
> You might run into difficulties if your operands are Linked geometry. If the ProBoolean fails, try merging the geometry instead of linking it into the scene.

8. One of the best features of a ProBoolean is the ability to change the way the faces are built in the object using the Quadrilateral Tessellation function. In the Layer dialog box, right-click on the layer **VIZ-1-Walls** and select **Object Properties**. In the Object Properties dialog box, in the *Display Properties* area, click By Layer to toggle it to By Object. Clear **Edges Only** and click OK.

9. Press <F4> to display the edges of the newly created faces, as shown in Figure 5–38. Note the way long skinny faces are created on some of the walls.

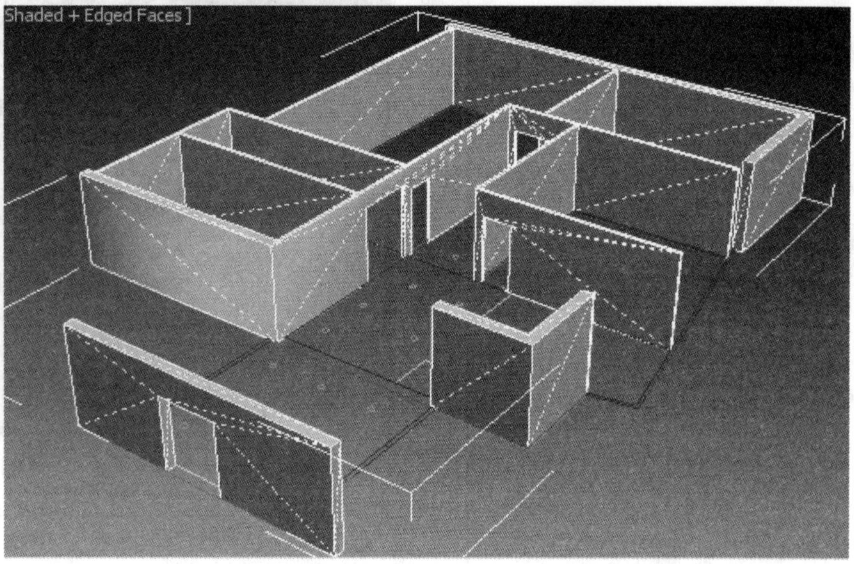

Figure 5–38

10. In the Command Panel, in the *Modify* panel ( ), note that the ProBoolean is displayed in the Modifier Stack. Expand the Advanced Options rollout (bottom of the list). In the *Quadrilateral Tessellation* area, select **Make Quadrilaterals**. Note the way the geometry has changed. There are no long triangular faces, as shown in Figure 5–39.

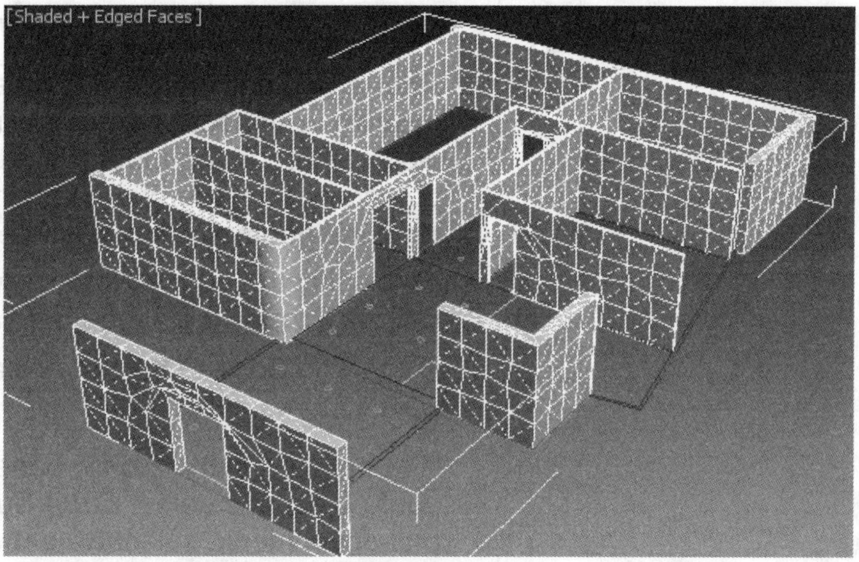

Figure 5–39

11. Increase the *Quad Size %* to **10.0**. This modifies the geometry so that the polygons are bigger, as shown in Figure 5–40.

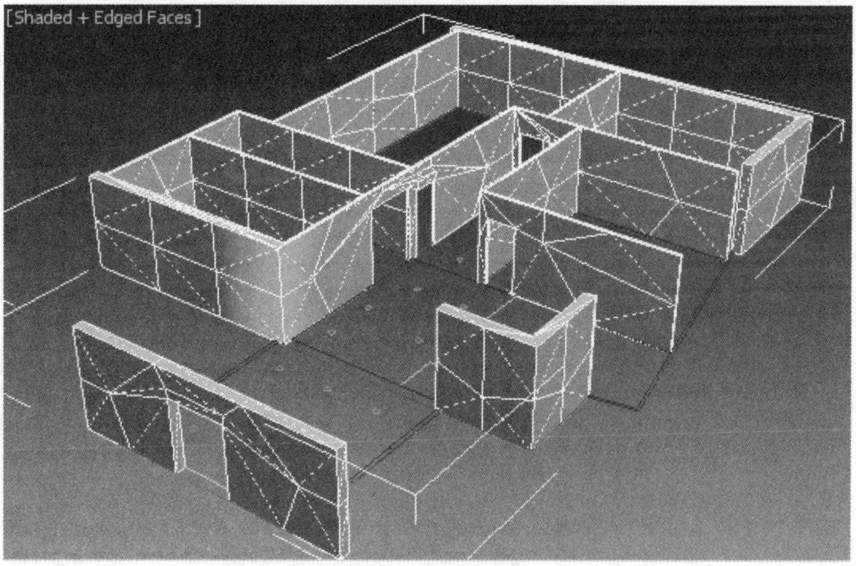

Figure 5–40

12. You can collapse the ProBoolean to a simple mesh. In the Modifier Stack, right-click on ProBoolean and select **Editable Poly**.
13. Save your work as **MySpline Walls Bound.max**.

Hint: Controlling Edge Line Visibility

After a Boolean or other complex operation, there might be missing or unnecessary edge lines in a wireframe or shaded viewport rendering mode. There are edges all across your 3D objects but only certain ones are visible, so that you can easily read the geometry on the screen.

To display the edges, right-click on the object and select **Object Properties**. In the *Display Properties* area, clear **Edges Only**. The **Edges Only** is available in [By Object]. Click [By Layer] to change it to [By Object].

Alternatively, in the *Modify* panel, add an **Edit Mesh** modifier to your object and select **Edge** Sub-object mode. In the **Edit** pull-down menu, select **Select All**. In the *Modify* panel, in the Surface Properties rollout, click [Invisible] to make all edges invisible. Click [Auto Edge] to show only those edges with 24°+ separation. To get required results on curved objects (including curved walls), you might have to enter different separation angles.

5.6 Using Snaps for Precision

Learning Objectives

- Understand how the snap options can be used to create and manipulate objects with precision.
- Understand the different snaps available in the software.

Snaps enable you to create, move, rotate, and scale objects with precision. Many functions are similar to their AutoCAD Object Snap counterparts. Snaps are activated using the buttons in the Main toolbar, as shown in Figure 5–41. Press <S> to toggle Snaps on and off while drawing lines, creating primitives, or transforming objects.

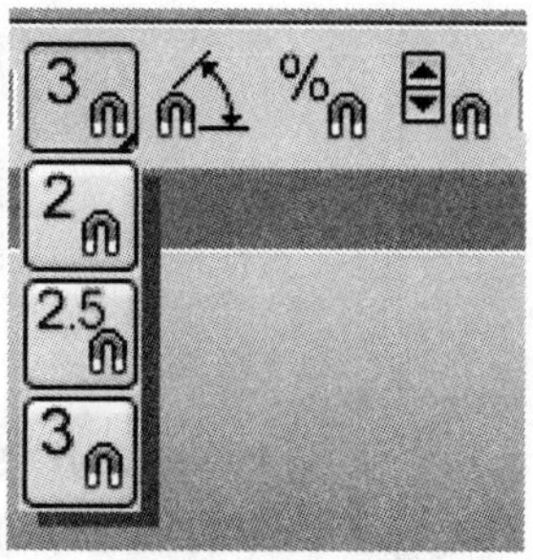

Figure 5–41

The Autodesk 3ds Max Design Snap Toggles are as follows:

	**3D Snap:** This mode snaps to objects in 3D. It is the default option and is similar to AutoCAD's Running object snaps.
	**2.5D Snap:** This mode snaps to a projection of the selected point at elevation 0 on the current grid.
	**2D Snap:** This mode enables you to snap to points at elevation 0 on the current grid.
	**Angle Snap:** This mode enables you to set rotational values (such as a Rotate Transform amount) in angle increments.
	**Percent Snap:** This mode enables percentile-based values (such as a Scale Transform amount) in percent increments (5%, 10%, etc.).
	**Spinner Snap:** This mode causes all spinner controls to increment at a set value with a single click. Transform and a host of parameter values can be adjusted by spinners ().

*Press <Shift> and right-click to open the **Snap** options menu, in which you can open the Grid and Snap Settings dialog box and also select the active snaps.*

Snap settings, such as the increment values for angle and percent snap, can be set by right-clicking on the **2D**, **2.5D**, **3D**, **Angle**, or **Percent Snap** buttons to open the Grid and Snap Settings dialog box and selecting the *Options* tab, as shown in Figure 5–42. You can also access the Grid and Snap Settings by selecting **Tools>Grids and Snaps>Grid and Snap Settings**.

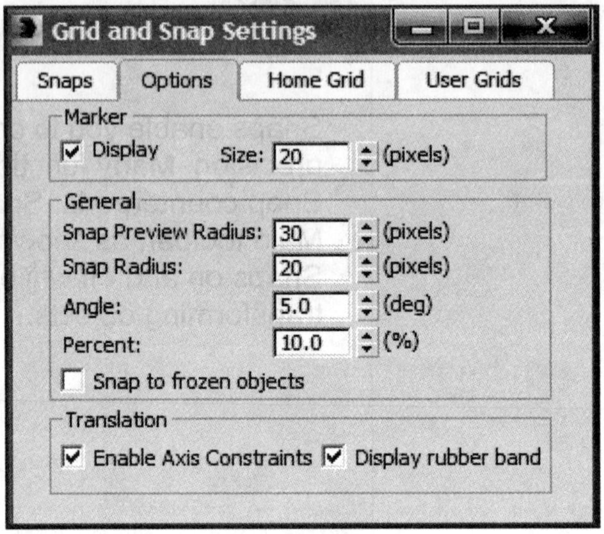

Figure 5–42

The active snaps are selected in the *Snaps* tab of the Grid and Snap Settings dialog box, as shown in Figure 5–43.

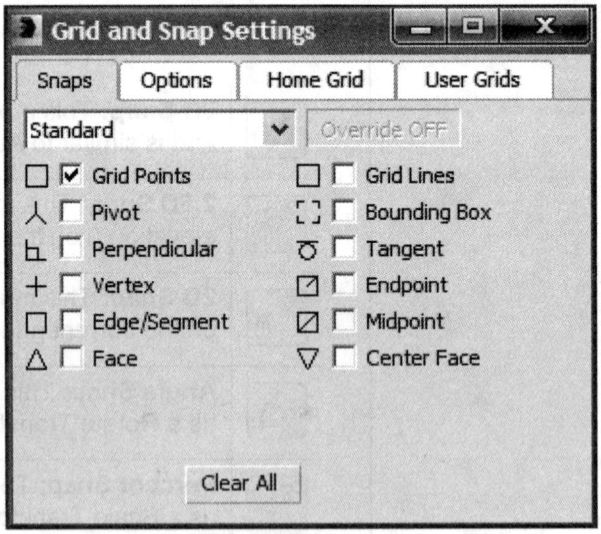

Figure 5–43

Right-click on empty space in the Main toolbar and select ***Snaps*** *in the menu to open the Snaps toolbar.*

You can specify the active snaps by selecting buttons in the Snaps toolbar, as shown in Figure 5–44, (hidden by default). The toolbar contains buttons for the most common snap settings.

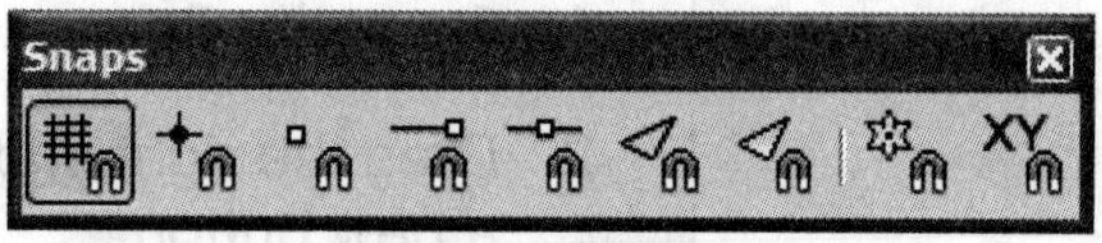

Figure 5–44

Below are brief descriptions of the Standard Snaps.

Grid Points: Snaps to grid intersections.

Pivot: Snaps to the pivot point of an object.

Vertex: Snaps to vertices on splines, meshes, or similar geometry.

Endpoint: Snaps to the vertices at the end of a spline segment, mesh edge, or similar geometry. Similar to Vertex except that not all vertices are at the endpoints of spline segments and mesh edges.

Midpoint: Snaps to the middle of spline segments, mesh edges, or similar geometry.

Edge/Segment: Snaps to anywhere along spline segments, mesh edges, or similar geometry. (Similar to the AutoCAD nearest object snap.)

Face: Snaps anywhere on the surface of a face.

Snap to Frozen Objects: Enables other snaps to reference frozen objects.

Snaps Use Axis Constraints: Forces result along the selected axis constraints set in the Axis Constraints toolbar.

There are two additional snap functions available in the Autodesk 3ds Max Design software: Ortho and Polar Snapping.

Ortho Snapping: Forces a transform in the horizontal or vertical directions based on the active grid.

Polar Snapping: Forces results to the angle increment set in the Grid and Snap Settings dialog box.

Neither of these snapping methods are included in the Snaps toolbar by default. To add these to a toolbar complete the following:

1. Open the Snaps toolbar.
2. Drag the right end of the toolbar to the right to make room for a new button.
3. Select **Customize>Customize User Interface**. The Customize User Interface dialog box opens.
4. Select the *Toolbars* tab.
5. Scroll through the Action list and select **Ortho Snapping Mode**. (You can jump to the O section by clicking any item in the list and then pressing <O>.)
6. Drag the Ortho Snapping Mode item from the list to the empty section in the Snaps toolbar to add it.
7. Repeat the process for the **Polar Snapping Mode** item.
8. Close the Customize User Interface dialog box.

The toolbar is automatically saved in its revised state and adds the buttons to the user interface. The following snaps do not display in the Snaps toolbar and are only available in the Snap and Grid Settings dialog box.

- **Grid Lines:** Snaps to anywhere along a grid line.
- **Bounding Box:** Snaps to the corners of an object's bounding box.
- **Perpendicular:** Snaps perpendicularly to a spline segment.
- **Tangent:** Snaps tangent to a curved spline segment.
- **Center Face:** Snaps to the center of triangular faces.

You can use a snap by pressing <Shift>, right-clicking and selecting **Standard** and selecting the required snap from the shortcut menu that opens, as shown in Figure 5–45. This can be useful when multiple snaps are displayed close together and you are having difficulty picking the correct one.

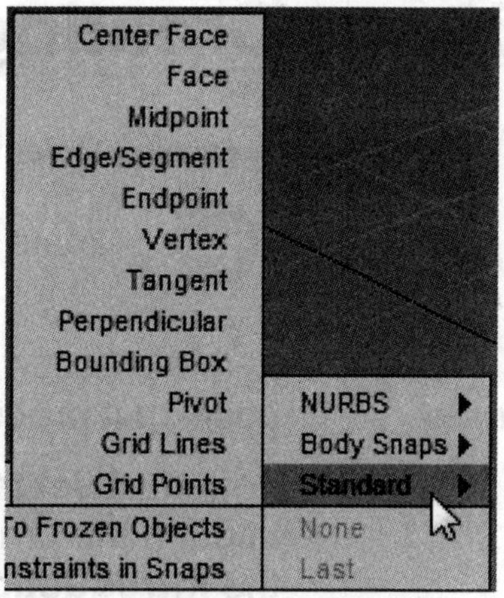

Figure 5–45

> **Hint: Snap to XRef Objects**
>
> You can snap to XRef objects just like any other object. In the earlier versions, XRef objects were displayed in the scene, but were not recognized by the snap functions.

Practice 5e Creating a Door with Snaps

Learning Objective

- Create doors at precise locations using snaps.

Estimated time for completion: 10 minutes

In this practice you will add a door to an opening, using snaps to position it precisely.

You must set the paths to locate the External files and Xrefs used in the practice. If you have not done this already, return to the **Introduction to Autodesk 3ds Max Design** chapter and complete Task 1 to Task 3 of the **Organizing Folders and Working with the Interface** practice. You only have to set the user paths once.

If a dialog box opens prompting you about a Mismatch, click OK *to accept the default values.*

1. Reset the scene and open **Creating a Door.max** from your *Class Files* folder.
   - The scene contains extruded walls with openings and extruded carpet and tile areas. A camera has also been added.
2. Verify that the Perspective viewport is active and use (Maximize Viewport Toggle) to maximize it.
3. In a Perspective viewport, use (Zoom) and (Orbit) to display the west side of the model (where the space for the outer door is located), as shown in Figure 5–46. Verify that the Perspective viewport displays as **Shaded+Edged Faces**.

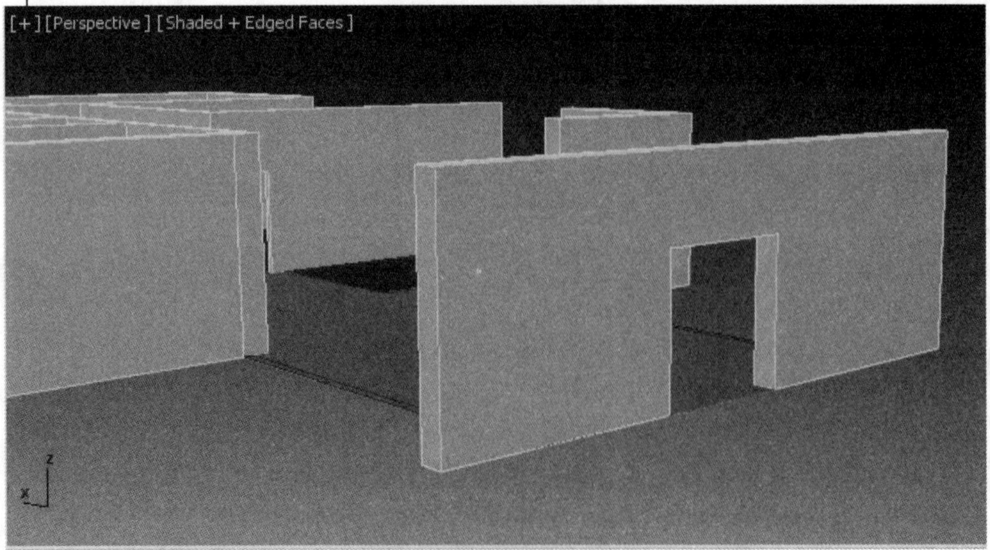

Figure 5–46

4. Using (Zoom) and **Pan**, zoom into the doorway opening as shown in Figure 5–47, to display the points for snapping.

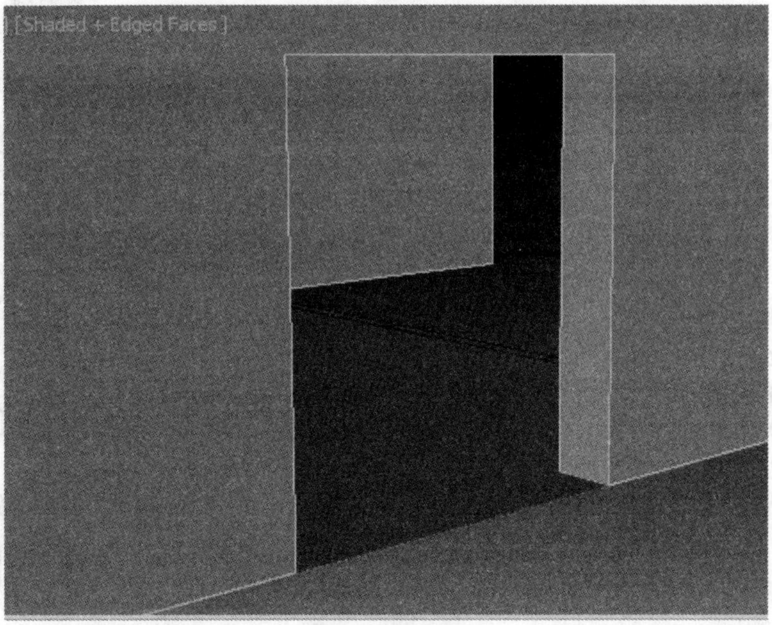

Figure 5–47

5. In the Main toolbar, click (3D Snaps) to activate it, if not already active. In the Command Panel, verify that *Create* panel> (Geometry) is open. In the Standard Primitives drop-down list, select **Doors**.

> **Hint: Create Window and Door Objects**
>
> By default Autodesk 3ds Max Design Doors and Windows are created by:
>
> - **Clicking and dragging:** To define the width of the door/ window.
> - **Releasing and picking:** A point to define the depth of the wall opening.
> - **Releasing and picking:** A point to define the height of the opening.

6. In the Object Type rollout, click Pivot, as shown in Figure 5–48, to start the door creation process.

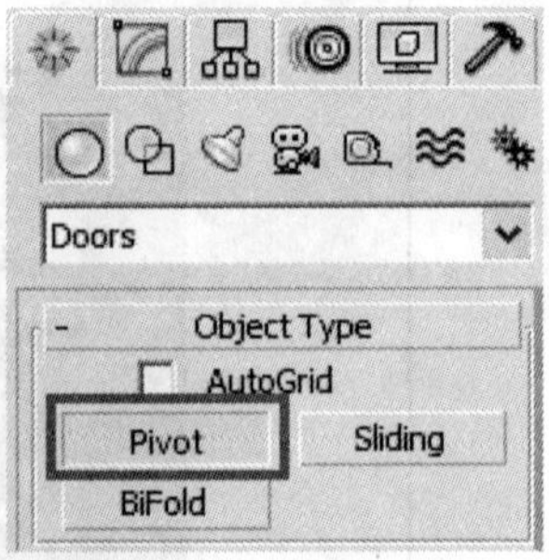

Figure 5–48

*You can also press <Shift> and right-click to open the **Snaps** quad menu and select **Standard>Endpoint**.*

7. Open the Snaps toolbar, and click  (Snap to Endpoint Toggle) as shown in Figure 5–49.

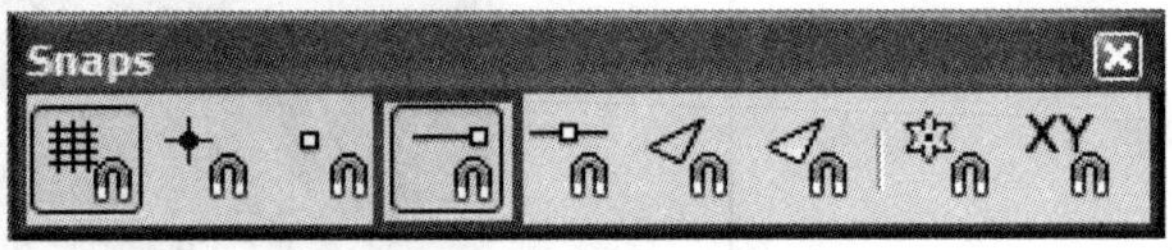

Figure 5–49

8. Hover the cursor at the bottom left corner of the door opening. Note that when the cursor hovers over the endpoint (corner), it snaps to that point and a small yellow square (endpoint marker) displays, as shown in Figure 5–50.

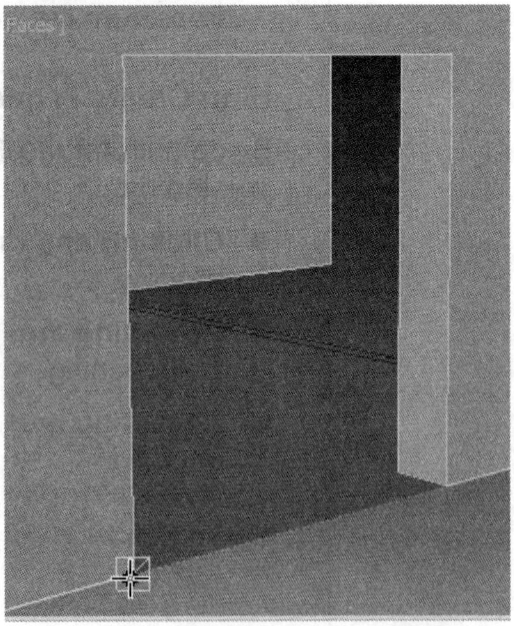

Figure 5–50

9. Click and hold at this point and then while still holding, drag your cursor over to the lower right corner. Once it snaps to the lower right corner, as shown in Figure 5–51, release the mouse button to define the width of the door.
   - If you have difficulty with this, change the orientation of the Perspective viewport, as shown below. You might also want to change to Wireframe display.

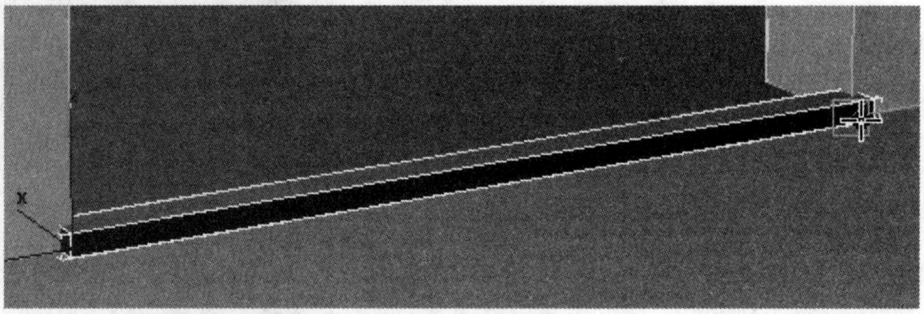

Figure 5–51

10. Move the cursor to the back corner of the door opening and click (not click and drag) to define the depth of the opening, as shown in Figure 5–52.

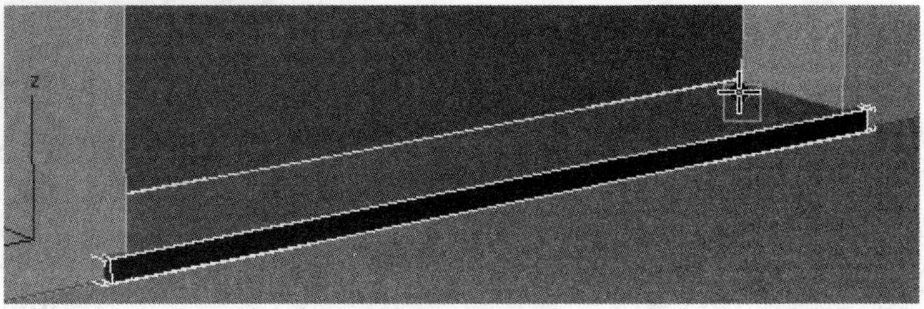

Figure 5–52

11. Move the cursor to the upper right corner of the door opening and click (not click and drag) to define the height, as shown in Figure 5–53. Sometimes this is difficult to do, depending on the angle of your view. You can toggle off the Snap by pressing <S>, then adjust the height using the Parameters rollout.

Figure 5–53

12. With the door still selected, in the Command Panel, select the *Modify* panel (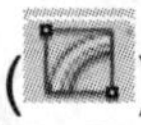). In the Parameters rollout, select **Double Doors**. Set the *Open* angle to **45°**. In the Leaf Parameters rollout, in the *Panels* area, select **Beveled**. Note that in the viewport, the door will change to double doors with beveled panels and will be open at a **45°** angle, as shown in Figure 5–54.

Figure 5–54

13. Set the *Open* angle to **0°** to display the panels as closed.

14. Save your work as **MyCreating a Door.max**.

Hint: Holes in Walls using Window and Door Objects

When you use Autodesk 3ds Max Design Wall objects combined with Window or Door objects, you can automatically create holes for the doors and windows. Create the walls and create the windows or doors using snaps to align them in place. If you create the door or window away from the wall, you can move it so it intersects with the wall. Use the **Select and Link** button to link the door or window to the wall to automatically create the hole. You can use Edge snap to align the doors with the walls.

The advantage to this is that if you move the door or window, the hole moves with it. However, this only works when you create Autodesk 3ds Max Design wall objects. This functionality is not available when you are extruding linked geometry.

Certification

Topic:

✓Modeling

Objectives:

✓Use object creation and modification workflows

5.7 The Sweep Modifier

Learning Objectives

- Create a 3D geometry by extruding a cross-section along a selected spline using the Sweep modifier.
- Understand the different parameters to extrude the shape along a spline.

The Sweep modifier is a simple and effective option to create 3D geometry based on a 2D section that follows a series of spline segment paths (including imported or linked AutoCAD lines and polylines).

- This modifier can very quickly create 3D pipe networks, curbing, moldings, and similar types of geometry.
- Sweeps are created by adding the Sweep modifier to the path, followed by adjusting cross-section settings and other parameters in the *Modify* panel.
- You can select a pre-defined cross-section shape such as, boxes, pipes, tees, and angles, or you can use a custom shape.
- Although this functionality is also available through the Loft compound object, the Sweep modifier is easier to configure.

To use the Sweep modifier, select a spline and then in the *Modify* panel (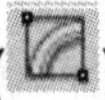), select **Sweep** from the Modifier List. A wall baseboard created using the Sweep modifier is shown in Figure 5–55.

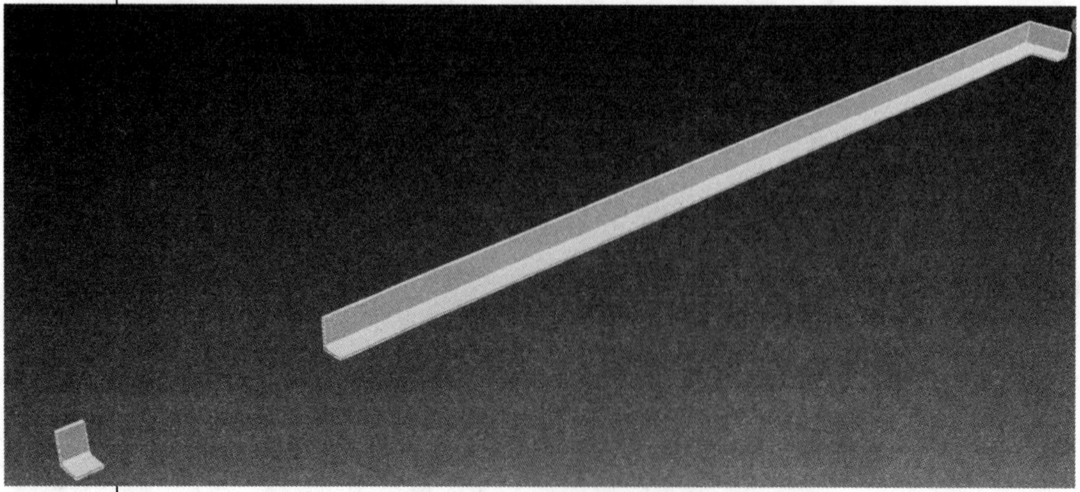

Figure 5–55

Sweep Parameters

Section Type

In the Section Type rollout, you can select the type of profile that you want to sweep along the spline segments.

- If you selected **Use Built-In Section**, a list of pre-created cross-sections is available as your profile, as shown in Figure 5–56. The **Angle** is the default cross-section.

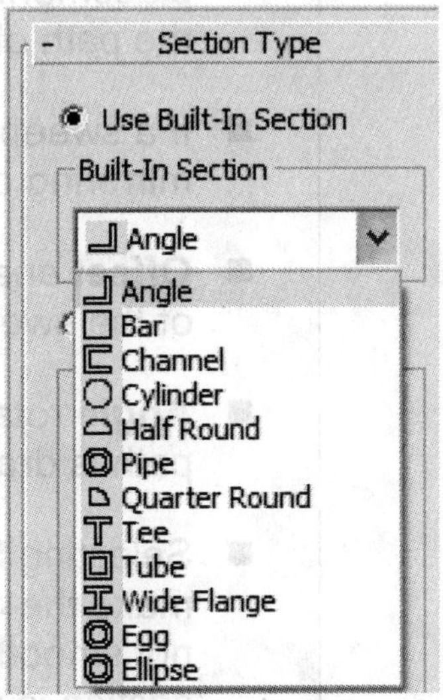

Figure 5–56

- You can select **Use Custom Section** to use a custom shapes as your section. You can either create your section in the current scene or obtain it from another .MAX file.

Interpolation

In the Interpolation rollout, you can control the smoothness of the cross-section by adding or removing vertices.

- Steps can be set to 0 for cross-section shapes that have sharp edges (no curves). Otherwise this value should be kept low to reduce complexity.
- The **Optimize** option groups the supplemented vertices closer to the corners rather than spaced evenly along the shape.
- The **Adaptive** option tessellates (break into segments) curves in the section shape. Select Adaptive results in a wireframe rendering mode to reduce complexity.

Parameters

In the Parameters rollout, you can control the size and shape of the pre-defined cross-sections.

Sweep Parameters

- In the Sweep Parameters rollout, you can control the placement and orientation of the cross-section shape along the path object.
- If a sweep result is backwards or upside down, use the two mirroring options to correct it.
- **Offset** enables you to shift the horizontal and vertical position of the sweep geometry away from the spline path.
- **Angle** rotates the section relative to the plane. The spline path is drawn as defined by its pivot point.
- Selecting **Smooth Section** and **Smooth Path** enables you to make the object smooth, even if the path object or shape are not smooth. In the case of the swept wall baseboard, the section is smoothed to make the cross-section display as filleted, not because the baseboard follows the angled corners of the wall.
- The **Pivot Alignment** enables you to anchor the cross-section shape to the path based on the shape's pivot point.
- **Banking** rotates a cross-section shape assigned to a 3D path, similar to an airplane rolling during a turn.

Practice 5f

Sweeping the Wall Baseboard

Learning Objective

Create a wall baseboard by extruding a pre-created cross-section along a selected spline using the **Sweep** modifier.

Estimated time for completion:15 minutes

In this practice you will create a vinyl baseboard object around the walls using the **Sweep** Modifier.

You must set the paths to locate the External files and Xrefs used in the practice. If you have not done this already, return to the **Introduction to Autodesk 3ds Max Design** chapter and complete Task 1 to Task 3 of the **Organizing Folders and Working with the Interface** practice. You only have to set the user paths once.

Task 1 - Sweep the path.

If a dialog box opens prompting you about a Mismatch, click OK to accept the default values.

1. Open **Sweep Modifier.max** from your *Class Files* folder.
   - The scene contains the extruded walls and main door in the closed position. A camera has also been added. In the Main toolbar, click (Manage Layers) to open the Layer dialog box. Select **VIZ-1-Floor Baseboard Path** and click (Select Highlighted Objects and Layers). This layer contains a series of lines and polylines that define the base of the wall with gaps at the openings. Close the Layer dialog box.

*You can also right-click in the viewport and select **Isolate Selection** or press <Alt>+<Q> to activate the Isolate Selection.*

2. To only display the sweep path (2D line), in the Status Bar, click (Isolate Selection Toggle) to isolate the selection. Click anywhere in the Perspective viewport to clear the selection. Zoom in so that the path (lines) are displayed as shown in Figure 5–57.

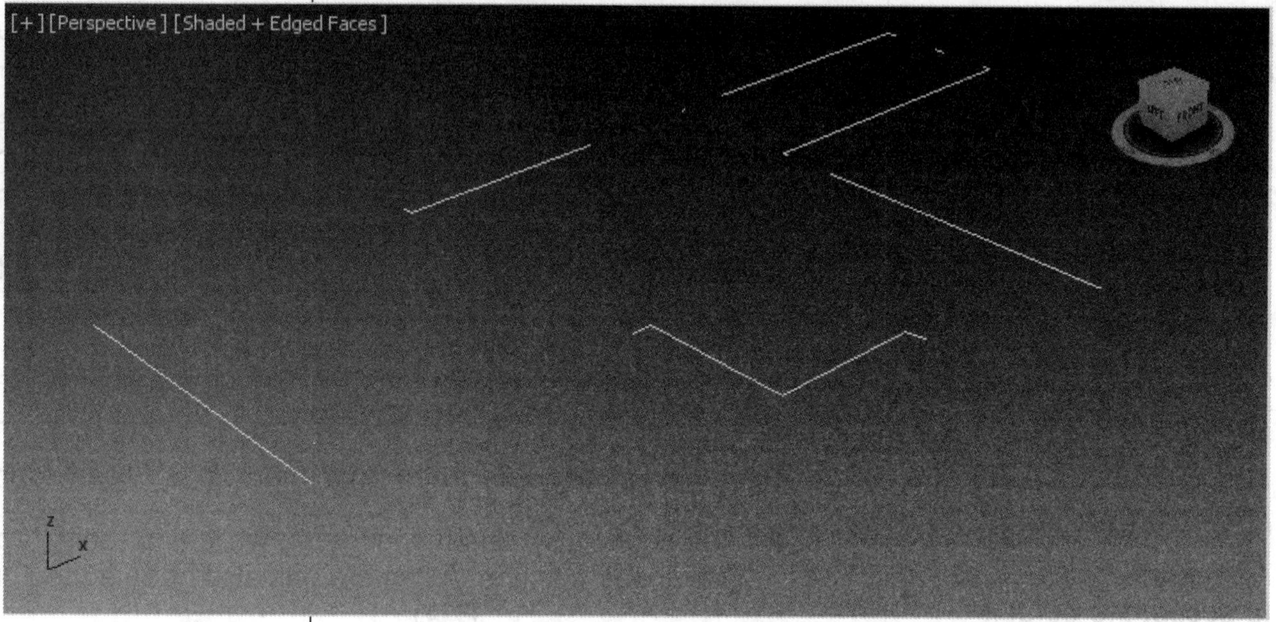

Figure 5–57

3. In the Perspective viewport, click anywhere on the 2D line to select it.

You can also create a custom profile to be swept along the sweep spline.

4. In the Command Panel, select the *Modify* panel ( ). The name **VIZ-1-Floor Baseboard Path** is displayed. In the Modifier List, select **Sweep**. The Sweep modifier displays in the Modifier Stack. In the Perspective viewport, zoom in on the left side baseboard. Note that the lines have extruded along an angled cross-section, as shown on the left in Figure 5–58. The shape of the extrusion depends on the selected **Built In Selection** in the Section Type rollout. The Angle type is the default selection, as shown on the right in Figure 5–58.

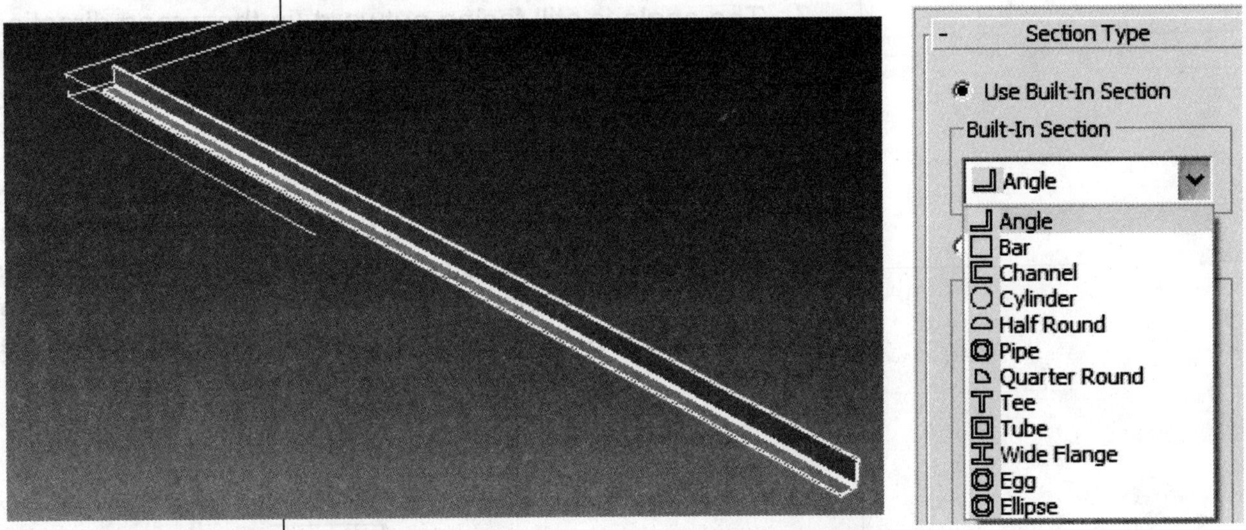

Figure 5–58

5. In the Interpolation rollout, set *Steps* to **0**. (Since all of the wall corners are square, there are no curves needed to interpolate along the path.)

6. In the Parameters rollout, set the values as shown in Figure 5–59. This shape is meant to create a baseboard with minimal detail. In the viewport, note how the baseboard detail changes.

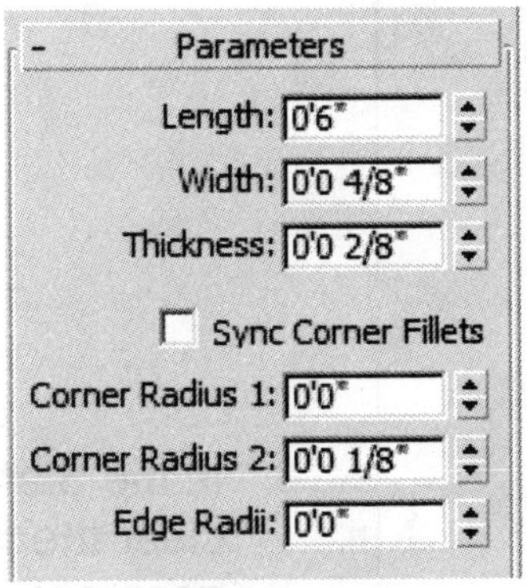

Figure 5–59

7. The angle is still facing outward (in the wrong direction). In the Sweep Parameters rollout, select **Mirror on XZ Plane** to reverse the angle face. Clear **Smooth Path** (all of the corners are square and should not display as rounded). Anchor the **Pivot Alignment** option by clicking  in the lower right corner. This option creates the 3D geometry object by sweeping the lower left corner of the baseboard cross-section along the baseboard path. Select **Gen. Mapping Coords.** and **Real-World Map Size** as well as shown in Figure 5–60.

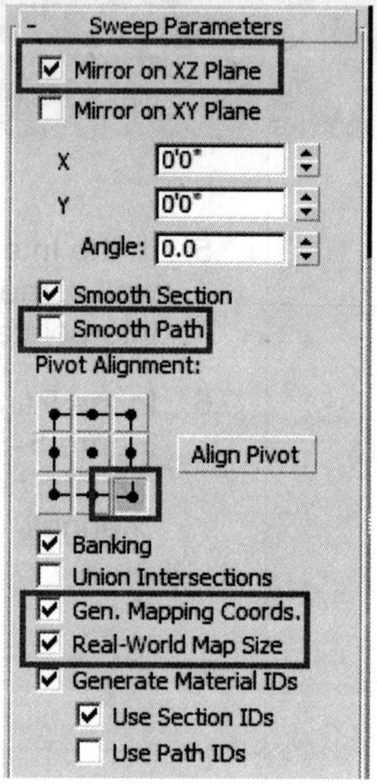

Figure 5–60

8. In the Status Bar, click  (Isolate Selection Toggle) again to clear the **Isolate Selection** option. The walls and other geometry are now displayed.

9. In the Front viewport, select the **Front** Point of View label and select **Cameras>Camera002-Door**. This displays the door from the inside. Select the **Visual Style** label and select **Shaded+Edged Faces**. Note that the baseboard runs along the entire wall, including the door, as shown in Figure 5–61

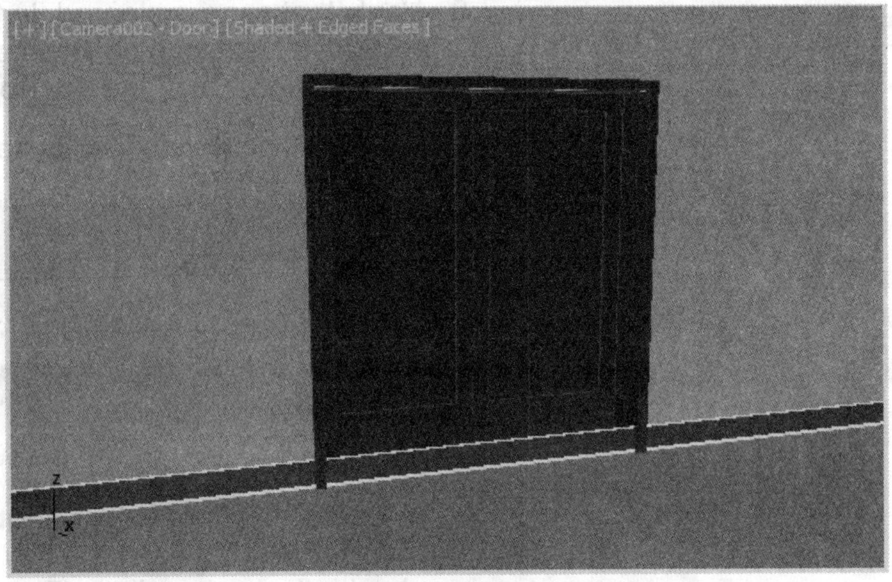

Figure 5–61

Task 2 - Modify the path.

1. Click (Maximize Viewport Toggle) to maximize the Camera002-Door viewport.
2. Click anywhere on the baseboard to select it. In the *Modify* panel ( ), verify that *Name* displays **Layer:VIZ-1-Floor Baseboard**.
3. In the Modifier Stack, in Editable Spline, select **Vertex,** as shown on the left in Figure 5–62. In the viewport, note that the baseboard is not displayed because you have selected an option before the Sweep modifier.
4. In the Geometry rollout, click Refine as shown on the right in Figure 5–62.

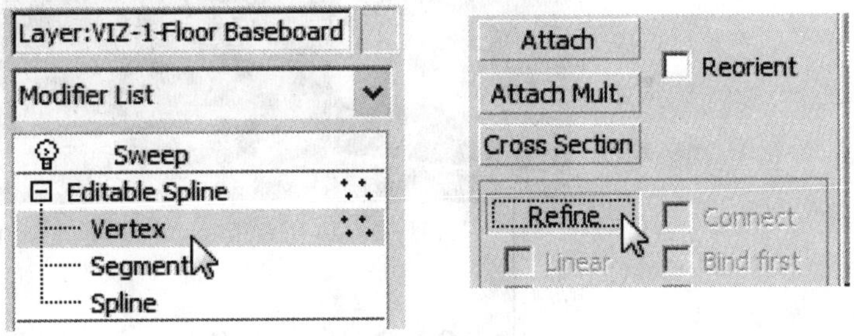

Figure 5–62

5. Verify that snap is cleared. In the viewport, click on the spline to place a vertex on either side of the door frame, as shown in Figure 5–63. Once the two vertices have been placed, click Refine again to clear its selection.

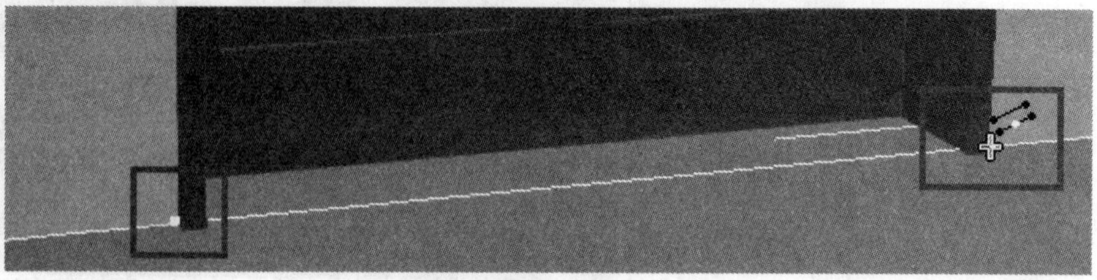

Figure 5–63

6. In Editable Spline, select **Segment**. In the viewport, click on the segment between the two vertices, in front of the door. It should display in yellow. (The segment might not be visible anymore, which is an issue with the software.) Note that the selection tripod in the center of the segment indicates that it is selected, as shown in Figure 5–64.

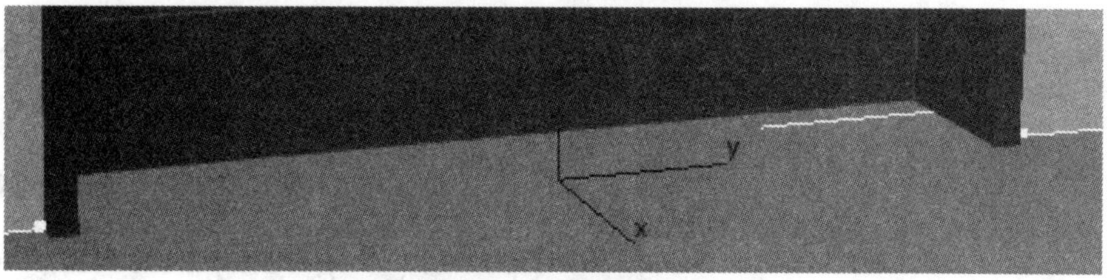

Figure 5–64

7. With the segment selected, press <Delete> to delete the segment. Note that the tripod is not visible anymore.

8. In the Modifier Stack, select **Sweep**. In the viewport, note that the baseboard has been modified and does not pass in front of the door, as shown in Figure 5–65.

Figure 5–65

9. Click  (Maximize Viewport Toggle) to open the four viewports display.

10. Expand , expand Import, and select **Merge**. In the Merge File dialog box, select **Interior Furnishings and Detail.max** from your *Class Files* folder. Click Open. In the Merge dialog box, click All at the bottom left to select all of the objects and click OK.

11. In the Perspective viewport, select the **Perspective** Point of View Viewport label and select **Cameras>Camera001 – Lobby1**. This changes the display to look through the newly merged **Camera – Lobby1**, as shown in Figure 5–66.

Figure 5–66

12. Select **Edit>Select None** to clear the object selection.

    - Note that the desk, chairs, and other furnishings are AutoCAD Architecture 3D blocks. The curtain walls, stairs, and doors are examples of architectural objects that can be created. Autodesk 3ds Max Design walls, doors, and windows are not as configurable as those in the AutoCAD Architecture or Autodesk Revit software, but they still can be a handy alternatives.

13. Save your work as **MySweep Modifier.max**.

Hint: Pre-created Objects

Instead of modeling all of your scene content from scratch, look for royalty-free or low-cost objects posted on the Internet. Consider 3D blocks from software, such as AutoCAD Architecture, Autodesk Revit, AutoCAD Civil 3D, or directly from manufacturer's web sites. You can also get your models from TurboSquid, a website devoted to 3D content. A popular alternative to using highly complex models (for people, trees, etc.) is to use 3rd party plug-ins.

Chapter Review Questions

1. While editing a spline at the vertex sub-object level, which tool enables you to manipulate the handles on one side of the curve separately from the other handle?
   a. **Bezier**
   b. **Bezier Corner**
   c. **Smooth**
   d. **Smooth Corner**
2. To combine shapes using the 2D Boolean operations, which sub-object level in the **Edit Spline** modifier should be selected?
   a. Vertex
   b. Segment
   c. Spline
3. Which **Sweep** modifier option in the Sweep Parameters rollout rotates a cross-section shape assigned to a 3D path?
   a. **Offset**
   b. **Angle**
   c. **Banking**
   d. **Pivot Alignment**
4. Which of the following Snap mode enables you to snap to points at elevation 0 on the current grid?
   a.  (Angle Snap)
   b. 

   (3D Snap)
   c. 

   (2.5D Snap)
   d. 

   (2D Snap)
5. You cannot snap to XRef objects as with any other object because the XRef objects are not recognized by the snap functions.
   a. True
   b. False

Command Summary

Button	Command	Location
	3D Snap	■ **Main Toolbar:** Snaps flyout
	2.5D Snap	■ **Main Toolbar:** Snaps flyout
	2D Snap	■ **Main Toolbar:** Snaps flyout
	Angle Snap	■ **Main Toolbar**
	Isolate Selection	■ **Status Bar** ■ **Keyboard:** <Alt>+<Q>
	Manage Layers	■ **Main Toolbar** ■ **Layers Toolbar**
	Merge	■ **Application Menu:** Import
	Offset Mode	■ **Status Bar**
	Percent Snap	■ **Main Toolbar**
	Shapes	■ **Command Panel:** *Create* panel ■ **Create:** Shapes
	Snap to Edge/Segment	■ **Snaps Toolbar**
	Snap to Endpoint	■ **Snaps Toolbar**
	Snap to Frozen Objects	■ **Snaps Toolbar**
	Snap to Grid Point	■ **Snaps Toolbar**
	Snap to Midpoint	■ **Snaps Toolbar**
	Snap to Pivot	■ **Snaps Toolbar**
	Snap to Vertex	■ **Snaps Toolbar**
	Snaps use Axis Constraints	■ **Snaps Toolbar**

Chapter 6

Materials

In this chapter you learn to use the different materials and maps. You learn to create, edit, and manage materials using the Slate Material Editor. You also work with Standard materials, such as architectural materials and multi/sub-object materials and how to manage and assign those materials. You learn to assign the opacity, bump, and reflection maps to objects in a scene. You also learn to work with the mental ray materials and how to manage them in a scene.

This chapter contains the following topics:

- ✓**Introduction to Materials**
- ✓**Understanding Maps and Materials**
- ✓**Managing Materials**
- ✓**Standard Materials**
- ✓**Material Shaders**
- ✓**Assigning Maps to Materials**
- ✓**Opacity, Bump, and Reflection Mapping**
- ✓**mental ray Materials**
- ✓**The Material Explorer**

6.1 Introduction to Materials

Learning Objective

- Understand the role of materials and maps in visualization.

Taken by itself, the geometry in your scenes MIGHT not convey enough detail to adequately describe your designs. Creating believable visualizations almost always involves using materials to dress up geometry so that it resembles objects in the real world.

Materials give the magic to the visualization process. In the strictest sense, materials control how light interacts with surfaces in 3D models. The surfaces of the models in the viewport interact with the light sources based on the material assignments. If an object is shiny it reflects the light, with transparency applied, the light passes through the object. The renderer determines what the pixel's RGB (red, green, blue) values are in the image based on the material assignments.

Materials control color, texture, transparency, and a host of other physical properties that you can adjust. The same polygons can take on different appearances instantly with a simple change to material. Materials use Maps to paint the surfaces with all types of textures to resemble the actual construction materials for your design.

It is important to understand the role materials play in the 3D visualization process. To create an image in the viewport or in a file, a *renderer* is employed. The viewport display is the work of an interactive viewport renderer. The images you create are made by an *image* (production) renderer. In the Autodesk® 3ds Max® Design 2014 software, you can use the scanline, quicksilver, iray renderer, or mental ray renderers as image renderers. You can also use 3rd party plug-in renderers, such as Brazil (made by Splutterfish), finalRender (made by Cebas), Maxwell (made by Next Limit Technologies), or V-Ray (made by Chaos Software). The viewport renderer can use Nitrous Direct 3D 11 (default), Nitrous Direct3D 9, Nitrous Software, Legacy Direct3D, or Legacy OpenGL graphics drivers to create the real-time interactive display.

Materials are deeply interconnected with the renderers. There is a range of different material types. The standard material type is associated with the Autodesk 3ds Max Design scanline renderer. Mental ray materials (*Autodesk Material Library/Arch & Design* materials) work with the mental ray renderer.

Whatever the material type, whatever the renderer, the rendering process is more or less the same. The viewport provides a frame around the image and the output resolution determines the number of pixels to be created within that frame. The renderer then examines the geometry in the scene, first looking at the face normals, removing the faces whose normals face away from the camera (face normals are directional vectors perpendicular to the surface of the face). The remaining faces are z-sorted, the faces in front covering up the ones further away. Once the faces are determined, the color, transparency, shininess, texture, reflection, bumpiness, and other values are defined based on the material type, shaders, and map channels. The visible faces are calculated using the UVW mapping coordinates and the scene illumination. This determines RGB values, which are applied to the pixels in the image. In short, the combination of geometry, materials, and lighting creates the illusion of reality.

Different material types use different material shaders to generate their work. Shaders are algorithms that create the image. Each shader has its own set of parameters. A language is associated with materials that can be daunting, but once understood, can provide great power in image creation. As with anything powerful, it can seem complicated and complex at first and then become simple and easy to use.

6.2 Understanding Maps and Materials

Learning Objectives

- Understand the physical components of materials.
- Understand the different types of maps that can be used while creating materials.

Materials have several fundamental components. Standard materials in the Autodesk 3ds Max Design software have *Ambient*, *Diffuse*, and *Specular Color* channels, which determine the color applied in the calculation based on the lighting interaction. The *Diffuse* channel represents those faces that are receiving illumination, and the *Ambient* channel paints the faces that are in darkness, as well as contributing color to all faces in the scene. The *Specular* channel determines color based on shininess and lighting information.

The Shininess is controlled by various parameters, such as **Specularity** and **Glossiness**. Shininess also plays a part in reflection and refraction.

A Transparency quality is determined by *opacity* values, which can have advanced features such as *falloff* and *additive* or subtractive behavior.

The key components of most materials are maps. Maps are based on either 2D image files (bitmaps) or are formula-based, computer-generated images called procedural maps. Some maps can be configured as composites or adjustments to other maps.

- Materials are defined by maps and other physical properties (diffuse, ambient, shininess, etc.).
- Materials can include multiple maps to serve different purposes.
- Beyond materials, a map can serve in other roles, such as an environment background or a lighting projection (a gobo).

When a material containing a map is applied to an object, mapping coordinates are required for the software to render correctly.

- Maps cannot be applied directly to objects in a scene; instead, they are assigned to materials. These materials are then directly applied to objects, as shown in Figure 6–1.

Figure 6–1

Two of the most commonly used maps types are diffuse color and bump. Diffuse Color define the color of objects under normal lighting.

- Diffuse Color maps are often the most important consideration in creating realistic materials.
- Digital or scanned photographs can be used as Diffuse Color maps.
- Figure 6–2 displays a brick diffuse map (left) and a rendering of an object with a brick material that uses it (right).

Figure 6–2

Bump maps make objects appear to have texture without adding to or modifying object geometry.

- Bump maps are used to describe indentations, relief, and roughness.

- In bump maps the lighter-colored areas display projected away from the surface while the darker areas display recessed.
- Figure 6–3 displays a brick bump map (left) and a rendering of an object with a brick material that uses it (right).

Figure 6–3

- You can apply both the diffuse and bump map to a single object, as shown in Figure 6–4.

Figure 6–4

In addition to these two map types, the Autodesk 3ds Max Design software can use maps to control many different material parameters that might vary across a surface, including shininess, transparency, and more.

Certification

Topic:

✓*Materials/Shading*

Objectives:

✓*Use the Material Editor*

6.3 Managing Materials

Learning Objective

Create, manage, and edit materials using the Slate Material Editor.

Autodesk 3ds Max Design materials are managed through the Material Editor (Slate or Compact). The Slate Material Editor has the Material/Map Browser included within it whereas the older Compact Material Editor has an option for accessing the Material/Map Browser. You can use the Slate Material Editor when you need to design and build materials. It graphically displays all of the components that you want to include in the material and enables you to easily move, position, and modify them in the parent material. You can use the Compact Material Editor when the materials have already been created and you just need to apply them.

Slate Material Editor Interface

The Slate Material Editor is a graphical interface for listing, creating, modifying, and assigning different kinds of materials. It enables you to graphically create and modify complex materials by wiring the maps and materials to different channels of the parent material. It also enables you to edit and modify the parameters of already created materials. In the Main toolbar, hold down

 (Compact Material Editor) or  (Slate Material Editor) to expand the Material flyout, as shown in Figure 6–5. Click

 (Slate Material Editor) to open the Slate Material Editor.

Figure 6–5

Alternatively, you can select **Rendering>Material Editor>Slate Material Editor** to open the editor. Pressing <M> opens the last material editor that was used.

The interface of the Slate Material Editor has the following main areas:

Material/Map Browser

The Material/Map Browser area, as shown in Figure 6–6, contains an extensive list of pre-defined materials and maps that you can use. You can use the pre-defined materials directly or as a base for modifying them to get the required material affect.

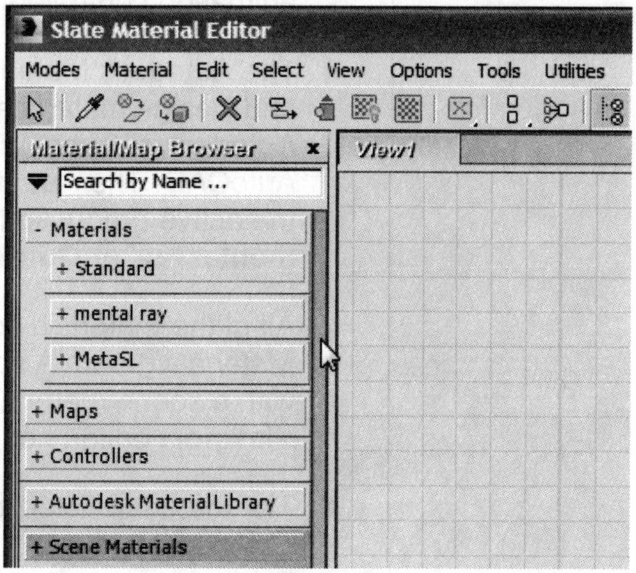

Figure 6–6

*You can also open the Material/Map Browser independent of the Material Editor by selecting **Rendering> Material/Map Browser** in the menu bar.*

- The Browser is displayed by default and you can use **x** to temporarily close it. You can open the Material/Map Browser by selecting **Tools>Material/Map Browser** in the Slate Material Editor's menu bar, or by pressing <O> when the Slate Material Editor is the active window.
- At the top of the Material/Map Browser, click ▼ to open the drop-down list (options menu) containing the options to control the display of the libraries, materials, maps, and other groups of materials. It also enables you to create and manage new custom libraries and groups.
- In the *Search by Name* box, you can enter the first few characters of the material/map name to display the list of materials/maps that you want to use.

The materials and maps listed in the Material/ Map Browser are dependant on the active renderer.

- The materials in the Browser are organized in the form of libraries and groups. The groups are organized on the basis of their attributes such as Maps, Materials, etc. The groups are further divided into subgroups (For example, **Materials> Standard**). Each library or group has a +/- sign, to expand or contract, along with its heading.

- The *Materials* and *Maps* groups contain the type of materials and maps that can be used as templates for creating custom materials and maps. The *Controller* group contains the animation controllers that can be used for material animation.

- The Autodesk Material Library contains the mental ray Arch and Design materials. These materials are also used in other Autodesk software, such as Autodesk Revit Architecture and AutoCAD. The Autodesk Material Library only displays when the active production renderer is set to **NVIDIA iray**, **NVIDIA mental ray**, or **Quicksilver Hardware Renderer**.

- All of the materials used in the scene are listed in the *Scene Materials* group. A solid wedge shaped red band displayed with a scene material name indicates that the **Show Map In Viewport** option has been selected.

- The materials listed in the Browser are dependent on the type of renderer you are currently using. If you want to see all of the materials independent of the renderer, select **Show Incompatible** option in the Material/Map Browser drop-down list (click ▼ to open the options menu).

Active View

The Active View is an area in the Slate Material Editor that displays the expanded view of materials with all its elements shown as nodes, as shown in Figure 6–7. You can graphically create and modify complex materials by wiring their nodes together, and further edit their parameters through this view.

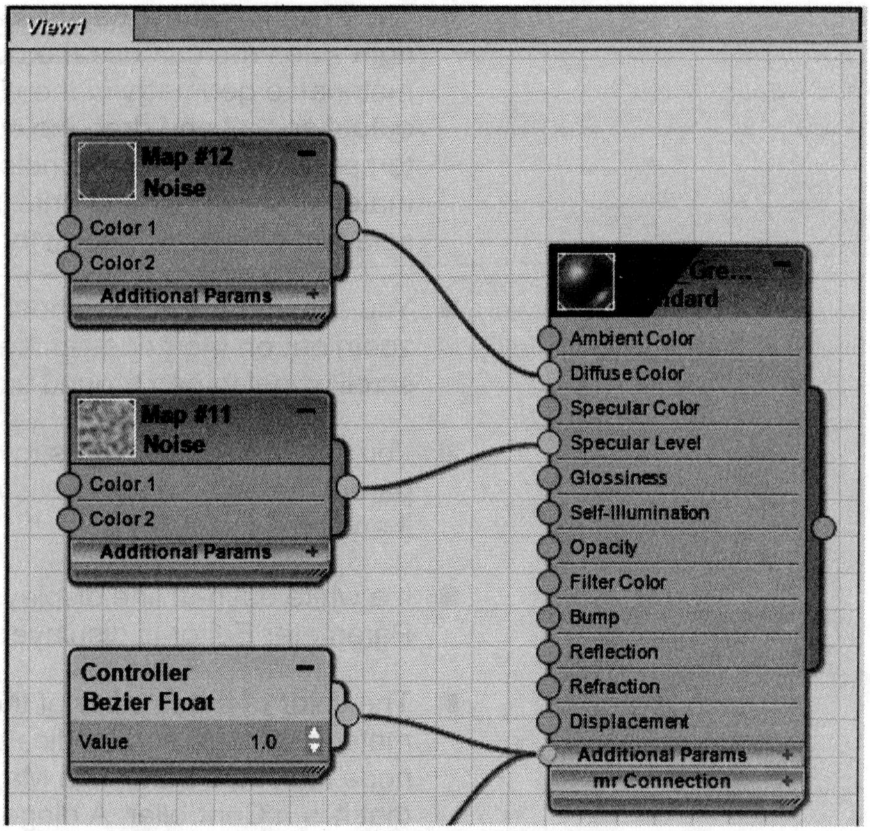

Figure 6–7

- To display a material in the active view (*View1*, by default), locate the material in the Map/Material Browser and then drag and drop the material on the *View1* sheet. You can also double-click on the material in the Map/Material Browser to automatically place it on the *View1* sheet. These are called the nodes.

- Once the material node is loaded on the active view, the title bar with a preview icon is displayed and the list of various channel slots are listed, as shown in Figure 6–7. You can wire each of these slots to another map or material. On the left side, each node has a number of input sockets (small circles) for each slot. On the right side of each node is a single output socket. These can be wired to the sockets of other material. If a map or material is wired to a channel, the slot displays in green. This material with its input sockets wired becomes the parent material and the materials and maps that are wired to the slots become the children. You can further wire the children to other materials to create complex material trees.

- You can also right-click in an empty area of the active view to open a menu containing options for selecting any material/ map/controller listed in the Material/Map Browser.

- The main material node has a blank output socket on the right side. You can use the output socket to assign this material to geometry in the viewport. Click and hold the output socket and drag the cursor on to the object. A temporary wire displays indicating that you are assigning the material. Assigning material in this way ignores already selected objects or geometry in the viewport.
- You can use the scroll wheel on your mouse to zoom in or zoom out on the nodes in the *View1* sheet. Hold down the scroll wheel to pan around to display the details of each node.
- You can also delete wires to cut the connection between the parent material and the child material. To delete a wire, select it and press <Delete>.
- If a white dashed line displays as a border around a node, its Parameter Editor is displayed in the active view.
- The color of the title bar of the node indicates the type of material. A blue node indicates that it is a material, a green node indicates that it is a Map, and a yellow node indicates that it is a Controller. A diagonal line dividing the title bar into two colors (red and blue) indicates that the **Show Map In Viewport** option is selected for that material.
- Right-clicking on a title bar of a node displays a specific right-click menu containing the options for managing that material or map. The options enable you to control the display of the material or map in the viewport or how you want the preview to be displayed on the active sheet. You can also use the right-click menu to organize all of the material nodes and their children in a more efficient manner.
- You can select multiple material/map nodes together and then right-click to open the combined menu. You can then select an option to apply it to all of the nodes at the same time.
- You can toggle between a large and small material preview icon by double-clicking on the icon in the node title bar.
- The outline of a preview icon indicates whether the material is assigned or not (hot or cold) to objects in the viewport.

	No white boundary around the icon indicates that the material is not used in the scene and is cold.
	Outlined white triangles at the four corners indicate the material is hot and is being used in the scene. Modifying this material interactively displays the modifications in the scene.
	Solid white triangles at the four corners indicate the material is applied to the currently selected object on the scene.

- Additional sheets can be added to the View area to organize materials. Right-click on the default *View1* tab and select **Create New View**. Using this menu, you can also rename and delete your views. Once multiple sheets exist you can select the appropriate tab to make it active and work with custom material.

Hint: Active View

It is recommended that you delete materials from the Active view once you have completed modifying the material. You should also delete the unused materials from the Active view to organize your working space. Once the material has been applied, it is listed in the *Scene materials* category in the Material/Map Browser. Deleting it from the Active view does not delete the material from the Scene materials list. You can drag and drop (or double-click) the material back to the Active view.

- After you have created and applied materials to a scene, the *View* sheets are saved with the .MAX file. When you open the file again, the sheets display the material nodes as they were saved. When you load a file in which materials have been assigned but nodes are not displayed in the *View* sheet, this indicates that the model was originally created in a version before 2011 when the Slate Material Editor did not exist or that the scene file was linked or imported with materials.

The Navigator window is displayed by default giving you a quick layout of the nodes in the active sheet, as shown in Figure 6–8. It can be used to pan around in the Active view by dragging the outlined red box. Similar to a sheet, a blue node indicates that it is a material, a green node indicates that it is a Map, and a yellow node indicates that it is a Controller. A red and blue node indicates that the **Show Map In Viewport** option is selected for that material.

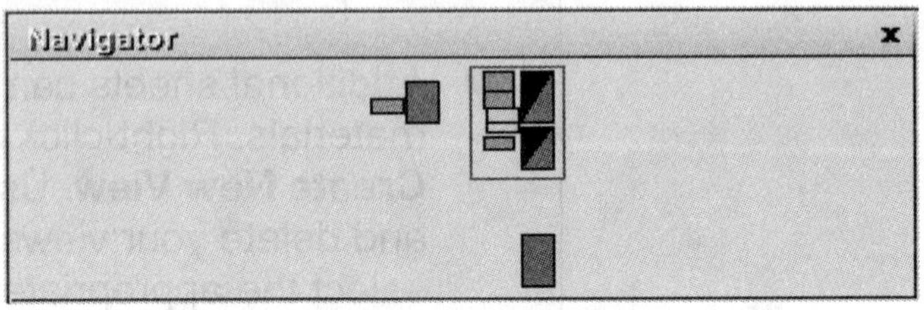

Figure 6–8

Parameter Editor

You can modify a material or a map by adjusting their parameters. All of the parameters are displayed in the material's Parameter Editor. In the Active View sheet, double-click on the material's title bar heading to display the Parameters, as shown in Figure 6–9. A white dashed line border displays around the node indicating that its Parameter Editor is displayed. The parameters are grouped in rollouts and you can click **+** on the rollout name bar to expand the rollout and access its parameters. You can rename the material by entering a new name in the *Name* field of the Parameter Editor.

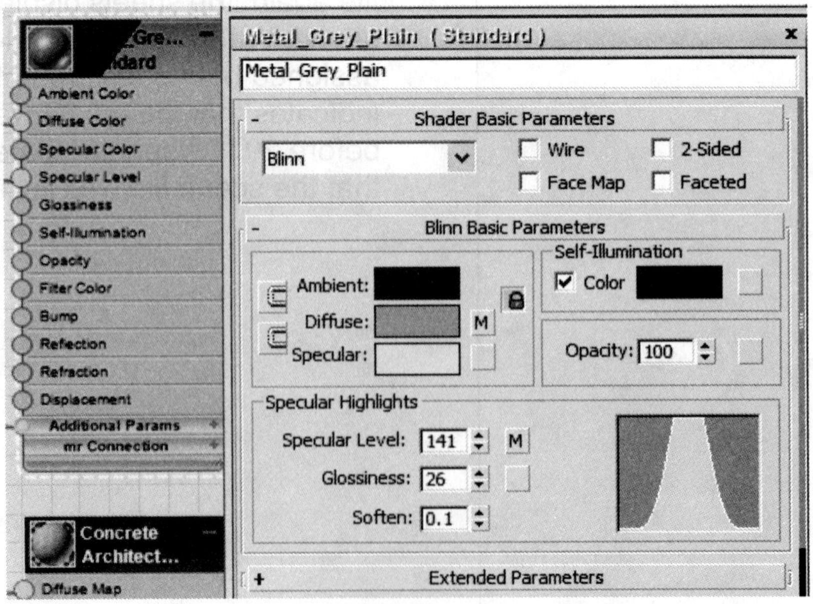

Figure 6–9

Floating the Parameter Editor and hiding the Navigator can help reduce the footprint of the Slate Material Editor on the screen.

- As with any other window, you can move, dock, float, or close the Parameter Editor. To float the Parameter Editor, drag its header outside the Slate Material Editor. To dock it again, double-click on its header.

Toolbar

The Slate Material Editor includes a toolbar, as shown in Figure 6–10, at the top left corner of the window. It contains tools related to materials and enables you to assign and manage the materials.

Figure 6–10

- (Select Tool) enables you to select a material node in the Active View. It is the tool that is selected by default.
- (Pick Material from Object) enables you to pick a material that is assigned to an object in the scene and display it in the active view.
- (Put Material to Scene) enables you to update objects having an older material whose copy has been edited after it was applied.
- (Assign Material to Selection) enables you to assign a selected material to selected objects in the viewport.
- (Move Children) enables you to move the complete material tree when you move the parent material node in the Active View. Clearing this tool, moves the Parent individually and extends the wires as you move the parent.
- / (Show Shaded Material in Viewport/Show Realistic Material in Viewport) enables you to display the maps for the active material. This is helpful when you are modifying the map in the View sheet, you can see the changes interactively in the viewport. You do not have to render to see the map changes.
- / (Lay Out All-Vertical/Horizontal) enables you to organize all of the material nodes and their children in the View sheet either vertically or horizontally.

- (Lay Out Children) enables you to lay out the children of the currently selected node without changing the position of the parent node.

- (Material/Map Browser) and (Parameter Editor) enable you to control the display of these tools in the Slate Material Editor.

- (Select by Material) enables you to select objects based on the active material.

Menu Bar

The Slate Material Editor displays a menu bar along the top of the window, as shown in Figure 6–11. It contains menus related to materials and enables you to assign and manage the materials. The menus enable you to toggle between editors, create new and assign materials, gain access to various selection techniques, navigate the view sheet, among other commands.

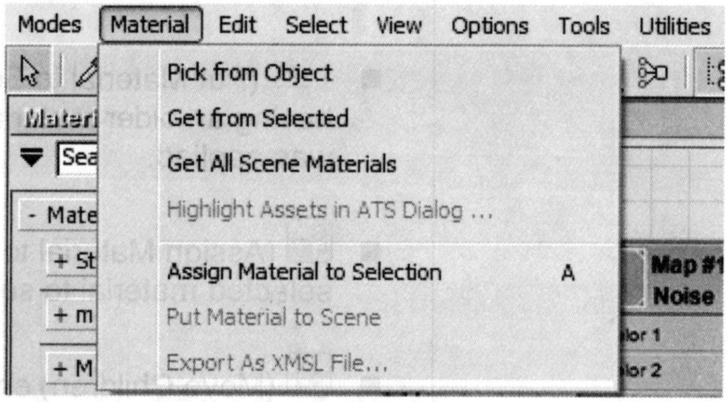

Figure 6–11

- **Modes:** Enables you to toggle between the two editors (Slate and Compact).

- **Material:** Options in the menu bar enable you to select a material by picking it from the object in the viewport, by selecting an object in the viewport, or selecting all of the materials used in the scene. You also have the options for assigning materials.

- **Edit:** Options in the Edit menu bar enable you to edit the active view and update the preview windows.

- **Select:** Provides you with different selection options that can be used in the active view.

- **View:** Provides you with different zoom and pan options and contains options for the layout of the nodes in the active view.

- **Options:** Enables you to further manage the Slate Material Editor.

- **Tools:** Controls the display of the Material/Map Browser, Parameter Editor, and Navigator.

- **Utilities:** Provides you with the render and object selection options and has options for managing the materials.

Practice 6a Introduction to Materials

Learning Objectives

- Assign previously created materials to different objects on the scene.
- Load a material library and change the display of material preview in the Slate Material Editor.
- Create and edit a new material using the Parameter Editor of the Slate Material Editor and assign it to objects in the scene.

Estimated time for completion: 20 minutes

In this practice you will add materials to the scene and render the Light Pole model.

You must set the paths to locate the External files and Xrefs used in the practice. If you have not done this already, return to the **Introduction to Autodesk 3ds Max Design** chapter and complete Task 1 to Task 3 of the **Organizing Folders and Working with the Interface** practice. You only have to set the user paths once.

Task 1 - Assigning materials in the Slate Material Editor.

If a dialog box opens prompting you about a Mismatch, click OK *to accept the default values.*

1. Open **Intro to Materials and Rendering.max** from your *Class Files* folder.
   - The Light pole model is displayed in the viewport.
2. In the Main toolbar, click (Slate Material Editor) to open the Slate Material Editor. Alternatively, you can select **Rendering>Material Editor>Slate Material Editor**.
   - The button displayed in the Main toolbar depends on the last selection. Hold down (Compact Material Editor) or (Slate Material Editor) to expand the Material flyout, if required.
   - If you start a new scene file, materials are not listed in the *View1* sheet of the Material Editor.
3. In the Slate Material Editor, in the *View1* sheet, four materials nodes are displayed, as shown in Figure 6–12. Note that the materials are listed in the *Scene Materials* group in the Material/Map Browser.

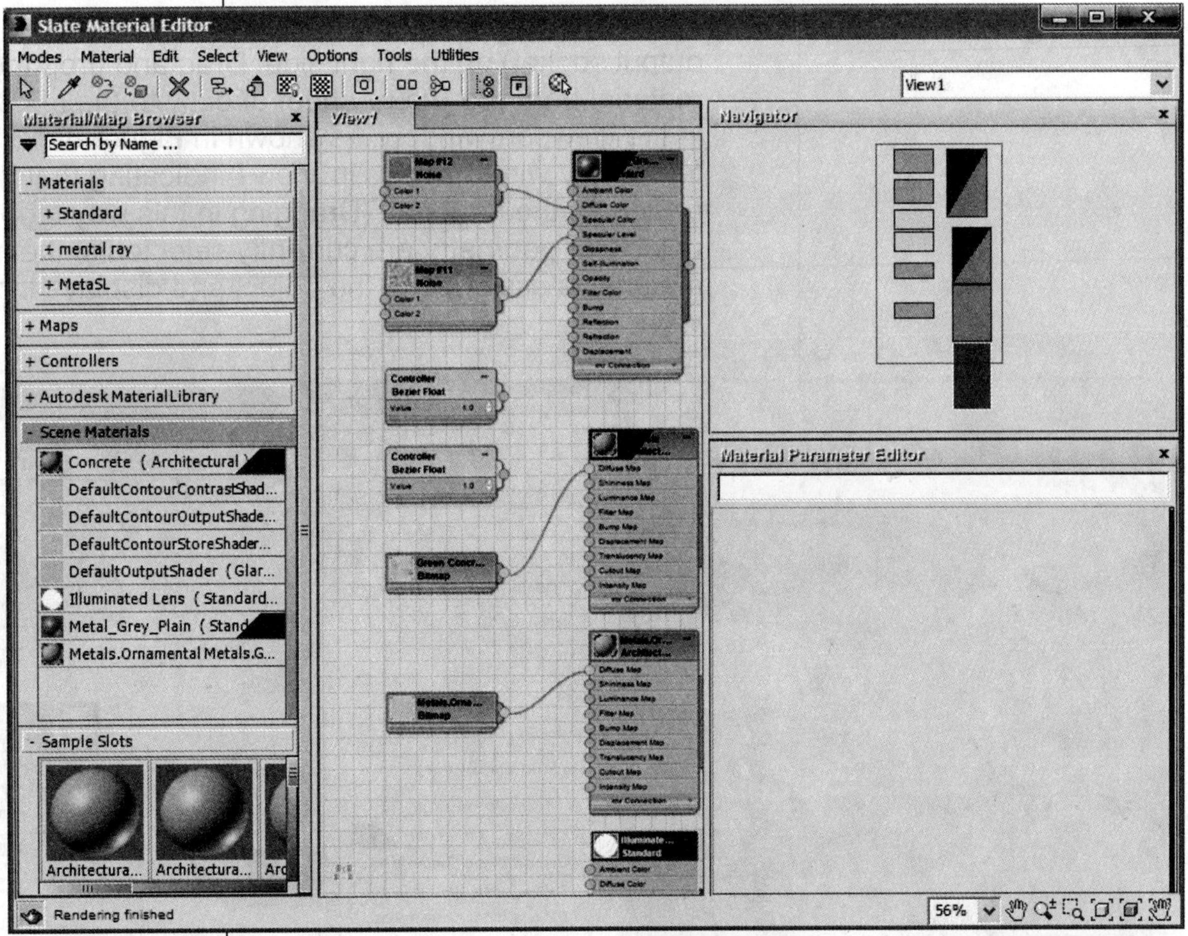

Figure 6–12

- A blue node indicates that it is a material, a green node indicates that it is a Map, and a yellow node indicates that it is a Controller. A diagonal line dividing the title bar into two colors (red and blue) indicates that the **Show Map In Viewport** option is selected for that material

4. Using the scroll wheel on your mouse, zoom into the nodes in the *View1* sheet. Hold down the scroll wheel to pan around to see the details of each node. The red bounding box in the *Navigator* area can also be dragged around to quickly access specific areas within the *View1* sheet.

5. Locate the **Concrete** material (second material node from the top).

You can close the Navigator and Parameter Editor to create more space for displaying the nodes in the active sheet.

6. Move and size the Slate Material Editor in the Drawing window so that you can see both the Material Editor and the model in the viewport window.

7. In the **Concrete** material, click and hold down (material output socket) on the right side. Drag and drop the **Concrete** material from the *View1* sheet directly to the LP Base object in the viewport window, as shown in Figure 6–13. A temporary wire displays in *View1* indicating that you are assigning the material. (Dragging in this way ignores which objects or geometry are currently selected in the model.) The material is assigned to the object and displays in the viewport.

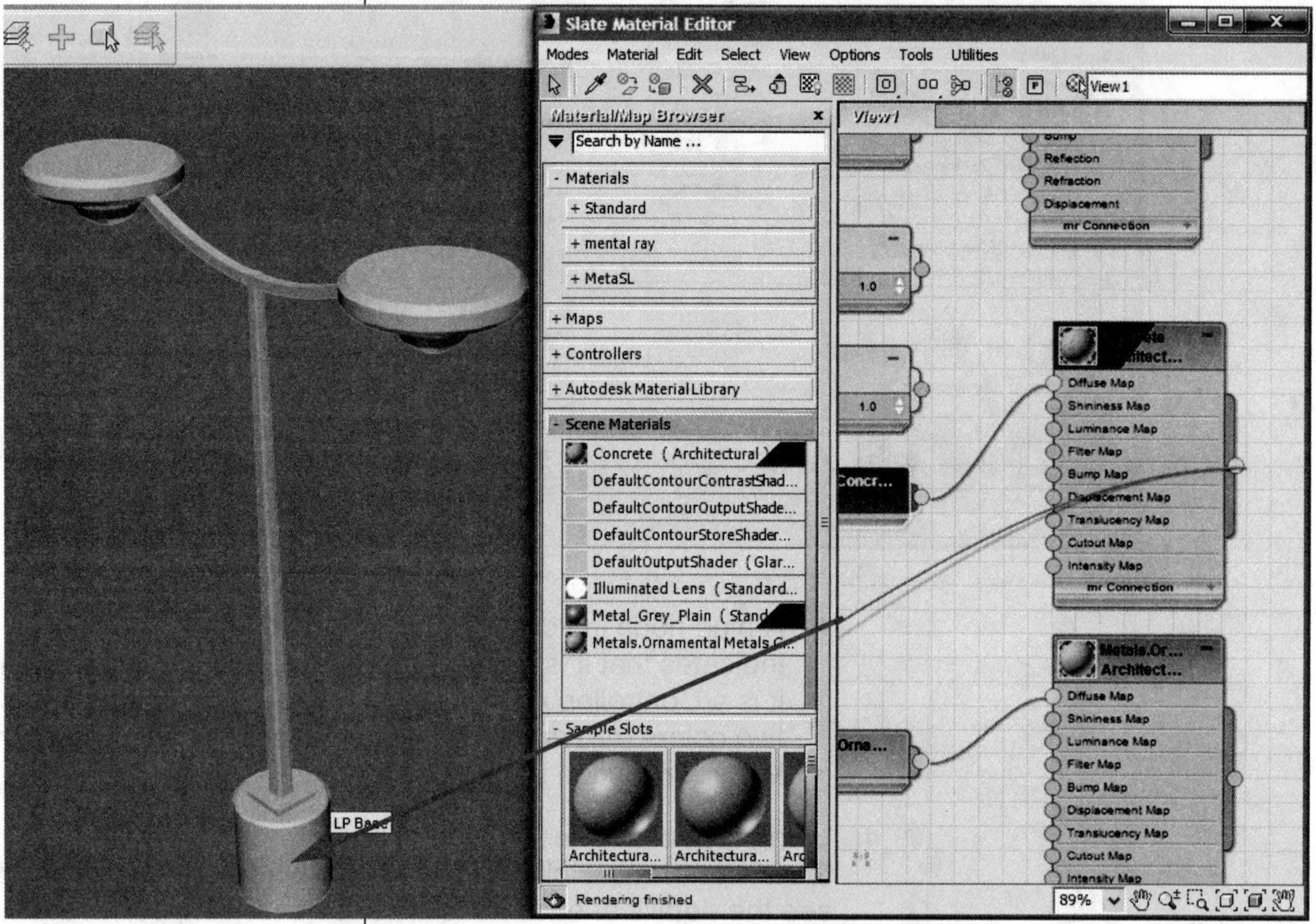

Figure 6–13

- Dragging materials can be challenging in highly complex scenes. Alternatively, you can first select objects in the viewport or select them by name, select the material, and then click (Assign Material to Selection) in the Slate Material Editor toolbar. You can also select the objects in the viewport and the in *View1* sheet, right-click on the material and select **Assign Material to Selection** from the drop-down list.

8. Select the two **LP Fixture Housings** (the groups containing fixture, globe, and mounting arm).

9. In the Slate Material Editor, in the *View1* sheet, locate **Metal_Grey_Plain** (the first material node). Right-click on the title bar of the material and select **Assign Material to Selection**. The material is applied to all of the objects in the two **LP Fixture Housings** groups.

> **Hint: Group Objects**
>
> To assign a material to individual objects in a group, select the group, select **Group>Open**, and then select the individual object in the group. Drag the material on the selected object. To close the group, select the pink bounding box and select **Group>Close**.

10. Use  (Orbit) to orbit the model so that you can see the LP Globe objects. Currently **Metal_Grey_Plain** is assigned to them. Click anywhere in the empty space to clear any selection.

11. You can also assign materials directly from the Material/Map Browser of the Slate Material Editor. Scroll to the bottom of the Material/Map Browser and expand the *Scene Materials* category, if required, as shown on the left in Figure 6–14. Click and drag **Illuminated Lens** to one of the LP Globe objects in the model. Both globes have **Illuminated Lens** material assigned to them, as shown in Figure 6–14. This method only assigns the material to the object on which you are dropping the material.

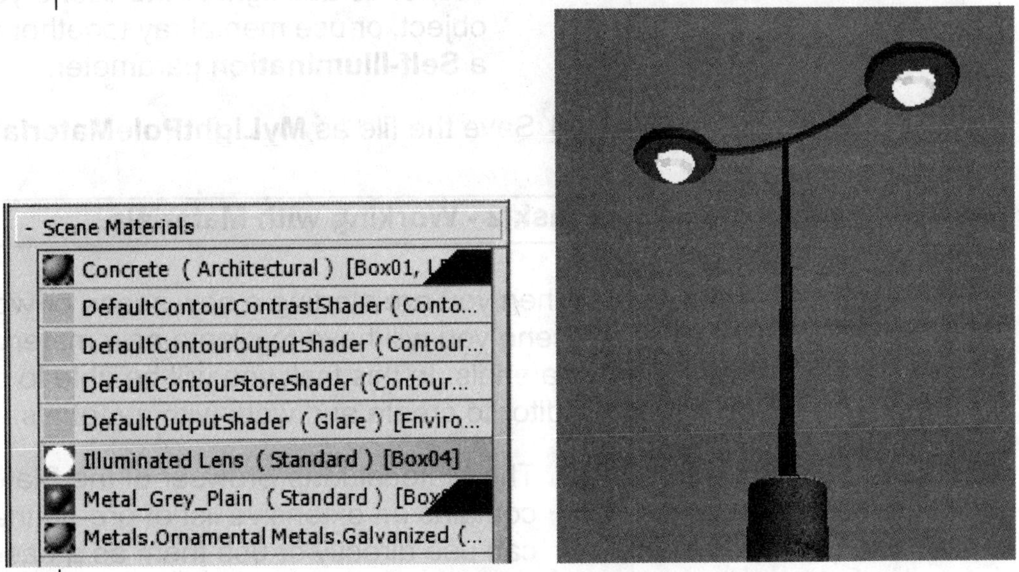

Figure 6–14

12. Assign the **Metal_Grey_Plain** material to both the LP Base Plate and LP Pole objects using any of the assigning materials method.

13. In the Main toolbar, click  (Render Production) to render the scene. The scene is rendered as shown in Figure 6–15.

Figure 6–15

- A Gradient background was added for visual clarity during rendering.
- The globe material was made to look as if it was illuminated, but it does not actually add any light to the scene. To add light to the scene you need to add a light object, or use mental ray together with a material that has a **Self-Illumination** parameter.

14. Save the file as **MyLightPoleMaterials.max**.

Task 2 - Working with Materials.

When you are starting a new scene or working in an existing scene you will have to create new materials or edit existing materials. In this task you will be able to use the Slate Material Editor to create and work with materials.

1. The Material/Map Browser of the Slate Material Editor contains an extensive list of pre-defined materials that you can use directly or use them as a base for creating your custom materials. You can also import your own material library. Scroll through the list of materials that are available in the list.

2. At the top of the Material/Map Browser, click ▼ to open the **Materials/Map Browser Options** menu. These options enable you to control the display of the material categories within the Material/Map Browser or to load a custom Material Library.

If the material libraries were not installed, there will be no files in the project folder in the \materiallibraries subdirectory.

3. In the **Materials/Map Browser Options** menu, select **Open Material Library**. The *materiallibraries* subdirectory will open because it was set as part of the User Paths. If you did not set it, browse to the path under the root installation (usually *C:\Program Files\Autodesk\3ds max Design 2014*). Open the *\materiallibraries* subdirectory. Select and open **AecTemplates.mat**. A list of materials is added to the top of the Material/Map Browser with **AecTemplates.mat** listed as the title, as shown in Figure 6–16.

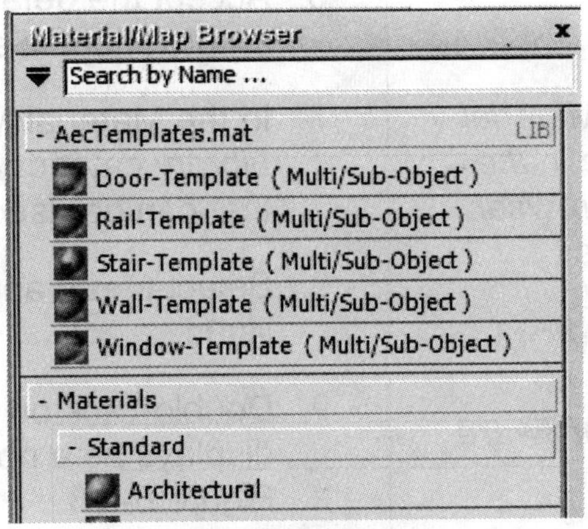

Figure 6–16

- You can remove a library by right-clicking on the category heading and selecting **Close Material Library**. Do not close this library.

4. In the Material/Map Browser, expand the *Materials>Standard* categories. A list of materials is displayed. Right-click on the *Standard* category and select **Display Group (and Subgroups) As**. Select **Medium Icons**. All of the materials in the *Standard* category now display as thumbnail images. Right-click on the *Standard* category again and select **Display Group (and Subgroups) As>Icons and Text** to display the materials in the icons and name format.

Double-clicking on a material in the Material/Map Browser also displays the material in the View1 sheet. Once in the View1 sheet you can customize the material, as needed. Materials do not have to be placed in the View1 sheet unless they are being customized. Standard materials can be assigned directly from the Material/Map Browser.

The Autodesk Material Library displays in the Material/Map Browser only if the active renderer is set to ***NVIDIA iray, NVIDIA mental ray****, or* ***Quicksilver Hardware Renderer****.*

5. The *View1* sheet already displays the materials used in the scene. You will create additional views to help organize your custom materials. To create a new view, right-click on the View1 label and select **Create New View**, as shown in Figure 6–17.

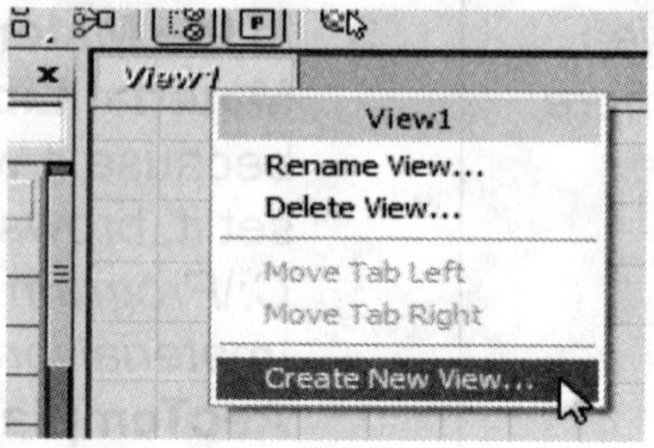

Figure 6–17

6. Accept the default name, *View2*, and click OK. A new empty sheet is added.

7. In the Material/Map Browser, select the *Autodesk Material Library* category to display the list of pre-defined materials that can be used.

8. Select **Metal** and then select **Steel** to display the materials listed.

9. Double-click on the **Galvanized** material. The material displays as a node on the *View2* sheet, as shown in Figure 6–18.

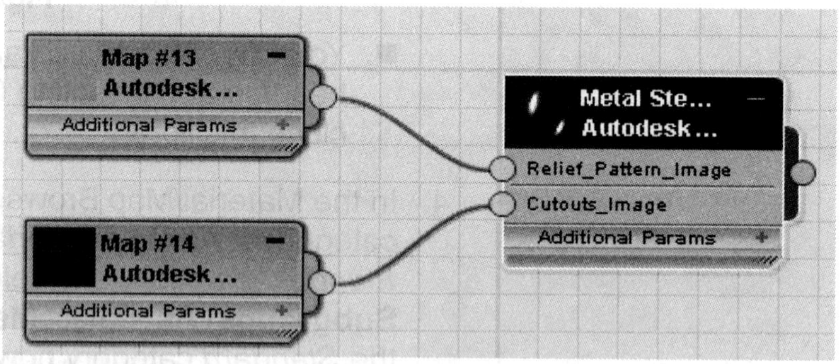

Figure 6–18

> **Hint: Add Materials to Sheets**
>
> You can add materials to sheets if they are going to be modified. If the material is simply going to be assigned to an object in the scene, you can select and drag it directly onto an object.

10. Double-click on the title bar of the **Metal/Steel Galvanized** material.

Note that in the active sheet (View2), the material node is surrounded by a dashed white border, indicating that the Parameter Editor for this material is displayed.

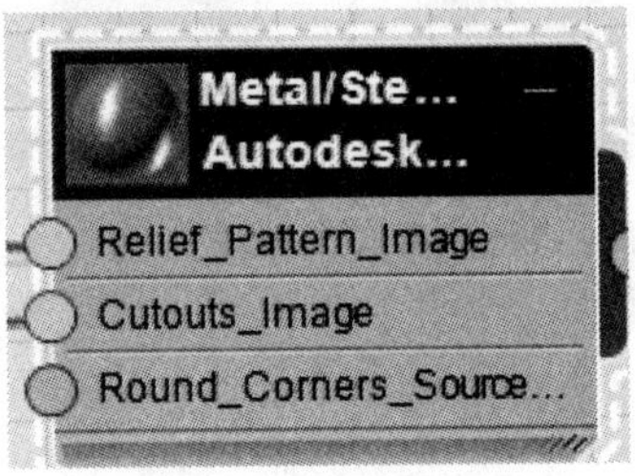

11. The Parameter Editor for this material opens in the Slate Material Editor. In the Relief Pattern rollout, the **Image** button displays the map name as **Metals.Metal Fabrications.Metal Stairs. Galvanized.png**, as shown in Figure 6–19.

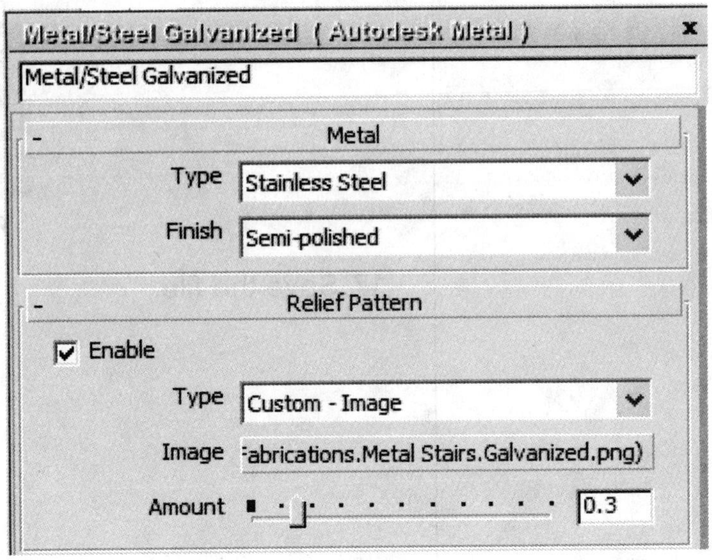

Figure 6–19

> **Hint: Parameter Editor**
>
> You can customize the materials by making changes in the Parameter Editor.

12. In the Relief Pattern rollout, use the *Amount* slider to change it to **0.5**. You can also enter the value directly in the edit box.

13. Review the preview icon for the material. Note that there is no outline around the icon, as shown in Figure 6–20, indicating that it is not assigned to any object and is a cold material.

Figure 6–20

14. Using the drag and drop method from the output socket, assign the **Galvanized** material to the **LP Fixture Housings** (the chamfer cylinders) and **LP Mounting Arms** (the arms holding the fixtures to the post).

15. Replace the existing material for the **LP Base Plate** and **LP Pole** with the **Galvanized** material.

16. Review the preview icon for the material. Note that there is now a white outline around the thumbnail, as shown in Figure 6–21. This indicates that the material has been assigned to an object in the scene.

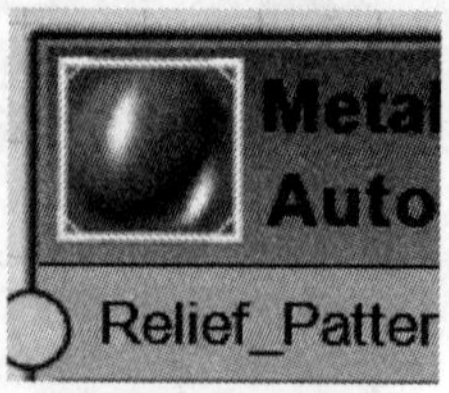

Figure 6–21

17. Save the file.

Certification

Topic:
✓*Materials/Shading*
Objectives:
✓*Identify standard materials*

6.4 Standard Materials

Learning Objectives

- Understand the standard materials provided with the Autodesk 3ds Max Design software.
- Create and work with the Multi/Sub-Object materials.

The most basic material in the Autodesk 3ds Max Design software is the Standard material, which can be accessed by expanding the *Materials>Standard* categories in the Material/Map Browser, as shown in Figure 6–22. The software provides a number of other Standard materials, which are located in the *Materials>Standard* categories as shown in Figure 6–22. All of these materials can be used directly or modified to further customize them.

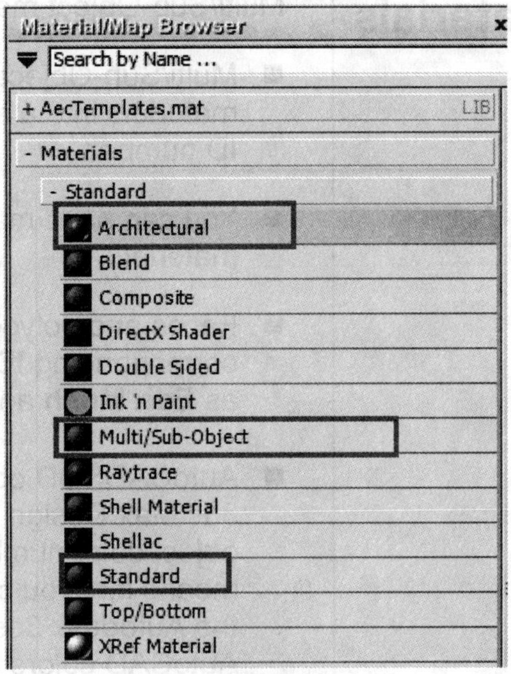

Figure 6–22

Any of the Standard materials can be used by selecting them in the Material/Map Browser and assigning them to objects in the scene. To modify the Standard materials, double-click on the material name or drag the material on to an active sheet. Double-click on the materials title bar to open its Parameter Editors and customize it as required.

Architectural Materials

Architectural materials are Standard materials, as shown in Figure 6–22, with the user interface updated for design visualization usage and are appropriate for scenes with physically based lighting. The same features have been renamed and rearranged to suit CAD users. They offer a streamlined interface that highlights the parameters and maps that (in many cases) you are most likely to change. (Architectural materials are applicable to many different kinds of visualization projects, not only Architectural or Civil/Site projects.) This streamlining makes Architectural materials easier to navigate in some respects, in exchange for giving up control of some properties. Architectural materials also offer other controls not directly available to Standard materials, such as refraction, luminance, and advanced lighting overrides.

Multi/Sub-Object Materials

Sometimes objects require different materials on each face. For example, a door or window might need different materials for front and back frames, mullions, and glazing. For this, Multi/Sub-Object materials, as shown in Figure 6–22, are used.

- Multi/Sub-Object materials enable you to stack multiple materials into a single *parent* material, each with a material ID number.
- You can have many materials in one Multi/Sub-Object material.
- Faces and polygons of individual objects can have a corresponding ID number assigned through modifiers such as **Edit Mesh** and **Edit Poly**.
- AutoCAD® 3D objects imported or linked into the Autodesk 3ds Max Design software automatically have their AutoCAD object color numbers recorded as material ID numbers. This means that you can configure **Multi/Sub-Object** materials for the Autodesk 3ds Max Design software corresponding to AutoCAD colors.
- Objects brought into the Autodesk 3ds Max Design software from vertical applications, such as the AutoCAD Architecture software and the AutoCAD Civil 3D software are normally divided into multiple objects by material. Therefore, they do not require Multi/Sub-Object materials.

- The Slate Material Editor provides a convenient view that enables you to visually identify all of the materials that make up a Multi/Sub-Object material. Initially when the material is created the parent material node opens with 10 default slots. You can wire sub-materials to each slot. Each of the sub-materials can be modified or you can add new materials to the view and rewire into any of the slots. Figure 6–23 displays **Material #70** as a Multi/Sub-Object material that is wired to ten default materials. Double-click on the title of the Multi/Sub-Object material to display its basic parameters.

  Slots can be added or deleted using the Add or Delete options in the Multi/Sub-Object Basic Parameters rollout.

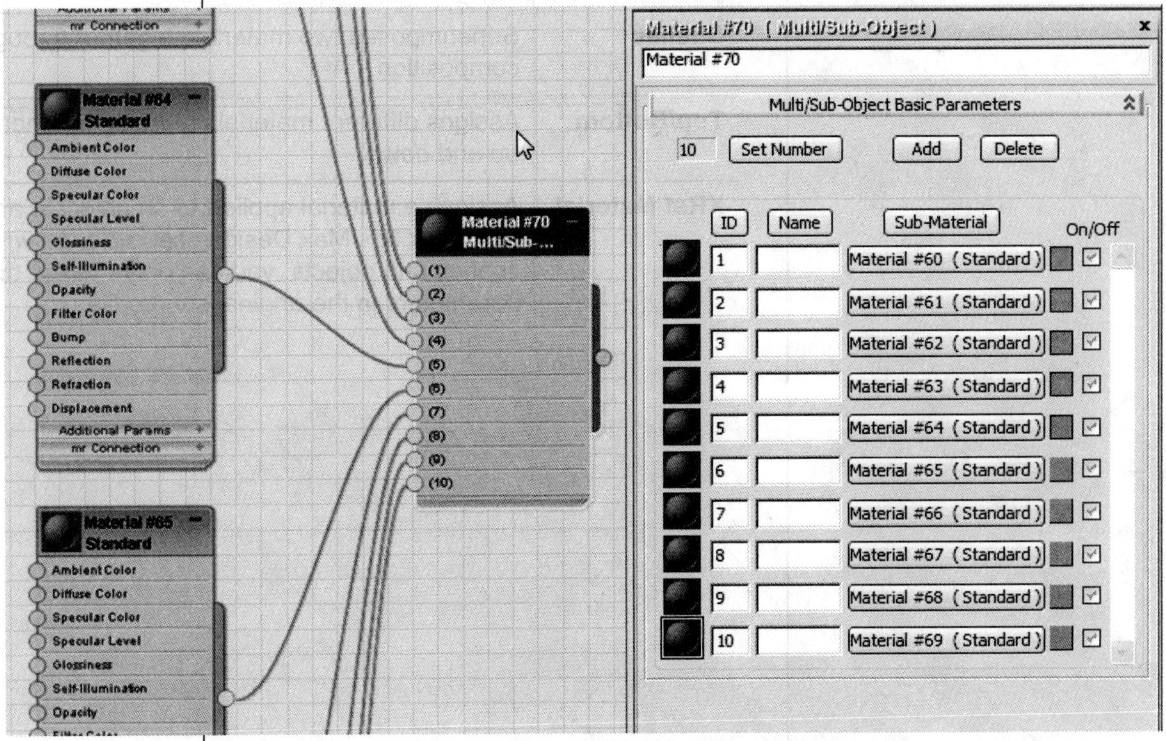

Figure 6–23

Additional Standard Materials

The following additional Standard materials are also available for use in the Autodesk 3ds Max Design software.

Blend	Combines two materials to create a third.
Composite	Enables multiple materials to be combined into a single, composite material through additive colors, subtractive colors, or opacity mixing.
DirectX Shader	Enables you to shade objects in the viewport to more accurately display how objects look when exported to real-time viewing.

Double Sided	Enables you to have one material assigned to the outside of objects and another to the inside (the back-facing sides).
Ink 'n' Paint	Creates a flat shaded cartoon rendering with the contours or edges as ink lines.
Raytrace	Used to create highly configurable, extremely realistic reflections and refractions. They also support fog, color density, translucency, fluorescence, and other effects. Some Architectural materials (such as ones with the mirror template) automatically generate raytraced results.
Shell Material	Used with *texture baking*, which is the process of creating replacement color maps that include the scene illumination (illumination is *baked in*).
Shellac	Superimposes two materials together through additive composition.
Top/Bottom	Assigns different materials to faces with normals pointing *up* and *down*.
XRef Material	Assigns a material applied to an object to another Autodesk 3ds Max Design scene file. As with XRef scenes and objects, you can only change the material parameters in the original source file.

Certification

Topic:

✓*Materials/Shading*

Objectives:

✓*Identify Shader parameters*

6.5 Material Shaders

Learning Objectives

- Understand how to control the color, highlights, self-illumination, and other attributes of a material using its Shaders.
- Control the parameters of the material shaders to accomplish the required affect on the materials.

Material Shaders are complex algorithms that describe how light interacts with surfaces. The material color, highlights, self-illumination, and many other features are dependant on the material shaders.

- Standard and mental ray materials enable you to select or use a shader. When using mental ray, a wide range of shaders are available for specific advanced effects. At the other extreme, Architectural materials do not provide any shader choice at all.
- In Standard materials the shader type is selected through the Shader Basic Parameters rollout, as shown in Figure 6–24.

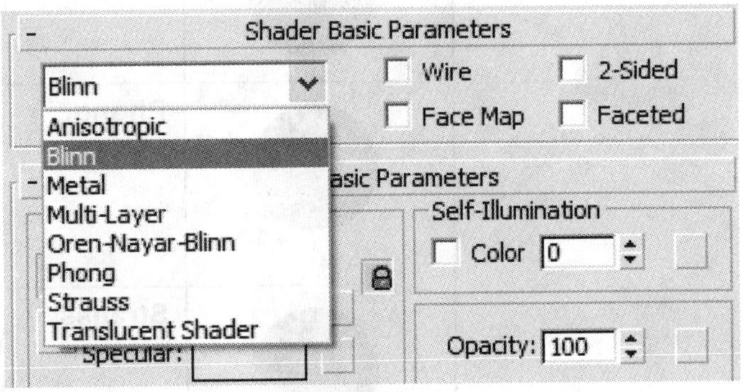

Figure 6–24

- In mental ray materials, shaders can be applied anywhere you might place a map. Generally they are located using the Material/Map Browser. In mental ray you can also apply shaders directly to cameras and lights.

Below is a brief description of the standard shader types. Many shader properties relate to highlights, the bright areas caused by the specular reflection of a light source on the surface of an object.

	**Anisotropic**	Shader for materials with elliptical highlights, such as hair, glass, or brushed metal.
	**Blinn**	General purpose shader for shiny, smooth objects with soft, circular highlights. Blinn is the default shader for Standard materials.
	**Metal**	For luminous metallic surfaces.
	**Multi-Layer**	Enables two sets of anisotropic controls for complex or highly polished surfaces.
	**Oren-Nayar-Blinn**	A variation of the Blinn shader that provides additional controls for matte surfaces such as fabric or terra cotta.
	**Phong**	Related to the Blinn shader, also used for shiny, smooth surfaces with circular highlights. The Phong shader generates harder, sharper (often less realistic) highlights than Blinn.
	**Strauss**	For metallic and similar surfaces, Strauss offers a simpler interface than the Metal shader.
	**Translucent Shader**	Enables you to control translucency, which is the scattering of light as it passes through the material. Appropriate for Semi-transparent materials, such as frosted glass.

- When using the mental ray renderer, you can apply mental ray shaders to materials. The mental ray shaders display with a yellow parallelogram, instead of the green symbol used for maps. The mental ray materials display as yellow spheres.

- The mental ray also enables you to attach shaders directly to lights and cameras for a variety of rendering effects such as contour rendering. If the mental ray render is NOT selected, the various mental ray shaders are not shown as a possible choice. However, in the Material/Map Browser options, when the **Show Incompatible** option is selected it displays incompatible materials to that renderer in gray.

Shader (Specific) Basic Parameters

Each material shader has a unique combination of parameters, as shown in Figure 6–25, that can be controlled.

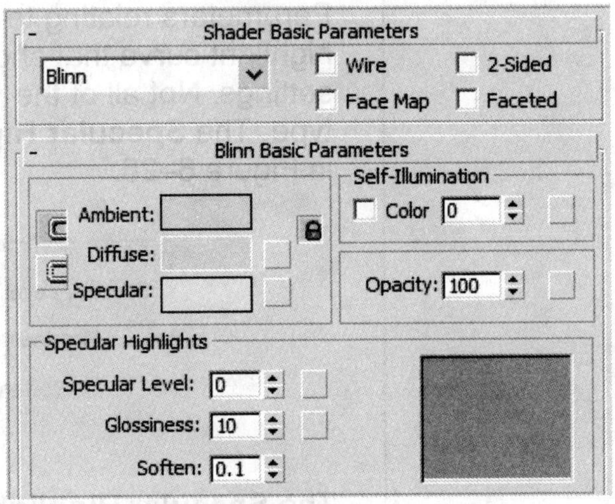

Figure 6–25

- Most of these parameters can be replaced by a map when their values are not constant across the surface. For example, a Diffuse Color Map can be used to replace a single diffuse color for a brick material.
- Colors can be selected by picking on the color swatch next to a color parameter, which opens the interactive Color Selector.

Ambient Color	The color of a material under ambient (background) lighting. It can be assigned globally and through standard lights set to cast ambient light. Ambient and diffuse colors can be locked at the same values, if necessary.
Diffuse Color	The color of a material under direct lighting. This is the base color of a material (outside of highlights).
Specular Color	The color of material's highlights. It is calculated automatically for the Metal and Multilayer shaders.

Self-Illumination	Values greater than 0 cause materials to appear to be illuminated, but surfaces with this material do not illuminate other objects. This parameter is useful for materials used in light fixtures. Self-illuminated objects do not automatically glow; glows need to be assigned as a special effect (**Rendering>Effects**).
Opacity	This is a percentage measurement of opacity, the opposite of transparency. Materials that have 0% opacity are completely see-through. As an example, a typical clear glass material could have an Opacity between 0-10%.

Parameters relating to Specular Highlights are listed next to a highlight curve that shows a graphical representation of these settings. Not all of the parameters are available for each shader type. The **Specular Highlights** parameters for Blinn are shown in Figure 6–26.

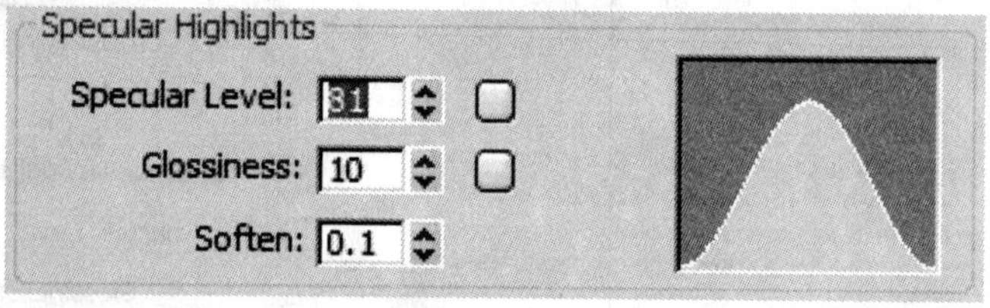

Figure 6–26

The **Specular Highlights** parameters for Anisotropic shaders are shown in Figure 6–27.

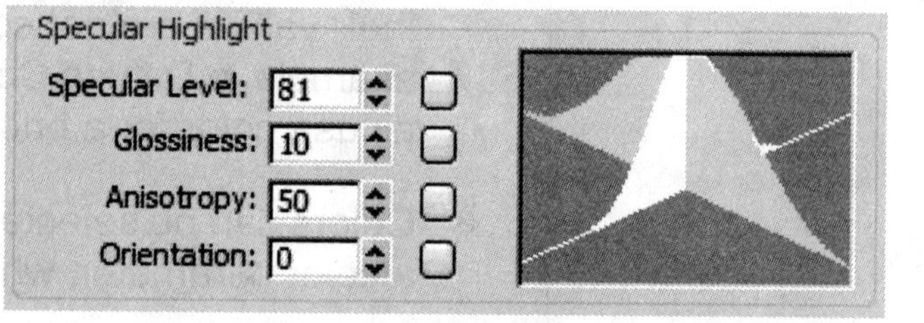

Figure 6–27

Specular Level	A relative measurement of the overall highlight intensity.
Glossiness	A relative measurement of the overall size of highlights. The more glossy an object the smaller and more intense the highlights.
Soften	A relative measurement used to soften the edges of highlights.
Anisotropy	Defines the elliptical shape of Anisotropic highlights, where 0 = round and 100 = a very tight ellipse.
Orientation	Defines the degrees of rotation for an Anisotropic highlight.

6.6 Assigning Maps to Materials

Learning Objective

Understand how to assign bitmaps or procedural maps to replace the shader parameters in materials.

Maps are often assigned to replace the shader parameters, especially Diffuse Color. Maps can be assigned to Standard materials through the Maps rollout, as shown in Figure 6–28. Maps include the Diffuse Color, Bump maps, Opacity etc.

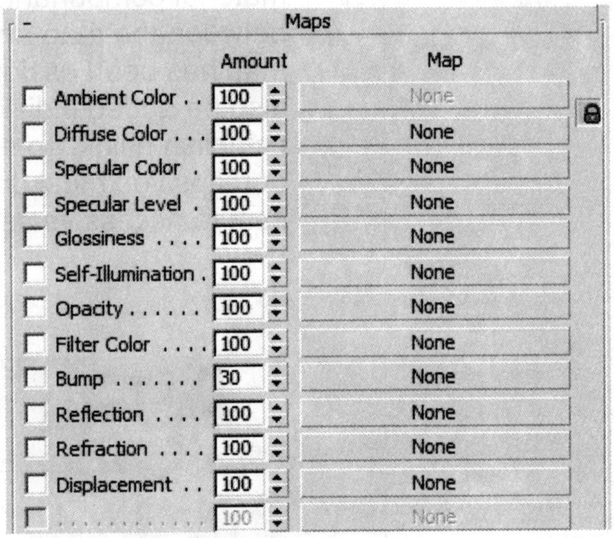

Figure 6–28

By clicking 

next to a channel, opens the Material/Map Browser, as shown in Figure 6–29, where you can select a map and assign it or change a map and its settings.

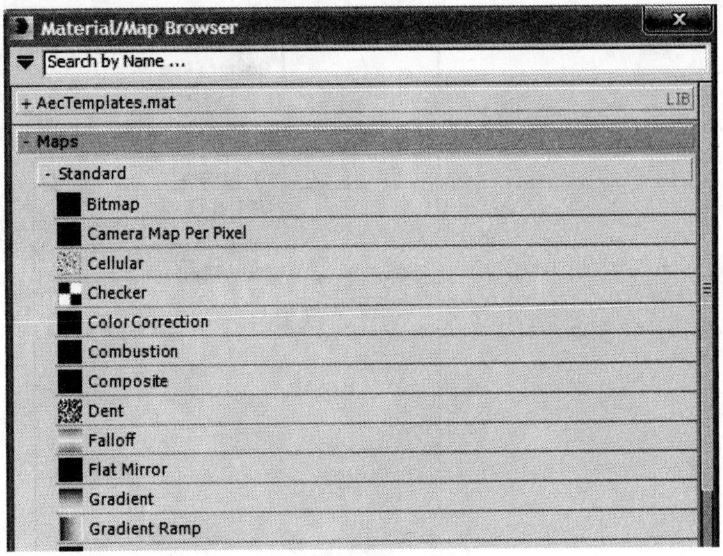

Figure 6–29

- The Bitmap map type enables you to assign an external image as a map. Many different kinds of image files can be used as maps including Windows Bitmaps, JPEGs, PNGs, Targas, TIFFs, and more.

- The remainder of map types available are all Autodesk 3ds Max Design **Procedural** maps. These maps are automatically generated mathematically rather than from image files.

- When you assign (or edit) a map to a material, individual nodes are created and display the maps assigned to the material components. Wires are created automatically between the map and the material component to which the map has been assigned, as shown in Figure 6–30. Maps can also be added individually and wired into a material to establish a link. To edit any of the parameters in the material or maps you must double-click on the title bar heading for the item to access its associated Parameter Editor.

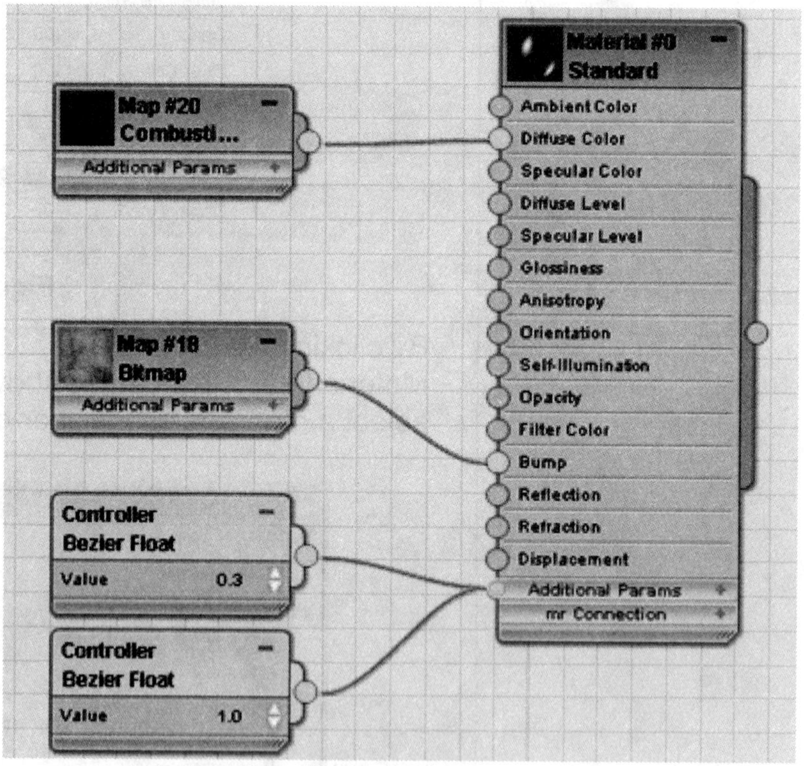

Figure 6–30

Practice 6b Working with Standard Materials and Maps

Learning Objectives

- Assign a Standard material to an object and apply parameter changes to it.
- Apply a procedural map to the Diffuse Color of the material.
- Apply an image file to the Diffuse Color of the material and add color correction to it.

Estimated time for completion: 20 minutes

In this practice you will work with Standard materials in a product design visualization.

You must set the paths to locate the External files and Xrefs used in the practice. If you have not done this already, return to the **Introduction to Autodesk 3ds Max Design** chapter and complete Task 1 to Task 3 of the **Organizing Folders and Working with the Interface** practice. You only have to set the user paths once.

Task 1 - Load Materials into the Material Editor.

If a dialog box opens prompting you about a Mismatch, click OK *to accept the default values.*

1. Open the file **Standard Materials.max** from your *Class Files* folder. A model of a guitar displays in the Perspective viewport.
2. In the Main toolbar, click (Slate Material Editor icon) to open the Slate Material Editor.

3. In the Slate Material Editor, in the Material/Map Browser, expand the *Scene Materials* category, if required. There are currently nine materials available in this scene, as shown in Figure 6–31.

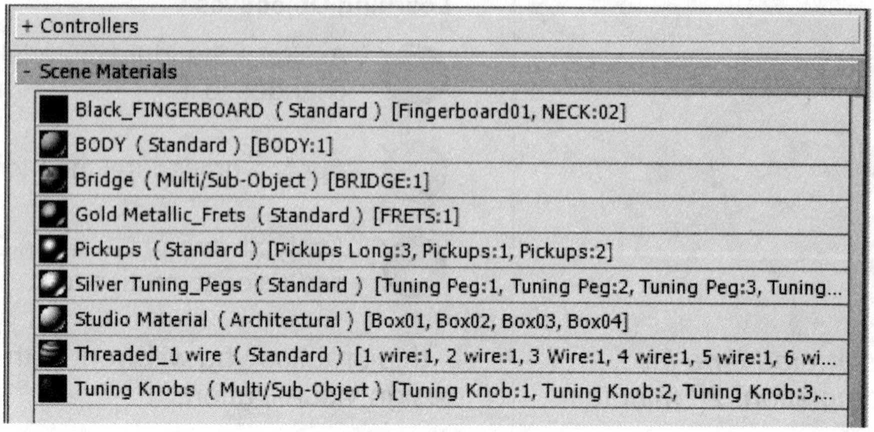

Figure 6–31

4. Each material name is listed and is followed by its material type that is listed in parentheses ( ). The square brackets [ ] at the end of the row indicates the scene object to which the material has been assigned.

You might need to expand (Lay Out All).

5. Note that all of these materials are also displayed in the *View1* sheet and are overlapping each other, as shown in Figure 6–32. In the Slate Material Editor toolbar, click (Lay Out All -Vertical) to display the materials vertically in the *View1* sheet.

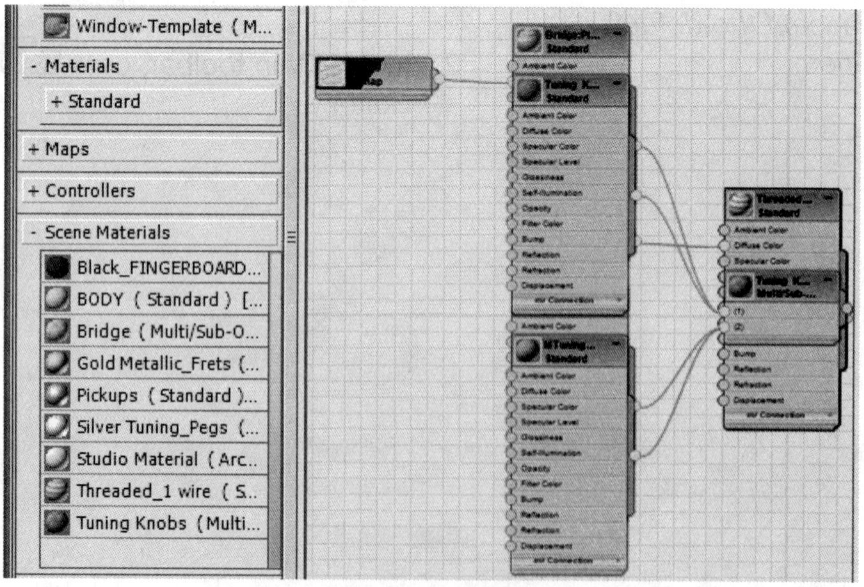

Figure 6–32

Task 2 - Change the material parameters.

1. In the *View1* sheet, use the mouse wheel to pan and zoom and locate the BODY Standard node. Verify that it displays **BODY Standard** in the title bar, as shown on the left in Figure 6–33. Double-click on the title bar heading to open its Parameter Editor, as shown on the right in Figure 6–33. Note that a white dashed border displays around the node in the *View1* sheet

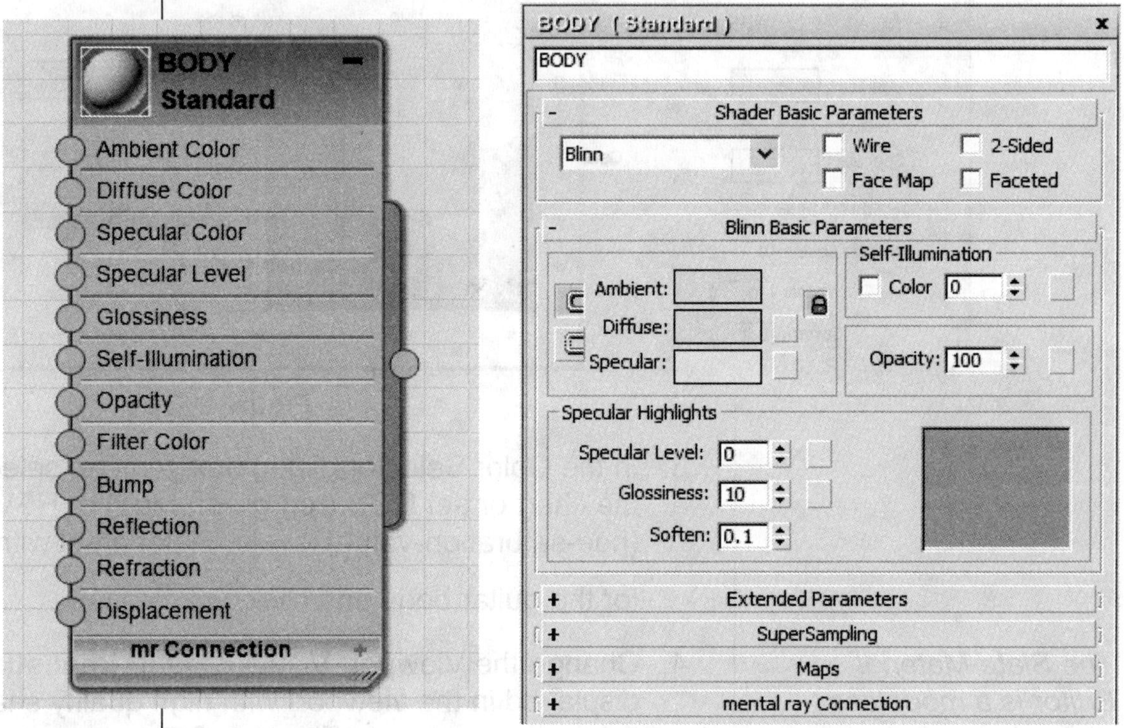

Figure 6–33

2. Note that the **Body** material is a Standard material that uses the Blinn shader. In the Blinn Basic Parameters rollout, select the Diffuse color swatch (currently gray) to open the Color Selector dialog box, as shown in Figure 6–34.

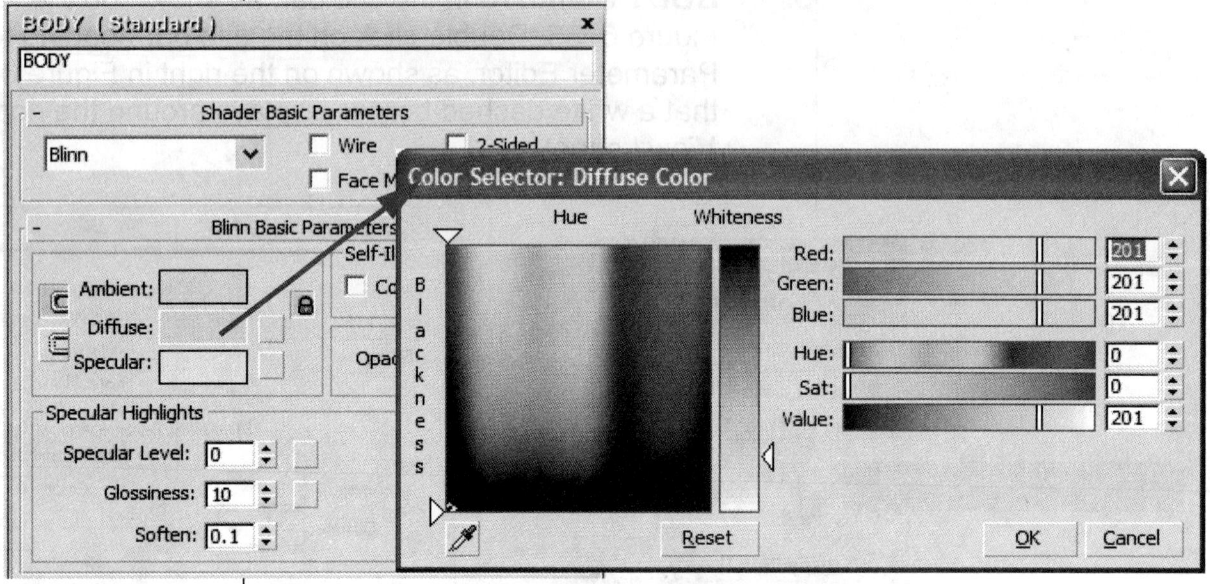

Figure 6–34

3. In the Color Selector dialog box you can select a color from the chart or set RGB (red-green-blue) or HSV (hue-saturation-value) levels. Experiment with different colors for the guitar body and click OK.

The Slate Material Editor is a modeless dialog box, which means it can remain open when you are working in the viewport or performing other operations that do not pertain to the dialog box.

4. Change the Viewport Visual Style to **Realistic**. The guitar is displayed in the viewport with high quality shading and lighting, as shown in Figure 6–35.

Figure 6–35

5. In the *Specular Highlights* area, the material's *Specular Level* is set to **0**, which is appropriate for a material that is not shiny. To simulate a shiny coating increase the *Specular Level* to **100,** as shown in Figure 6–36. Note the shiny coating on the guitar body.

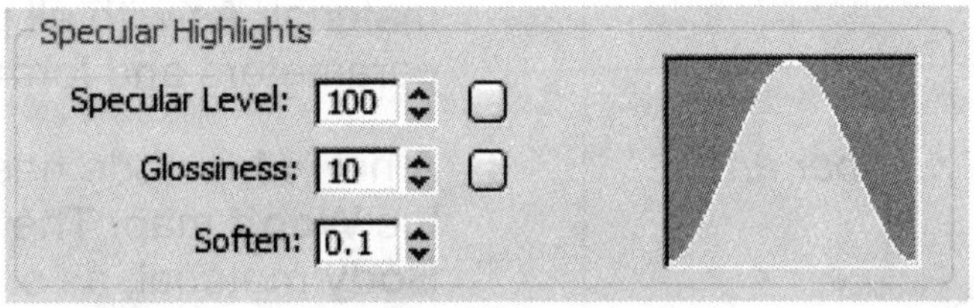

Figure 6–36

6. Change the *Glossiness* to **25**. Increasing the glossy value focuses the highlighting in a smaller area. You can also click  (Render Production) in the Main toolbar to see a more realistic rendered image. To render, you can also select **Rendering>Render**. Close the dialog box.

Task 3 - Applying a procedural map and image file.

A Procedural Map is generated algorithmically. It is not a digital photo or painting. Procedural Maps are useful for terrains or other objects where the texture should not repeat in a tiled pattern.

1. You will replace the Diffuse Color with a procedural map that represents a wood grain. In the Parameter Editor, expand the Maps rollout, as shown in Figure 6–37. Next to the **Diffuse Color** option, click None.

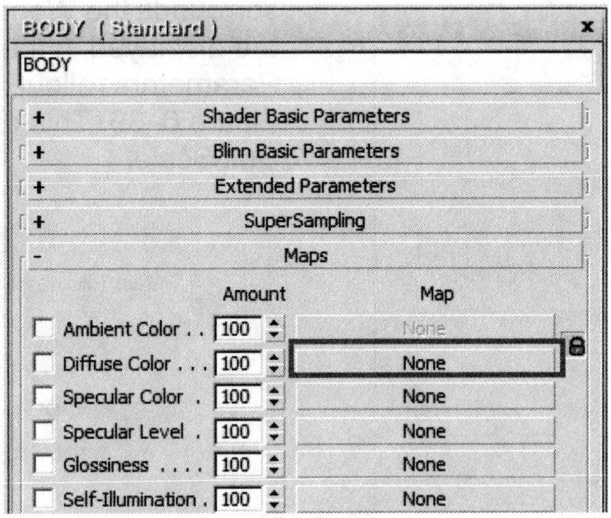

Figure 6–37

2. A separate Material/Map Browser opens displaying the custom library (if any), the *Maps* category, and the *Scene Materials* listing only the materials that contain maps. Expand the *Maps>Standard* categories and select **Wood**. Click 

to assign it as a map to the **BODY** Standard material. As with all procedural maps, **Wood** is defined by parameters and formulas, not an image file.

The Map number and name 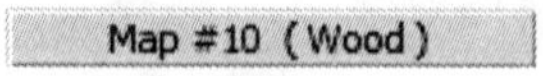

replaces 

for the Diffuse color in the Parameter Editor.

3. A new Map node has been added to *View1* that represents the **Wood** map. The node is wired to the Diffuse Color in the **Body** material, as shown in Figure 6–38. Note that the title bar of this node is green, indicating that the node is a Map node.

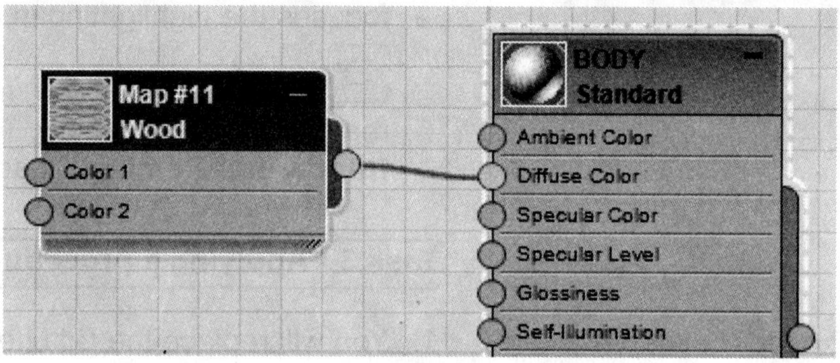

Figure 6–38

4. Double-click on the title bar heading for the Wood map to open its Parameter Editor. Note that a white dashed border surrounds the Wood Map node, indicating that its parameters are displayed in the Parameter Editor. In the Wood Parameters rollout, set *Grain Thickness* to **8**, as shown in Figure 6–39. This distance is measured in the file's System Unit Scale.

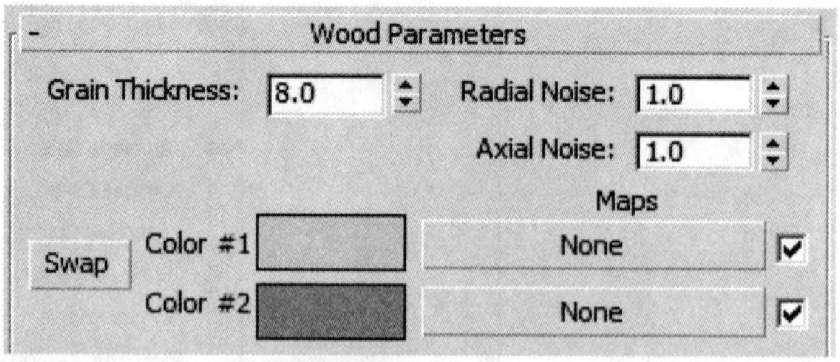

Figure 6–39

*A red and blue node indicates that the **Show Shaded Material in Viewport** option is selected for that material. A red and green node indicates that the **Show Shaded Material in Viewport** option is selected for that map.*

5. The wood grain does not display on the guitar body in the viewport. To display the map in the viewport, near the top of Slate Material Editor, click (Show Shaded Material in Viewport). The wood grain displays on the guitar body in the viewport but it is not accurate. Note that the title header of this node has changed to a half diagonal red area and the rest is green.

6. In the Main toolbar, click (Render Production) to render. The wood map is displayed on the body of the guitar, as shown in Figure 6–40. You can leave the Render dialog box open because it is a modeless dialog box.

Figure 6–40

- Note that the display in the viewport is not identical to the rendered display. This is typical of procedural maps. Procedural maps offer some interesting parameter-driven maps, which maintain the wood grain into the third dimension (across the top of the guitar body).

7. You will replace the procedural **Wood** map with an image file. In the *View1* sheet, double-click on the title bar heading for the **BODY** material to open its Parameter Editor. Expand the Maps rollout, if required. Right-click on Map #10 (Wood), and select **Clear**. Alternatively, you can drag any None onto it. Note that in the *View1* sheet, the wiring between the BODY material node and the Wood map node has been deleted.

8. Click None next to the **Diffuse Color** to open its specific Material/Map Browser.

9. In the Material/Map Browser, double-click on Bitmap in the *Maps>Standard* categories, as shown in Figure 6–41.

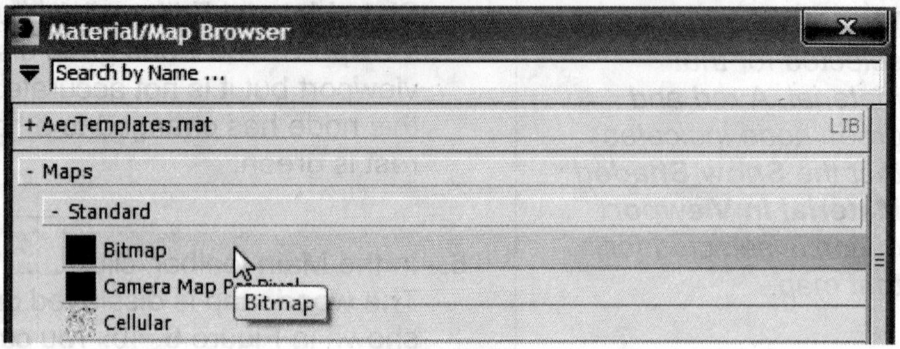

Figure 6–41

You can delete the unused node by clicking its title bar heading and pressing <Delete>. This keeps the active sheet clean. It also removes the material from the active sheet only.

10. The Select Bitmap Image File dialog box opens. Browse to your *Class Files* folder and open the *Maps* folder. Select **GuitarDiffuse.jpg** and click Open. A new node for Bitmap is added to the *View1* sheet. The new Bitmap node and Wood Map node might overlap. Select the header of one of the nodes to move them apart. Note that the wire from the Diffuse Color input socket of the BODY material node is connected to the output socket of the new Bitmap node, as shown in Figure 6–42.

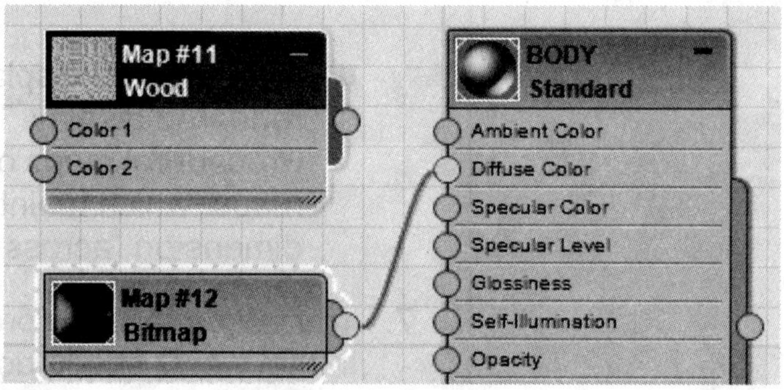

Figure 6–42

11. Double-click on the Bitmap node title bar to display its Parameter Editor. In the Coordinates rollout, clear the **Use Real-World Scale** and set the *Tiling* to 1.0 in both **U** and **V**, as shown in Figure 6–43.

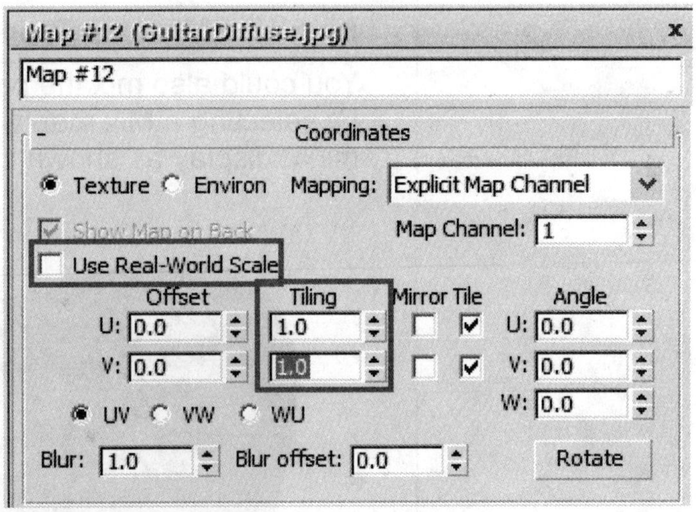

Figure 6–43

12. Click  (Show Shaded Material in Viewport) again to display the **BODY** material with the new map in the viewport.

13. In the Render dialog box, click , which is located near the top right corner, to display the effect, as shown in Figure 6–44. If you closed the Render dialog box, open it again from the Main toolbar by clicking  (Render Production). Leave the dialog box open.

Figure 6–44

Hint: Use Mix Map Type

You could also mix the procedural wood grain with the bitmap by selecting a Mix map type. The mix material on the guitar might display as shown in Figure 6–45.

Figure 6–45

14. You will use a Color Correction map along with the Bitmap. In the Material/Map Browser, open the *Maps>Standard* categories. Double-click on the Color Correction map. A new node for Color Correction is added to *View1*, as shown in Figure 6–46. To relocate a node in the active sheet, hold and drag the title bar heading.

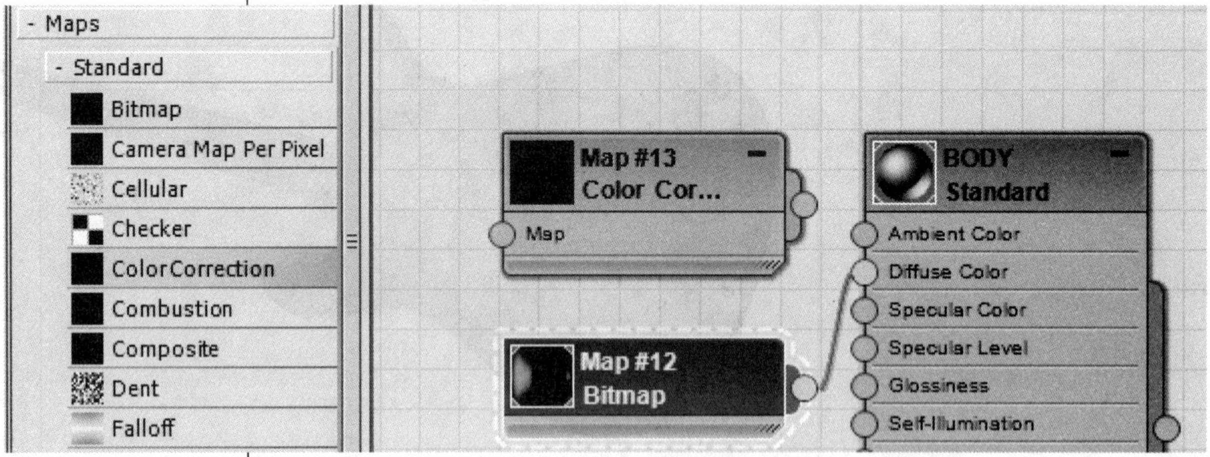

Figure 6–46

15. Select the red wire that connects the Bitmap node to the Diffuse Color of the **BODY** material, press <Delete>.

The input socket of Color correction is used for a Map.

16. For the Bitmap node (**Map # Bitmap**), select the material output socket (right socket) and drag/drop the wire to the material input socket (left socket) for the Color Correction node (**Map # Color Correction**), as shown in Figure 6–47. Note that the wired slots display in green.

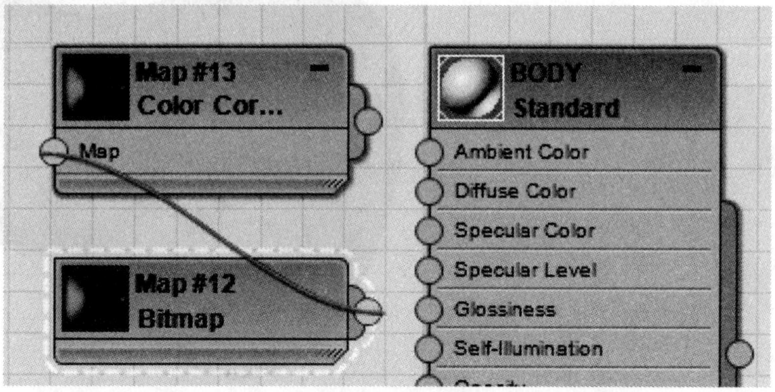

Figure 6–47

17. Select (material output socket) for the Color Correction node and drag the wire to the material input socket for the Diffuse Color entry in the BODY material node, as shown in Figure 6–48.

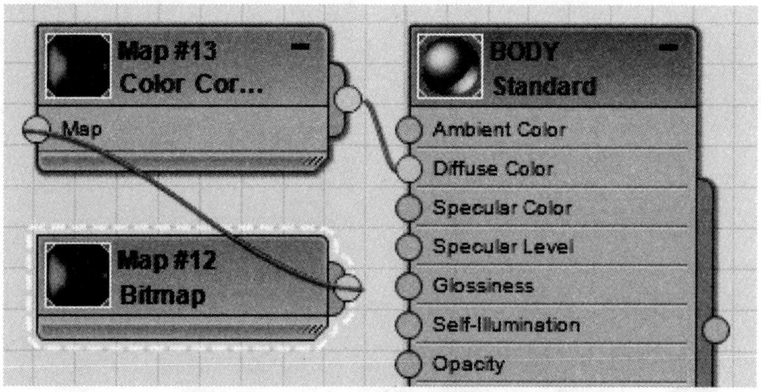

Figure 6–48

18. Select the Color Correction heading and then click (Show Shaded Material in Viewport) to display the map on the guitar in the viewport.

19. Double-click on the Color Correction heading to open its Parameter Editor. In the Color rollout, change the *Hue Shift* slider and note that the guitar changes color interactively in the viewport. Set the slider at any color (such as a green color hue).

20. In the Render dialog box, click Render to render the scene, as shown in Figure 6–49.

Figure 6–49

21. Save your work as **MyGuitar.max**.

Practice 6c Working with Multi/Sub-Object Materials

Learning Objectives

- Create a Multi/Sub-Object material having different materials on different material ID's.
- Assign different materials to specific faces of a single object using material ID numbers.

Estimated time for completion: 20 minutes

In this practice you will work with Multi/Sub-Object materials.

You must set the paths to locate the External files and Xrefs used in the practice. If you have not done this already, return to the **Introduction to Autodesk 3ds Max Design** chapter and complete Task 1 to Task 3 of the **Organizing Folders and Working with the Interface** practice. You only have to set the user paths once.

Task 1 - Identify and Apply Multi/Sub-Object Materials.

If a dialog box opens prompting you about a Mismatch, click OK *to accept the default values.*

1. Open **Interior Model.max** from your *Class Files* folder.
2. In the Main toolbar, click to open the Slate Material Editor.
3. In the Material/Map Browser, expand the *Scene Materials* categories (scroll down to the bottom of the list). Note that six of the materials in the scene are Multi/Sub-Object materials.

4. Click, drag, and drop the **Curtain Wall Doors** material on **PivotDoor07** (door on the left side of the model), as shown in Figure 6–50. Hover the cursor over the object to display its name as a tooltip. You can leave the Slate Material Editor open because it is a modeless dialog box.

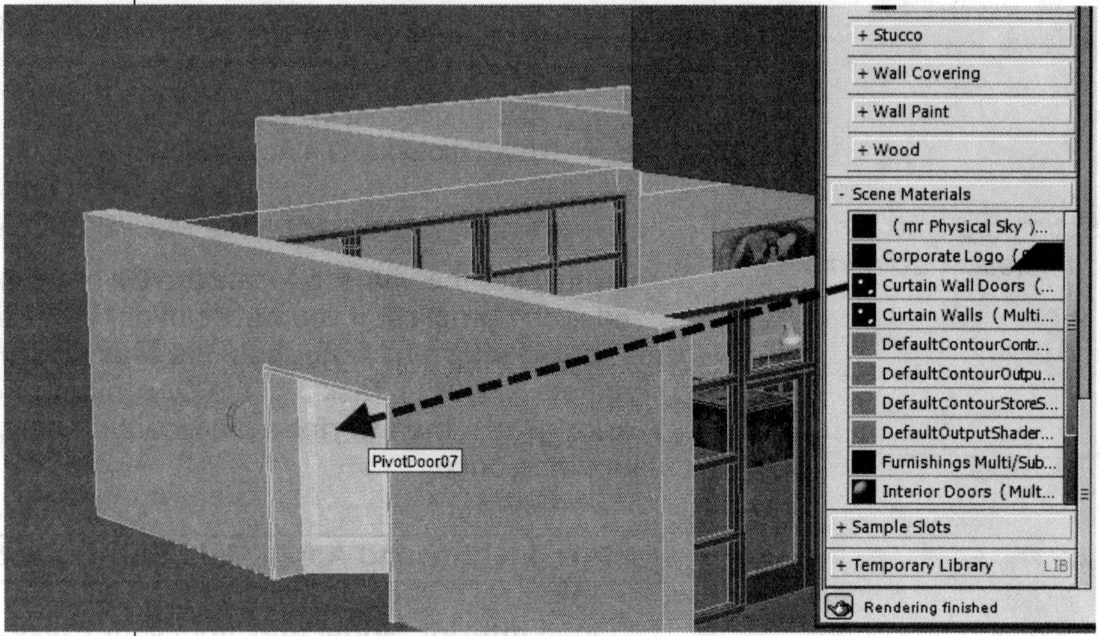

Figure 6–50

5. Select **PivotDoor07** object and click (Zoom Extents Selected) to zoom into the selected object. The doors have glass panels and solid frames, as shown in Figure 6–51.

Figure 6–51

Task 2 - Create a Multi/Sub-Object Material.

In this task, you will create your own Multi/Sub-Object material for your wall system. Most of the walls will have the **Paint – Beige Matte** material. In addition some of the outside faces will be assigned an Autodesk material while other interior faces will be given an accent paint color.

1. In the Material/Map Browser, expand the *Materials> Standard* categories. Double-click on Multi/Sub-Object or drag an instance of it to add it to the *View1* sheet, as shown in Figure 6–52.

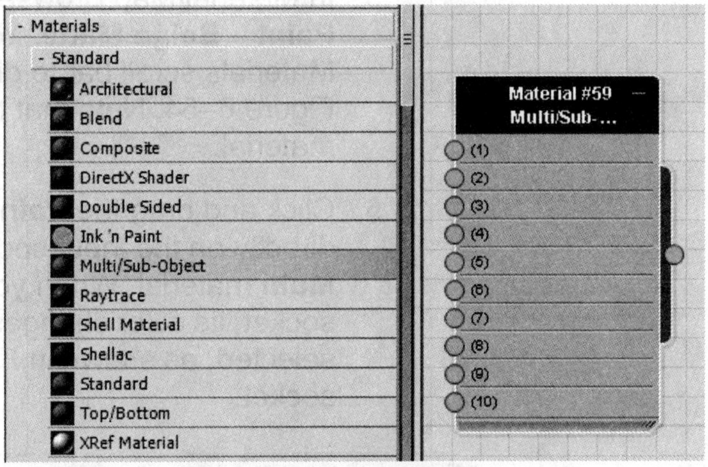

Figure 6–52

2. Right-click on the title bar heading for the new material, and select **Rename**, as shown in Figure 6–53.

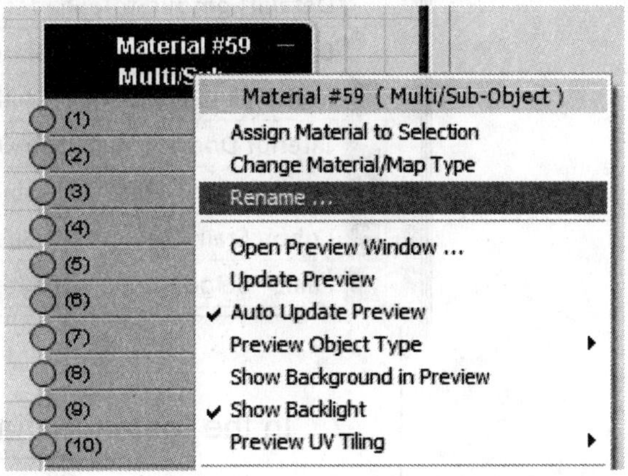

Figure 6–53

3. Enter **Wall Multi** and click OK.

4. There are ten default slots in a Multi/Sub-Object material. This material only requires five slots. You can set the number of materials by double-clicking on the Wall Multi material title bar to open its Parameter Editor. Click Set Number, enter **5** in the *Number of Materials* edit box and click OK.
   - You will use an instanced copy of the **Paint – Beige Matte** material present in the scene for your sub-material 3. (This material displays dark brown in this practice but will look more like beige when lights are added to the scene.)

5. In Material/Map Browser, in *Scene Materials* category, locate **Paint – Beige Matte**. You might need to use the Scene Materials scroll bar to display all of the materials as shown in Figure 6–54. Note that this material is an Architectural material.

6. Click and drag the **Paint – Beige Matte** material and place it directly on the input socket 3 (for sub-material 3) in the **Wall Multi** material. When you move your cursor on top of the socket, its color changes to green indicating that the socket is selected, as shown in Figure 6–54. Drop the material on this socket.

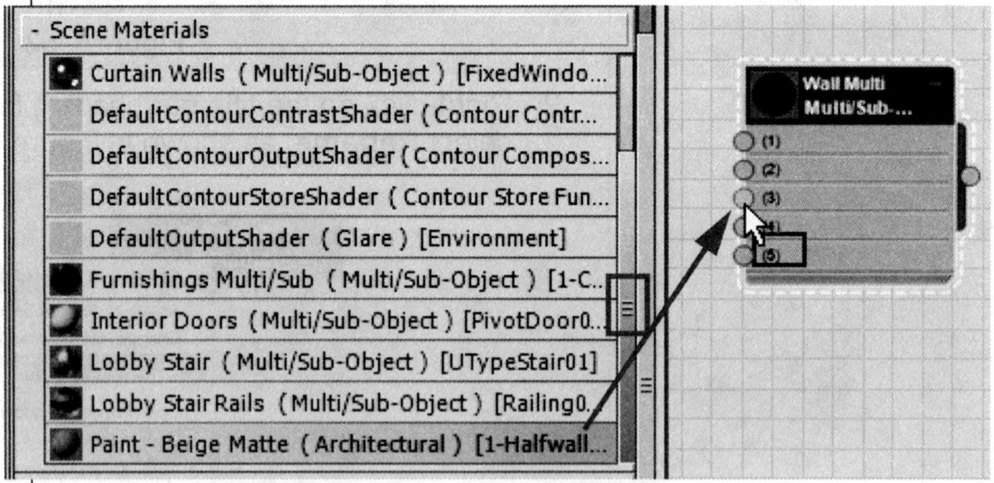

Figure 6–54

7. In the Instance dialog box, verify that **Instance** is selected and click OK. Instance will use the same material that is already applied to other objects in the scene. If you select **Copy**, a separate copy of the material is created with no link to the original material.

8. The Paint – Beige Matte material node is wired to slot 3 of **Wall Multi** material. Use the pan and zoom (middle mouse button) to display both the material nodes in the *View1* sheet.

9. Verify that the Wall Multi (Multi/Sub-Object material) node has a white dashed boundary indicating that its Parameter Editor is displayed. Note that the **Paint – Beige Matte** material is displayed on the 3 ID slot, as shown in Figure 6–55.

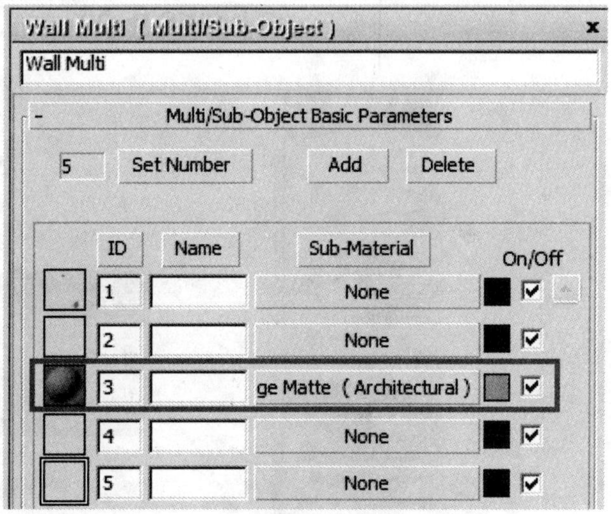

Figure 6–55

10. In the Material/Map Browser, expand the *Autodesk Material Library>Finish* categories and browse for the **Paint- Varnish** material.

11. You will place this material on ID 5 of the **Wall Multi** (Multi/Sub-Object) material. Click and drag the **Paint-Varnish** material onto the Wall Multi Parameter Editor and release it over None next to *ID* slot **5**. Note that the **Paint- Varnish** material is wired to slot 5 of the **Wall Multi** material. Alternatively, you can place the **Paint-Varnish** material on the *View1* sheet and wire it to slot 5.

    - Note that you cannot drag and drop Autodesk materials on the input socket for sub-material 5 directly in the *View1* sheet as you did with the **Paint-Beige Matte** scene material. You need to use the Parameter Editor.

12. All of the nodes might not be visible and might be overlapping each other in the active sheet (View1). In the Slate Material Editor toolbar, click (Lay Out All - Vertical) to arrange all of the sub-materials vertically, as shown on the left in Figure 6–56. Note that in the active view, the input socket 5 of Wall Multi material node is wired to the output socket of the Finish (Paint Varnish) material node. Also, note that in the Parameter Editor of the **Wall Multi** material, the ID5 slot now displays **Finish (Autodesk Generic)**, as shown on the right in Figure 6–56.

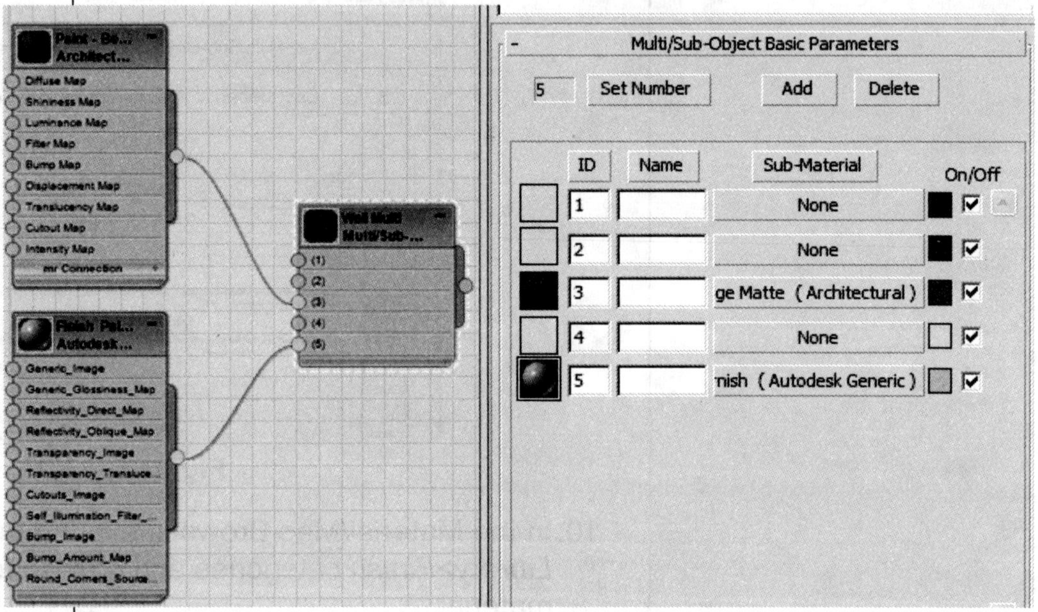

Figure 6–56

13. You will copy and adjust the **Paint – Beige Matte** material into an accent paint material. In Material/Map Browser, in *Scene Materials* category, click and drag the **Paint – Beige Matte** material and place it on the input socket for sub-material 4 in the **Wall Multi** material.

14. In the Instance dialog box, select **Copy** and click OK.

15. In the Slate Material Editor menu bar, click (Lay Out All - Vertical), if required.

16. Double-click on the title bar heading for the new **Paint – Beige Matte** material (slot 4) to open its Parameter Editor.

17. Change the material name to **Paint – Accent**, as shown in Figure 6–57.

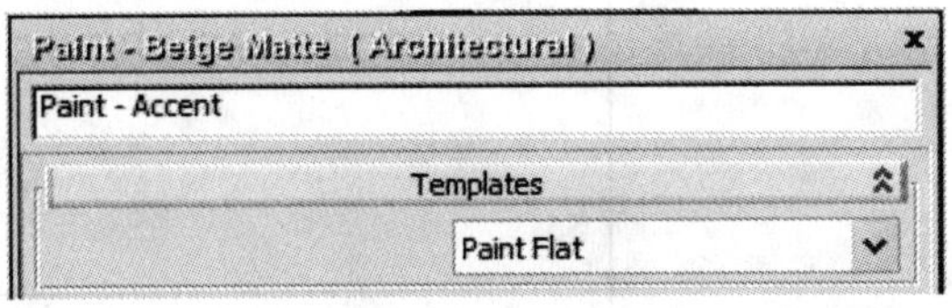

Figure 6–57

18. In the Physical Qualities rollout, select the Diffuse Color swatch. In the Color Selector set *Value* as **255** and press <Enter>. The color changes, as shown in Figure 6–58, and click .

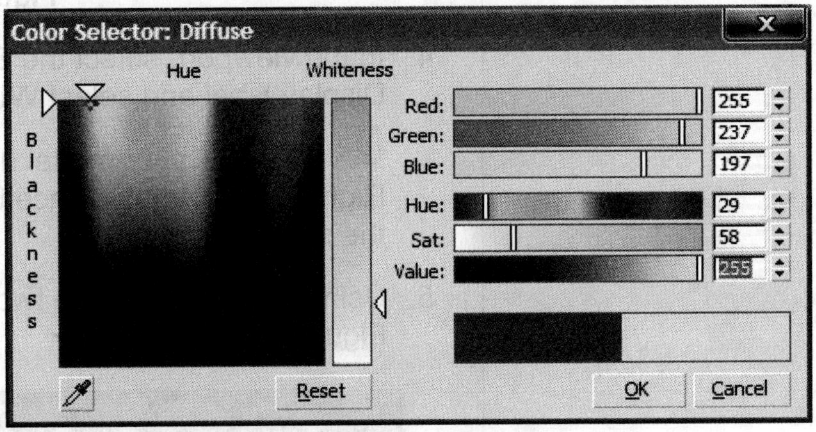

Figure 6–58

19. Close the Slate Material Editor.

Task 3 - Assign Material ID Numbers to the Wall System.

In this task, you will assign material ID numbers to certain faces that correspond with your Multi/Sub-Object material IDs.

1. Verify that the Perspective viewport is active. Zoom out and pan so that the entire model is displayed in the viewport.

2. Click in empty space to clear any selection. Press <H> to open the Select From Scene dialog box. In the dialog box toolbar, click  (Display None) and then click  (Display Geometry). Select **Layer:VIZ-1-Walls** and click . All of the walls in the lower floor are selected.

3. Select the *Modify* panel () and note that it is an Editable Mesh in the Modifier Stack. Select the **Polygon** Sub-object mode, as shown in Figure 6–59.

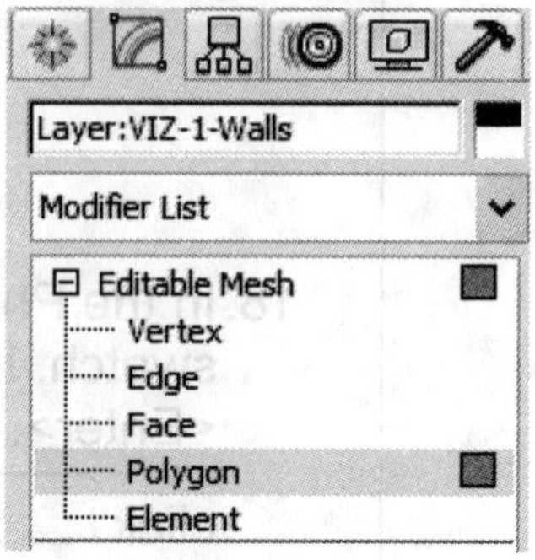

Figure 6–59

4. In the viewport, select the **Shaded + Edged Face** Visual Display label and select **Wireframe** in the menu. Also use  (Orbit) till your model displays as shown in Figure 6–60. Right-click in empty space to exit the command and maintain the selection.

5. Using <Ctrl>, select the two polygons as shown in Figure 6–60.

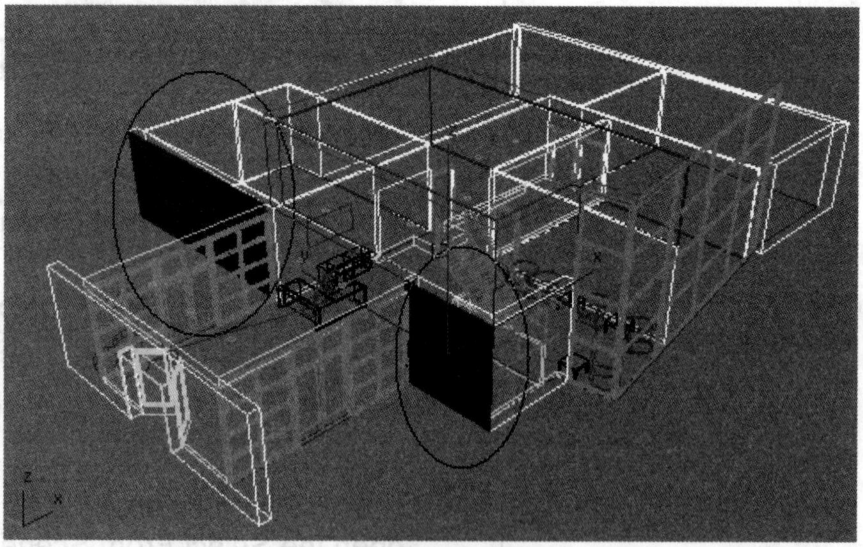

Figure 6–60

6. In the Command Panel, in the Surface Properties rollout, in the *Material* area, set *Set ID* to **5** and press <Enter>. *Select ID* also changes to **5**, as shown in Figure 6–61. This sets the selected polygons to ID 5. This will associate the Finish (Autodesk Material) with those two walls.

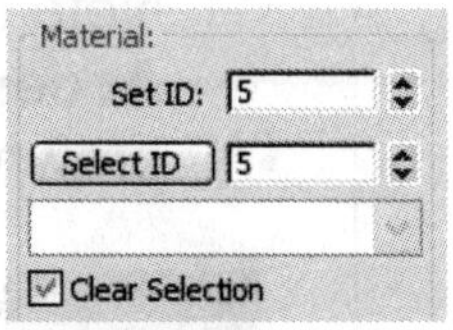

Figure 6–61

7. Clear the selection of the two walls, select the polygon as shown in Figure 6–62, set *Set ID* to **4**, and press <Enter>. This will associate the **Beige - Accent** material with this wall.

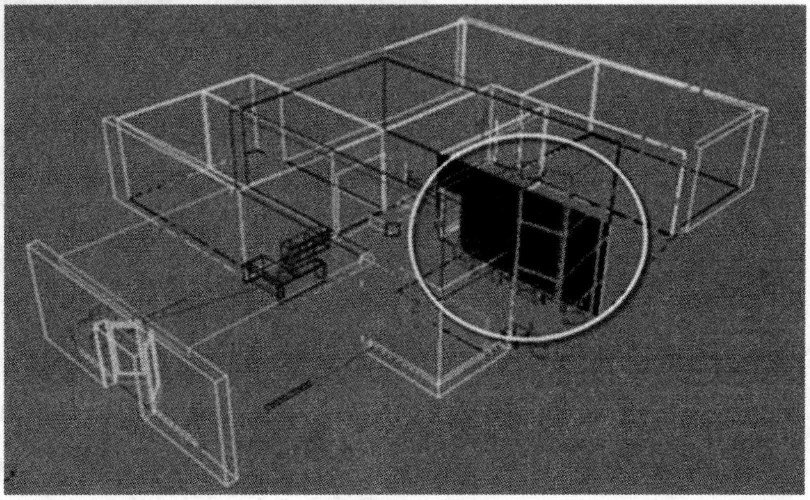

Figure 6–62

8. In the Command Panel, select **Editable Mesh** to exit Sub-object mode.
9. Change the visual display to **Shaded + Edged Faces** by selecting the **Wireframe** label and selecting **Shaded**. There is no change in the model because the material has not yet been assigned.
10. With the wall object (**Layer:VIZ-1-Walls**) still selected, open the Slate Material Editor, select the Wall Multi material title bar heading in the *View1* sheet. In the Slate Material Editor toolbar, click  (Assign material to Selection), as shown in Figure 6–63.

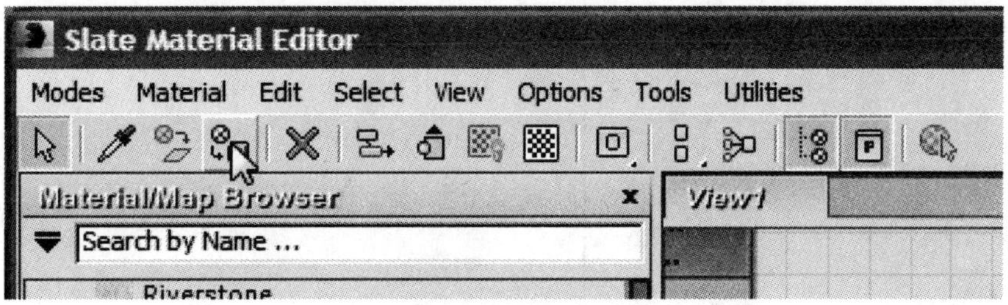

Figure 6–63

11. Note that the interior wall displays in light beige (**Paint – Accent**) and the two exterior brick walls display in grayish brown (**Paint- Varnish**), as shown in Figure 6–64.

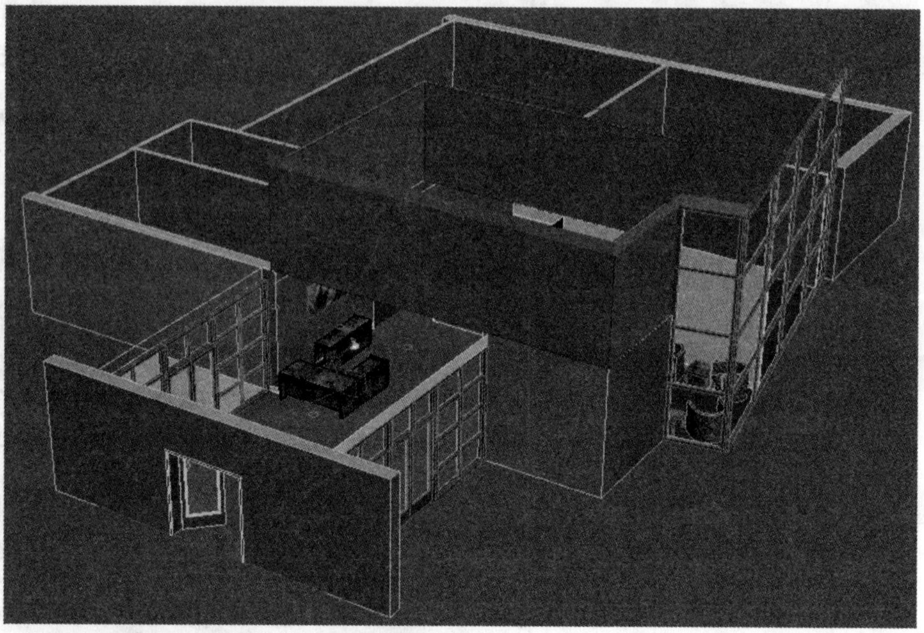

Figure 6–64

12. Open the Slate Material Editor and double-click on the Finish Paint - Varnish title node to open its Parameter Editor.

13. In the Generic rollout, select the Color bar to open the Color Selector. Change the color to a different one, such as red. In the viewport, note that only the color of the two walls that have ID 5 changes. This indicates that your **Multi-Sub -Object** materials have been applied.

14. Save the file as **MyInteriorModelMultiMaterials.max**.

6.7 Opacity, Bump, and Reflection Mapping

Learning Objectives

- Understand how transparency is controlled using Opacity mapping.
- Understand how an embossed or pitted appearance is obtained using Bump mapping.
- Understand how a glass or mirror effect is obtained using the Reflection mapping.

To add detailed objects to a scene, it is recommended to use a simple object with materials and textures applied to it rather than using a complex geometry object. For example, leaves on trees or a chain link fence can be generated using a simple model with mapped textures and materials rather that creating it with complex geometry.

Opacity Mapping

Opacity mapping controls the transparency, as shown with the lace curtains in Figure 6–65.

Figure 6–65

To create an Opacity map, simply add a map to the *Opacity map* channel, under the Maps rollout of the material.

The black to white values are mapped to the transparent state, where black creates a hole (completely invisible) and white makes a surface (100% opaque). Grays create a semi-transparent effect, good for clouds and fabrics. If a color image is used as an opacity map, the RGB color is ignored and only the Luminance value is used. Opacity maps are usually created by taking digital photos and manipulating them in other programs.

Hint: Two-sided Opacity Mapped Material

When you create an opacity mapped material, make the material two-sided to see the backsides of faces if looking inside/through an object.

Bump Mapping

Bump mapping gives the illusion of an embossed or pitted surface without actual geometry having to be present on the model, as shown for a braided carpet in Figure 6–66. As with Opacity mapping, it uses black to white values to generate the appearance of a raised surface. The white value raises the surface fully and the black value does not raise the surface at all. When combined with texture mapping it helps the scene lighting integrate with the textures to place shadows in cracks, and generally add a veneer of three-dimensionality to the surfaces. It is the hidden detail that creates the most striking effects.

Figure 6–66

Reflection Mapping

Reflection mapping gives a surface the ability to mirror the world surrounding the object, as shown on the glass on the right in Figure 6–67. The environment and objects in the scene are visible. The clouds on the windows of a high rise are a typical example. Reflection mapping can be generated by a number of different methods. Using Standard materials, you can place a bitmap or a reflection map type in the *Reflection map* channel. If you add a bitmap to the *Reflection map* channel, the faces reflect the bitmap based on shininess and scene lighting. If you add a Reflect/Refract or Raytrace map, the objects in the scene reflect along with the environment. Raytrace and mental ray materials also can be used to generate realistic reflections in your scene.

Figure 6–67

Practice 6d Opacity and Bump Mapping

Learning Objectives

- Assign a Diffuse Color texture map to an object.
- Assign an Opacity map to an object to display the cutouts.
- Assign a Bump map to an object to make the texture display realistic.
- Add a map to the *Specular Level* channel to add shininess to the texture.

Estimated time for completion: 15 minutes

In this practice you will create a chain link fence using opacity and bump mapping.

You must set the paths to locate the External files and Xrefs used in the practice. If you have not done this already, return to the **Introduction to Autodesk 3ds Max Design** chapter and complete Task 1 to Task 3 of the **Organizing Folders and Working with the Interface** practice. You only have to set the user paths once.

Task 1 - Assign the texture map.

If a dialog box opens prompting you about a Mismatch, click OK to accept the default values.

1. Open **start_chainlink.max** from your *Class Files* folder.
2. In the viewport, select the object Line01 (yellow fence object).
3. In the Main toolbar, click to open the Slate Material Editor.
4. In the Material/Map Browser, expand the *Materials>Standard* categories. In the list, double-click on the Standard material to add it to the *View1* sheet.
5. Assign this Standard material to the selected fence object by clicking (Assign Material to Selection) in the Material Editor toolbar. Verify that the fence object displays in gray in the viewport.

6. In the *View1* sheet, double-click on the Standard material title bar heading to open its Parameter Editor. In the Blinn Basic Parameters rollout, next to *Diffuse* swatch, click (None), as shown in Figure 6–68, to open a separate Material/Map Browser.

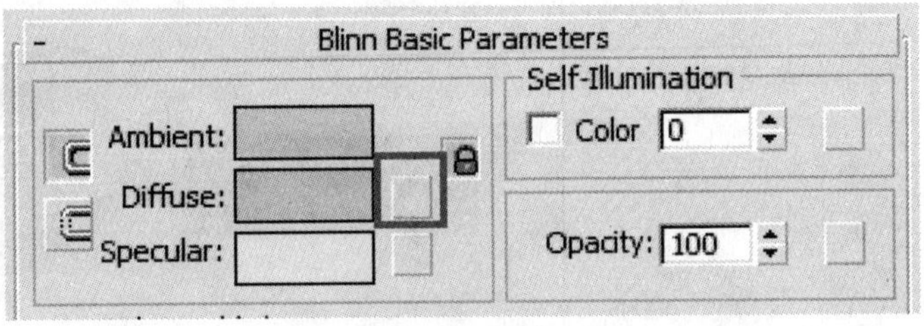

Figure 6–68

7. Expand the *Maps>Standard* categories and double-click on Bitmap, as shown in Figure 6–69.

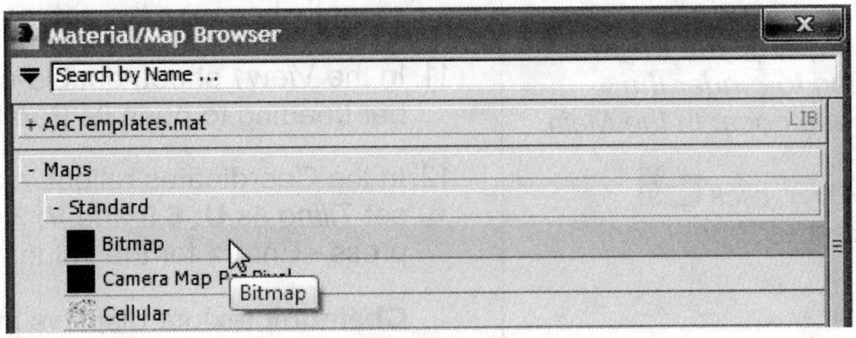

Figure 6–69

8. In the Select Bitmap Image File dialog box, in your *Class Files* folder, open the *Maps* subfolder.

> **Hint: Autodesk Maps**
>
> The Autodesk Maps are also available and can be found under *C:\Program Files\Autodesk\3ds Max Design 2014\maps*.

9. Select **Chain-link.bump.jpg** and click Open. Note that in the Parameter Editor the icon changes to M, as shown in Figure 6–70. Also note that in *View1* sheet, the output socket of the Bitmap node is wired to the Diffuse Color input socket of the Standard material, as shown in Figure 6–70.

Figure 6–70

If the texture does not display in the viewport after clicking (Show Shaded Material in Viewport), you might need to render the scene once. In the Main toolbar, click (Render Production).

10. In the Slate Material Editor toolbar, click (Show Shaded Material in Viewport). The **Chainlink** texture should display on the Line01 object in the viewport, but does not display properly because the settings need to be changed.

11. In the *View1* sheet, double-click on the Map #0 Bitmap title bar heading to open its Parameter Editor.

12. In the Coordinates rollout, clear **Use Real-World Scale** and set *Tiling* as **U: 6.0** and **V: 3.0**, as shown in Figure 6–71 and press <Enter> for the values to take affect. Note how the **Chainlink** texture displays in the viewport. Click (Show Shaded Material in Viewport) to display the map in the viewport.

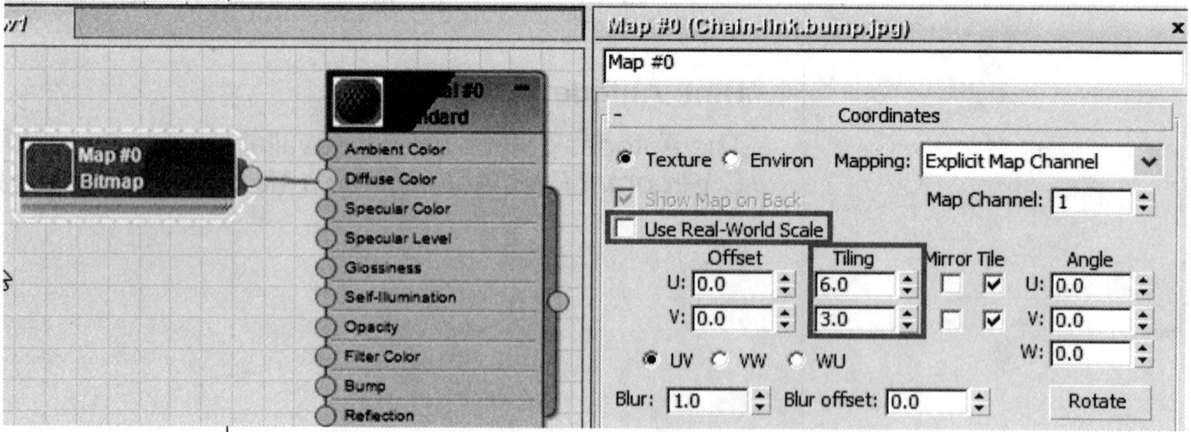

Figure 6–71

13. In the Main toolbar, click (Render Production). The map displays in the rendered window. Leave it open.

14. Change the background color of the rendering by selecting **Rendering>Environment**. In the *Background* area, select the color swatch as shown in Figure 6–72. In the Color Selector, select a new color (cyan) and click **OK**. Close the Environment and Effects dialog box.

Figure 6–72

15. In the Render dialog box, click **Render**. The Render window should display as shown in Figure 6–73. Leave the Render dialog box open.

Figure 6–73

Task 2 - Assign the Opacity map.

1. In the Slate Material Editor, in the *View1* sheet, double-click on the Standard material title bar heading to open its Parameter Editor, if required.

2. Expand the Maps rollout and note that chainlink map has already been applied to the *Diffuse* channel. To control the transparency you need to apply the map to the *Opacity* channel. Click [None] for **Opacity**, as shown in Figure 6–74.

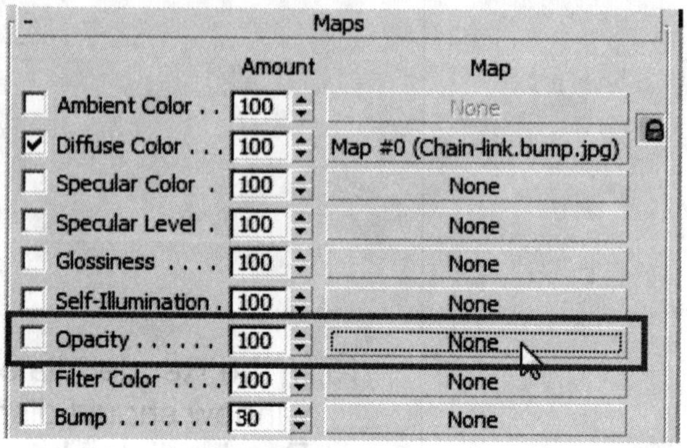

Figure 6–74

3. In the Material/Map Browser, expand the *Maps>Standard* categories. Double-click on Bitmap to open the Select Bitmap Image File dialog box. Open **Chain-link.cutout.jpg** (from your *Class Files* folder>*Maps* subfolder) and click [Open]. Note that this bitmap is wired to **Opacity** in Standard material. It also replaces [None] in the Maps rollout of the Parameter Editor.

The Tiling settings for the Diffuse map and the Opacity map should be the same so that they overlap each other for the cutout to display properly.

4. In the *View1* sheet, double-click on Map #1 Bitmap (Opacity) title bar heading to open its Parameter Editor. In the Coordinates rollout, clear **Use Real-World Scale** and set the *Tiling* to **U: 6.0** and **V: 3.0**, as shown in Figure 6–75 and press <Enter>.

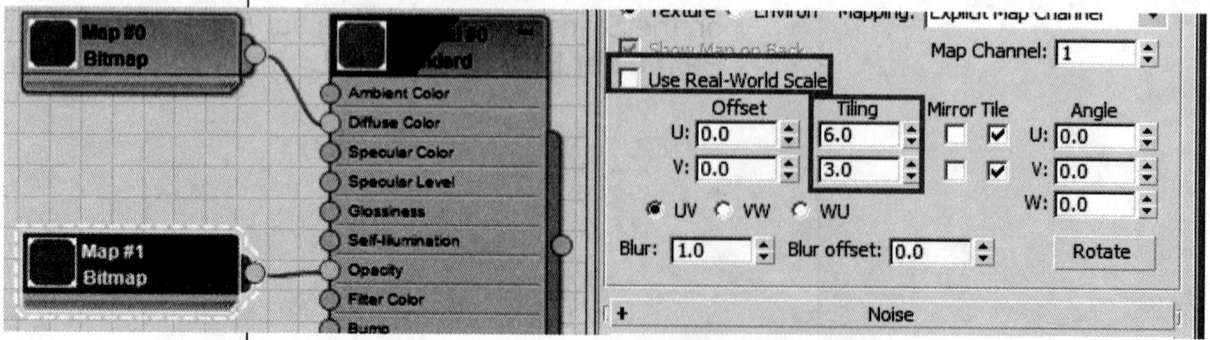

Figure 6–75

5. In the Render dialog box, click **Render** to render the scene. Note that the background is displayed through the fence, as shown in Figure 6–76. This is caused by the map on the *Opacity* channel. The chainlink in your rendering might display a little lighter in color than that shown in Figure 6–76.

Figure 6–76

6. Close the Render Window.

Task 3 - Assign the Bump map.

1. In the Slate Material Editor, in the *View1* sheet, double-click on the Standard material title bar heading to open its Parameter Editor. In the Maps rollout, click **None** for **Bump**.

*You can also drag and drop the map from the Diffuse channel onto the Opacity channel and select **Copy** in the dialog box.*

2. In the Material/Map Browser, expand the *Maps>Standard* categories and double-click on Bitmap to open the Select Bitmap Image File dialog box. Open **Chain-link.bump.jpg** (from your *Class Files* folder>*Maps* subfolder). Note that this bitmap is displayed on the **Bump** button, as shown in Figure 6–77 (the same map was used on the *Diffuse Color* channel). Note that in the *View1* sheet, it is wired to **Bump** in Standard material, as shown in Figure 6–77.

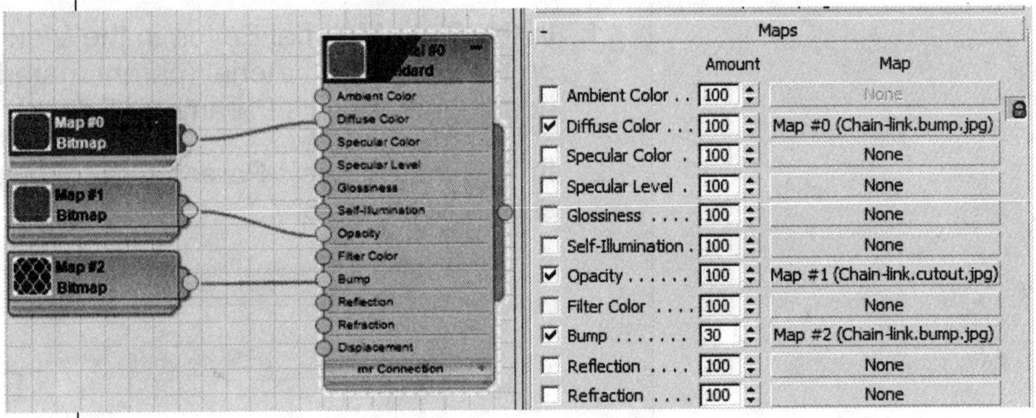

Figure 6–77

If you copied the map, the settings are also copied and you are not required to enter the Tiling values.

3. In the *View1* sheet, double-click on the Map #2 Bitmap (*Bump* channel) title bar heading to open its Parameter Editor. In the Coordinates rollout, clear **Use Real-World Scale** and set the *Tiling* to **U: 6.0** and **V: 3.0**. Click (Render Production) to render the scene.

4. To make the chain link more realistic (smaller cutouts), set the *Tiling* values for the three maps to **U: 18** and **V: 11**. Double-click on each map title bar heading to open its Parameter Editor and change the values.

5. Click (Render Production) to render the scene. The rendered scene is shown in Figure 6–78.

Figure 6–78

6. Click (Orbit) and navigate in the viewport to the other side of the chain link fence. Click (Render Production) to render again. The chain link has disappeared. The material needs to be two-sided to render on both sides. Leave the Render window open.

Task 4 - Make the material 2-sided.

1. In the Slate Material Editor, in the *View1* sheet, double-click on the Standard material (parent material node) title bar heading to open its Parameter Editor.

2. In the Shader Basic Parameters rollout, select **2-Sided**, as shown in Figure 6–79.

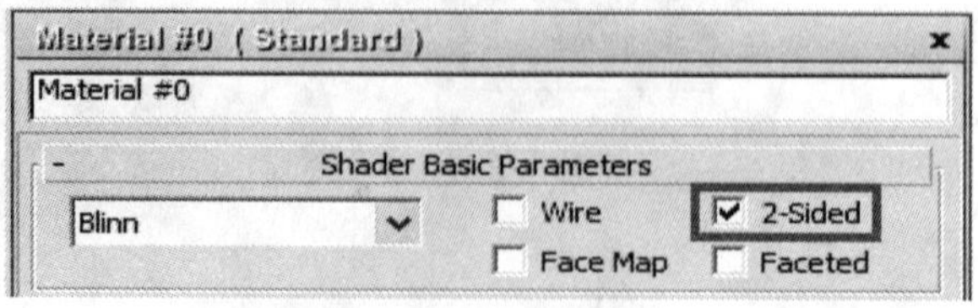

Figure 6–79

3. In the viewport, use (Orbit) to navigate to the back side of the chain link fence, if you are not already on that side. In the Render dialog box, click Render to render the scene. It should render correctly, as shown in Figure 6–80. There is no light on this side, so the rendering might display dark.

Figure 6–80

4. In the viewport, navigate back to the front side of the fence.

Task 5 - Assign the Specular Level Map.

1. In the Slate Material Editor, in the *View1* sheet, double-click on the Standard material (parent material node) title bar heading to open its Parameter Editor, if not already open.

2. In the Blinn Basic Parameters rollout, in the *Specular Highlights* area, set the *Specular Level* to **100**. Render again. The entire fence becomes shiny, as shown in Figure 6–81. You need to use Specular Level mapping instead. Change the *Specular Level* back to 0.

Figure 6–81

3. Expand the Maps rollout, click and drag the map **Chain-link.bump.jpg** from the *Diffuse Color* channel and drop it on the *Specular Level* channel, as shown in Figure 6–82.

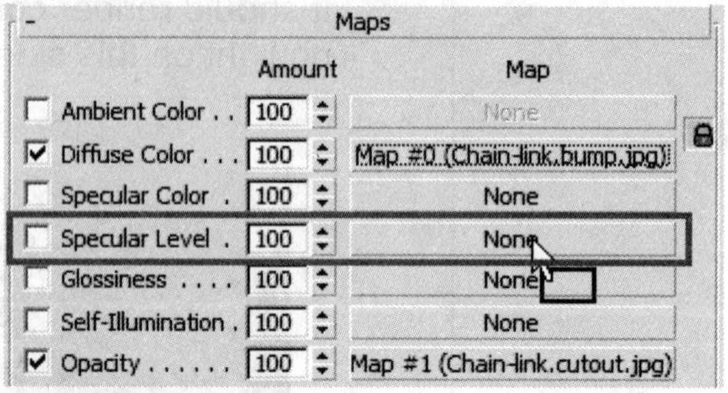

Figure 6–82

4. In the Copy dialog box, select **Instance** and click OK.

   Click (Render Production). The chainlink fence displays with shininess in the correct way, as shown in Figure 6–83.

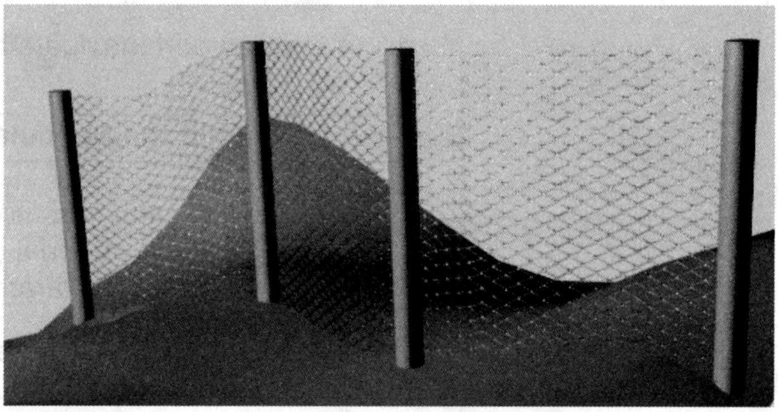

Figure 6–83

5. Save your work as **MyChainLinkFence.max**.

6.8 mental ray Materials

Learning Objectives

- Understand the mental ray materials present in the software.
- Understand the attributes of different types of mental ray materials.

The mental ray materials have been created to be used with mental ray renderer. The mental ray renderer is created by NVIDIA and has been used for years in the film industry. You can achieve high-quality images using mental ray with the capability of generating accurate lighting effects.

The mental ray material list is displayed in the Material/Map Browser if the NVIDIA mental ray, NVIDIA iray, or Quicksilver Hardware Renderer is assigned to be the current renderer. To make the mental ray renderer current, select **Rendering> Render Setup**. In the *Common* tab, expand the Assign Renderer rollout. Click [...] next to the *Production* field and select **NVIDIA mental ray**.

The material types for mental ray are available in the Material/Map Browser, in the *Materials>mental ray* categories, as shown in Figure 6–84.

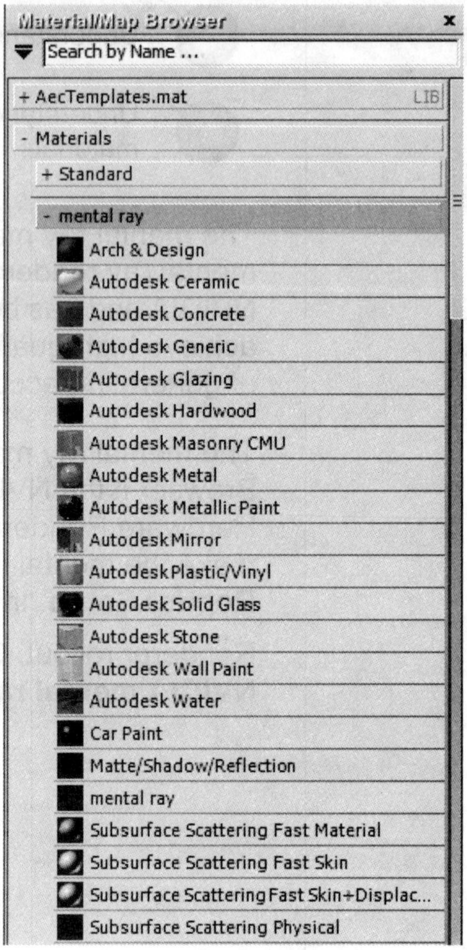

Figure 6–84

You can modify any of the mental ray materials in the same way as the Standard materials are modified.

Arch & Design Materials

The Arch & Design material type is the most commonly used; it can be used to create most design visualization materials. Within the Arch & Design material you can select from over 20 different templates for Appearance and Attributes, Finishes, Transparent Materials, and Metals. There are also Advanced Tools for detail enhancement. The Arch & Design templates have default texture bitmaps already assigned when you select them. The templates include the following:

■ Matte, Pearl, or Glossy Finish	■ Physical Frosted Glass
■ Satin or Glossy Varnished Wood	■ Translucent Plastic Film with Light Blur

■ Rough or Polished Concrete	■ Translucent Plastic Film with Opalescent Effect
■ Glazed Ceramic/Glazed Ceramic Tiles	■ Water, Reflective Surface
■ Glossy or Matte Plastic	■ Chrome
■ Masonry	■ Brushed Metal
■ Rubber	■ Satined Metal
■ Leather	■ Copper
■ Thin or Solid or Physical Glass	■ Patterned Copper

To create a new Arch & Design material, select it as a Material Type and assign values, as necessary, to the material properties. For example, adjust the color in the *Diffuse* channel and add any texture maps, making sure the tiling is correct for the scene.

Arch & Design materials enable you to:

- Adjust the reflection, refraction, and transparency of the material.
- Control the blurriness of the reflections by using Fast Reflection.
- Control the distance that reflects in a surface.
- Adjust the strength of the reflection based on the angle of viewing (BDRF).
- Mental ray materials have additional special effects. These all work together to create the effect on the surface of an image.
- Self-Illumination can be used to add light into the scene. The self-illumination used with mental ray materials emits illumination in the scene instead of faking the effect, like standard lights.
- Round corners through a post-production pixel shader and an Ambient Occlusion setting that adds subtle detail enhancement to surface corners, cracks, and crevices. The Autodesk 3ds Max Design software has the ability to display Ambient Occlusion in the viewport. To toggle it on, select the **Shading** label and select **Lighting and Shadows>Ambient Occlusion**.

- It is recommended to use mental ray Arch & Design materials with mental ray lighting and rendering; however, it is not always practical. For example, if you import a file from Inventor or AutoCAD Architecture materials might already be assigned. When imported into the Autodesk 3ds Max Design software these are Architectural materials and have to be changed to Arch & Design materials. In some situations changing the type might be practical and in other situation it might not.

Autodesk Materials

Fourteen mental ray materials are available directly in the *mental ray* category. These materials are identified with the word **Autodesk** appended to the beginning of the material name. The Autodesk mental ray materials include the following:

Autodesk Ceramic	Autodesk Metallic Paint
Autodesk Concrete	Autodesk Mirror
Autodesk Generic	Autodesk Plastic/Vinyl
Autodesk Glazing	Autodesk Solid Glass
Autodesk Hardwood	Autodesk Stone
Autodesk Masonry CMU	Autodesk Wall Paint
Autodesk Metal	Autodesk Water

In addition to the list of Autodesk materials in the *mental ray* category there are an additional 22 categories of Autodesk materials present in the *Autodesk Material Library* category offering a variety of additional materials that can be used directly or modified for use in your scenes.

The Autodesk Material Library materials are simplified versions of the Arch & Design materials. It has presets that permit faster selection of specific material parameters as well as have pre-assigned bitmaps.

- The Autodesk Material Library was designed specifically for architectural visualization and includes material categories for *Ceramic*, *Concrete*, *Fabric*, *Finish*, *Flooring*, *Glass*, *Liquid*, *Masonry*, *Metal*, etc.
- These materials are aligned with the latest release of the Autodesk Revit software, so the materials applied in the Autodesk® Revit® Architecture software display as Autodesk Material Library materials inside the Autodesk 3ds Max Design software.

- Autodesk mental ray materials also display on objects that are imported from the Autodesk Revit Architecture software.

Car Paint Material

A layered material that provides for four layers combining to create one surface treatment. A base paint layer, an embedded metal flake layer, a clear-coat layer, and a Lambertian dirt layer each have their own parameters and rollouts. It enables you to create complex highly reflective surfaces. By using your own texture maps with these base materials, and tweaking the various parameters within each, you can achieve an unlimited variety of materials.

Matte/Shadow/ Reflection Material

This is a mental ray version of the Standard Matte/Shadow material. You can create matte objects by using the Matte/Shadow/Reflection (mi) material included in the Production Shaders library. Here a photographic plate, that has real-world objects is used as the scene background. The material provides various options for combining the photographic background plate with the 3D scene. The options include ambient occlusion, bump mapping, and indirect illumination.

mental ray Material

This is your basic mental ray material. It provides rollouts for assigning component shaders for materials used with the mental ray renderer. With the addition of the new Arch & Design Materials, you would have to have a very specific reason to start with this type of material, instead of using the new ones.

Subsurface Scattering (SSS) Materials

Enables you to create organic materials like skin that do not reflect light at the surface, but scatter or absorb light below in the surface. There are four different types of Subsurface Scattering materials available for use with the mental ray renderer.

> **Hint: Output Rollout**
>
> The Output rollout of the texture bitmap can be used to great advantage when using mental ray materials. Lighten and brighten the output of the texture by enabling the color map or increasing the Output Amount.

Practice 6e Working with mental ray Materials

Learning Objectives

- Assign a mental ray material template to an object.
- Assign a mental ray material to an object and modify the material using a map and a color mapping.

Estimated time for completion: 20 minutes

In this practice you will explore the mental ray materials, shaders, and templates.

You must set the paths to locate the External files and Xrefs used in the practice. If you have not done this already, return to the **Introduction to Autodesk 3ds Max Design** chapter and complete Task 1 to Task 3 of the **Organizing Folders and Working with the Interface** practice. You only have to set the user paths once.

Task 1 - Assign the NVIDIA mental ray renderer.

If a dialog box opens prompting you about a Mismatch, click OK to accept the default values.

1. Open **candleholder.max** from your *Class Files* folder. The candle holder is displayed in the four viewports layout. A Camera view has already been set up.

The Slate Material Editor is a modeless dialog box and can be left open. Use (minimize) to minimize the dialog box if you need to work in the viewports.

2. In the Main toolbar, click (Slate Material Editor) to open the Slate Material Editor. Note that no mental ray materials are listed in the Material/Map Browser. To work with mental ray materials, you need to set the renderer to mental ray.
3. In the Main toolbar, click (Render Setup) or select **Rendering>Render Setup** to open the Render Setup dialog box.

You need to scroll down to the bottom of the dialog box to display the Assign Renderer rollout. You can collapse the Common Parameters rollout or other expanded rollouts to display the Assign Renderer rollout.

4. In the *Common* tab, scroll down to the Assign Renderer rollout.

5. Expand the Assign Renderer rollout. Click next to the *Production* field to open the Choose Renderer dialog box.

   Select **NVIDIA mental ray** and click OK. **NVIDIA mental ray** displays in the *Production* field as shown in Figure 6–85. Close the Render Setup dialog box.

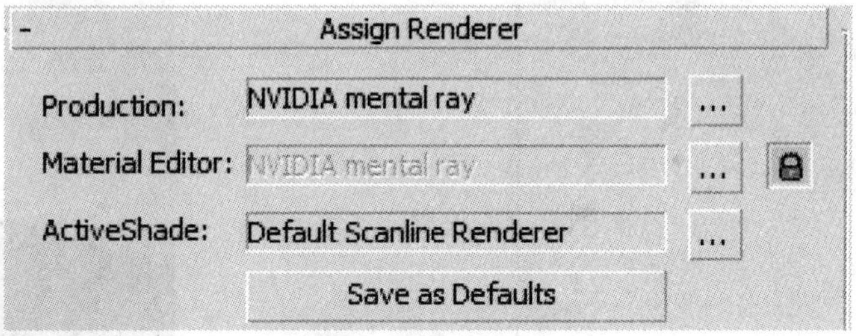

Figure 6–85

Task 2 - Assign the Arch & Design materials.

1. Open the Slate Material Editor, if not already open, note that the mental ray materials are now listed. Expand the *Scene Materials* category at the bottom of the Material/Map Browser. Four gray Standard materials are being used in the scene.

2. Double-click on each of the four gray materials (**CandleHolder**, **Countertop**, **Left Wall**, and **Right Wall**) to place them on the *View1* sheet. They are placed on top of each other. In the Material Editor toolbar, click (Lay Out All - Horizontal) to display the four materials horizontally in the *View1* sheet.

3. Change the color on each of these scene materials. Double-click on each material node to open the Parameter Editor. In the Blinn Basic Parameters rollout, select the Diffuse swatch, and select a color in the Color Selector. You can use any color (**Countertop** - dark pink, **Right Wall** - blue, **CandleHolder** - dark blue, or **Left Wall** - green).

4. Verify that the Camera01 viewport is active (yellow border) and in the Main toolbar, click (Render Production) or press <F9> to render the scene, as shown in Figure 6–86. Note the shadow cast by the candleholder. There is a shadow casting mental ray spotlight already set up in the scene. Leave the Render dialog box open as well.

Figure 6–86

5. In the Material/Map Browser in the Slate Material Editor, expand the *Materials>mental ray* categories. Double-click on Arch & Design, as shown in Figure 6–87, to add a new material node to the *View1* sheet.

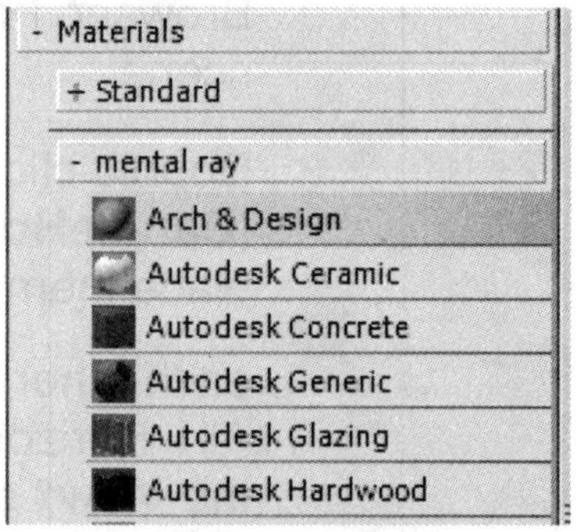

Figure 6–87

6. Double-click on the Material # Arch & Design title bar heading to open its Parameter Editor.
7. In the Templates rollout, expand the (Select a template) drop-down list and in the *Metals* sub-category, select **Copper**, as shown in Figure 6–88. The **Copper** material displays as the sample sphere in the material's title bar.

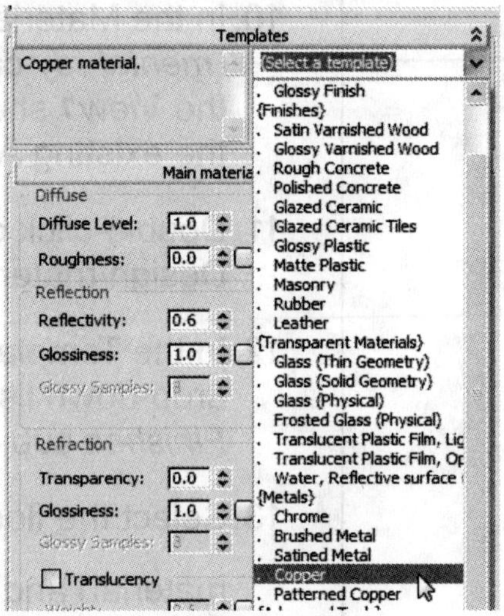

Figure 6–88

You can select the object in any other viewport but you must activate the Camera - 01 viewport before rendering the view.

8. In the Camera - 01 viewport, select the **candleholder** object and in the Slate Material Editor toolbar, click (Assign Material to Selection).

Render is located at the bottom right corner of the Settings panel because of the mental ray renderer.

9. Click Render or click (Render Production) (if the Render window was closed) to render the Camera01 viewport, as shown in Figure 6–89. The **Copper** material reflects the colors of the walls around it, as well as the lighting in the scene. The rendering time is a little slower due to the calculations for reflections.

Figure 6–89

10. In the Material/Map Browser, double-click on Arch & Design (*mental ray* category) again to add another material node to the *View1* sheet. Place this new material node to the left of the existing Arch & Design (Copper) node.

11. Double-click on the title bar heading for the new Arch & Design material to access its Parameter Editor.

12. In the Templates rollout, expand the (Select a template) drop-down list and select **Glazed Ceramic Tiles** in the *Finishes* sub-category.

13. Select the floor object (Box01 which has the countertop material) and in the Slate Material Editor toolbar, click [icon] to assign the new ceramic tile to the floor.

14. Click [icon] (Show Shaded Material in Viewport) to see the tiles displayed on the floor in the viewport.

15. Render the Camera01 viewport, as shown in Figure 6–90. The **Copper** and **Glazed Tile** materials both display in the scene. The rendering is slower (possibly due to the shadow of the candlestick reflecting on the tiles).

Figure 6–90

16. Double-click on the title bar heading for the Arch & Design material (Copper template). In the Templates rollout, expand the (Select a template) drop-down list and select **Frosted Glass (Physical)** in the *Transparent Materials* category. This material is automatically assigned to the Candlestick and render the Camera 01 view again, as shown in Figure 6–91. The render time is significantly slower. The **Translucent** material enables the light to pass through it. The light is casting a ray-traced shadow, rather than a shadow map shadow.

Figure 6–91

17. Save your work as **Mycandleholder.max**.

Task 3 - Assign a Car Paint material.

To explore the **Car Paint** material you will load a different file.

1. Open **MR_guitar.max**. This is the guitar with a plain gray material applied to the body.
2. Click  to open the Slate Material Editor. In the Material/Map Browser, expand the *Materials>mental ray* categories. Double-click on the **Car Paint** mental ray material to add it to the *View1* sheet.

3. Select the **BODY:1** object in the viewport and in the Slate Material Editor toolbar, click (Assign Material to Selection) to assign the **Car Paint** material. In the Main toolbar, click (Render Production). The **Car Paint** material is applied to the body as shown in Figure 6–92. Your rendering might not display as shown in Figure 6–92. It depends on your monitor display and the Gamma and LUT settings.

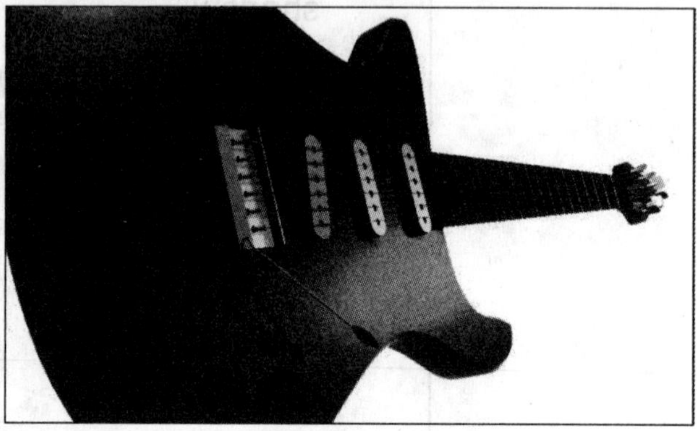

Figure 6–92

4. Note that the pickups and strings reflect in the guitar body, but the body looks a little dull. You can brighten it by changing the *Ambient/Extra Light* value. In the *View1* sheet, double-click on the Material# Car Paint title bar heading to open its Parameter Editor. In the Diffuse Coloring rollout, select the *Ambient/Extra Light* color swatch to open the Color Selector. Set the *Value* slider to **100**. Click OK.

5. Click Render or click (Render Production) (if the Render window was closed) to render and note the change in brightness.

6. To add a texture map to a mental ray material, in the Diffuse Coloring rollout, click for **Base Color** as shown in Figure 6–93.

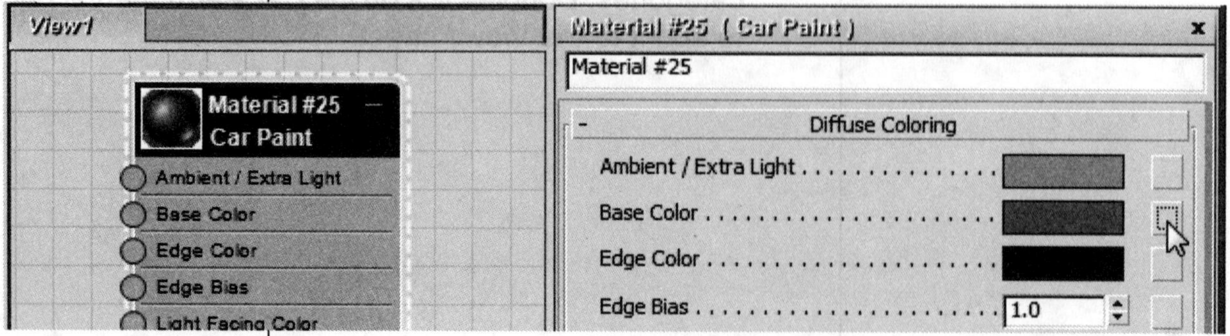

Figure 6–93

7. In the Material/Map Browser, expand the *Maps>Standard* categories and double-click on Bitmap. In the Select Bitmap Image File dialog box, browse to your *Class Files* folder, and in *Maps* directory, select **BURLOAK.JPG**. Click Open.

8. Render the viewport again. The wood texture is displayed on the guitar body, as shown in Figure 6–94.

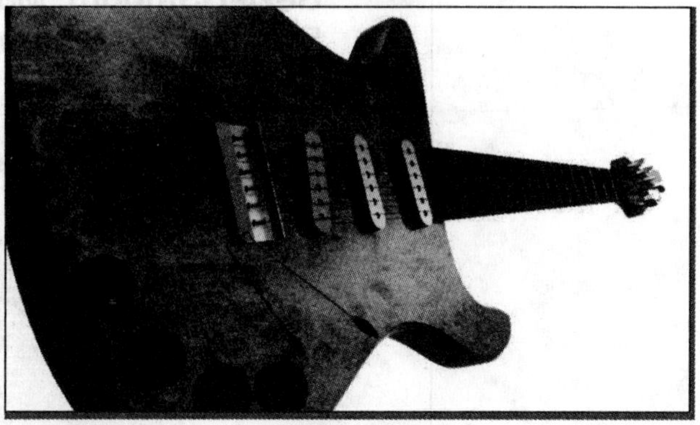

Figure 6–94

9. To brighten up the wood texture, in the *View1* sheet, double-click on the Map # Bitmap title bar (wired to the Base color of **Car Paint** materials) to open its Parameter Editor.

10. Expand the Output rollout and select **Enable Color Map**. In the Color Map toolbar, click (Add Point) and add a point to the diagonal line at its midpoint, as shown in Figure 6–95.

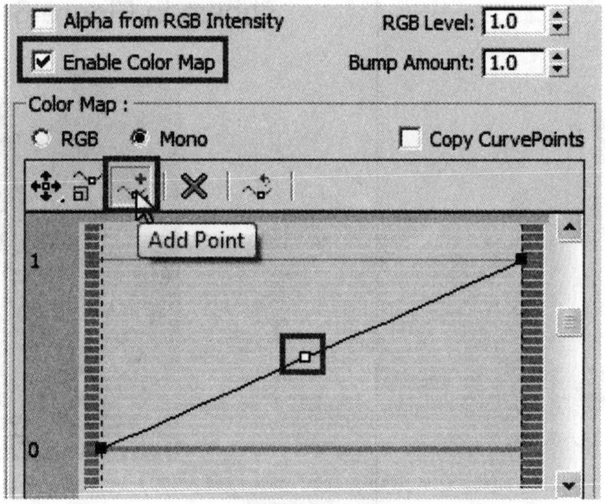

Figure 6–95

11. In the Color Map toolbar, click (Select and Move) and drag the right-most point to a *value* of about **2**. You can enter **2** in the right text box at the bottom of graph. Use the **Zoom** tool (located in the lower right corner of the graph window) of the graph to display the point.

12. Move the middle point to 1, right-click on it and select **Bezier-Smooth**. Move the point and/or handles, as shown in Figure 6–96. The sample sphere for the bitmap updates.

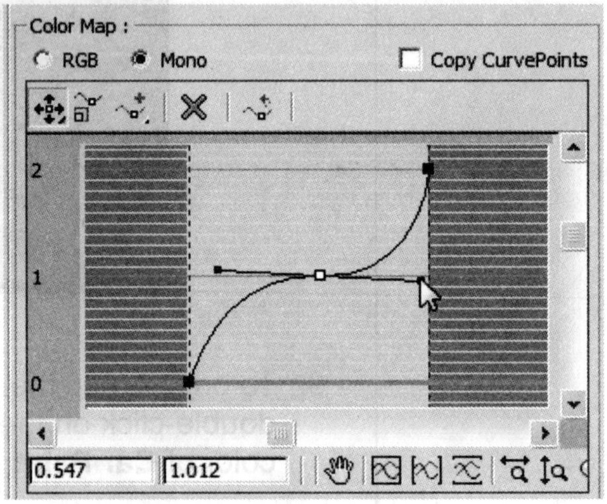

Figure 6–96

13. In the viewport, use (Field-of-View) to zoom in on the pickups. Render the scene and note the reflections, as shown in Figure 6–97.

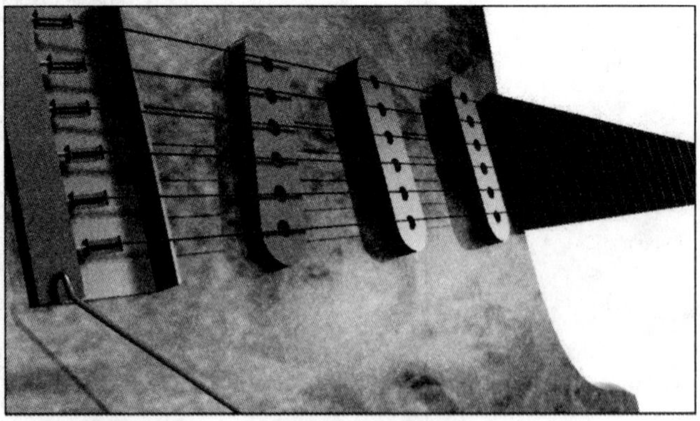

Figure 6–97

14. Save your work as **My_MR_guitar.max**.

6.9 The Material Explorer

Learning Objective

- Understand how to display and manage all of the materials used in a scene using the Material Explorer.

In the Autodesk 3ds Max Design software you can manage all of the materials used in a scene using the Material Explorer. You can open it by selecting **Rendering>Material Explorer**. The Material Explorer displays all of the materials used in the scene and also displays the material's *Name*, *Type*, *Show in Viewport* setting, and *Material ID*, as shown in Figure 6–98.

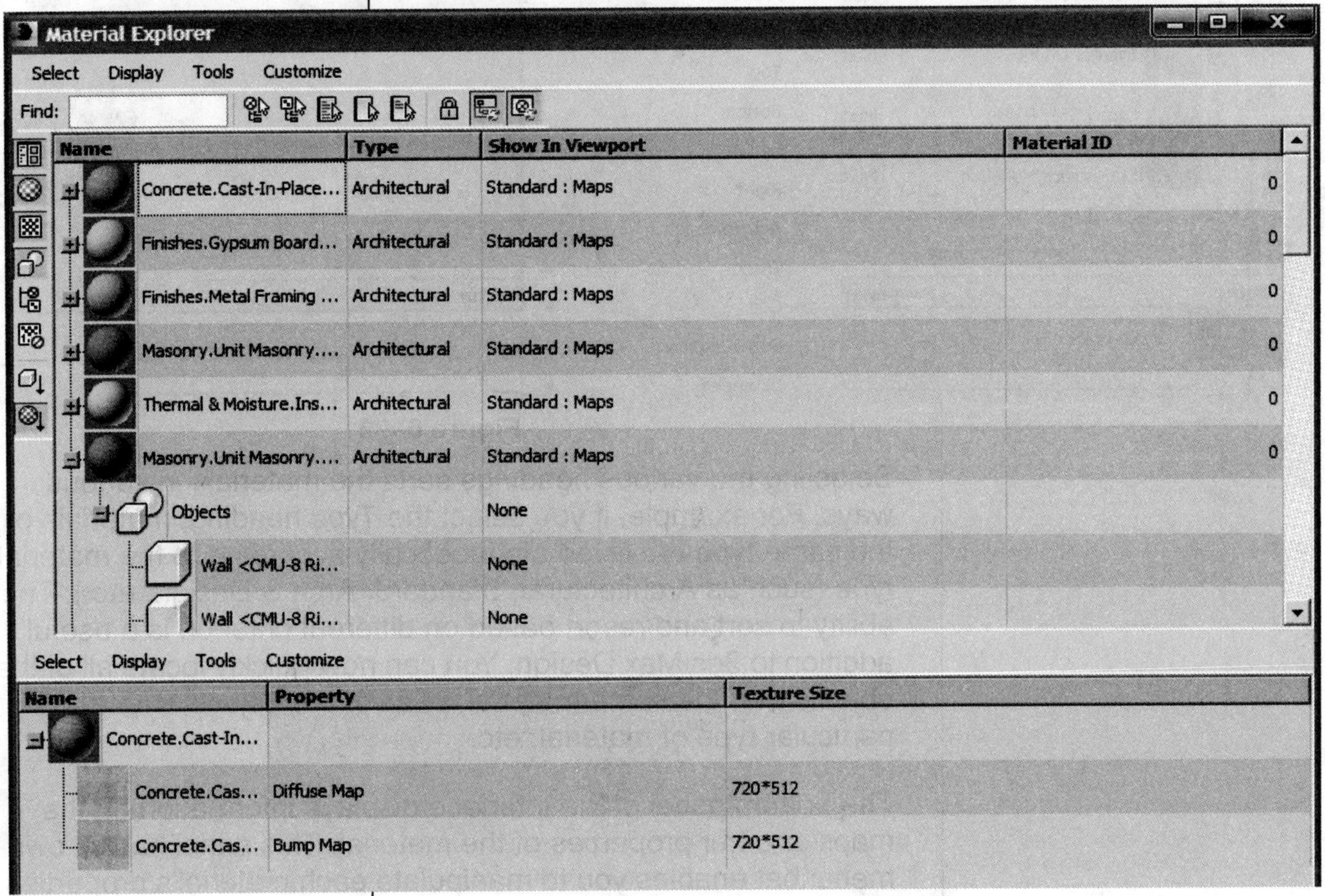

Figure 6–98

Alternatively, you can select the Point of View label (Perspective, Top, etc.) in a viewport and then select **Extended Viewports> Material Explorer** in the label menu. This replaces the viewport with the Material Explorer. To display the viewport with the models again, right-click anywhere in empty space on the Material Explorer menu bar and select the required Point of View, as shown in Figure 6–99.

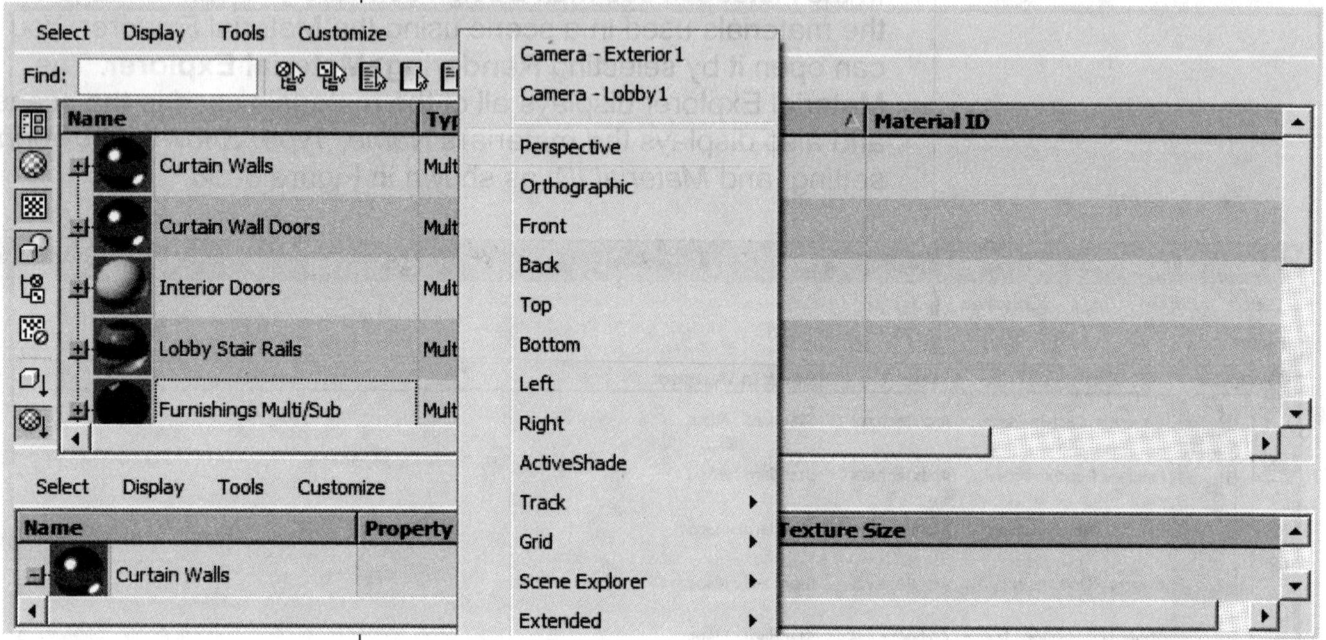

Figure 6–99

Selecting the various headings sorts the materials in various ways. For example, if you select the *Type* heading, materials of the same type are listed alphabetically according to the material type (such as Architectural, Standard, Arch & Design, etc.). The ability to sort and resort based on different criterion is a useful addition to 3ds Max Design. You can now quickly locate all of the objects with the same material, or all of the objects with a particular type of material, etc.

The bottom panel of the interface displays information on the maps or other properties of the material. This panel has its own menu that enables you to manipulate each material's properties; you can even remove all sub-maps applied to individual materials.

From the Material Explorer you can save directly to a new material library, as shown in Figure 6–100, or perform a variety of tasks depending upon the type of the material.

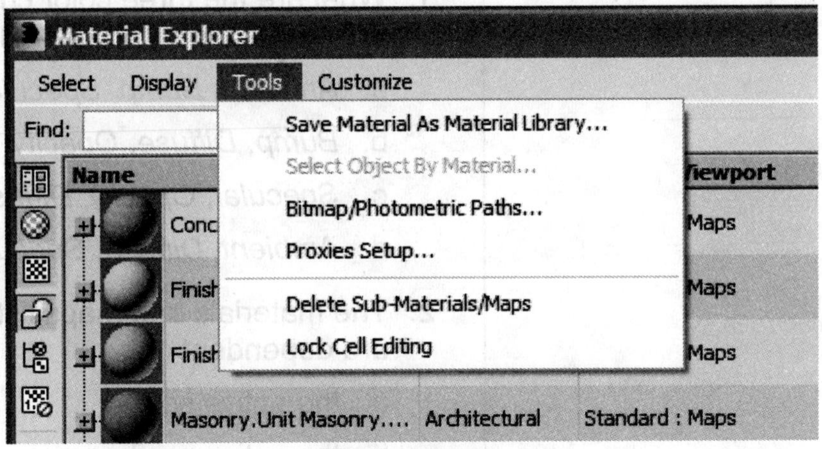

Figure 6–100

Chapter Review Questions

1. What are the three color channels in Standard materials that determine the color applied to an object?
   a. *Ambient*, *Bump*, *Specular*
   b. *Bump*, *Diffuse*, *Opacity*
   c. *Specular*, *Opacity*, *Diffuse*
   d. *Ambient*, *Diffuse*, *Specular*
2. The materials and maps listed in the Material/Map Browser are dependent on...
   a. the active scene.
   b. the active renderer.
   c. the active viewport.
   d. the active material editor.
3. In the active view sheet of the Slate Material Editor, the green color (title bar) of a node indicates that it is a...
   a. Material
   b. Map
   c. Controller
   d. Material with the **Show Map In Viewport** option applied.
4. In the active view sheet of the Slate Material Editor, a dashed white border around a material node indicates that the...
   a. Material is being used in the scene.
   b. Map is assigned to one of the channels (socket) of the material.
   c. Parameters of the material are displayed in the Parameter Editor.
   d. Material is a customized material.
5. The Phong shader generates softer, smoother (often more realistic) highlights than the Blinn shader.
   a. True
   b. False

6. Which type of standard material enables you to stack multiple materials into a single parent material, each with a material ID number.
   a. Multi/Sub-Object material
   b. Architectural material
   c. Raytrace material
   d. Shell material
7. Which type of mapping gives the illusion of an embossed or pitted surface without actual geometry having to be present on the model?
   a. Opacity mapping
   b. Bump mapping
   c. Reflection mapping
8. Which type of mental ray material is a layered material that provides for four layers (base paint layer, embedded metal flake layer, clear-coat layer, and Lambertian dirt layer) combining to create one surface treatment?
   a. Arch and Design material
   b. Matte/Shadow/Reflection material
   c. Subsurface Scattering (SSS) material
   d. Car Paint material

Command Summary

Button	Command	Location
	**Compact Material Editor**	■ **Main Toolbar** ■ **Rendering:** Material Editor>Compact Material Editor
	Material Explorer	■ **Rendering:** Material Explorer
	**Orbit**	■ **Viewport Navigation Toolbar (Non-Camera Views):** Orbit flyout
	**Render Production**	■ **Main Toolbar:** Render flyout ■ **Rendering:** Render
	**Render Setup**	■ **Main Toolbar** ■ **Rendering:** Render Setup
	**Slate Material Editor**	■ **Main Toolbar** ■ **Rendering:** Material Editor>Slate Material Editor

Chapter 7

Mapping Coordinates and Scale

In this chapter you learn to manipulate and position the maps correctly and accurately with mapping coordinates. You also learn to use the explicit map scaling and continuous map scaling. You learn about using spline mapping to generate mapping coordinates that follow the path of extrusion.

This chapter contains the following topics:

- ✓**Mapping Coordinates**
- ✓**Mapping Scale**
- ✓**Spline Mapping**

7.1 Mapping Coordinates

Learning Objectives

- Understand the mapping coordinates required for objects with texture maps.
- Assigning mapping coordinates using the Slate Material Editor, MapScaler modifier, and the UVW Map modifier.

Most of the sample materials provided with the Autodesk® 3ds Max® Design software are assigned image texture maps, especially the Diffuse Color and Bump maps. Objects that are assigned materials with maps require mapping coordinates to control how the map is projected onto the object. For example, a rectangular sign can use planar or box mapping and a cylindrical can uses cylindrical mapping.

- Mapping is referenced by its own local coordinate system described by UVW coordinates. (UVW is used instead of XYZ to indicate that the mapping does not need to be aligned with the world XYZ coordinates.)

- Many objects (including primitives) are automatically assigned mapping coordinates. This is controlled by **Generate Mapping Coords** in the Command Panel, in the object's Parameters rollout, as shown in Figure 7–1.

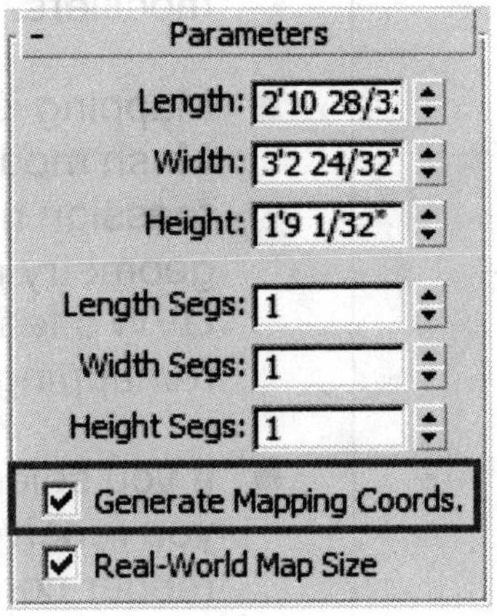

Figure 7–1

- Linked or imported objects with materials assigned in AutoCAD® automatically have mapping coordinates if the **Generate coordinates for all objects** is selected in the import or link preset options, as shown in Figure 7–2. This is recommended unless you are not using materials with maps or would prefer to add mapping manually.

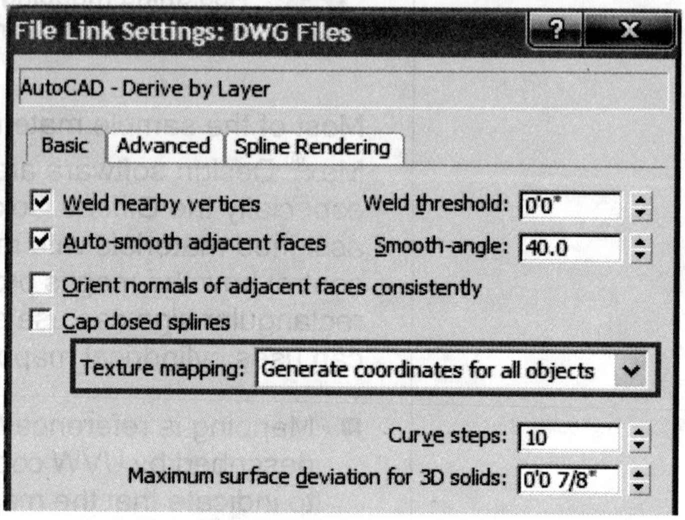

Figure 7–2

- Regardless of whether mapping is automatically applied or not, you can (and often need to) reassign mapping manually in the Autodesk 3ds Max Design software. There are a number of different modifiers that can be used to accomplish this, including **UVW Map**, **Unwrap UVW**, and **MapScaler** modifiers.

- Mapping is often disturbed by editing (as through an Edit Mesh modifier) and by Boolean operations. You often need to reassign mapping coordinates for objects that have their geometry modified. The Edit Poly modifier has a Preserve UVW's feature that can be toggled on to prevent the need for remapping.

- If you select to render an object without mapping coordinates you receive a warning message that the maps might not render correctly.

Mapping Controls in Slate Material Editor

At the map level of the Slate Material Editor there are controls to manipulate the positioning of a map with mapping coordinates. These controls are available through the Parameter Editor of the map, as shown in Figure 7–3 and apply to all objects showing this map. (Some of these controls are duplicated in the UVW Map modifier, which controls only the object it is applied to.)

Use Real-World Scale On

The **Use Real-World Scale** attempts to simplify the correct scaling of textures by specifying the actual height and width, as shown in Figure 7–3, as represented by the 2D texture map. This option requires that the object use UV texture mapping set to Real World Map Size and that the Material also have Use Real-World Scale selected. It replaces the *Tiling* fields with a Size value for Width and Height.

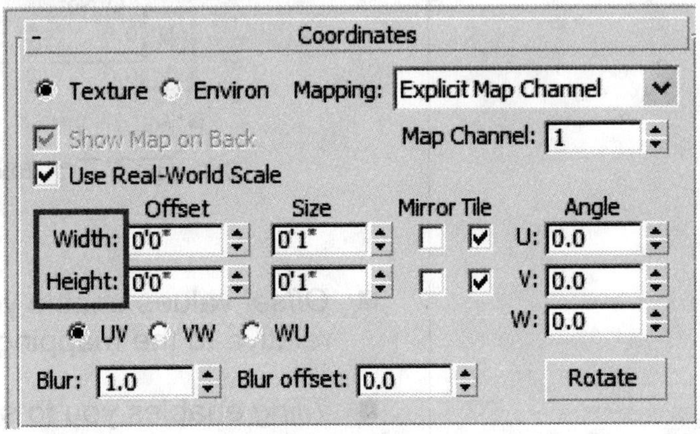

Figure 7–3

Hint: Importing with Use Real-World Scale

Using the **Use Real-World Scale** option when importing from earlier versions of the Autodesk 3ds Max software might cause textures to display wrong. It can be due to **Real World Map Size** and **Use Real-World Scale** trying to create an extreme texture. If you leave these on, you need to reset *Tiling* to a different value. You might try **0.01** or a similar small value before you can see the bitmap texture, or go larger and try 10 or 20. If the texture does not display correctly, it might be easier to toggle off **Use Real-World Scale** and set *Tiling* to **1.0** x **1.0**.

Use Real-World Scale Off

When the **Use Real-World Scale** is toggled off, the map texture is placed with respect to the UV values, as shown in Figure 7–4.

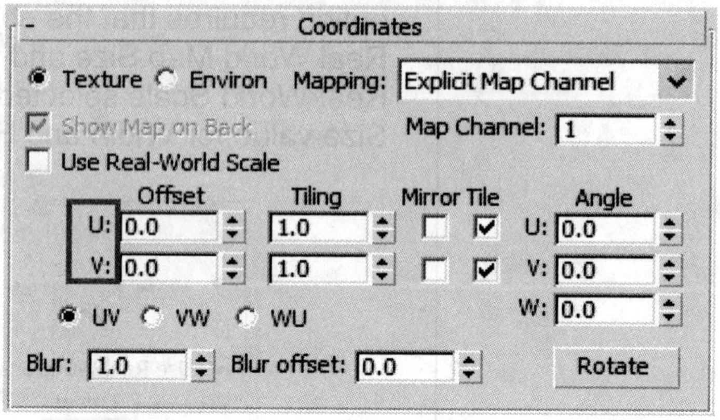

Figure 7–4

- *Offset* values enable you to move the map on an object relative to the mapping coordinates.
- *Tiling* enables you to specify whether the map is repeated or tiled across the surface, in either the U (often width) or V (often height) direction.
- *Mirror* causes tiled maps to be mirrored end-to-end as they tile.
- The *W-rotation* field (angle) controls rotation of the map about the W (local Z) axis. For 2D maps (such as with an image file) this value typically is used to rotate the map on the surface of an object.

MapScaler Modifier

A simple way to add mapping coordinates is through the MapScaler Modifier. It projects a map perpendicular to each face of an object. The MapScaler is available through the Modifier List in the *Modify* panel ().

- In the Autodesk 3ds Max Design software there are two MapScalers: a World Space Modifier (WSM), as shown on the left in Figure 7–5, and an Object Space Modifier (OSM), as shown on the right in Figure 7–5. The World Space Modifier keeps the map scale constant if the object size changes with the Scale transform. The Object-Space Modifier scales the map proportionally.

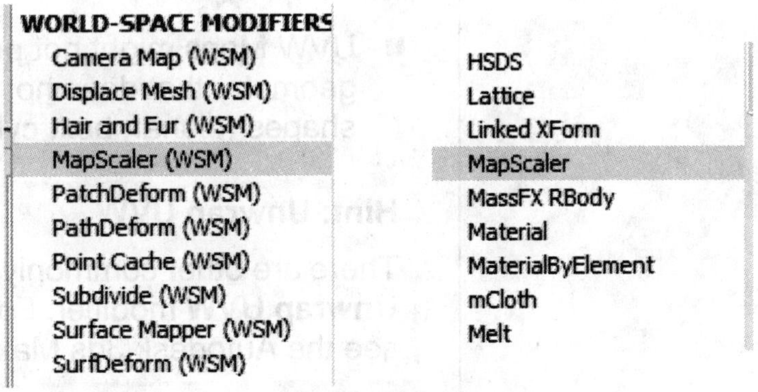

Figure 7–5

- MapScalers enable automatically generated, continuous tiling across complex geometry that might be difficult with UVW Maps. They tend to work well with geometry imported from the AutoCAD Architecture and the Autodesk Revit software.

- One method of repositioning a map on an object assigned a MapScaler is to adjust the U- and V-offset settings in the Bitmap Parameters rollout in the Material Editor. Otherwise apply a UVW XForm modifier to the object and apply the offsets there instead.

- MapScalers sometimes do not project well on curved surfaces.

Objects displaying tiling material maps that do not have a defined beginning or end point are often a good choice for MapScaler modifiers, including concrete pads, metals, asphalt, grass, and sometimes brick.

UVW Map Modifier

The UVW Map modifier (*Modify* panel ()>Modifier List) enables you to explicitly apply a map to an object, where you select a specific shape and location to project the map onto.

- The UVW Map modifier offers more for locating maps than the MapScaler Modifier. It has a gizmo for transforming in Sub-object mode.
- UVW Maps might not project as well as MapScalers on geometry that does not lend itself to the standard projection shapes (planar, box, cylinder, etc.).

Hint: Unwrap UVW

There are other commonly used mapping methods, such as the **Unwrap UVW** modifier. For more information on *Unwrap UVW*, see the Autodesk 3ds Max Design 2014 Help files.

Practice 7a Applying Mapping Coordinates

Learning Objective

- Adjust the placement of a map on an object using the UVW Map and MapScaler (WSM) modifiers.

Estimated time for completion: 10 minutes

In this practice you will adjust the material mapping in the light pole scene you started earlier.

You must set the paths to locate the External files and Xrefs used in the practice. If you have not done this already, return to the **Introduction to Autodesk 3ds Max Design** chapter and complete Task 1 to Task 3 of the **Organizing Folders and Working with the Interface** practice. You only have to set the user paths once.

If a dialog box opens prompting you about a File Load: Mismatch, click OK to accept the default values.

1. Open **Light Pole Mapping.max** from your *Class Files* folder.
2. In the viewport, select the concrete **LP Base** object and then click (Zoom Extents Selected) to zoom into the base object as shown in Figure 7–6. When this cylinder was created, the mapping coordinates were generated automatically and the Edit Poly modifier has disturbed its placement.

Figure 7–6

You need to scroll down the list to select the ***UVW Map*** *modifier.*

3. With the **LP Base** object selected, in the Command Panel, select the *Modify* panel ( ). In the Modifier drop-down list, in the *OBJECT-SPACE MODIFIERS* group, select **UVW Map**, as shown in Figure 7–7.

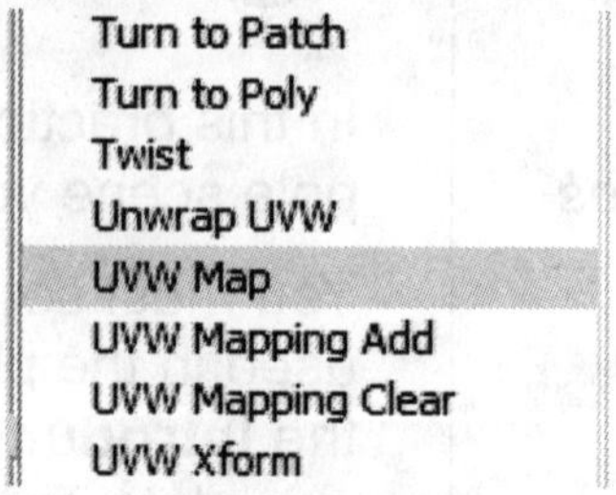

Figure 7–7

4. In the Parameters rollout, in the *Mapping* area, select **Box**. This projects the concrete map onto the object from all six sides of an imaginary box, causing a seam to form in places as shown in Figure 7–8.

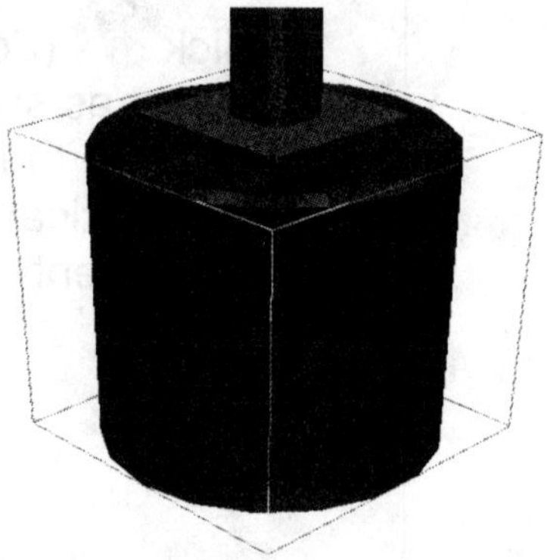

Figure 7–8

5. Change the projection to *Cylindrical* and then *Planar*, noting the differences. The Cylindrical projection is not handling the beveled top very well, as shown on the left in Figure 7–9. The Planar projection is not displaying the cylindrical base properly (as shown on the right in Figure 7–9), because it is intended for 2D objects or 3D objects in which the edge pixels can be permitted to project into the third dimension.

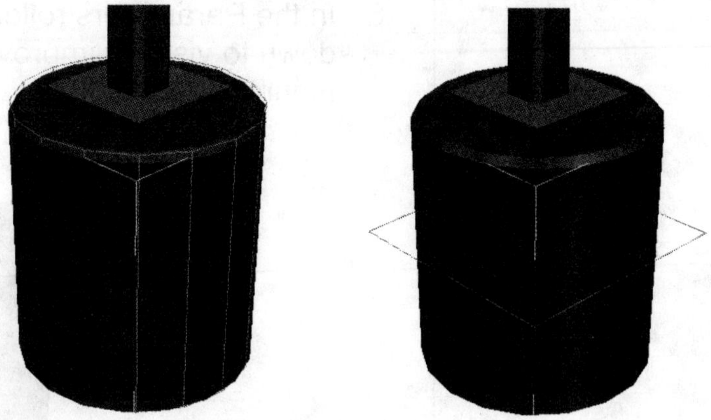

Figure 7–9

6. Remove the UVW Map modifier from the Modifier Stack by clicking  (Remove modifier from the stack), as shown in Figure 7–10.

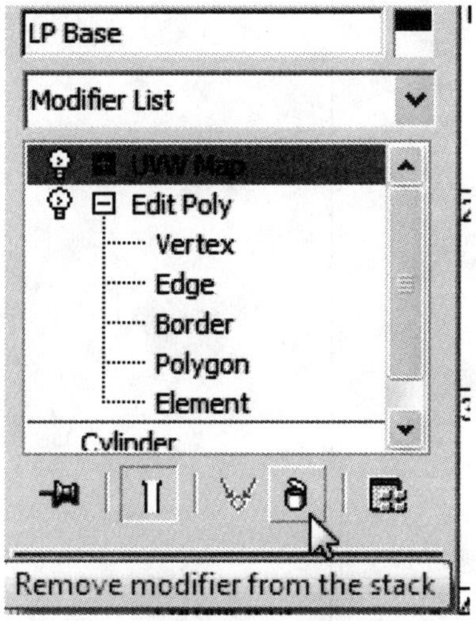

Figure 7–10

7. In the Modifier drop-down list, in the WORLD-SPACE MODIFIERS, select **MapScaler (WSM)**. The MapScalers are automatically projected perpendicular to each face of an object.

8. In the Parameters rollout, adjust the *Scale* spinner up or down to visually improve the look of the map, as shown in Figure 7–11.

Figure 7–11

9. Save your work as **MyLight Pole Mapping.max**.

Practice 7b Mapping a Large Scale Image

Learning Objectives

- Assign a map to a model and apply the mapping coordinates using the Slate Material Editor.
- Apply the mapping coordinates using the UVW Map modifier to adjust the map.

Estimated time for completion: 10 minutes

In this practice you will apply a scanned image to a terrain model and map it accurately.

You must set the paths to locate the External files and Xrefs used in the practice. If you have not done this already, return to the **Introduction to Autodesk 3ds Max Design** chapter and complete Task 1 to Task 3 of the **Organizing Folders and Working with the Interface** practice. You only have to set the user paths once.

If a dialog box opens prompting you about a File Load: Mismatch, click OK *to accept the default values.*

1. Open the file **Mapping a large scale image.max** from your *Class Files* folder.
2. If your Units setup is maintained for Imperial, a Units Scale Mismatch dialog box opens. Click OK to accept the defaults. The units for this file are set to **Meters** and the *System Unit Scale* is **1 Unit=1 Meter**. This is required because the map that will be used is set for Metric units as well.
3. In the Main toolbar, click (Material Editor) to open the Slate Material Editor. In the Material/Map Browser, expand the *Materials>Standard* categories. Double-click on the Standard material to add it to the *View1* sheet. Double-click on the title bar heading for this new material to open the Parameter Editor. Change the material name to **Quad Map**.
4. Expand the Maps rollout and for *Diffuse Color*, click None, as shown in Figure 7–12. The Material/Map Browser opens.

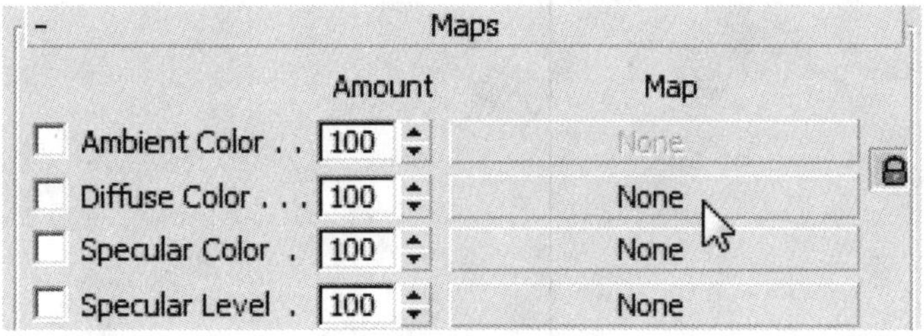

Figure 7–12

5. You will browse for a scanned USGS (United States Geological Survey) Quad Map to show on the surface. In the Material/Map Browser, expand the *Maps>Standard* categories. Double-click on Bitmap to open the Select Bitmap Image File dialog box. In your *Class Files* folder in the *Maps* subfolder, open the image **q257938.tif**.

6. In the *View1* sheet, note that the **Map # Bitmap** is wired to the Input socket of *Diffuse Color* of the Quad Map material. Double-click on the Bitmap title bar heading to open its Parameter Editor. In the Bitmap Parameters rollout, in the *Cropping/Placement* area, click View Image to open the bitmap. Close the Specify Cropping/Placement window.

7. In the Coordinates rollout, clear **Use Real-World Scale**. Clear *Tile* for both **U** and **V**, as shown in Figure 7–13, because you want this map to display only once and in a specific location.

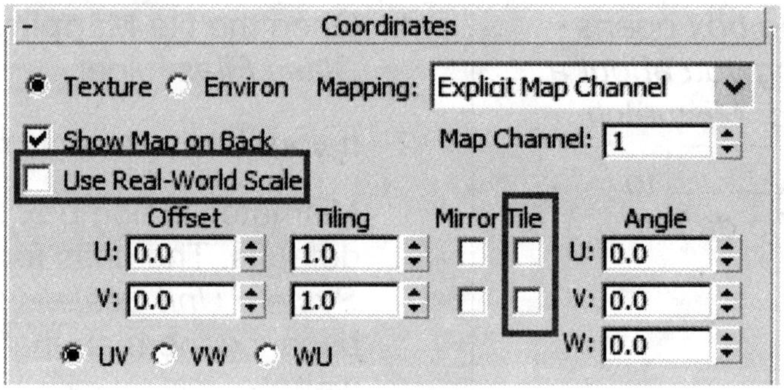

Figure 7–13

8. In the viewport, select the **Terrain01** object. In the *View1* sheet, select the **Quad Map** material and in the Material Editor toolbar, click (Assign Material to Selection). The material does not preview in the viewport.

9. In the viewport, right-click on the Terrain01 object and select **Object Properties**. In the *Display Properties* area, clear **Vertex Channel Display** and click OK. Now the gray color of the material is visible on the terrain, but no texture map.

10. This means that there might be a mapping problem on that object. In the Main toolbar, click to render the scene and note the warning message of missing map coordinates. You need a **UVW Map** or a **MapScaler** modifier for this object. Click Cancel in the Missing Coordinates dialog box and close the render window.

11. In the viewport, select the **Terrain01** object, if not already selected. In the Command Panel, select the *Modify* panel ( ), and in the Modifier List, select **UVW Map**. In the Parameters rollout, verify that **Planar** is selected and clear **Real-World Map Size**, as shown in Figure 7–14, because the diffuse map is not meant to tile.

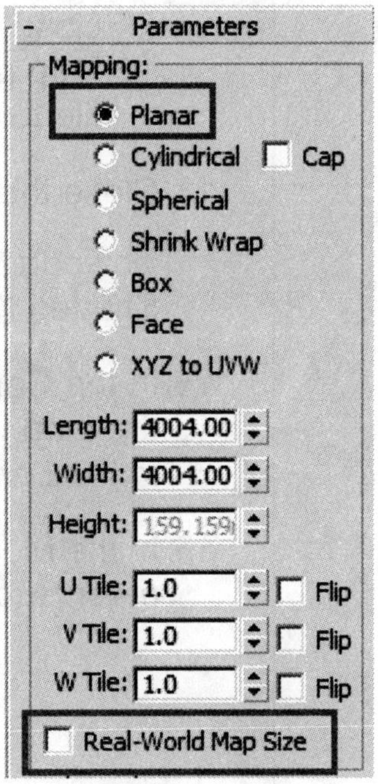

Figure 7–14

12. Click to render the scene. The terrain model should now resemble a 3D map, as shown in Figure 7–15.

Figure 7–15

- Without any direct manipulation it appears that this texture map is being applied correctly. This is because the contours used to create the surface were trimmed very close to the geographic boundary of the image file. **UVW Map** parameters can be used to explicitly locate an image file to be precise when necessary.

13. Close the Render window. If the map does not display in the viewport, in the Slate Material Editor toolbar, click (Show Shaded Material in Viewport).

14. In the Command Panel, in the Parameters rollout, note that the map was automatically scaled to 4004 x 4004 displayed in the *Length* and *Width* values, as shown in Figure 7–14.

15. In the Modifier Stack, expand UVW Map and select **Gizmo** to enter Sub-object mode, as shown in Figure 7–16.

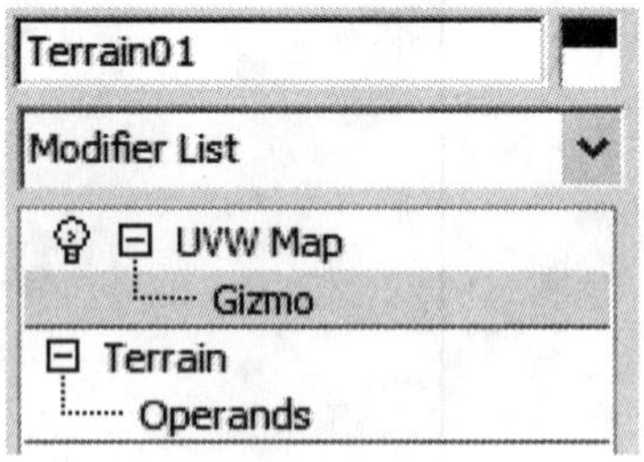

Figure 7–16

16. In the Main toolbar, click (Select and Move) and move the image map on the terrain object. You can adjust the map more precisely using the UVW Map gizmo.

17. Save your work as **MyLargeScaleProjectMapped**.

7.2 Mapping Scale

Learning Objective

- Adjust the size of the image maps using the explicit map scaling and the continuous map scaling options.

Mapping Scale is directly related to mapping coordinates and both are often addressed at the same time. Objects that use materials with image maps need to have them sized appropriately. (Procedural maps need to be scaled also, but they are normally controlled by scale parameters at the Map level of the Material Editor and not through the controls discussed here.)

Explicit Map Scaling

Maps that need to display an exact number of times (such as only once) might be most easily controlled through the size parameters of the UVW Map modifier. Examples of this include maps used in materials for 3D models of signs, billboards, computer screens, paintings, etc. This is exactly how you approached the **Terrain Quad Map** material in a previous practice. In the Quad Map practice you applied the map once across the surface with an exact size of 4004 x 4004.

- These kinds of maps normally are not assigned a real-world scale since they often need to be sized manually for each object. In these situations it is important to clear the **Use Real-World Map Scale** option in the Map Coordinates rollout and clear the **Real-World Map Size** in the **UVW Map** parameters, as shown in Figure 7–17.

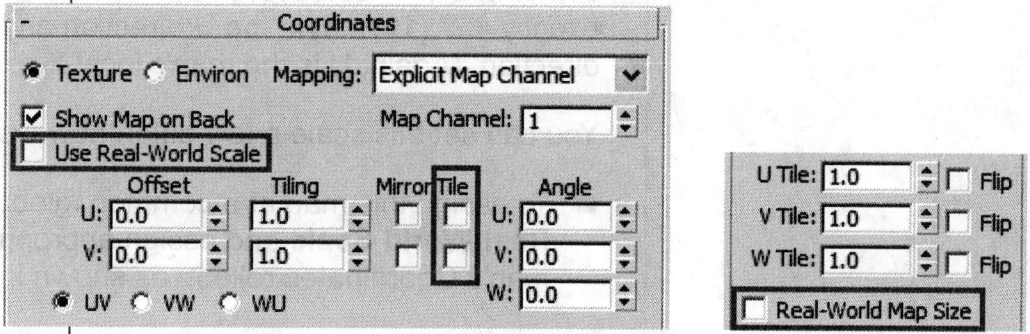

Figure 7–17

- If the map should display only once then the U and V tile values should be set to 1.0 in both the Map Coordinates rollout of the Material Editor and the **UVW Map** modifier parameters. To make the map display twice in the V-direction, for example (the map's local Y-direction), set the V tile value to **2** in one of these locations, but not both.

Continuous Map Scaling

When material maps are meant to tile continuously across an object (instead of exactly once, twice, etc.), a continuous approach can be used. The size of these maps can be controlled by a Real World scale that affects all objects using the map, or they can be sized directly using **UVW Map** or **MapScaler** size parameters for each object. Setting a Real World scale makes it easier to effect a global map scale change to multiple objects. Either way you might need to determine the physical size you want to display an image file map in your scene. Although many of the materials in the architectural libraries already include Real World scales the example below describes how to calculate them when necessary.

The **Brick** material uses an image file for a diffuse color map, as shown in Figure 7–18.

Figure 7–18

This image map represents a section of wall that is five bricks wide (measured along the long edges) and 16 courses tall. If you want to use this material to represent bricks that are 11" on center laid in 4" courses, this brick map should be scaled to exactly 4'7" (11" x 5) in the U direction and 5'4" (4" x 16) in the V direction. (Again, U is the map's local X-axis and V is the local Y.)

You can set this scale a few different ways:

- To assign this map at a common, global scale, enable **Use Real-World Scale** and assign appropriate size values in the map's Coordinates rollout, as shown in Figure 7–19.

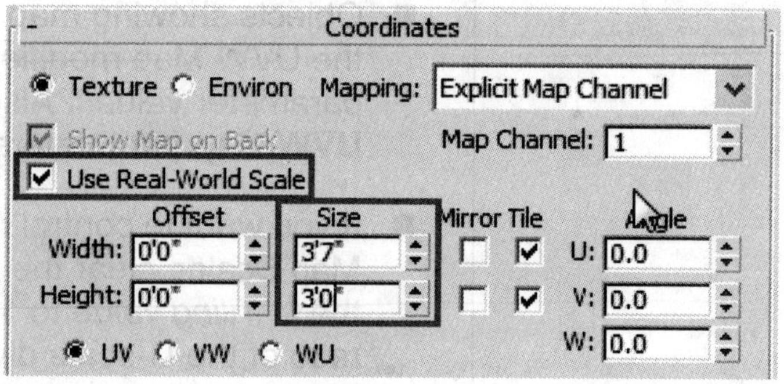

Figure 7–19

- If mapping coordinates are necessary, apply UVW Maps or Map Scalers to objects displaying this map. UVW Maps should have the **Real World Map Size** option enabled as shown on the left in Figure 7–20. The Map Scalers should be set to a size of one scene unit (such as 1"), as shown on the right in Figure 7–20, in the Parameters rollout of WSM modifier.

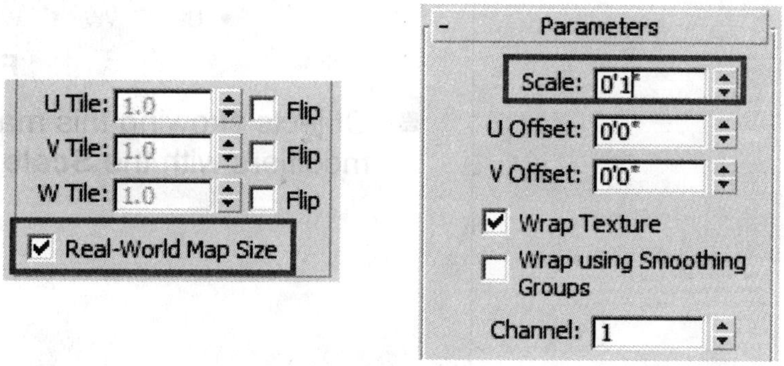

Figure 7–20

- If you want to control map scaling of individual objects through a UVW Map, clear the **Use Real-World Scale** option in the Coordinates rollout and set the *Tiling* values to **1.0** as shown in Figure 7–21.

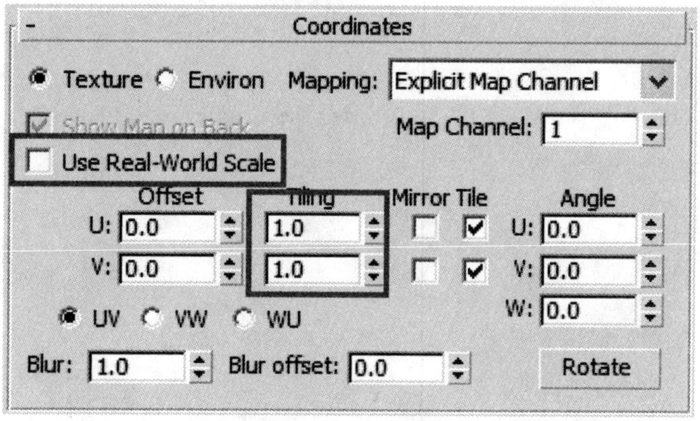

Figure 7–21

- Objects showing map can be assigned sizes directly through the UVW Map modifier's **Length**, **Width** and **Height** parameter values. Also clear **Real-World Map Size** in the **UVW Map** parameters.
- If you want to control map scaling on individual objects with a Map Scaler, clear the **Use Real-World Scale** option and set the *U-Tiling* value to **1.0** and the *V-Tiling* value equal to the ratio of the U-scale divided by the V scale, as shown in Figure 7–22.

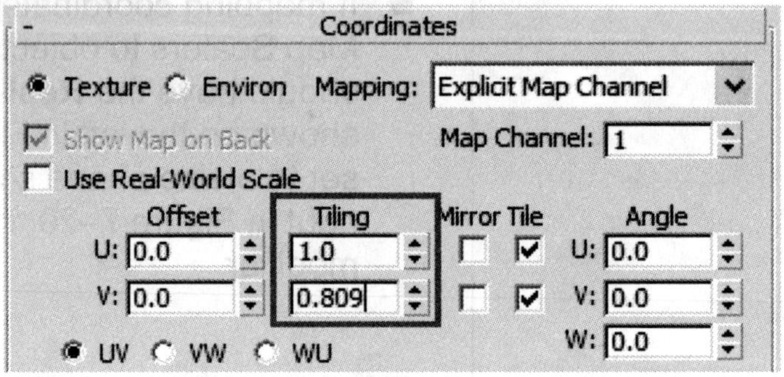

Figure 7–22

- Objects showing this map can be assigned MapScaler modifiers with the **Scale** parameter value set to the U scale.

Practice 7c Assigning Map Scales

Learning Objectives

- Assign a material, which contains an image map, to objects in a scene.
- Adjust the size of the image maps using the MapScaler (WSM) modifier and use the scaling options to position it correctly.

Estimated time for completion: 15 minutes

You must set the paths to locate the External files and Xrefs used in the practice. If you have not done this already, return to the **Introduction to Autodesk 3ds Max Design** chapter and complete Task 1 to Task 3 of the **Organizing Folders and Working with the Interface** practice. You only have to set the user paths once.

Task 1 - Position and Scale the Brick Maps.

The wall objects in the interior model assigned the **Wall Multi** material are all square (orthogonal to each other) so they would be a good candidate for either a UVW Map set to box mapping or a MapScaler.

If a dialog box opens prompting you about a File Load: Mismatch, click OK to accept the default values.

1. Open the file **Interior Mapping.max** from your *Class Files* folder. A Units Scale Mismatch dialog box opens, because the *Units* were changed to **Metric** in the Terrain Mapping practice. Click OK to accept the defaults and adopt the file's units (Imperial).

2. In the Main toolbar, click (Select by Name). In the Select From Scene dialog box, click (Display None) to clear any selection, and click (Display Geometry). Select **Layer:VIZ-1-Walls** and click OK.

3. In the *Modify* panel ( ), in the Modifier List, select **MapScaler (WSM)**. In the Parameters rollout, verify that the *Scale* value is set to one system unit **0'1"**, as shown in Figure 7–23.

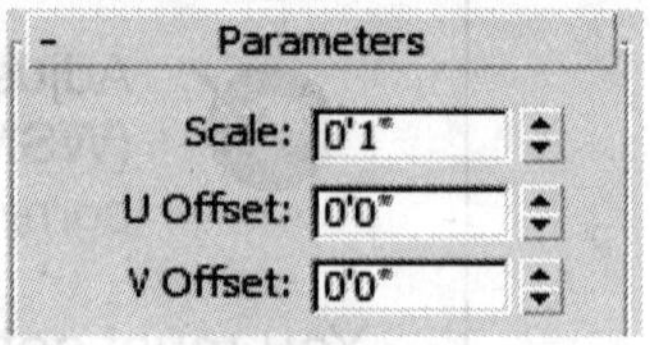

Figure 7–23

4. In the Main toolbar, click (Material Editor) to open the Slate Material Editor.

5. In the *Scene Materials*, double-click on the **Wall Multi Multi/Sub-Object** material to open it on the *View1* sheet. Locate the **Masonry** material, wired to input socket 5 of the **Wall Multi** material, as shown in Figure 7–24. Note that this material has a bitmap in the *Diffuse* and *Bump* channels. Double-click on the Masonry Bitmap wired to the **Masonry** material's Diffuse Map, to open its Parameter Editor.

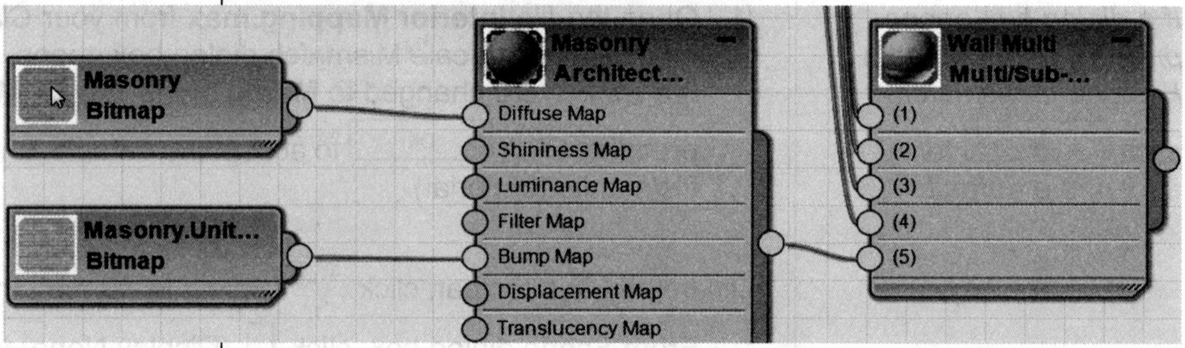

Figure 7–24

6. In the Coordinates rollout, verify that **Use Real-World Scale** is selected and set the *Width* and *Height Size* values to **4'7"** and **5'4"** respectively, as shown in Figure 7–25.

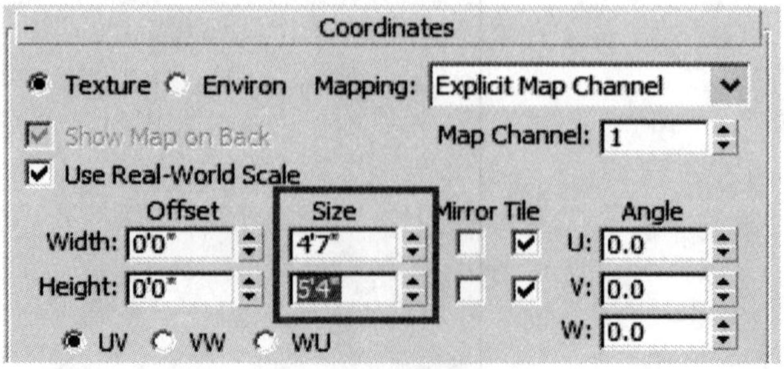

Figure 7–25

The Slate Material Editor is a modeless dialog box and can remain open while you are working in the viewport or other commands. You can minimize it if it is in the way and maximize it when you need it again.

7. In *View1* sheet, select the **Masonry Architect** material and click (Assign Material to Selection) to apply it to the selected wall objects (**Layer:VIZ-1-Walls**). In the Material Editor toolbar, click (Show Shaded Material in Viewport). Note that the **brick** material has been assigned to the walls.

8. In the Perspective viewport, use the various navigation tools, such as (Zoom), (Pan), (Orbit), and (Field-of-View) to zoom into and obtain the required orientation of one of the brick walls. The brick texture displays at the correct scale on the wall objects displaying the brick sub-material, as shown in Figure 7–26.

Figure 7–26

Hint: Map Visibility

If the brick is not visible in the viewport, try the following: drag a Standard material onto the wall object, add a diffuse map to that material, and click (Show Shaded Material in Viewport). The Standard material with texture map displays on the wall. Drag the original material back onto the wall, and the multi-sub architectural brick displays.

- For the most part the brick texture terminates in acceptable positions along the wall edges. If this were not the case you could move the texture along the wall with the **U-** and **V-** offset parameters in the map's Coordinates rollout or with a UVW XForm modifier.

9. When a material has multiple image maps that are meant to be aligned with each other (as in this case), all of their mapping coordinates' parameters should match. In the Slate Material Editor, double-click on the title bar heading for the **Masonry.Unit** bitmap, wired to the Bump Map of the **Masonry** material. In the Coordinates rollout, set the *Width* and *Height Size* values that were used for the Diffuse Map. This makes the bitmap texture display more realistic.

Hint: Multiple Sets of Mapping Coordinates

In the example you scaled a Multi/Sub-Object material map with a single MapScaler Modifier. What if another material's map in Wall Multi needed a **UVW Map** or different **MapScaler Scale** parameter?

Material maps can be assigned to separate channels in the Material Editor, so that each can be controlled by separate UVW Maps or MapScaler Modifiers. In this case you can apply multiple UVW Maps or MapScaler Modifiers to the same object and assign each the applicable channel identified in the **Map** parameters, as shown in Figure 7–27.

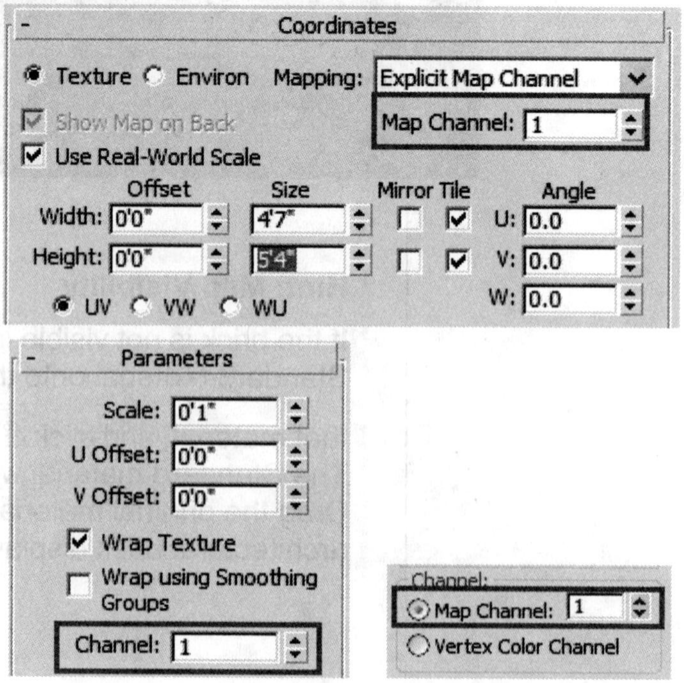

Figure 7–27

Task 2 - Assign the Ceiling Material.

1. Change your current view to the **Camera - Lobby1** camera view, by selecting the **Perspective** POV label and selecting **Cameras>Camera - Lobby1**.

The production renderer should be NVIDIA mental ray, NVIDIA iray, or Quicksilver Hardware Renderer to display the Autodesk Material Library.

2. You will use a material with an image map from the Autodesk Material Library. In the Material/Map Browser in the Slate Material Editor, the Autodesk Material Library might not be displayed. In the Main toolbar, click (Render Setup) to open the Render Setup dialog box. Alternatively, select **Rendering>Render Setup**. Close the Common Parameters rollout or scroll down to expand the Assign Renderer rollout. Next to the *Production* field, click (Choose Renderer) and select **NVIDIA mental ray**. Click OK and close the Render Setup dialog box.

3. In the Material/Map Browser in the Slate Material Editor, note that the Autodesk Material Library is displayed. Right-click on the View1 label and select **Create New View**. Accept the default view name (View2) and click OK. The *View2* sheet, which is empty, is the active sheet now.

4. Expand the Autodesk Material Library and the *Miscellaneous* category. Double-click on the **Acoustic Tile - 2x2 White Pebbled** material to display it in *View2* sheet, as shown in Figure 7–28.

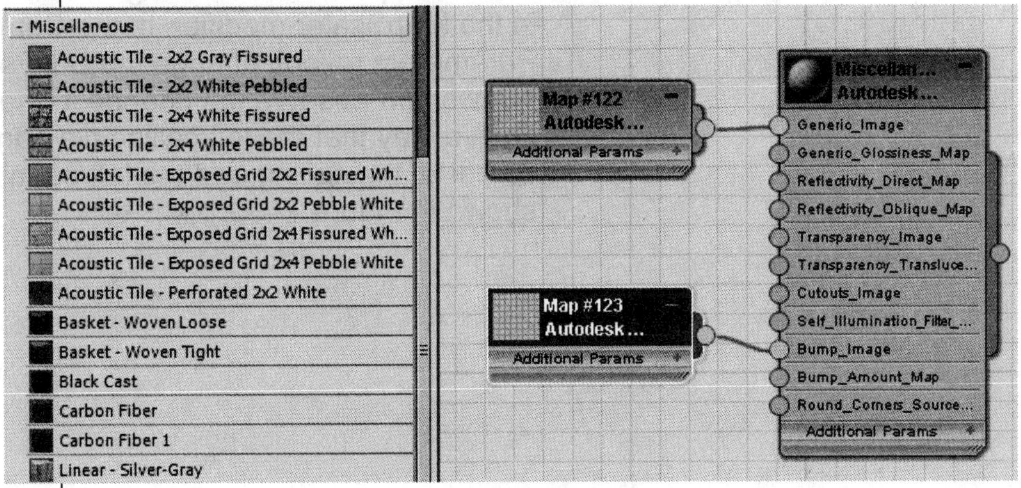

Figure 7–28

5. In the viewport, select the **Layer:VIZ-1-Ceiling** object, and in the Command Panel, apply a **MapScaler (WSM)** modifier by selecting it from the Modifier List. In the Parameters rollout, verify that *Scale* is set to **0'1"**.

6. In the Slate Material Editor, in the *View2* sheet, select **Miscellaneous** material by clicking on its title bar. In the Slate Material Editor toolbar, click (Assign Material to Selection) to assign it to the ceiling object (**Layer:VIZ-1-Ceiling**).

7. Note that the ceiling displays in gray in the viewport. In the Slate Material Editor toolbar, click (Show Shaded Material in Viewport) to preview the diffuse map in the viewport, as shown in Figure 7–29. The ceiling tiles have been sized using the Real-World Map Size that was defined for this material in the Autodesk Material Library (to a 2'x2' grid).

Figure 7–29

8. You can reposition the ceiling texture through the *Offset* fields in the MapScaler modifier. In the Command Panel, in the Parameters rollout, change the *U Offset* and *V Offset* spinner arrows and observe the change in the viewport. Move it in such a way that the left ceiling tile edge coincides with the corner of the ceiling and the left curtain wall window, as shown in Figure 7–30.

Figure 7–30

9. Save your work as **MyInterior Mapping.max**.

7.3 Spline Mapping

Learning Objective

- Apply spline mapping to a curved object using the Unwrap UVW modifier.

When you create a loft object you have the ability to generate mapping coordinates that follow the path of extrusion. This is an important and useful feature if you need a texture to follow the curvature of the lofted object. Spline mapping can be applied using the **Unwrap UVW** modifier. It enables you to select a spline for the basis of the mapping coordinates. You can also use the Mapping gizmo to modify the mapping along the cross-section. The spline mapping is applied at a sub-object level (Polygon or Face), as shown on the left in Figure 7–31, and is present in the Wrap rollout of the **Unwrap UVW** parameters, as shown on the right in Figure 7–31.

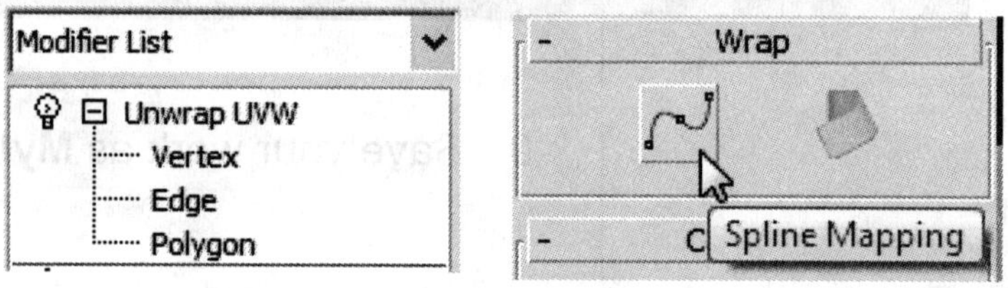

Figure 7–31

Practice 7d Spline Mapping

Learning Objective

- Apply spline mapping to a curved object using the Unwrap UVW modifier.

Estimated time for completion: 15 minutes

You must set the paths to locate the External files and Xrefs used in the practice. If you have not done this already, return to the **Introduction to Autodesk 3ds Max Design** chapter and complete Task 1 to Task 3 of the **Organizing Folders and Working with the Interface** practice. You only have to set the user paths once.

Task 1 - Position and Scale the Checker Map.

If a dialog box opens prompting you about a File Load: Mismatch, click OK to accept the default values.

1. Open **Spline Mapping.max**. There are two curved objects. The one on the right has been mapped with spline mapping and the one on the left does not have mapping. You will apply spline mapping to the object on the left and adjust the scale and position to match the one on the right.
2. Select the object on the left, named **Roadshape01**. A spline has already been prepared in this file, it runs (yellow line) through the center of the curved object. You can change the Visual Style to **Wireframe** to display the spline more clearly and then change it back to **Shaded**.
3. Expand the *Modify* panel ( ) and in the Modifier Stack verify that a Line object and an Extrude modifier are listed.
4. In the Main toolbar, click (Material Editor) to open the Slate Material Editor.
5. In the Material/Map Browser, scroll down to the *Scene Materials* category, locate the **02 - Default** Standard material. Double-click on this material to place it in the *View1* sheet. This material has already been assigned to the Roadshape01 object.
6. Double-click on the 02 Default title bar to open its Parameter Editor. In the Blinn Basic Parameters rollout, you can change the Diffuse color to verify that the material is assigned to the selected object (the Roadshape01 object interactively changes to the new color in the viewport). Click Cancel in the Color Selector dialog box.

7. In the Blinn Basic Parameters rollout, click (None) for the *Diffuse color* channel, as shown in Figure 7–32.

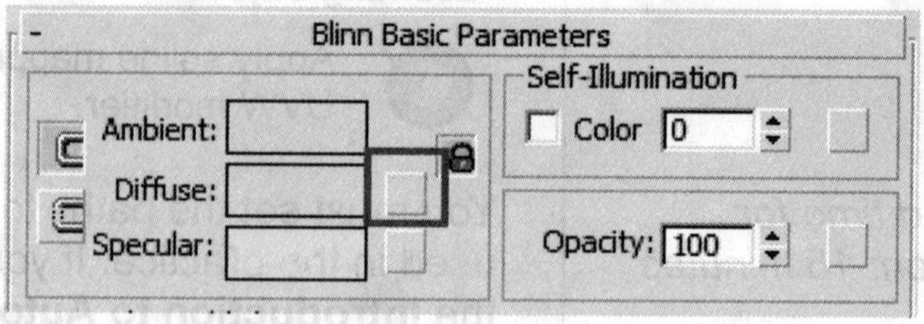

Figure 7–32

8. In the Material/Map Browser that opens, in the *Maps> Standard* categories, double-click on Checker. In the *View1* sheet, note that the Checker node is wired to the input socket of Diffuse Color of the **02- Default** material.

A checker board mapping material is useful for identifying map scaling and orientation issues, which can then be corrected before applying the actual texture map so that it displays correctly.

9. In the Slate Material Editor toolbar, click (Show Shaded Material in Viewport) to display the checker texture on the road shape in the viewport, as shown in Figure 7–33.

Figure 7–33

You can minimize the Slate Material Editor so that it is not in the way while you are working in the Command Panel and the viewport and maximize it when you need it again.

- Note that the checker map is projected as a single sheet on top of the rectangular object and not generated to follow the curvature of the spline.

10. To generate the checker map so that it follows the curvature of the spline, you need to apply the **Unwrap UVW** modifier. In the Command Panel, in the *Modify* panel ( ), in the Modifier List, select **Unwrap UVW**. Note that the Unwrap UVW is listed above Extrude in the Modifier Stack.

11. In the Modifier Stack, expand Unwrap UVW and select **Polygon**, as shown in Figure 7–34.

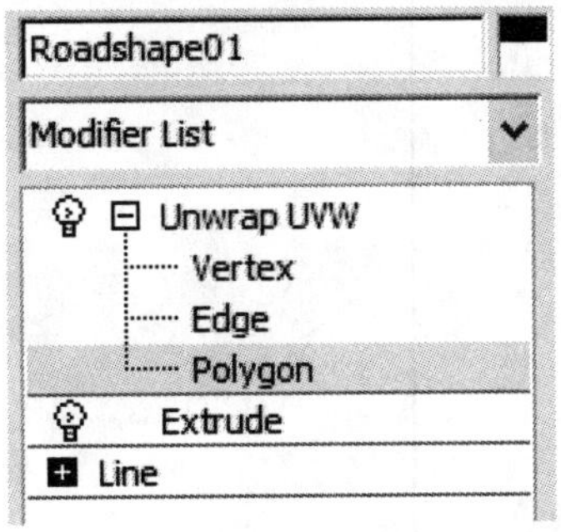

Figure 7–34

12. In the viewport, select the top face along the curve of the Roadshape01 object. Note that the checker is displayed in a red hue indicating that the face is selected.

13. In the Command Panel, scroll down to the Wrap rollout. Click (Spline Mapping), as shown in Figure 7–35.

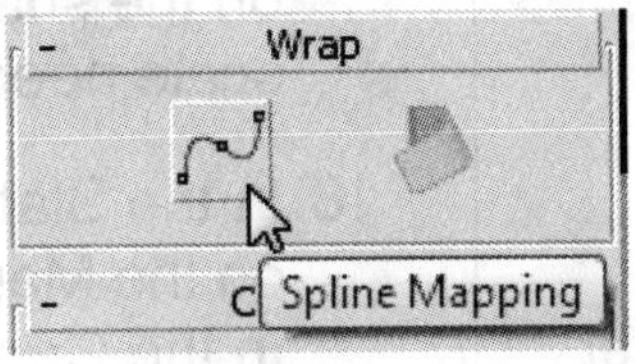

Figure 7–35

*Apply **Planar** for roads and planar surfaces with a line cross-section. Use **Circular** Mapping for objects with a circular cross-section.*

14. In the Spline Map Parameters dialog box, click - Pick Spline - and set the *Mapping* to **Planar**, as shown in Figure 7–36.

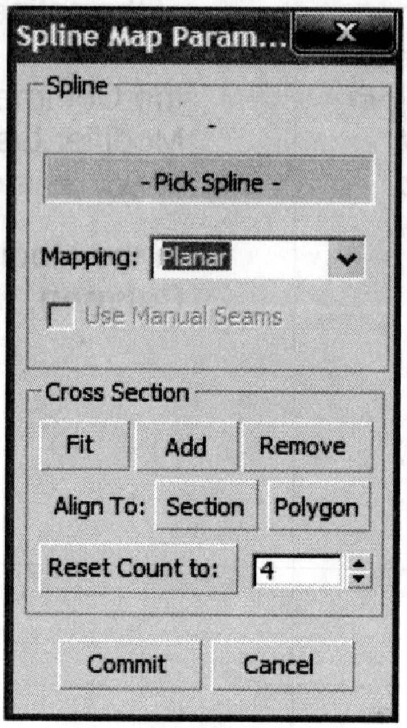

Figure 7–36

15. In the viewport, select the end of the spline, which is displayed at either end of the Roadshape01 object.

16. In the Spline Map Parameters dialog box, click Commit.

17. In the Modifier Stack, select **Unwrap UVW** to clear the selection and exit Sub-object mode. The texture is displayed on the shape as a single color indicating that the position and scale need to be corrected.

It is possible that by applying the values given here, the checker map might not display as required. Use the spinner for the Size Width to increase or decrease the value and note the interactive changes in the viewport. The checker line should pass through the center, following the curve line.

18. In the Slate Material Editor, in the *View1* sheet, double-click on the Map # Checker title bar to display its Parameter Editor. In the Coordinates rollout, set the *Size Width* to **0'0.8"**, and the *Size Height* to **0'0.08"**, and press <Enter>, as shown in Figure 7–37. Verify that the *Offset* values are **0'0.0"** for both *Width* and *Height*. It is recommended that you use the spinners to increase and decrease the *Size Width* while checking the interactive display of checker in the viewport.

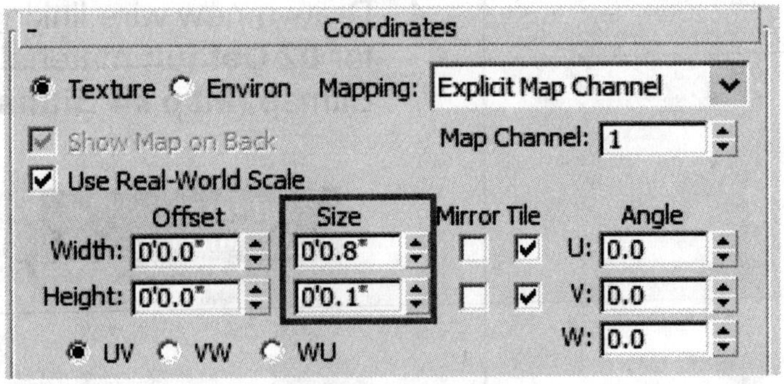

Figure 7–37

19. The checker map displays as shown in the Figure 7–38. This is the correct position and scale of the **checker** material.

Figure 7–38

Task 2 - Assign the Road Material.

1. In the Material/Map Browser, expand the *Maps>Standard* categories. Double-click on Bitmap to open the Select Bitmap Image File dialog box. In your *Class Files* in the *Maps* subfolder, open **TextureForRoad.jpg**.

2. Note that a new node for this bitmap is added in the *View1* sheet.

3. Delete the wire that currently exists between the **Checker** Map and the Diffuse Color of **02 Default** material by selecting the wire and pressing <Delete>.

4. Draw a new wire linking the input socket of the Diffuse Color for **02 Default** material to the output socket of the new Bitmap (**Map #4 Bitmap**), as shown in the Figure 7–39.

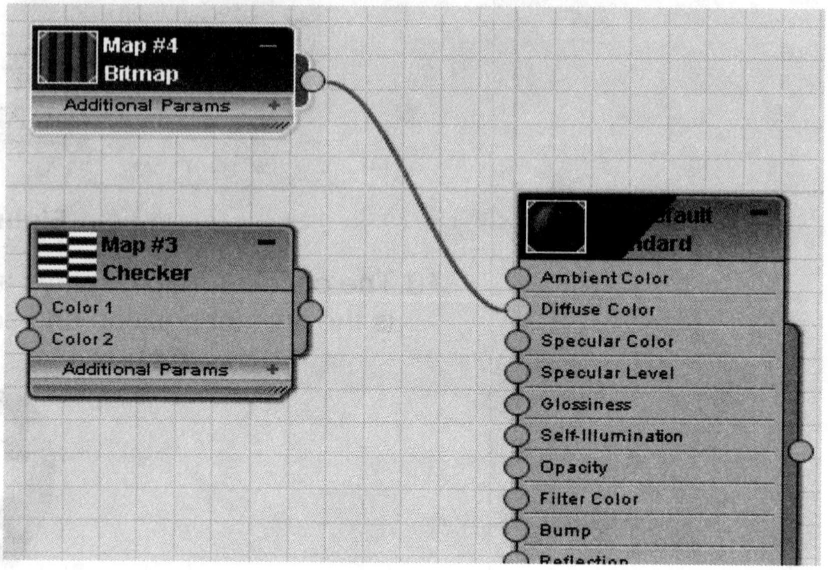

Figure 7–39

5. Select the **02 Default** material title bar and click (Show Shaded Material in Viewport) to display the road texture on the face on **Roadshape01** object.

6. Double-click on the new **Map # Bitmap (TextureForRoad)** material to open the Parameter Editor. In the Coordinates rollout, clear **Use Real-World Scale**.

7. Set *Tiling* for **U: 2** and **V: 8**. Use the **Offset U** and **V** sliders to center the road. Increasing the V tiling brings the dashes closer to the middle of the road while decreasing it makes the dashes longer and farther apart along the center curve. Use the *Offset U* spinner to increase or decrease the value so that the dashed line is placed along the center of the road. The road shape on the left should now match the road shape on the right as shown in Figure 7–40.

Figure 7–40

8. Save your work as **MyStartSplineMapping.max**.

Chapter Review Questions

1. Which option manipulates a map with mapping coordinates at the map level of the Slate Material Editor?
   a. Generate coordinates for all objects.
   b. Generate Mapping Coords
   c. Unwrap UVW
   d. Use Real-World Scale
2. The MapScaler in the World Space Modifier keeps the map scale constant if the object size changes with the Scale transform.
   a. True
   b. False
3. In the **UVW Map** modifier, which mapping parameter option (Parameter rollout>*Mapping* area) is intended for 2D objects or 3D objects where the edge pixels are permitted to project into the third dimension?
   a. **Box**
   b. **Planar**
   c. **Spherical**
   d. **Shrink Wrap**
4. Which of the following is the correct method for controlling map scaling of individual objects using a UVW Map? These options are accessed in the Parameter Editor of the map in the Slate Material Editor.
   a. Select **Use Real-World Scale** and assign the appropriate size (*Width* and *Height*) values.
   b. Select **Use Real-World Scale** and assign both the *Width* and *Height Size* values to the U-scale value.
   c. Clear **Use Real-World Scale** and set the *Tiling U* and *V* values to **1.0**.
   d. Clear **Use Real-World Scale** and set the *U-Tiling* value to **1.0** and the *V-Tiling* value equal to the ratio of the U-scale divided by the V scale.

5. Which mapping modifier is used to generate a map to follow the curvature of the spline along which the object was extruded (Spline mapping)?
    a. UVW Map
    b. Unwrap UVW
    c. MapScaler (WSM)
    d. MapScaler (OSM)

Chapter 8

Introduction to Lighting

In this chapter you learn the concept of local and global illumination. You learn the different types of lights provided with the software. You learn to create standard lights, the different types of standard lights that you can use, and the parameters to control the settings for each of them. You also learn to use the different types of shadow casting methods and how to modify their parameters.

This chapter contains the following topics:

- ✓**Local vs. Global Illumination**
- ✓**Standard Lighting**
- ✓**Types of Standard Lights**
- ✓**Shadow Types**

Certification

Topic:

✓Lighting

Objectives:

✓Differentiate light functions in a scene

8.1 Local vs. Global Illumination

Learning Objectives

- Understand the default lighting that is provided with the software.
- Understand the concept of local illumination.
- Understand how light interacts with multiple surfaces using global illumination.

A strength of the Autodesk® 3ds Max® Design software is that it provides several different kinds of scene lighting. Each method can be used to create results of the highest quality, but certain approaches are better for certain situations. As with all aspects of the Autodesk 3ds Max Design software, lighting results vary depending on the time spent configuring a scene and the experience level of the user. A significant difference between lighting methods is whether they provide local or global illumination.

Default Illumination

First, the Autodesk 3ds Max Design software automatically adds light to unlit scenes with invisible, un-selectable light objects referred to as default lighting. A key light is located in the front and left of a scene and a fill light behind and to the right. These lights act as omni lights, which are lights that illuminate in all directions. When user-defined light objects are added to a scene, the default lighting is automatically disabled for rendering.

Local Illumination

With a traditional local illumination approach, light sources only affect those objects that they can directly illuminate. Local illumination algorithms do not account for the diffuse light that bounces off of one surface to illuminate another nor do the effects of this reflected light become mixed together.

- Since the world is filled with illumination that transfers between surfaces and mixes with light bounced from other surfaces, local illumination strategies usually require arbitrary fill or ambient lights to simulate this indirect lighting.
- Ray traced materials in a scene lit by standard lighting permit the calculation of specular reflections between surfaces. Specular reflections create mirrored effects and highlights on shiny surfaces.

- Using a local illumination strategy in the Autodesk 3ds Max Design software is often referred to as Standard Lighting.

When a scene is illuminated with standard lighting (local illumination) without ambient or indirect light, the ceiling and shadows are dark as there are no lights pointed directly at those areas, as shown in Figure 8–1.

Figure 8–1

When the ambient lights are added with standard lighting, the ceiling and shadows become softer, as shown in Figure 8–2.

Figure 8–2

Global Illumination

Global Illumination (GI) algorithms describe how light interacts with multiple surfaces. The illumination and rendering methods that take into account GI include mental ray, radiosity, and raytracing.

- Ray tracing is not used as a stand-alone rendering method in the Autodesk 3ds Max Design software as it can be computationally intensive. Instead it is used to compliment the other rendering methods when called for by ray traced materials and certain shadow types.
- Radiosity and mental ray are two different lighting/rendering strategies that calculate diffuse inter-reflections of light, automatically generating ambient illumination and light mixing.
- Because they accurately calculate ambient light levels (rather than you approximating them) Radiosity and mental ray can produce stunningly realistic results, especially when daylight is involved.
- Radiosity and mental ray are designed to work with physically based (photometric) lights that have parameters derived from real-world lighting properties. Global Illumination calculations can be rendered as a lighting analysis to reveal illumination levels. The Autodesk 3ds Max Design software has the Lighting Analysis Assistant that generates light meter objects and image overlays based on mental ray physical lighting and materials. This information can be used for green building LEED certification credit 8.1.
- There are also 3rd party renderers available like Maxwell, Brazil, finalrender, and VRay that give spectacular global illumination results. VRay has dominated the architecture market in the past and can be considered a standard in high-end visualization.

Figure 8–3 was created with global illumination, showing an interior scene with night time lighting.

Figure 8–3

Figure 8–4 was created with global illumination, showing an interior scene with daytime lighting.

Figure 8–4

In Figure 8–5, the indoor scene uses mental ray lit by physical lighting.

Figure 8–5

Selecting a Lighting Strategy

- Generally, Global Illumination (GI) approaches tend to require more time overall than a standard approach but the results are often more realistic.
- Nearly all of the renderings showcased in the Autodesk 3ds Max Design product literature are produced with a GI lighting approach.
- In terms of total time spent configuring, calculating, and rendering, standard lighting tends to be less time consuming than the GI approaches (although there are exceptions).
- For simple scenes with a small number of objects or surfaces (such as a small mechanical model), there might be little added benefit from a GI approach.
- GI approaches are very popular in architecture, interior design, and related fields. However, standard lighting still has a place in these industries for conceptual tasks, projects with short timeframes, or those that do not require extreme photorealism.

Types of Lights

There are two types of lights provided with the software. You can have standard lights or photometric lights in a scene and both types are placed as light objects. Different parameters are provided when you create either type of light and both Standard lights and Photometric lights have many similar parameters. The lights can be created using the Command Panel. In the *Create* panel ( ), click (Lights), and select the type of light you want to create in the drop-down list, as shown in Figure 8–6. Alternatively, you can select **Create>Lights** and then select the type you want to create.

Figure 8–6

8.2 Standard Lighting

Certification

Topic:

✓Lighting

Objectives:

✓Compare Attenuation and Decay

Learning Objectives

- Understand how the standard lights are created and the strategy behind using the standard lighting type.
- Understand the General Parameters that are common to all of the types of Standard lights.

Standard lights are objects that are based on computer calculations, which imitate lights that are used in everyday life. Standard lights are not the default option when creating lights in the Autodesk 3ds Max Design software. You are required to select the **Standard** option in the Command Panel. The following specifics apply to working with a standard lighting strategy in the Autodesk 3ds Max Design software.

- Standard lighting strategies use standard light objects, such as **Spot**, **Directional**, **Omni**, and **Skylights**.
- Standard lights are highly configurable, but are not based on real-world lighting parameters. Standard lighting requires arbitrary adjustments to achieve the required effect.
- Objects illuminated with standard lighting can use any material type.
- Scenes lit by standard lighting almost always require ambient (fill) lights to be added, either through a global ambient value or ambient light objects. Ambient light should be added carefully. Rough or approximate fill lighting can lead to flat or washed out effects that detract from the final result.
- Lighting results are calculated at render time and are not stored on the objects. Processing standard lights does not increase file size and mesh subdivision is not required (as with Radiosity).
- Standard lighting does not require exposure control. Exposure control is a method of balancing illumination levels in rendered output. It is essential to working with global illumination, using mental ray or Radiosity. When doing standard lighting ensure exposure control is not on by default. If there is a strong difference between the viewport display and the rendering result, this might be the symptom of exposure control being active.

- Standard lighting is designed for use with the Default Scanline Renderer. Standard lighting will also work with mental ray, but the results will not be physically accurate. When working with mental ray, photometric lights are the preferred lighting technique.

Common Parameters

All standard lights share common General Parameters and Intensity/Color/Attenuation settings. These parameters can be set while creating each type of standard light, as shown in Figure 8–7. Once the lights have been created, you can access these parameters in the *Modify* panel () in the Command Panel.

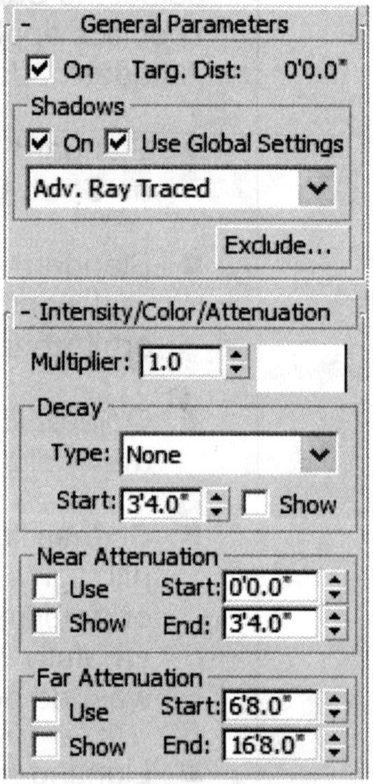

Figure 8–7

General Parameters

- The General Parameters rollout enables you to turn the light on and off in the scene using the **On** option, change the light type (**Spot**, **Directional**, or **Omni**), select to work with a target, and select shadow settings. Lights cast illumination even if they are on a hidden layer. The simplest way to turn off a light is using this option. You can also right-click on any light and turn it off from the **Tools 1** quad menu.

- Several types of lights (and some cameras as well) can have a target object. A light always points directly at its target, enabling you to change the direction of the light by moving the target. Manipulating a target is sometimes easier than transforming and orienting a light. Lights with targets are called Target lights and those without targets are called Free lights.

Intensity/Color/Attenuation Parameters

- The **Multiplier** option is the brightness control for standard lights. This is an arbitrary value that needs to be evaluated by eye to achieve the required results. The color swatch to the right enables you to select a color to filter the light with. Start with the **Multiplier** option at 1.0 and adjust, as necessary. Avoid using high Multiplier values, or you get overly bright lighting.
- The *Decay* area offers techniques for simulating how light fades over distance.
- The *Far Attenuation* area provides a similar kind of fading based on explicitly set distances. The *Start* value is where fading begins and the *End* value is the point at which the light fades to zero illumination. Typically you would use either the options in the *Decay* or *Far Attenuation* areas, not both.
- The *Near Attenuation* area enables you to define a distance from the light where the light starts casting faint illumination and then end with full illumination. Near attenuation does not occur in the real world and is included here as a computer graphics lighting effect.
- The **Show** option for attenuation enables a graphical representation of these distances to remain visible after the object is cleared.

All of the standard lights except for directional lights, are considered Point lights, which means their light is cast from a single point rather than along a line or from an area.

Certification

Topic:
✓Lighting
Objectives:
✓Differentiate light functions in a scene

8.3 Types of Standard Lights

Learning Objective

Work with different types of standard light objects and learn about their specific parameter settings.

The type of standard light objects that can be created are **Spot**, **Directional**, **Omni**, and **Skylights**. You can select the required type of standard lights in the Object Type rollout, as shown in Figure 8–8.

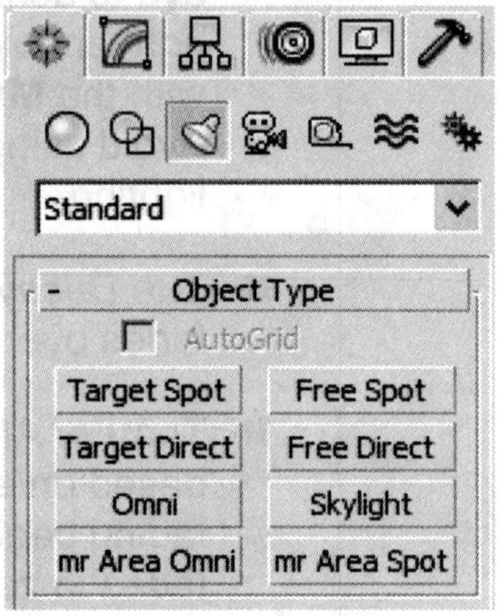

Figure 8–8

Omni Lights

Omni lights, as shown in Figure 8–9, are used to represent point lights that cast light equally in all directions, such as an idealized light bulb. Omni lights are also commonly used for ambient fill lights. A single omni light requires six times the computational effort of a single spotlight, so use spotlights in place of omni lights whenever possible.

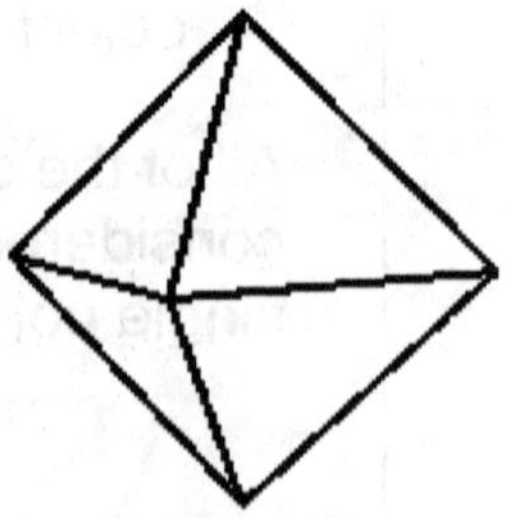

Figure 8–9

Spotlights

Spotlights are used to represent point light sources that cast focused beams of light in a cone with a circular or square base. A spotlight with a circular base in 2D is shown on the left in Figure 8–10, and 3D is shown on the right in Figure 8–10. Most real world lighting fixtures are more appropriately represented by spotlights rather than omnis or directional lights.

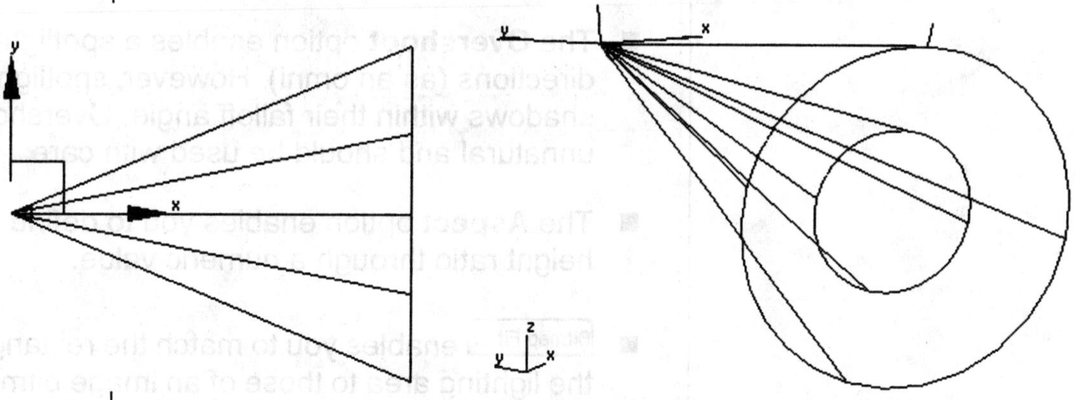

Figure 8–10

Two types of spotlight objects are available: **Target Spot** and **Free Spot**. **Target Spot** light objects cast focused beams of light pointing directly at a target, whereas the **Free Spot** light object casts focused beams of light pointing anywhere without a target object. In addition to the Common Standard Parameters, spotlights have specific parameters, as shown in Figure 8–11, to control the distribution of the light they cast.

Figure 8–11

- The *Hotspot/Beam* value is the angle over which the full lighting intensity is projected. It is represented in the graphics above as the inner cone.
- The *Falloff/Field* value is the outer angle that illumination projects. It is represented in the graphics above as the outer cone.

- The light fades from full intensity to zero intensity between these two angles. Therefore when these angles have similar values the light creates a sharp, defined pool of light. Widely separated angles create a soft, gradual fade.

- The hotspot and falloff values almost always need to be adjusted from the default settings.

- The **Overshoot** option enables a spotlight to cast light in all directions (as an omni). However, spotlights only cast shadows within their falloff angle. Overshoot generally looks unnatural and should be used with care.

- The **Aspect** option enables you to define the width and height ratio through a numeric value.

- Bitmap Fit... enables you to match the rectangular proportions of the lighting area to those of an image bitmap file directly. This is very useful if you are also projecting the bitmap.

Directional Lights

Directional lights are used to represent light sources that cast parallel rays, as shown in Figure 8–12. The best example of parallel light would be the light cast from the sun to an Architectural-scale project or smaller. (The sun could be considered an omni light when dealing with massive visualizations at the continental or global scale.)

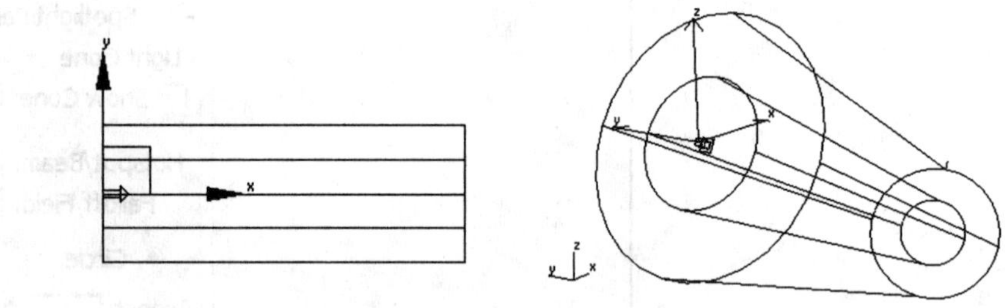

Figure 8–12

Two types of directional light objects are available: **Target Direct** and **Free Direct**. In addition to the Common Standard Parameters, directional lights have specific options available through the Directional Parameters rollout, as shown in Figure 8–13. The Directional Parameters options are nearly identical to those in the Spotlight Parameters rollout options. The only difference is the *Hotspot/Beam* and *Falloff/Field* values. These are measured in terms of a width parameter rather than an angle.

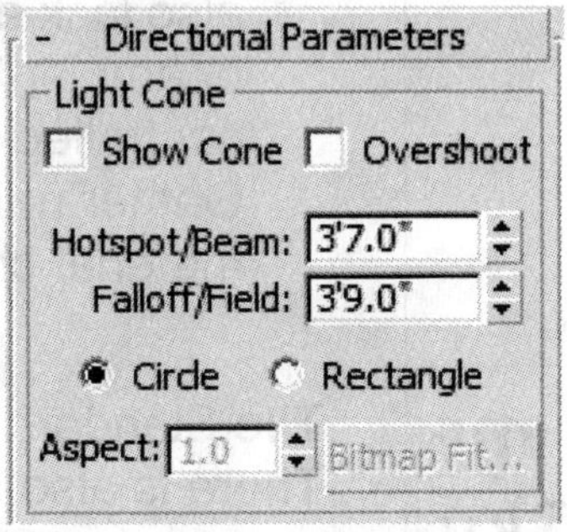

Figure 8–13

Fill Lights

Any light can be used to approximate indirect lighting, which is referred to in this text as a fill light. Fill lights can act as normal lights or they can be specifically set to cast ambient light, by selecting the **Ambient Only** option in the Advanced Effects rollout in the **Standard lights** parameters, as shown in Figure 8–14.

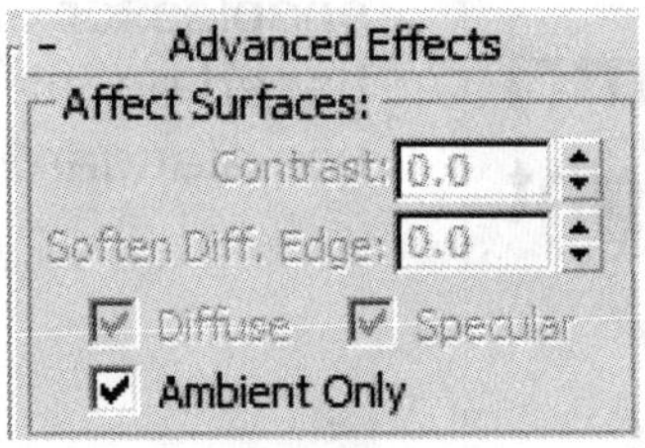

Figure 8–14

- Standard materials have an **Ambient color** parameter that can be used when illuminated using ambient lights. This color can be different from the diffuse color produced by normal (non-ambient) lights. The Ambient color is normally locked to the diffuse or it can be set darker than the diffuse color for emphasis.

- Setting a fill light to cast ambient light automatically disables shadow casting. The reason for this is that only real-world light sources (the sun and lighting fixtures) are normally permitted to cast shadows.

- If you would prefer that your fill lights cast normal light (which illuminates a material's diffuse color instead of ambient), do not select the **Ambient Only** option. In this case you would need to manually disable shadow casting.
- Architectural materials were designed for Radiosity and do not have an **Ambient color** parameter. Otherwise they function similarly to Standard materials with standard lighting.
- Arch & Design materials were designed for mental ray and also lack an ambient color channel. In mental ray the concept of ambient lighting is replaced with bounced lighting. It is controlled by the number of diffuse bounces in the Final Gather rollout, as well as reflectivity/transparency, and other material choices.

Skylight and mr Sky

The Standard light category also includes a Skylight object. There is also a mental ray skylight (mr Sky) used with an mental ray sun (mr Sun) to create a sky when rendering with the mental ray renderer. The mr sky is found in the Photometric category. Both the Skylight and the mr Sky serve as a type of ambient lighting adding global illumination to the scene.

mental ray (mr) Area Omni Light and mental ray (mr) Area Spotlight

Also included in the standard light category are these two area light objects (as opposed to point light objects). They are intended specifically for use with mental ray. You can combine the use of mental ray materials and mental ray lighting. This enables for energy-conserving lighting, which is calculated based on the 1st Law of Thermodynamics. Mental ray can also use standard lights for rendering.

Practice 8a Standard Lighting for an Interior Scene

Learning Objectives

- Create standard lights in a scene and adjust their parameters to make the scene realistic.
- Create ambient fill lighting to approximate the indirect illumination that would be present in the real world.

Estimated time for completion: 30 minutes

In this practice you will model interior lighting conditions without daylight. You will add a spotlight to represent each interior light and omni lights for ambient lighting.

You must set the paths to locate the External files and Xrefs used in the practice. If you have not done this already, return to the **Introduction to Autodesk 3ds Max Design** chapter and complete Task 1 to Task 3 of the **Organizing Folders and Working with the Interface** practice. You only have to set the user paths once.

Task 1 - Create, Array, and Instance Light Objects.

If a dialog box opens prompting you about a File Load: Mismatch, click OK *to accept the default values.*

1. Open **Standard Lighting – Interior.max** from your *Class Files* folder.

Hold down <Win> and press <Shift> repeatedly to cycle through all of the viewports. Release <Win> when the viewport that you want maximized is highlighted.

2. To represent the ceiling lights, you will add free spotlights in the Top viewport. Adding lights in this view causes them to point toward the floor. Hold down <Win> and press <Shift> (do not hold down <Shift>). This opens an overlay displaying all of the available viewports in the layout, with the Top viewport highlighted. Release <Win> to display the maximized Top viewport. Click (Zoom Extents) to refit the model in the Top viewport.

3. In the *Create* panel ( ), click (Lights). In the drop-down list, select **Standard** and in the Object Type rollout, click Free Spot, as shown in Figure 8–15.

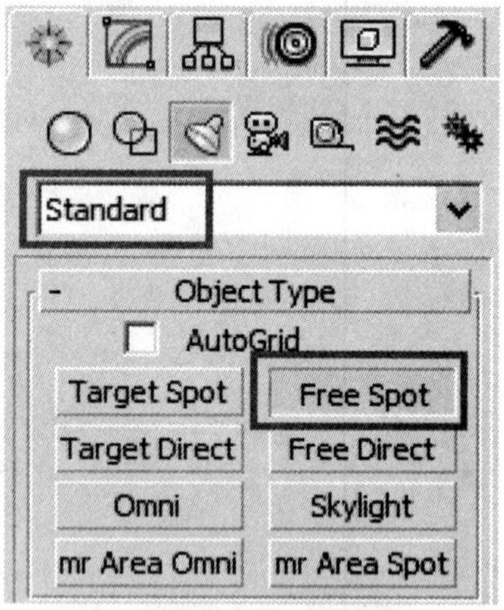

Figure 8–15

4. You will add a light near the approximate center of the upper left circle representing the opening for recessed lighting. Click to place a free spotlight as shown in Figure 8–16.

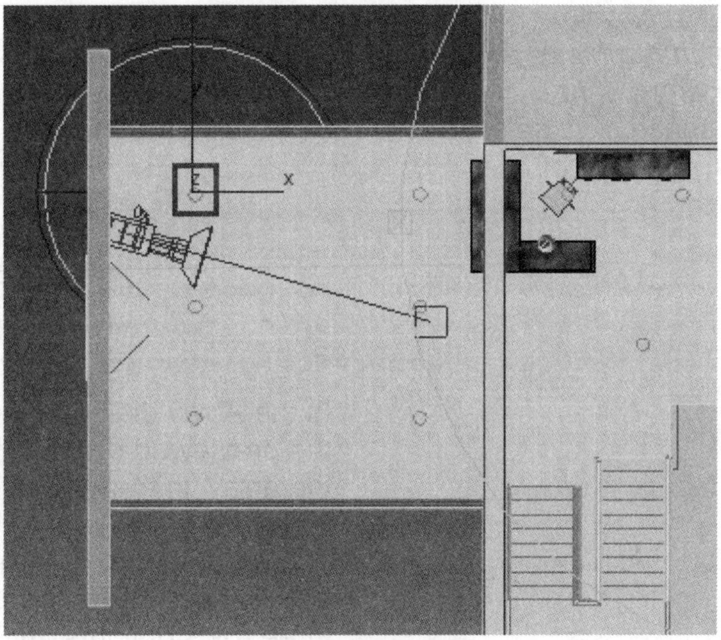

Figure 8–16

5. With the light object still selected, click (Select and Move).

6. In the Status Bar, verify that (Absolute Mode Transform Type-In) is displayed and in the *X, Y,* and *Z* edit boxes, enter **84'7"**, **126'10"**, and **9'11"** respectively, as shown in Figure 8–17. Press <Enter>.

Figure 8–17

- In addition to placing the light at the exact center of the recessed fixture, it places the light at a height of 9'11", which is 1" below the ceiling height.

7. In the Command Panel, select the *Modify* panel ( ) and name the light **Ceiling Downlight 00**.

- The way this scene has been set up, there is no convenient snap to automatically locate your light objects to the center of the circles representing the recessed fixtures. Instead you have to enter the exact coordinates, which need to be previously determined through Autodesk 3ds Max Design Utilities, such as the **Measure** tool. The six lights in the foyer area are 12' apart along the world X-direction and 6' apart along the world Y-direction. You will instance these lights using the **Array** option.

If the Extras toolbar is hidden, in the Main toolbar area, right-click in empty space, and select ***Extras*** *in the list of toolbars*

8. With the light selected, in the Extras toolbar, click (Array), as shown in Figure 8–18, or in the Menu bar select **Tools>Array**.

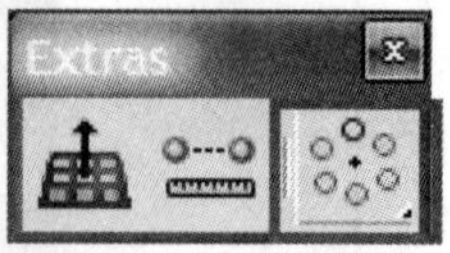

Figure 8–18

9. In the Array dialog box, click Preview to enable the previewed display in the scene. For the first dimension of the array, in the *Array Transformation* area, enter *X Incremental* value of **12'0"**. In the *Array Dimensions* area, set *1D Count* to **2** to create two columns of lights. Select **2D** and set *2D Count* to **3** and *Incremental Row Y* to **-6'0"** to create three rows of lights. In *Type of Object* area, verify that **Instance** is selected so that the parameters of all of the lights can be adjusted at the same time. Note that *Total in Array* is automatically set to **6** (two lights in each of the three rows), as shown in Figure 8–19.

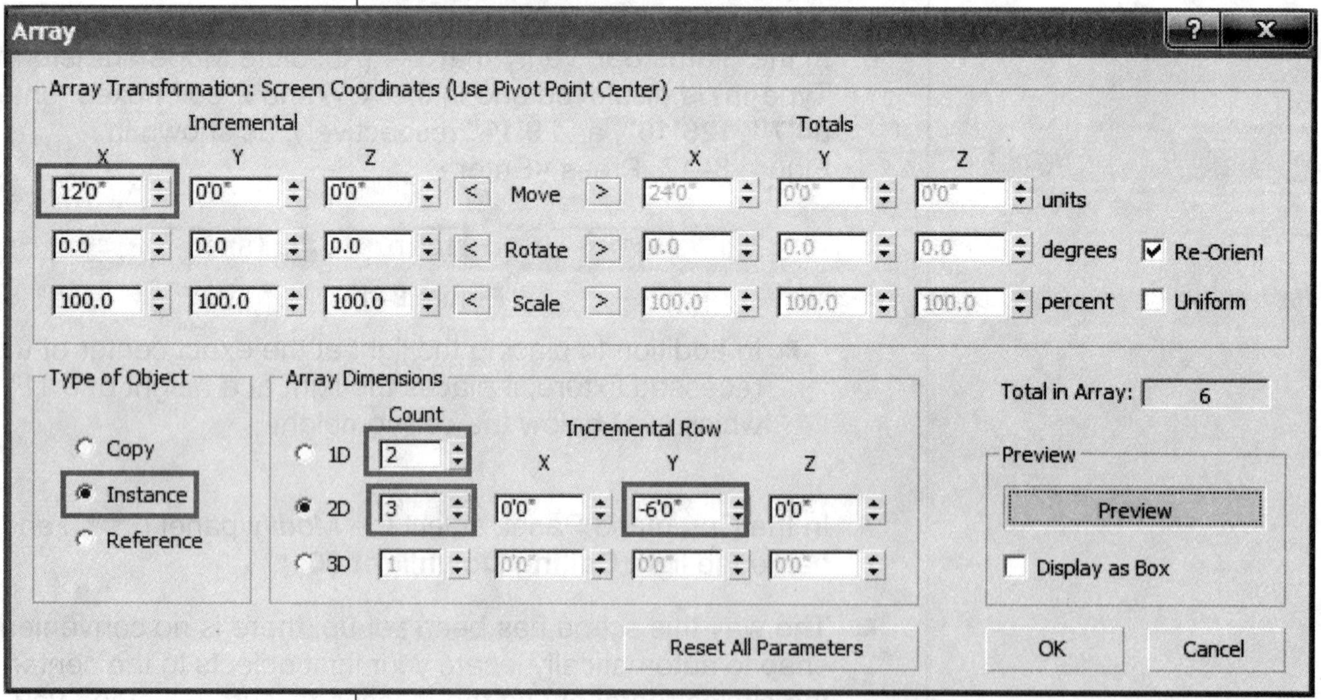

Figure 8–19

- The six lights will be displayed in the viewport because of Preview selected.

- You can leave the Array dialog box open (it is modeless) and pan and zoom in the viewport to verify that the lights are placed in the required position.

10. If the lights preview is in the correct positions, as shown in Figure 8–20, click OK in the dialog box.

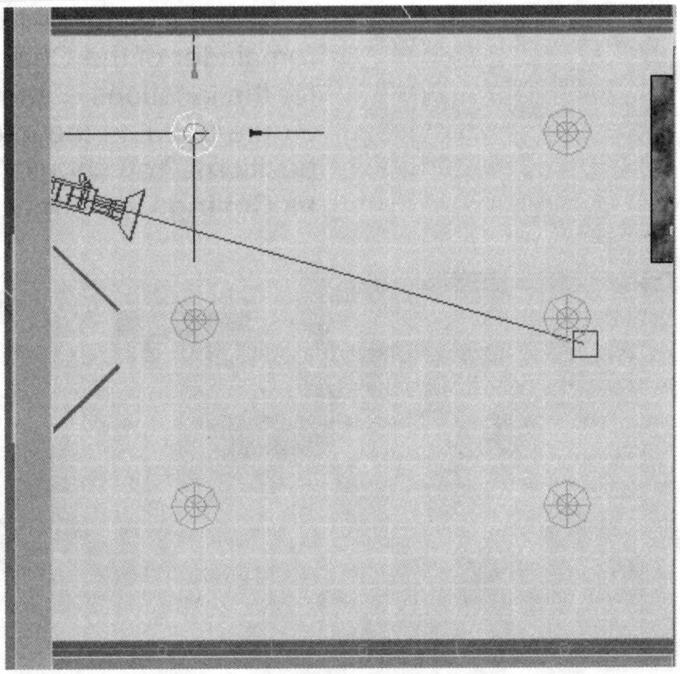

Figure 8–20

When arraying the objects, the software automatically increments the name by 1.

11. Select the light in the upper right corner (**Ceiling Downlight 001**). Click (Select and Move), and hold down <Shift> while dragging along the Transform gizmo's X-axis to locate the light over the desk area, almost on top of the chair, as shown in Figure 8–21. In the Clone Options dialog box, verify that **Instance** is selected and click OK.

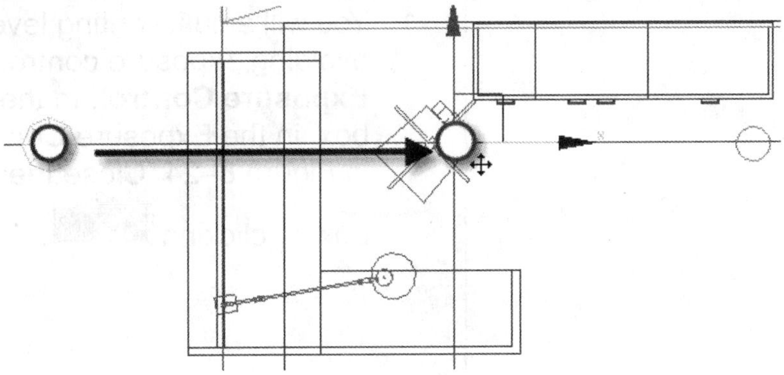

Figure 8–21

12. With this light still selected, in the Status Bar, in the *X, Y,* and *Z* edit boxes, set the exact coordinates as **104'7"**, **126'10"**, and **9'11"**, as shown in Figure 8–22.

Figure 8–22

13. Continue to <Shift> + click and drag to instance the remainder of the Ceiling Downlights, to the circles provided for the locations of the recessed lighting, as shown in Figure 8–23. In the interest of time, approximate their positions. You should have 14 lights with the last one named as **Ceiling Downlight 013**.

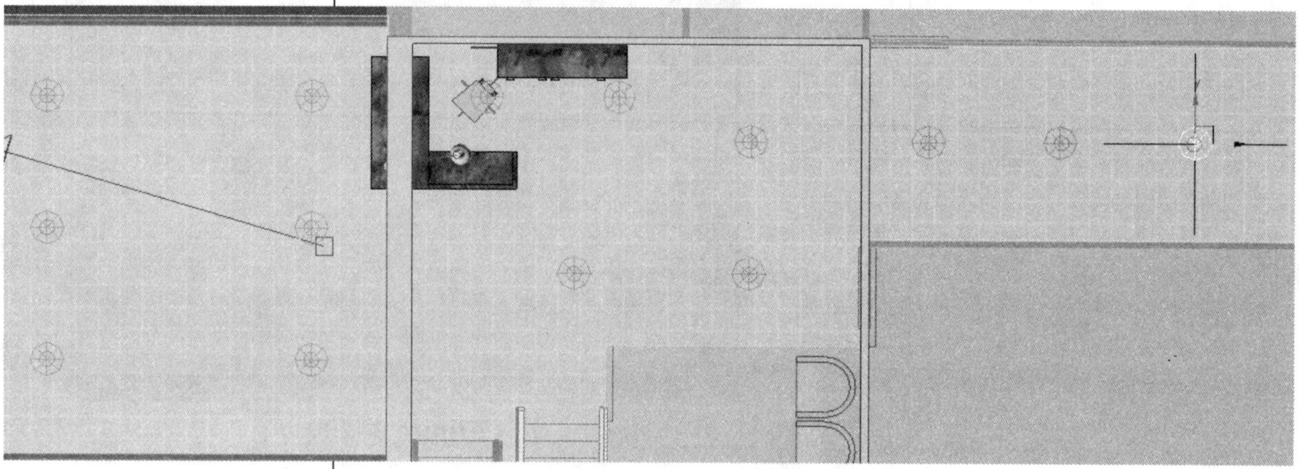

Figure 8–23

Task 2 - Adjust Standard Light Parameters.

In Task 1, you made instances of each of the lights so that their parameters can be adjusted together. If you want different light fixtures in the scene, you might not want to instance them.

1. You will adjust lighting levels through light object parameters, avoiding exposure control for now. Select **Rendering> Exposure Control**. In the Environment and Effects dialog box, in the Exposure Control rollout, clear **Active**, as shown in Figure 8–24. Close the Environments and Effects dialog box by clicking .

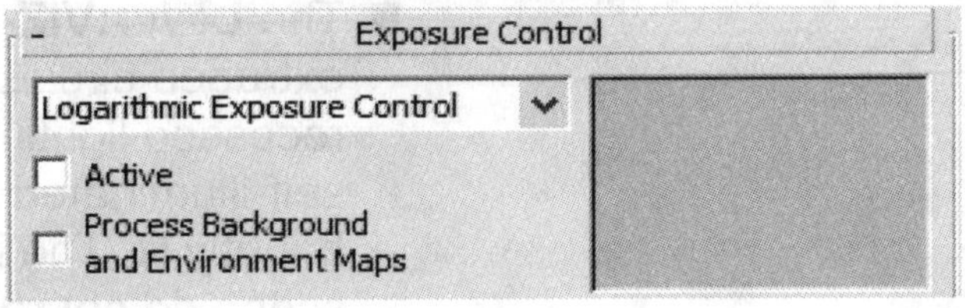

Figure 8–24

2. Select any of the instanced lights. In the Command Panel, verify that the *Modify* panel () is open and that **Ceiling Downlight** (any number) name is displayed. In the Spotlight Parameters rollout, set *Hotspot/Beam* to **45**, press <Enter> and verify that **Circle** is selected. The *Falloff/Field* updates automatically, as shown in Figure 8–25.

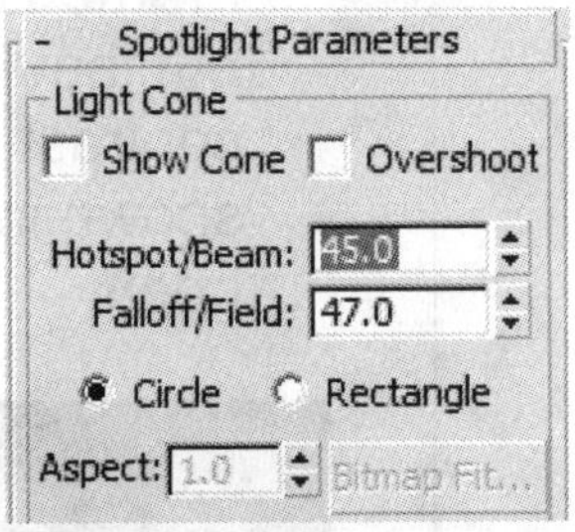

Figure 8–25

3. Change to the Camera – Lobby1 view by selecting the **Top** POV label and selecting **Cameras>Camera - Lobby 1**. In the Main toolbar, click  (Render Production). At this point your light objects are only illuminating small pools of light on the floor, as shown in Figure 8–26, due to their current hotspot and falloff values.

Figure 8–26

- The **Layer:VIZ-1-Ceiling Lights** object is made up of extruded circles representing the openings for your recessed lighting. They have been assigned a self-illuminated material to make the openings display brightly lit. The light objects you have just added to the scene do not render.

4. Select one of the instanced lights, if not already selected. In the Spotlight Parameters rollout, set the *Falloff/Field* value to **170** degrees and press <Enter>

If you need to change some of the parameters and render again, you can leave the Rendered Frame Window open because it is a modeless dialog box. After changing a parameter, click 

in the Rendered Frame Window to render the viewport again.

5. Click  (Render Production) if you closed the Rendered Frame Window or click 

if the Rendered Frame Window is open. The illumination now spreads out, but the floor is being lit too brightly and has lost all of its contrast (sometimes referred to as being washed out), as shown in Figure 8–27. Leave the Rendered Frame Window open.

Figure 8–27

6. In the Intensity/Color/Attenuation rollout, in *Far Attenuation* area, select **Use**. Set *Start* and *End* as **0'0"** and **16'0"** respectively, as shown in Figure 8–28.

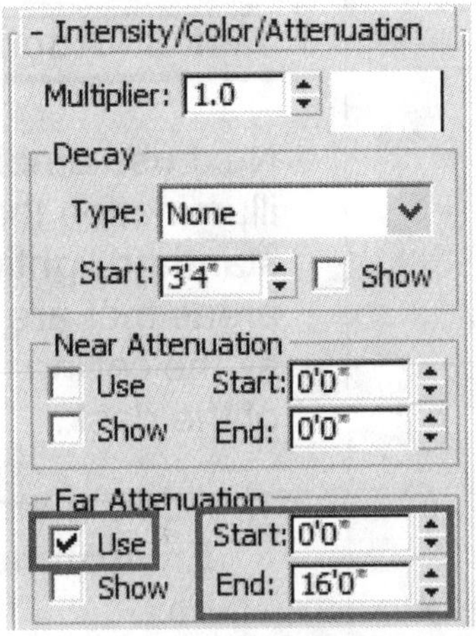

Figure 8–28

7. Click Render. The washed out effect is removed but the overall render looks dark, as shown in Figure 8–29.

Figure 8–29

*As with most **Standard Lighting** parameters, attenuation settings are arbitrary and require trial and error to achieve the required result.*

8. Adjust the overall brightness of the lights using the Multiplier. In the Intensity/Color/Attenuation rollout, set *Multiplier* to **2.0**.

   Click Render in the Rendered Frame Window. The surfaces under direct illumination should now become brighter.

Task 3 - Add Ambient Fill Light.

Next use ambient fill lighting to approximate the indirect illumination that would be present in the real world. With a standard lighting approach, fill light is necessary to brighten areas that are not directly illuminated by your light objects, such as the ceiling, the underside of the curtain wall rails, and the front of the desk.

1. Add the ambient light globally. Select **Rendering> Environment** to open the Environment and Effects dialog box.

2. In the *Environment* tab, in the Common Parameters rollout, in the *Global Lighting* area, select the **Ambient** color swatch, as shown in Figure 8–30.

Figure 8–30

3. In the Color Selector dialog box, change the *Value* to **25**, and press <Enter>, as shown in Figure 8–31. Leave both the Environment and Effects dialog box and Color Selector dialog box open and in the Rendered Frame Window, click 

to render the scene.

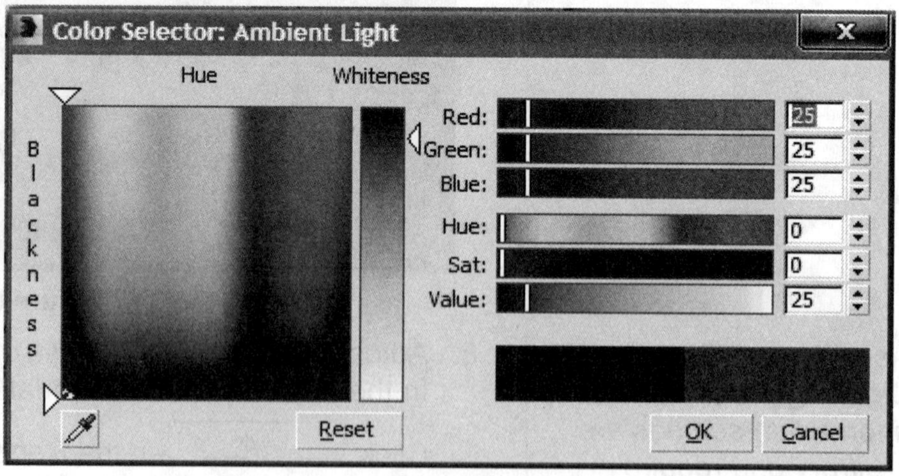

Figure 8–31

4. In this rendering many areas have become lighter but the ceiling is still too dark. In the Color Selector dialog box, change the *Value* to **50** and press <Enter>. In the Rendered Frame Window, click Render. The ceiling is brighter but objects under direct illumination have lost some contrast, as shown in Figure 8–32. The front of the half-wall behind the stairs looks flat because the ambient lighting is so uniform. (This is a pitfall of adding too much global ambient light.)

Figure 8–32

5. This scene might respond better with manually configured ambient light rather than the global settings. First, in the Color Selector dialog box, set the ambient color *Value* to **0** and press <Enter>. Close all dialog boxes.

6. In the viewport, change to the Top viewport by pressing <T> and click (Zoom Extents) to see the floorplan. In the *Create* panel ( ), click (Lights) and verify that **Standard** is displayed. Click Omni to create an omni light. You use this light to simulate ambient light reflected off the floor and lower walls.

7. Click once in the center of the six lights in the foyer to add an omni light. In the Name and Color rollout, enter **Lobby Fill Light 00** as the name of the light.

8. Click (Select and Move) and in the Status Bar, change its absolute Z-elevation to **2'0"**.

9. Hold down <Shift>, and drag and click to create two instances of the omni light, as shown in Figure 8–33.

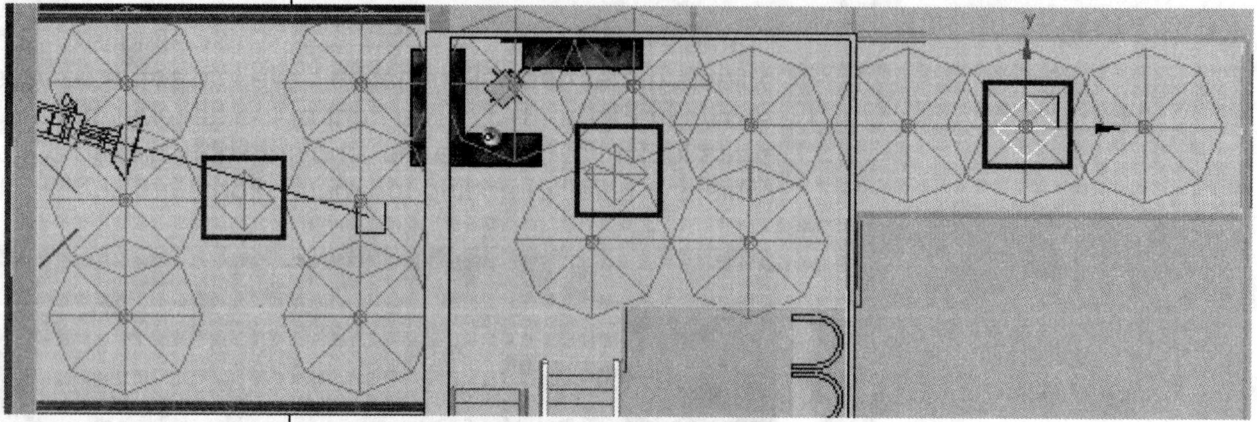

Figure 8–33

10. With one of the omni lights selected, in the *Modify* panel (), in the Advanced Effects rollout, select **Ambient Only**, as shown in Figure 8–34. This setting causes the light to illuminate the ambient color of standard materials and not to cast shadows.

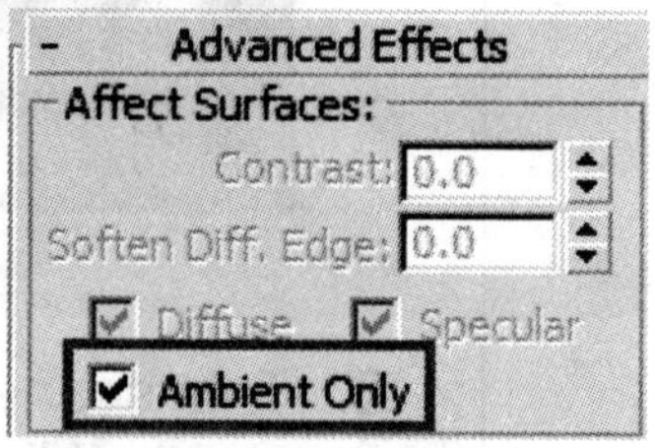

Figure 8–34

11. Change to **Camera – Lobby 1** viewport, render the scene by clicking (Render Production). Ambient lights can wash out a scene with their default settings. Leave the Rendered Frame Window open.

12. With the omni light still selected, in the Intensity/Color/Attenuation rollout, set *Multiplier* as **0.75** and in *Far Attenuation* area, select **Use**. Set *Start* and *End* as **0'0"** and **16'0"** respectively, as shown in Figure 8–35.

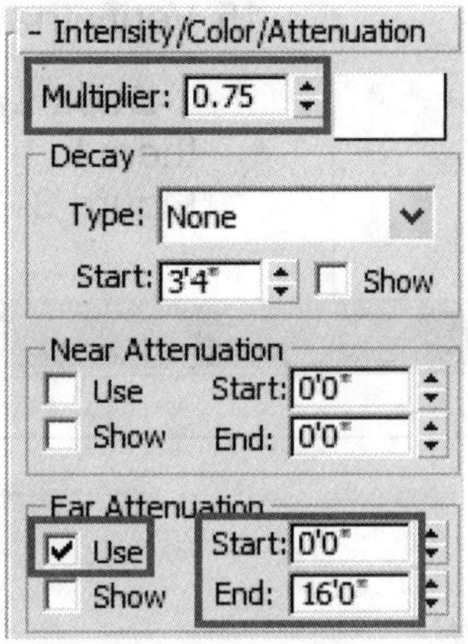

Figure 8–35

Your rendering might not be exactly the same because of your monitor display. You can adjust your Gamma and LUT correction (Preference Settings dialog box> Gamma and LUT tab) to get a similar rendering.

13. In the Rendered Frame Window, click Render. The ambient lighting does not look flat but the floor and desk lamp are illuminated too brightly, as shown in Figure 8–36.

Figure 8–36

14. To resolve the brightness issue, you can exclude these objects from the ambient light. With one of the omni (ambient) lights still selected, in the *Modify* panel ( ), in the General Parameters rollout, click Exclude.... The Exclude/Include dialog box opens.

15. Verify that **Exclude** is selected. In the list on the left, select **1-Desk Lamp** and **Layer:VIZ-1-Floor-Tile**. Click >> to add them to the Exclude list on the right, as shown in Figure 8–37.

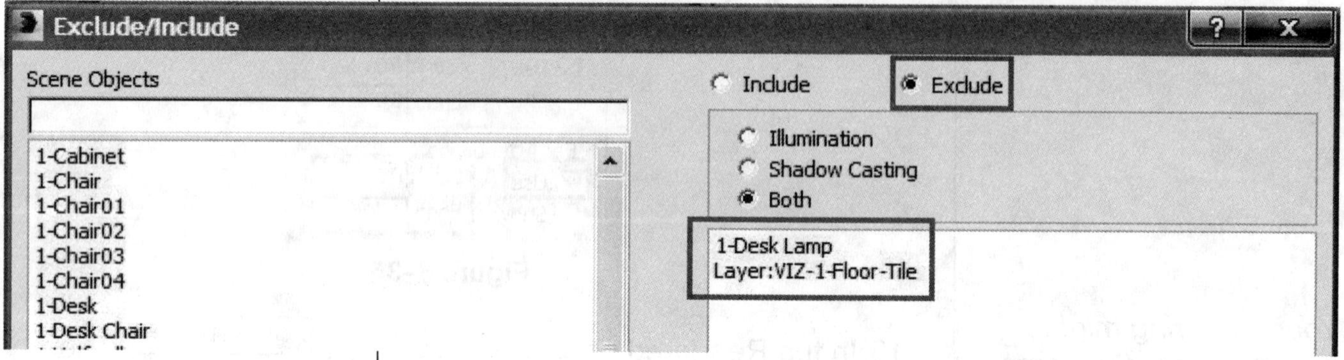

Figure 8–37

16. Click OK to close the dialog box.

17. In the Rendered Frame Window, click Render. The brightness of the lamp and the floor is removed, as shown in Figure 8–38. Close the Rendered Frame Window.

Figure 8–38

18. Save your work as **MyStandard Lighting – Interior.max**.

Certification

Topic:

✓Lighting

Objectives:

✓Identify parameters for modifying shadows

8.4 Shadow Types

Learning Objectives

- Understand the different types of shadows casting methods available in the Autodesk 3ds Max Design software.
- Understand the common parameters that can be used to control the common settings of all types of shadow casting methods.
- Understand how to control and set the specific parameters for each type of shadow casting method.

As with lights in the real world, Autodesk 3ds Max Design lights are able to cast shadows from opaque objects. Believable, realistic shadows are critical for producing a convincing visualization.

The Autodesk 3ds Max Design software offers several different shadow-casting methods, such as Shadow Mapped, Ray Traced, Area, etc. While creating light objects, you can set the type of shadow by selecting it in the drop-down list (as shown in Figure 8–39), in the *Shadows* area of General Parameters rollout. In the same area you can also set the various aspects of the shadows. Alternatively, after creating the light objects, you can control or change them using the *Modify* panel ( ) parameters of light objects. Individual lights might cast different kinds of shadows in the same scene and shadow casting can be disabled for specific lights.

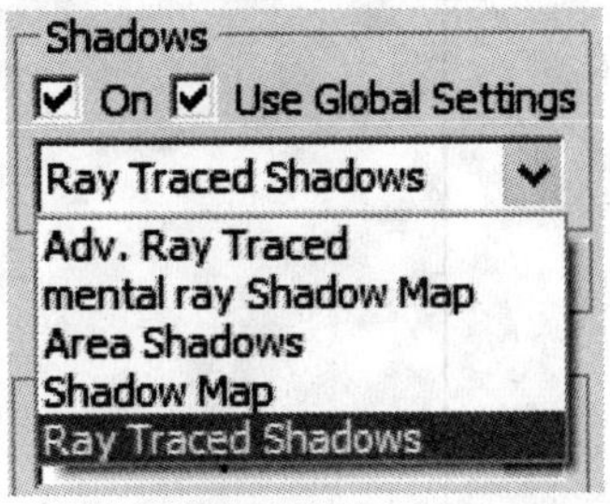

Figure 8–39

The shadow-casting methods, such as **Shadow Mapped**, **Ray Traced Shadows**, **Advanced Ray Traced Shadows**, and **Area Shadows** are shown in Figure 8–40.

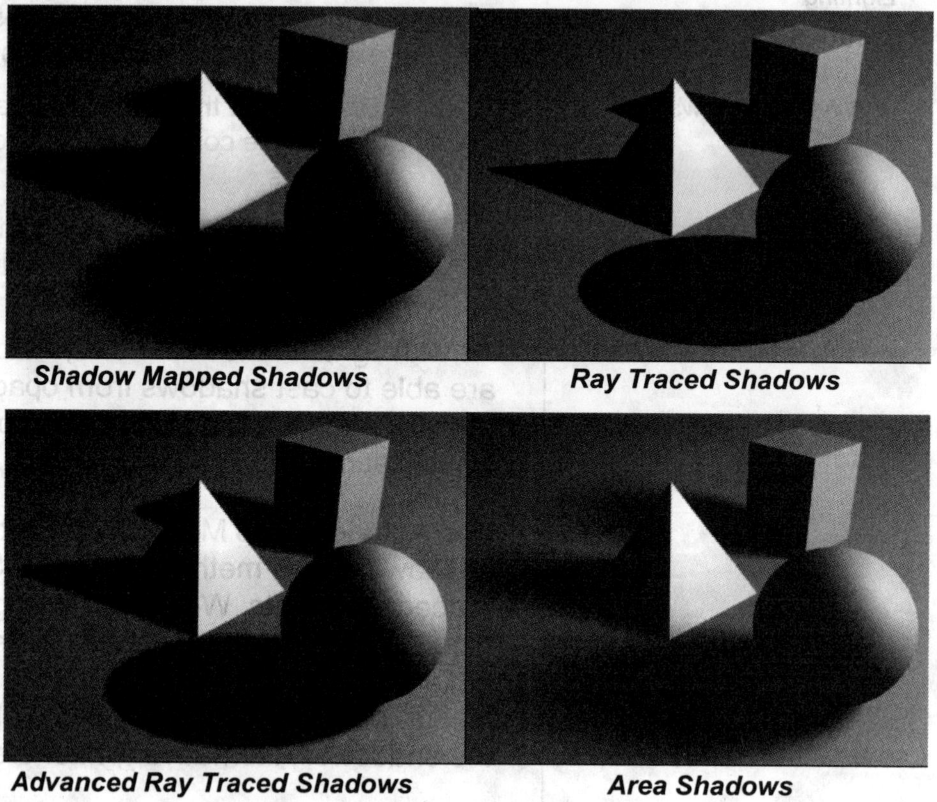

Figure 8–40

Shadow Type	Description, Advantages	Disadvantages
Shadow Map	Traditional approach, shadow mapping is relatively fast and creates soft-edged shadows. **Animation:** Shadows only need to be calculated once when scene geometry is not animated. Most efficient shadow type for omni lights.	Not as accurate as other methods; might not be appropriate for shadow studies. Uses a lot of RAM. Does not support materials with transparency or opacity maps.

Ray Traced Shadows (RT)	More accurate than shadow maps, supports transparency and opacity mapping. **Animation:** Shadows only need to be calculated once when scene geometry is not animated. In these cases, RT might be best for animations (including animated shadow studies) in terms of rendering time.	Slower than shadow maps, and shadows have sharp edges. Avoid omni lights with RT shadows whenever possible, as they require 6x the processing time of spot and directional lights.
Advanced Ray Traced (ART)	A good, general-purpose shadow type that is an improvement on RT shadows. It is more accurate than Shadow Maps, supports transparency and opacity mapping. Uses less RAM than standard raytraced shadows, therefore is generally faster for producing still renderings. Offers several parameters that can help soften and smooth shadows.	Slower than shadow maps. **Animation:** Shadows must be calculated at every frame, regardless of whether scene geometry is animated or not. Avoid omni lights with ART shadows whenever possible, as they require 6x the processing time of spot and directional lights.
Area Shadows	Enables a simulation of shadows cast from an area light (the other methods assume point light sources). Supports transparency and opacity mapping, uses relatively little RAM.	Generally slower than shadow maps, RT and ART. **Animation:** Shadows must be calculated at every frame, regardless of whether scene geometry is animated or not.
mental ray Shadow Maps	A shadow type optimized for the mental ray renderer. This is not covered in this training course.	Not as accurate as RT or ART shadows.

Common Shadow Parameters

The most commonly used shadow parameters in the Autodesk 3ds Max Design software are:

General Shadow Parameters

All lights have certain general parameters (*Shadows* area in *General Parameters* area) common to all shadow types, as shown in Figure 8–41.

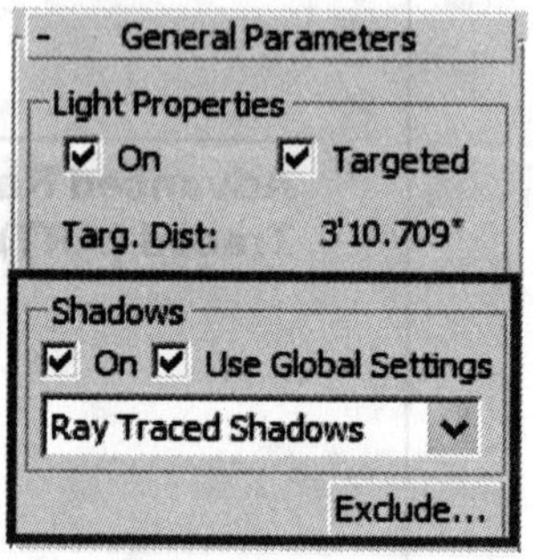

Figure 8–41

- The **On** option enables you to select whether to cast shadows from this light or not and the type of shadows to use.
- The **Use Global Settings** option controls whether the scene's global shadow generator or the light's own individual shadow generator is used.
- The drop-down list contains all of the different types of shadows that are available in the Autodesk 3ds Max Design software. Selecting the type provides a shadow specific rollout that can be used to control the advanced settings in the selected shadow type.

Shadow Parameters Rollout

The Shadow Parameters rollout (shown in Figure 8–42), contains settings that are common to all types of shadows.

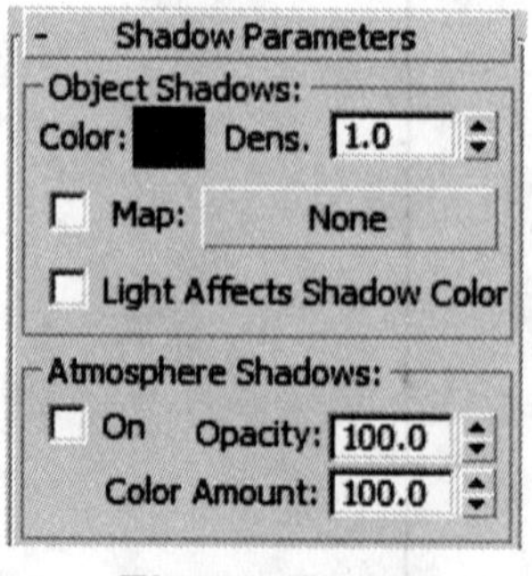

Figure 8–42

Color	Use this swatch to set a shadow to display as a color other than black.
Density	Controls the overall darkness of the created shadows. A density below 1.0 makes shadows lighter, greater than 1.0 makes them darker.
Map	Use this option to have an image map project inside your shadow.
Light Affects Shadow Color	Enables colored light to blend with the assigned shadow color when generating shadows.
Atmosphere Shadows	Enables atmospheric effects to cast shadows.

Shadow Map Parameters

In the General Parameters rollout, in the *Shadows* area, selecting **Shadow Map** in the drop-down list provides a Shadow Map Params rollout, as shown in Figure 8–43. Lights set to cast shadow mapped-shadows have additional controls that are specific to the Shadow Map type of shadow.

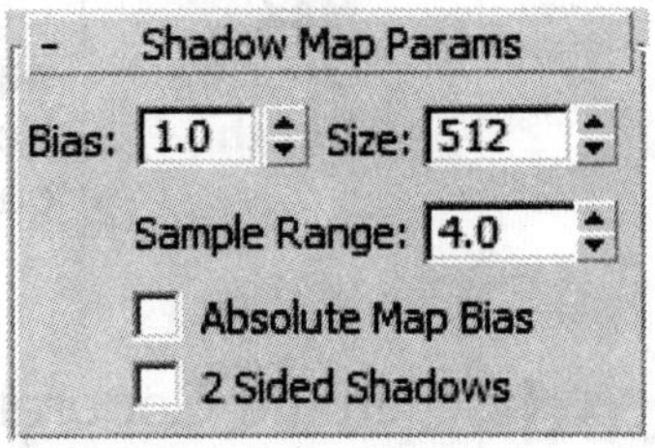

Figure 8–43

Bias	A relative adjustment that can move the shadow closer to or further away from the objects casting them. This value sometimes needs to be adjusted with large scenes.
Size	The height and width (in pixels) of the image map used to create the shadows. Shadow detail and computation time increase as the size increases.
Sample Range	Controls the amount of blending and smoothing. If shadow mapped-shadows appear grainy, increase this value.
Absolute Map Bias	Enables the Bias to be fixed to a value measured absolutely in scene units rather than a relative, normalized value. This option should normally not be used unless shadows flicker and disappear during an animation.
2 Sided Shadows	Enables both sides of a face to cast shadows. Double-sided mode is discussed in the rendering information.

Ray Traced Shadows

In the General Parameters rollout, in the *Shadows* area, selecting **Ray Traced Shadow** in the drop-down list provides a Ray Traced Shadow Params rollout, as shown in Figure 8–44. This rollout contains additional settings for lights set to cast (standard) ray traced shadows.

Figure 8–44

Ray Bias	Similar to shadow map bias, ray bias is a relative adjustment to move a shadow closer or further away from an object casting them. This value might need to be adjusted for large scenes.
2 Sided Shadows	Enables both sides of a face to cast shadows.
Max Quadtree Depth	Controls ray-tracing performance. Increasing the quadtree depth can speed up ray-tracing time but requires more RAM. You need to experiment to determine the most efficient quadtree settings for individual scenes (default = 7).

Advanced Ray-Traced Shadows

In the General Parameters rollout, in the *Shadows* area, selecting **Adv. Ray Traced** in the drop-down list provides an Adv. Ray Traced Params rollout, as shown on the left in Figure 8–45 and the Optimizations rollouts, as shown on the right in Figure 8–45. Both rollouts contains additional settings for lights set to cast advanced ray-traced shadows.

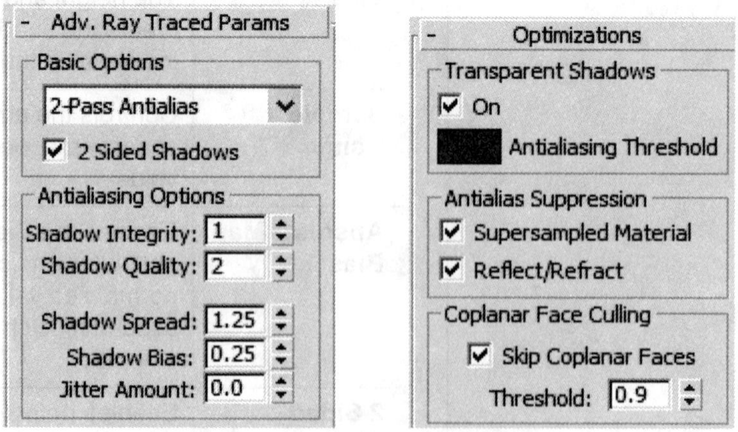

Figure 8–45

Adv. Ray Traced Params Options

Basic Options	The pull-down menu assigns either a mode without antialiasing (simple), a single or double-pass antialiasing mode. Antialiasing is an additional calculation made to smooth pixilated edges of shadows.
2 Sided Shadows	Enables both sides of a face to cast shadows.
Shadow Integrity and Quality	Controls the number of rays cast in the calculation. Increasing these values can enhance the final result at the expense of longer calculation time.
Shadow Spread	A parameter to blur or soften shadows, measured in pixels.
Shadow Bias	The minimum distance required to cast a shadow. This parameter should be increased as shadow spread is increased.
Jitter Amount	Blurred shadows sometimes cause artifacts to form. Increasing jitter can help break up the patterns of these artifacts and make them less noticeable.

Optimizations Options

Transparent Shadows	When enabled, transparent objects cast colored shadows based on their transparency and diffuse color.
Antialias Suppression	When using supersampling, reflections or refractions, this option disables the second pass in two-pass antialiased mode. This is a good idea to save time since the second pass often adds little in these situations. (Supersampling is discussed in the rendering and animation material.)
Skip Coplanar Faces	Prevents coplanar faces from shading each other (those that lie overlapped in the same plane).

mental ray Shadow Maps

In the General Parameters rollout, in the *Shadows* area, selecting **mental ray Shadow Map** in the drop-down list provides a mental ray Shadow Map rollout, as shown in Figure 8–46. The options should be used with mental ray lights. Generally, you only use these for interior shots that render with mental ray and require physical lighting effects, such as caustics or global illumination.

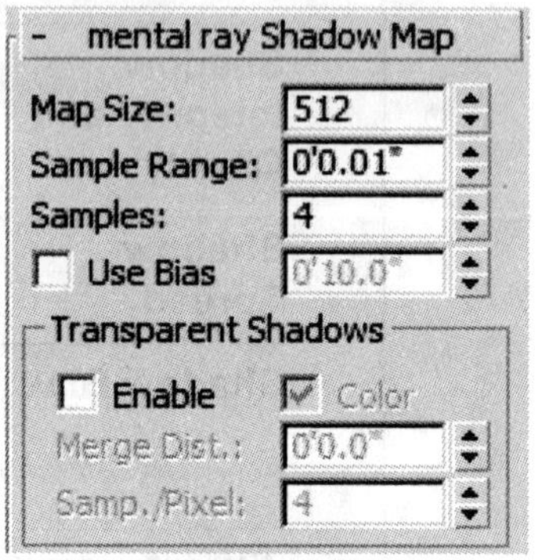

Figure 8–46

Map Size	Determines the resolution of the shadow bitmap. The size of the map is actually the square of this value. It should be in powers of 2 – 256, 512, 1024, 2048 etc.
Sample Range	Used to create soft-edged shadows when using mental ray lights. You must increase this value AND the Samples values greater than zero to get soft shadow effects.
Samples	Determines the number of samples that are removed from the map to make the shadows soft.
Use Bias	Moves the shadow closer or farther from the object.
Transparent Shadows	Provides controls for finer looking shadows. When enabled, you can add transparency and control shadow color. The *Merge Dist* and *Samp./Pixel* fields enable you to increase shadow quality (this result in additional memory consumption and slower renderings).

Practice 8b Working with Shadow Parameters

Learning Objective

Understand the different types of shadows casting methods available in the Autodesk 3ds Max Design software.

Estimated time for completion: 10 minutes

In this practice you will adjust parameters to refine the shadows.

You must set the paths to locate the External files and Xrefs used in the practice. If you have not done this already, return to the **Introduction to Autodesk 3ds Max Design** chapter and complete Task 1 to Task 3 of the **Organizing Folders and Working with the Interface** practice. You only have to set the user paths once.

If a dialog box opens prompting you about a File Load: Mismatch, click OK to accept the default values.

1. Continue working with **MyStandard Lighting – Interior.max** file or open **Shadow Parameters.max** from your *Class Files* folder.

2. In the Main toolbar, click (Select by Name). In the Select From Scene dialog box, click (Display None) to clear any selections and click (Display Lights). Select one of the Ceiling Downlight objects, such as **Ceiling Downlight 06**. Click OK.

3. In the Command Panel, select the *Modify* panel ( ), and examine its parameters. These lights are using the default Advanced Ray Traced shadow type. In the General Parameters rollout, in the *Shadows* area, note that **Adv. Ray Traced** is displayed, as shown in Figure 8–47.

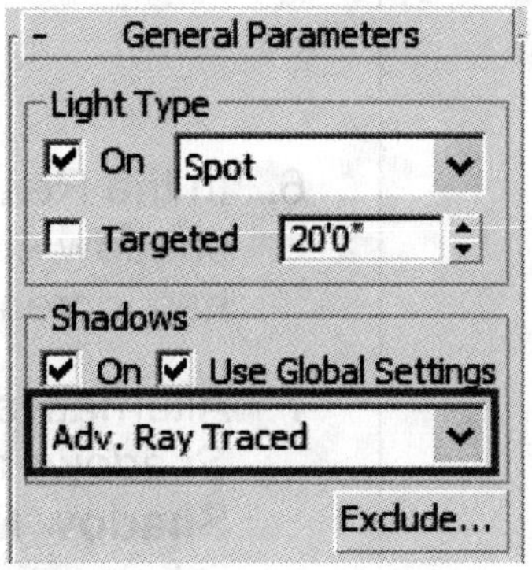

Figure 8–47

4. In the Main toolbar, click (Render Production) to render the scene. In the Rendered Frame Window, zoom and pan to the desk area, as shown in Figure 8–48. The edges of the shadow under the desk display jagged. Leave the Rendered Frame Window open.

Figure 8–48

5. In the *Modify* panel ( ), expand the Adv. Ray Traced Params rollout and in the *Basic Options* area, select **2-Pass Antialias** in the drop-down list. In the *Antialiasing Options* area, set the *Shadow Integrity* to **2** and the *Shadow Quality* to **3** and press <Enter>, as shown in Figure 8–49.

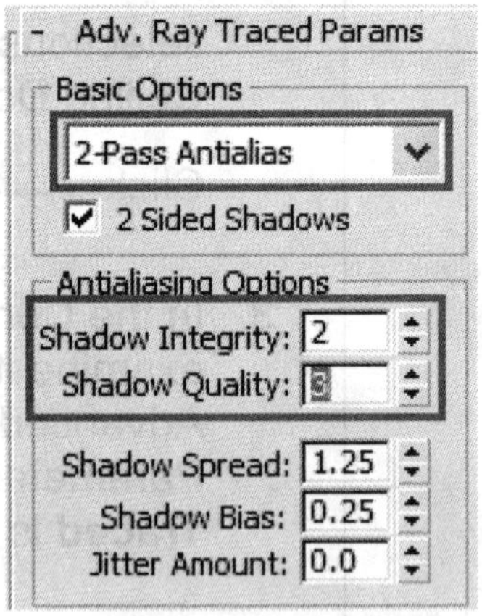

Figure 8–49

6. In the Rendered Frame Window, click Render. The shadow edges display more smoothly, but the rendering time has increased.

7. Alternatively, in the General Parameters rollout, in the *Shadows* area, change the type from *Adv. Ray Traced* to **Shadow Map** by selecting **Shadow Map** in the drop-down list.

8. In the Rendered Frame Window, click Render. These shadows are fuzzier and less accurate, as shown in Figure 8–50, but significantly faster to render. When soft shadows are required or speed is critical, Shadow maps make a good alternative.

Figure 8–50

9. To make the shadow-mapped shadows better defined, increase the map size. In the Shadow Map Params rollout, double the *Size* from 512 to **1024**, as shown in Figure 8–51.

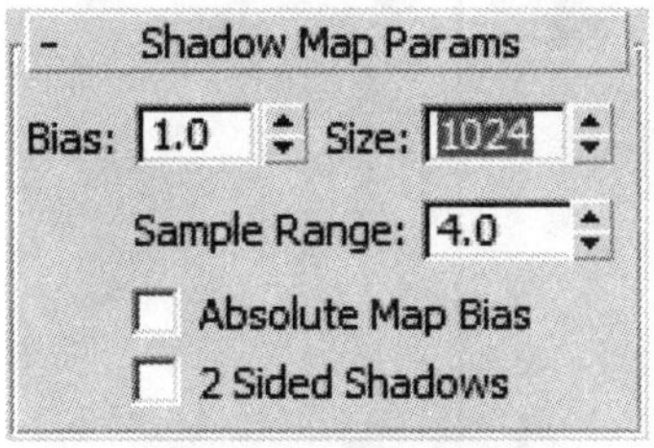

Figure 8–51

10. In the Rendered Frame Window, click Render. There might not be a huge difference in shadows under the desk.

11. Zoom into the right side and note that the shadow maps are causing rendering artifacts along the curtain wall, as shown in Figure 8–52.

Figure 8–52

12. Adjust the Shadow map *Size* to **2048** and set the *Bias* to **0.01**. Click 

to render the scene again. These settings reduce the problem, but can increase rendering time.

13. Save your work as **MyShadow Parameters.max**.

Chapter Review Questions

1. The default lights (key light and fill light) provided by default in the Autodesk 3ds Max Design scene, act as:
   a. Omni lights
   b. Spotlights
   c. Directional lights
   d. mental ray area omni light
2. Which type of standard lights are used to represent light sources that cast parallel rays?
   a. Omni lights
   b. Spotlights
   c. Directional lights
   d. mental ray area omni light
3. In the Intensity/Color/Attenuation rollout, which has common parameters for all of the standard lights, which option does not occur in the real world and is only included as a computer graphics lighting effect? An example of the Intensity/Color/Attenuation rollout is shown in Figure 8–53.

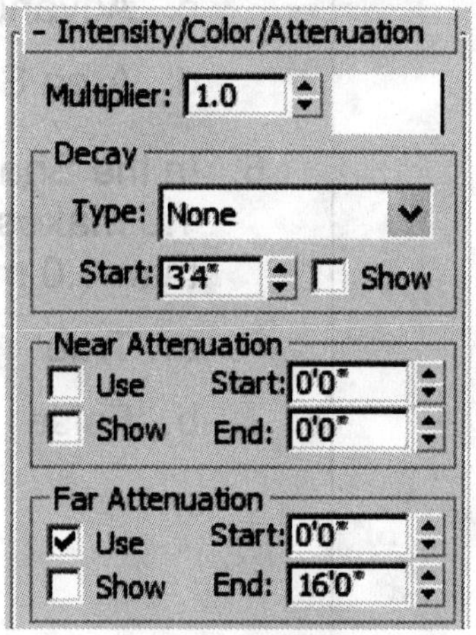

Figure 8–53

   a. Multiplier
   b. Decay options
   c. Near Attenuation options
   d. Far Attenuation options

4. In the Spotlight parameters rollout (shown in Figure 8–54), which option enables a spotlight to cast light in all directions and behave like an omni light? (Hint: Setting this option generally looks unnatural and it should be used with care.)

Figure 8–54

   a. Show Cone
   b. Overshoot
   c. Hotspot/Beam
   d. Falloff/Field

5. Which one of the following shadow types does not support materials with transparency and opacity maps?
   a. Shadow Map
   b. Ray Traced Shadows
   c. Advanced Ray Traced
   d. Area Shadows

6. In the Shadow Map type of shadows, a density value below 1.0 makes the shadow darker and a density value of greater than 1.0 makes the shadow lighter.
   a. True
   b. False

Command Summary

Button	Command	Location
	**Array**	■ **Extras toolbar** ■ **Tools:** Array
	**Lights**	■ **Command Panel:** *Create* panel ■ **Create:** Lights
	**Render Production**	■ **Main toolbar** ■ **Rendering:** Render

Chapter 9

Lighting and Rendering

In this chapter you learn to create photometric light types and modify their parameters. You learn the concept of Exposure Control and how to use the exposure control methods with NVIDIA mental ray renderer. You also learn to create sunlight and skylight and to create a daytime scene.

This chapter contains the following topics:

- ✓**Photometric Light Objects**
- ✓**Exposure Control**
- ✓**Daytime Lighting**

Certification

Topic:
✓Lighting
Objectives:
✓Identify parameters for modifying shadows

9.1 Photometric Light Objects

Learning Objectives

- Understand how to use photometric lights in a scene.
- Create photometric lights and modify them by changing their parameters.

Photometric lights are a type of light that attempts to correspond to real-world lighting. These light objects have parameters based on quantitative measurements of light levels and distribution. They provide accurate scene illumination when used together with mental ray and other global illumination solutions. In the Autodesk® 3ds Max® Design software, photometric lights are the default choice for creating lights. It provides you with templates to make it easy to select the color temperature of the light, and new attenuation controls for manual manipulation of the light falloff.

- Photometric lights take advantage of physically-based color, intensity, and distribution properties. They can be defined with real-world lighting parameters in engineering units.
- Since photometric lights are based on real-world calculations of light energy, they are **scale-specific**. Scenes using photometric lights and mental ray/Radiosity should have an appropriate system unit scale.
- All photometric lights automatically decay (attenuate) with an inverse-square relationship. Far attenuation can now be controlled manually, to save calculation time and energy.
- Photometric lights work for both the scanline renderer and mental ray renderer.

- The key to getting good results from Photometric Lights is to use Exposure control to adjust the brightness of the scene. You can also independently manipulate the Shadow/ Midtones and Highlight areas of the image. It is common to place Photometric lights in a scene, render and see nothing but black. This is because Exposure control is not on by default. If the Exposure Control is not on and you select a Photometric light type in the Command Panel, a Photometric Light Creation dialog box opens and prompts you to use the Logarithmic Exposure Control (for Default Scanline renderer) or the mr Photographic Exposure Control (for the mental ray renderer).

Photometric Light Types

In the Command Panel, in the *Create* panel ( ), clicking (Lights) opens the *Light* panel. The **Photometric** is the default light type and the object types for photometric lights are **Target Light** and **Free Light**, as shown in Figure 9–1. The **mr Sky Portal** is also included in the Object Type rollout but is not a standard photometric light type.

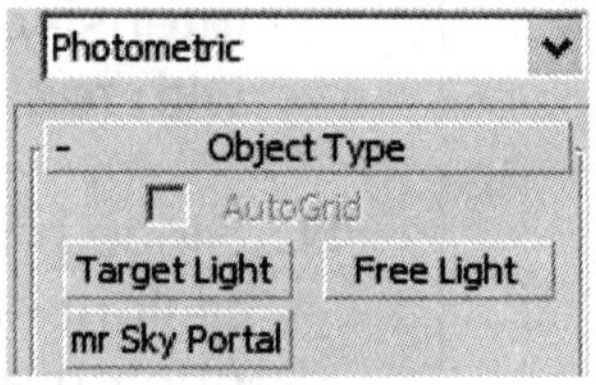

Figure 9–1

While creating a Target Light or a Free Light, you can set different parameters to illuminate the scene accurately and effectively. Once the lights have been created, you can modify the parameters using the *Modify* panel in the Command Panel.

Templates Rollout

Once you create either a Target or Free light there are Templates to select from, as shown in Figure 9–2. Here you can select from a list of preset real-world lighting choices. Selecting a template controls the intensity and color temperature of the light.

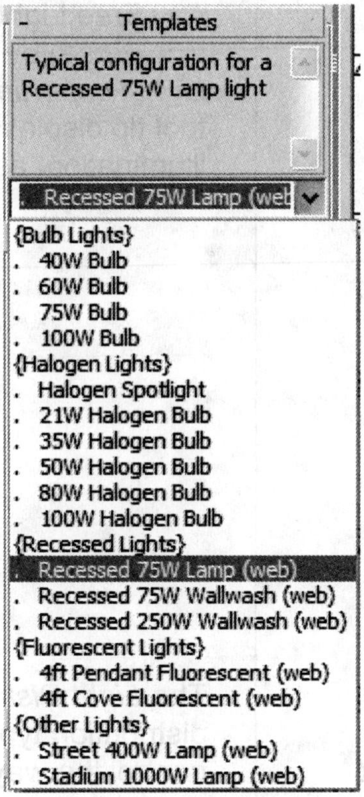

Figure 9–2

General Parameters Rollout

The General Parameters rollout controls some of the basic settings for turning the light on and off in the scene and the different shadow casting methods (Ray Traced, Adv. Ray Traced, mental ray, Shadow Map, etc.). The options found in the *Light Properties* area and *Shadows* area are similar to the options found in Standard Lights and can be used in the same manner.

Any Free Light can be turned into a Targeted Light (and vice-versa) by selecting or clearing the **Targeted** option in the *Light Properties* area. When the Targeted option is enabled, a tool tip displays as you move the target indicating the illumination, as shown in Figure 9–3.

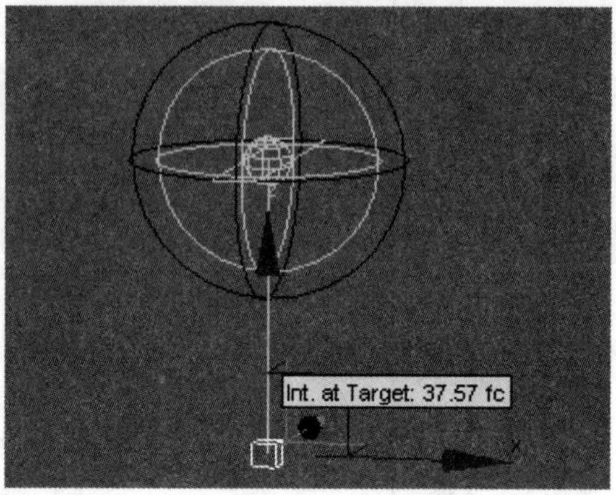

Figure 9–3

In the General Parameters rollout, many options (Light Properties area options, Shadows area options, and ***Spotlight*** *parameters) are identical or similar to the options used when creating Standard Lights.*

The *Light Distribution* area has a list of photometric light distribution types that are available in the software. These control the way the light illuminates the surrounding space. The available options in Light Distribution type are:

- **Uniform Spherical:** Casts light in all directions like a standard Omni light.
- **Uniform Diffuse:** Casts light in one hemisphere only and mimics the way light emits from a surface. This was previously called Diffuse.
- **Spotlight:** Provides hotspot and falloff parameters identical to standard spotlights.
- **Photometric Web:** Casts light according to a 3D representation of light intensity as determined by a lighting file type, such as IES, LTLI, or CIBSE. These are files provided by lighting manufacturers, usually available via the Internet.

Distribution (Photometric Web) Rollout

If you select Photometric Web in the Light Distribution type list, the Distribution (Photometric Web) rollout is displayed, as shown in Figure 9–4. Real-world luminaries (lighting fixtures) nearly always cast light in varying amounts in different directions. The Web distribution method enables the Autodesk 3ds Max Design software to simulate the laboratory-determined light distribution of specific lighting fixtures.

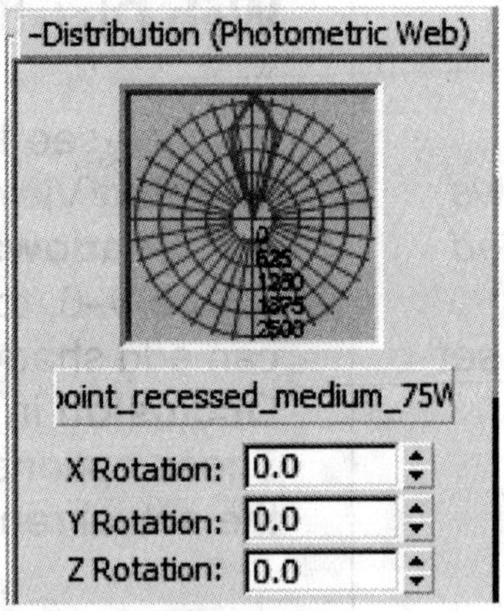

Figure 9–4

- Photometric lights can make use of web distribution information from IES, LTLI, or CIBSE photometric web data files.
- These photometric web data files can be obtained from lighting manufacturers for specific light fixture models. They are often available directly from manufacturers' web sites.
- Lights with Web distributions are indicated with photometric web icons, as shown in Figure 9–5, that graphically represent the 3D distribution of light cast from the light fixture.

Figure 9–5

Web Distribution in Viewports

*The options in the Lighting and Shadows submenu are disabled (grayed out) if the viewport shading is set to **Shaded**.*

You can see the web distribution in the viewport. Select the **Shading** Viewport label (such as **Realistic**) and select **Lighting and Shadows>Illuminate with Scene Lights**, as shown in Figure 9–6, to enable you to see the lights in the viewport. You can add shadows by selecting **Shadows** and toggle on **Ambient Occlusion** in the viewport to add subtle detail enhancement. These options only take effect in viewport and have no effect on the actual renderings.

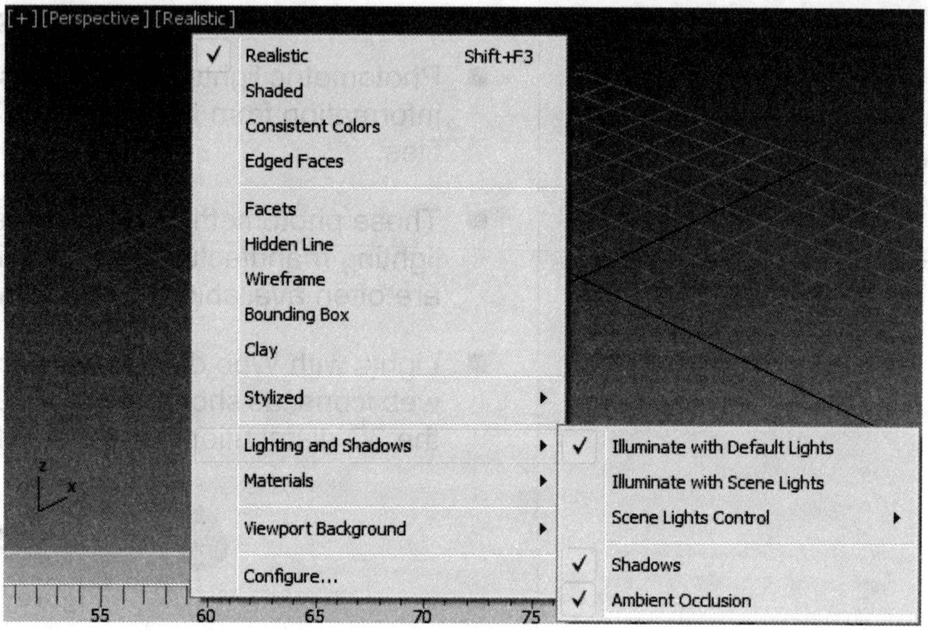

Figure 9–6

Shape/Area Shadows Parameters

These controls are used to generate a shadow casting shape. The different shapes calculate shadows as if they were coming from that particular shape. The different shapes have different parametric controls. In the Shape/Area Shadows rollout, in the *Emit light from (Shape)* area, you can select between **Point**, **Line**, **Rectangle**, **Disc**, **Sphere**, and **Cylinder**, as shown in Figure 9–7.

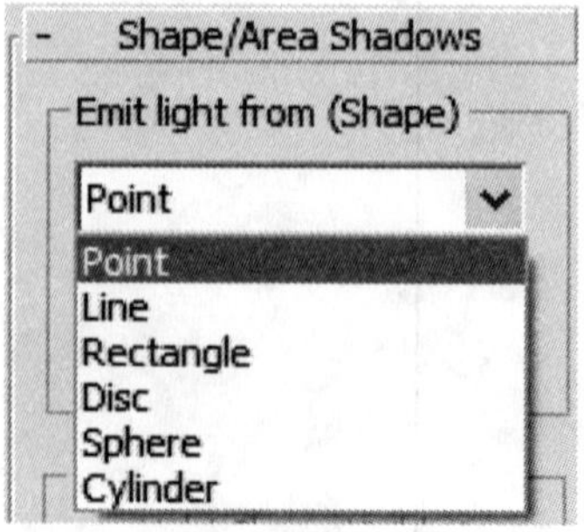

Figure 9–7

- **Point:** Shadows are created as if the light was one single point, as shown in Figure 9–8.

Figure 9–8

- **Line:** Shadows are created as if the light was one single line, as shown in Figure 9–9. The size of the line is controlled with the **Length** parameter.

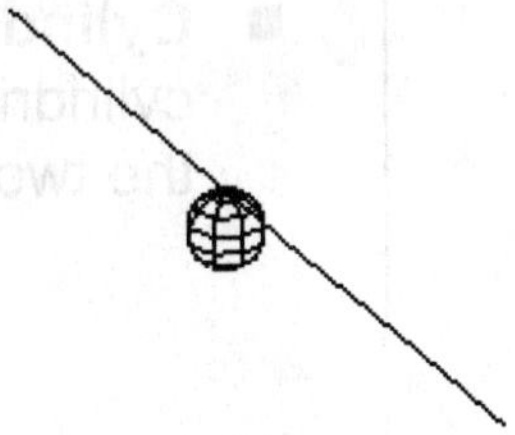

Figure 9–9

- **Rectangle:** Shadows are created as if the light was a rectangular area, as shown in Figure 9–10, governed by **Length** and **Width** parameters. Use this for fluorescent tubes or rectangular ceiling lights.

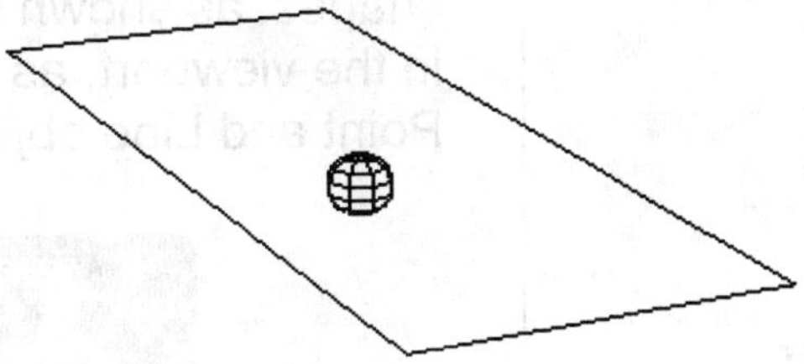

Figure 9–10

- **Disc:** Shadows are created as if the light was a flattened sphere, as shown in Figure 9–11. A radius control determines the size of the disc.

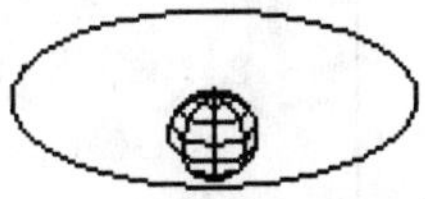

Figure 9–11

- **Sphere:** Shadows are created as if the light was a round ball or globe, as shown in Figure 9–12. Again a radius control determines the size of the sphere.

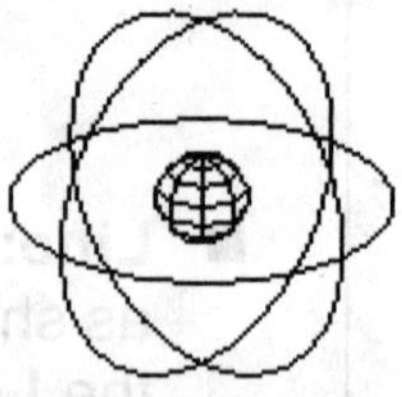

Figure 9–12

- **Cylinder:** Shadows are created as if the light emitter is cylindrical, as shown in Figure 9–13. **Radius** and **Length** are the two parameters to control the cylinder proportions.

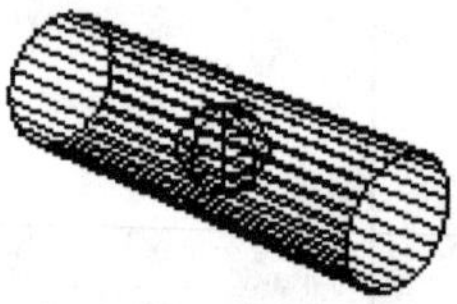

Figure 9–13

In the Shape/Area Shadows rollout, in the *Rendering* area, you can also select the **Light Shape Visible in Rendering** option. This permits the Cylinder, Disc, Sphere, and Rectangle light shapes, as shown on the top in Figure 9–14, to render as objects in the viewport, as shown on the bottom in Figure 9–14. The Point and Line objects do not work with this feature.

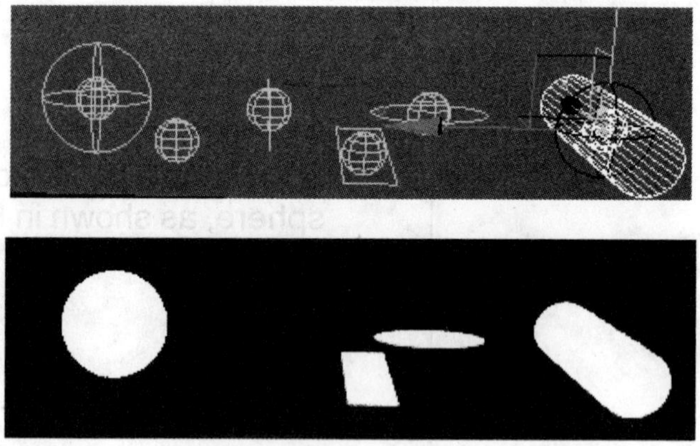

Figure 9–14

Intensity/Color/Attenuation Rollout

Photometric light color can be assigned through a lamp specification (such as fluorescent, halogen, incandescent, etc.) or through a temperature specified in degrees Kelvin. This color can also be filtered (tinted) through a color swatch. All of these options can be selected in the *Color* area of the Intensity/Color/Attenuation rollout, as shown in Figure 9–15.

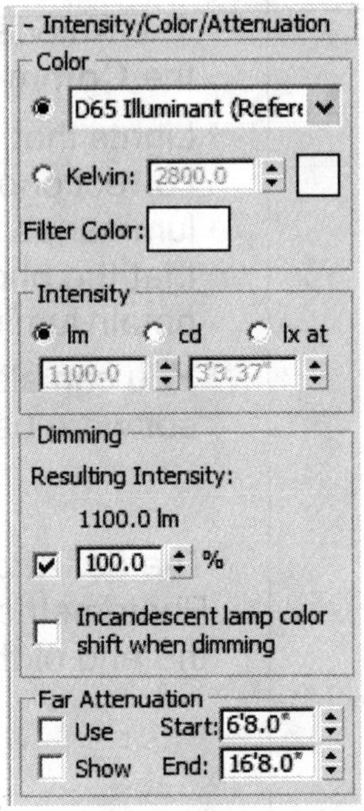

Figure 9–15

The overall brightness of Photometric lights can be specified as one of three intensity values (*Intensity* area):

- **Luminous flux:** The overall output strength of the lamp measured in lumens (lm).
- **Luminous intensity:** How much light energy is released over time, measured in candelas (cd).
- **Illuminance:** A measurement of how much illumination reaches a surface a set distance away from a lamp with a certain facing. Illuminance is measured in foot-candles (fc, lumens/ft2) or lux (lumens/m2). When using this option, specify both the **Luminous flux** (lumens) and the distance at which that brightness occurs.

Hint: Photometric Lights Data

You are not required to know all of the above technical data or be a lighting expert to use Photometric lights and mental ray. You are also not required to search for dozens of IES files for each scene. The Autodesk 3ds Max Design software ships with a host of sample lighting templates you can use out-of-the-box.

The Autodesk 3ds Max Help lists a number of sample fixtures in the **Common Lamp Values for Photometric Lights** section.

Lights that combine the geometry of a light fixture with the correct photometric light distribution model are referred to as luminaries. These are assemblies with a hierarchy created so that the photometric light is linked to the geometry. You can obtain luminaries from manufacturer websites (such as ERCO).

You can also import lighting fixtures from the Autodesk® Revit® software using FBX import.

The *Far Attenuation* area provides control over exactly where the Photometric light ends as well as the area that is graduated as the end of the range is approached, as shown in Figure 9–16.

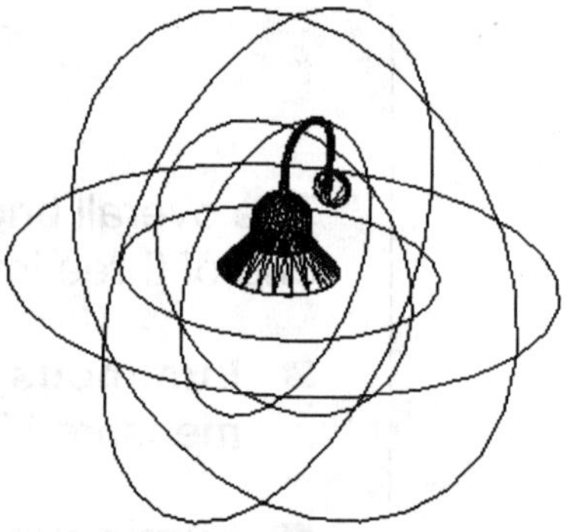

Figure 9–16

Practice 9a Working with Photometric Lights

Learning Objectives

- Create photometric lights in a scene and change their parameters to achieve a required lighting affect.
- Use different preset lamps and their provided data to achieve a required lighting affect.

Estimated time for completion: 10 minutes

In this practice you will create and adjust photometric lights for use with mental ray. You will apply a realistic lighting to the lobby model.

You must set the paths to locate the External files and Xrefs used in the practice. If you have not done this already, return to the **Introduction to Autodesk 3ds Max Design** chapter and complete Task 1 to Task 3 of the **Organizing Folders and Working with the Interface** practice. You only have to set the user paths once.

If a dialog box opens prompting you about a File Load: Mismatch, click OK to accept the default values.

1. Open **Photometric Lighting start.max** from your *Class Files* folder.
2. Using <Win> and <Shift>, display the Top viewport as the maximized viewport. Click (Zoom Extents) to display the floorplan. Change to Wireframe mode by pressing <F3>.
3. In the *Create* panel ( ), click (Lights) and verify that **Photometric** is displayed in the drop-down list. In the Object Type rollout, select **Free Light**, as shown in Figure 9–17.

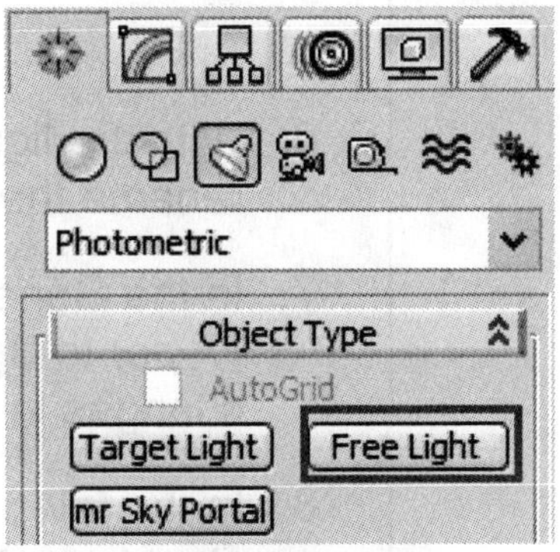

Figure 9–17

4. Click over the upper left light fixture circle to place a light, as shown in Figure 9–18.

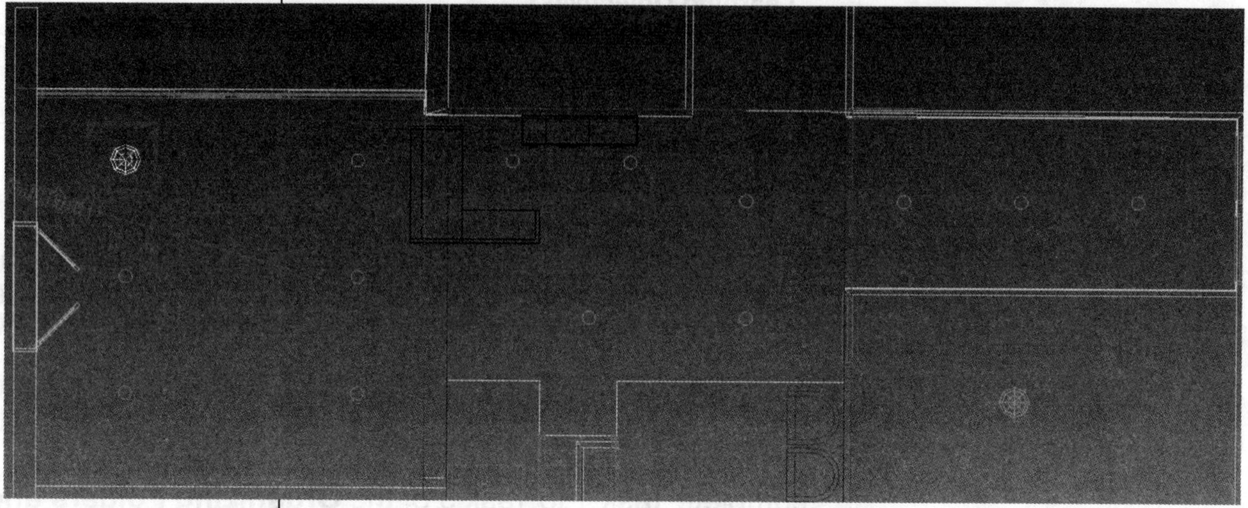

Figure 9–18

Alternatively, right-click on (Select and Move) in the Main toolbar to open the Transform Type-In dialog box. You can also enter the values in the Status Bar.

5. In the viewport, right-click on the new light and in the Quad menu, next to **Move**, select (Settings). In the Move Transform Type-In dialog box, in the *Absolute:World* area, set *X* as **84'7"**, *Y* as **126'10"**, and *Z* as **9'11"** (elevation), as shown in Figure 9–19. Close the dialog box.

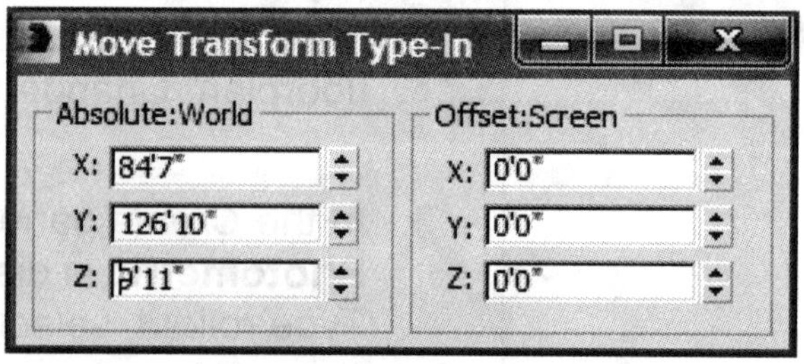

Figure 9–19

6. With the light object selected, in the *Modify* panel ( ), rename the light object as **Light – Downlight A 00**.

7. In the General Parameters rollout, set *Light Distribution (Type)* to **Spotlight**. Note that the shape of the light object changes in the viewport.

8. In the Intensity/Color/Attenuation rollout, set *Color* to **HID Quartz Metal Halide**, as shown in Figure 9–20.

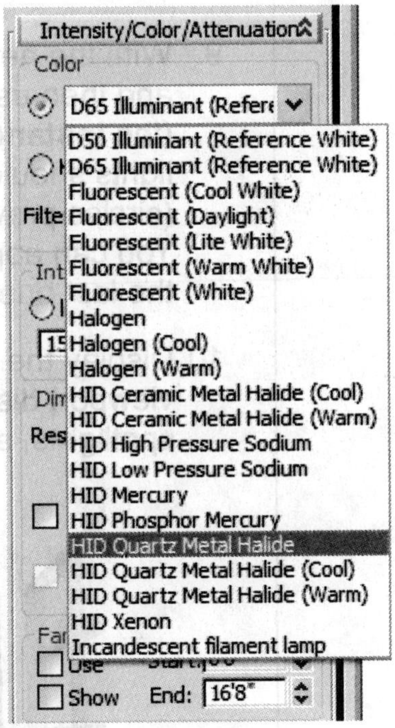

Figure 9–20

Hint: Accessing Photometric Lights Data

In this example you are using metal halide lamps. You can find suggestions for their photometric light parameters in the Help system. In the InfoCenter, click in and select **3ds Max Design Help**. Select the *Search* tab and enter **Common Lamp Values** in the search box. Select **Common Lamp Values for Photometric Lights**. Scroll down to **Par38 Line Voltage Lamps**. The **Medium Beam** has intensities between 1700-4000 candelas as shown in Figure 9–21. The values for beam and field angles are also displayed.

Par38 Line Voltage Lamps

Class.	Watts	Type	Intensity	Beam	Field
Narrow Beam	45	Spot	4700	14	28
Narrow Beam	75	Spot	5200	12	25
Narrow Beam	150	Spot	10500	14	28
Medium Beam	45	Spot	1700	28	60
Medium Beam	75	Spot	1860	30	60
Medium Beam	150	Spot	4000	30	60

Figure 9–21

9. With the new light still selected, click (Select and Move) and then use <Shift> + click and drag to instance the light (the **Instance** option in the Clone Options dialog box). The lights should correspond to the symbols for Ceiling Lights (circles provided for the locations of the recessed lighting). You can approximate their positions and have 14 lights with the last one named **Light - Downlight A 013**.

10. Display the **Camera-Lobby1** viewport and change the viewport display to **Shaded + Edged Faces** to display the 14 spotlights, as shown in Figure 9–22.

Figure 9–22

11. Select **Rendering>Exposure Control** to open the Environment and Effects dialog box. Note that this being a legacy file, **Logarithmic Exposure Control** is selected in the Exposure Control rollout.

12. In the Exposure Control rollout, select **Active**. Click Render Preview. Note the render preview in the preview window.

13. In the Logarithmic Exposure Control Parameters rollout, increase the *Brightness* to **88**, press <Enter>, and watch the render preview update. Close the dialog box.

14. Click (Render Production) to render the viewport. Note that the scene is quite dark. Leave the Rendered Window open.

15. With one light still selected, in the Command Panel, in the Distribution (Spotlight) rollout, note that *Hotspot/Beam* and *Falloff/Field* have default values of **30°** and **60°** as stated in the Autodesk 3ds Max Help.

When changing the Light Distribution Type, the shape of the light object (in the viewport) changes accordingly.

16. If you have access to a photometric data file for a light fixture, you can use it for this light. In the General Parameters rollout set *Light Distribution (Type)* to **Photometric Web**, as shown in Figure 9–23.

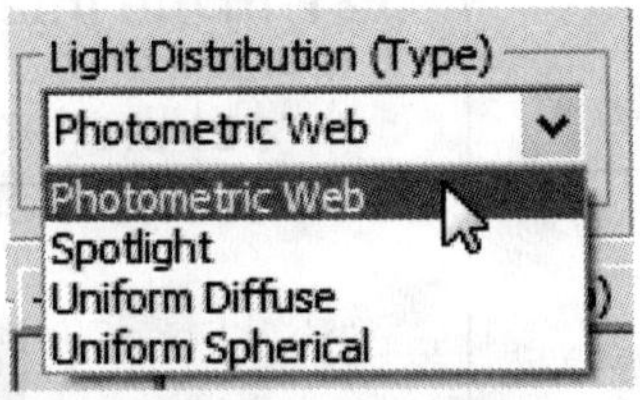

Figure 9–23

17. In the Distribution (Photometric Web) Parameters rollout, click < Choose Photometric File > and in your *Class Files* folder, *sceneassets* subfolder, *photometric* subfolder, open **sample_downlight.ies**. The thumbnail diagram of the selected web file is displayed, as shown in Figure 9–24.

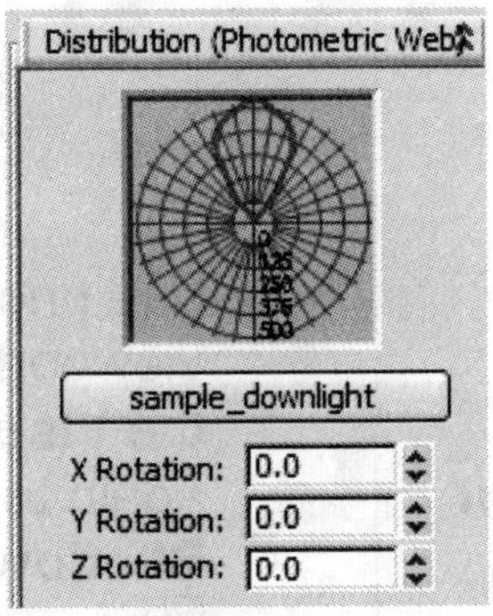

Figure 9–24

- The red shape displays the beam.

18. Note that in the Intensity/Color/Attenuation rollout, in the *Intensity* area, the intensity of the light has been updated to **3298.0 cd**.

19. In the General Parameters rollout, in the *Shadows* area, select **Shadow Map** in the drop-down list, as shown in Figure 9–25.

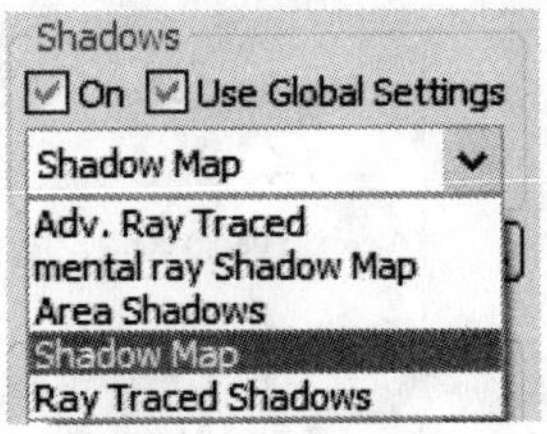

Figure 9–25

20. Click [Render] in the Rendered Window. Note that the dark areas on the floor have been removed and the floor looks washed out (too bright).

21. In the Intensity/Color/Attenuation rollout, in the *Intensity* area, set the intensity to **1100** cd and click [Render] again. The scene displays as shown in Figure 9–26.

Figure 9–26

*Selecting **Illuminate with Scene Lights** automatically clears **Illuminate with Default Lights** and vice-versa.*

22. The photometric lights representation is displayed in the viewport and you can control their effects individually. Select the **Visual Display** label and set it to **Realistic**. Select it again to display the label menu and select **Lighting and Shadows** and **Illuminate with Scene Lights**. In the menu, also expand Scene Lights Control and select **AutoDisplay Selected Lights**, as shown in Figure 9–27.

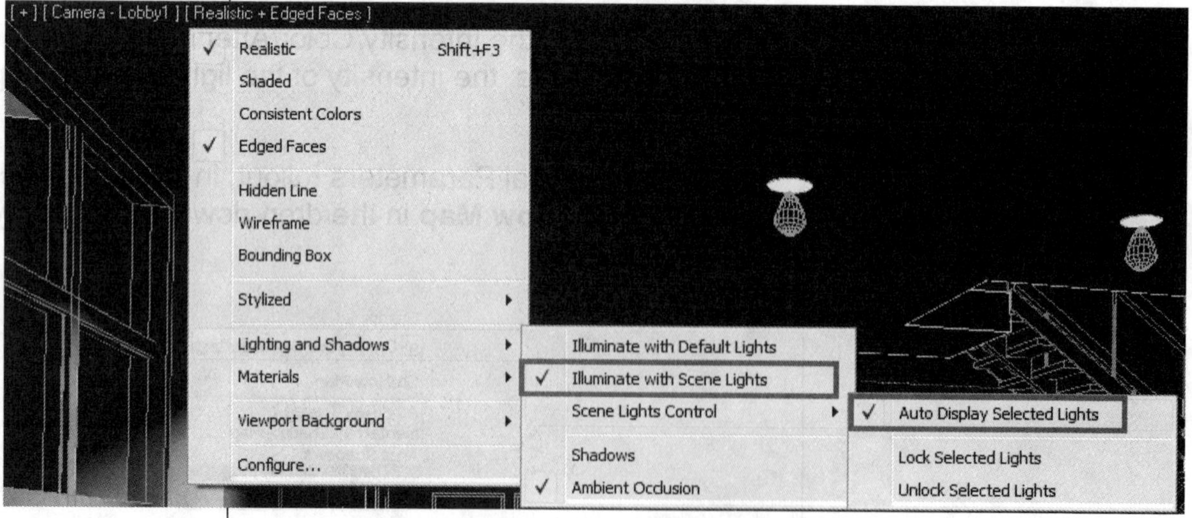

Figure 9–27

If the lights in the viewport are not easily selectable use the Select From Scene dialog box to select the lights.

23. In the viewport, select one of the lights to enable it. You will see the affect of that light in the viewport. Using <Ctrl>, select a few more lights to activate the lights and visually see the affects.

The display of shadows in the viewport is dependant on the driver you are using. The shadows are previewed in the viewport if you are using Nitrous or the Direct 3D drivers.

24. In the **Visual Style** Viewport label menu, verify that **Lighting and Shadows>Shadows** is selected to display the shadows that are cast along with the lighting affect of the light selected.

25. With one of the lights selected, in the Command Panel, in the Templates rollout, select **75 W Bulb**. Note the changes, as shown in Figure 9–28.

Figure 9–28

26. Click  to render the scene. Since the light distribution is spherical, the lighting now illuminates the ceiling as well as the upper walls, as shown in Figure 9–29.

Figure 9–29

27. In the Templates rollout, select **Recessed 75W Lamp (web)**. This uses a different IES file. Render again. The lighting is dark and moody.

28. Save your work as **MyLightingformentalray.max**.

Hint: Using Light Lister

The Autodesk 3ds Max Design software includes a utility called the Light Lister, as shown in Figure 9–30, (**Tools>Light Lister** or in the **Tools 1** Quad menu) that enables you to view and change many light properties without having to select them first. You can change the settings for all lights together or for the selected lights.

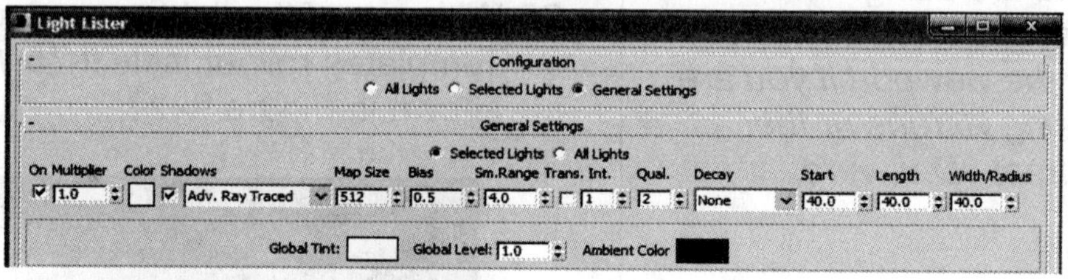

Figure 9–30

Hint: Using mental ray with Standard Lights

The mental ray renderer was designed to be used with photometric light objects. Standard lights can also be used with mental ray, but since they are not physically-based it can be more difficult to achieve accurate results. It is better not to mix standard and photometric lights in the same scene if the goal is accuracy. Consider mixing their use when you want to take artistic license with the scene. Keep these points in mind:

- The luminous intensity of standard lights is equal to the light's multiplier parameter times the Physical Scale value in Logarithmic Exposure Control. (The default Physical Scale value is 1500 candelas in the Logarithmic Exposure Control Parameters rollout in the Environments and Effects dialog box.) You can make drastic changes to the Physical Scale value to compensate for scale problems in lighting a scene. Some experts change this value to 80,000 or 150,000 to brighten a scene.
- To limit the effects of exposure control (i.e., not have the exposure control affect the direct lighting) use the **Affect Indirect Only** option.
- There is an Exposure Control type called **mr Photographic Exposure Control**. In the mr Photographic Exposure Control rollout, in the *Physical scale* area, you can change the scale by selecting **Unitless** and adding a Physical scale value.

Practice 9b Materials that Create Lighting

Learning Objective

- Create a self illuminating material and apply it to an object for illuminating the scene.

Estimated time for completion: 5 minutes

In this practice you will learn how to turn on self-illumination materials that illuminate the scene.

You must set the paths to locate the External files and Xrefs used in the practice. If you have not done this already, return to the **Introduction to Autodesk 3ds Max Design** chapter and complete Task 1 to Task 3 of the **Organizing Folders and Working with the Interface** practice. You only have to set the user paths once.

If a dialog box opens prompting you about a File Load: Mismatch, click OK to accept the default values.

1. Open **LightPoleSelfIllumination start.max** from your *Class Files* folder.
2. Verify that the Camera01 viewport is active and in the Main toolbar, click (Render Production). The rendered image is displayed as shown in Figure 9–31. Close the Render Frame Window.

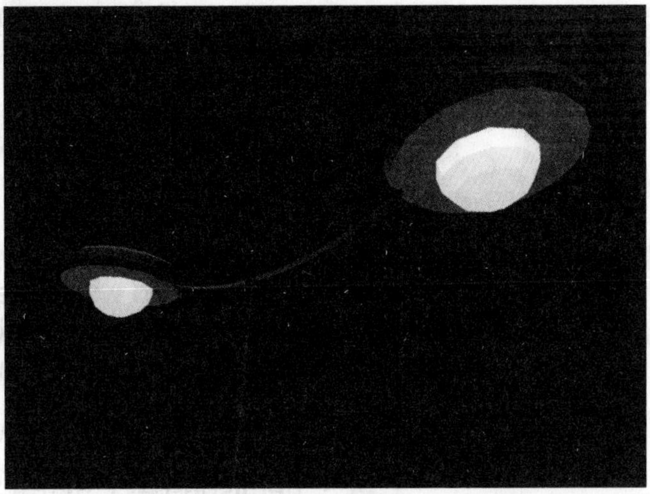

Figure 9–31

3. The globes have a standard material with 100% self-illumination. You will replace the standard material with an Arch & Design Material. In the Main toolbar, click (Material Editor) to open the Slate Material Editor.

4. In the Material/Map Browser, expand the *Materials>mental ray* categories, double-click on Arch & Design to create a new material node in View1 sheet.

5. Double-click on the title bar heading of the new material to open its Parameter Editor. Rename the material **mr Illuminated Lens**, as shown in Figure 9–32.

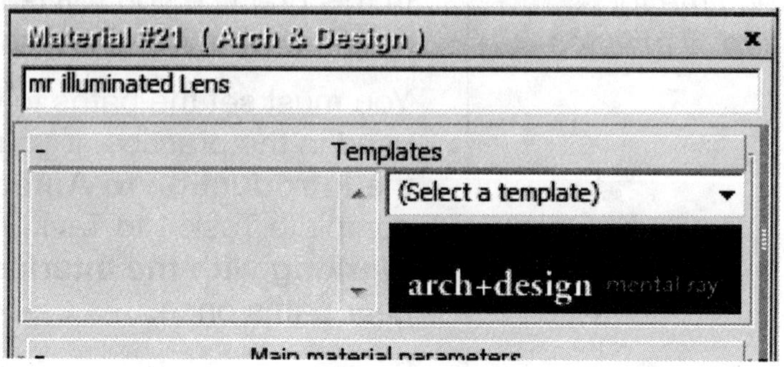

Figure 9–32

Minimize the Slate Material Editor for use again.

6. Scroll down and expand the Self Illumination (Glow) rollout. Select **Self-Illumination (Glow)**, as shown in Figure 9–33.

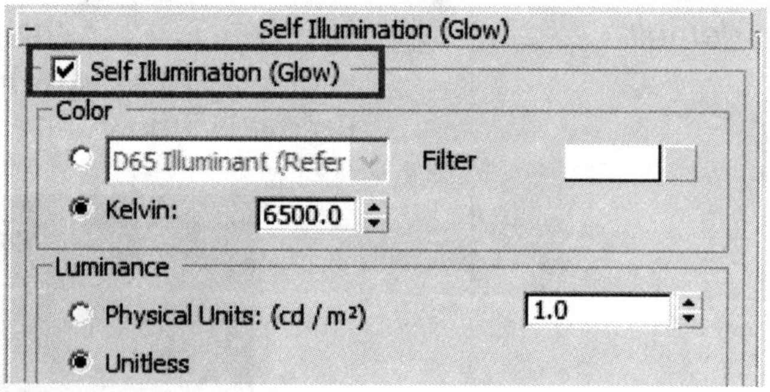

Figure 9–33

7. You will apply the new material to the globes. As the globes are grouped with other objects, ungroup each globe. In the viewport, select a globe group and in the Menu bar, select **Group>Ungroup**. Ungroup the second globe group.

8. In the Camera01 viewport, select the two globes (inverted hemispheres). In the Slate Material Editor, click (Assign Material to Selection) to apply the material to the globes.

9. Click (Render Production). The rendering should be identical to the first rendering before applying the new material.

10. In the Slate Material Editor, in the **mr Illuminated Lens** Parameter Editor, in the Self-Illumination (Glow) rollout, in the *Glow options* area, select **Illuminates the Scene (when using FG)**, as shown in Figure 9–34.

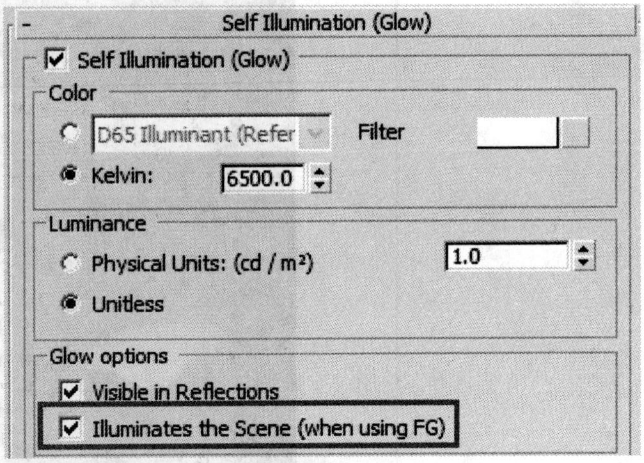

Figure 9–34

11. Click 

if the Rendered Frame Window is open or click  to render the Camera01 viewport again. The illumination is still not visible. Leave the Rendered Frame Window open.

12. In the Slate Material Editor, in the Self-Illumination (Glow) rollout, in the *Luminance* area, verify that **Unitless** is selected, and increase its multiplier to **10**, as shown in Figure 9–35.

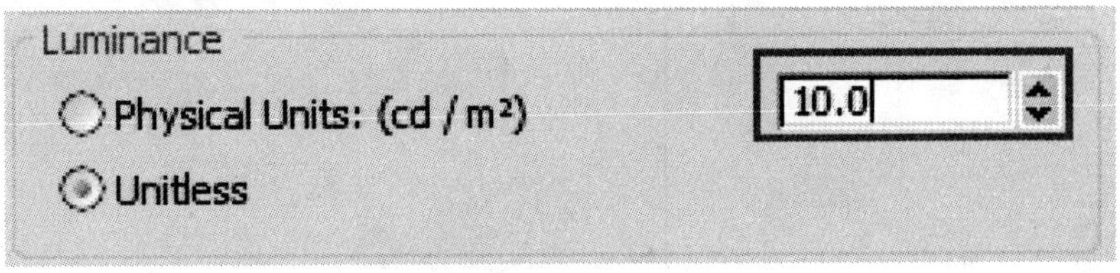

Figure 9–35

13. In the Rendered Frame Window, click . The illumination is displayed around the globe as shown in Figure 9–36.

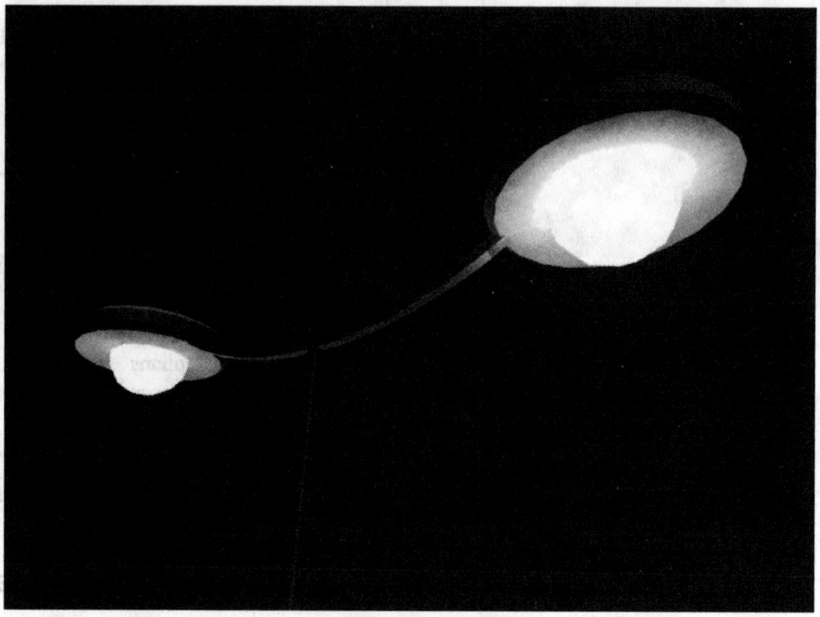

Figure 9–36

14. Save your work as **MymrIlluminatedMaterials.max**.

9.2 Exposure Control

Learning Objectives

- Understand the concept of Exposure Control and how it should be used to produce a real-world rendering.
- Work with different methods of Exposure Control and understand how to use the parameters of **Logarithmic Exposure Control** and **mr Photographic Exposure Control**.

Lighting, Materials, and Exposure Control are all used together in a workflow to produce a real-world rendered image.

- In the Autodesk 3ds Max Design software, **Exposure Control** parameters are a global adjustment used to modulate the output levels and color range of renderings and viewport display to expected values. Although the exposure control methods are optional when using scanline renderer, they are mandatory when working with mental ray. This is an image effect that manipulates the pixel values to adjust the image to fit within a given range.
- In the real world, your eyes automatically adapt to changes in brightness levels by contracting or dilating the pupils, enabling more or less light into your eyes. The same principle applies to aperture controls on real-world cameras.
- The Autodesk 3ds Max Design software has the ability to incorporate exposure control in the viewport. This is dependant on the driver you are using and can be displayed in the viewport if you are using the Nitrous or Direct 3D display drivers. You can tune the interactive rendering of the viewport just like you do for rendering an image.
- The Autodesk 3ds Max Design software calculates real-world illumination values through mental ray. Computer monitors (and printed media) are only able to show a tiny fraction of the total brightness range visible to your eyes.
- Exposure control enables you to adapt the often large dynamic range (the variation of lighting levels) calculated by mental ray into the relatively small dynamic range that can be displayed on a computer screen or printed on paper.

Exposure Control Methods

The exposure control parameters can be found in the *Environment* tab in the Environment and Effects dialog box (**Rendering>Environment** or **Rendering>Exposure Control**). In the Exposure Control rollout, open the drop-down list to select a method of applying exposure control, as shown in Figure 9–37. Exposure Control is used when the **Active** option is enabled.

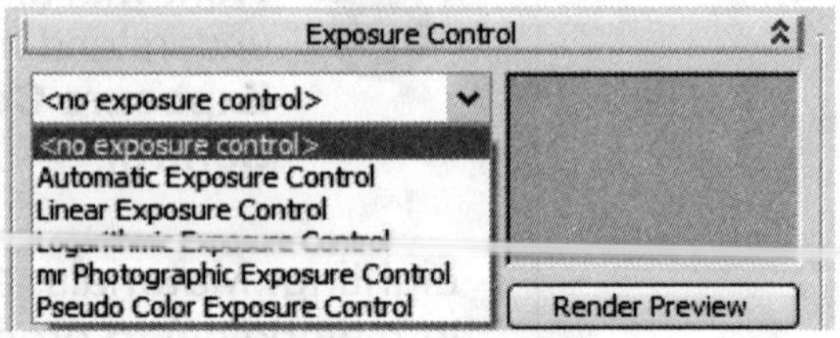

Figure 9–37

- **Automatic Exposure Control** attempts to automatically adjust the sample range of lighting levels. It is appropriate for still renderings with very large dynamic ranges. This method can cause flashing when animating, because different frames could be modulated differently.
- **Linear Exposure Control** interprets and adjusts the lighting levels linearly, which might provide better results when working with low dynamic ranges (small variations in lighting levels).

Only Logarithmic, mr Photographic, and Pseudo-Color exposure controls are supported by the mental ray renderer.

- **Logarithmic Exposure Control** interprets and adjusts the lighting levels with a logarithmic distribution. The logarithmic method provides additional controls that make it a good, general purpose exposure control method. New scenes have this method assigned to them (and active) by default.
- **mr Photographic Exposure Control** gives you the same type of control found in Logarithmic Exposure control, only using terms derived from physical cameras and film. Values like *Shutter Speed*, *Aperture* (fstops), and *Film speed* can be used. In addition, there is a section that allows for *Shadow*, *Midtone*, and *Highlight* manipulation similar to the type of work done in a darkroom with an enlarger. A variety of Presets automatically adjust the settings, but it is highly recommended to verify these values. If you use the Presets, and your rendering is overly bright or too dark, you'll need to adjust the *Physical scale* setting to **Unitless**, and adjust its value.

- **Pseudo Color Exposure Control** is used to generate a lighting analysis rendering colorized by luminance (light source brightness) or illuminance (the amount of illumination that arrives at a surface). The different colors in the render, as shown in Figure 9–38, give a representation of lighting levels. The red areas depict overlit areas, blue are underlit, and the green areas are at a good lighting level.

Figure 9–38

Many designers prefer to avoid exposure control when using a standard lighting approach (without mental ray) to reduce the number of variables they have to juggle. On the other hand, most find that exposure control with standard lighting is an excellent way to adjust output levels. In most real-world productions, some type of post-render processing, usually done in Adobe Photoshop to control brightness and saturation, is a standard workflow.

Logarithmic Exposure Control Parameters

When you select the **Logarithmic Exposure Control** as the Exposure Control method, a corresponding rollout with parameters that are specific to this method is displayed, as shown in Figure 9–39.

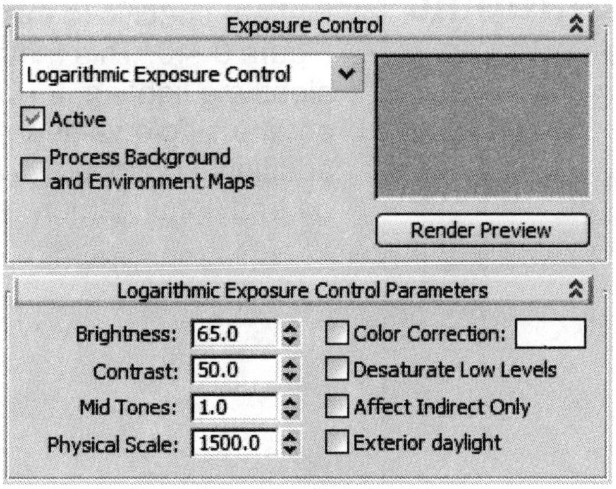

Figure 9–39

Brightness/ Contrast	Adjust the overall brightness and contrast of the rendered image. Brightness controls the perceived illumination of surfaces. Contrast can be used to adjust the difference between light and dark portions of the image. Images that appear washed out (with only a small difference in brightness levels) often benefit from increasing contrast.
Mid Tones	Enables you to shift the brightness levels of the middle portion of the color range. Increasing the midtones value brightens the middle tones of an image and lowering its value darkens them.
Physical Scale	Sets the real-world luminous intensity value of standard lights used with mental ray (multiplied by their multiplier parameter), measured in candelas. This value has no effect on scenes that have only Photometric or IES lights.
Color Correction	Enables you to adjust the color caste of an image so that the color in the swatch displays as white in the final rendering. This adjustment takes place automatically in human vision and is manually adjusted in some real-world cameras using balancing.
Desaturate Low Levels	Converts dark colors to shades of gray, simulating what happens to human vision under dim lighting.
Affect Indirect Only	Enables you to apply exposure control only to indirect lighting, not the direct lighting of your light objects. When working with standard lights this is a helpful option that enables you to manipulate the light object's direct illumination separate from the calculated ambient light.
Exterior daylight	Indicates that you are working with outdoor illumination values, which are much higher than is normally used indoors. When rendering with a camera outside in daylight this option is essential to avoid overexposure.

mr Photographic Exposure Control Parameters

Selecting **mr Photographic Exposure Control** as the Exposure Control method, a corresponding rollout containing parameters that are specific to this method is displayed, as shown in Figure 9–40. This method offers basic presets for daytime/ nighttime lighting, for both interior and exterior scenes. You can enter a single value to control exposure or use any of the additional options available. These additional options are based on traditional camera and darkroom functionality.

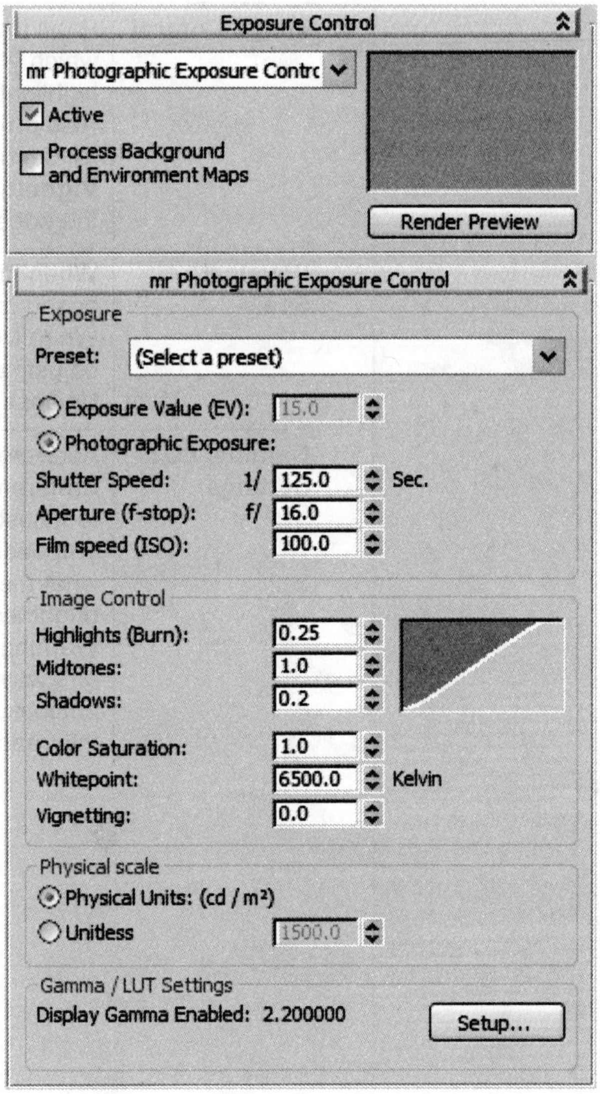

Figure 9–40

Preset	Provides you with predefined sets of values. Lets you select from Physically Based Lighting for Indoor or Outdoor for Daytime or Nighttime, or Non-Physically Based Lighting.
Exposure Value (EV)	Provides you with two options for defining exposure. Exposure Value (EV) is a single value to control the Exposure. Photographic Exposure provides a combination of 3 values to control the Exposure (Photographic Exposure).
Photographic Exposure:	Provides three fields (*Shutter Speed*, *Aperture*, and *Film speed*) to control the exposure. The faster the shutter speed, the less light that is admitted into the camera. The lower the aperture (fstop) the wider the opening in the camera lens and thus the more light admitted. With film speed, the higher the number the faster the film, thus more light required.

Image Control	Provides controls similar to a darkroom technique in which you can burn and dodge to control shadows, highlights, and midtones independent of one another. Also provides tools for **Color Saturation** (use 0 for B&W renderings), **Whitepoint** to affect color tinting, and **Vignetting** to create a fuzzy elliptical gradation around the edges of the rendering.
Physical Scale	When this is set to Physical Units, the calculations occur based on the physical lighting and materials in the scene. When Unitless is set, you can enter a numeric adjustment to increase the energy in the scene. Use Unitless whenever the scene seems too dark or bright.
Gamma/ LUT Settings	Accesses the *Gamma and LUT* tab of the Customize> Preferences Viewports dialog box. Gamma is a method to adjust the rendering to suit a particular monitor or output device. Display Gamma, when enabled, controls what the monitor displays. Output gamma controls the brightness and contrast going to the output rendering. Warning: Changing gamma results in images that look one way within the Autodesk 3ds Max Design software, but look different in other programs like Photoshop. For this reason be cautious when changing the Gamma.

Practice 9c Working with Exposure Control

Learning Objectives

- Assign NVIDIA mental ray renderer to the scene.
- Apply mr Photographic Exposure Control to the scene and modify the parameters to adjust lighting levels.

Estimated time for completion: 10 minutes

In this practice you will prepare an interior scene for global illumination with mental ray. You will also begin saving the Quick Renders for future reference.

You must set the paths to locate the External files and Xrefs used in the practice. If you have not done this already, return to the **Introduction to Autodesk 3ds Max Design** chapter and complete Task 1 to Task 3 of the **Organizing Folders and Working with the Interface** practice. You only have to set the user paths once.

Task 1 - Assign NVIDIA mental ray Renderer.

If a dialog box opens prompting you about a File Load: Mismatch, click OK to accept the default values.

1. Open **mentalray_ExposureControl_start.max** from your *Class Files* folder.
2. Verify that the Camera – Lobby1 viewport is active. In the Main toolbar, click (Render Production). The scene is dark without any calculated ambient light or exposure control, as shown in Figure 9–41.

Figure 9–41

- The object named **Layer:VIZ-1-Ceiling Lights** consists of extruded circles representing the openings for the downlights. The openings display as lit in the renderings because a self-illuminated material has been assigned to them.

3. In the Rendered Frame Window, in the upper left area, click (Save Image) to save this rendering as a JPEG image file. In the Save Image dialog box, save the file in the *renderings* subfolder of your *Class Files* folder with the name **1_No_Exposure_Control**. In the Save as type drop-down list, select **JPEG File (*.jpg,*.jpe,*.jpeg)**, as shown in Figure 9–42. Click Save.

Figure 9–42

4. In the JPEG Image Control dialog box, drag the slider to set *Quality* to **Best** (100) and click OK. Leave the Rendered Frame Window open for the rest of the practice.

You can also press <F10> to open the Render Setup dialog box.

5. In the Rendered Frame Window, click (Render Setup).

   Alternatively, in the Main toolbar, click (Render Setup) or select **Rendering>Render Setup** to open the Render Setup dialog box.

You might need to scroll down to the bottom of the dialog box to display the Assign Renderer rollout. You can also collapse the Common Parameters rollout or other expanded rollouts to display the Assign Renderer rollout.

6. Verify that the *Common* tab is selected. Scroll to the bottom of the dialog box and expand the Assign Renderer rollout. Click ... (Choose Renderer) next to *Production,* as shown in Figure 9–43. In the Choose Renderer dialog box, select **NVIDIA mental ray** and click OK. The **NVIDIA mental ray** is displayed in the Production box, as shown in Figure 9–43.

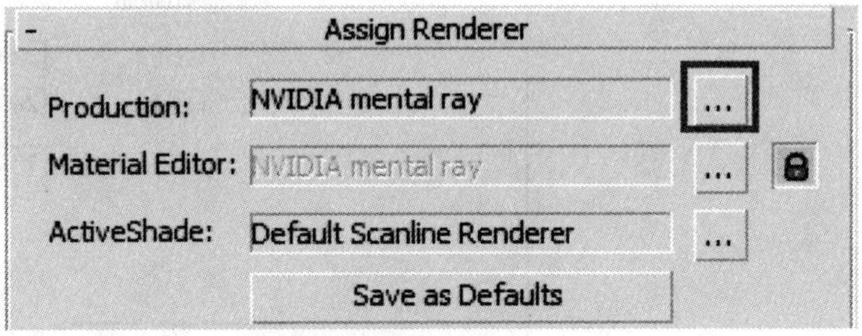

Figure 9–43

The additional panel only displays when NVIDIA mental ray is selected as the production renderer.

7. Note that an additional panel displays at the bottom of the Rendered Frame Window, as shown in Figure 9–44. This panel contains some of the settings for final gather, reflection, etc., which are available in the Render Setup dialog box. This enables you to change the settings easily.

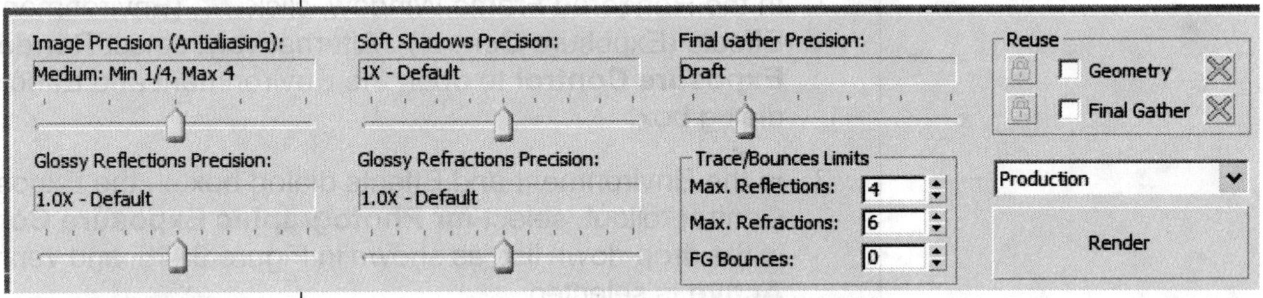

Figure 9–44

8. Click Render in the Render Setup dialog box or in the bottom panel of the Rendered Frame Window. The rendering takes a little longer but it still looks dark.

9. The rendering might be too slow. If the Render Setup dialog box is not already open, click (Render Setup) in the Main toolbar to open it. In the Common Parameters rollout, in the *Output Size* area, click 320x240, as shown in Figure 9–45. Close the dialog box.

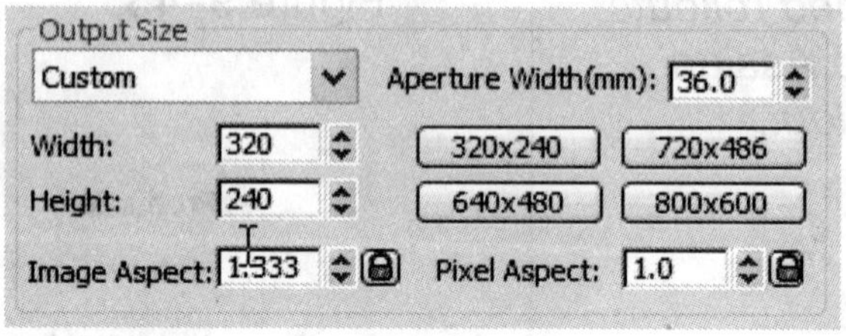

Figure 9–45

10. Click Render in the bottom panel of the Rendered Frame Window. The rendered image is smaller and takes lesser time to render.

Task 2 - Work with Exposure Control.

1. In the Rendered Frame Window, click (Environment and Effects (Exposure Control)). Alternatively, select **Rendering> Exposure Control** to open the Environment and Effects dialog box.

2. In the Environment and Effects dialog box, in the Exposure Control rollout, select **mr Photographic Exposure Control** in the drop-down list, as shown in Figure 9–46, and verify that **Active** is selected.

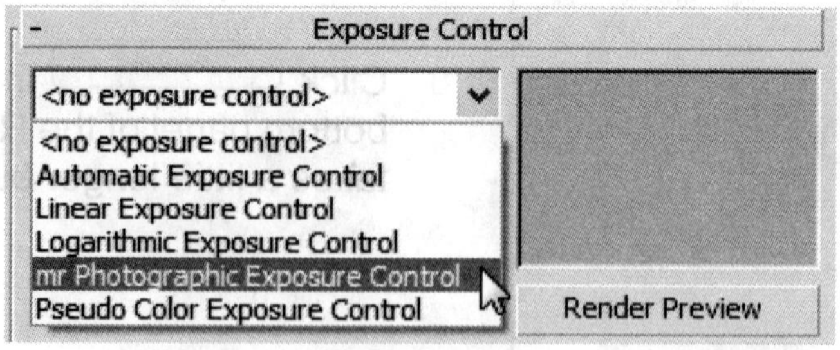

Figure 9–46

3. Click Render Preview and the preview displays. Nothing is visible as everything is black.

Use the spinner to reduce the Exposure Value EV and note the Render Preview. It updates interactively as you change this value.

4. In the mr Photographic Exposure Control rollout, in the *Exposure* area, select **Exposure Value (EV)** and adjust the Exposure value, as shown in Figure 9–47, until you have a good view of the tile floor in the preview window. You might try a value like EV = **6** or **7**.

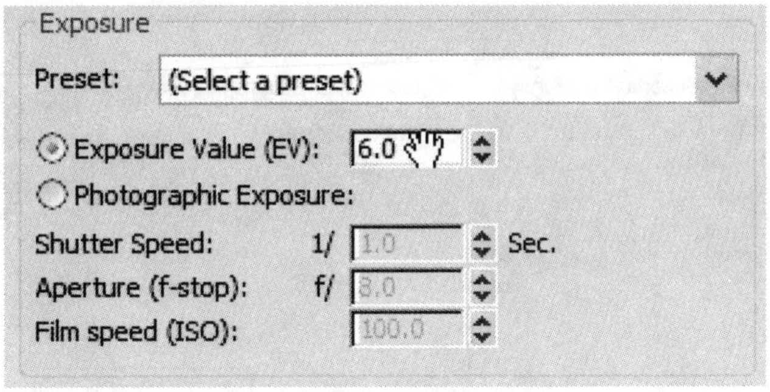

Figure 9–47

5. Click Render in the information panel of the Rendered Frame Window. With Exposure Control applied, the scene displays much brighter than before, as shown in Figure 9–48, under the same lighting conditions. Close the Environment and Effects dialog box.

Figure 9–48

6. In the Camera - Lobby1 viewport, select any of the **Light–Downlight A-#**. In the Command Panel, select the *Modify* panel ( ). In the Intensity/Color/Attenuation rollout, in the Color area, select **HID Ceramic Metal Halide (Cool)**.

7. In the Rendered Frame Window, click Render.

8. In the bottom panel of the Rendered Frame Window, in the *Final Gather Precision* area, verify that the slider is set to **Draft**. Set the *FG Bounces* to **8**, as shown in Figure 9–49.

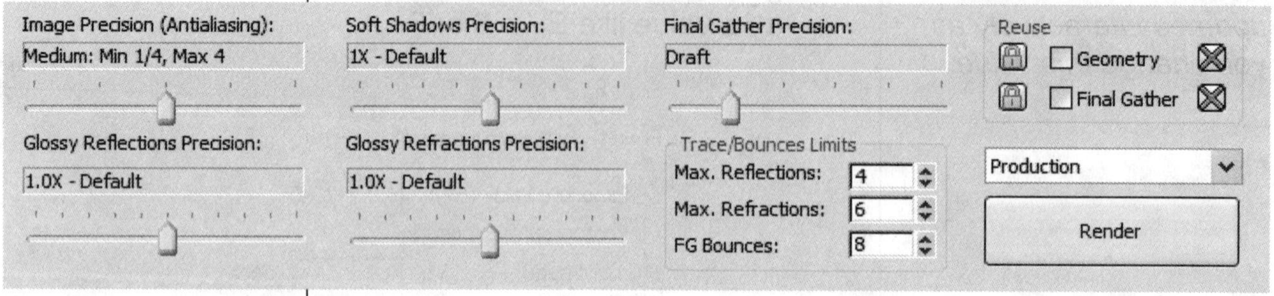

Figure 9–49

9. Click Render. Note that there are subtle differences in the lighting in the back of the room, as shown in Figure 9–50.

Figure 9–50

10. In the Rendered Frame Window, click (Save Image) and save this rendering as **2_Exposure_Control.jpg** in your *Class Files* folder, *renderings* folder.

11. Save your work as **mymentalray_ExposureControl_start.max**.

Certification

Topic:
✓Lighting
Objectives:
✓Use the Daylight System

9.3 Daytime Lighting

Learning Objective

Create Sunlight and Skylight and use their parameters to enhance the lighting in the scene.

Standard lights can be used to illuminate a nighttime interior scene or a scene that does not have openings to allow in daylight. Nighttime exterior scenes can be lit similarly, where outside light sources are represented by light fixtures and dim fill lights, as necessary.

Both interior and exterior scenes can be lit with specialized light objects during daytime. You begin by distinguishing between sunlight and skylight.

Sunlight and Skylight (Scanline and mental ray Renderers)

In the Autodesk 3ds Max Design software, sunlight represents the direct illumination of the sun, as shown in Figure 9–51 with the thick parallel arrows. On clear days a great deal of sunlight is reflected off of the earth's surface and then back down again from the atmosphere. The light that returns to the earth from the atmosphere (as well as the light that diffuses through the atmosphere on overcast days) is represented in the Autodesk 3ds Max Design software as skylight. Skylight illuminates a scene as if it were cast down from a hemispherical dome, as shown in Figure 9–51 with the smaller, solid white arrows.

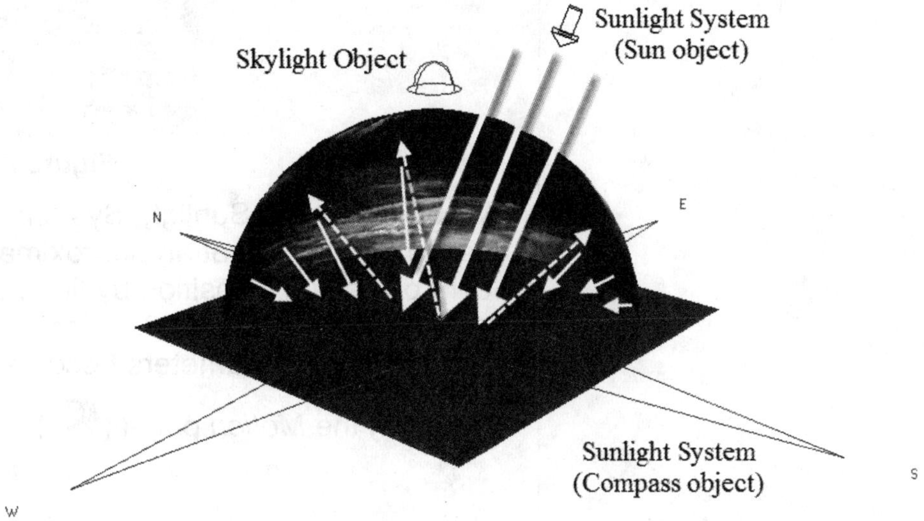

Figure 9–51

You can also create a **Daylight System** that combines both Sunlight and Skylight. If you are using the NVIDIA mental ray renderer, you can create an mental ray daylight system to render a physically based sun and sky lighting.

Sunlight can be modeled with a Sunlight System that includes a sun object (a direct light) and a compass object used to orient the sun in the scene. The angle of the sun's light can be controlled through date, time, and location parameters. The position of the sun can be animated over time for shadow studies.

A skylight object is not a part of the Sunlight system and is an entirely separate object. With a standard lighting approach, the illumination of a skylight object is not controlled by date, time, and location settings of the sunlight system. The skylight's brightness (multiplier) parameter can be set manually and animated to change over time.

Sunlight Parameters

Sunlight and **Daylight** objects are created as System objects.

They are created by selecting the *Create* panel ( ) and clicking (Systems), as shown in Figure 9–52.

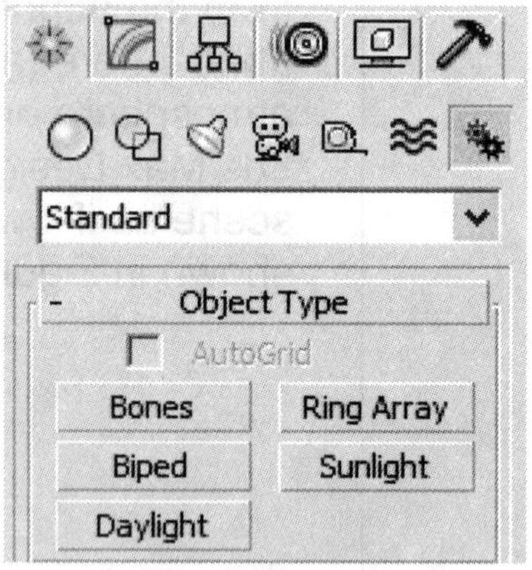

Figure 9–52

When creating a Sunlight System, locate the compass over the center of your site at an approximate ground elevation. You can control the sun's position by time, day, and location parameters, as shown in Figure 9–53. Once a sun object has been created, these Control Parameters become available in the Command Panel, in the *Motion* panel ( ).

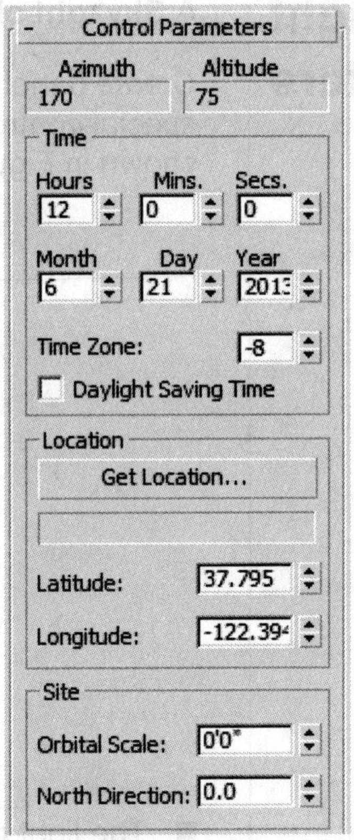

Figure 9–53

- Parameters in the *Time* and *Location* areas enable you to interactively position the sun in the correct location over the scene.
- The angle that indicates north in the current coordinate system can be entered in the *North Direction* field. This is used to orient the sunlight to your project geometry.
- The *Orbital Scale* value is the distance from the sun object to the compass (and the ground). The orbital scale should be large enough so that there are no objects behind the sun.

Sun objects are directional lights. Their *Modify* panel () parameters are the same as those for directional lights. To generate shadows correctly, it is sometimes necessary to clear the **Overshoot** option in Directional Parameters rollout and increase the *Hotspot/Beam* value until it encompasses the entire site.

Skylight Parameters

A **Skylight** object is created as a standard light object in the *Create* panel (), click  (Lights). Skylight objects have special controls available in the Skylight Parameters rollout, as shown in Figure 9–54.

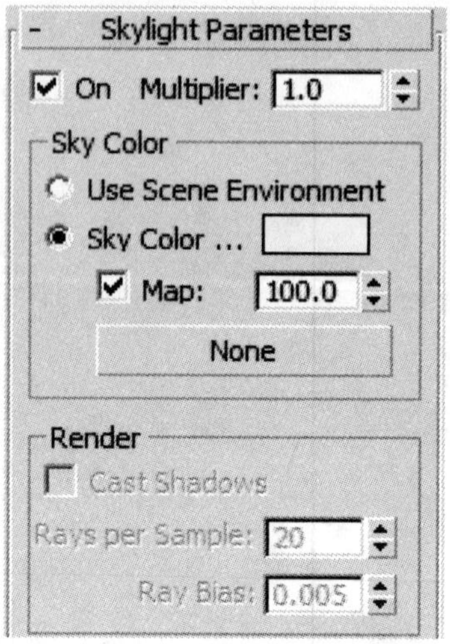

Figure 9–54

- The light cast from skylights can be colored based on the scene environment map. The **Use Scene Environment** option uses the environment that has been set up in the *Environment* tab in the Environment and Effects dialog box (**Rendering>Environment**).
- You can use a single color or a map using the **Sky Color** option.
- The Sky Color maps provided with the Autodesk 3ds Max Design software come with the illumination capabilities with all renderers.

Since skylight is cast down from many directions simultaneously, the shadows it creates are complex and can take a long time to render. These skylight shadows can be extremely realistic and can significantly enhance scenes lit with natural lighting.

The following settings help control the overall quality (and calculation time) of sky shadows:

- **Rays per Sample:** The number of illuminated rays collected at each sampling point. Lower values result in faster renderings but grainier shadows. Set this value low for test renderings but increase it for the final product (try 15 for still images, but animations might need as much as 20 or 30 to avoid flickering).

- **Ray Bias:** This is the minimum distance between two points for one to cast sky shadows on the other. Increasing this value in scenes with a lot of small detail might dramatically speed up rendering time without significantly lowering rendering quality.

Sun and Skylight Options

The following table displays the scene with different sun and skylight options:

	Scene with default lighting (no light objects or shadow casting).
	Scene with Sun (no skylight or ambient light). Note the pitch black shadows.
	Scene with Sun and Skylight; no ambient fill lights or Radiosity calculations have been added. Number of Rays = 4.
	Scene with Sun and Skylight; no ambient fill lights or Radiosity calculations have been added. Note that the shadows here are less grainy than the ones rendered above. Number of Rays = 10.
	Scene with Sun and Skylight; no ambient fill lights or Radiosity calculations have been added. Note that the shadows here are even less grainy than the ones rendered above. Number of Rays = 30. This result took 10x longer to render than the 4 Rays sample.

Image Based Lighting

Image Based Lighting (IBL) is a rendering technique that involves a scene representation of real-world light information as a photographic image. The image used is typically in a high dynamic range file format, such as, .HDR or .EXR. In the Autodesk 3ds Max Design software, this image is displayed as an environment map and used to simulate the lighting for the objects in the scene. This enables detailed real-world lighting to be used to light the scene, instead of trying to simulate the lighting information with standard or photometric lights. In addition to the Autodesk 3ds Max Design software, other Autodesk software, such as Autodesk Maya, Autodesk Softimage, and Autodesk Showcase offer some type of image based lighting.

New in 2014

Image Based Lighting is only available when **NVIDIA mental ray** is the active Production renderer. You can control the IBL settings in the *Global Illumination* tab>Skylights & Environment Lighting (IBL) rollout in the Render Setup dialog box, as shown in Figure 9–55. The **Skylight Illumination from IBL** is the default option used to provide the lighting information for the mental ray renderer. You can set the *Shadow Quality* by entering a value between 0.0 to 10.0 (the higher value creates crisper shadows and longer render times). You can select a *Shadow Mode* between **Transparent** (better quality and longer render time) and **Opaque**.

Once the options have been set, you need to add a skylight (Command Panel, click  (Lights)>**Skylight**) to the scene and select **Use Scene Environment** (Skylights Parameters rollout) to use the lighting from the image.

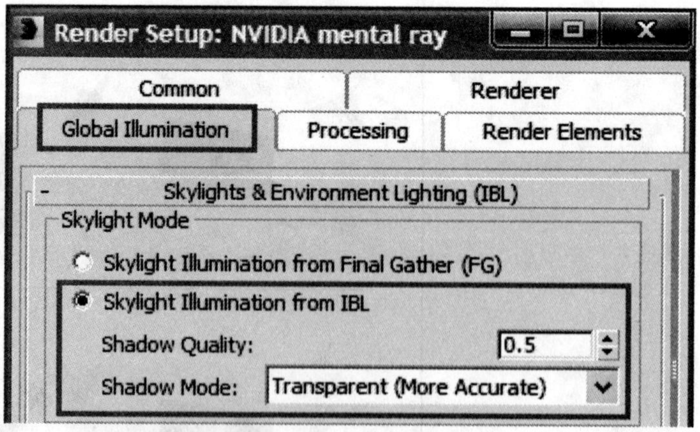

Figure 9–55

Exterior Daylight with mental ray

The mental ray Daylight System includes a physical sun and sky. This can be seen in the Daylight Parameters in the *Modify* panel (). Mental ray daylight calculates indirect illumination, so that you can illuminate an exterior scene with only a single light source. Early morning and late evening sunlight are tinged with color to create authentic looking renderings. Figure 9–56 shows a mental ray rendering using exterior daylight to illuminate the interior scene.

Figure 9–56

Practice 9d Lighting Using Image Based Lighting

Learning Objective

- Light a scene using the light in an environment map image.

Estimated time for completion: 15 minutes

In this practice you will learn to light an exterior scene using an HDR image in the Image Based Lighting (IBL) technique for mental ray.

You must set the paths to locate the External files and Xrefs used in the practice. If you have not done this already, return to the **Introduction to Autodesk 3ds Max Design** chapter and complete Task 1 to Task 3 of the **Organizing Folders and Working with the Interface** practice. You only have to set the user paths once.

If a dialog box opens prompting you about a File Load: Mismatch, click OK to accept the default values.

1. Open **Retail Exterior.max** from your *Class Files* folder.

You might need to scroll down to the bottom of the dialog box to display the Assign Renderer rollout. You can also collapse the Common Parameters rollout or other expanded rollouts to display the Assign Renderer rollout.

2. You need to have NVIDIA mental ray set as your Production Renderer to work with IBL. In the Main toolbar, click (Render Setup) or select **Rendering>Render Setup**. In the Render Setup dialog box, open the Assign Renderer rollout. Click ... (Choose Renderer) next to *Production,* select **NVIDIA mental ray**, and click OK. Close the Render Setup dialog box.
3. Select **Rendering>Environment** or press <8> to open the Environment and Effects dialog box.
4. In the Common Parameters rollout, in the *Background* area, click None for Environment Map.
5. In the Material/Map Browser, expand the *Maps>Standard* categories. Double-click on Bitmap.

CountryRoad.hdr *has been taken from the Environments folder in the Autodesk Showcase software.*

6. In the Select Bitmap Image File dialog box, navigate to the *sceneassets\images* in your *Class Files* folder and open **CountryRoad.hdr**. This image will provide the lights for the scene.

7. In the HDRI Load Settings dialog box, in the *Internal Storage* area, verify that **Real Pixels** and **Def. Exposure** are selected, as shown in Figure 9–57. Click OK.

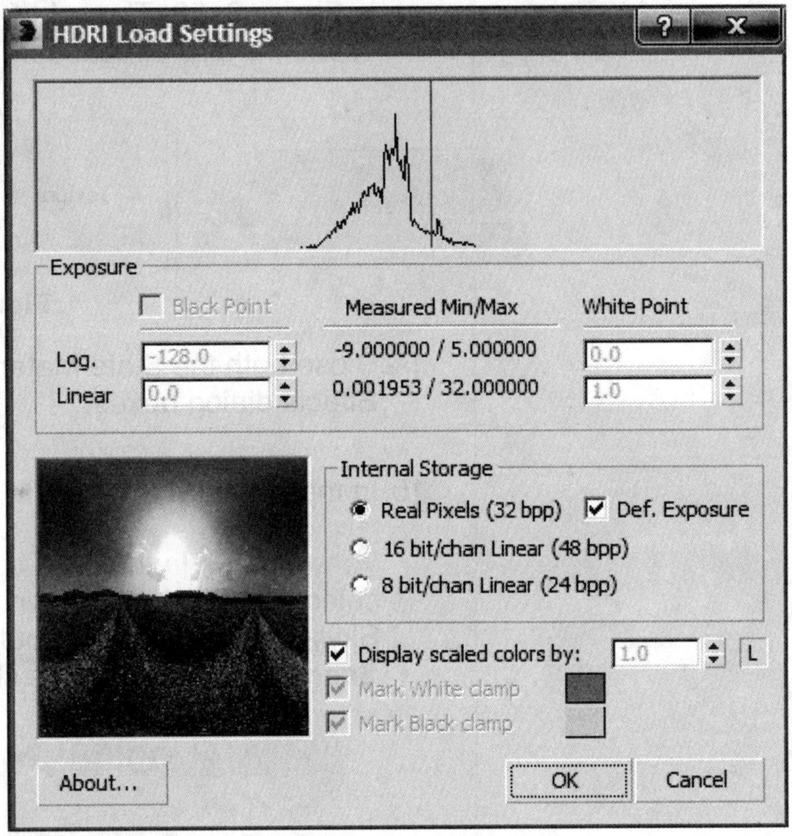

Figure 9–57

8. In the Environments and Effects dialog box, note that None has been replaced with Map #9 (CountryRoad.hdr). Do not close the dialog box.

9. In the Main toolbar, click (Slate Material Editor) to open the Slate Material Editor.

10. In the Environments and Effects dialog box, drag and drop Map #9 (CountryRoad.hdr) onto the *View1* sheet in the Slate Material Editor.

11. In the Instance (Copy) dialog box, verify that **Instance** is selected and click OK. The Map # Bitmap node is placed on the View1 sheet.
12. In the *View1* sheet, double-click on the Map # Bitmap title bar to open its Parameter Editor.
13. In the Parameter Editor, in the Coordinates rollout, note that **Spherical Environment** is selected for *Mapping*, as shown in Figure 9–58. The light from the image will illuminate the scene from all directions.

Figure 9–58

14. Close both the Slate Material Editor and Environment and Effects dialog boxes.
15. In the Command Panel, in the *Create* panel ( ), click (Lights). In the drop-down list, select **Standard** and then select **Skylight**, as shown on the left in Figure 9–59. In the Skylight Parameters rollout, in the *Sky Color* area, select **Use Scene Environment**, as shown on the right in Figure 9–59.

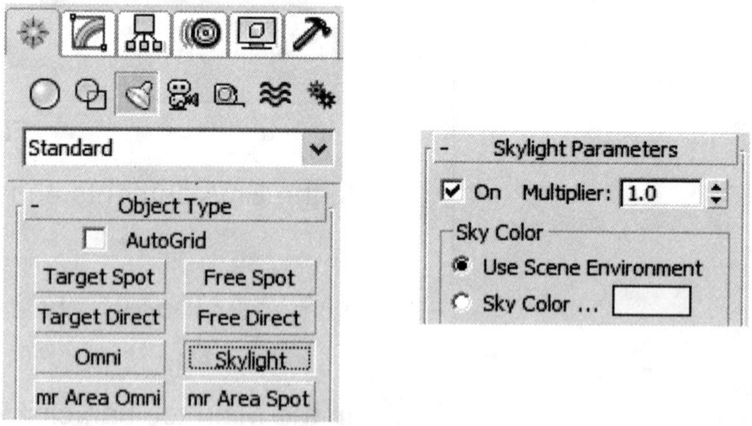

Figure 9–59

It does not matter where you place the skylight because it is only a helper object.

16. In the Camera - Southeast View (the top left viewport), click in one of the parking lines to place the skylight as shown in Figure 9–60.

Figure 9–60

You do not require Final Gather if the scene is using the IBL image for lighting.

17. In the Main toolbar, click (Render Setup) to open the Render Setup dialog box. In the *Global Illumination* tab, in the Final Gathering (FG) rollout, clear **Enable Final Gather**. Close the dialog box.

18. Verify that Camera - Southeast View is active. Click  (Render Production) to render the scene, as shown in Figure 9–61. Note the environment background that was used and the lighting in the scene.

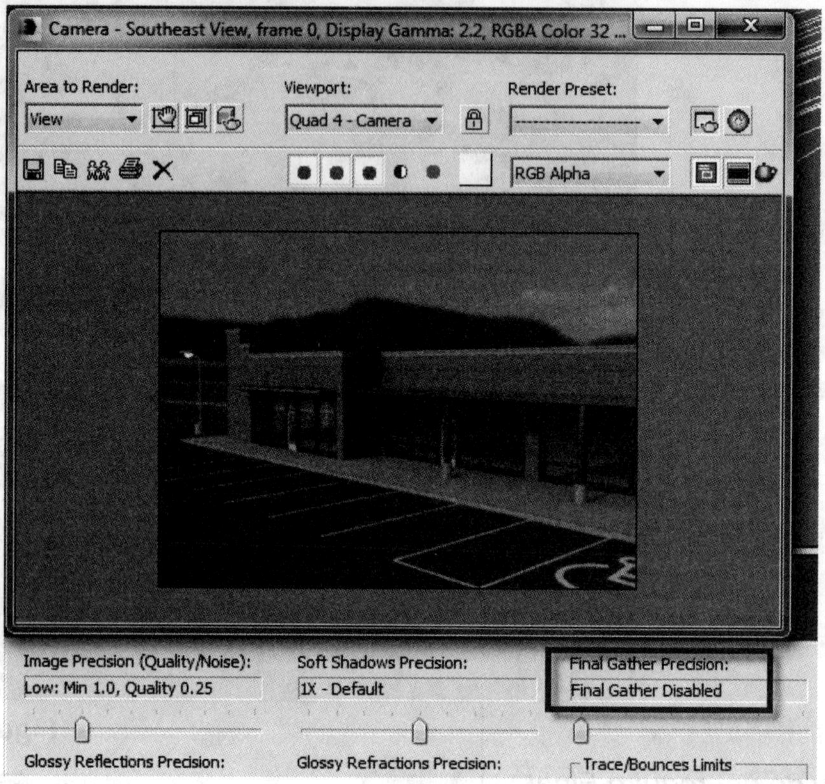

Figure 9–61

19. Close the Render Frame Window and save the file as **MyIBL.max**.

Practice 9e

Lighting for an Exterior Scene with mental ray Daylight

Learning Objective

Create a Daylight system with NVIDIA mental ray renderer and modify the parameters to get a realistic rendering of the scene.

Estimated time for completion: 15 minutes

In general, if you want a daylight system, you should use the mental ray daylight. In this practice you will learn the simple steps of creating a mental ray daylight simulation.

You must set the paths to locate the External files and Xrefs used in the practice. If you have not done this already, return to the **Introduction to Autodesk 3ds Max Design** chapter and complete Task 1 to Task 3 of the **Organizing Folders and Working with the Interface** practice. You only have to set the user paths once.

If a dialog box opens prompting you about a File Load: Mismatch, click OK to accept the default values.

1. Reset the scene and open **Retail Exterior.max** from your *Class Files* folder.

You might need to scroll down to the bottom of the dialog box to display the Assign Renderer rollout. You can also collapse the Common Parameters rollout or other expanded rollouts to display the Assign Renderer rollout.

2. In the Main toolbar, click (Render Setup) or select **Rendering>Render Setup**. In the Render Setup dialog box, open the Assign Renderer rollout. Click (Choose Renderer) next to the *Production,* select **NVIDIA mental ray** and click OK. Close the Render Setup dialog box.

3. Activate the Top viewport and click (Maximize Viewport) or press <Alt>+<W>. Click (Zoom Extents).

4. In the *Create* panel ( ), click (Systems). In the Object Type rollout click Daylight, as shown in Figure 9–62.

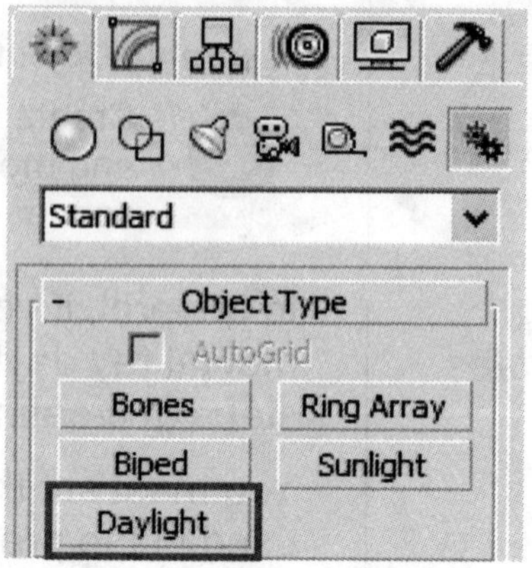

Figure 9–62

The first click is the location of the compass rose. Keep holding down the cursor and drag the mouse to resize the compass rose.

5. In the center of the Top viewport, click and drag out to create a compass rose to the size as shown in Figure 9–63, and release the mouse button to complete the creation. You are still in the **Daylight** command.

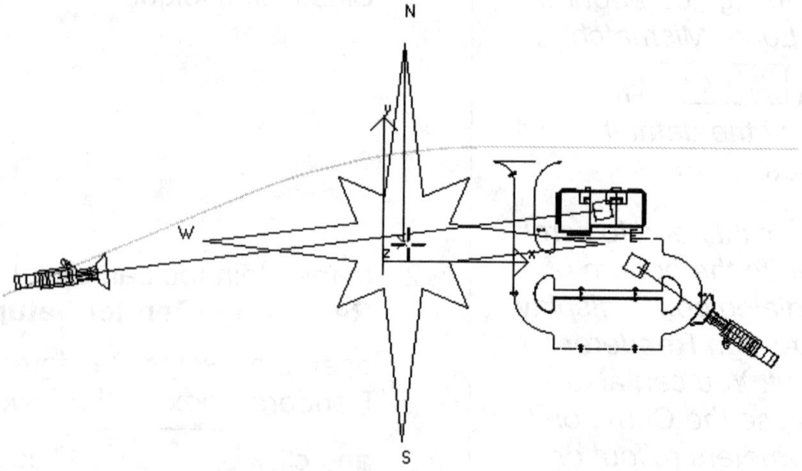

Figure 9–63

6. In the mental ray Sky dialog box, click Yes.
7. Press <L> to change to a Left view. You are still in the sunlight system creation mode. Move the cursor up and down to graphically set the initial orbital scale of the sun object. Click when the sun is at a position as shown in Figure 9–64.

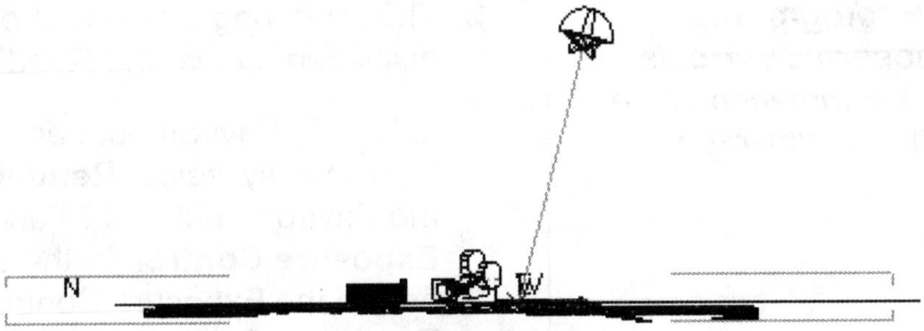

Figure 9–64

Once the Daylight System has been created, these parameters are located in the Motion panel () in the Command Panel.

8. Sun objects should be placed back from the scene for the shadows to be generated correctly. In the Control Parameters rollout, in the *Model Scale* area, set *Orbital Scale* to **250'0"**, as shown in Figure 9–65.

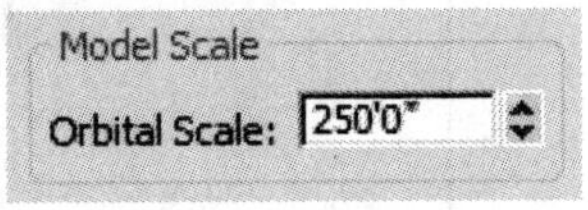

Figure 9–65

9. In the Control Parameters rollout, in the *Location* area, click Get Location... and in the Geographic Location dialog box, select **Portland, ME**, and click OK.

10. In the Control Parameters rollout, in the *Time* area, set the time to **14** *Hours* and leave the date as *Month* **6**, *Day* **21**, and *Year* **2013**, as shown in Figure 9–66. The location of the sun object changes based on the time and date. Press <Esc> to exit the **Daylight creation** command.

Figure 9–66

11. Click  (Maximize Viewport) to show all four views. Activate the **Camera - Southeast View** viewport and click  (Render Production).

mr Photographic Exposure Control *is the recommended type for the mental ray renderer.*

12. The rendering looks washed out because not much is displayed. Leave the Rendered Frame Window open and click (Environment and Effects (Exposure Control)). Alternatively, select **Rendering>Exposure Control** to open the Environment and Effects dialog box. Select **Rendering>Exposure Control**. In the Environment and Effects dialog box, in the Exposure Control rollout, select **mr Photographic Exposure Control**. In the mr Photographic Exposure Control rollout, select **Exposure Value (EV)** and set it to **13.5**, as shown in Figure 9–67. Close the dialog box.

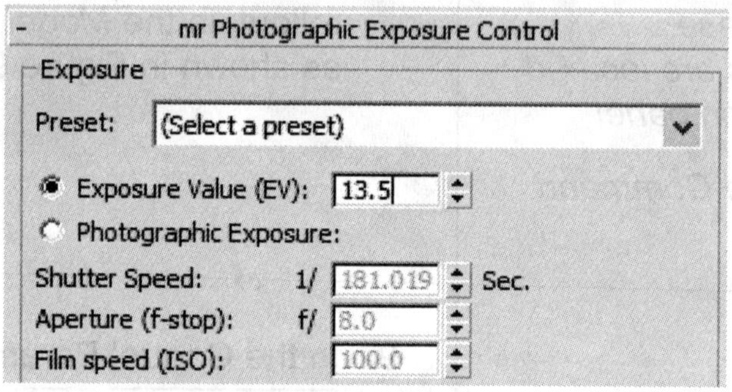

Figure 9–67

13. In the Rendered Frame Window, click Render. The rendering should look better, but the shadow areas are dark.

14. In the bottom panel, in the *Trace/Bounces* area, set *FG Bounces* to **2**, as shown in Figure 9–68.

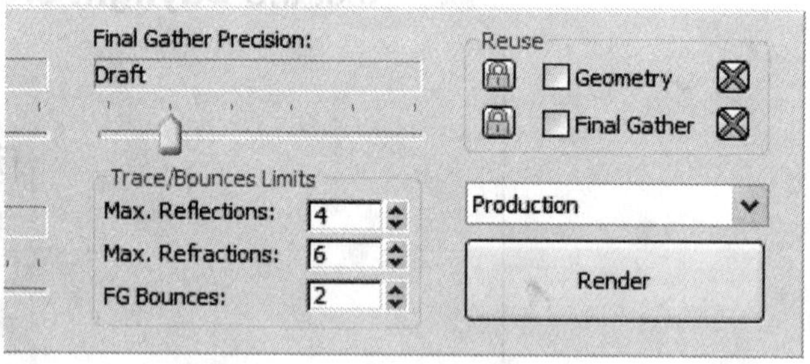

Figure 9–68

15. Click Render. Now the shadow areas are not as dark, as shown in Figure 9–69.

Figure 9–69

16. Activate the Perspective view and use (Orbit) to orbit to the north direction. Press <Ctrl>+<C> to create another camera viewport. You can also change the time of day to 7 am. In any viewport, select **Daylight001**, which is the sun object. In the Command Panel, select the *Motion* panel ( ). In the Control Parameters rollout, in the *Time* area, set *Hours* to **7**. Activate the new Camera viewport and render the scene, as shown in Figure 9–70.

Figure 9–70

17. Save your work as **Mymr Daylight.max**.

Practice 9f Viewport Lighting and Shadows

Learning Objective

- Set the different shading modes to display the shadows in the viewport.

Estimated time for completion: 5 minutes

In the Autodesk 3ds Max Design software you can view shadows directly in the viewport, without having to render. In this practice you will learn how to enable Viewport Shading in your models.

You must set the paths to locate the External files and Xrefs used in the practice. If you have not done this already, return to the **Introduction to Autodesk 3ds Max Design** chapter and complete Task 1 to Task 3 of the **Organizing Folders and Working with the Interface** practice. You only have to set the user paths once.

If a dialog box opens prompting you about a File Load: Mismatch, click OK to accept the default values.

1. Open **ViewportShadows_start.max** from your *Class Files* folder.

- This file has a mental ray daylight system already added and the renderer is also mental ray in this file.

2. In the Perspective Viewport, note that the Visual Style label is set to **Shaded + Edged Faces**. Select the **Visual Style** label and select **Realistic**. Note that the shadows are displayed in the viewport.

For the shadows to be displayed in the viewport, your graphics card should support the Shader Model (2.0 or 3.0) and the display driver should be set to Nitrous Direct3D 11, Nitrous Direct3D 9, or Nitrous Software.

3. Select the **Visual Style** label again and select **Lighting and Shadows**. Clear the **Shadows** selection and note how the shadows disappear. Select Shadows to display the shadows in the viewport.

4. Select the **Visual Style** label again and select **Lighting and Shadows>Illuminate with Scene Lights**. The Perspective viewport might be washed out as the shadows are based on the Scene Lights and not the default lights.

Use the spinner to change the Exposure Value (EV) and note the interactive changes in the viewport.

5. Select **Rendering>Exposure Control** or press <8> to open the Environment and Effects dialog box. Set the *Exposure Value (EV)* to a number between **13.5** and **14.0**, depending on the brightness of your display. Now the shadows are displayed properly as shown in Figure 9–71.

Figure 9–71

6. In any viewport, select the **Daylight01** object. In the Command Panel, select the *Motion* panel (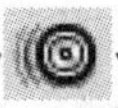). In the Control Parameters rollout, in the *Location* area, change the **North Direction** (using the spinner) and watch the shadows move in the viewport. Note that the **Daylight01** object also moves.

7. In the Control Parameters rollout, note that the month is set to **2** (Feb). Zoom in on the corner of the retail shop to get a closer look at the shadows.

The shadows get longer in winter months and shorter in summer months.

8. Change the month to **7** (July) and review the shadows, as shown in Figure 9–72. The shadows get shorter.

Figure 9–72

9. Select the **Visual Style** label and select **Lighting and Shadows**. Toggle **Ambient Occlusion** on and off (select and clear). Note the subtle change to the shadows in the viewport.

10. Save your work as **MyViewportShadows_start.max.**

Chapter Review Questions

1. With a Photometric light type, which type of Exposure Control is recommended for the Default Scanline Renderer?
   a. Automatic Exposure Control
   b. Linear Exposure Control
   c. Logarithmic Exposure Control
   d. Pseudo Color Exposure Control
2. Which photometric light distribution type only casts light in one hemisphere and mimics the way light emits from a surface?
   a. Uniform Spherical
   b. Uniform Diffuse
   c. Spotlight
   d. Photometric Web
3. Since photometric lights are based on real-world calculations of light energy, they are not scale-specific.
   a. True
   b. False
4. While using the **Logarithmic Exposure Control** as your exposure control method, which option converts dark colors to shades of gray, simulating what happens to human vision under dim lighting?
   a. Mid Tones
   b. Color Correction
   c. Desaturate Low levels
   d. Affect Indirect Only
5. Which of the following statements is correct?
   a. The angle of the sun's light cannot be controlled using date, time, and location parameters.
   b. The illumination of a skylight object is controlled by date, time, and location settings of the sunlight system.
   c. Skylight objects are directional lights and their modify parameters are the similar as those for directional lights.
   d. Sunlight objects are directional lights and their modify parameters are the similar to those for directional lights.

6. Which renderer should be the active Production renderer for the Image Based Lighting (IBL) rendering technique to become available?
    a. Default Scanline Renderer
    b. NVIDIA mental ray
    c. NVIDIA iray
    d. Quicksilver Hardware Renderer
    e. VUE File Renderer

Command Summary

Button	Command	Location
	**Lights**	■ **Command Panel:** Create panel ■ **Create:** Lights
	**Motion panel**	■ **Command Panel**
	**Render Production**	■ **Main toolbar** ■ **Rendering:** Render
	**Render Setup**	■ **Main toolbar** ■ **Rendering:** Render Setup
	**Systems**	■ **Command Panel:** Create panel

Chapter 10

mental ray Rendering

In this chapter you learn to use the NVIDIA® mental ray® renderer for global illumination. You learn the concept behind Photon Mapping and how to use Final Gather to generate a smooth render. You learn to add Exposure Control, Sampling Controls, and Ambient Occlusion to further refine the renderings. You also learn about Sky Portal objects and mental ray Proxy objects.

This chapter contains the following topics:

- ✓**Fundamentals of mental ray**
- ✓**mental ray Interior Rendering**
- ✓**Controlling mental ray Quality**
- ✓**mental ray Proxies**

Certification

Topic:
✓Rendering
Objectives:
✓Differentiate Renderers

10.1 Fundamentals of mental ray

Learning Objective

- Understand the concept and working of the NVIDIA mental ray renderer.

The Autodesk® 3ds Max® Design software contains the high-end renderer NVIDIA® mental ray®. It is a global illumination system, and has been used in the film industry for many years. In the Autodesk 3ds Max Design software, mental ray has been customized specifically for work with design visualization. It calculates physically based lighting using physically correct lights, such as the mr daylight system, and physically based materials, such as the Autodesk materials or Arch & Design materials.

Essentially the mental ray renderer traces the paths of beams of light from their source (the CG light source) to the 3D surface and from the 3D surface onwards to the eye. It computes whether light reflects off the surface, passes through the surface, or is absorbed by the surface based on material definition.

To spread the light through the scene accurately, mental ray scatters points through the scene, which shoot out rays. Averaging occurs over these points with ray calculations to create the color for the pixels in the image. In Figure 10–1 you can see a mental ray rendering in process. On the right is the rough calculated final gather display and on the left is the finished rendered image.

Figure 10–1

Two basic methods for distributing light and color through the scene are available in mental ray: *Photon Map* and *Final Gather*.

Photon Mapping is the original method that mental ray used to calculate the pixels in a rendering. It creates overlapping circular areas based on photon particles distributed by light energy through the scene. These circular areas blend together to create the lighting information in the scene. After calculation, the photon map file can be saved. Photons are essential when caustic lighting effects are required. Photon mapping can be useful when rendering interiors that are lit by Photometric lights with intricate detail in low light areas. Photon mapping is view independent, so you can calculate it once and then use it throughout an animation using a moving camera.

Final Gather is the most recent method, which is faster and easier to set up and control. In general, Final Gather is the method to use for exterior renderings or interiors that are lit by exterior daylight coming through windows. Final Gather can be used in combination with Photon Mapping or without the photon map calculation. In earlier versions of the Autodesk 3ds Max software, the workflow started with Photon Mapping and added Final Gather as a second step. This workflow has been replaced with Final Gather being the first pass and Photon Mapping only used to solve specific problems.

mental ray Rendering

A mental ray rendering can approximate the real-world behavior of light. Its calculations are performed before rendering, during rendering, or both. By taking advantage of photometric lights and physically-based material parameters (those based on real-world illumination and material properties), mental ray can accurately predict ambient lighting. Therefore, the light/color mix looks very realistic. Light calculations in mental ray can even be used for lighting analysis to provide certification data for government approval of energy compliance. Some specifications of mental ray rendering are as follows:

- The mental ray renderer is intended to work with Photometric light objects: **Target Lights**, **Free Lights**, the **mr Sun**, and **mrSkylight** objects. You can also work with Standard lights if you attenuate them.
- The mental ray renderer can work with any material type. However, the Arch & Design materials have built-in mental ray adjustment controls, such as self-illuminance, reflectance, and transmission of light energy. The Autodesk materials simplify the Arch & Design UI.

The Autodesk® Revit® and AutoCAD software use Autodesk materials and can share files with the Autodesk 3ds Max Design software.

- Since mental ray calculates ambient light, theoretically, ambient light objects are not required. Therefore, using mental ray can reduce the time spent configuring ambient lights. (Manually configured ambient light can be added as needed, although it is an artistic fix and not a physically based solution.)
- Exposure control, a method of balancing illumination levels, is always required when lighting with mental ray. In 3ds Max Design scenes rendered with mental ray should use the **mrPhotographic Exposure Control**. Older scenes open with Logarithmic exposure control.
- The mental ray results can be stored as an .FGM (Final Gather Map) file. By generating and saving a final gather map file, you can speed up iterative renders by reusing the calculation. However, Final Gather is view dependent and when using an animated camera you need to calculate the final gather map over the course of the animation (usually every 10 or 20 frames).
- The mental ray renderer can use huge amounts of memory. The challenge is to find the point between the least memory usage and acceptable lighting results. It is easy to overload a system by simply setting the quality to **High** in Final Gather or by using too much reflection or transparency with a large number of objects.
- The mental ray Final Gather results are view-dependent. A mental ray solution can be rendered for multiple viewpoints, but each one must recalculate the Final Gather map for each frame where new geometry is revealed to the eye. While very useful for still images, Final Gather is a challenge for animation.

Hint: Using .FGM Files

To speed up the process, consider calculating the .FGM (Final Gather Map) file using a much smaller resolution. Once complete, use the .FGM file for the larger resolution rendering. In addition, you can lower the *Sample per Pixel* **Minimum** and **Maximum** values to save time when calculating the .FGM file. These options are found in the Render Setup dialog box in the Sampling Quality rollout in the *Renderer* tab.

Certification

Topic:

✓Rendering

Objectives:

✓Identify rendering parameters

✓Identify pass types

✓Use Render to render an effect pass

10.2 mental ray Interior Rendering

Learning Objectives

- Add global illumination to an interior scene with daylight using the mental ray renderer.
- Apply photon mapping to the scene and then add Final Gather to generate a smooth render.
- Use Exposure Control to balance illumination levels.
- Use Sampling Controls for antialiasing the rendered image and add Ambient Occlusion for detail enhancement effect.

If you are creating interiors without exterior lighting, you can use Photometric lights rather than standard lights. In this case, you do not need to use mental ray lights because photometric lights are the recommended light objects. However, when you create daylight and then render an interior scene (as shown in Figure 10–2), there is initially no indirect illumination. There is only direct light from the sun object, which does not look very realistic. To realistically illuminate the interior scene and generate accurate lighting effects, you need to add indirect illumination with the mental ray renderer.

Figure 10–2

Hint: Autodesk Library Materials

It is recommended that you use Autodesk Library materials (which are based on Arch & Design materials) or Arch & Design materials with mental ray to save substantial time and generate the best quality surfaces.

You might need to scroll down to the bottom of the dialog box to display the Assign Renderer rollout. You can also collapse the Common Parameters rollout or other expanded rollouts to display the Assign Renderer rollout.

To use mental ray, you should assign the NVIDIA mental ray as your renderer. In the Main toolbar, click (Render Setup) or select **Rendering>Render Setup** to open the Render Setup dialog box. Verify that the *Common* tab is selected. Scroll to the bottom of the dialog box and expand the Assign Renderer rollout. Click (Choose Renderer) next to *Production,* as shown in Figure 10–3. In the Choose Renderer dialog box, select **NVIDIA mental ray** and click OK. **NVIDIA mental ray** is displayed in the *Production* field, as shown in Figure 10–3.

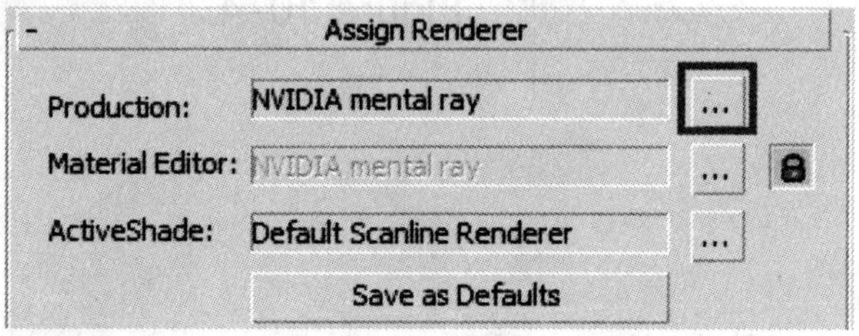

Figure 10–3

Global illumination is included in mental ray as part of generating indirect illumination in interior scenes. It can be obtained by either **photon tracing** or **final gathering**. Both methods use the photon mapping technique.

Photon Mapping

Photons are light particles that reflect, refract, and scatter across the diffuse surfaces based on materials applied to objects. Photons distribute energy quickly in the scene as they bounce from surface to surface.

Hint: Practice for Students

There is no practice using this Photon mapping. However, you can follow along with this lecture by opening **Mental_Interior_Photons_Start1.max**.

*You should have assigned **NVIDIA mental ray** as your production renderer to display the Global Illumination options.*

To generate photons, you need to work in the Render Setup dialog box. In the Main toolbar, click  (Render Setup) or select **Rendering>Render Setup** to open the Render Setup dialog box. Select the *Global Illumination* tab and expand the Caustics & Photon Mapping (GI) rollout. In the *Photon Mapping (GI)* area, select **Enable**. By setting *Maximum Num. Photons per Sample* to a small number (1 or 2) and selecting **Maximum Sampling Radius**, as shown on the left in Figure 10–4, you generate (click Render in the dialog box) swarms of small white circles the cover the surfaces, as shown on the right in Figure 10–4.

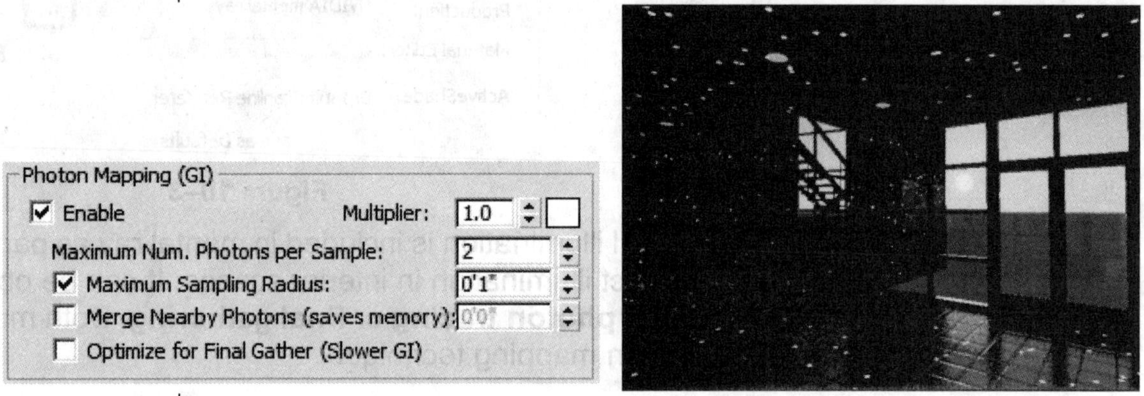

Figure 10–4

Slowly increase the **Maximum Sampling Radius** and the circles begin to join and overlap. On the left in Figure 10–5, the **Maximum Num. Photons per Sample** and **Maximum Sampling Radius** are set to **1** and **0'2"** respectively and on the right in Figure 10–5, the values are set to **5** and **0'5"** respectively.

Figure 10–5

Increase the number of photons per sample by an order of magnitude. Continue increasing until you have a smooth photon-based solution. On the left in Figure 10–6, the **Maximum Num. Photons per Sample** and **Maximum Sampling Radius** are set to **50** and **5'0"** respectively and on the right in Figure 10–6, the values are set to **500** and **5'0"**.

Figure 10–6

You might want to reduce the radius and increase the number of photons. The general rule is that when you decrease the radius by 2, you increase the maximum number of photons per sample times by **5.6 (4 x 1.4)**, and in the *Light Properties* area, increase the **Average GI Photons per Light** number by **1.4** photons.

To make the scene smoother, you should add final gathering to it. Expand the Final Gathering (FG) rollout (*Global Illumination* tab), in the *Basic* area, toggle on **Enable Final Gather**, and set *Diffuse Bounces* to **2**, as shown in Figure 10–7.

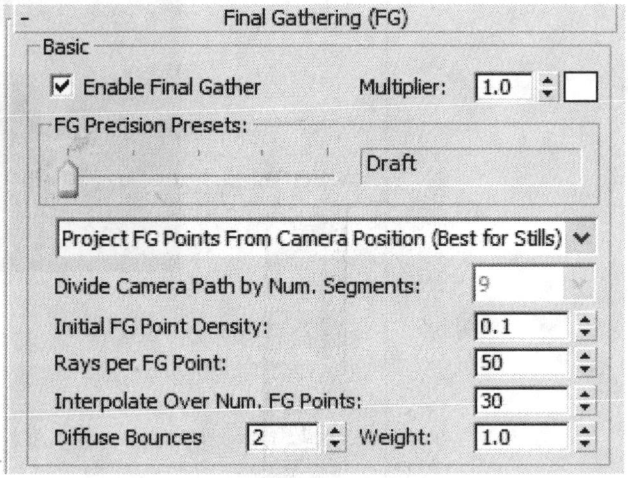

Figure 10–7

***mr Photographic Exposure Control** is the recommended exposure control method for the mental ray renderer.*

After rendering, note that the scene is still dark because the exposure control options have not been set. Select **Rendering>Exposure Control** or, in the Rendered Frame Window, click (icon) to open the Environment and Effects dialog box to set the exposure controls. In the Exposure Control rollout, select **mr Photographic Exposure Control** in the drop-down list, verify that **Active** is selected, and click Render Preview. The preview displays very darkly because no exposure value has been set. In the mr Photographic Exposure Control rollout, activate **Exposure Value (EV)** and lower the EV value (**6.5**) until the lighting is improved in the Render Preview, as shown in Figure 10–8.

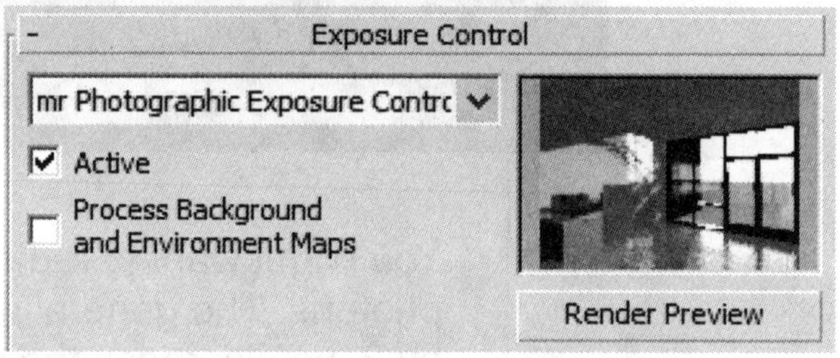

Figure 10–8

Render the scene as shown in Figure 10–9.

Figure 10–9

When you get the required photon solution, you can save a photon map. This calculation is scene-based rather than specific to a viewport. To save a photon map, in the Render Setup dialog box, in the *Global Illumination* tab, expand the Reuse (FG and GI Disk Caching) rollout. In the *Caustics and Global Illumination Photon Map* area, click [...] and specify a folder and filename. Verify that **Read/Write Photons to Photon Map Files** is selected in the drop-down list, and click [Generate Photon Map File Now], as shown in Figure 10–10. The file is saved as a binary .PMAP file (photon-map file).

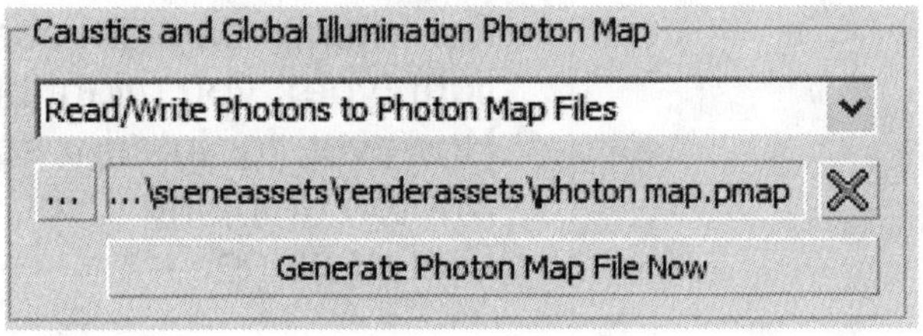

Figure 10–10

In many animations, especially with locked-down (non-moving) camera shots, a photon map saves you considerable rendering time. For interior renderings, photon mapping helps generate light in the scene and can smooth out flashing and shimmering problems in animations.

Photon Merging

Photon merging is similar to adaptive tessellation in radiosity. You can set a merge radius and the photons within that area are merged to conserve memory and calculation time.

Generally, the workflow for this is to set the merge radius less than 5 percent of the maximum sampling radius, and increase the number of photons drastically. For example if you have two million photons in your scene, you might increase it to 10 million. You can save the photon map once your photon merging calculations are satisfactory and your image looks smooth.

To enable Photon Merging, in the Caustics & Photon Mapping (GI) rollout, in the *Photon Mapping (GI)* area, toggle on **Merge Nearby Photons (saves memory)** and enter a radius, as shown in Figure 10–11.

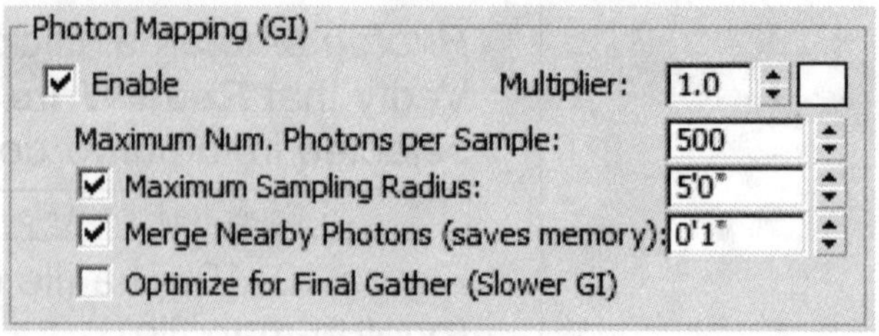

Figure 10–11

For interior daylight scenes using mr Sky Portals (a photometric light type), you might be able to skip Photon Mapping entirely. However, for interior scenes with artificial illumination, use Photon Mapping if you cannot get suitable results with Final Gather alone.

Final Gather

Final Gather is a viewport-based pixel computation that calculates indirect lighting by shooting rays throughout the scene. It creates Final Gather points that produce these rays, which are used to compute the brightness of the lighting. Final Gather uses Bucket Rendering, which enables you to see different portions being rendered. If they are not rendered correctly, you can cancel the rendering, make the required modifications, and render again. In Render Setup dialog box, *Global Illumination* tab, in Final Gathering (FG) rollout, you can control the **Initial FG Point Density** and **Rays per FG Point**, as shown in Figure 10–12, to develop a smooth rendering. The Final Gather Presets set these numbers for you automatically.

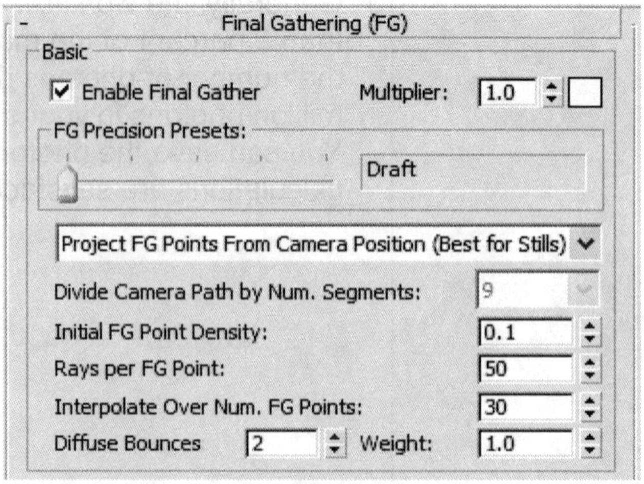

Figure 10–12

It is possible to display the final gather points in the renderings. In the Render Setup dialog box, in the *Processing* tab, expand the Diagnostics rollout. In the *Visual* area, select **Enable** and **Final Gather**, as shown in Figure 10–13.

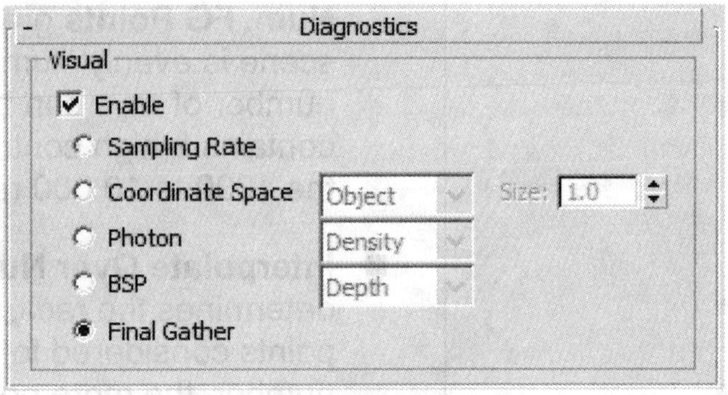

Figure 10–13

Render the scene and note that your rendering displays with green dots, as shown in Figure 10–14. Each dot represents a FG point.

Figure 10–14

The important **Final Gather** parameters are present in the *FG Precision Presets* area, as shown in Figure 10–15, (*Global Illumination* tab>Final Gathering (FG) rollout).

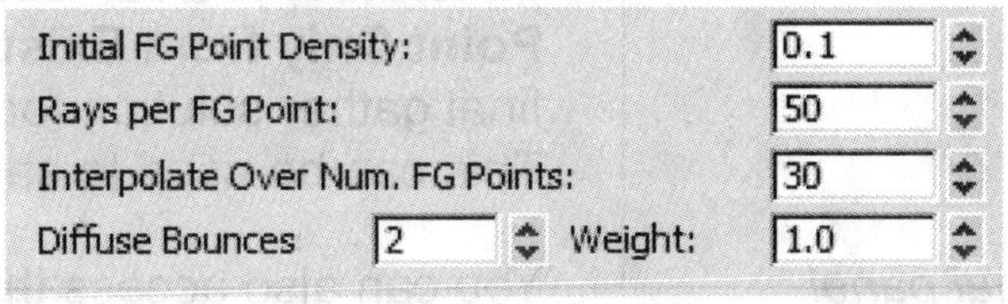

Figure 10–15

- **Initial FG Point Density:** This sets the grid spacing. Using too much density might introduce noise into the image. Remember that each point shoots rays in the scene.

- **Rays per FG Point:** Controls the number of rays shot into the scene from the FG point. If you set the **Interpolate Over Num. FG Points** to **1**, you have a one to one correspondence between Rays and Points. Increase the number of Rays and render to observe the effects. Increase the **Interpolate Over Num. FG Points** gradually to smooth the image. If your scene is evenly illuminated, you can use low values. The number of rays can be set from 50 to 500. If your scene contains a high contrast, you can use much higher values, in the 1000 to 10,000 range.

- **Interpolate Over Num. FG Points:** Setting this value determines the radius for smoothing, based on the number of points considered for the light calculation. The larger the number, the more points are considered in a single calculation. Setting this value to something high (between 100 and 250) should result in extremely realistic, artifact-free images. The workflow is to find the minimum radius that achieves realistic results, while maintaining detail in the scene.

- **Diffuse Bounces:** Defines the number of times the light bounces from surface to surface. Typical values range from 5 to 10, depending on the brightness required in the scene. Presets do not affect the *Diffuse Bounces* value.

Final Gather Map

Just like the Photon Map, you can write a Final Gather Map using the Render Setup dialog box. In the *Global Illumination* tab, expand the Reuse (FG and GI Disk Caching) rollout. In the *Final Gather Map* area, select **Incrementally Add FG Points to Map Files** from the drop-down list and specify a path and filename by clicking [...]. Then click [Generate Final Gather Map File Now]. Once the final gather map is generated, you can set the final gather map option to **Read FG Point Only from Existing Map**. This enables you to reuse the final gather solution for future renderings without recalculation. This can be used to save time for long renderings.

An additional panel displays at the bottom of the Rendered Frame Window when NVIDIA mental ray is selected as the active production renderer.

You can also access this functionality directly from the Rendered Frame Window. In the bottom panel, select **Final Gather** in the *Reuse* area and click [lock icon] (Lock) next to Final Gather, as shown in Figure 10–16.

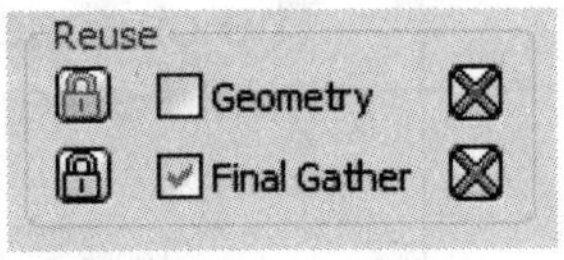

Figure 10–16

Exposure Control

Exposure Control (**Rendering>Exposure Control**, Exposure Control rollout) is recommended as part of the mental ray workflow. Select the **mr Photographic Exposure Control** (recommended exposure control method with mental ray), as shown in Figure 10–17. In the mr Photographic Exposure Control rollout, enable **Exposure Value (EV)** and click Render Preview to display an image in the thumbnail view. When the image is visible, make adjustments to the **Exposure Value (EV)** spinners and watch the image update interactively in the preview window. Selecting the spinner arrows adjusts the setting in increments of 10. You can also manually enter a numeric value. Controlling one number changes the entire range of values.

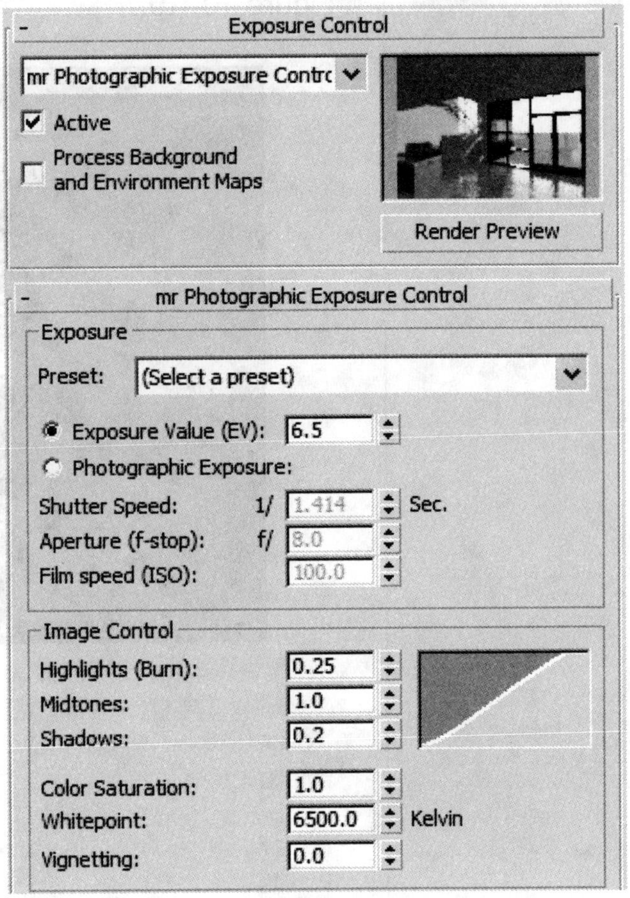

Figure 10–17

The changes can be applied to the whole scene to brighten the whole area, as shown in Figure 10–18.

Figure 10–18

You can also apply Exposure control specifically to the midtone or shadow areas to brighten only those areas, as shown in Figure 10–19.

Figure 10–19

Hint: Photographic Exposure

If you are experienced with photography, you can consider using the **Photographic Exposure** option. This is the combination of *Shutter Speed*, *Aperture*, and *Film speed* values consistent with what is used with a traditional 35 mm camera, as shown in Figure 10–20.

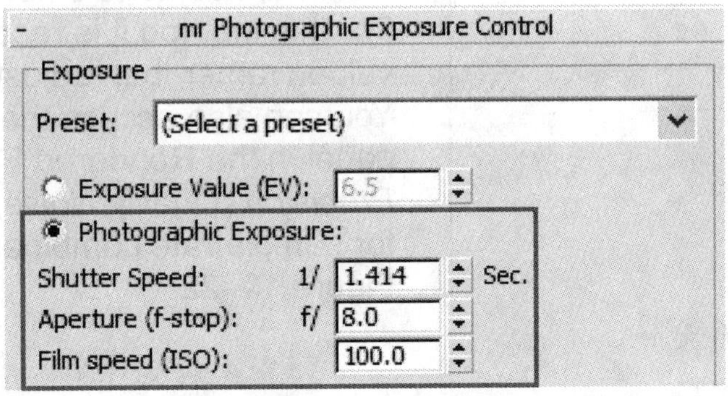

Figure 10–20

Sampling Quality

With mental ray renderer, you can use the Sampling Controls for antialiasing the rendered images. In the Render Setup dialog box, select the *Renderer* tab and expand the Sampling Quality rollout, as shown in Figure 10–21.

You can perform different kinds of sampling, by selecting the *Sampling Mode* in the drop-down list, as shown in Figure 10–21

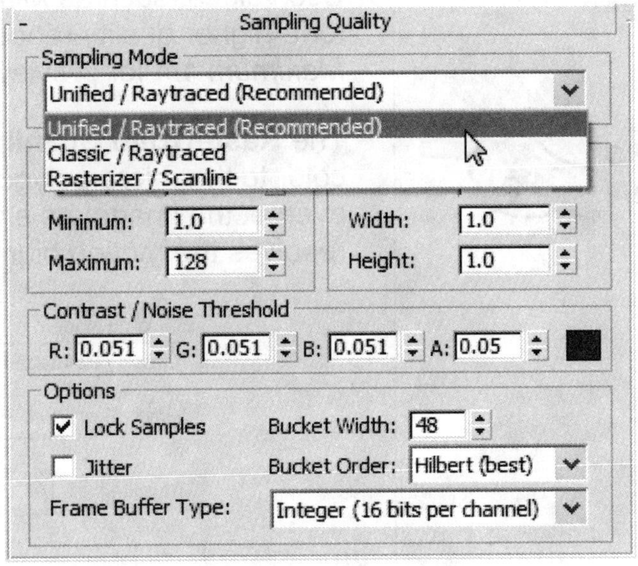

Figure 10–21

***New* in 2014**

Use the **Unified / Raytraced (Recommended)** method when you need a quick rendering because it uses the same sampling method for antialiasing and motion blur. Set the *Quality* of rendering to a range of **0.1 - 20.0** (the higher quality has lesser noise), as shown on the left in Figure 10–22. The *Minimum* and *Maximum* values in the *Samples per Pixel* area provide controls similar to Supersampling in the scanline renderer. Increase the *Maximum* value to smooth out any jagged edges on diagonals. For this method it is recommended that you adjust the *Quality* values rather than adjusting the *Minimum* and *Maximum* values. You can also access these settings in the bottom additional panel in the Rendered Frame Window and use the *Image Precision (Quality/Noise)* slider, which provides various presets for sample rate combinations, as shown on the right in Figure 10–22

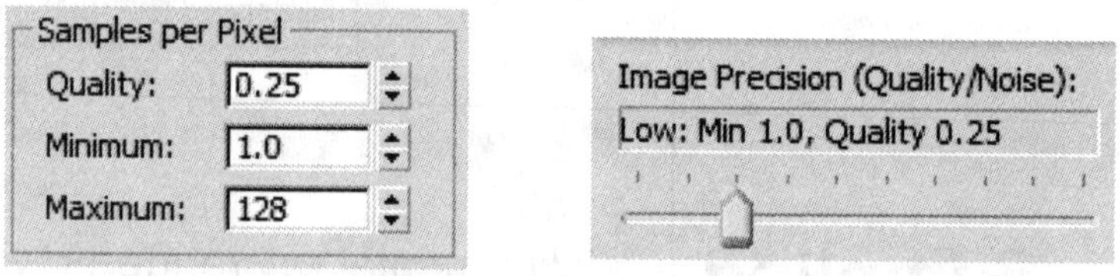

Figure 10–22

Do not assign the same value to Minimum and Maximum. The ratio of Minimum to Maximum is typically approximately 1:16.

The **Classic / Raytraced** method controls the antialiasing for the render. This method only uses the *Minimum* and *Maximum* sample rates, as shown on the left in Figure 10–23. Consider using low values while determining the initial lighting. Increase these values when you are close to a more finished rendering. Use values, such as *Minimum* **4**, and *Maximum* **64** (or smaller) for a higher quality rendering and values of *Minimum* **1/16**, *Maximum* **1/4** for preview quality.

***Enhanced* in 2014**

The **Rasterizer / Scanline** method uses *Shading* to assign a color to the micro-polygons and uses the *Visibility* samples to overset the image, as shown on the right in Figure 10–23. This resolves the motion blur using many samples.

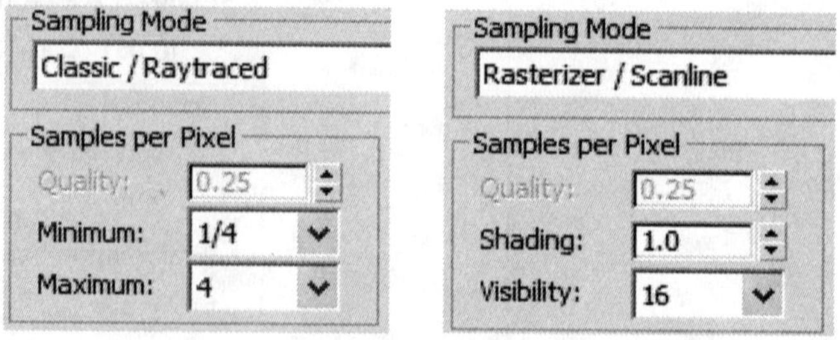

Figure 10–23

Ambient Occlusion (A0)

Ambient Occlusion is a type of light calculation that adds a detail enhancement effect to an image or rendering. It adds gradient shading that brings out subtle differences. It is a material effect that is part of the Arch & Design materials and some of Autodesk Material Library materials. This is enabled in the Special Effects rollout in the Parameter Editor of the material, in the Slate Material Editor, as shown in Figure 10–24.

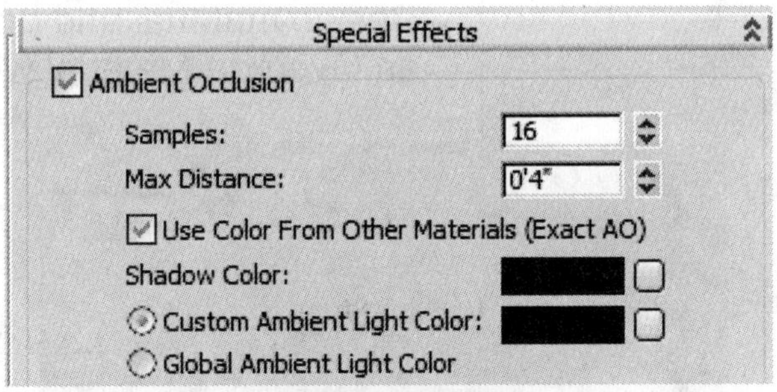

Figure 10–24

Ambient Occlusion uses shaders to calculate the extent an area is inhibited by incoming light. It brings out detail in dark corners, along edges, and in bright places exposed to too much light.

It has a *Max Distance* setting to speed up the rendering by limiting the radius considered. You can combine an extremely low final gather density (e.g., 0.1) with a small AO local radius (e.g., 4") to create quick renderings with good detail and smoothing.

In the film industry, it is common to create a separate Ambient Occlusion pass (called a dirt pass or beauty pass) on top of the rendering to enhance the details. You can create this kind of render pass using **Material Override**. You can enable Material Override in the Render Setup dialog box, in the *Processing* tab, in the Translator Options rollout. Placing an Arch & Design material in that slot temporarily overrides all materials in the scene. On the left in Figure 10–25, the teapot has the Arch & Design material and on the right in Figure 10–25, the teapot has an Override Material with an AO map.

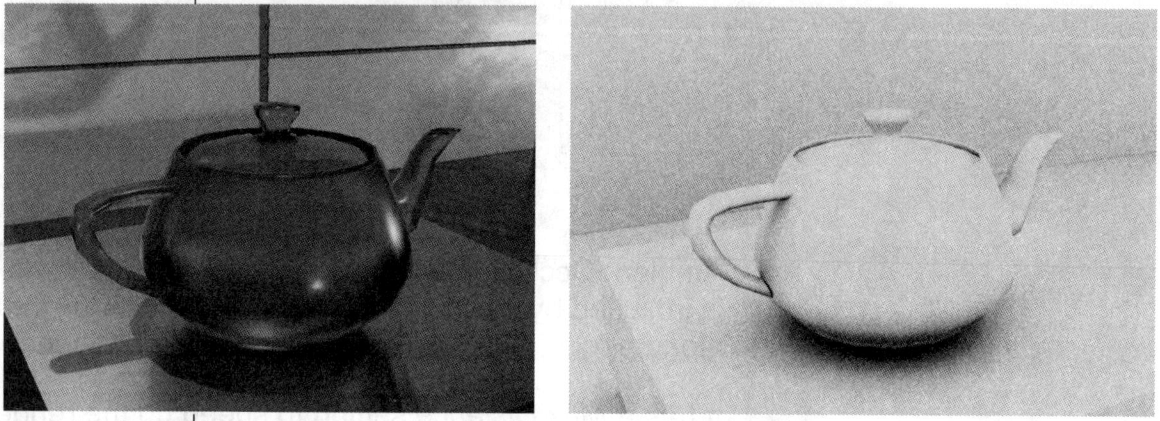

Figure 10–25

Hint: Override Material

The **Override Material** can be used to remove the materials temporarily so that you can examine the lighting in your scene in isolation and make changes as required.

Use **Final Gather** first and see how it looks. If the image has problems, generate a Photon solution to transport light energy into the scene. You can think of this as painting a broad light into the scene. Save a photon map. Use **Final Gather** again. It uses the Photon information and smooths it out into medium size details. Then use **Ambient Occlusion** in the materials to bring out the small details. This can create quick, smooth, but detailed renderings.

Hint: Ambient Occlusion for Materials

You can apply Ambient Occlusion to the material. In the Slate Material Editor, open the material's Parameter Editor and in the Templates rollout, select **Enable Detail Enhancement**, as shown in Figure 10–26.

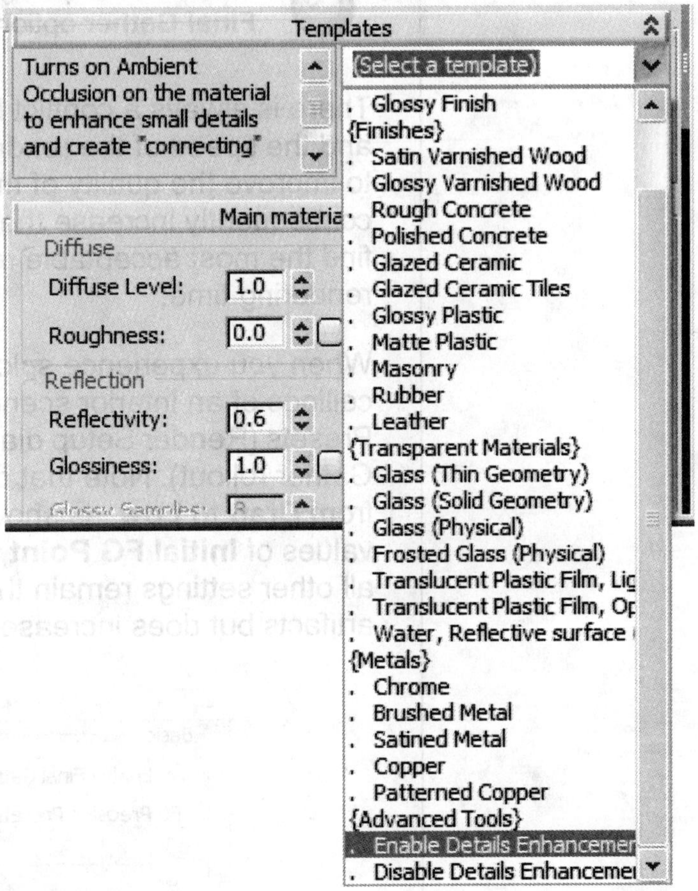

Figure 10–26

10.3 Controlling mental ray Quality

Learning Objective

- Enhance the quality of the rendered image using additional **Final Gather** options.

There is always a conflict between the quality of the rendering and the speed of the rendering. There are controls you can use to improve the quality of the rendering; however, it does consequently increase the rendering time. The challenge is to find the most acceptable rendering quality in the quickest rendering time.

When you experience splotchiness on the walls, floors, or ceilings of an interior scene, you can increase the Final Gather Presets (Render Setup dialog box>*Indirect Illumination* tab>Final Gather rollout). Note that changing the *FG Precision Presets* from **Draft** to **Low**, as shown in Figure 10–27, changes the values of **Initial FG Point Density** and **Rays per FG Point** but all other settings remain the same. This eliminates some of the artifacts but does increase the rendering time.

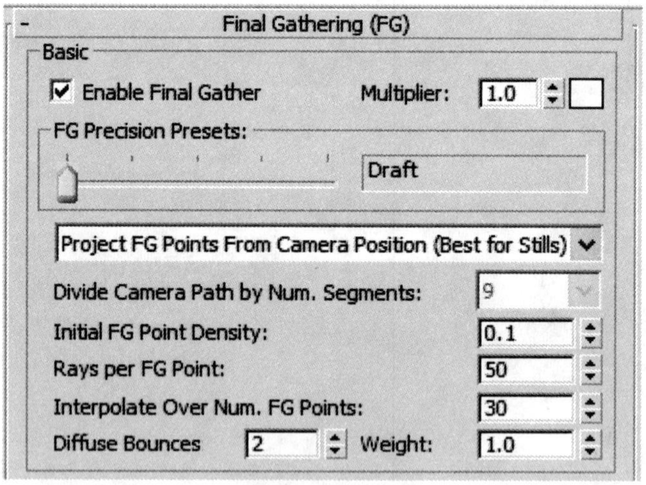

Figure 10–27

Changing to **Medium** should eliminate almost all artifacts, but doubles or triples rendering times. You should not use the **High** setting except if you are doing large scale print work.

The preset values for **Low**, **Medium**, and **High** vary in two settings: **Initial FG Point Density** and **Rays per FG Point**. By default, all other settings are set the same. However, you can make changes as needed.

You can also use the Final Gather Precision slider directly in the bottom panel of the Rendered Frame Window, as shown in Figure 10–28.

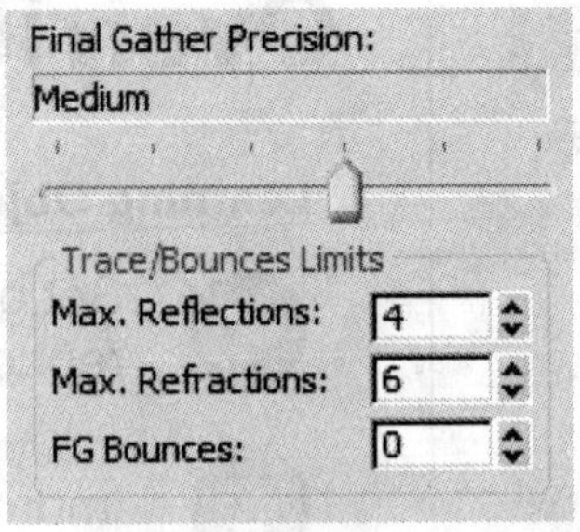

Figure 10–28

Hint: Additional Options in Rendered Frame Window

A panel at the bottom of the Rendered Frame Window is only available when the production renderer is set to **NVIDIA mental ray**. In addition to controlling the Sampling Quality and Final Gather Precision, sliders are available for setting the *Precision of Glossy Reflections*, *Glossy Refractions*, and *Soft Shadows*. This is a quick global override to speed up rendering in the design stages.

Practice 10a Improving mental ray Speed, Quality, and using Material Overrides

Learning Objectives

- Set options in the Render Setup dialog box and save the render as a Final Gather Map file for reuse later.
- Improve the render quality and reuse the existing .FGM file.
- Apply **Material Override** to temporarily remove the materials for examining the lighting in the scene.

Estimated time for completion: 35 minutes

In this practice you will set various Render Setup options and learn a technique to speed up iterative renderings. Iterative rendering enables you to repeatedly render the same camera view while adjusting lighting, materials, or other settings to achieve the optimal image.

You must set the paths to locate the External files and Xrefs used in the practice. If you have not done this already, return to the **Introduction to Autodesk 3ds Max Design** chapter and complete Task 1 to Task 3 of the **Organizing Folders and Working with the Interface** practice. You only have to set the user paths once.

Task 1 - Working with Render Setup and Exposure Control.

If a dialog box opens prompting you about a File Load: Mismatch, click OK to accept the default values.

1. Open **Final Gather Map Start.max** from your *Class Files* folder.

Leave the Rendered Frame Window open for the rest of the practice.

2. Verify that the **Camera - Lobby1** viewport is active. In the Main toolbar, click (Render Production) to render the viewport. Note that the rendering is washed out and the ceiling is dark. In the Rendered Frame Window bottom panel, note that **Final Gather** is disabled and **Image Precision (Antialiasing)** is the selected Sampling option, as shown in Figure 10–29.

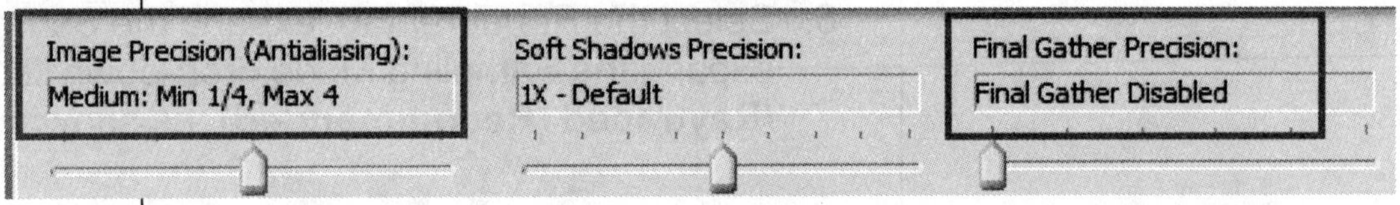

Figure 10–29

- While rendering, a Rendering window displays indicating the progress of the rendering, as shown in Figure 10–30. Once the rendering is complete, the window closes automatically. You can cancel the rendering anytime and do not have to wait until it completes.

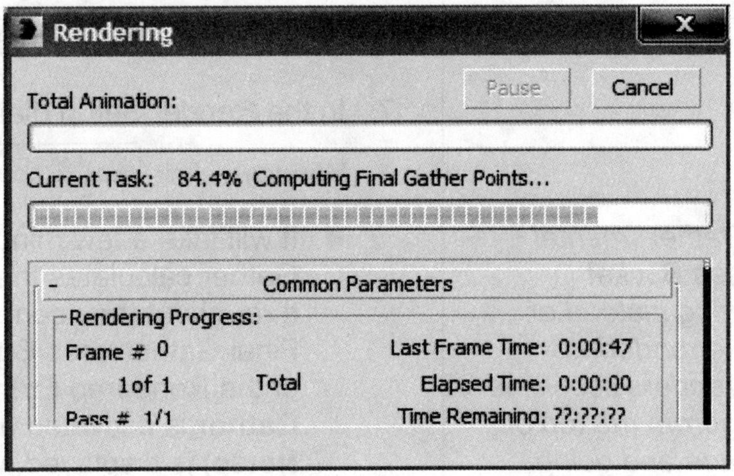

Figure 10–30

You can also press <F10> to open the Render Setup dialog box. Leave the Render Setup dialog box open for the rest of the practice.

3. In the Rendered Frame Window, click (Render Setup).

   Alternatively, in the Main toolbar, click (Render Setup) or select **Rendering>Render Setup** to open the Render Setup dialog box.

4. In the *Global Illumination* tab, open the Final Gathering (FG) rollout. In the *Basic* area, select **Enable Final Gather**.

5. In the *Global Illumination* tab, expand the Skylights & Environment Lighting (IBL) rollout. Verify that **Skylight Illumination from Final Gather (FG)** is selected.

6. Select the *Renderer* tab, expand the Sampling Quality rollout, expand the Sampling Mode drop-down list and select **Unified /Raytraced (Recommended)**, as shown in Figure 10–31.

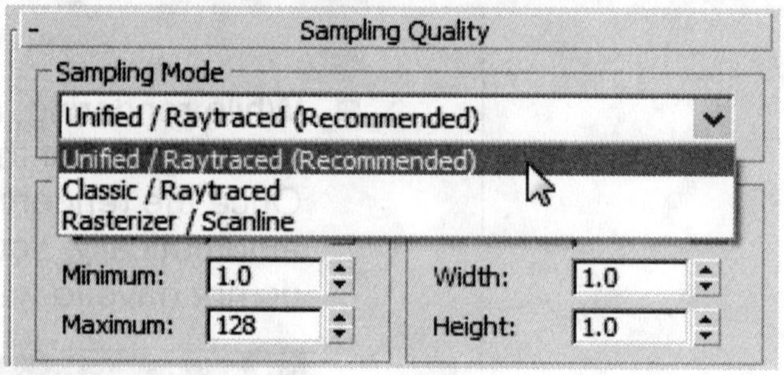

Figure 10–31

7. In the Render Setup dialog box or in the Rendered Frame Window, click .

Final Gather (mental ray) uses Bucket Rendering instead of scanline rendering, which renders scanlines starting from the top of the image and going down.

- It will take a few minutes to render because the Final Gather calculates the indirect lighting by shooting rays throughout the scene. Different portions are rendered as Final Gather uses Bucket Rendering. In the bottom panel of the Rendered Frame Window, note that the **Final Gather** is activated and **Image Precision (Quality/ Noise)** is displayed, which is the **Unified /Raytraced (Recommended)** Sampling option, as shown in Figure 10–32.

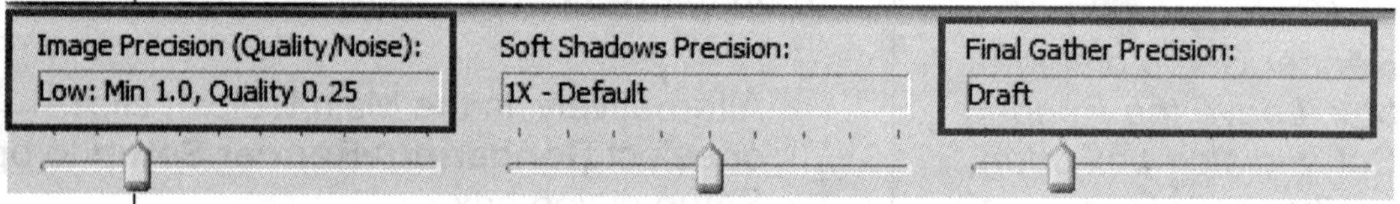

Figure 10–32

8. The rendering is too bright because the Exposure Controls have not been set. In the Rendered Frame Window, click  (Environment and Effects (Exposure Control)). Alternatively, you can select **Rendering>Exposure Control** to open the Environment and Effects dialog box.

9. In the Environment and Effects dialog box, in the Exposure Control rollout, in the drop-down list, select **mr Photographic Exposure Control** and verify that **Active** is selected.

10. In the mr Photographic Exposure Control rollout, in the *Exposure* area, select **Exposure Value (EV)** and set the *Exposure value* to **14**, In the Exposure Control rollout, click Render Preview, as shown in Figure 10–33. The preview looks better so the render will look better as well. If you have time, you can render it and see the effect of the changes, otherwise y skip it now because you will render it later. Close the Environment and Effects dialog box.

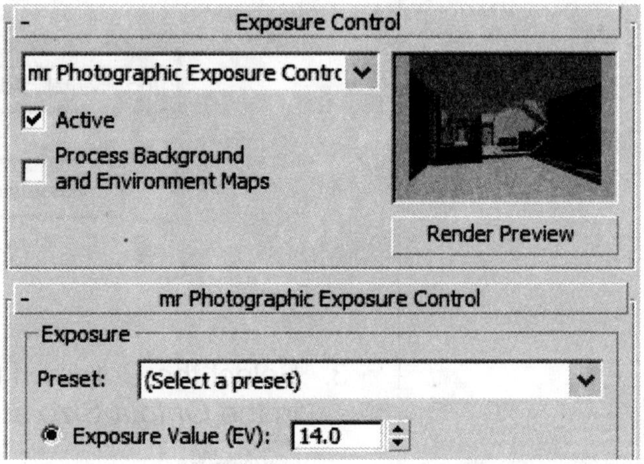

Figure 10–33

Task 2 - Improve rendering speed.

Rendering the **Camera01 - Lobby** view in this scene at 640 x 480 can take almost four minutes on a Dell Precision M90 with 2 GB Ram. Much of the rendering time is used for the Final Gather calculations. You will save these calculations to a final gather map and reuse them. To save time you can also use an output size that is smaller than the actual required rendering.

In the Rendered Frame Window, click  *(Render Setup). Alternatively, in the Main toolbar, click*  *(Render Setup) or select* ***Rendering> Render Setup*** *to open the Render Setup dialog box.*

1. In the Render Setup dialog box, open the *Global Illumination* tab. Expand the Reuse (FG and GI Disk Caching) rollout.

2. In the *Final Gather Map* area, click ... as shown in Figure 10–34. In the Save As dialog box, enter **MyFinalGatherMap** as the name of the file. Note that *Save as type* displays **Final Gather Maps (*.fgm)**. Click Save. In the Render Setup dialog box, note that **Incrementally Add FG Points to Map Files** is automatically set and that the save location for the .FGM file is displayed, as shown in Figure 10–34.

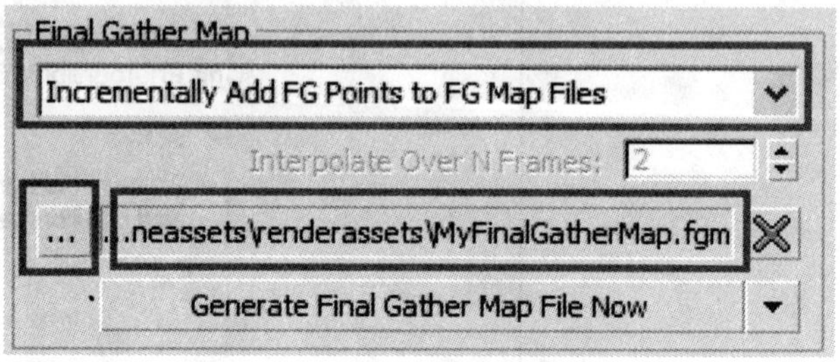

Figure 10–34

3. Select the *Common* tab. In the Common Parameters rollout, in the *Output Size* area, change the resolution by clicking 320x240.

4. Return to the *Global Illumination* tab. In the Reuse (FG and GI Disk Caching) rollout, in the *Mode* area, select **Calculate FG/GI and Skip Final Rendering** and click Generate Final Gather Map File Now, as shown in Figure 10–35.

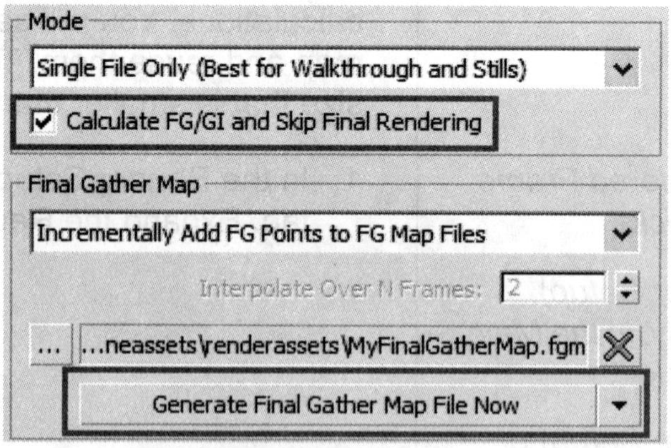

Figure 10–35

- Note that the completed rendering is smaller and does not look like a final rendered image because **Calculate FG/GI and Skip Final Rendering** is selected. It is used to save the Final Gather calculations, which are used in future renderings.

5. When the Final Gather Map calculation is finished, in the Render Setup dialog box, in the Reuse (FG and GI Disk Caching) rollout, clear the **Calculate FG/GI and Skip Final Rendering** option.

6. In the Rendered Frame Window, in the *Reuse* area, verify that **Final Gather** is selected and click next to it. This signals the renderer to skip the step of calculating the final gather map, and reuse the saved final gather map. Note that in the Render Setup dialog box, in the *Final Gather Map* area, the option has been automatically changed to **Read FG Points Only from Existing Map Files**, as shown in Figure 10–36.

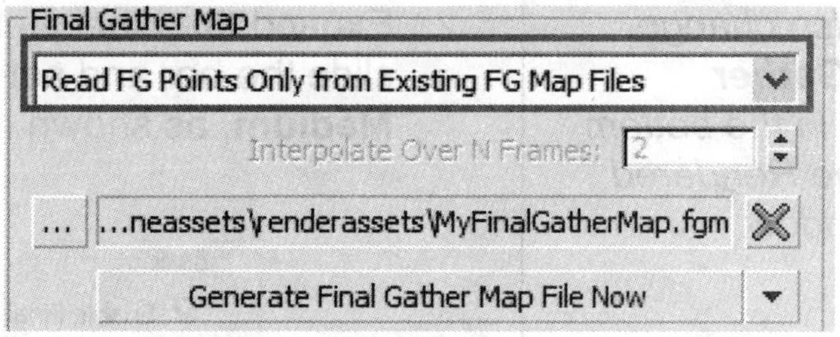

Figure 10–36

7. In the Render Setup dialog box, select the *Common* tab, click 640x480 to change the resolution.

8. Click Render in the Rendered Frame Window or in the Render Setup dialog box. Note that a bucket rendering is not displayed while rendering because it skips the Final Gather Map calculation. The rendering is displayed as shown in Figure 10–37.

Figure 10–37

- The rendering is faster but the quality needs improvement. As long as you do not change the camera view you can use the final gather map over and over again. If you change to a different view, you should create another .FGM file.

Task 3 - Improve Rendering Quality.

1. In the Render Setup dialog box, open the *Global Illumination* tab. In the Reuse (FG and GI Disk Caching) rollout, in the *Final Gather Map* area, click [...]. In the Save As dialog box, enter **MyFinalGatherMap2** as the name of the file and click [Save].

*You can also change the **Final Gather Precision** in the bottom panel of the Rendered Frame Window.*

2. Expand the Final Gathering (FG) rollout. In the *Basic* area, slide the bar and set the *FG Precision Presets* value to **Medium**, as shown in Figure 10–38.

Figure 10–38

3. Select the *Common* tab and manually enter a custom output size with values of **160** (*Width*) x **120** (*Height*), as shown in Figure 10–39.

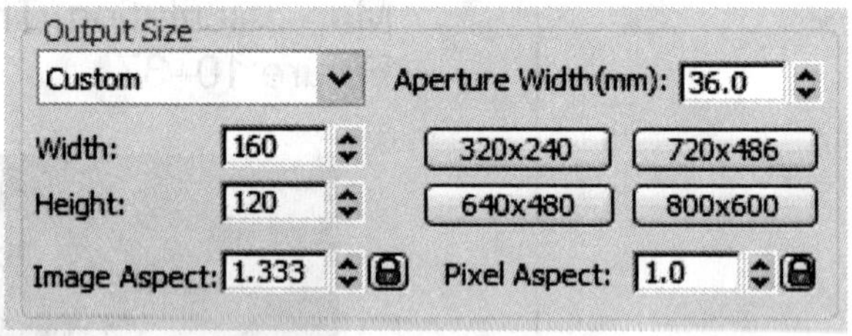

Figure 10–39

4. Return to the *Global Illumination* tab, in the Reuse (FG and GI Disk Caching) rollout, click [Generate Final Gather Map File Now]. This could take some time to calculate (about 5 minutes).

5. When the Final Gather Map calculation is finished, verify that in the Render Setup dialog box, in the *Final Gather Map* area, **Read FG Points Only from Existing Map Files** is set, as shown in Figure 10–40. This indicates that the renderer needs to skip the step of calculating the final gather map, and reuse the saved final gather map in the future.

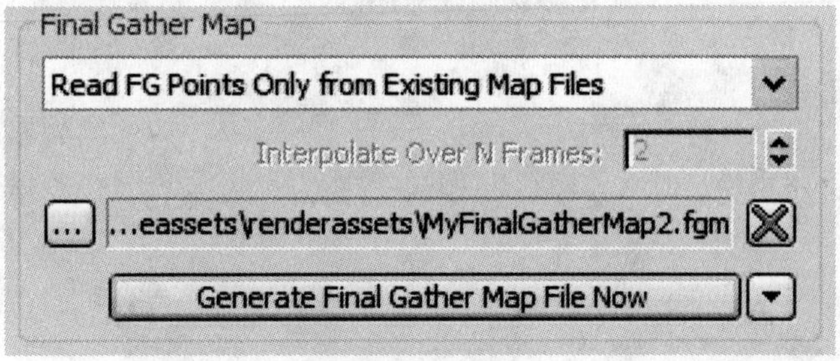

Figure 10–40

6. In the *Common* tab, click 640x480 and render. The rendering only takes little over a minute because it uses the Final Gather points from the saved file. The splotchiness on the ceiling is much less, as shown in Figure 10–41, than when the final gather map was set to *Draft*.

7. The image still looks jagged. In the bottom panel of the Rendered Frame Window, in *Image Precision (Quality/ Noise)*, drag the slider to **Medium: Min 1.0, Quality 1.0**, as shown in Figure 10–41. Render again. The rendering is less jagged as shown in Figure 10–41.

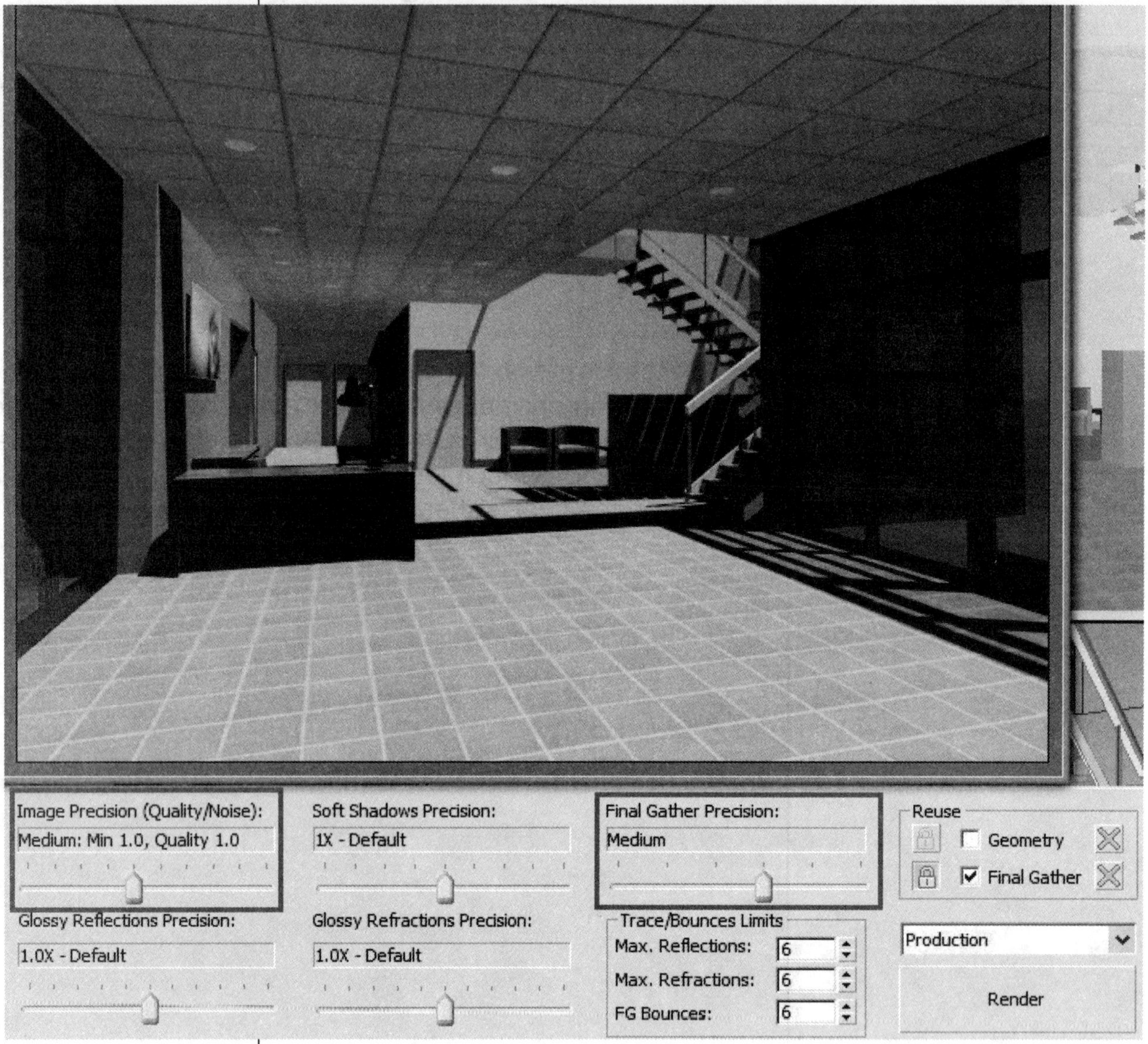

Figure 10–41

Task 4 - Set Material Override.

Materials have a dramatic effect on the rendering; therefore, sometimes you will want to isolate lighting from materials. You can use the Material Override to do this.

1. Open the Slate Material Editor.
2. In the Material/Map Browser, in the *Materials>mental ray* category, double-click on Arch & Design to add it as a node to the *View1* sheet.
3. Double-click on the title bar heading for the new Arch & Design material to open its Parameter Editor.
4. Change the material name to **Override**. In the *Diffuse* area, set *Color* to **white**. In the *Reflection* area, set the Reflectivity to **0**, as shown in Figure 10–42.

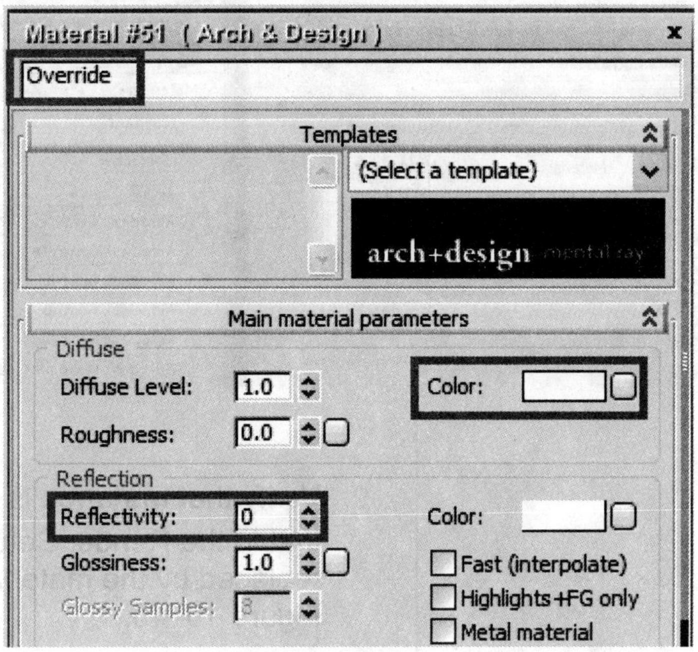

Figure 10–42

5. Expand the Special Effects rollout and select **Ambient Occlusion**, as shown in Figure 10–43.

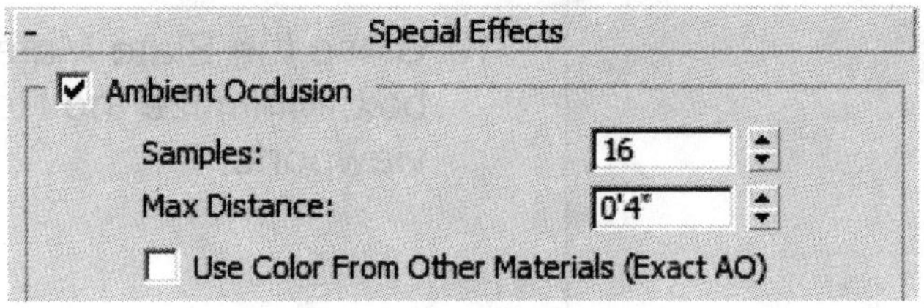

Figure 10–43

The Render Setup dialog box, the Slate Material Editor, and the Rendered Frame Window are modeless dialog boxes and can remain open at the same time.

6. Move the Render Setup dialog box and place it next to the Slate Material Editor. Verify that the Override material node (View1 sheet) is visible in the Slate Material Editor, as shown in Figure 10–44.

7. In the Render Setup dialog box, select the *Processing* tab. In the Translator Options rollout, in the *Material Override* area, select the **Enable** option.

8. In the Slate Material Editor, in the *View 1* sheet, click and drag the **Override** material's output socket and drop it in the Render Setup dialog box, in the *Material Override* area, on *Material* [None], as shown in Figure 10–44.

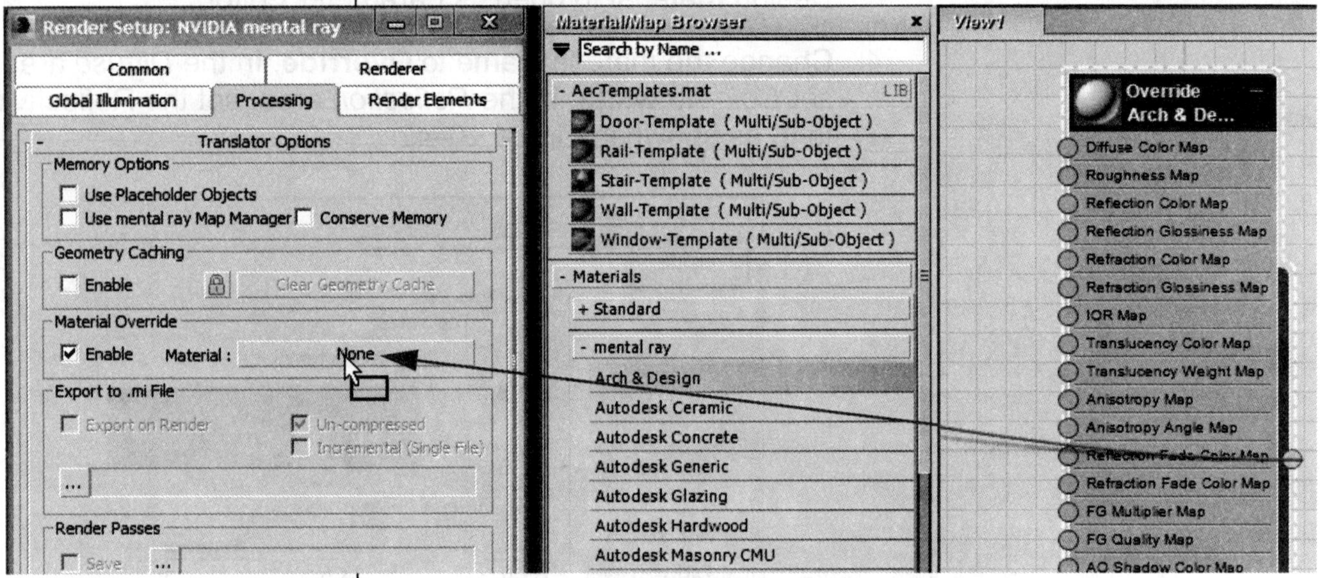

Figure 10–44

9. Verify that **Instance** is selected and click [OK]. Note that in the Render Setup dialog box, [None] is replaced by the material **Override** button, as shown in Figure 10–45.

Figure 10–45

10. Close the Slate Material Editor and the Render Setup dialog box. Minimize the Rendered Frame Window to display the viewports.

11. In the Main toolbar, click (Select by Name). In the Select From Scene dialog box, click (Display None) and click (Display Lights). In the list, select **Light Downlight A00** and click OK. In the **Camera-Lobby 1** view, right-click and select **Light On** in the Quad menu, as shown in Figure 10–46. Note that in the viewport all of the downlights are displayed in (yellow) because the lights are instanced.

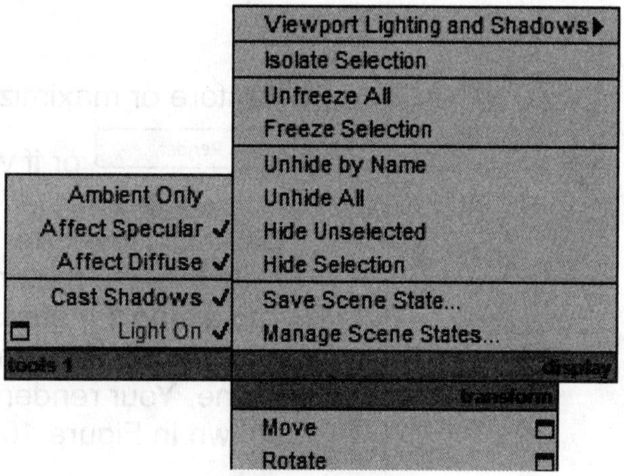

Figure 10–46

12. In the Command Panel, select the *Modify* panel ( ). In the General Parameters rollout, in the *Light Distribution (Type)* drop-down list, select **Spotlight** as shown in Figure 10–47.

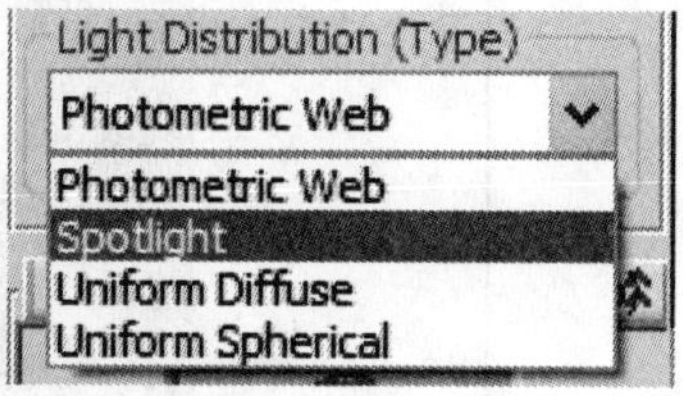

Figure 10–47

13. In the Intensity/Color/Attenuation rollout, in the *Dimming* area, enable **Resulting Intensity** by selecting the box before the % edit box and set the *% value* to **1000**, as shown in Figure 10–48.

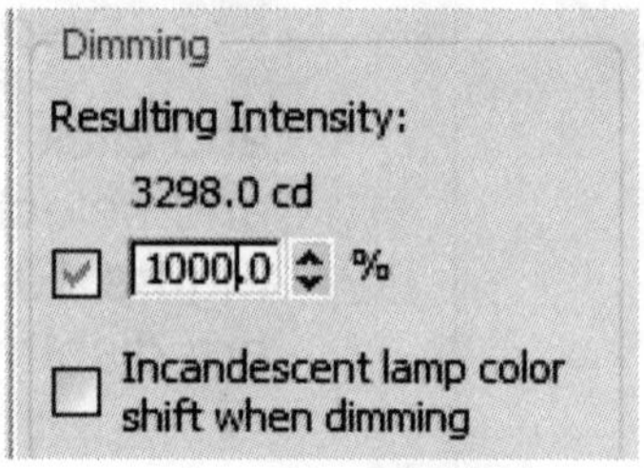

Figure 10–48

14. Restore or maximize the Render Frame Window and click 

or if you closed the Rendered Frame Window click  to render the scene, as shown in Figure 10–49. Note that the materials have been overridden in this scene and a single material is used throughout. This enables you to remove the materials temporarily to examine lighting in your scene. Your rendering might be slightly different than that shown in Figure 10–49.

Figure 10–49

15. Save your work as **MyFinal Gather Map Start.max**.

Practice 10b Adding a Sky Portal for Interior Lighting from Daylight

Estimated time for completion: 20 minutes

Learning Objective

Add a Sky Portal to incorporate more light to the interior scene from the daylight system.

The Sky Portal object is a photometric area light that magnifies the outdoor daylight and focuses it into the room. You must have a Skylight object (outdoor mr Sun and Sky Daylight system, Skylight, or IES Sky light) in the scene for Sky Portal to add light to the rendering. Sky Portal is dependent on the exterior lighting energy.

You must set the paths to locate the External files and Xrefs used in the practice. If you have not done this already, return to the **Introduction to Autodesk 3ds Max Design** chapter and complete Task 1 to Task 3 of the **Organizing Folders and Working with the Interface** practice. You only have to set the user paths once.

In this practice, the Sky Portal object will be applied to the surface of the window frame, using **AutoGrid**. You will also verify the direction in which the light should be pointing towards the inside of the scene.

If a dialog box opens prompting you about a File Load: Mismatch, click OK to accept the default values.

1. Open **SkyPortal_Start.max** from your *Class Files* folder.
2. Activate the **Camera01** viewport and in the Main toolbar, click (Render Setup) or select **Rendering>Render Setup** to open the Render Setup dialog box. In the *Common* tab, in the Common Parameters rollout, in the *Output Size* area, click 320x240. Click Render

- Note that Final Gather has been set for the render because the bucket rendering is being performed. The completed render is displayed, as shown in Figure 10–50. Note that light is already coming through the windows.

Figure 10–50

3. In the Rendered Frame Window, use the wheel on your mouse to zoom into the rendering for a closer look at the lamp, as shown in Figure 10–51. You can press, hold, and move the wheel to pan. The desk lamp is completely black without any lights being reflected. Close the Rendered Frame Window and the Render Setup dialog box.

Figure 10–51

4. Activate the Perspective viewport and maximize it. Verify that the complete window is displayed in the viewport. Use **Zoom** and **Pan** to position the window, if required.

5. In the Command Panel, in the *Create* panel ( ), click (Lights) and verify that **Photometric** is the default lighting type. In the Object Type rollout, click mr Sky Portal and select **AutoGrid**, as shown in Figure 10–52.

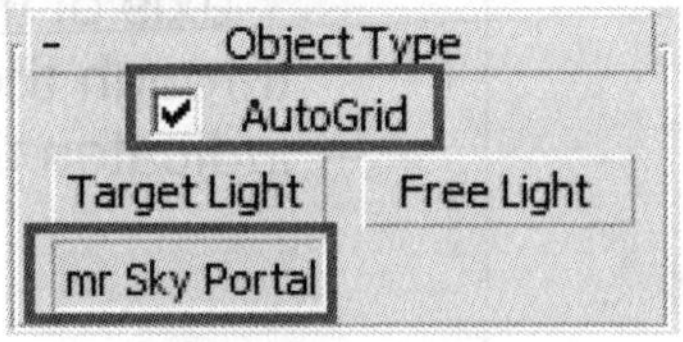

Figure 10–52

The rectangular wireframe window is the Sky Portal object and a perpendicular white arrow in the center of this window indicates the direction of the light.

6. Position the cursor over the bottom left corner of FixedWindow04. The Transform gizmo displays. Verify that the Y-axis is displaying upward. (You might need to move the cursor slightly to point the gizmo in the right direction). Click at this point and drag the cursor to the upper right corner, as shown in Figure 10–53, to create a window. Release the cursor to display the white portal window. This creates a Sky Portal object that approximately matches the size of the frame.

Figure 10–53

7. To verify that the light is pointing toward the correct direction (toward the inside of the room), with the skyportal still selected, click  (Select and Move) to display the move Transform gizmo at the center of the skyportal. Zoom into the Transform gizmo and note that a white arrow, overlapping the Y-axis of the gizmo, is pointing toward the building (i.e., through the window), as shown in Figure 10–54. This indicates the light direction and is pointing correctly.

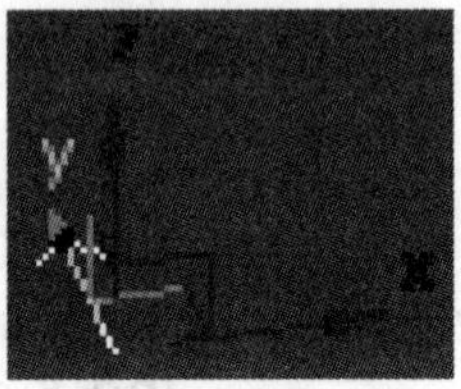

Figure 10–54

- If the light direction arrow is pointing towards the wrong direction, you can change it in the mr Skylight Portal Parameters rollout (**Sky Portal Modify** parameters), as shown in Figure 10–55. Use the **Flip Light Flux Direction** option.

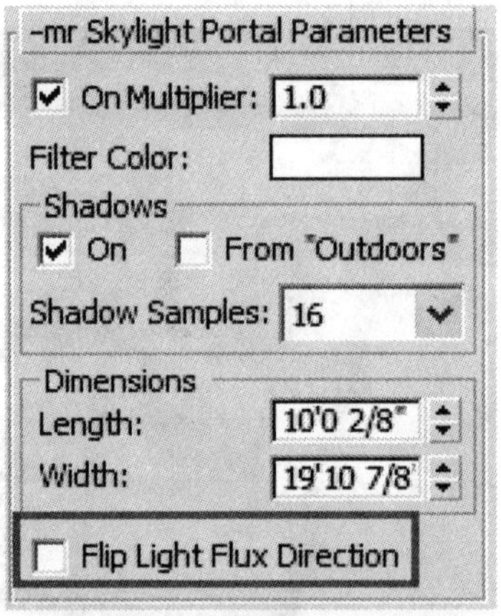

Figure 10–55

8. Zoom out and move the sky portal slightly away from the wall.

9. Hold down <Win> and press <Shift> to display the viewport overlay. Keep pressing <Shift> until the **Camera01** viewport is highlighted. Release <Win> to display Camera01 as the maximized viewport.

In the Render Setup dialog box, you can click 640x480 to set a higher resolution and display the effect of the sky portal clearly, although the rendering time will increase substantially.

10. Click (Render Production). Zoom in on the lamp, as shown in Figure 10–56, and note the reflectivity and brightness on the lamp.

Figure 10–56

11. Save your work as **MySkyPortal_Start.max**.

- Typically you will add Sky Portal lights wherever there is glass, that lets in light. In the **SkyPortal_Start.max**, the materials used are Architectural materials rather than Arch & Design materials. Because of that, the Sky Portal effect might not be drastically different.

There is a tremendous difference between Architectural materials and Arch & Design materials in responding to illumination.

- The Sky Portal has a Multiplier that can be used. As shown in Figure 10–57, the materials were converted to Arch & Design and the rendering has the *sky portal Multiplier* set to **30** to bring more light into the room.

Figure 10–57

10.4 mental ray Proxies

Learning Objective

- Create mental ray proxy objects.

The Autodesk 3ds Max Design software includes mental ray proxy objects. These objects enable you to render large quantities of complex objects as instances so that they are only loaded into memory, as needed, per bucket during the rendering process. Scenes that used to freeze and die in early releases now render quickly. This is handy for trees and other kinds of vegetation or any object that has a lot of detail and are repeated many times in the scene. These are proxy objects and should be rendered with mental ray. These objects are created using

mental ray selection in the *Create* panel ( )> (Geometry).

Practice 10c mental ray Proxies

Learning Objective

- Create mental ray proxy objects.

Estimated time for completion: 10 minutes

You must set the paths to locate the External files and Xrefs used in the practice. If you have not done this already, return to the **Introduction to Autodesk 3ds Max Design** chapter and complete Task 1 to Task 3 of the **Organizing Folders and Working with the Interface** practice. You only have to set the user paths once.

If a dialog box opens prompting you about a File Load: Mismatch, click OK *to accept the default values.*

1. Open **mentalray_proxies_start.max** from your *Class Files* folder. This is the far corner of the parking lot of the Retail Exterior file.

2. The scene is displayed in the Perspective view. Press <F3> to change to Wireframe mode.

3. In the Command Panel, in the *Create* panel ( ), click (Geometry), in the Standard Primitives drop-down list, select **mental ray**, as shown in Figure 10–58.

Figure 10–58

4. In the Object Type rollout, click mr Proxy.

5. In the viewport, beside the plant, click and drag to create the mr proxy object (a bounding box will be created), as shown in Figure 10–59.

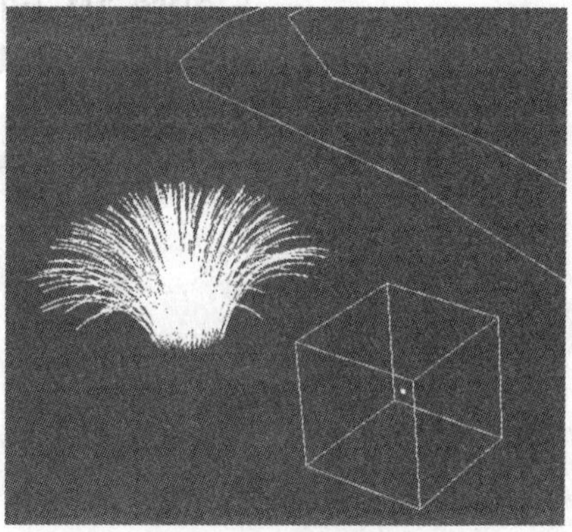

Figure 10–59

6. With this mr proxy object selected, in the Command Panel, select the *Modify* panel ( ). In the Parameters rollout, in the *Source Object* area, click None. In the viewport, select the **Foliage01** object (the plant). The name **Foliage01** displays on the **None** button, as shown in Figure 10–60.

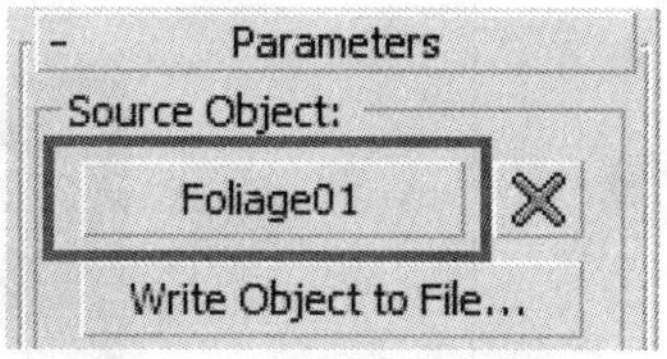

Figure 10–60

7. Click Write Object to File.... In the Write mr Proxy file dialog box save the file as **RetailExteriorPlanting**. Note that this proxy object will be saved as an **mr Proxy Files (*.mib)** file. Click Save.

8. In the mr Proxy Creation dialog box, accept the defaults and click OK. In the *Display* area of the Parameters rollout, note that a thumbnail of the plant is displayed, as shown in Figure 10–61. Also, note that the vertices of the image are displayed in the viewport.

Figure 10–61

9. In the *Display* area, increase the *Viewport Verts* value to **1000** and press <Enter>. The number of vertices have increased in the proxy display, as shown in Figure 10–62.

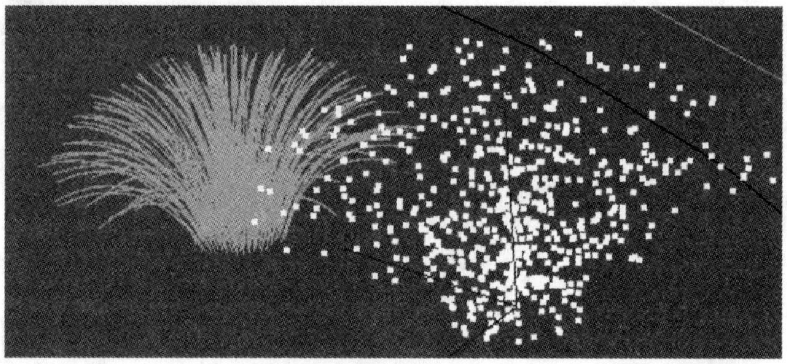

Figure 10–62

You can open the Extras toolbar by right-clicking in an empty area in the Main toolbar and selecting ***Extras****.*

10. You can use the **Spacing** tool to plant a row of these proxies. Open the Extras toolbar, in the Array flyout, click  (Spacing Tool), as shown in Figure 10–63.

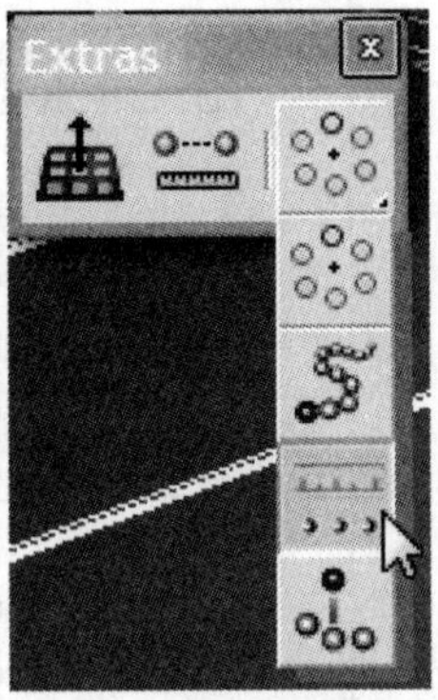

Figure 10–63

11. In the Spacing Tool dialog box, click Pick Path and select the green line (Line01) drawn on the grassy area, as shown in Figure 10–64. Note that the **Pick Path** button is replaced by **Line 01** button. In the *Parameters* area, verify that **Count** is selected, increase the *Count* to **25** and press <Enter>. Click Apply and close the dialog box.

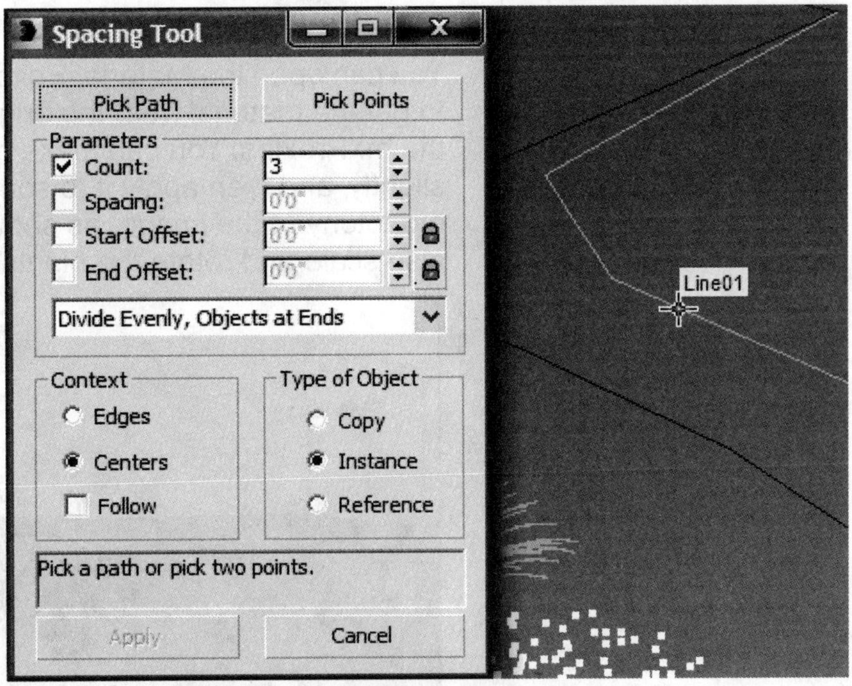

Figure 10–64

12. The plant proxies are placed along the Line01 path.

13. Click  to render the scene, as shown in Figure 10–65.

Figure 10–65

14. Save your work as **Mymentalray_Proxies.max**.

Hint: Modify the Proxies to Add Variety

You can open the Material Editor and use the **Eyedropper** icon to get the material from the original object and then apply it to the mr Proxies. You can make copies of this material, change it slightly, and then apply it to some of the proxies to break the monotony of the image, as shown in Figure 10–66. You can also scale and rotate the plants to add variety.

Figure 10–66

Chapter Review Questions

1. In mental ray, which option can be used to obtain global illumination?
   a. **Final Gather**
   b. **Exposure Control**
   c. **Sampling Controls**
   d. **Ambient Occlusion**
2. Which Sampling Mode uses *Quality*, *Maximum*, and *Minimum* values for adjusting antialiasing and motion blur?
   a. Unified / Raytraced (Recommended) mode
   b. Classic / Raytraced mode
   c. Rasterizer / Scanline mode
3. What does Ambient Occlusion use to calculate the extent of an area that is inhibited by the incoming light?
   a. Photons
   b. Materials
   c. Shaders
   d. Diffuse
4. What type of light object is required for the mr Sky Portal object to add and gather light in the scene?
   a. Omni light
   b. Spotlight
   c. Directional light
   d. Skylight
5. mental ray proxy objects enable you to render large quantities of only simple objects as instances?
   a. True
   b. False

Command Summary

Button	Command	Location
	**Environment and Effects dialog box**	■ **Rendered Frame Window** ■ **Rendering:** Exposure Control
	**Render Setup**	■ **Main toolbar** ■ **Rendering:** Render Setup
	**Spacing Tool**	■ **Extras Toolbar:** Array flyout

Chapter 11

Rendering and Cameras

In this chapter you learn to work with the rendering options provided with different renderers and how to use them to improve the rendering of a scene. You learn to use iterative rendering and to resolve face normal issues to create double-sided renderings. You create cameras and learn to a place a background image in a viewport and in the rendering. You also learn to use the Print Size Wizard to print the rendered image.

This chapter contains the following topics:

- ✓**Rendering Options**
- ✓**Rendering Presets**
- ✓**Single vs. Double-Sided Rendering**
- ✓**State Sets**
- ✓**Cameras**
- ✓**Background Images**
- ✓**The Print Size Wizard**

Certification

Topic:

✓*Rendering*

Objectives:

✓*Differentiate Renderers*

✓*Identify rendering parameters*

11.1 Rendering Options

Learning Objectives

- Understand the common options available in all of the renderers.
- Understand the renderer specific options for NVIDIA iray and the Default Scanline Renderer.

You can set, modify, and change the different options in the Render Setup dialog box as shown in Figure 11–1.

The dialog box can be opened by selecting **Rendering>Render Setup** or by clicking  (Render Setup) in the Main toolbar. The shortcut is <F10>.  (Render Setup) is also displayed in the Rendered Frame Window for quick access to the dialog box. To quickly re-render the last rendering, press <F9>. This eliminates the use of the Render Setup dialog box or of  (Render Production). This feature renders the last rendered viewport and disregards which viewport is actually active.

The tabs in the dialog box change per the active renderer. You should first assign the renderer and then set the options in the different tabs. The *Common* tab and *Renderer* tab are present for all of the renderers.

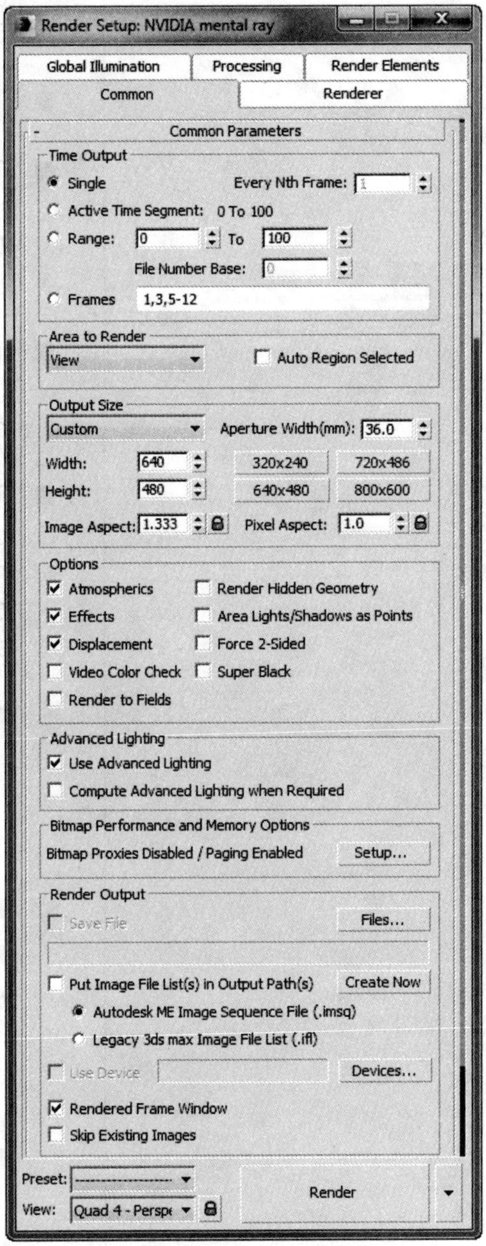

Figure 11–1

Common Tab

The *Common* tab contains settings applicable to all rendering systems. Some of the options in the rollouts are given below:

Common Parameters rollout

- The *Time Output* area designates whether you are rendering a still frame (Single) or an animation. When rendering an animation you can specify to render the entire animation (Active Time Segment), a certain range (Range) or a list individual frames (Frames).
- The *Area to Render* area enables you to define what portion of the scene is rendered. The options include, View, Selected, Region, Crop, or Blowup.
- The *Output Size* area contains the render size options.
- The *Options* area enables you to select the objects and effects to render (**Atmospherics**, **Render Hidden Geometry**, etc.). You can also select the overrides (**Area Lights/Shadows as Points**, **Force 2-Sided**).
- The *Advanced Lighting* and *Bitmap Performance and Memory Options* areas provide additional options to further customize the rendering.
- The *Render Output* area enables you to specify a file name before rendering. Always determine the file format that is required by the designer using the rendering. Some of the commonly used file formats in which the rendering images are saved are as follows:
    - **JPEG:** When saving a single rendering keep in mind that JPEG is a lossy format, which means it sacrifices quality in exchange for a smaller file size. To preserve the highest level of quality in your still renderings you should consider other formats.
    - **BMP:** Windows Bitmap (24 bit, 16.7 Million Colors).
    - **TGA:** Targa (as 24 or 32 bit uncompressed).
    - **PNG:** Portable Network Graphics (as 24 or 48 bit color, no interlacing). This is the best choice regarding file size to quality ratio. It offers the highest color depth with a smaller compression.
    - **TIFF:** Tagged Image File Format (24 bit color without compression). If renderings are to be printed, using TIFF is a safe choice. You need to distinguish between Mac or PC as the Autodesk 3ds Max Design software can produce either version.

Assign Renderer Rollout

The Autodesk 3ds Max Design software ships with five different rendering systems. You can switch rendering systems in the Render Setup dialog box, in the *Common* tab, in the Assign Renderer rollout. Other, third-party rendering systems can be purchased separately and plugged into the Autodesk 3ds Max Design software.

- The **Default Scanline Renderer** is intended to be used with both standard lighting (local illumination) and Radiosity-based lighting.
- The **NVIDIA iray** uses the NVIDIA® iray® rendering technology and was integrated in the Autodesk 3ds Max Design 2012 software. It is a physically accurate renderer and renders by tracing light paths.
- The **NVIDIA mental ray** renderer, is a separate lighting and rendering system that determines illumination through the distribution of photons.
- The **Quicksilver Hardware Renderer** uses the system's graphics hardware (GPU) to produce high-quality images in a much shorter time. In order to use this renderer your graphics hardware must support Shader Model 3.0 (SM3.0) or a later version.
- The **VUE File Renderer** is legacy functionality from 3D Studio for DOS and is not a graphical renderer. It uses ASCII text files to describe the position and transformation of objects, lighting, etc.

Email Notifications Rollout

The options in this rollout are useful when the render is run without being monitored, in the case of lengthy renders. In this rollout, you can set the option of having an email notification sent to you or another user whose email address has been specified. For example, an email notification can be sent after the system has rendered a specific number of frames, if an error occurred during the rendering process, or after the rendering process has been completed.

Scripts Rollout

In this rollout you can enable the software to run a selected script before a rendering process has begun or you can set the script to be run after the rendering process has been completed. The valid scripts that can be run here are: MAXScript file (.MS), macro script (.MCR), batch file (.BAT), and executable file (.EXE).

Renderer Tab

The *Renderer* tab displays renderer-specific options. It is provided for all of the renderers with options specific to their types.

iray Renderer

The NVIDIA iray renderer was created out of the rendering revolution, an integral part of XBR initiative. It first appeared in the Autodesk Subscription Advantage Pack for the Autodesk 3ds Max Design 2011 software. In the Autodesk 3ds Max Design 2014 software, the iray renderer has been upgraded to iray v2.1. The new iray completely supports Sky Portal objects, translucency, and glossy refractions. The physically accurate renderer renders by tracing the light paths. Different from mental ray renderer that renders in buckets, iray renders by progressively refining the image until it has completed the render. Setup compared to other renderers is minimal and is simple, like a point and shoot camera.

The approach of the iray renderer is based on any of the three forms of time, that can be set in the *Renderer* tab, in the iray rollout, as shown in Figure 11–2, of the Render Setup dialog box.

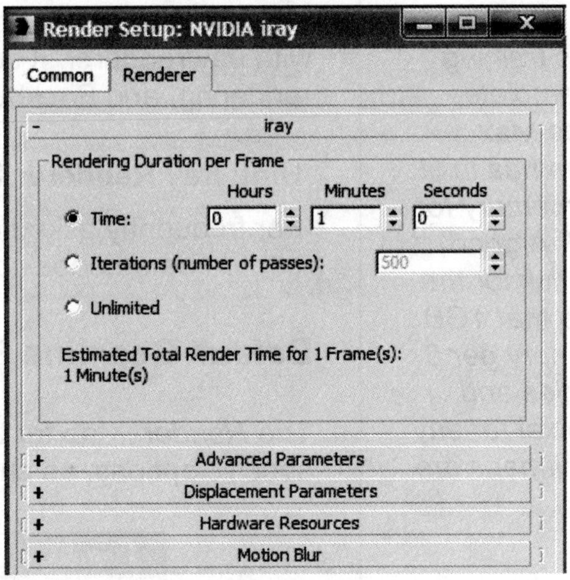

Figure 11–2

You specify the length of time in hours, minutes, and seconds, or specify the number of iterations to complete, or you can launch the rendering for an unlimited amount of time, only stopping when you want.

In the Motion Blur rollout you can enable the **Motion Blur** option to apply it to objects in a scene. You can specify the Shutter Duration that imitates the shutter speed of a camera. You can also set the number of segments for the blur and the number of iterations before the scene is updated to the next time sample.

The Hardware Resources rollout displays information about your system's graphics support, as shown in Figure 11–3.

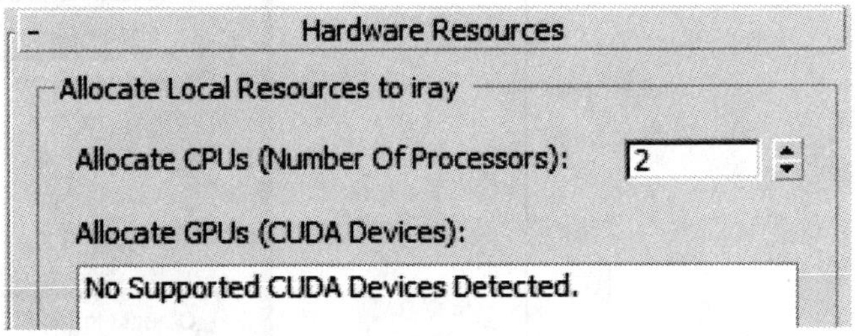

Figure 11–3

The NVIDIA iray is the first CPU/GPU renderer of its kind. A graphics card with CUDA enabled Graphics Processing Unit (GPU) can be used to speed up rendering. These cards are made solely by NVIDIA currently.

The fact that you have a CUDA enabled GPU does not mean that it is used in your render calculations. As of the writing of this training guide, the complete Autodesk 3ds Max Design scene has to fit in the GPU memory for it to be used. A good measuring stick for the calculation is that 1GB of video memory per 8 million triangles and 3bytes per pixel for any referenced bitmaps are required.

The iray renderer only supports a subset of Standard materials and all mental ray materials, such as Arch & Design and Autodesk Library materials with the exception of Autodesk Metallic Paint. Only photometric lights, including mental ray daylight, and mr Photographic Exposure Control can be used with iray renderer. It supports Batch rendering, Command Line rendering, and Backburner.

> **Hint: iray Renderer Information**
>
> For frequently asked questions on iray, refer to http://area.autodesk.com/blogs/shane/the_iray_faq.

Default Scanline Renderer Tab

The *Renderer* tab for the Default Scanline Renderer displays its specific options, as shown in Figure 11–4.

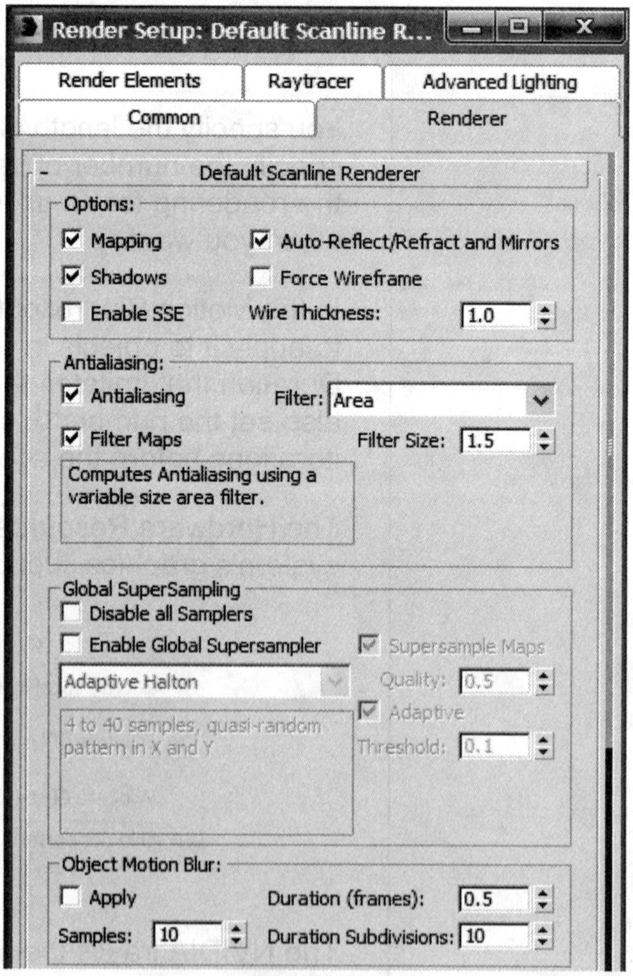

Figure 11–4

- The *Options* area enables you to globally enable or disable the use of all image maps (**Mapping**) or the calculation of all shadows (**Shadows**). The **Force Wireframe** option causes the scene geometry to render as wireframe objects with the **Wire Thickness** parameter listed below.
- The *Antialiasing* area contains options for antialiasing. Antialiasing is the process of smoothing jagged diagonal lines and curves that display in renderings. Disabling antialiasing speeds up rendering substantially but quality suffers. In Figure 11–5, the images were rendered with antialiasing (left) and without antialiasing (right). If diagonals and curves appear too edgy with the default options you could experiment with the other antialiasing methods and values in the *Antialiasing* area.

Figure 11–5

- SuperSampling (*Global SuperSampling* area) is an additional antialiasing pass applied to material textures. SuperSampling is a powerful rendering adjustment that can dramatically cut down on noise, flickering, and moire patterns caused by dense material maps. It is often most efficient to enable SuperSampling at the material level for those materials that need it. The example on the left in Figure 11–6, shows a scene without Supersampling. The example on the right in Figure 11–6, shows the same scene with Supersampling. Note that in the moire pattern is reduced and the highlight areas are more antialised.

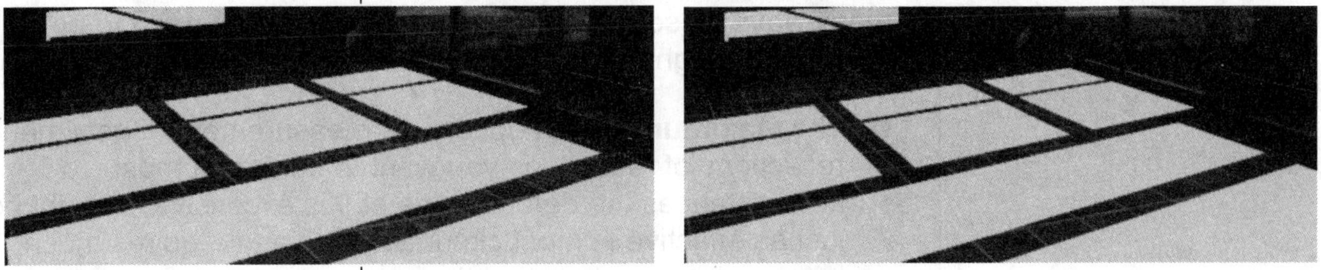

Figure 11–6

Raytracer Tab (Scanline Renderer)

Raytracing is a rendering method used to calculate accurate reflections, refractions, and shadows. Although both the Default Scanline and mental ray renderers use raytracing, the options in this tab, as shown in Figure 11–7, only apply to the Default Scanline Renderer (mental ray has its own set of controls). Generally speaking, mental ray is now recommended when a raytrace effect is required, rather than using the earlier Raytrace features. However, if you are using scanline renderer, radiosity and raytracing can add beauty to your work.

Raytracing is used for raytrace materials and some Architectural materials with shiny, transparent, or mirrored templates (glass, mirror). Raytraced and area shadows cause raytracing to take place. These shadows are also managed by the parameters in this tab.

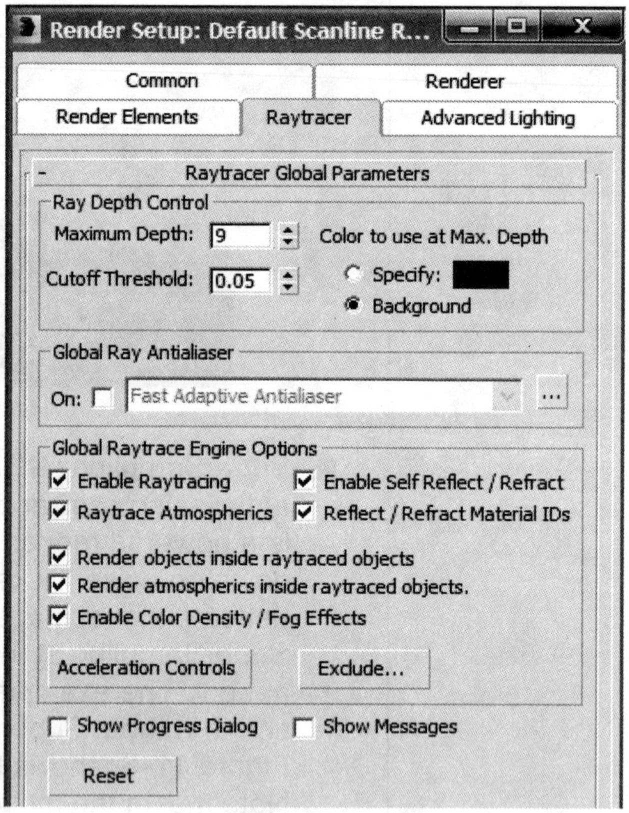

Figure 11–7

Several of these options relate to rendering performance. In many ways these are black box parameters that need to be adjusted through trial and error for individual scenes.

- The **Maximum Depth** option is a measurement of how many reflections of reflections you want to permit. In most circumstances the default value of **9** is excessive; **3** might be just as effective in most circumstances and requires much less rendering calculation time.

- The **Cutoff Threshold** option is a percent value that causes the Autodesk 3ds Max Design software to ignore rays that only contribute that percent or less of a pixel's color in the final rendering. This value can be increased to significantly reduce rendering time, at a cost of less accurate raytracing calculations.
- If you find that your raytraced reflections or shadows are edgy (have jagged diagonal lines or curves) you can enable **Global Ray Antialiasing** in this dialog box. Once enabled, individual raytrace materials can have overrides applied to control their specific performance. Remember that certain shadow types (like Advanced Raytraced) have antialiasing options as well.
- If cleared, the **Enable Raytracing** option in the *Global Raytrace Engine Options* area, disables all raytracing in the scene.

Practice 11a Working with Rendering Options

Learning Objective

- Set various rendering options to improve the rendering of the scene.

Estimated time for completion: 10 minutes

In this practice you will set some of the Rendering options. This practice uses the Default Scanline Renderer as the active renderer.

You must set the paths to locate the External files and Xrefs used in the practice. If you have not done this already, return to the **Introduction to Autodesk 3ds Max Design** chapter and complete Task 1 to Task 3 of the **Organizing Folders and Working with the Interface** practice. You only have to set the user paths once.

If a dialog box opens prompting you about a File Load: Mismatch, click OK to accept the default values.

1. Open **Rendering Options.max** from your *Class Files* folder.
2. In the Main toolbar, click  (Render Setup) or select **Rendering>Render Setup** to open the Render Setup dialog box.
3. In the *Common* tab, in the Common Parameters rollout, in the *Advanced Lighting* area, verify that **Use Advanced Lighting** is enabled, as shown in Figure 11–8. Clear **Compute Advanced Lighting when Required**, if necessary. (If this option is enabled, the Autodesk 3ds Max Design software wants to recalculate Radiosity for the material adjustments you make. Your changes are going to be very subtle, and you can ignore the recalculations for this practice.)

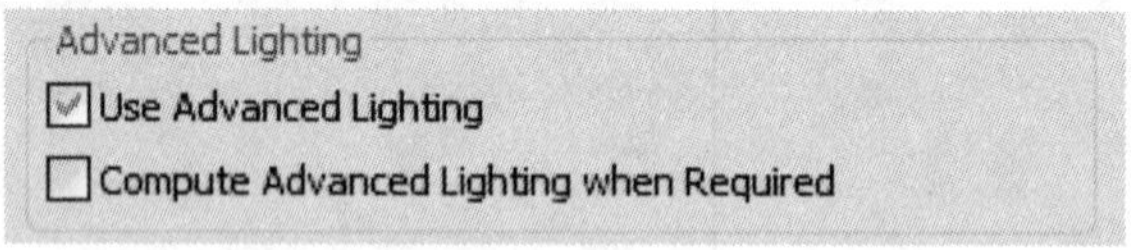

Figure 11–8

You can also click  (Render Production) in the Main toolbar.

4. Verify that Camera – Lobby1 viewport is active and click Render in the Render Setup dialog box. In the Rendered Frame Window, use the mouse wheel to zoom into the floor. Note that a circular moire pattern has formed on the tile floor, as shown in Figure 11–9.

Figure 11–9

5. Select the *Renderer* tab, in the Default Scanline Renderer rollout, in the *Global SuperSampling* area, verify that **Enable Global Supersampler** is cleared, as shown in Figure 11–10. Leave this setting off because you do not want to calculate Supersampling for all materials.

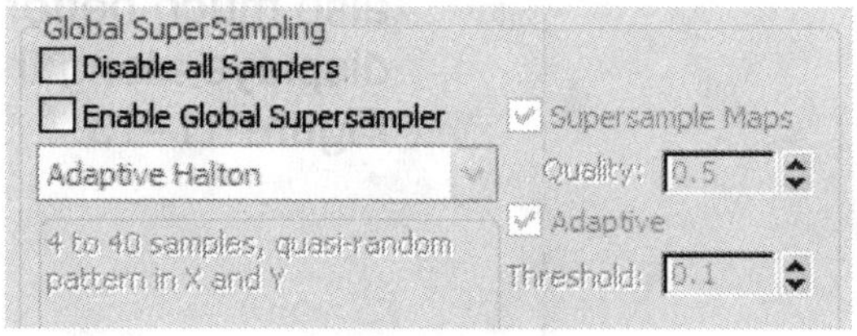

Figure 11–10

6. Open the Slate Material Editor. In the Material/Map Browser, expand Scene Materials and double-click on **Finishes.Flooring.Tile.Square.Terra Cotta** to display it in *View1* sheet, as shown in Figure 11–11.

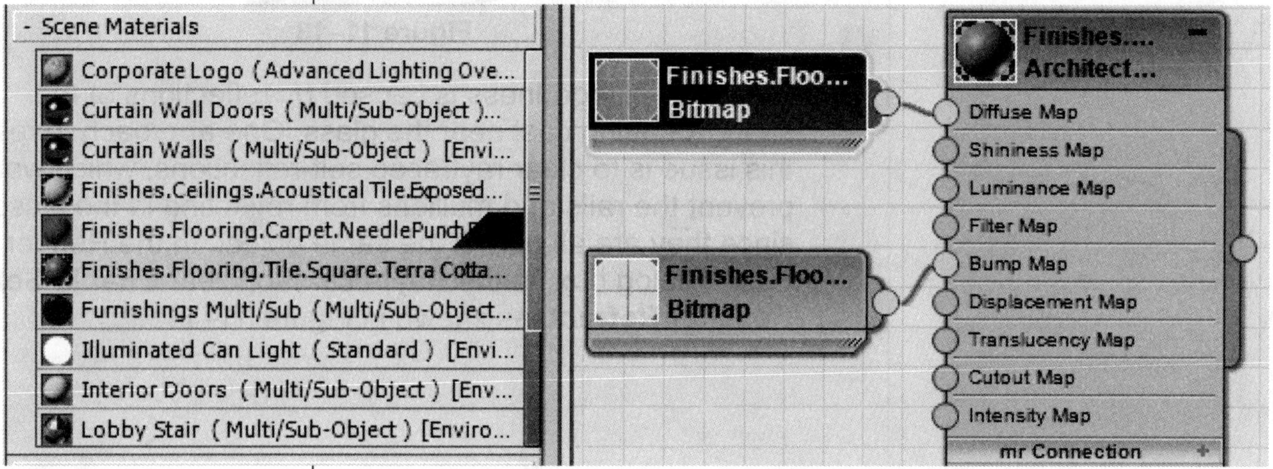

Figure 11–11

7. Double-click on the title bar of the material to open its Parameter Editor.

8. Expand the SuperSampling rollout and clear **Use Global Settings**, as shown in Figure 11–12. (Clearing this option only enables **Supersampling** for the floor material.) Use the default parameters including **Adaptive Halton** as the local supersampler.

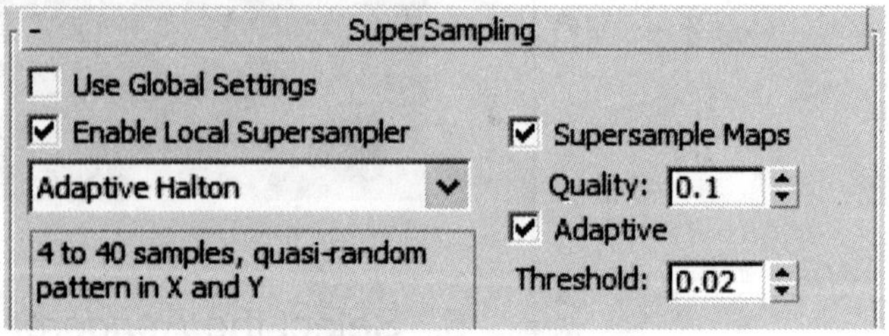

Figure 11–12

9. Render the Camera – Lobby1 and note that the moire pattern is virtually eliminated, but that the rendering time has increased. The visible edges of the sun's highlight area are also much better defined and antialiased. Some jaggedness displays along the rails in the curtain wall, as shown in Figure 11–13.

Figure 11–13

10. Part of this jaggedness is caused by reflections of the shadows being cast near the glass. One approach to resolve this issue is to clear raytraced self-reflections, which would prevent the rails and mullions from reflecting in the glass since they are all part of the same object. In the Render Setup dialog box, in the *Raytracer* tab, clear **Enable Self Reflect / Refract**, as shown in Figure 11–14.

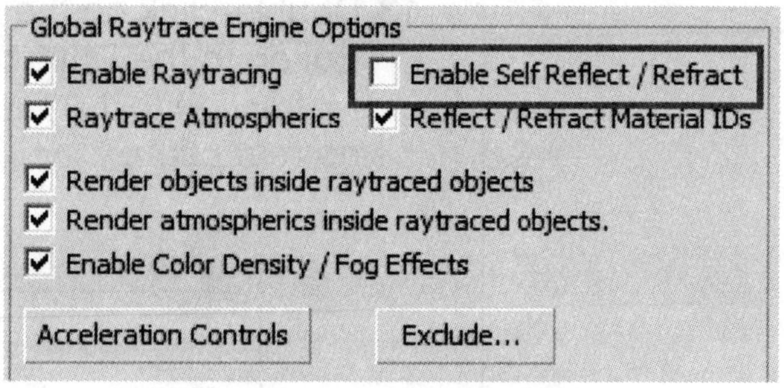

Figure 11–14

11. Render the scene. The rendering shows an unexpected side effect; there is a significant refraction of the outside walls through the glass. Note that the outside wall is jagged, and half of it is turned dark. With a Raytrace material you could disable refraction, but for an Architectural material reduce the Index of Refraction.

12. You will modify the curtain wall materials separately. In the Slate Material Editor, in the Material/Map Browser, in the Scene Materials, double-click on Curtain Walls and Curtain Wall Doors to display in the *View1* sheet. Click (Lay Out All - Vertical) to arrange all of the materials vertically, as shown in Figure 11–15.

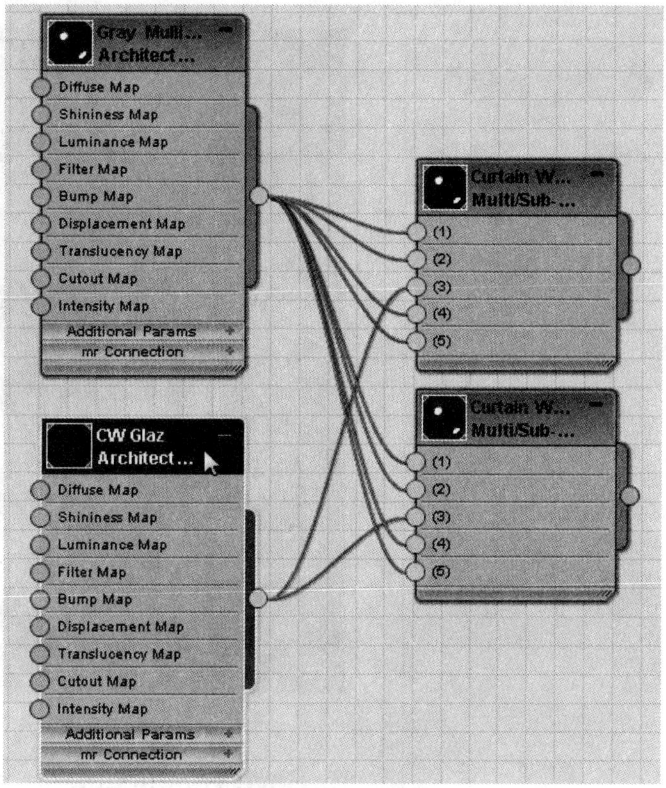

Figure 11–15

13. Double-click on the title CW Glaz to open its Parameter Editor. In the Physical Qualities rollout, set the *Index of Refraction* to **1.0**, as shown in Figure 11–16, which results in no refraction.

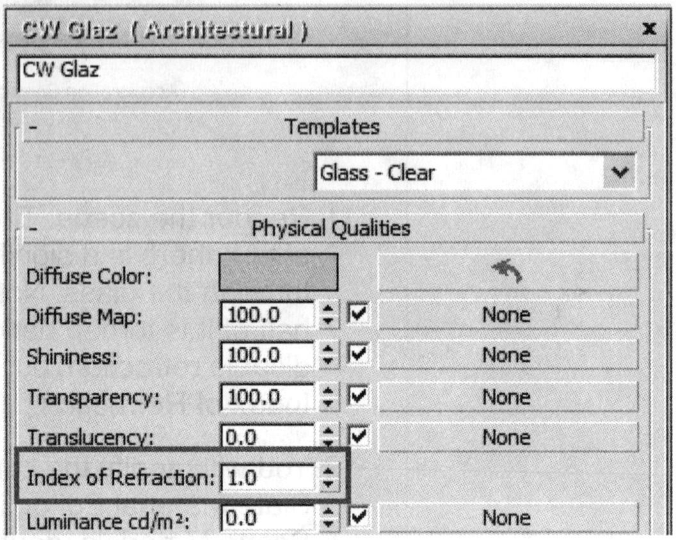

Figure 11–16

14. Render the scene again, as shown in Figure 11–17. The outside wall and rails are less jagged and the glass is less shiny than before.

Figure 11–17

15. Save your scene file as **MyRendering Options.max**.

11.2 Rendering Presets

Learning Objective

Create, load, and save the render presets using the Render Setup dialog box, the Render Shortcuts toolbar, or the Rendered Frame Window.

When a single scene file is configured to create more than one kind of output you might find yourself swapping render options quite often, especially when you configure still renderings and animations in the same file. Render Presets enable you to save some or all of your rendering options as .RPS files.

Keep in mind that changing a render preset causes a Radiosity solution to be reset.

- In the Render Setup dialog box, at the bottom of the dialog box, you can create, load, save, and swap between the preset files. Click next to the Preset selection to open the drop-down list, as shown in Figure 11–18. You can select from a list of preset options or use the **Load Preset** and **Save Preset** options to create a custom preset.

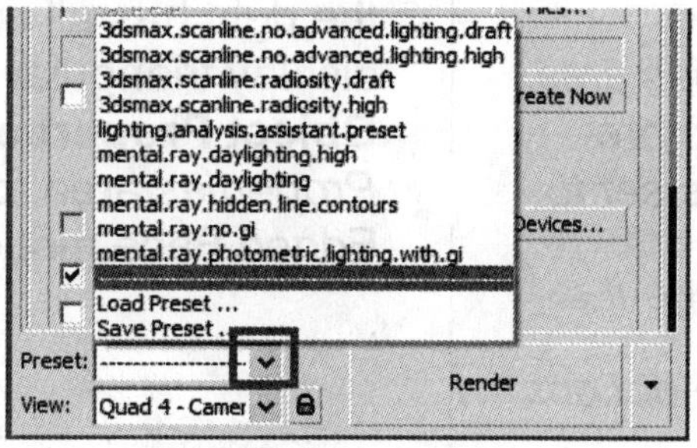

Figure 11–18

*You can open the Render Shortcuts toolbar by right-clicking in an empty area in the Main toolbar and selecting **Render Shortcuts**.*

- There is a Render Shortcuts toolbar, (shown in Figure 11–19), enabling you to access these presets. When using the toolbar, you can save the current rendering settings as preset A, B, or C by selecting one of the corresponding buttons in the toolbar while holding down <Shift>.

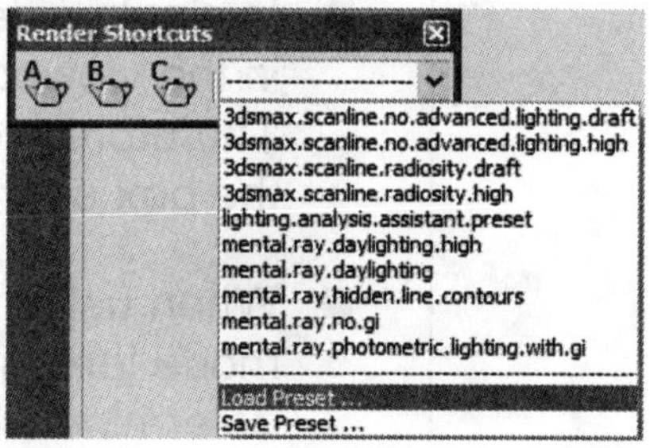

Figure 11–19

- Render Presets are available in the Rendered Frame Window.

Certification

Topic:

✓Rendering

Objectives:

✓Identify rendering parameters

11.3 Single vs. Double-Sided Rendering

Learning Objectives

- Understand surface normals and their effects while rendering objects.
- Understand how to resolve face normal issues while importing/linking .DWG and .DXF files.
- Understand how to resolve face normal issues using double-sided materials and rendering modes.

Surface Faces and Rendering Modes

In the Object Properties dialog box, in the Display Properties area, all of the options are grayed out if it is set to By Layer*. Change it to* By Object *for the options to be available.*

Autodesk 3ds Max Design's 3D objects are treated as surface models rather than solids to make calculations faster. 3D geometry is resolved into triangular faces when rendered. Even Boolean operations result in surface models, although they appear to add or subtract one solid to (or from) another.

Figure 11–20 displays two identical Box objects with the one on the right has all of its edges display its triangular faces. To display triangular faces, right-click on the object, and select **Object Properties**. In the *Common* tab, in the *Display Properties* area, clear **Edges Only**. If the viewport is set to Edged Face mode (<F4>), the triangular faces are displayed.

Figure 11–20

- In single-sided rendering mode the faces are only displayed in the viewport and in renderings from the outside of the box. Therefore, no time is spent on calculating the inner faces of the box as the inside does not affect the final rendering.
- When using the scanline renderer, rendering in double-sided mode forces the Autodesk 3ds Max Design software to determine what the inside and the outside of each face looks like, adding significant rendering time.

Therefore, working in single-sided mode is a more efficient way to render. You should use single-sided mode whenever possible.

Surface Normals

The Autodesk 3ds Max Design software determines which side of a face is visible in single-sided rendering mode using surface normals.

- Normals are imaginary vectors located perpendicular to one side of each face. The side that the normals project from is considered the front side or outside of the face.
- In single-sided mode, the Autodesk 3ds Max Design software renders faces whose vectors point towards the camera, as shown in Figure 11–21, even if at very oblique angles.

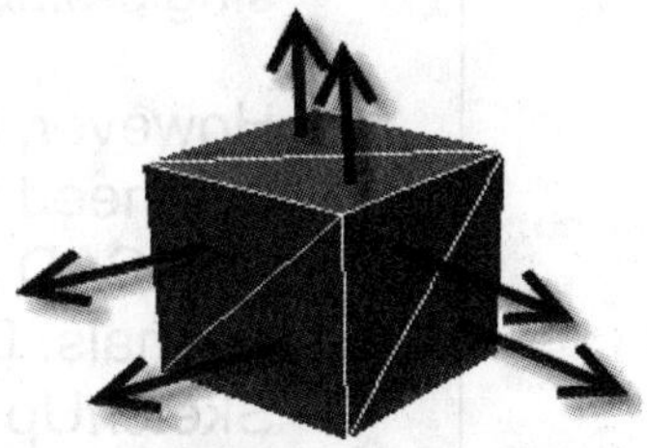

Figure 11–21

- 3D objects created by the Autodesk 3ds Max Design software (such as primitives like these boxes) automatically have their face normals pointing to the outside. It is a common problem to have flipped face normals when importing geometry from other programs, such as SketchUp, where the face normal direction is not known.
- Single-sided rendering mode can cause problems when object normals are inconsistent (inverted). In Figure 11–22, the box on the right has its top face normals pointing down instead of up. This can cause the box with missing faces. (The back-facing edge lines are shown here for clarity but normally would not be visible.)

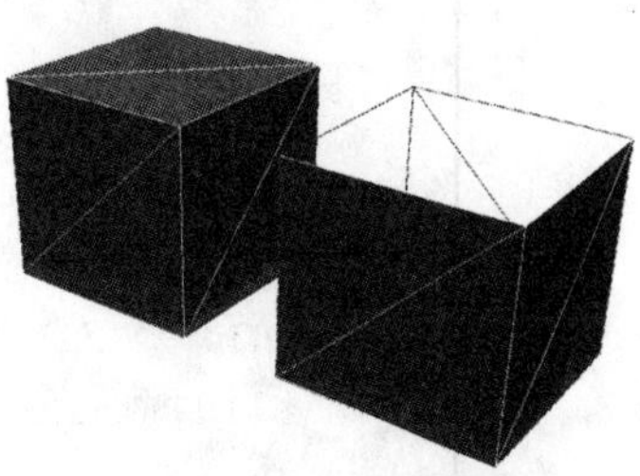

Figure 11–22

Inconsistent face normals are a common result of importing 3D data from other applications.

- CAD software packages generally do not assign surface normals to 3D geometry. When you import this data into the Autodesk 3ds Max Design software, surface normals are automatically assigned to faces based on the order in which the vertices were created, which can result in inconsistent facings.
- Later versions of AutoCAD® (2002+) and other Autodesk vertical applications generate 3D geometry in more consistent ways, enabling many objects to link or import into the Autodesk 3ds Max Design software correctly for single-sided rendering.
- However, inconsistent face normals are occasionally present, and need to be corrected. The 3D blocks provided by AutoCAD Architecture do sometimes have inconsistent face normals. Drawings from non-Autodesk programs such as SketchUp can have inconsistent face normal. These normal can be inverted, but are time-consuming and difficult to repair or replace.

Steps to Resolve Face-Normal Issues

If you would prefer to work in single-sided rendering mode but have missing faces because of inconsistent normals, here are some ways to resolve these issues.

If the troublesome data was imported or linked (.DWG or .DXF file), delete and re-import or reload the linked file and in the Import Options dialog box, select **Orient normals of adjacent faces consistently**, as shown in Figure 11–23. This option should be left off unless face-normal issues are present. (Enabling this option might cause problems where none would otherwise exist.)

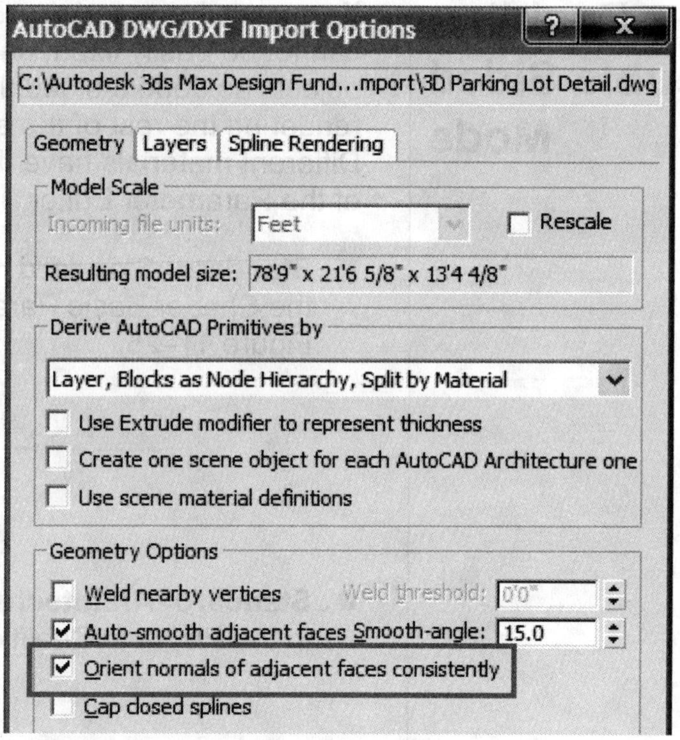

Figure 11–23

If re-importing or reloading data is not feasible (or the data was not imported/linked) the Normal modifier can be used to unify faces. This object-space Modifier also has the ability to flip all of the face normals when an object is completely inside out.

If you have a small number of faces with normals pointing the wrong way (or a large number and some time to spend) you could manually flip and unify face normals. Using the Edit Mesh and Edit Poly modifiers, select the inverted polygon and then in the Surface Properties rollout use the **Flip** and **Unify** options as shown in Figure 11–24.

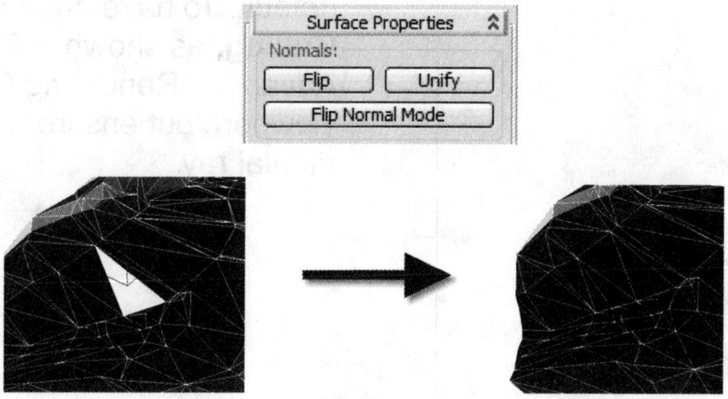

Figure 11–24

Enabling Double-Sided Mode

If you only have certain objects with face-normal issues that cannot be easily fixed, use **2-sided** materials. This renders the objects as double-sided that have double-sided materials, while rendering the rest of the scene geometry as single-sided. Different materials have the 2-sided options in different rollouts of the Parameter Editor.

- **Standard>Standard** materials have the **2-Sided** option in the Shader Basic Parameters rollout, as shown in Figure 11–25.

Figure 11–25

- **Standard>Architectural** materials have the **2-Sided** option in the Physical Qualities rollout, as shown in Figure 11–26.

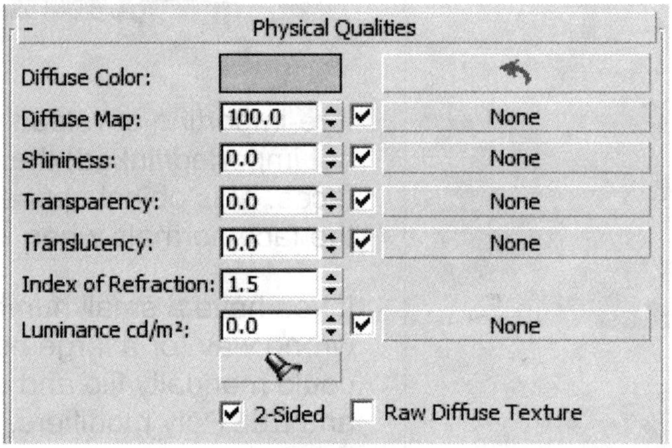

Figure 11–26

- **mental ray>Arch & Design** materials are two-sided by default. To have one-sided behavior, select **Back Face Culling**, as shown in Figure 11–27, in the material's Advanced Rendering Options rollout. This can be handy in a viewport, but ensure the faces are the right direction if using mental ray.

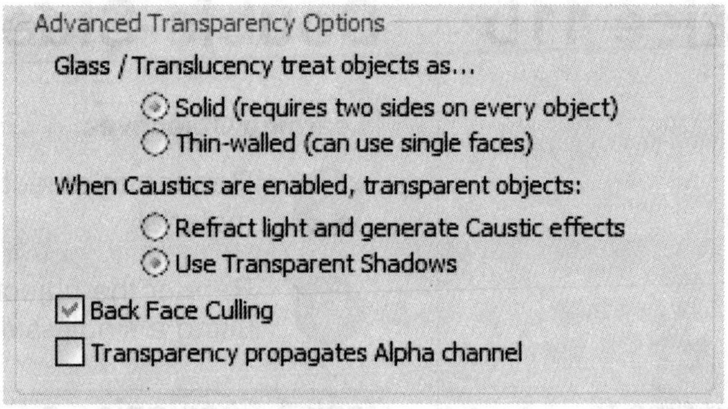

Figure 11–27

You can also enable double-sided mode globally to display the missing faces.

- To render a scene double-sided, in the Render Setup dialog box, in the *Common* tab, in the *Options* area, enable **Force 2-Sided**, as shown in Figure 11–28. (When not selected, the Autodesk 3ds Max Design software renders in single-sided mode, regardless of any viewport settings.)

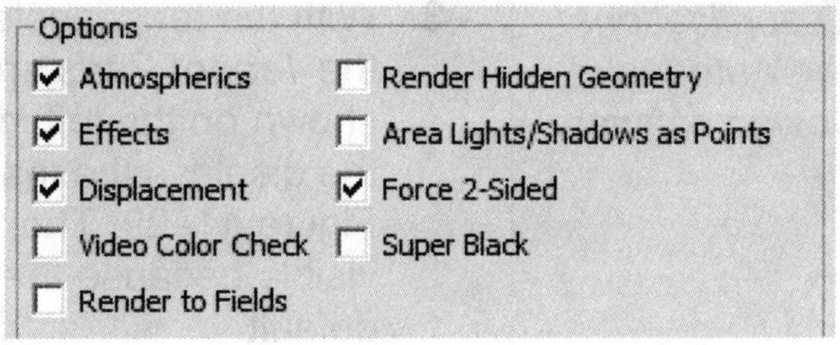

Figure 11–28

- The double-sided options are specific to each individual scene file.

In earlier versions of the Autodesk 3ds Max Design software, faces with inverted face normals would be invisible in the viewport. The new behavior displays those faces in black in the viewport, but still invisible in the rendering. The viewport behavior might also vary depending on your video driver. To return to the earlier behavior of seeing through the faces that point away, right-click on the object and select **Object Properties**. In the *Display Properties* area, select the **Backface Cull** option.

Practice 11b Double-Sided Rendering Mode

Learning Objectives

- Render an object as double-sided using a double-sided material.
- Render the objects on the scene as double-sided while using a single-sided material.

Estimated time for completion: 5 minutes

Task 1 - Assigning a Double-Sided Material.

1. Reset by expanding (Application Menu) and selecting **Reset**.

At the university of Utah in 1975, Professor Martin Newell developed the teapot object. It was used for testing rendering algorithms. Today, the (Newell) teapot still exists in many 3D applications, including the Autodesk 3ds Max Design software.

2. In the Command Panel, in the *Create* panel,( ), click (Geometry), and in the Object Type rollout, click Teapot. In the Perspective viewport, click and drag to create the teapot object.

3. With the teapot selected, select the *Modify* panel ( ) and in the *Teapot Parts* area of the Parameters rollout, clear **Lid**, as shown on the left in Figure 11–29. This removes the lid and the displays the inside of the teapot, as shown on the right in Figure 11–29. The faces on the inside of the teapot are visible because the **Backface Cull** option is not set by default.

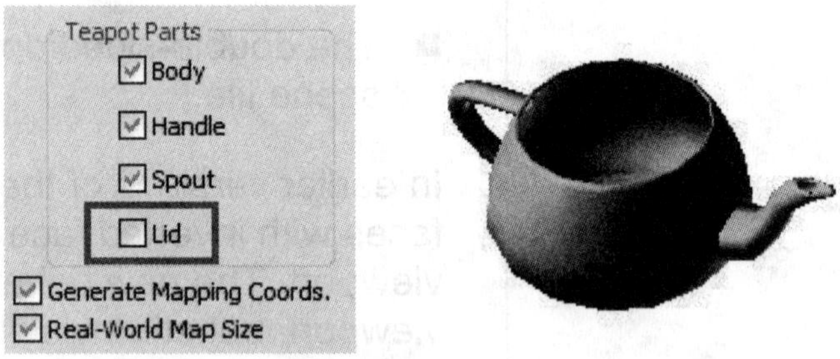

Figure 11–29

- The teapot selection has been cleared and its orientation has been changed to display the inside clearly.

4. Use (Orbit) to change the orientation of the teapot so that the inside is displayed.

In the Object Properties dialog box, in the Display Properties area, all of the options are grayed out if it is set to By Layer*. Change it to* By Object *for the options to become available.*

5. Right-click on the selected teapot and select **Object Properties**. In the *General* tab, in the *Display Properties* area, click By Layer to change it to By Object, if required. Select **Backface Cull** (as shown in Figure 11–30), and click OK. The inside faces of the teapot become invisible.

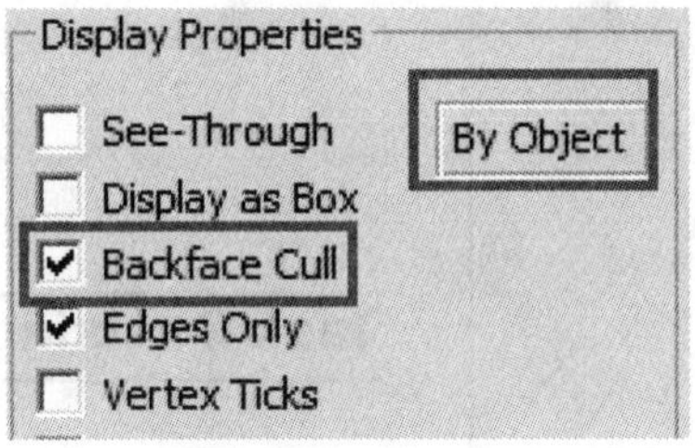

Figure 11–30

6. Click to render the scene. Note that the inside of the teapot is black, due to the black background, as shown in Figure 11–31. Leave the Rendered Frame Window open.

Figure 11–31

*You can also open the Environment and Effects dialog box by selecting **Rendering> Environment**.*

7. Change the background color in the rendering. In the Rendered Frame Window, click to open the Environment and Effects dialog box. In the Common Parameters rollout, in the *Background* area, click the **Color** swatch. In the Color Selector, change the color to white. Click OK and close the Environment and Effects dialog box.

8. Render the scene again. The faces inside the teapot are missing and display as white because of the background color.

9. Open the Slate Material Editor. In *Materials>Standard* categories, select the material **Double Sided**. Drag and drop it onto the teapot. Alternatively, double-click on the material to place it on the *View1* sheet. Verify that the teapot is selected in the viewport and click to assign it.

10. Render the scene. The inside faces are now visible in the rendering as shown in Figure 11–32. The Object properties are overridden by the double-sided material.

Figure 11–32

Task 2 - Using the double-sided Rendering option.

1. In the Slate Material Editor, select **Shellac** in the *Materials>Standard* list. The **Shellac** material is not double-sided. Drag and drop this material on top of the teapot. Close the Slate Material Editor.

2. Render the scene. The faces inside the teapot are missing and display as white because of the background color.

Alternatively, click (Render Setup) in the Main toolbar, or select ***Rendering >Render Setup*** *to open the Render Setup dialog box.*

3. To make all scene objects double sided, enable the option in the Render Setup dialog box. In the Rendered Frame Window, click to open the Render Setup dialog box. In the *Common* tab, in the Common Parameters rollout, in the *Options* area, select **Force 2-Sided,** as shown in Figure 11–33.

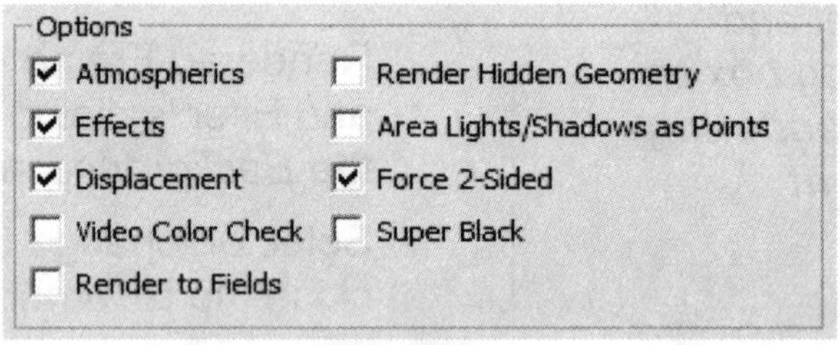

Figure 11–33

4. Render the scene. The teapot renders double-sided, as shown in Figure 11–34, because you have set the Rendering option to **Force 2-sided**.

Figure 11–34

5. Save your work as **MyTeapot.max**.

Enhanced in 2014

11.4 State Sets

Learning Objective

- Create scene states and render pass states using the State Sets feature in the Autodesk 3ds Max Design software.

State Sets is a scene management/render pass manager in the Autodesk 3ds Max Design 2014 software. The State Sets Manager enables you to record the changes made to the scene at different intervals and saves them in an hierarchical form. Select **Rendering>State Sets** to open the State Sets dialog box, as shown in Figure 11–35. It opens in the tree view called *States* in which the states are recorded and managed. You can also use the Compositor View, which can be displayed by selecting **Compositor>Compositor View** in the dialog box menu bar. The Compositor View has similar functionality to the View sheet in the Slate Material Editor.

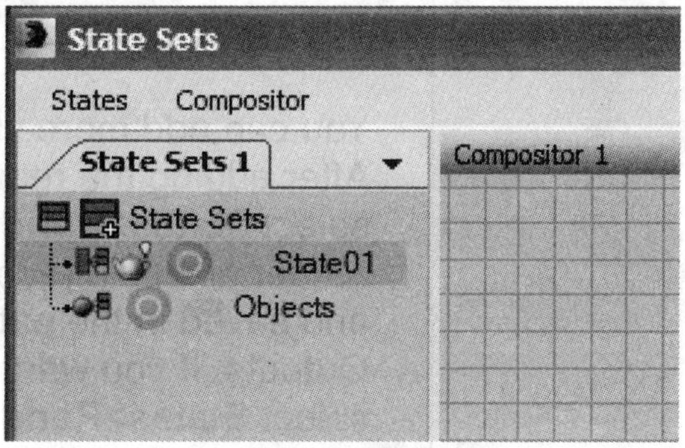

Figure 11–35

The tree view opens with the master state at the top displayed as (State Sets) and contains the **State01** state. You can add a new state by clicking (icon) next to the master state or by selecting **States>Add State**. A new state with the name State02 is added in the tree view, as shown in Figure 11–36.

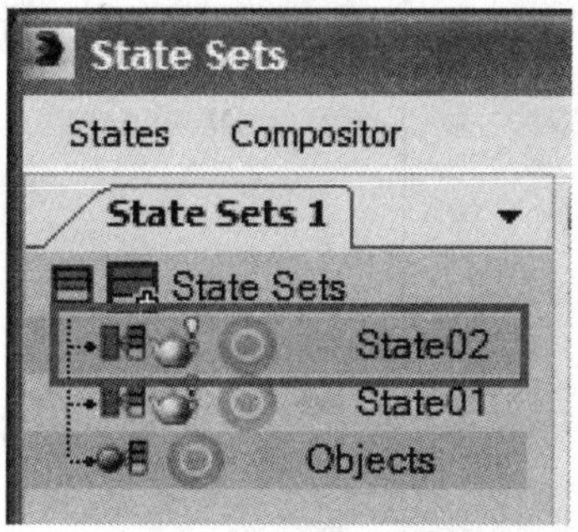

Figure 11–36

Some of the changes, such as using transforms, are not recordable by State Sets. See the Autodesk 3ds Max Design Help for a list of properties that can be used with the State Sets.

Start to record changes to this state by clicking next to State02. The icon displays in red indicating that the state is being recorded. Start making changes to the scene. Once completed, click again to stop recording. The icon then displays in gray indicating that nothing is currently being recorded. The recorded change is displayed as a child for this state, as shown in Figure 11–37.

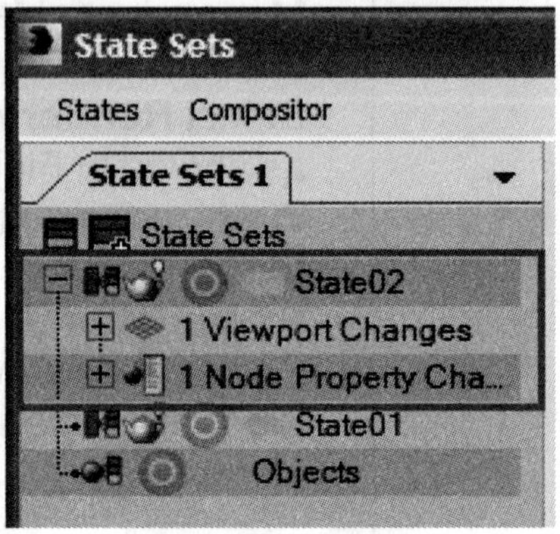

Figure 11–37

You can add more states and record changes in those states. After adding the required states, in the State Sets Menu bar, select **States>Render All States** (as shown in Figure 11–38), to render all of the recorded states. The states are rendered to files and saved in the path and filename provided in the Render Outputs. If you want to set a name and path for the output files, select **States>Render Outputs** to display the render outputs panel at the bottom of the State Sets dialog box. Double-click on Render Outputs to open the Render Outputs dialog box in which you can browse and set the path for the files.

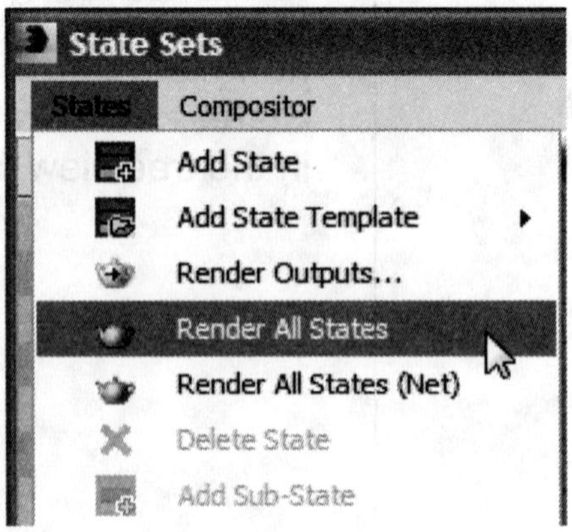

Figure 11–38

State Sets can bi-directionally interoperate with the Adobe After Effects CS4 (32-bit) and Adobe After Effects CS5/CS5.5 (64-bit). This requires that the files are copied from the Autodesk 3ds Max Design install folder into the After Effects install folder.

Note that in the Compositor View, all of the wired states are displayed. You can modify the composition by modifying the nodes. You can select **Compositor>Compositor Link** to output the composition to the After Effects software or select **Compositor>Create PSD** to output the composition to an Adobe Photoshop .PSD file, as shown in Figure 11–39.

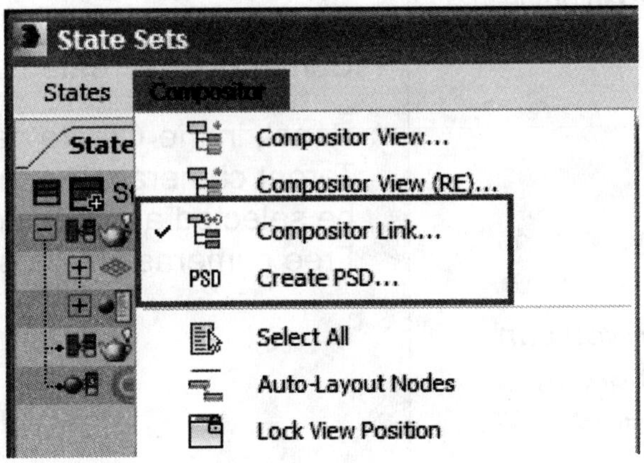

Figure 11–39

Certification

Topic:
✓*Cameras*
Objectives:
✓*Differentiate camera types*
✓*Edit FOV (Field of View)*

11.5 Cameras

Learning Objective

Create different types of cameras and understand the associated parameters.

Cameras are created using (Cameras), in the Command Panel, in the *Create* panel ( ), as shown in Figure 11–40. Target cameras, like target lights, have a target object that can be selected and transformed separately from the camera itself. Free cameras are those that do not have a target object.

*Alternatively, you can create a camera by selecting **Create> Cameras**.*

Figure 11–40

Cameras can also be created on the fly to match a Perspective viewport using the **Views>Create Camera From View**. The shortcut for this is <Ctrl>+<C>.

Camera Parameters

The **Camera** parameters are available in the *Modify* panel ( ) in the Command Panel, as shown in Figure 11–41.

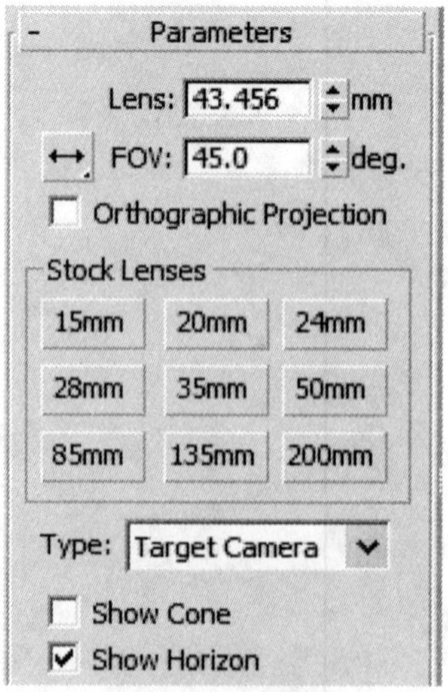

Figure 11–41

The **Camera** parameters found in the Parameters rollout are:

- The focal length of real-world cameras is the distance between the focus point (the film or light-sensitive media) and the optical center of the lens. Autodesk® 3ds Max® Design cameras have a **Lens** option that governs how much of the scene is visible to the camera. This corresponds to the focal length of real-world cameras.

- Autodesk 3ds Max Design camera focal lengths are directly related to that camera's field of view (FOV): an angular measurement of how much of the horizon can be seen by the camera. The field of view can be measured horizontally, vertically, or diagonally using the different field of view options, as shown in Figure 11–42.

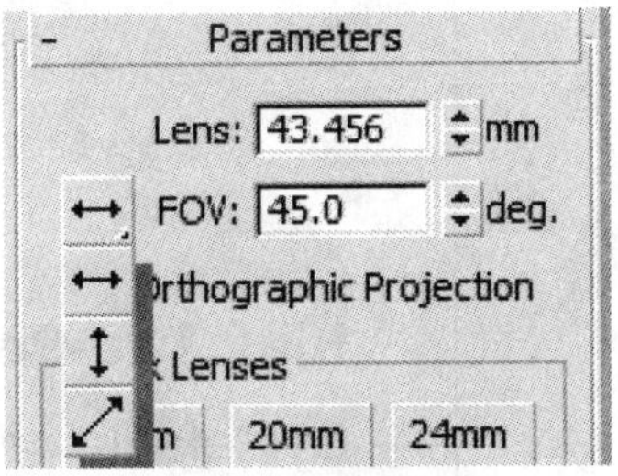

Figure 11–42

- Human vision is often approximated with a 45° field of view; it in fact varies from 60 degrees above to 75 degrees below the horizontal meridian. A focal length of 50mm is very commonly used in real-world cameras, which relates to about a 40° field of view in the Autodesk 3ds Max Design software.

- Other stock focal lengths are provided in the Autodesk's 3ds Max Design software as button presets. Focal lengths below 50mm are considered short or wide-angle lenses, while those above 50mm are called telephoto lenses.

- The **Orthographic Projection** option, as shown in Figure 11–43, causes a camera view to display as an orthographic or user view (axonometric rotated) rather than a three-point perspective.

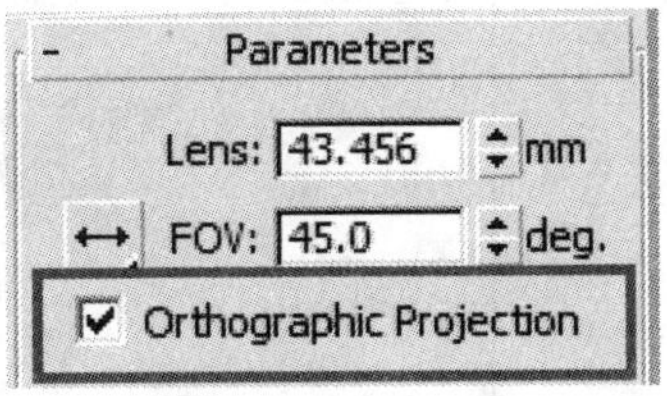

Figure 11–43

- The camera's cone of vision is visible when the camera is selected, as shown in Figure 11–44. The **Show Cone** option causes it to remain visible after the camera is not selected.

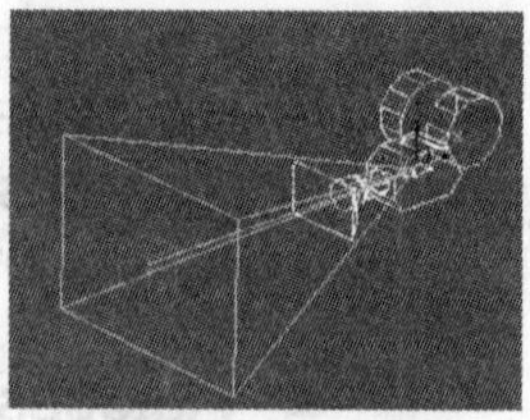

Figure 11–44

- The **Show Horizon** option, as shown in Figure 11–45, displays a dark gray line in the camera viewport representing the horizon in the camera view. It can be helpful when aligning a camera to a background image.

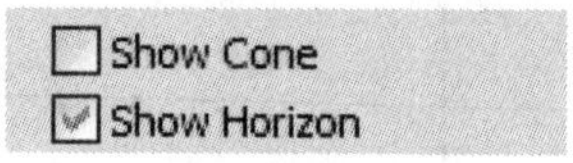

Figure 11–45

Hint: Two-Point Perspectives Through Cameras

By default, camera and perspective viewports show three-point perspective views. You can display a two-point perspective by adding a Camera Correction modifier to the camera object; select **Camera Correction** in **Modifiers>Cameras**, as shown in Figure 11–46. Two-point perspective causes vertical lines to remain vertical rather than converge over distance.

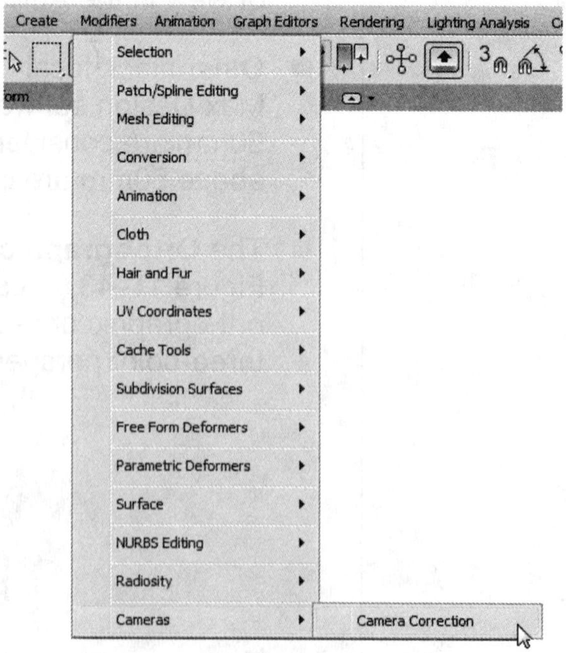

Figure 11–46

There are some additional **Camera** parameters, as shown in Figure 11–47.

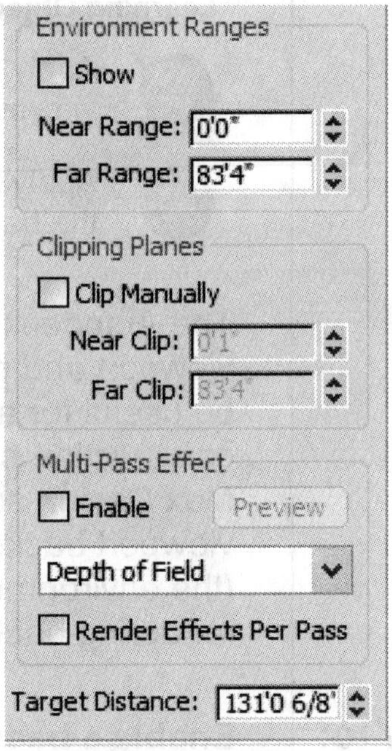

Figure 11–47

- The *Environment Ranges* area contains the distances measured from the camera between which you want to show any atmospheric effects assigned in the Atmosphere rollout of the *Environment* tab in the Environment and Effects dialog box (**Rendering>Environment**).

- The *Clipping Planes* area contains the cutoff distances for the geometry that displays in the camera. When enabled, only geometry between the clip distances is visible.

Depending on the selected effect, a Parameters rollout specific to that effect (Depth of Field Parameters or Motion Blur Parameters) opens below the Cameras Parameters rollout.

- The *Multi-Pass Effect* area (default is Depth of Field) is a camera-specific rendering effect that causes distance blurring, where only a certain point is in focus. This effect simulates how areas away from the focal point display blurred in human vision and photography. You can either select **Depth of Field (mental ray)**, **Depth of Field**, or **Motion Blur**, as shown in Figure 11–48, as an effect to be used in the rendering. You can also select the native Depth of Field effect of either mental ray, iray, or Quicksilver renderer.

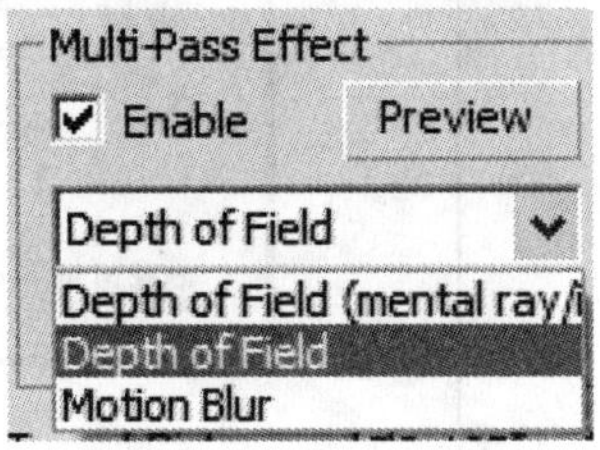

Figure 11–48

11.6 Background Images

Learning Objectives

- Apply **Background Images** to a single viewport or all of the viewports.
- Apply **Aspect Ratio** and **Safe Frames** to correctly display the background image in the viewport.

The Autodesk 3ds Max Design software can use image files as viewport and rendering backgrounds. Background images can be useful for adding detail to a scene or showing a proposed construction project in its real-world context. The Autodesk 3ds Max Design software enables you to load an image into the viewport background, independent of the rendering background (the environment map) or load it to both the viewport and rendering backgrounds.

How to:

Enable a background image to viewports

1. Select **Views>Viewport Background>Configure Viewport Background** (<Alt>+<B>).
2. The Viewport Configuration dialog box opens with the *Background* tab selected, as shown in Figure 11–49.

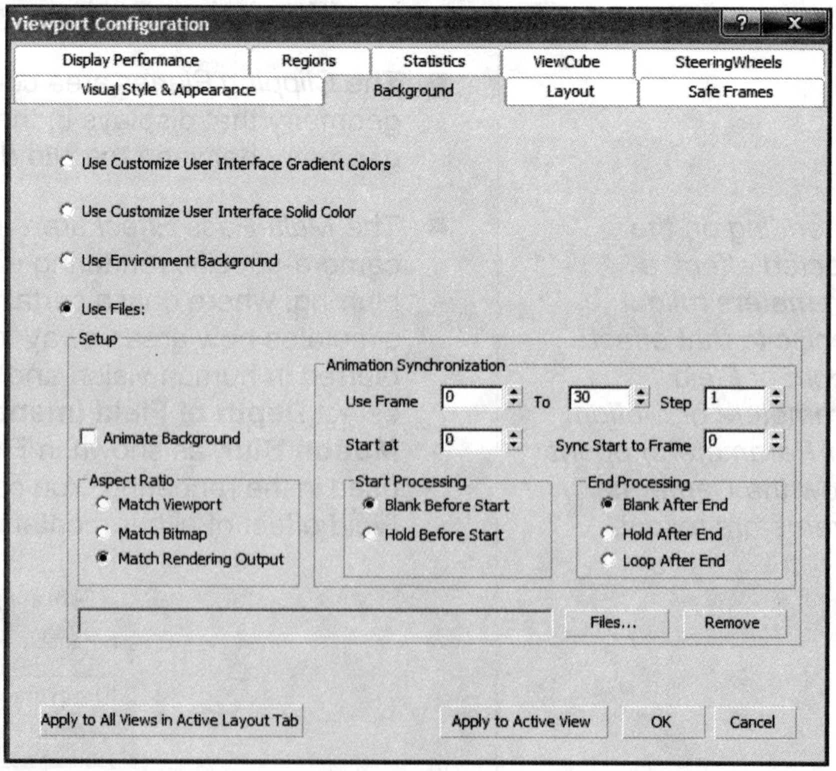

Figure 11–49

*If any option other than the **Use Files** option is selected, the Setup area is grayed out.*

3. Select **Use Files** to make the *Setup* area available for use.
4. In the *Aspect Ratio* area, select **Match Bitmap** to keep the aspect ratio of the image file constant.
5. Click **Files...** to browse for the image file and open it.
6. Click **Apply to Active View** or click **Apply to All Views in Active Layout Tab** to only display the image in the active viewport or to display it in all of the viewports.
7. Click **OK**.

How to: Assign an environment map to a viewport

*Select **Rendering >Environment** to open the Environment and Effects dialog box.*

1. To enable an environment map to display in a viewport, you need to select the **Use Map** option and load a map using the *Environment Map* slot in the Environment and Effects dialog box, as shown in Figure 11–50. You can adjust the map parameters using an Instance of the map in Slate Material Editor, and opening its Parameter Editor.

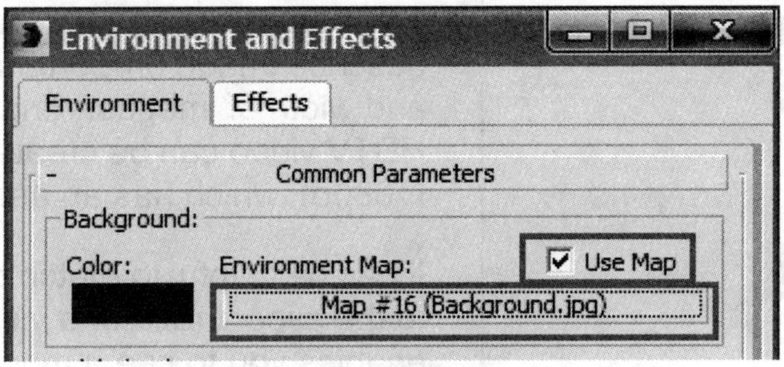

Figure 11–50

*Select **Views>Viewport Background> Configure Viewport Background** or press <Alt>+<B>.*

2. Select the viewport in which you want to display the map.
3. In the Viewport Configuration dialog box (*Background* tab), select **Use Environment Background** and click **OK**.

> **Hint: Updating a Background Image**
>
> Certain changes (e.g., change in resolution or aspect ratio) do not update the background image automatically. You should use <Alt>+<Shift>+<Ctrl>+<B> to update the background image in the active viewport. This command is not available if the active viewport does not display a background image.

Hint: Assign Background Image from Windows Explorer

You can also assign a background image directly from Windows Explorer by dragging and dropping the image file onto a viewport. A Bitmap Viewport Drop dialog box opens prompting you to select it as a viewport background or an environment map or both, as shown in Figure 11–51.

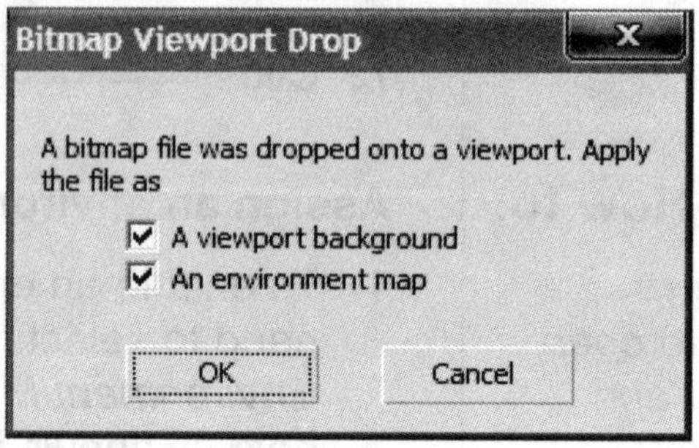

Figure 11–51

Aspect Ratio

The Autodesk 3ds Max Design software uses an aspect ratio to describe image proportions. It is the relationship between length and width of images, renderings, and viewports. For example, HDTV video can be created at a resolution of 1920 x 1080 pixels (1080p), which has an aspect ratio of 1.78 (1920 / 1080 = 1.78).

It can be helpful to match the aspect ratio of a background image to the aspect ratio of a viewport and the rendered output. This enables you to see a more accurate representation of the final output in the viewports. In Figure 11–52, the composition of a massing study displays different in the viewport (left) than it does in the rendered output (right) when their aspect ratios do not match.

Figure 11–52

You can maintain the aspect ratio of the viewport background using the options in the *Aspect Ratio* area in the Viewport Configuration dialog box, in the *Background* tab, as shown in Figure 11–53.

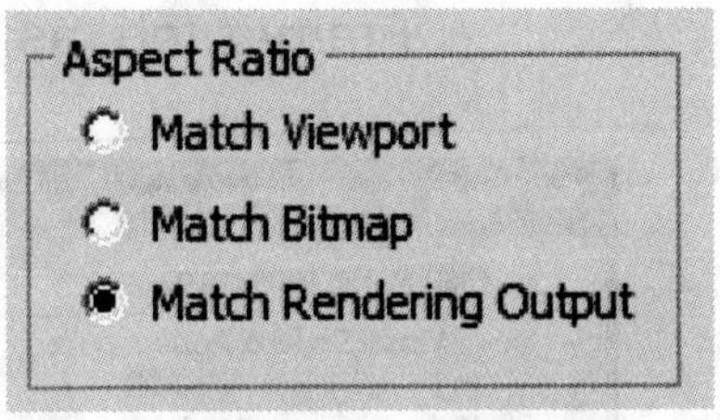

Figure 11–53

- **Match Viewport:** Enables you to match the aspect ratio of the image to the aspect ratio of the viewport,
- **Match Bitmap:** Enables you to lock the original aspect ratio of the image.

Enhanced in 2014

- **Match Rendering Output:** Enables you to match the aspect ratio of the image to the active rendering output device.

Safe Frames

Safe Frames is a viewport display option that defines the portions of the viewport for rendered display. To enable this option, select the Viewport **+** label, and select **Configure Viewports** or select **Views>Viewport Configuration**. When the Viewport Configuration dialog box opens, select the *Safe Frames* tab, as shown in Figure 11–54.

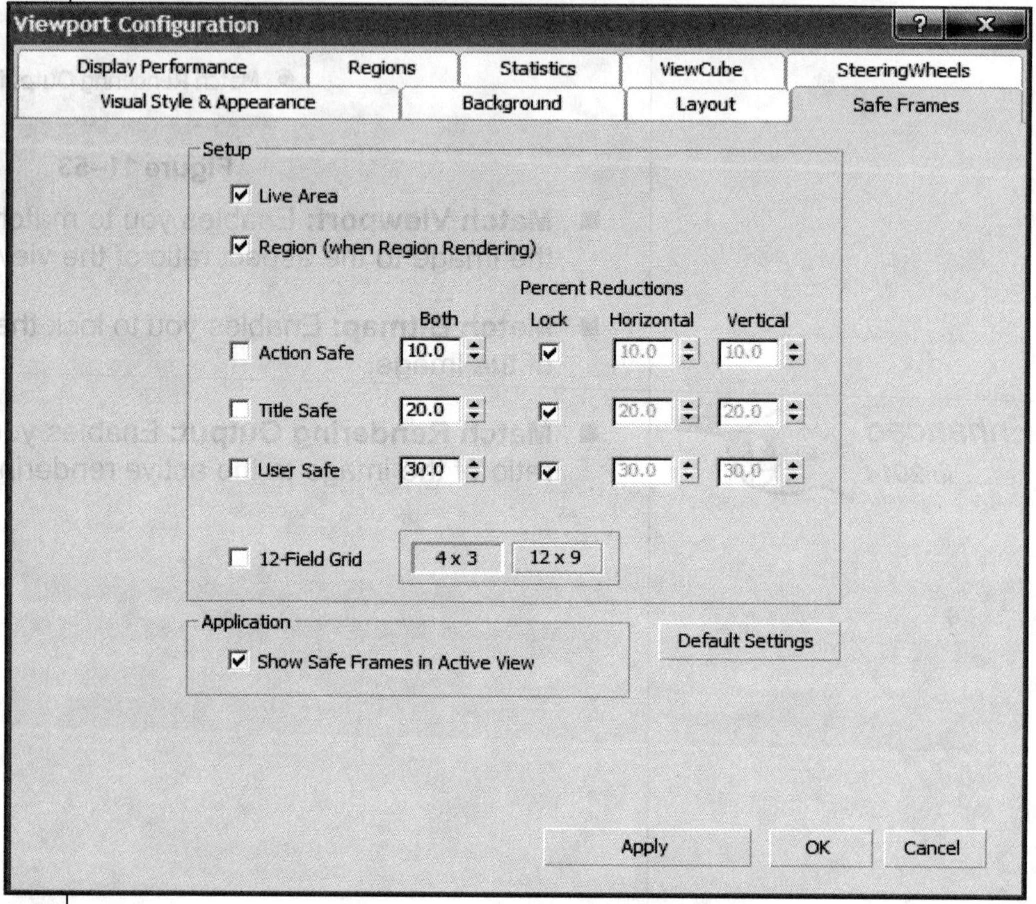

Figure 11–54

The *Safe Frames* tab provides setup options that relate to safe areas for animated action and titles when creating graphics for television. When set, these are displayed as rectangles in the active view:

- The outer rectangle, as shown in Figure 11–55, is the *Lve area*; the limits of what is rendered.
- The middle rectangle, as shown in Figure 11–55, is the *Action safe area*, the recommended area for any animated action when creating graphics for television.
- The inner rectangle, as shown in Figure 11–55, is the *Title safe area*, the recommended area for titles when creating graphics for television.

Figure 11–55

- The *User Safe* frame can be enabled, if required. It can be turned on and customized to any proportion.
- The *12-Field Grid* frame displays a grid of cells (or fields) in the viewport. The 12-field grid yields either 12 (4x3) or 108 (12x9) cells and is used mainly by directors to reference specific areas of the screen.

Assigning Size and Aspect Ratio for Rendered Output

The rendering size (in pixels) and the aspect ratio of rendered output can be assigned in the *Output Size* area of the Render Setup dialog box, as shown in Figure 11–56 (**Rendering> Render Setup**>*Common* tab). There are several different presets available for output size.

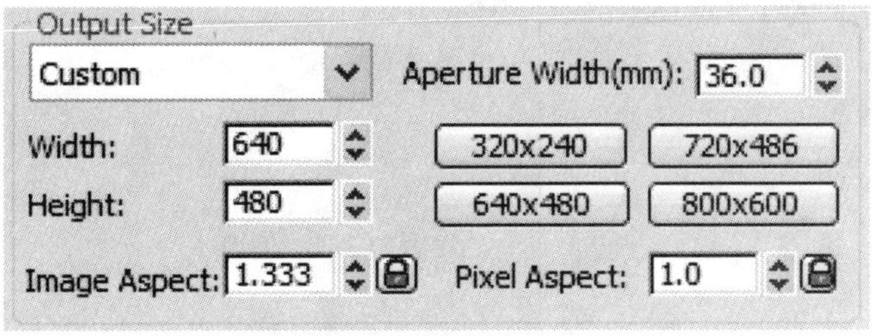

Figure 11–56

Do not confuse the Image Aspect Ratio with the Pixel Aspect ratio. In the Autodesk 3ds Max Design software, you can define the proportions of the pixel rectangle independent from the image. Consider the pixels to be individual tiles in a mosaic. The tiles can be narrow, long, or short and wide. Most programs do not make this distinction; the pixel aspect ratio is determined by the image width and height.

Hint: Use Standard Aspect Ratios

Be cautious about selecting random width and height values. Most output has a required width and height value for a particular media type. Problems occur because non-standard choices have been made for the rendering aspect ratio.

Practice 11c

Cameras and Background Images

Learning Objectives

- Apply a bitmap image and assign it as an Environment Map to display it in a rendered scene.
- Apply the bitmap image as a Background Image to display it in the viewport.
- Create a Target Camera and modify the Camera and Target Parameters so that the scene objects are reasonably located over the background image.

Estimated time for completion: 20 minutes

You must set the paths to locate the External files and Xrefs used in the practice. If you have not done this already, return to the **Introduction to Autodesk 3ds Max Design** chapter and complete Task 1 to Task 3 of the **Organizing Folders and Working with the Interface** practice. You only have to set the user paths once.

Task 1 - Apply an Environment Map.

You will first configure an Environment Map to serve as a viewport and rendering background.

If a dialog box opens prompting you about a File Load: Mismatch, click OK to accept the default values.

1. Open **Rendering and Animation.max** from your *Class Files* folder. This is the retail exterior scene with standard exterior lighting. The **Sunlight System** parameters are set to match the date and time of a site photo to be used as an environment map.
2. In the Menu Bar, select **Rendering>Environment**. The Environment and Effects dialog box opens.
3. In the *Environment* tab, you will set the background image for the screen or rendering. In the Common Parameters rollout, in the *Background* area, click None.
4. In the Material/Map Browser, open the *Maps>Standard* categories and double-click on Bitmap.
5. In the Select Bitmap Image File dialog box, in your *Class Files* folder, in the *Maps* folder, open **Background.jpg**.

6. Note that in the Environment and Effects dialog box, the **None** button is replaced with 

and **Use Map** is automatically enabled, as shown in Figure 11–57. Close the dialog box.

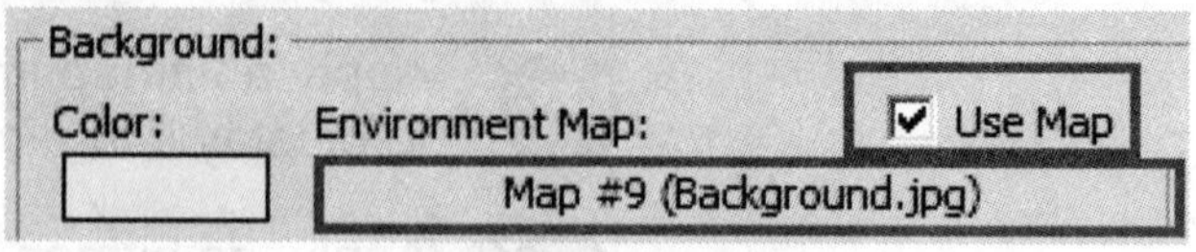

Figure 11–57

7. Activate the Perspective viewport and click  (Render Production). The tree line displays behind the model, as shown in Figure 11–58.

Figure 11–58

- Note that the image file is only displayed in the rendering as a background and not in the viewport.
- The position of the background image is not correct.

8. Close the Rendered Frame Window.

You can also press <Alt>+<B> to open the Viewport Configuration dialog box.

9. To display the image file in the Perspective viewport, verify that it is the active viewport, and select **Views>Viewport Background>Configure Viewport Background** to open the Viewport Configuration dialog box with the *Background* tab displayed.

10. Select **Use Environment Background**, as shown in Figure 11–59 and click OK.

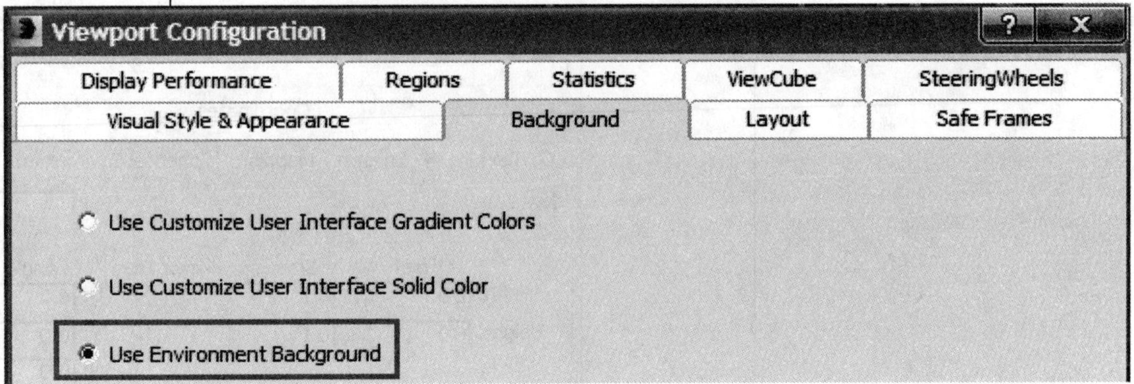

Figure 11–59

- Note that the image displays behind the scene in the Perspective viewport, but is not in the correct position.

11. To modify the image, open the Slate Material Editor.

12. In the Material/Map Browser, expand the *Scene Materials* category, locate **Map # (Background.jpg) [Environment]**, and double-click on it. The Map # Bitmap node is placed on the *View1* sheet, as shown in Figure 11–60.

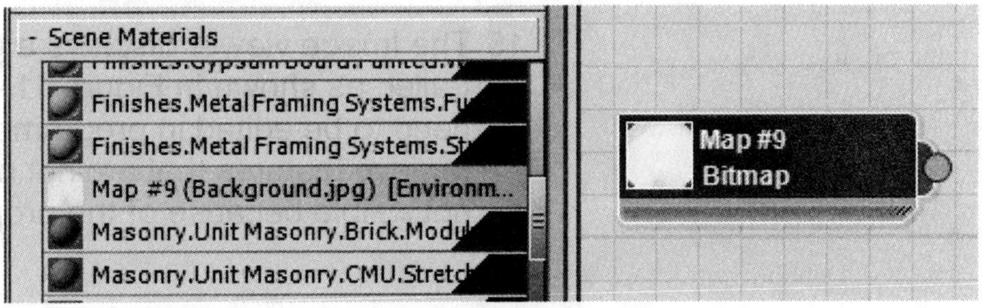

Figure 11–60

13. Double-click on the Map # Bitmap title bar to open its Parameter Editor.

14. In the Bitmap Parameters rollout, click View Image, as shown in Figure 11–61.

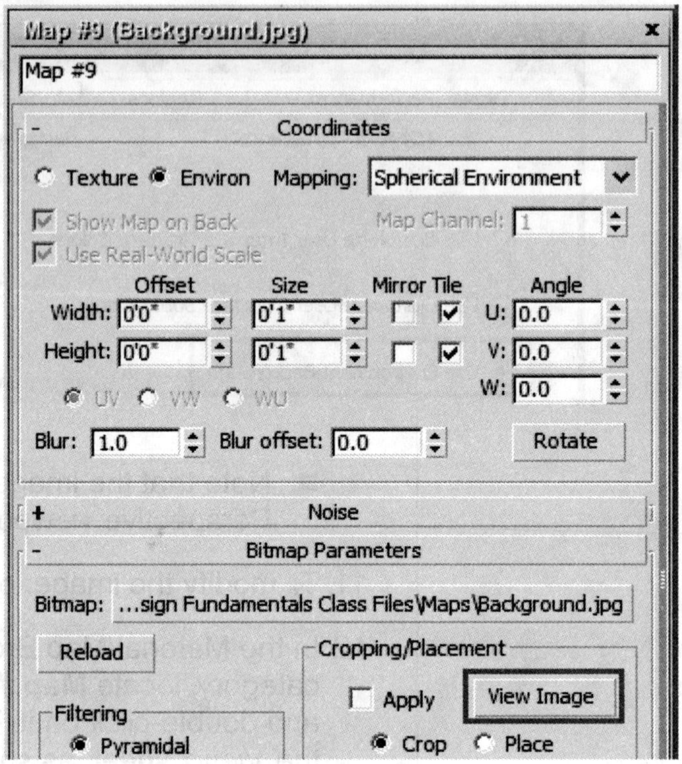

Figure 11–61

15. The Image viewer displays a grassy field with the top of a trailer, as shown in Figure 11–62. Often background images need to be edited in programs like Adobe Photoshop to remove features that are not needed. In this case the trailer is not visible because of the proposed grading so you ignore it.

Figure 11–62

- In the Image viewer, you can specify the image cropping (the limit of the area to be displayed) by re-sizing the red rectangle around the image. When required, cropping is enabled in the Bitmap Parameters rollout, in the *Cropping Placement* area, using the **Apply** option.

The Aspect value indicates if the image is being stretched or not.

16. Right-click and hold over the image to access the color and other image data information, as shown in Figure 11–63. The image is currently 1200 pixels wide by 750 pixels high. The Aspect value of 1.00 shows that this image is displaying normally. Close the Image viewer.

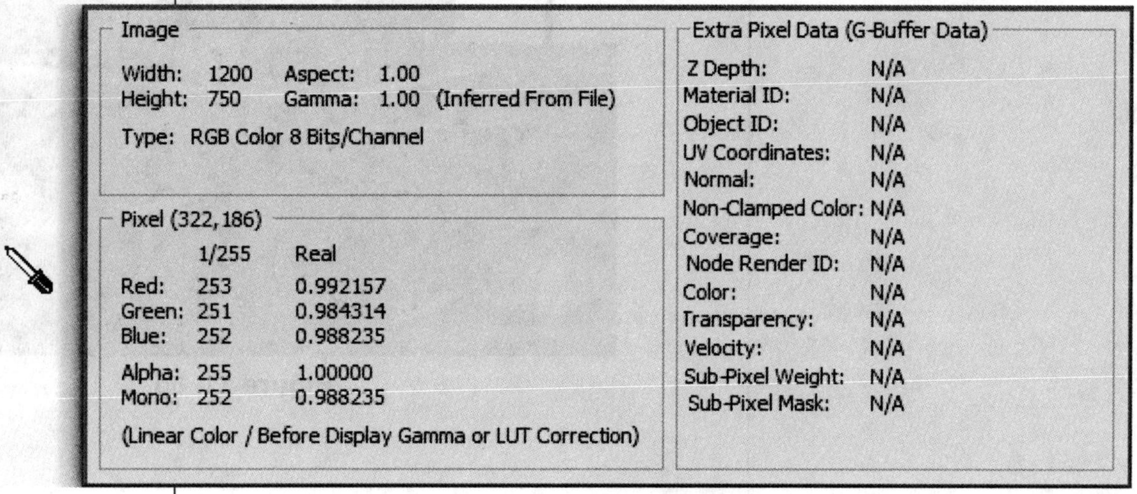

Figure 11–63

17. In the Map Parameter Editor, in the Coordinates rollout, verify that **Environ** is selected. This indicates that the map is used as a 2D backdrop. Note that the **Mapping** option is set to **Spherical Environment**. This is the default option and is the reason the image is not displayed correctly. In the Mapping drop-down list, select **Screen**, as shown in Figure 11–64. Close the Slate Material Editor.

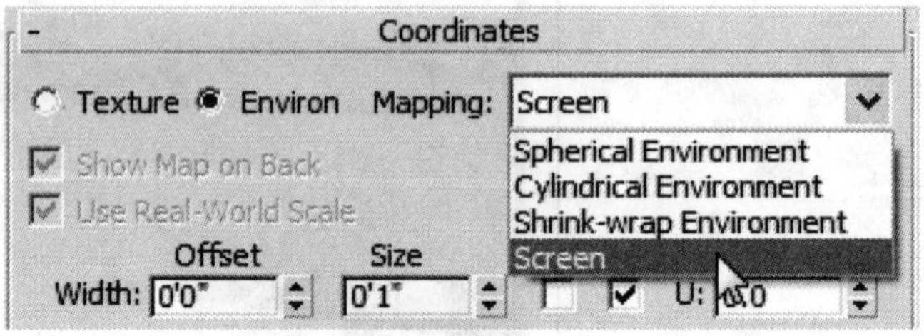

Figure 11–64

- In the Perspective viewport, note that the background image has updated and that a small portion of the tree line displays behind the right side of the building.

18. Render the Perspective viewport. The tree line in the image should display partially behind the model, as shown in Figure 11–65, (although the image is not yet in the correct position). Close the Rendered Frame Window.

Figure 11–65

Task 2 - Create a Camera.

The background photograph was taken from about the center of the westerly end of the proposed parking lot curb island location. The camera was approximately eleven feet above the proposed first floor elevation (on a ladder). The camera was pointed horizontally towards a proposed interior wall corner and vertically to the level of the horizon. In this task you will create a camera approximately lined up with the background image. This type of approximation is necessary when exact measurements of camera position and other existing features are not available.

1. Activate the Top viewport. Click  (Maximize Viewport) and zoom into the parking lot and the building area.

2. In the Command Panel, in the *Create* panel (), click  (Cameras), and click 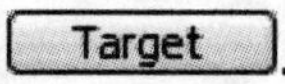. Starting at the approximate camera location (to the left of the middle double parking lot), click and drag to locate the target approximately over the model's back wall, as shown in Figure 11–66, and release to place the target.

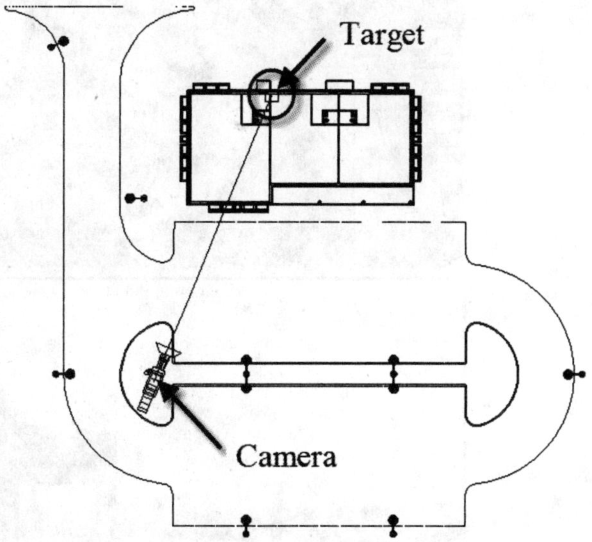

Figure 11–66

3. Click  (Maximize Viewport) again. Press <Esc> to exit the **Cameras** command and then activate the Perspective viewport.

4. Select the **Perspective** POV label to open the label menu and select **Cameras>Camera001**. Note that the background image is visible in the viewport with the top of the trailer visible in the front.

5. You will move the camera up so that the trailer top of the image is not visible in the viewport. With the camera object selected, in the Main toolbar, click  (Select and Move). In the Status Bar, note that Z elevation is 0.0. Set *Z* to **11'0"**. Note that the tree lining is now visible behind the building and the trailer top is not visible.

6. You can now adjust the camera to display the image with respect to the building. In the Top Viewport, move the Camera object and keep looking in the Camera001 viewport until you get the scene similar to that shown in Figure 11–67.

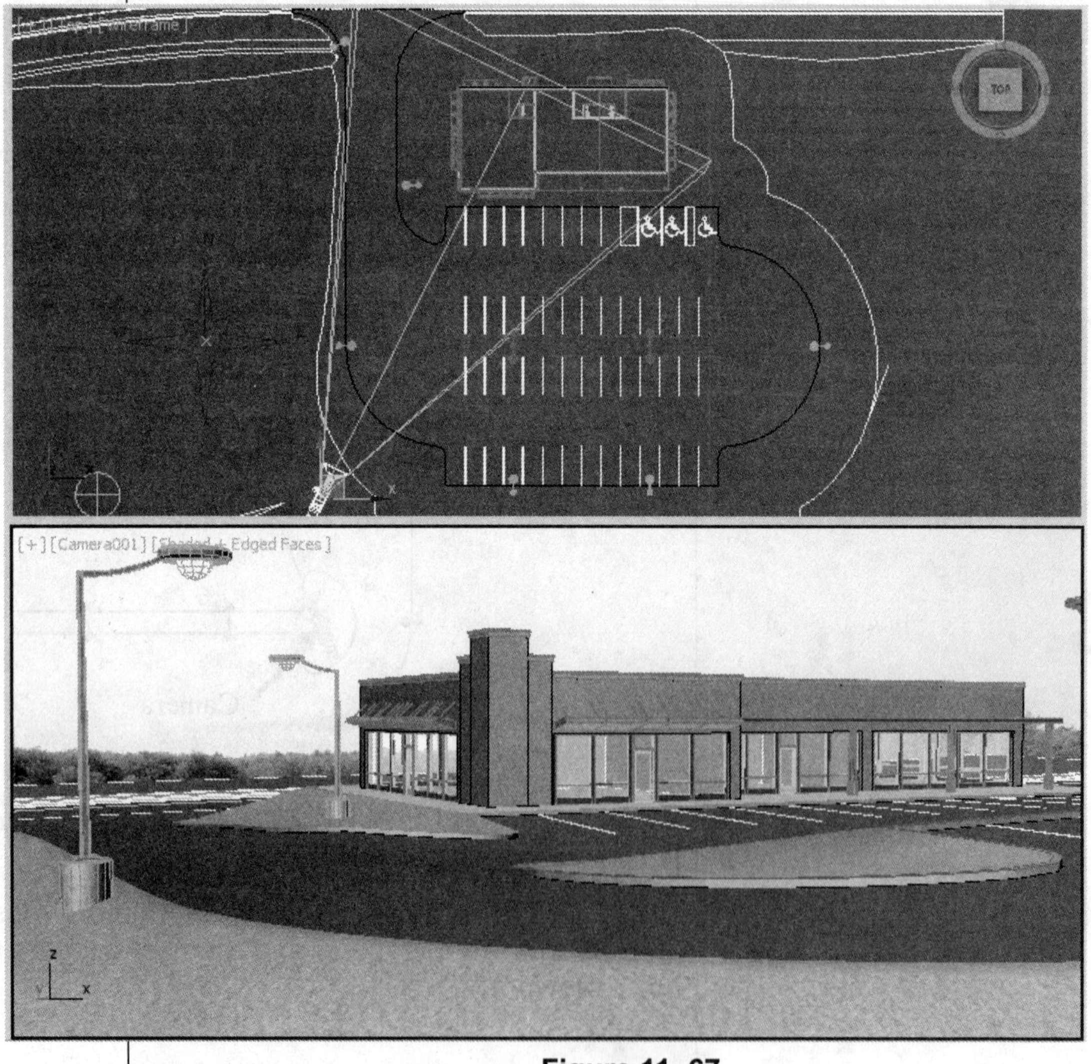

Figure 11–67

Task 3 - Approximately Match the Camera to the Background.

The background image has an aspect ratio of 1.6 (1200 pixels wide/750 pixels high). You will match the viewport and rendering to this aspect ratio.

1. In the Main toolbar, click  (Render Setup) or select **Rendering>Render Setup**.

2. In the Render Setup dialog box, in the Common Parameters rollout, in the *Output Size* area, set *Image Aspect* to **1.6** and click  next to it. Set the *Width* to **600** pixels and press <Enter>, as shown in Figure 11–68. Note that the *Height* is automatically set to **375** because the *Image Aspect* is locked at **1.6**.

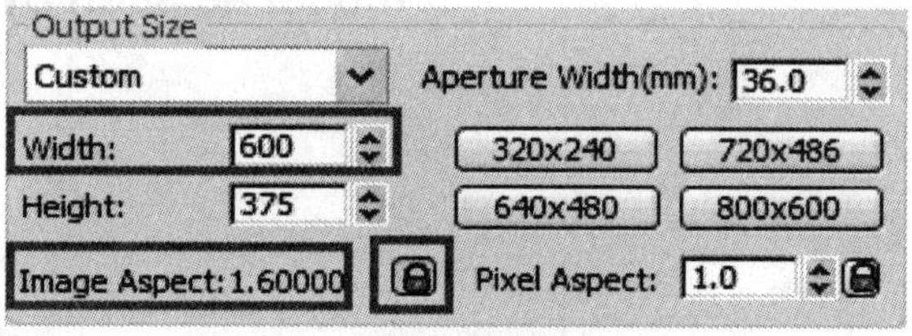

Figure 11–68

3. Activate the Camera001 viewport render the scene to see the results.

4. Select the **Camera001** label and select **Show Safe Frames**.

5. You will resize the viewports manually. Place the cursor on the center intersection point of the four viewports until the cursor displays as a **Move** icon. Drag the viewport corner as shown in Figure 11–69. Note that the viewport maintains the correct proportions as long as safe frames are active.

Figure 11–69

Real-world 35mm cameras are named because of the diagonal measurement of their film, not their focal length.

6. Select the camera in any viewport and in the Command Panel, select the *Modify* panel ( ). The photo was taken with a 35mm camera that had an adjustable lens set to a 28mm wide-angle zoom. In the Parameters rollout, in the *Stock Lenses* area, click 28mm, as shown in Figure 11–70.

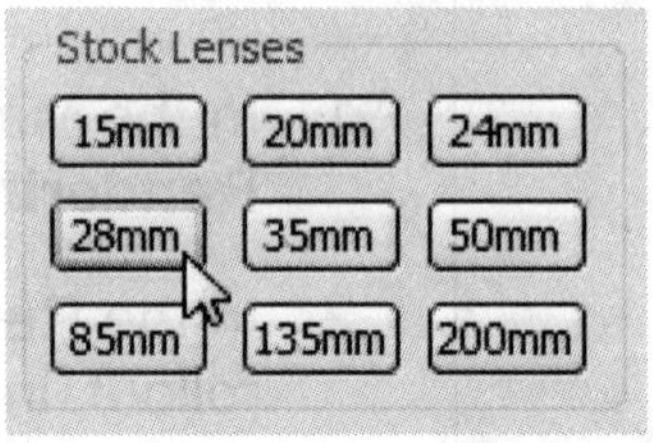

Figure 11–70

7. Select **Show Horizon**, as shown in Figure 11–71. In the Camera001 viewport, note that a black line displays across the middle of the viewport. It represents the horizon of the 3D model as seen by the camera.

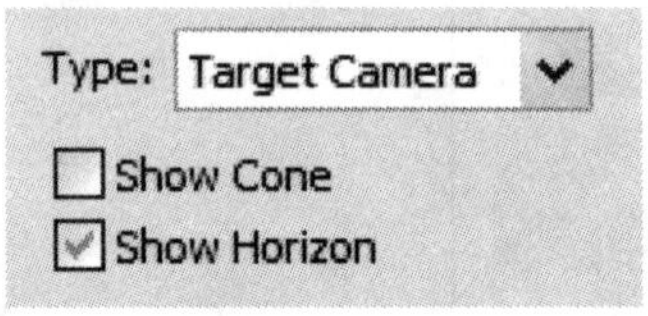

Figure 11–71

8. You will adjust the position of the horizon by changing the elevation of the target. In the Main toolbar, click .

9. In the Select From Scene dialog box, click (Display None) and click (Display Cameras), as shown in Figure 11–72, to only list the camera objects.

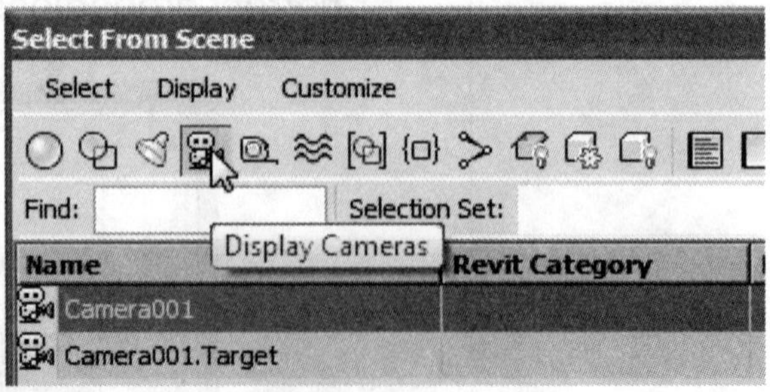

Figure 11–72

10. Select **Camera001.Target** and click OK. You can also select the camera target in a viewport by right-clicking on the camera object and selecting **Select Camera Target**.

11. In the Main toolbar, click  (Select and Move) and enter different Z-elevation for the target to place the horizon 1/3 of the way up the tree line (in the Status Bar, enter a *Z-elevation* of approximately **13'0"**). Your values might vary. Using the keyboard you can assign precise values to the target to match the photographic background.

12. Verify that Camera001 viewport is active and render the scene. Note that, with the help of some assumptions you have reasonably located the model over an existing photograph, as shown in Figure 11–73.

Figure 11–73

13. Save your work as **MyRenderingandAnimation.max**.

11.7 The Print Size Wizard

Learning Objective

Set the print resolution, paper size, and other options for a rendering using the Print Size Wizard.

When you create renderings for print, the Print Size Wizard, as shown in Figure 11–74, can help you select an appropriate rendering based on a required output resolution. To access the wizard, select **Rendering>Print Size Assistant**.

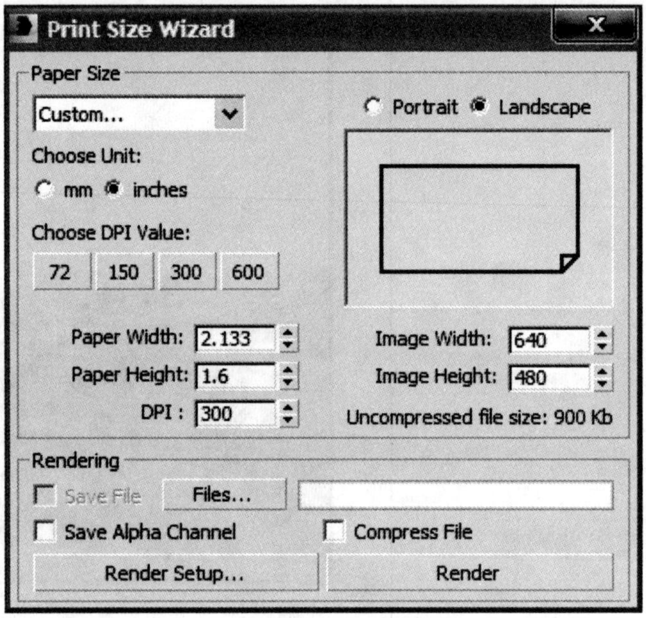

Figure 11–74

- A rendering's print resolution describes how many pixels show per printed inch, often referred to as pixels-per-inch on screen (ppi) or dots-per-inch on paper (DPI). Select the required dpi in the *Choose DPI Value* options.
- Rendering time increases exponentially with size, so select the lowest resolution that provides an acceptable result. Trial and error might be necessary to determine an appropriate resolution.
- Many laser printers and plotters output between 300-600 DPI, however, when rendering values such as 72-150 DPI you can also get good results. High-end equipment plotting at 1200 DPI or better creates outstanding prints at 200-300 dpi and on high-quality paper.
- Higher quality paper can get better results than increasing resolution.

Practice 11d Using the Print Size Wizard

Learning Objective

Set the print resolution, paper size, and other options for a rendering using the Print Size Wizard.

Estimated time for completion: 5 minutes

In this practice you will prepare a rendering for an A-size, 8.5"x11" print at 72 DPI. You want at least a 1/2" border around all sides and the aspect ratio of 1.6.

You must set the paths to locate the External files and Xrefs used in the practice. If you have not done this already, return to the **Introduction to Autodesk 3ds Max Design** chapter and complete Task 1 to Task 3 of the **Organizing Folders and Working with the Interface** practice. You only have to set the user paths once.

If a dialog box opens prompting you about a File Load: Mismatch, click OK *to accept the default values.*

1. Open **Print Wizard.max** from your *Class Files* folder.
2. Open the Print Size Wizard by selecting **Rendering>Print Size Assistant**. Verify that the printing units (*Choose Unit*) are set to **inches** and the orientation is set to **Landscape**.
3. In the Paper Size drop-down list, select **A – 11x8.5in**. Note in the viewport that this setting changes the aspect ratio (11"/8.5" = 1.29). Change the Paper Size back to **Custom**.

4. Set the *Paper Width* to **10** (11" minus a half-inch border on each side). When printing, the 1/2" border displays along both sides as long as you print this image centered on an 8.5" x 11" page at 72 DPI. On a hand-calculator work out the required rendered height 10"/1.6 = 6.25". Set the *Paper Height* to **6.25** and select the *DPI* value of **72**, as shown in Figure 11–75, and press <Enter>. Note that the rendering size changes to 720 x 450 pixels.

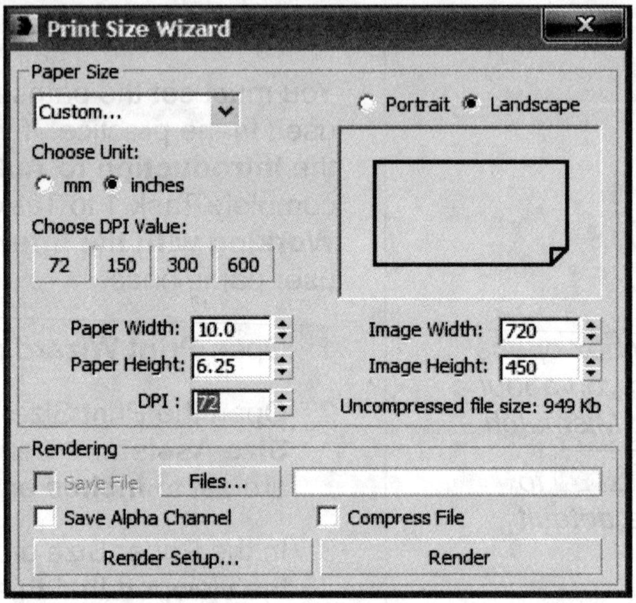

Figure 11–75

5. Click 
.

- Once rendered, you save the image and open it in an image editor or layout program to add your company logo, titles, labels, and other additional details.
- You can also print directly to the current system printer by clicking (Print Image) in the Rendered Frame Window.

6. Save the file as **MyPrint Wizard.max**.

Chapter Review Questions

1. Which renderer in the Autodesk 3ds Max Design software is not a graphical renderer and uses ASCII text files to describe the position and transformation of objects, lighting, etc.?
   a. Default Scanline Renderer
   b. VUE File Renderer
   c. Quicksilver Hardware Renderer
   d. NVIDIA mental ray renderer
2. Which renderer in the Autodesk 3ds Max Design software is a CPU/GPU renderer?
   a. Default Scanline Renderer
   b. VUE File Renderer
   c. NVIDIA iray renderer
   d. NVIDIA mental ray renderer
3. In rendering, which of the following is used to calculate accurate reflections, refractions, and shadows?
   a. Antialiasing
   b. SuperSampling
   c. Motion Blur
   d. Raytracing
4. In single-sided mode, the Autodesk 3ds Max Design software renders faces whose vectors point towards the camera.
   a. True
   b. False
5. What is the most commonly used focal length in real-world cameras?
   a. 30mm
   b. 50mm
   c. 70mm
   d. 90mm

6. For background images, which keys do you press to update the active viewport with the specific changes made to the image (the changes that do not update automatically)?
   a. <Alt>+<B>
   b. <Alt>+<Ctrl>+<B>
   c. <Alt>+<Shift>+<B>
   d. <Alt>+<Ctrl>+<Shift>+<B>

Command Summary

Button	Command	Location
	**Cameras**	■ **Command Panel:** *Create* panel ■ **Create:** Cameras
	**Effects and Environment dialog box**	■ **Rendered Frame Window** ■ **Rendering:** Environment
	**Render Iterative**	■ **Main Toolbar:** Render flyout
	**Render Setup**	■ **Main Toolbar** ■ **Rendering:** Render Setup
	Viewport Configuration dialog box> ***Background*** **tab**	■ **Views:** Viewport Background> Configure Viewport Background ■ **Keyboard:** <Alt>+<B>

Chapter 12

Animation

In this chapter you learn about the Animation and Time Controls that can be used in the Autodesk 3ds Max Design software to create an animation. You learn to animate and keyframe a camera to create a walkthrough animation. You also learn to create single-frame images and then assemble them to create a movie.

This chapter contains the following topics:

- ✓**Animation and Time Controls**
- ✓**Walkthrough Animation**
- ✓**Animation Output**

Certification

Topic:

✓Animation

Objectives:

✓Analyze the animation of an object using the Curve Editor

✓Identify Controller types

✓Identify playback settings

✓Locate the value of keys in the Time Slider

12.1 Animation and Time Controls

Learning Objectives

- Work with the Animation and Time Controls provided with the software.
- Set the options in the Time Configuration dialog box.

Animations in the Autodesk® 3ds Max® Design software are created by playing back a number of still frames in rapid succession using desktop animation files such as .AVIs and .MOVs. While traditional movies play back a sequence of still images in rapid succession, computer movie formats use a slightly different technique. They compile a sequence of still images into a compressed format, keeping track of the changes from frame to frame at the pixel level. The Autodesk 3ds Max Design animation system offers powerful controls to create animations, ranging from simple camera movements to extremely complex sequences.

Animation in the Autodesk 3ds Max Design software is based on Key Frames (or keys), which are time indexes at which objects change their position, rotation, scale, and/or a limited number of object parameters. The Autodesk 3ds Max Design software can generate animations by interpolating between a small number of user-defined key frames – smoothly or otherwise.

The animation controls, found at the bottom of the viewports, enable you to create and play back a preview animation in one or more viewports.

Time Slider and Track Bar: The time slider and the track bar, as shown in Figure 12–1, are found below the viewports. These enable you to scrub or manually advance and reverse along an animation forward or backwards in time. The numbers below the time slider indicate the current time or frame number. Use the greater than (>) and lesser than (<) keys as shortcuts for moving the time slider a frame at a time. The track bar comes with a right-click menu that contains the key properties and the controller properties. Selecting a key and then right-clicking displays all of the values for that key. Using the right-click menu, you can also delete keys and use filter options for the display of the track bar.

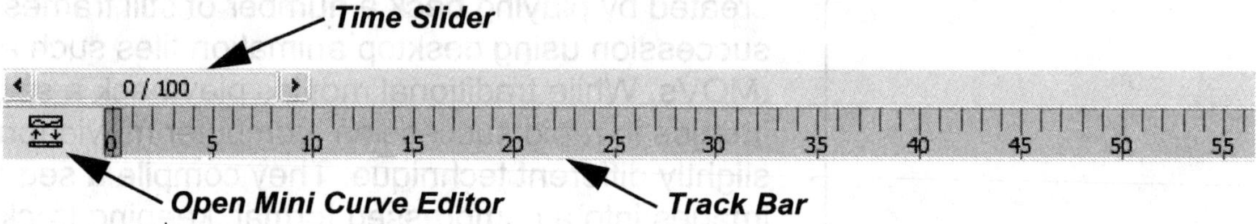

Figure 12–1

On the left side of the track bar, clicking  (Open Mini Curve Editor) opens the Curves Editor (as shown in Figure 12–2), which replaces the track bar and the time slider. The Curve Editor contains a menu bar, toolbar, controller window, and the key window. You can collapse the Curve Editor by clicking

at the left end of the Curve Editor toolbar.

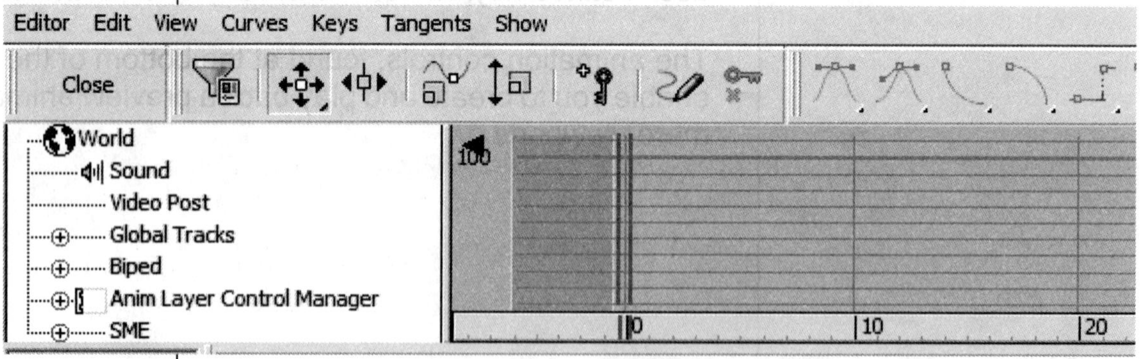

Figure 12–2

*When either **Auto Key** mode or **Set Key** mode is active, their corresponding buttons display in red indicating that you are in the animation mode.*

Animation and Time Controls: The Animation and Time Controls, as shown in Figure 12–3, are found at the bottom right corner next to the Navigation Controls.

Figure 12–3

The various Animation and Time controls are:

-  enables you to manually add an animation key at the time currently shown in the time slider.

- 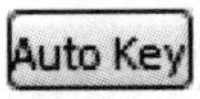 and  activate either Auto Key or Set Key Animation Modes. When **Auto Key** mode is active all movement, rotation, and scale changes are automatically stored as keys at the current frame. In the Autodesk 3ds Max Design software, parameter changes are saved as well. The **Set Key** mode offers more control over the kinds of keys you create through filters and by using . The **Set Key** mode enables you to create keys and when to set the key information. These modes offer two distinctly different methods of animating, generally the Auto Key method is more widely used by design visualizers. Set Key functionality was added primarily for character animators who used this methodology in other packages. Press <N> as a shortcut to toggle on Auto Key mode. <'> (single apostrophe) is the shortcut for Set Key mode.

- The **Previous**, **Play**, and **Next** buttons (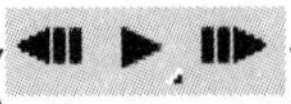) enable you to play an animation in your viewport(s) and advance to the next or previous frame/key. When you click  (Play Animation), the software plays the animation in the active viewport and replaces this icon with  (Stop Animation).  (Play Animation) is a flyout and contains  (Play Selected), which only plays the selected objects in the active viewport.

- (Key Mode Toggle) enables you to move between frames or keys. When you are in Key mode (**On**), the **Previous** and **Next** icons display as and enable you to jump to the previous or next keyframe. Keyframes are set in the Time Configuration dialog box (*Key Steps* area). When Key mode is off, the **Previous** and **Next** icons are displayed as and you can jump to the previous and next frame.

- (Go to Start) and (Go to End) enable you to move directly to the beginning or end of an animation. The time slider jumps to the selected location.

- (Current Frame) enables you to advance to a specific frame or time in the animation.

- Key Filters... opens the Set Key Filters dialog box, which enables you to select the tracks on which the keys can be created. The track sets are created with the **Set Key** mode.

  The drop-down list in Selected contains the created track sets and selection sets and enables you to select the required one quickly while working in the **Set Key** mode.

- (Default In/Out Tangents for New Keys) contains a list of tangent types, as shown in Figure 12–4. While creating a new animation key, you can set its tangent type by selecting the required type.

Figure 12–4

- (Time Configuration) opens the Time Configuration dialog box.

Time Configuration

Clicking  (Time Configuration) opens the Time Configuration dialog box, as shown in Figure 12–5, where you assign an animation, its length, playback rate, and other critical parameters. It is helpful to adjust these parameters before you start configuring an animation.

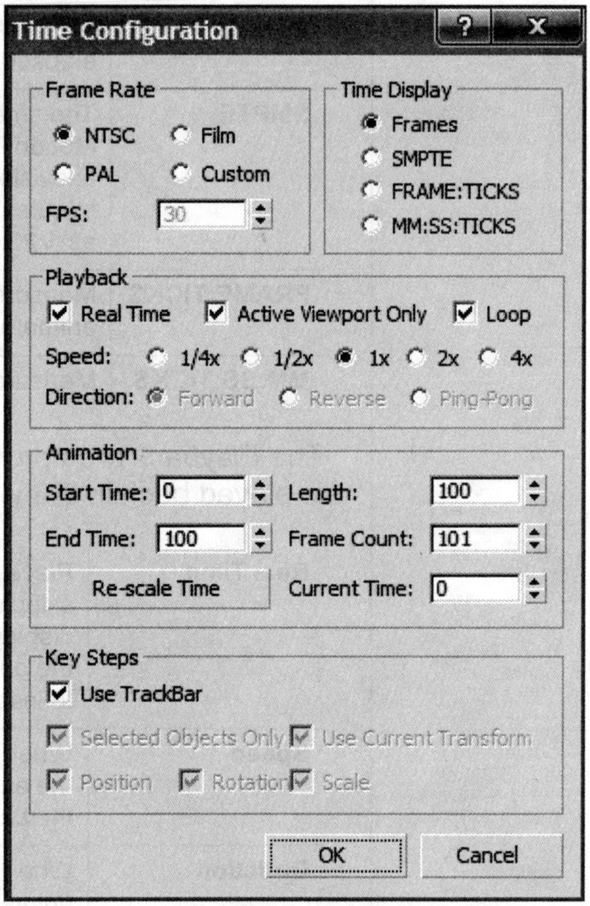

Figure 12–5

The *Frame Rate* area provides options to define how many still frames to show per second (FPS). When setting a frame rate, the goal is to create an animation that flows smoothly but does not require you to unnecessarily render thousands of additional frames. Often the best choice for frame rate depends on the medium where you intend to play your animation.

NTSC	**National Television Standards Committee:** the standard television frame rate used across most of the Americas and Japan: 30 FPS.
PAL	**Phase Alternate Line:** the standard used across Europe: 25 FPS.
Film	Assigns the frame rate used in film production: 24 FPS.

Custom	Enables you to select a specific frame rate. Animations created for desktop and web-based presentations are often set 12-25 FPS.

The *Time Display* area provides options to select how you want to measure time during your animation.

Frames	Measures time in the number of frames that have elapsed since the beginning of the animation.
SMPTE	The time measurement standard used by the Society of Motion Picture Technical Engineers for video and television productions. This standard measures time in minutes, seconds, and frames separated by colons (such as 1:22:43).
FRAME:TICKS	Measures time in frames and ticks only. A tick is a unit of animated time that equals 1/4800 of a second.
MM:SS:TICKS	Measures time in minutes, seconds and ticks.

The *Playback* area provides options to control how the animation is played back in the viewports.

Real Time	Plays the animation at the real world playback rate, skipping frames if necessary. Clearing this option displays all frames in sequence, even if it slows down the animation preview. This is used by most animators to inspect every frame for problems.
Speed	When **Real Time** is enabled, speed up or slow down the animation using this option or continually play using the **Loop** option.
Direction	When not using **Real Time** you can select to play the animation forwards, backwards, or ping-pong (forwards and backwards again) using the **Direction** option.
Active Viewport Only	Limits the animation preview to the active viewport, which might be necessary if system resources are taxed by the animation playback.

The options in the *Animation* area define the active time segment (the current animation length) between the starting and ending time.

Start Time	Can be equal to 0, a positive, or negative time value as needed.
End Time	Can be equal to 0, a positive, or negative time value as needed.
Length	The calculated time between the starting and ending points.

Frame Count	A value equal to the animation length + 1 frame, to account for the rendering of frame 0.
Current Time	Provides the frame you are on in the animation. Use this field to change to a different frame without exiting the dialog box.

When animation times are changed in this dialog box, the existing keys do not automatically scale to the new time. For example, if you lengthen an existing animation by increasing the end time the current animation still stops at the old end time (unless you then manually adjust the keys).

To expand or contract an animation's overall length, click Re-scale Time, to open the Rescale Time dialog box, as shown in Figure 12–6. Changing the animation times here spaces the existing keys along the new animation length.

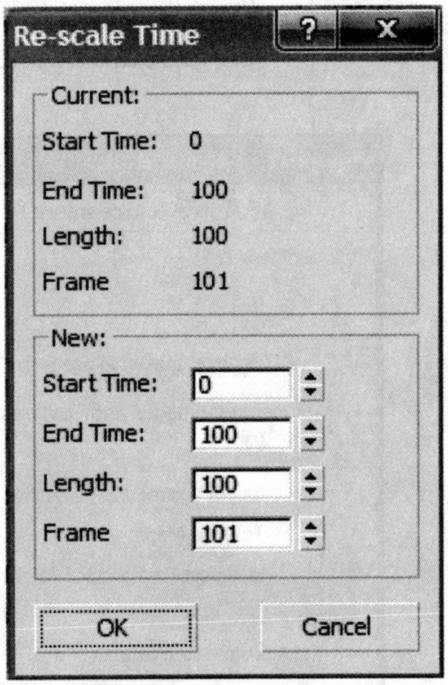

Figure 12–6

The *Key Steps* area provides options to limit how and which animation keys are created in Key mode. Leave the **Use TrackBar** option enabled to not limit key creation.

Progressive Display and Adaptive Degradation

Enhanced in 2014

If you are using one of the legacy display drivers (Direct3D or Open GL), the Adaptive Degradation tab replaces the Display Performance tab in the Viewport Configuration dialog box.

The Progressive Display (only for Nitrous drivers) and Adaptive Degradation is a display option that can be very useful when playing animations in the viewport or when navigating large files in the viewport. When enabled (in the Status Bar, click , or use <O> to toggle it on/off) it degrades an animation preview to a simpler display method to display the proper playback rate. Essentially it enables you to play a complex animation in a viewport at the correct speed, even if it means simplifying the display to a less detailed display mode, such as wireframe.

In the Status Bar, right-click on (Adaptive Degradation) to open the Viewport Configuration dialog box in the *Display Performance* tab, as shown in Figure 12–7. You can also open this dialog box by selecting **Views>Viewport Configuration**. Alternatively, in the Viewport label, click [+] to display the label menu and select **Configure Viewports**. Using the menu bar or the Viewport label menu opens the dialog box in the *Visual Style & Appearance* tab. Select the *Display Performance* tab.

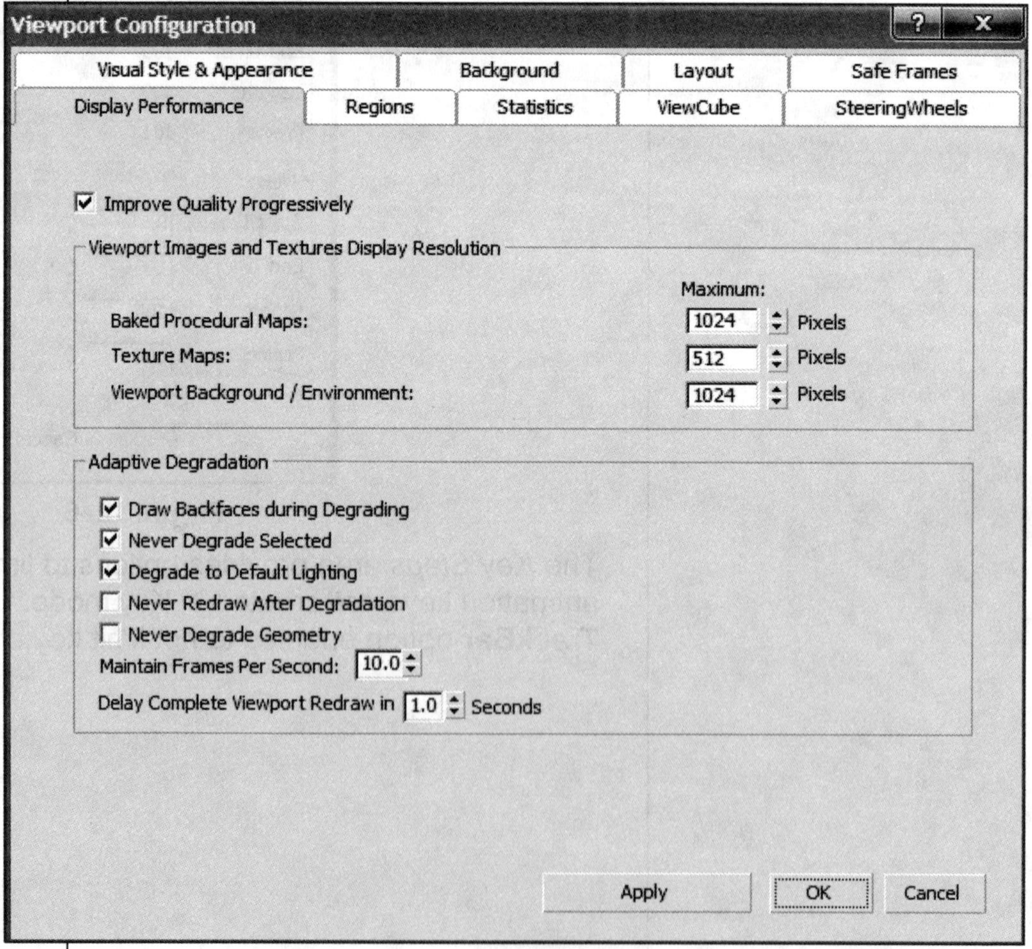

Figure 12–7

Improve Quality Progressively

This option (only available for Nitrous display drivers) enables you to improve the viewport quality through successive iterations. Once the iterations have been completed, a high quality rendered image is displayed in the viewport. You can also activate or clear this option in the Menu bar (**Views> Progressive Display**).

Viewport Images and Textures Display Resolution

- The **Baked Procedural Maps** option enables you set the resolution, in pixels, that is used to display the procedural maps in the viewports.

***New** in 2014*

- **Texture Maps:** Enables you to set the resolution in pixels, that is used to display the texture maps in the viewports.

***New** in 2014*

- The **Viewport Background / Environment:** Enables you to set the resolution in pixels, that is used to display the environment and background maps.

***New** in 2014*

Adaptive Degradation

> **Hint: Bitmap Proxy Images**
>
> Using Proxy images enables you to reduce the memory required for the 2D texture and increase the rendering speed.
>
> Expand [MXD], select **References**, and select **Asset Tracking** to open the Asset Tracking dialog box. Use **Bitmap Performance and Memory>Global Settings** to set the proxy resolution.

- When **Draw Backfaces during Degrade** is toggled on, the software draws the backface polygons while degrading the objects.
- When **Never Degrade Selected** is toggled on, the software does not degrade the selected objects.
- When **Degrade to Default Lighting** is toggled on, the software turns off all of the lights in the viewport with only the default lighting toggled on.
- When **Never Redraw after Degrade** is toggled on, the degraded objects display as is and do not redraw.

- When **Never Degrade Geometry** is toggled on, the geometry in the viewport is not degraded.
- The **Maintain Frames Per Second** enables you to set the frame rate. The software maintains this frame rate through degradation.
- The **Delay Complete Viewport Redraw** enables you to set a time in seconds, during which the viewports are not redrawn when degradation is complete.

Certification

Topic:

✓Animation

Objectives:

✓Create a path animation and evaluate an object along the path

12.2 Walkthrough Animation

Learning Objective

- Work with the Animation and Time Controls provided with the software.

When animating cameras it is often easier to have a camera follow a linear path than to configure the camera's position manually. For example, in Figure 12–8, you can animate a camera following a path going up a street to the house.

Figure 12–8

- In the Autodesk 3ds Max Design software, to animate a target camera following a path, you create a helper object called a Dummy object, as shown in Figure 12–9. While a Dummy object is not required, it is a good practice as it provides more control.
- The path can be a spline, as shown in Figure 12–9, created in the Autodesk 3ds Max Design software or a linked/imported line, polyline, spline, or similar object. You then create a target camera and Dummy object and align them so they share a similar orientation. Multiple paths can be assigned and weighted during an animation.

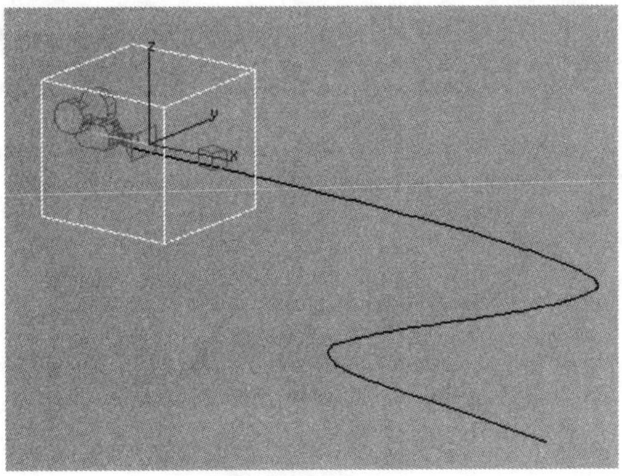

Figure 12–9

- To create a Dummy object, in the Command Panel, in the *Create* panel ( ), click (Helpers). In the Object Type rollout, click Dummy. A Dummy object is usually drawn in the Top viewport to ensure orientation with world space. Dummies have no parameters in the *Modify* panel and do not render in your final animation.

- In the Main toolbar, use (Select and Link) to link the Camera and Dummy.

- To animate the Dummy object and Camera, define a Path Constraint (**Animation>Constraints>Path Constraint**). A dotted line displays in the viewport, as shown in Figure 12–10. Select the spline to be used as the path. If you cannot see the path, you can press <H> to select the path by name from the Select From Scene dialog box.

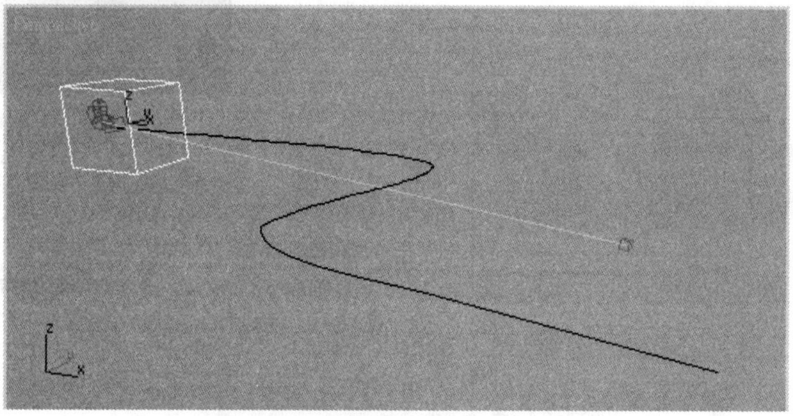

Figure 12–10

- Alternatively the target object can be positioned over the subject and left unanimated. In this case, the target stays fixed over the building and the Dummy and Camera back animate along the path.

- The Dummy can follow the path using the **Follow** checkbox in the *Motion* panel.

Practice 12a Creating a Turntable Animation

Learning Objectives

- Add a dummy object on the building and set the key frames to create an animation.
- Apply rotation at the key frames to animate the building.
- Add interpolation to the keys using the dialog box and the Mini Curve Editor.

Estimated time for completion: 20 minutes

In this practice you will animate a camera rotating around the retail exterior building. This creates the illusion that the viewer is standing still and the building is revolving as if on a turntable.

You must set the paths to locate the External files and Xrefs used in the practice. If you have not done this already, return to the **Introduction to Autodesk 3ds Max Design** chapter and complete Task 1 to Task 3 of the **Organizing Folders and Working with the Interface** practice. You only have to set the user paths once.

If a dialog box opens prompting you about a File Load: Mismatch, click OK to accept the default values.

1. Open **Turntable_Animation_Start.max** from your *Class Files* folder.

2. Verify that the Top viewport is active and click (Maximize Viewport).

3. Select the camera (**Turntable camera** is the only camera object) in the viewport. Click (Zoom Extents All Selected) to display the camera, its target, and the entire building, as shown in Figure 12–11.

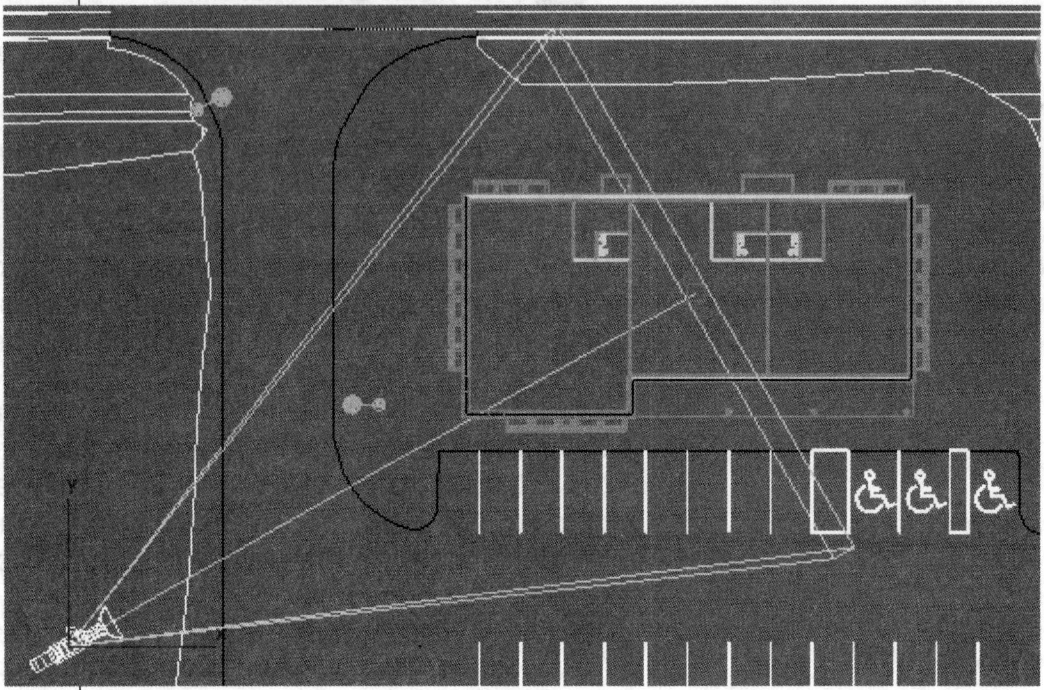

Figure 12–11

4. In the Command Panel, in the *Create* panel ( ), click (Helpers).

5. In the Object Type rollout, click Dummy. Starting from the camera target by clicking on the target (the small blue square in the center of the building), drag to create a dummy object (a square box) large enough to approximately extend beyond the two horizontal walls of the building, as shown in Figure 12–12.

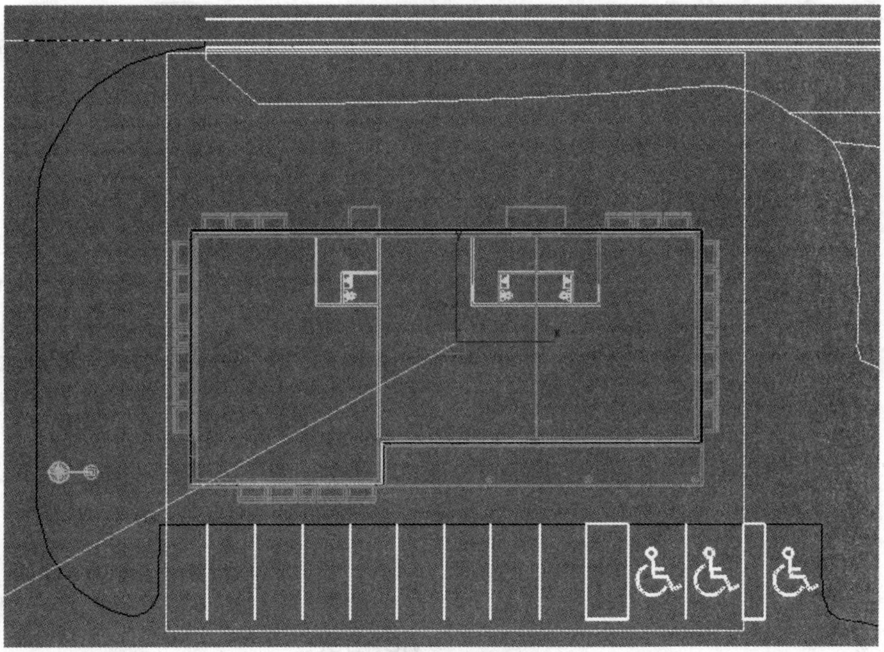

Figure 12–12

6. In the Main toolbar, click (Select and Link). In the viewport, select **Turntable camera** (camera object). Note that your cursor displays as two linked squares when you hover it over the selected camera. Starting from the camera, click and drag the cursor to the Dummy object (green square). A white dotted line displays, as shown in Figure 12–13, between the camera and the dummy. Release the mouse to link the camera to the dummy.

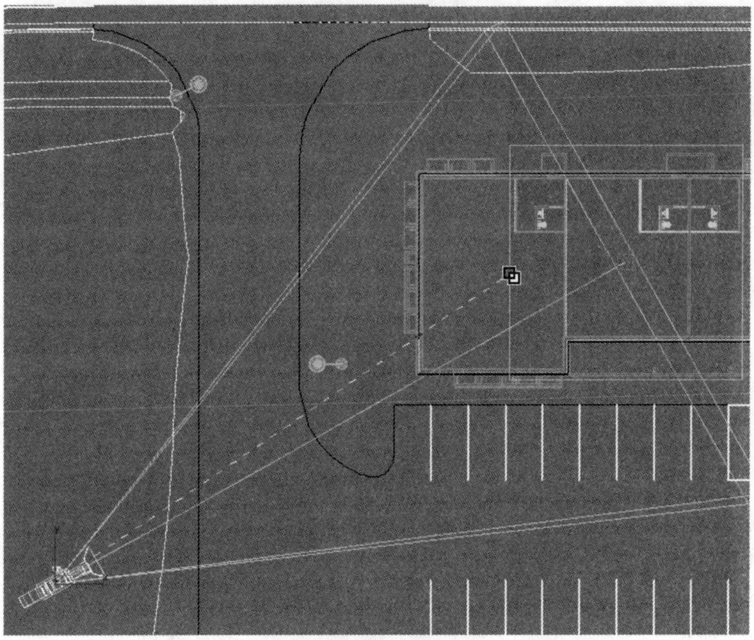

Figure 12–13

7. To test it, click (Select and Move) and move the Dummy object. The camera should move with it. Undo the move after the test and click (Select Object) to exit the **Move** command.

8. In the Animation playback controls, click (Time Configuration) to open the dialog box. Set the *Time Display* to **Frames**. In the *Animation* area, set the *End Time* to **99**. Click OK. Near the bottom of the viewport, note that the Time Slider displays as < 0 / 99 >.

9. Click (Maximize Viewport) or <Alt>+<W> to display all four viewports. Activate and maximize the **Turntable camera** viewport.

Click Auto Key. It displays in red, indicating that you are in the Auto Key animation mode. The slider bar area displays in red and a red border surrounds the current viewport.

10. To create the turntable animation, click Auto Key (it displays in red) and drag the Time Slider to **frame 33**. The Track Bar displays a blue rectangle at frame 33, as shown in Figure 12–14.

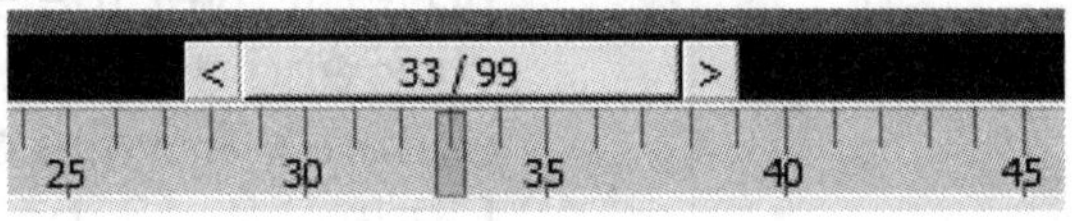

Figure 12–14

You can also use the Rotate gizmo to rotate the dummy object horizontally until the values on the screen display as [0.00, -0.00, -120.00].

11. Select the dummy object (green box). (Dummy001 should be displayed in the Name and Color rollout. You can also use (Select by Name) and select the Dummy object). Click (Select and Rotate). In the Status Bar, in the *Z* field, enter **-120** and press <Enter>, as shown in Figure 12–15. Note that the scene is rotated.

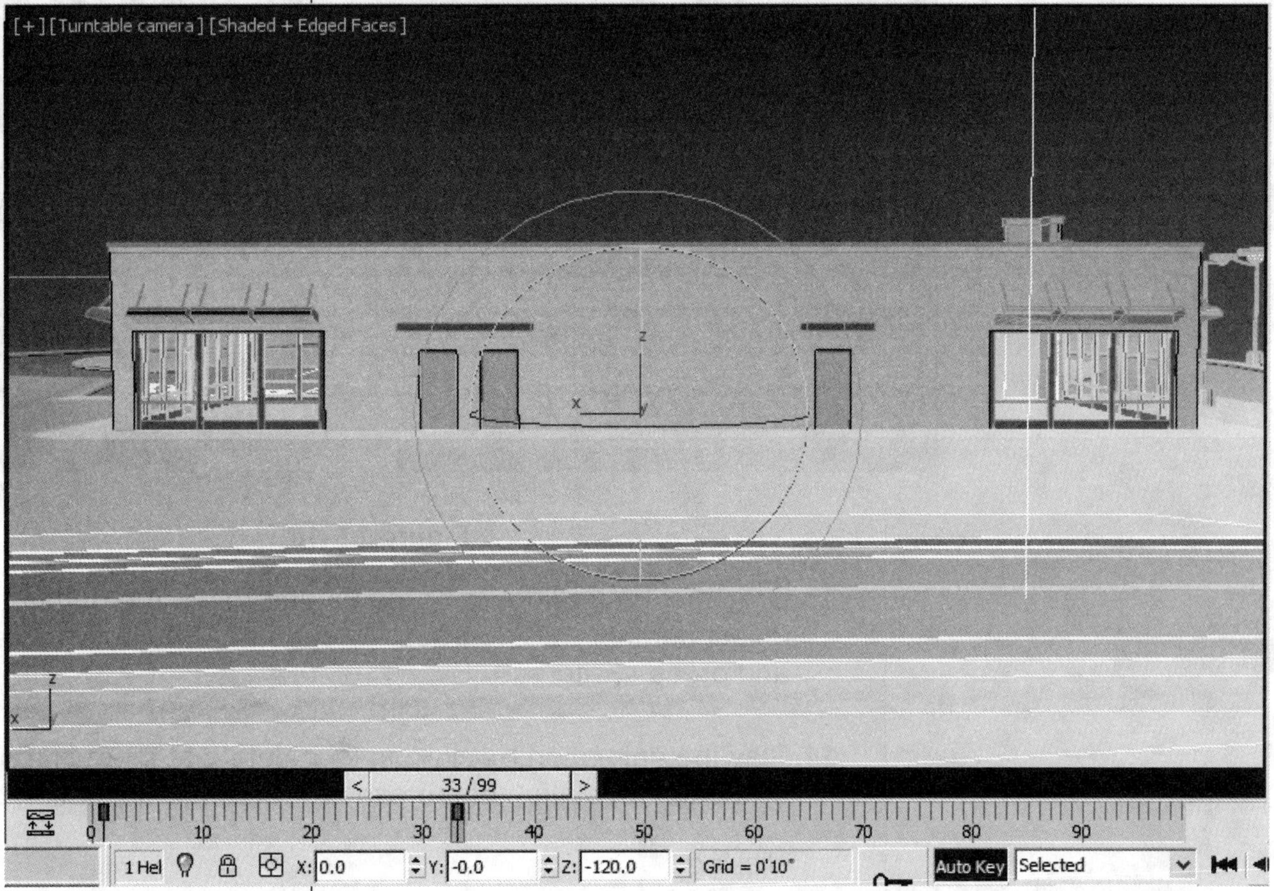

Figure 12–15

12. Drag the Time Slider to frame **66** and rotate the dummy object another 120 degrees, by entering **-240** in the *Z* field of the Status Bar and press <Enter>, as shown in Figure 12–16.

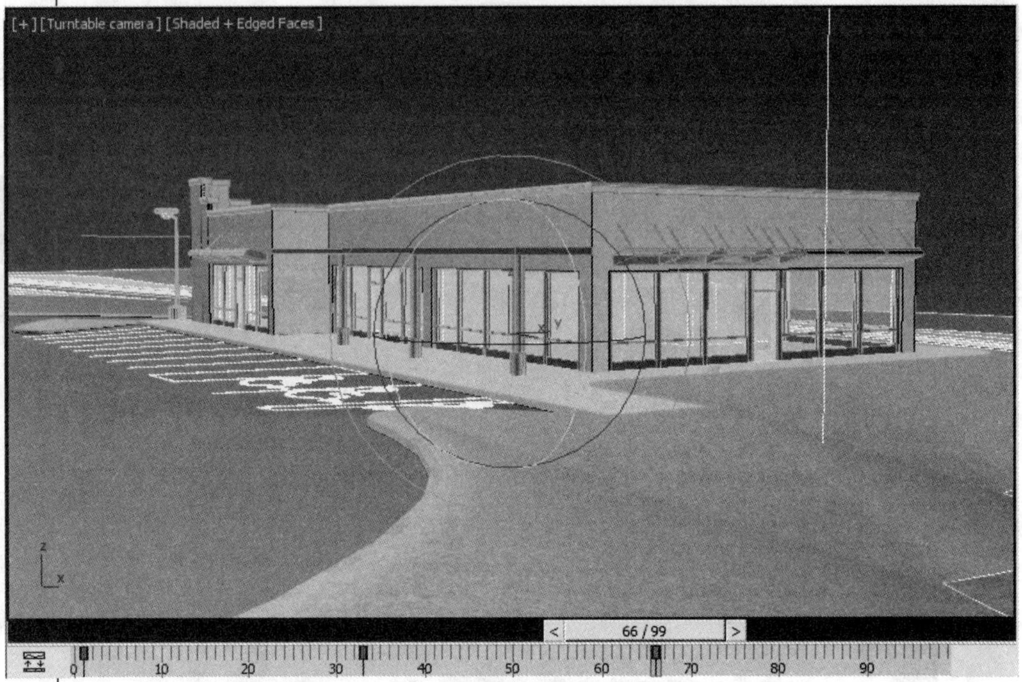

Figure 12–16

13. Drag the Time Slider to frame **99** and rotate the dummy object another 120 degrees, by entering **-360** in the *Z* field and press <Enter>.

14. Play the animation by clicking ▶. Note that there is a pause with each revolution of the camera. Stop the animation by clicking ❚❚.

15. If your animation has a lag, in the Status Bar, click (Adaptive Degradation).

When the degradation is being applied to the models, displays in aqua.

16. In the Animation controls, click ▶. Note that over time, the objects change into a wireframe model and animate smoothly. Stop the animation by clicking ❚❚. Note that the model is redrawn as shaded almost immediately.

17. Right-click on  (Adaptive Degradation) to open the Viewport Configuration dialog box in the *Display Performance* tab. In the *Adaptive Degradation* area, set *Delay Complete Viewport Redraw* to **5.0** seconds. Click  to close the dialog box

18. Click . Let the animation play in the viewport until the complete model has been degraded to a wireframe model and then click . Note that the model remains a wireframe for 5 seconds before it is redrawn as a shaded model.

19. To fix the pause at each revolution, right-click on the green key in the timeline at frame 99 and select **Dummy001: Z Rotation**, as shown in Figure 12–17. You can Pause the animation, if it is still running.

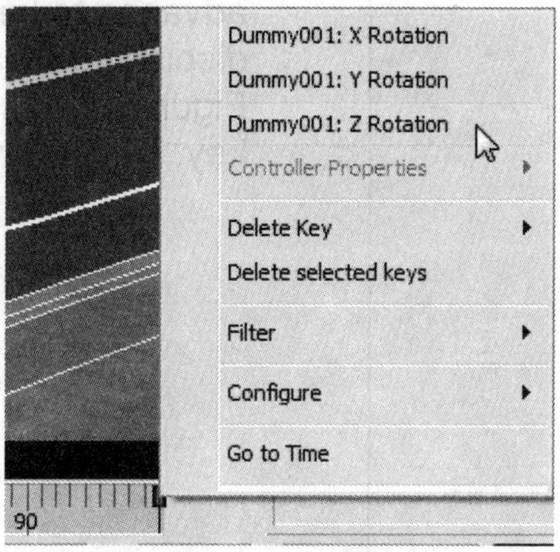

Figure 12–17

20. In the dialog box that opens, expand Interpolation to display the interpolation tools flyout, as shown in Figure 12–18.

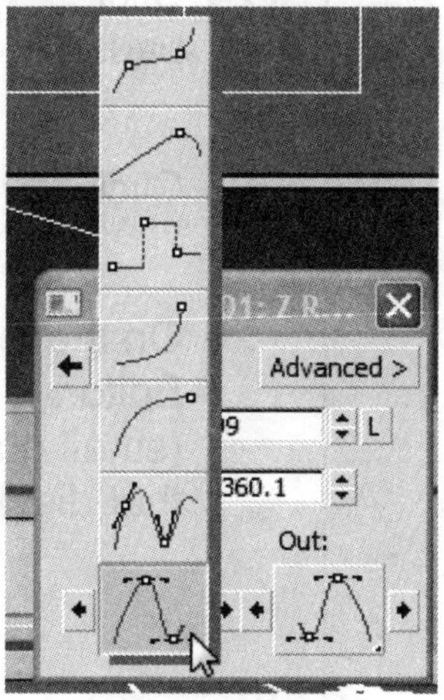

Figure 12–18

21. Click (Linear interpolation). Change the *Out* interpolation to **Linear** as well, as shown in Figure 12–19.

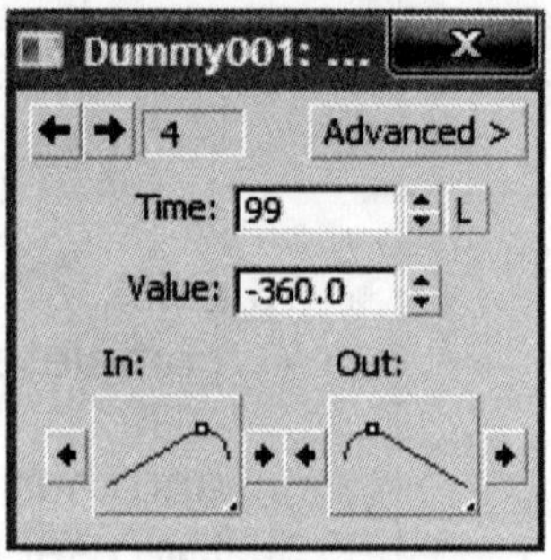

Figure 12–19

- This sets the interpolation to Linear at frame 4 (99).

22. You will set the interpolation to Linear for the other three frames (0, 33, 66). In the upper left corner, click to advance to key **1**, which is the key number. The *Time* displays as **1** and the *Value* displays as **0.0**, as shown in Figure 12–20. Set the *In* and *Out* Interpolation to **Linear** for key 1.

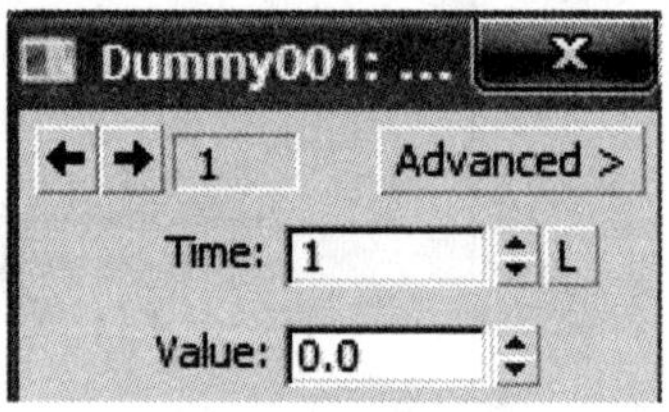

Figure 12–20

23. Repeat for the remaining keys **2** and **3** (frames 33 and 66), using to move to the required key. Close the dialog box.

24. Click to play the animation. It should loop without any pause.

25. Click to stop the animation.

26. On the left side of the track bar, click to open the Curves Editor. It displays the key window (right side) containing keys (small gray squares) and the linear slanting line (blue line) that displays the animation, as shown in Figure 12–21.

27. Hover the cursor over the Controller window (left side). It displays as a **Hand** icon. Hold and drag it up until the dummy object is listed with its applied Transforms, as shown in Figure 12–21.

28. In the Rotation node of the dummy object, select **X Rotation**, **Y Rotation**, and **Z Rotation**, if not already selected, as shown in Figure 12–21.

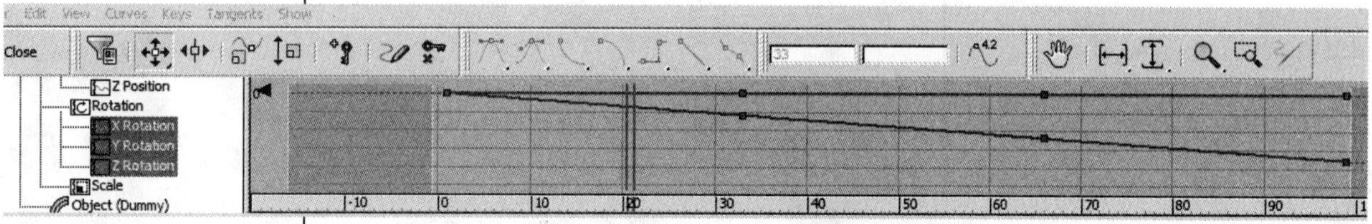

Figure 12–21

29. In the Key window, on the blue line, select the key (small gray square) at frame 33. It displays in white indicating that it has been selected, as shown in Figure 12–22. In the Curve Editor toolbar, click  (Set Tangents to Slow).

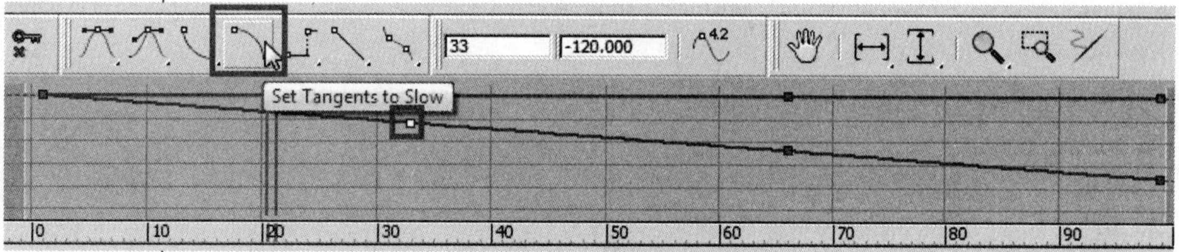

Figure 12–22

- Note that a slight curve is added at this frame 33.

30. Click  to play the animation and note that the animation slows down slightly when it reaches frame 33. Click  to stop the animation.

31. Add **Set Tangents to Slow** to the keys at frame 0, 66, and 99. Slight curves are added to these frames, as shown in Figure 12–23.

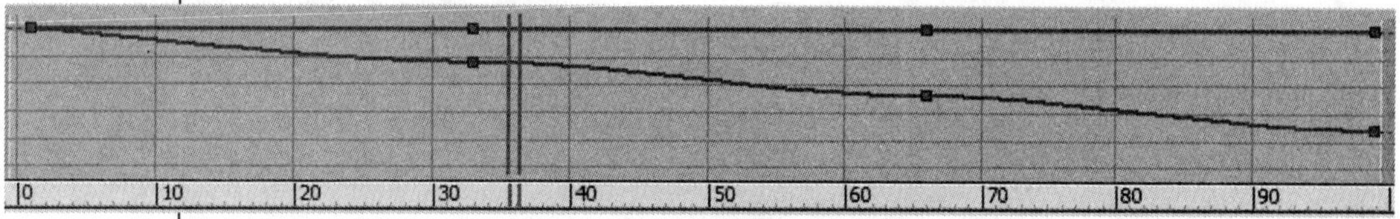

Figure 12–23

32. Click to play the animation and click to stop.

33. Click Close at the left end of the Curve Editor toolbar to close the Curve Editor.

34. Save your work as **MyTurntable_Animation.max**.

Practice 12b Keyframing a Camera Animation

Learning Objectives

- Add an new camera to a scene and set the animation for the camera.
- Modify the animation by creating a new key and modifying the camera position at this key.

Estimated time for completion: 20 minutes

In this practice you will animate a camera flying over the site. This approach is similar to manually configuring a walkthrough or driveby animation.

You must set the paths to locate the External files and Xrefs used in the practice. If you have not done this already, return to the **Introduction to Autodesk 3ds Max Design** chapter and complete Task 1 to Task 3 of the **Organizing Folders and Working with the Interface** practice. You only have to set the user paths once.

Task 1 - Save the Previous Render Options as a Preset.

If a dialog box opens prompting you about a File Load: Mismatch, click OK to accept the default values.

1. Open **Presets.max** from your *Class Files* folder.

*To display the toolbar, right-click anywhere in the blank area of the Main toolbar and select **Render Shortcuts**.*

2. Before you configure the animation you should save all of the rendering settings for the still rendering. In the Render Shortcuts toolbar, in the Presets drop-down list, select **Save Preset**, as shown in Figure 12–24.

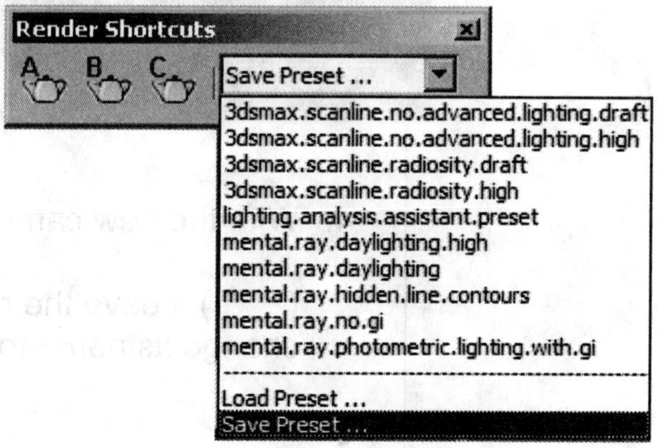

Figure 12–24

3. In the Render Presets Save dialog box, in the File name edit box, enter **Retail_Exterior_with_Background** to save your current render settings and click Save. In the Select Preset Categories dialog box that opens, leave all of the preset categories as highlighted and click Save.

Task 2 - Configure the Camera Animation.

1. Activate the Top Viewport and click (Maximize Viewports) to maximize it.

2. Zoom out till the building, parking lot, and the end of the road on the left side is displayed.

3. In the Command Panel, in the *Create* panel ( ), click (Cameras). In the Object Type rollout, click Target. Create a camera and the target in the approximate positions, as shown in Figure 12–25.

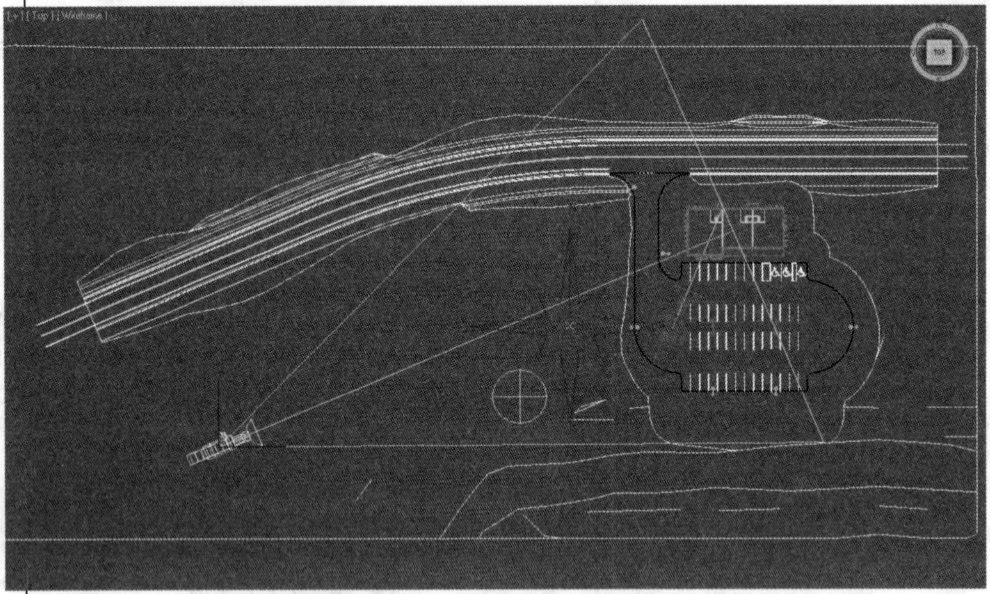

Figure 12–25

4. With the new camera selected, select the *Modify* panel ( ). Leave the camera with the default parameters but change its name to **Camera – Flyover**.

5. Click (Maximize Viewports) to display all four viewports. Right-click on the Front viewport to activate it. Change that view to show the Camera – Flyover view, as shown in Figure 12–26, by selecting the **Front** Point of View label and selecting **Cameras>Camera – Flyover**.

Figure 12–26

6. In the Animation controls, click (Time Configuration). In the *Frame Rate* area, select **Custom**, set *FPS* to **20**, and in the *Animation* area, set *End Time* to **0:30:0** and press <Enter>, as shown in Figure 12–27. Also verify that all of the other values match the values in Figure 12–27. Note that the *Length* and *Frame Count* also changes. Your animation is 30 seconds long and intended for desktop playback at 20 FPS. Click OK.

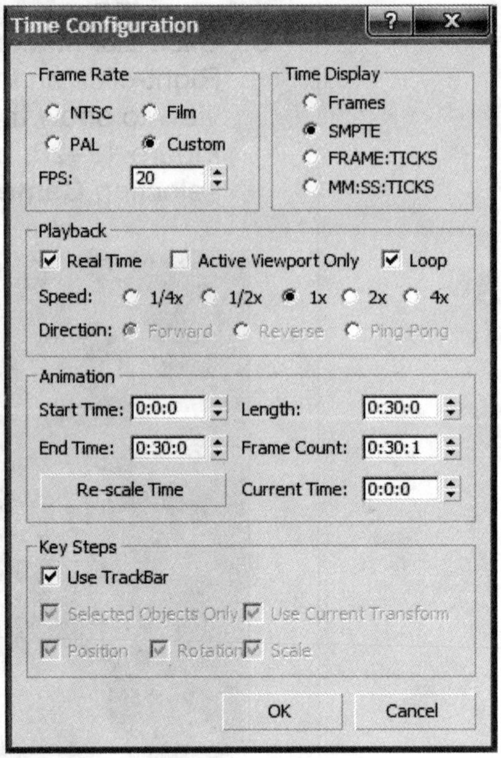

Figure 12–27

7. Verify that the Time Slider is currently located at time **0:0:0**, as shown in Figure 12–28.

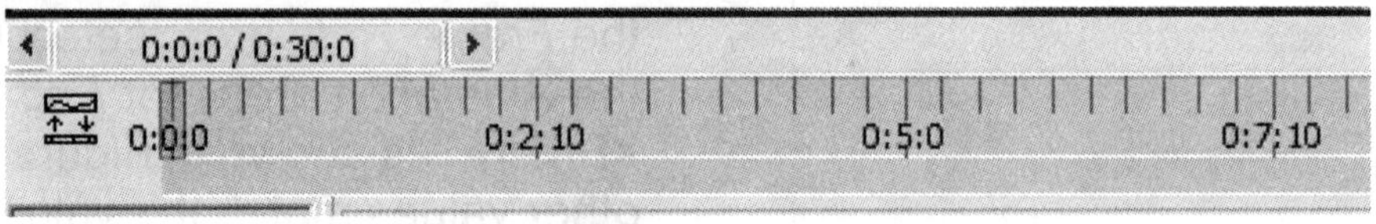

Figure 12–28

8. Click Auto Key. It displays in red. Note that the Time Slider and outline of Camera -Flyover viewport also display in red.

9. Drag the Time Slider all of the way to the *end time* of **0:30:0**, as shown in Figure 12–29. Note the blue marker on the scale.

Figure 12–29

10. Verify that the Camera - Flyover object is selected (note the name in the Modifier Stack). You can use (Select by Name) and select **Camera - Flyover**). Click (Select and Move) and in the Status Bar, in the *Transform Type-In* area enter **X = 300'0"**, **Y = 0'0"**, and **Z = 0'0"**, as shown in Figure 12–30. The roundoff error might change your X-coordinate to a value just below 300' (this often happens, but does not significantly affect this animation).

Figure 12–30

If you do not click Auto Key again to toggle off Auto Key mode, you create an unintended animation. The camera's animation keys are visible along the time slider as colored boxes (as long as the camera is selected). Right-click to modify or delete a key.

11. Click Auto Key again to toggle off Auto Key mode.
12. Slide (scrub) the Time Slider left and right and watch the camera move. With the Camera – Flyover viewport active, click to see a preview of the animation.
13. is changed while the animation is playing. Stop the animation by clicking . Move to the beginning by clicking .

Task 3 - Modify the Animation by Adding a New Key.

You are currently skimming at elevation 0 which makes you fly directly through some slopes of the terrain. To make the animation look more like a flyover you will add another key in the middle of the animation and raise the camera up in the Z-direction at that point.

1. Verify that the **Camera – Flyover** camera is selected.
2. Move the Time Slider to exactly **0:15:0** (the midpoint of the animation) and click (Set Keys). A new key is created at this point.
3. Right-click on this new key and select **Camera – Flyover: Z Position**. Set the *Value* to **30'0"**, press <Enter> and close the dialog box.

4. Click to return to the beginning and click to preview the animation. Note the vertical change has been adjusted but now the midpoint the camera is too close to the building. You will pull the camera back from the building at the midpoint. Stop the animation by clicking .

5. Drag the Time Slider to exactly **0:15:0** and click Auto Key.

6. Activate the Top viewport. Select **Camera – Flyover** camera, click (Select and Move) and in the Status Bar, in the *Transform Type-In* area, enter **X = 15'0"**, **Y = -120'0"**, and **Z = 30'0"**, as shown in Figure 12–31, to move the Camera – Flyover camera away from the building. Since this is done in **AutoKey** mode the camera's existing key at 0:15:0 is updated with this new position. (If done without being in Auto Key mode you would move the camera at frame 0 and at all other keys.)

Figure 12–31

7. Click Auto Key to toggle it off. Click to return to the beginning and click to preview the animation. Stop the animation by clicking .

8. Click (Render Setup) to open the Render Setup dialog box. In the *Common* tab, in the Common Parameters rollout, *Output Size* area, set *Width* to **300** and press <Enter>, as shown in Figure 12–32. With the aspect ratio locked at 1.6 a rendering *Height* of **188** is automatically calculated.

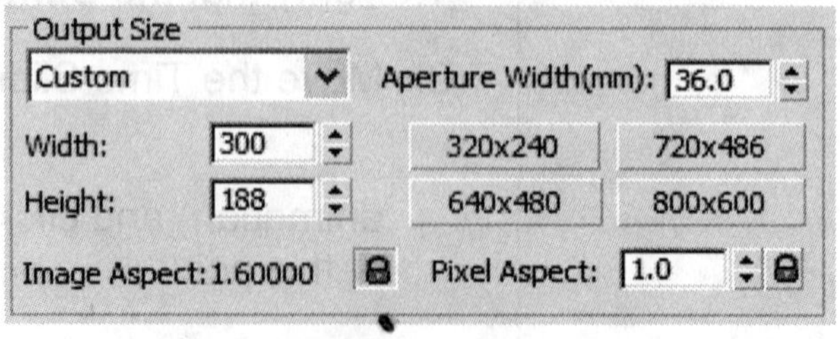

Figure 12–32

9. In the *Time Output* area select **Active Time Segment** (entire animation). Normally you select a filename and location to render to.

10. At the bottom of the dialog box, in the Preset drop-down menu, select **Save Preset** to save the rendering settings as **RetailExteriorAnimation.rps**. Save all preset categories.

11. Save the file as **MyCameraAnimationFlyover.max**.

Practice 12c Creating a Walkthrough Animation

Learning Objective

- Animate a camera object along a path in a scene, using a dummy object attached to the camera.

Estimated time for completion: 10 minutes

In this practice you will merge a .MAX file, which has a hemispherical dome with a simple sky texture and ground color applied to be used as a background for the current scene. You will also merge a file in which the path has been created.

You must set the paths to locate the External files and Xrefs used in the practice. If you have not done this already, return to the **Introduction to Autodesk 3ds Max Design** chapter and complete Task 1 to Task 3 of the **Organizing Folders and Working with the Interface** practice. You only have to set the user paths once.

If a dialog box opens prompting you about a File Load: Mismatch, click OK *to accept the default values.*

1. Open **Camera Animations.max** from your *Class Files* folder.
2. Expand , expand Import, and select **Merge**. In the dialog box, select **Sky and Ground Dome.max** from your *Class Files* folder. Click Open.
3. In the Merge dialog box, select **Sky and Ground Dome** and click OK. The Dome object has been turned inside-out by the normal modifier so that in single-sided rendering mode its surfaces can only be seen from the inside. This enables the dome to be seen in the renderings when a camera is inside the dome.
4. Expand , expand Import, and select **Merge** and select **Animation Path.max**. Click Open.

5. In the Merge dialog box, select **Animation Path 3D** and click OK. This 3D path is along the proposed ground surface of the access road, as shown in Figure 12–33.

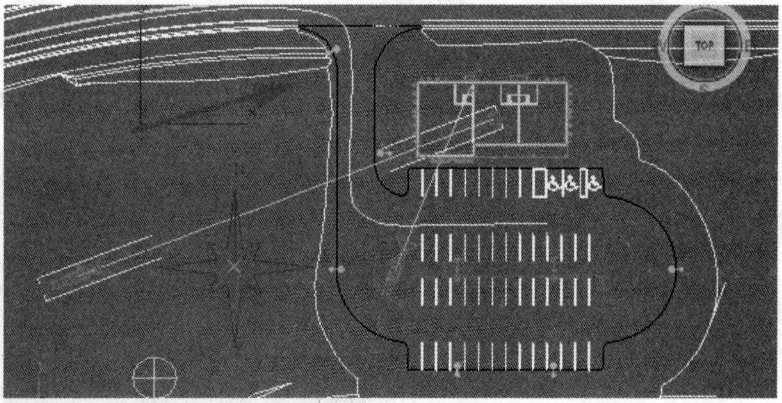

Figure 12–33

6. Maximize the Top viewport.
7. It is easier to work if you temporarily freeze the Site Model. Press <H> or click (Select by Name) to open the Select From Scene dialog box. Click (Display None) and click (Display Groups). Select the object group **_Site Model** and click OK.
8. Right-click in the viewport and select **Freeze Selection** in the quad menu. The Site model geometry displays in a dull gray color and you can easily see the blue path that travels along the street. If required, use **Pan** to display the complete path in the viewport.

9. In the Command Panel, in the *Create* panel ( ), click (Cameras). In the Object Type rollout, click Target. Click close to the left end of the path to place the camera, drag to the center of the building and release to set the target, as shown in Figure 12–34. In the Name and Color edit box, enter the name of the camera as **Walkthrough_Cam01**.

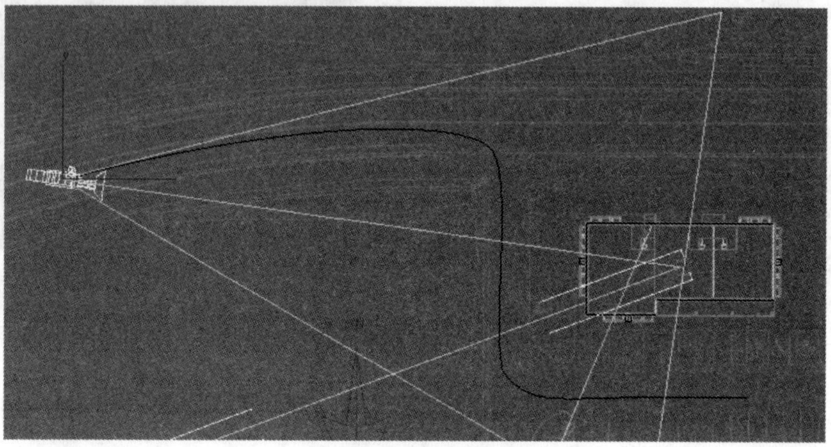

Figure 12–34

10. In the viewport, pan into the Camera object. In the Command Panel, in the *Create* panel ( ), click (Helpers). Click Dummy.

If you were flying a camera through the interior of a design you would align the camera to the dummy at this point. In this animation it is not required for this type of exterior flyby.

11. Click and drag to create the Dummy object over the Camera at the beginning of the animation path spline, as shown in Figure 12–35.

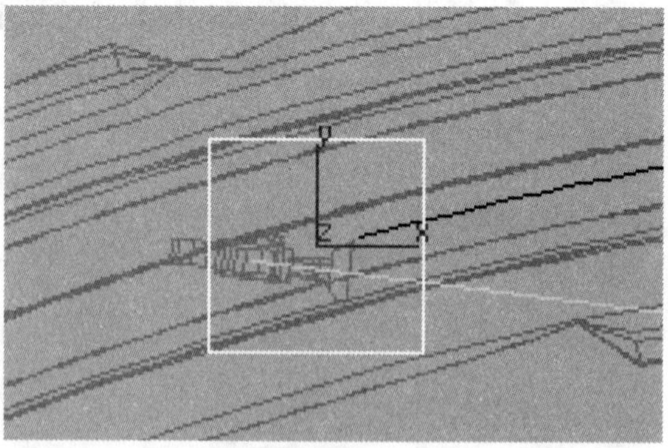

Figure 12–35

12. In the Main toolbar, click (Select and Link).

13. In the viewport, select and hold the newly created **Walkthrough_Cam01** object to define it as the child object. Drag your cursor to the outline of the Dummy. A dotted line displays between the cursor and the object, as shown in Figure 12–36. Release to link the camera to the Dummy.

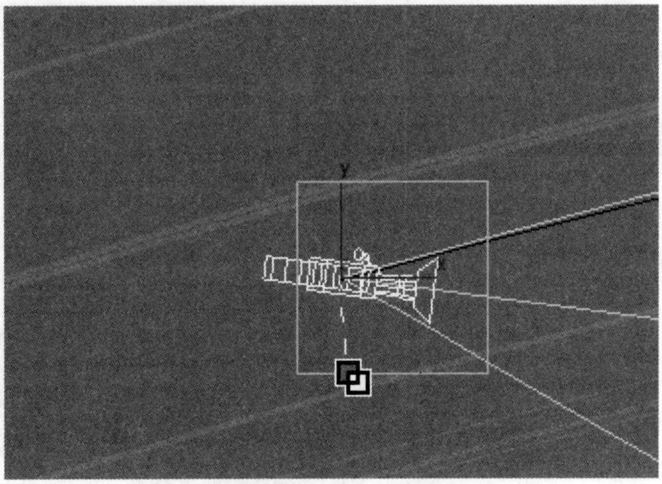

Figure 12–36

14. To check it, in the Main toolbar, click  and move the Dummy. You should see the Camera move with it. This confirms that the linkage is correct. Undo the move.

15. Now you will constrain the dummy to the path. Select the Dummy object in the viewport and select **Animation> Constraints>Path Constraint**. Your cursor is connected with a dotted line to the pivot point of the Dummy object. Click anywhere over the blue spline (Animation Path 3D) to select it as the animation path. The pivot point of the dummy automatically shifts to coincide with the start point of the path.

16. Zoom out till the entire blue path is displayed. Click ▶ to play the animation. The Dummy and the camera animates along the path, as shown in Figure 12–37. Click ⏸ to stop the animation.

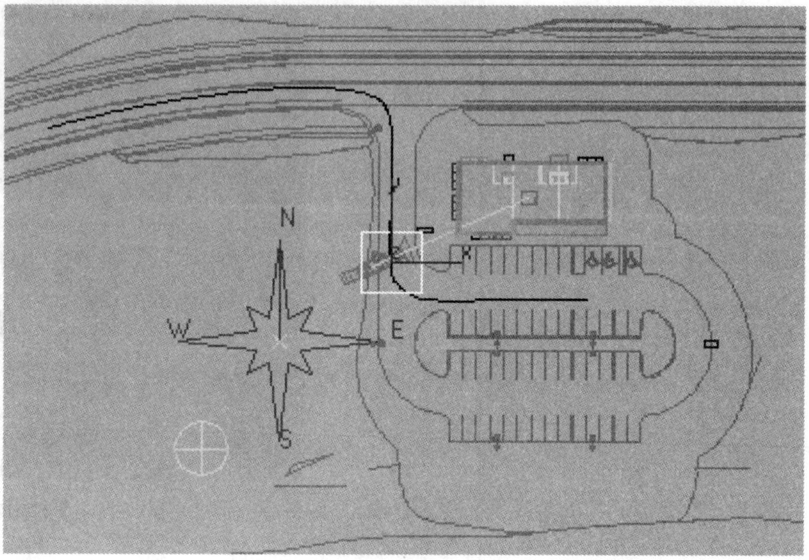

Figure 12–37

17. Press <Alt>+<W> or click (Maximize Viewports) to display all four viewports. Activate the Camera01 viewport and change it to the Walkthrough_Cam01 viewport (select the **POV** label and select **Cameras>Walkthrough_Cam01**).

18. Click ▶ to play the animation. The animation might be improved if the camera was higher off the ground. Since the Camera is a child of the Dummy you can add transforms to the Camera without affecting the Dummy's animation.

19. Click ⏮ to go to the start of the animation, at frame zero.

In the Select From Scene dialog box, click (Display Cameras) and select ***Walkthrough_Cam01****.*

20. Select Walkthrough_Cam01 object and in the *Modify* panel rename it as **Camera_Flyby**.

21. With the **Camera Flyby** object selected, in the Main toolbar, right-click on (Select and Move) to open the Move Transform Type-In dialog box.

22. In the Absolute:World, change the Z-value to **6'0"**. Close the dialog box. Since Auto Key is off this lifts the Camera for the entire animation.

23. Play the animation in the Camera_Flyby viewport. Stop the animation.

24. Right-click on the viewport and select **Unfreeze All**. The Site model is displayed with full color.

25. Save your work as **MyCameraAnimationFlyby.max**.

12.3 Animation Output

Learning Objective

- Understand the strategies for creating animation output and which approach to select.

There are two strategies for creating animation output:

- Render directly to a single, composite animation file such as a .MOV or .AVI. This is generally recommended for previews.
- Render each still image (such as .PNG, .JPEG, .BMP, .TIFF, etc.) and later combine the stills into a composite animation using the Autodesk 3ds Max Design RAM Player, Video Post, or 3rd party post-production software.

Generally speaking the second approach is far superior to the first. Some of the reasons are listed below:

- A lot of time is spent calculating the information to create a rendered frame. Do not throw that information away by rendering to a compressed animation format. Saving it as a sequence of still images gives you access to all of the information in the future.
- A system crash, disc error, power outage, or similar problem can invalidate a composite animation file, forcing you to re-render the entire animation. In contrast, if you render individual frames, all of the previously saved frames remain available after a catastrophic error. You could then render only the missing frames to complete your animation.
- Unexpected problems with materials, lighting, and even geometry present themselves through specific frames of an animation. It never happens that you only render an animation once. Compressed animation files cannot be easily adjusted and ALL of the frames must be re-rendered. However, when rendering to frames, you can fix such problems and then only re-render those frames that are affected.

- When rendering to an animation file you need to select the compression or video quality settings up front. If you do not like the results you need to select another value and re-render the entire animation. When rendering to stills, select a quality value after rendering is complete so if you do not like the results you can simply try different settings and save out another composite file from the same still renderings.

- Rendering to a still image file format that supports an alpha channel (transparency) enables you to use a compositing package like Combustion or Adobe After Effects for post-production processing and assembly.

You can select an animation output option in the Render Output File dialog box. To open this dialog box, open the Render Setup dialog box and expand the Common Parameters rollout in the *Common* tab. In the *Render Output* area, click Files..., as shown in Figure 12–38.

Figure 12–38

The Render Output File dialog box opens. In the Save as type drop-down list (shown in Figure 12–39), you can select to render to a single, compressed animation file (.MOV or .AVI) or to individual frames (such as .PNG, .JPEG, .BMP, .TIFF, etc.). If you select to render as individual frames, you need to provide the name once and the software automatically creates individual files for each frame, which are numbered sequentially.

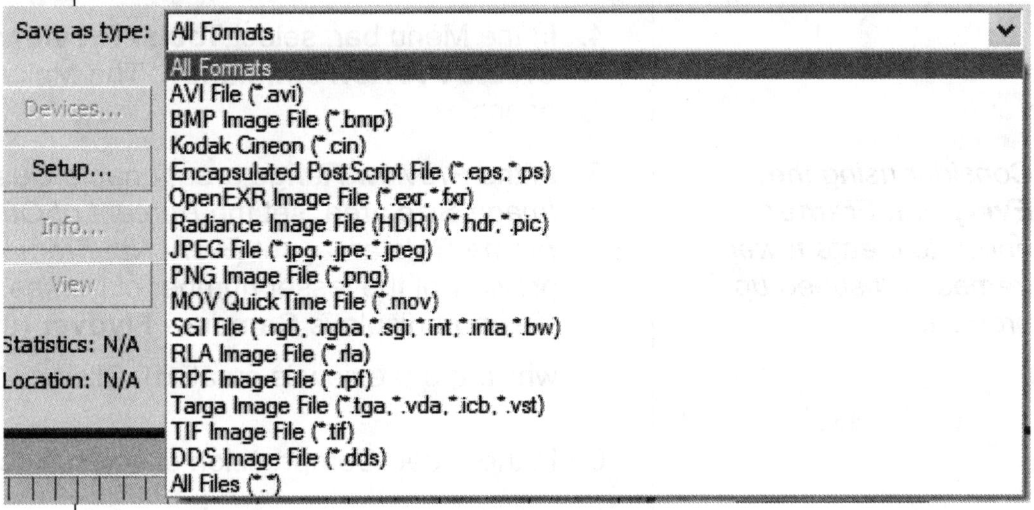

Figure 12–39

Practice 12d Creating Animation Output

Learning Objectives

- Create an animation preview.
- Create single-frame file images at every 5th frame to the .PNG format.
- Assemble the individual frame images to form a movie using the RAM Player.

Estimated time for completion: 15 minutes

You must set the paths to locate the External files and Xrefs used in the practice. If you have not done this already, return to the **Introduction to Autodesk 3ds Max Design** chapter and complete Task 1 to Task 3 of the **Organizing Folders and Working with the Interface** practice. You only have to set the user paths once.

Task 1 - Create a Preview.

If a dialog box opens prompting you about a File Load: Mismatch, click OK *to accept the default values.*

1. Open **Camera_Animation_Start_Render.max** from your *Class Files* folder.
2. Make the Camera - Flyover viewport active.
3. Click (Time Configuration) to open the Time Configuration dialog box. Change the *Time Display* to **Frames**. In the *Animation* area, note that the *End Time* is set to **600** indicating that you have a 600 frame animation. Click OK. The Time Slider displays as < 0 / 600 >.
4. In the Menu bar, select **Tools>Preview - Grab Viewport> Create Preview Animation**. The Make Preview dialog box opens.

*Consider using the **Every Nth Frame** option to create fewer frames and speed up production.*

5. In the *Preview Range* area, enable **Custom Range**. In the *Image Size* area, set the *Percent of Output* to **100**. In the *Frame Rate* area, set *Every Nth Frame* to **10** to create a preview of the lesser number of frames. Note that the Render Viewport displays **Camera - Flyover** (the active viewport for which the preview is created). Click Create.
6. In the Video Compression dialog box, click OK.

The Preview enables you to access the framing and timing of your animation. You are able to check it for any unplanned glitches such as cameras traveling through objects. At this point in a real production you would always make corrections to your camera timing or position.

- It takes a few minutes to create the preview. Note that while the preview is being created, a Status Bar for completion is displayed at the bottom of the viewports, displaying the percentage completed. A small preview window is also displayed with the preview at each specified frame being created.

7. When the preview is finished, a Media Player window automatically launches, playing the preview as shown in Figure 12–40. Hover the cursor over the preview window to display the controls. You can click the **Play** and **Stop** buttons to review what has been already created. Close the Media Player window.

Figure 12–40

- The automatic opening of the Media Payer after creating the preview is controlled by the **AutoPlay Preview File** toggle option in the Preference Settings dialog box>*General* tab>*UI Display* area.

Task 2 - Create the Still Frames.

Since there is not enough time to render 600 frames in class, you can select a shorter range and set the **Every Nth Frame** option to make this manageable.

1. Click (Render Setup) to open the Render Setup dialog box (**Rendering>Render Setup**). In the *Common* tab, verify that the Common Parameters rollout is expanded. In the *Time Output* area, select **Range**. Set a *Range* of **200** to **600** and set *Every Nth Frame* to **5**, as shown in Figure 12–41. This renders every 5th frame between 200 and 600, which is a total of 81 frames of animation.

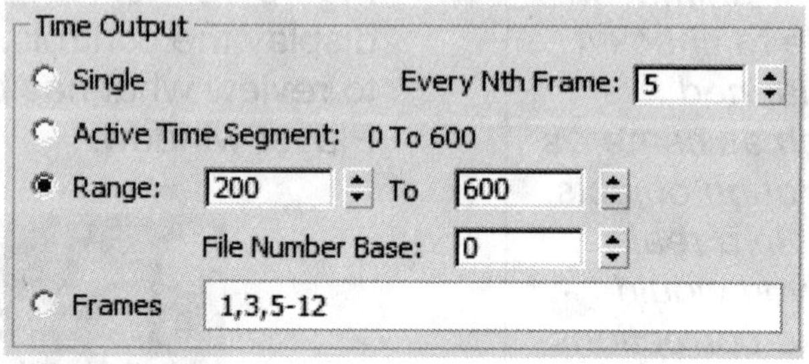

Figure 12–41

2. In the *Render Output* area, click Files....

In the Render Output File dialog box, in the Save as type drop-down list, you can select to render to a single, compressed animation file (.MOV, .AVI), or to individual frames. If you select a single-frame file format as you are doing here (such as .PNG, .JPEG, .BMP, .TIFF, etc.), then you will automatically create individual files for each frame, numbered sequentially.

3. The Render Output File dialog box opens. Locate your *renderings* folder in your *Class Files* folder. Set the *Save as type* to **PNG Image File (*.png)**, and in the *File name* enter the name **Animation.png**. Click Save.

4. In the PNG Configuration dialog box, select **RGB 24 bit** and leave **Alpha channel** enabled, as shown in Figure 12–42. Click OK.

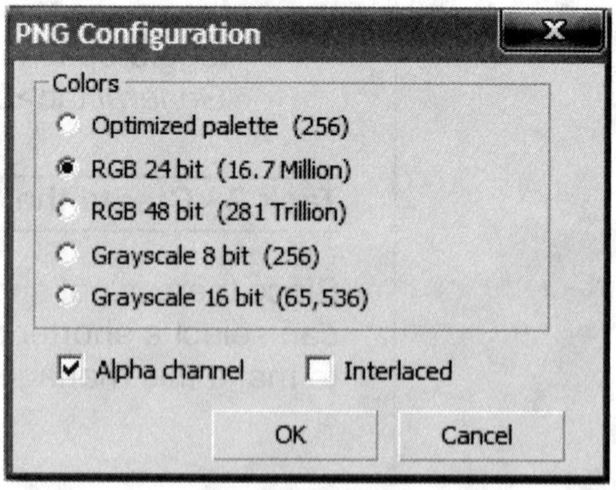

Figure 12–42

5. In the Render Setup dialog box, click Render to begin creating individual renderings for each frame.

6. The Rendered Frame Window opens with each frame being rendered and the Rendering dialog box opens (as shown in Figure 12–43), displaying information about the renderings, number of files to be rendered, estimate of the remaining rendering time, render settings, etc.

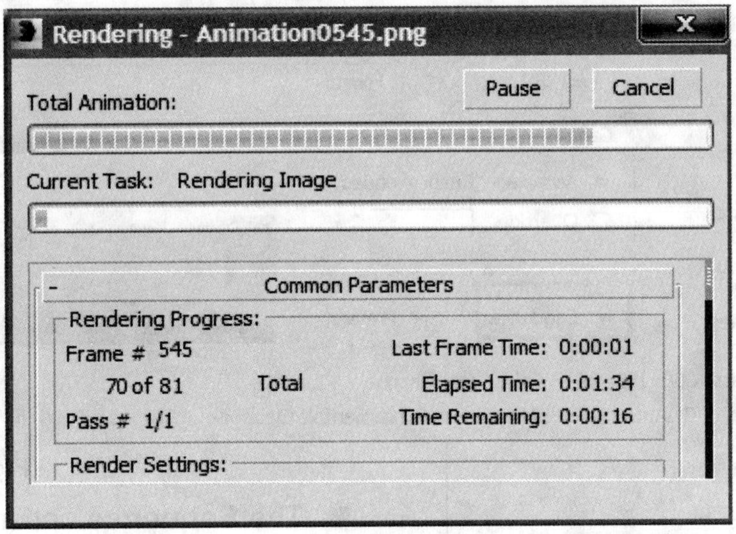

Figure 12–43

7. It might take some time to complete the 81 frames of the animation, so you can stop the process with some frames completed or let it continue until all of the frames have completed if you have time. Close the Rendered Frame Window and Render Setup dialog box.

Task 3 - Assemble the Final Animation.

1. In the Menu bar, select **Rendering>Compare Media in RAM Player** to open the RAM player. The RAM player is a utility used for comparing two images side-by-side or previewing and compiling animations. (It is called this because it loads these images into RAM.)

2. In the *Channel A* area, click  (Open Channel A), as shown in Figure 12–44.

Figure 12–44

3. In the Open File, Channel A dialog box, browse for your *renderings* folder in your *Class Files* folder. Select **Animation0200.png** and verify that **Sequence** is enabled, as shown in Figure 12–45. Click Open.

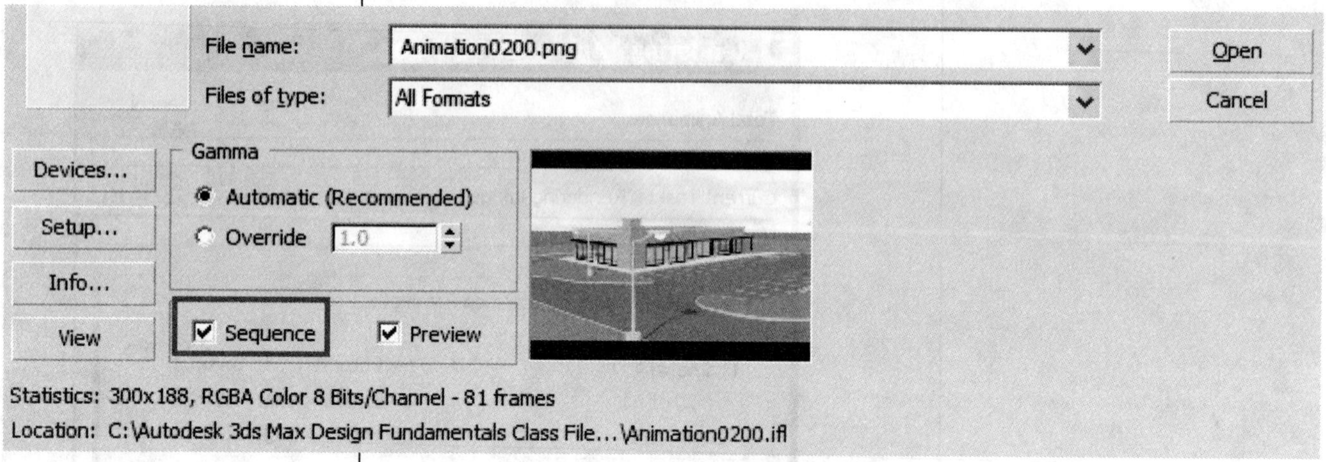

Figure 12–45

- The **Sequence** option enables the system to open all of the PNGs named **Animation*.png**.

4. The Image File List Control dialog box opens, as shown in Figure 12–46. It displays the folder where the image file list (.IFL) is being created (an ASCII list of which files were used and in which order). The dialog box also provides you with options to limit the animation to certain frames. Click OK.

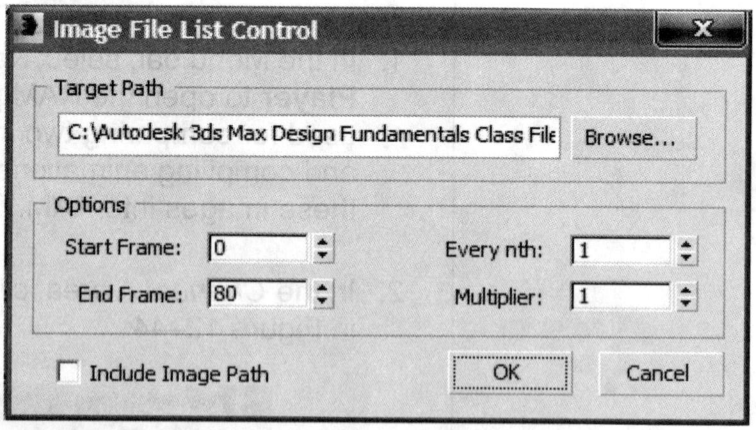

Figure 12–46

5. The RAM Player Configuration dialog box opens. It provides you with an option to change the image size or aspect ratio on import. Additionally, it enables you to limit the number of frames to use and the maximum amount of RAM you want to dedicate to this process. Click OK.

6. After the animation has loaded into the RAM player you can play back the animation at different frame rates by selecting a number in the drop-down list, as shown in Figure 12–47.

   Click to play the animation. Select different frame rates and play the animation to see the effect.

Figure 12–47

7. To save a desktop animation file, click (Save Channel A).

8. In the Save File, Channel A dialog box, browse to *renderings* folder of your *Class Files* folder. Set *Save as type* to **AVI File (*.avi)**. Save the animation as **FlybyAnimation**.

9. In the AVI File Compression Setup dialog box, for the *Compressor*, select **MJPEG Compressor**, set the *Quality* to **60**, and click OK.

10. Save your work as **MyCameraAnimation.max**.

11. Navigate to your **Flyby Animation.avi** or **.mov** file to watch the animation.

If the quality of the animation is not good, you could try other methods or qualities until you have an acceptable result.

Chapter Review Questions

1. Activating (toggling on) which option in the Animation Controls changes the **Previous**, **Play**, and **Next Frame** buttons ( ) to **Previous**, **Play**, and **Next Keyframe** buttons ( )?
   a. (Auto Key animation mode)
   b. (Set Key animation mode)
   c. (Key Mode)
   d. (Set Keys)
2. A frame rate of 30 frames per second (FPS) is best suited for which medium?
   a. NTSC
   b. PAL
   c. Film
   d. Custom
3. When animation times are changed in the *Animation* area in the Time Configuration dialog box, the existing keys automatically scale to the new time.
   a. True
   b. False
4. Which category in the *Create* panel ( ) contains **Dummy** as its Object Type?
   a. (Geometry)
   b. (Shapes)
   c. (Cameras)
   d. (Helpers)

5. If you render each still image (such as .PNG, .JPEG, etc.), which utility can you use to combine the stills into a composite animation?
   a. Media Player
   b. RAM Player
   c. Batch Render
   d. Panorama Exporter

Command Summary

Button	Command	Location
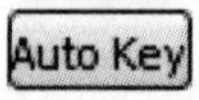	**Auto Key animation mode**	■ **Animation Controls Toolbar**
	**Cameras**	■ **Command Panel:** *Create* panel ■ **Create:** Cameras
	**Default In/Out Tangents for New Keys**	■ **Animation Controls Toolbar**
	**Go to Start**	■ **Animation Controls Toolbar**
	**Go to End**	■ **Animation Controls Toolbar**
	**Helpers**	■ **Command Panel:** *Create* panel
	**Key Mode**	■ **Animation Controls Toolbar**
	**Mini Curve Editor**	■ **Track bar**
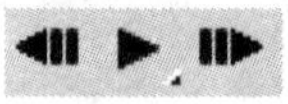	**Previous, Play, Next Frame**	■ **Animation Controls Toolbar**
	**Progressive Display**	■ **Status Bar**
	**Render Setup**	■ **Main Toolbar** ■ **Rendering:** Render Setup
	**Select and Link**	■ **Main Toolbar**
	**Set Keys**	■ **Animation Controls Toolbar**
	**Set Key animation mode**	■ **Animation Controls Toolbar**
	**Time Configuration**	■ **Animation Controls Toolbar**

Appendix A

Optional Topics

This appendix contains the following topics:

- ✓Getting Help with Autodesk 3ds Max Design
- ✓Compact Material Editor
- ✓Architectural Materials
- ✓Object Substitution
- ✓Lighting Analysis
- ✓Creating Hierarchies
- ✓Customizing the User Interface

Enhanced in 2014

A.1 Getting Help with Autodesk 3ds Max Design

Learning Objective

Understand how to access Autodesk 3ds Max Design Help and learn the different Help tools available in the software.

If this training guide was your first exposure to the Autodesk® 3ds Max® Design software, you were probably surprised by the level of detail that goes into visualization tasks. The many thousands of options and parameters available in the Autodesk 3ds Max Design software can be overwhelming at times, even to the most experienced users

Here are some places to look for more information. The Help menu contains an extensive list of help options, which are organized as submenus so that finding information is easy. Some of the available help options are as follows:

1. The **Autodesk 3ds Max Design Help** is robust, well illustrated, and logically laid out. It is often the fastest way to find what an option or parameter controls and how to use it. This help is in the form of HTML files at autodesk.com website. There are a variety of ways to access this help. In the InfoCenter, click (?) or expand and select **Autodesk 3ds Max Design Help**. You can also press <F1> or select **Help>Autodesk 3ds Max Help**.

2. The **Autodesk 3ds Max Design Tutorials** (select **Help> Tutorials**) offer thorough and comprehensive learning materials to get you started with almost all of the features in the Autodesk 3ds Max Design software. The tutorials are in the HTML format at autodesk.com website. You can download the Tutorials and the files required for the tutorials from http://www.autodesk.com/3dsmaxdesign-tutorials-scene-files-2014. Install the files on your local hard drive for use as you are completing the tutorials. The Design version of the software has tutorials geared for architectural visualization; the classic version of the software has tutorials geared for entertainment.

3. **3ds Max Communities:** Select **Help>3ds Max Communities>AREA Product Community** and **AREA Discussion Forums** and to connect to http://area.autodesk.com/, a community URL. It provides a single location for users to closely interact. It contains Autodesk 3ds Max and 3ds Max Design forums, as well as Mudbox, Motionbuilder, FBX, Maya, and forums for other entertainment products. The Autodesk 3ds Max Design forums are famous for the strength of the user community support.
4. **3ds Max Services and Support**: Select **Help>3ds Max Services and Support>SupportCenter** to connect to the support site. It has many frequently updated technical support articles available. If you have a question/problem there is a good chance someone else has as well, and Autodesk might have a document describing how to fix the problem or get around it. Autodesk Subscription customers also have access to email support directly from Autodesk. Speak to your organization's Autodesk coordinator or reseller for more information. You can also connect with other Autodesk 3ds Max users and share information using the Autodesk 3ds Max Design Facebook page.
5. **3ds Max Resources and Tools:** A collection of tools can be accessed by selecting **Help>3ds Max Resources and Tools**, as shown in Figure A–1. This provides access to White Papers, the downloadable Vegetation Library, a Keyboard Shortcut Map that opens a webpage displaying the keyboard shortcuts in an animation, etc.

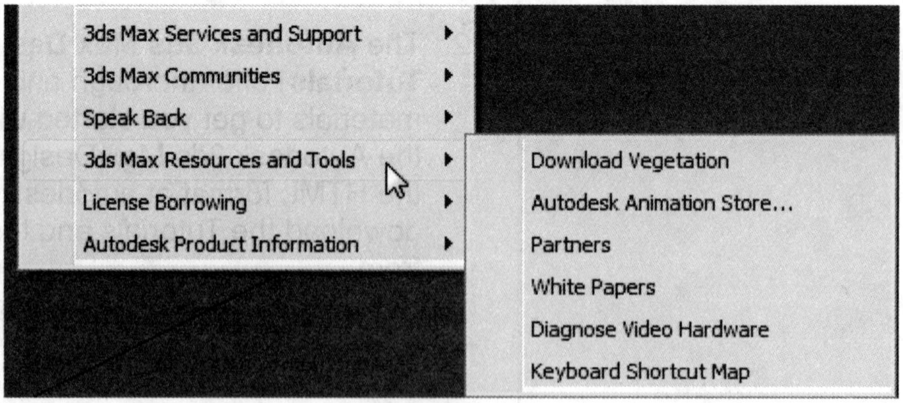

Figure A–1

6. **Feedback:** The Autodesk 3ds Max Design software provides various **Speak Back** options, as shown in Figure A–2. Selecting an option connects you to web pages for reporting a bug in the software or making a request for small enhancements and new features.

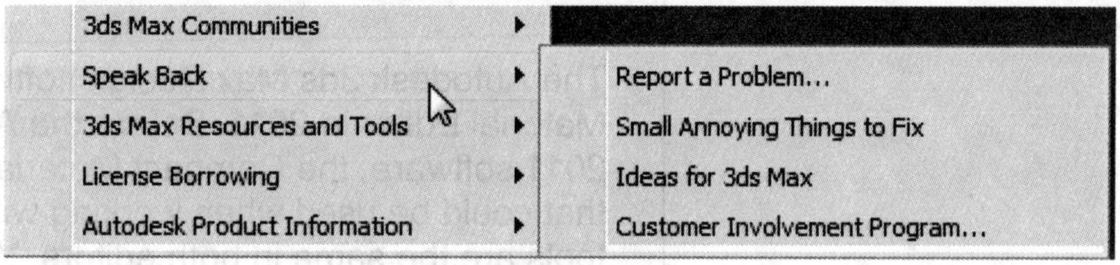

Figure A–2

7. **Other web communities:** There is a staggering amount of information available on the internet for the Autodesk 3ds Max Design software. Simple keyword searches can quickly find other sites that provide tutorials and helpful tips.

A.2 Compact Material Editor

Learning Objective

Understand how to use the Compact Material Editor.

The Autodesk 3ds Max Design software introduced the Slate Material Editor in 2011. Before the Autodesk 3ds Max Design 2011 software, the Compact Material Editor was the only editor that could be used when working with materials. Many of the tools are the same in both editors. You can use the Slate Material Editor when you need to design and build materials. It graphically displays all of the components that you want to include in the material and enables you to easily move, position, and modify them within the parent material. You can use the Compact Material Editor when the materials have already been created and you just need to apply them.

Compact Material Editor

The Compact Material Editor permits the creation of new maps and materials, as well as the scene assignment and adjustment of their many properties.

- The Compact Material Editor can be opened by clicking (Compact Material Editor) in the Main toolbar (Material Editor flyout), or by selecting **Rendering>Material Editor>Compact Material Editor**.
- It is possible to have a material in the scene that has not been loaded into the editor. One way to add a scene material to the editor is to use (Get Material), which opens the Material/Map Browser, scroll down to the Scene Material category and double-click on the scene material. You can also use (Pick Material from Object) in the Material Editor and select the object in the viewport.
- Additional options can be accessed in the Material Editor using the pull-down menus at the top of the dialog box and using the buttons. One useful option is **Utilities>Condense Material Editor Slots**. It moves all of the materials in use to the top of the editor.
- **Options>Options...** in the Material Editor dialog box offers controls that can help speed up performance when several large or complex materials are present in the editor.

The Material Sample Slots preview the maps and materials currently available for editing.

- A total of 6, 15, or 24 individual maps and materials can be displayed and adjusted in the editor at one time. The number to be displayed is set by right-clicking on a sample slot and selecting **3x2**, **5x3**, or **6x4**.
- Although you can view only 24 maps or materials, there is no limit to how many you can be present in a scene or in a library.
- A material shown in a sample slot is previewed as applied to a 3D object. A map previewed in a sample slot is shown as a flat 2D rectangle.

Right-click Menu Options

- Materials can be copied from one slot to another by dragging and dropping them within the editor as long as the **Drag/Copy** option is selected in the right-click menu, as shown in Figure A–3.

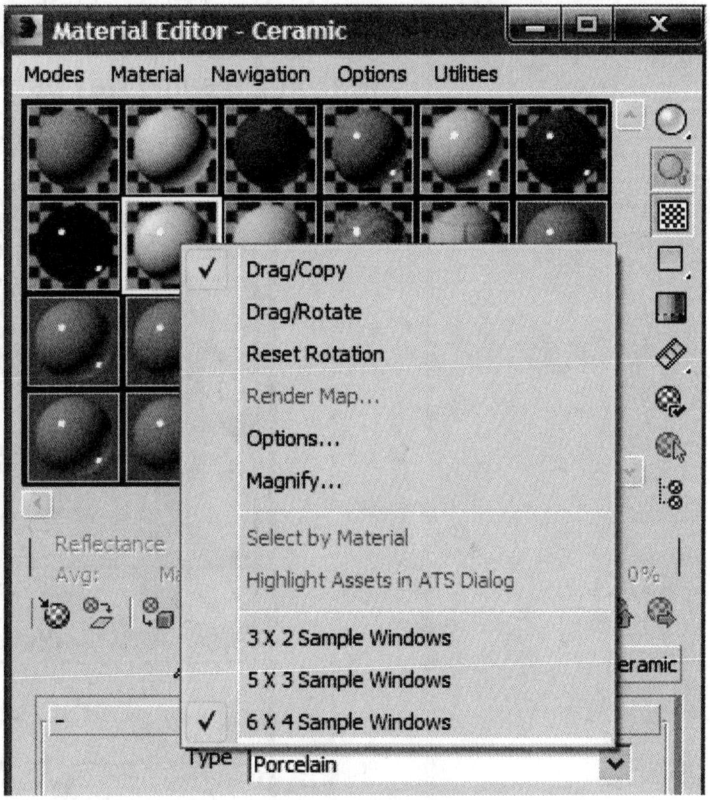

Figure A–3

- Material samples can be rotated in place by selecting **Drag/Rotate** in the right-click menu on a sample slot. They can be returned to the default position with **Reset Rotation**.
- **Render Map** is used to create a bitmap from a procedural texture.
- Selecting **Options** launches the Material Editor Options dialog box that controls the lighting in the sample slots, and additional items.
- Selecting **Magnify...** (or double-clicking on a sample slot) opens the selected material in a floating magnification window that can also be resized for a closer look.
- **Select by Material** opens the Select Object dialog box with all of the objects selected that share a material.
- **Highlight Assets in ATS Dialog** enables you to quickly see the selected material in the Asset Tracking dialog box.

*The sample material should contain a scene material for the **Select by Material** option to be available. The **Highlight Assets in ATS Dialog** is available if the material contains a map.*

Material Editor Toolbar

The Material Editor toolbar is located at the bottom and to the right of the sample slots, as shown in Figure A–4. These tools work in the same way as the tools present in the Slate Material Editor.

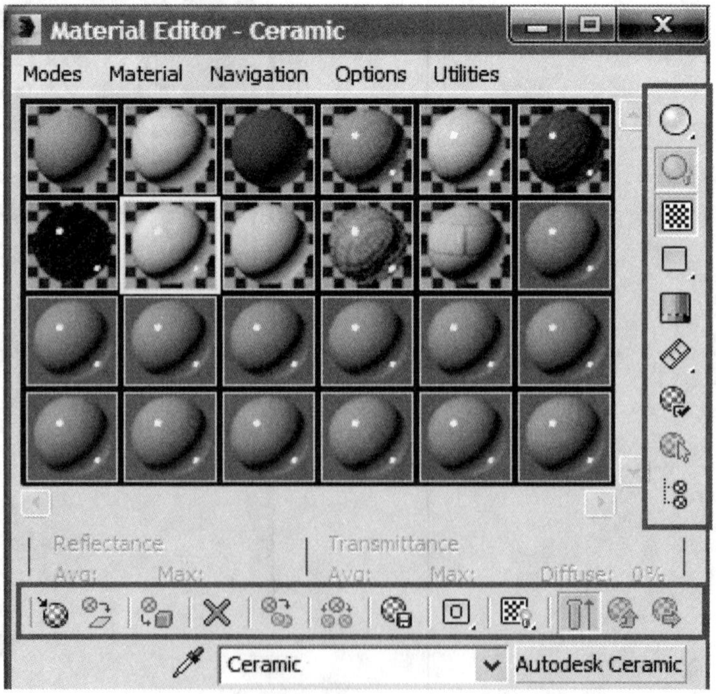

Figure A–4

Material/Map Browser

*The Material/Map Browser is embedded in the Slate Material Editor. You can also open the Material/Map Browser independently by selecting **Rendering> Material/Map Browser** in the Menu bar.*

- The Material/Map Browser can be accessed through the Compact Material Editor by clicking  (Get Material). Once you have located a required material in the browser, drag it from the browser to a scene object or to a sample slot in the Material Editor.
- Previews of the materials can be shown in a list or as buttons. To change the display, right-click on the category's heading and select **Display Group (and Subgroups) As**, as shown in Figure A–5. The available display options enable you to view the materials as small, medium, or large icons, as icons and text, or as just text.

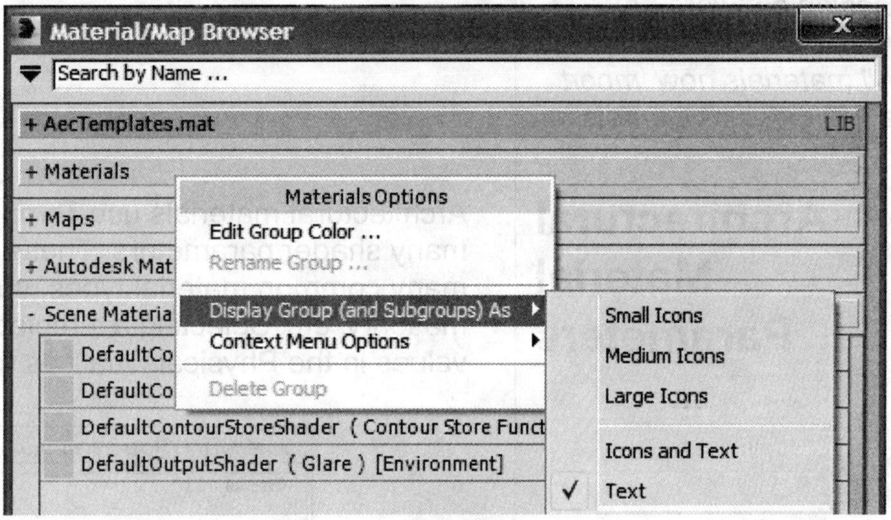

Figure A–5

- The materials listed in the browser are dependent on the type of renderer you are currently using. If you want to display all of the materials independent of the renderer, select **Show Incompatible** option in the Material/Map Browser drop-down list (click ▼ to open the options menu).

A.3 Architectural Materials

Learning Objective

- Work with Architectural materials.

Before 2011, materials assigned in legacy AutoCAD®, Autodesk® Revit®, and Autodesk® Inventor® software, all translated into the Autodesk 3ds Max Design software as Architectural materials. All materials now import as Autodesk Materials.

Architectural materials offer a simplified interface over Standard materials because they have limited control (directly selecting a shader, some specular parameters, etc.), they might best be used for visualizations where you do not need the finest level of control over shader parameters. Architectural materials offer additional, built-in controls for translucency, refraction, and global illumination renderers.

Architectural Material Parameters

Architectural materials use Templates to assign shaders and many shader parameters. These Templates are pre-defined with many common material types, such as metals, paint, plastic, masonry, etc. Selecting a template automatically populates other values in the Physical Qualities rollout, as shown in Figure A–6.

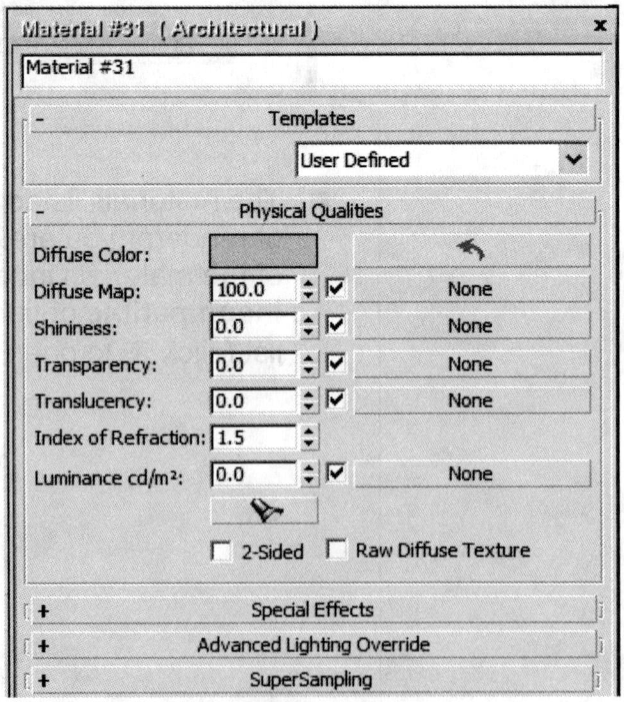

Figure A–6

- The *Diffuse Color* and the *Diffuse Map* controls are located at the top of the Physical Qualities rollout. These are identical to the controls for Standard materials.
- *Shininess* is similar to the Specular Level of Standard materials. Architectural material highlights are generated through the **Shininess** and **Index of Refraction** parameters.
- *Transparency* is the overall percentage that a material is transparent. For example, clear glass materials could be assigned transparencies between 90 and 100%.
- *Translucency* is a measure of how much light is scattered as it passes through the object.
- The *Index of Refraction* (IOR) controls refraction and reflection. Typical values include 1.0 for air (effectively no refractive distortion), 1.33 for water, 1.5-1.7 for thick glass, and 2.5 for diamond.
- *Luminance* is the amount of physically-based light the material emits. Unlike the **Self-Illumination** parameter of Standard materials, objects assigned Architectural materials can actually add light to scenes through this parameter as if they were light objects. (For example, illuminated materials are often used to represent neon tubes.)
- *Bump Maps* can be assigned in the Special Effects rollout.
- Architectural materials do not have Ambient Color controls because these materials are designed to work with Radiosity, which directly calculates ambient illumination. Mental ray will also provide the kind of global illumination previously available via the Radiosity system.

Configuring Architectural Materials for mental ray

Problems with images can frequently be traced back to material settings so it is important to ensure that certain material properties are within appropriate ranges. If not, renderings might appear overexposed, tinted, grainy, etc., and might contain distracting visual artifacts.

When light strikes a surface it is either reflected off of, absorbed by, or transmitted through the surface. **Reflectance** and **Transmittance** are derived properties that depend on other material parameters but can be overridden, as necessary. These two properties are included as additional parameters in the Architectural material. Click and hold the material title bar to display a list of additional parameters. Select **Reflectance Scale** and **Transmittance Scale** in the list, as shown on the left in Figure A–7. These are listed in the Additional Params rollout in the material's node, as shown on the right in Figure A–7. You can edit the value using the spinners or entering a value directly in its field. When an image file is used for certain map types (diffuse color, transparency, etc.) the average and maximum values reflect the color variation of the image file.

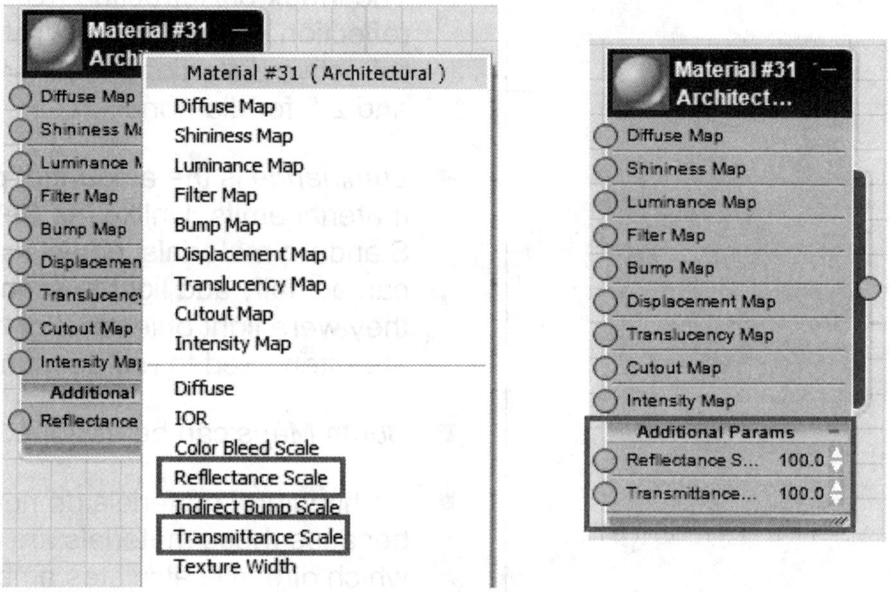

Figure A–7

Transmittance

The Transmittance property is based on the transparency parameter of Architectural materials or the inverse of the opacity value for Standard materials. This value is then adjusted by the light's filter color, translucency, and by an Architectural material's template type. (The diffuse transmittance value applies only to materials that use translucency through ray-traced materials or the translucent shader.) In most cases transmittance can be adjusted with the opacity or transparency parameter.

Reflectance

Reflectance values that are too high are a major cause of rendering problems that occur with mental ray.

- Reflectance is derived directly from the brightness of the diffuse color (specifically the **V** or **Value** parameter in the HSV color system). Therefore brighter colors reflect more light and absorb less light than darker colors, as occurs in the real world.

- Objects with bright colors (such as white walls) might default to excessively high reflectance values. In the real world bright white paint has a maximum reflectance value of 80%. Most other materials should be significantly lower.

- Materials that use image files for diffuse maps often have very high reflectance values because the camera flash or scanner light has illuminated them more brightly than they would appear in the scene.

A table of suggested material reflectances has been included from Autodesk 3ds Max Help. All scene materials should have reflectance values that fall within these ranges when using mental ray.

Typical Reflectance Values for Materials

Material	Minimum	Maximum
Ceramic	20%	70%
Fabric	20%	70%
Masonry	20%	50%
Metal	30%	90%
Paint	30%	80%
Paper	30%	70%
Plastic	20%	80%
Stone	20%	70%
Wood	20%	50%

Architectural materials indicate when a reflectance value is out-of-range by colorizing the value in the Material Editor (based on the selected material template). Values that are too low are shown in blue and those that are too high are shown in red. Reflectance values that are out-of-range can be adjusted in a number of ways:

- When using a simple diffuse color (no diffuse image map) lower the overall value (V) of the color. If this is not appropriate for your design you might need to follow one of the other suggestions listed below.

- The reflectance of Architectural materials can be reduced by entering a lower value for the *Reflectance Scale* in the Advanced Lighting Override rollout, as shown in Figure A–8. For example, 50 (50%) would cut the default reflectance in half. (Standard materials do not have this rollout.)

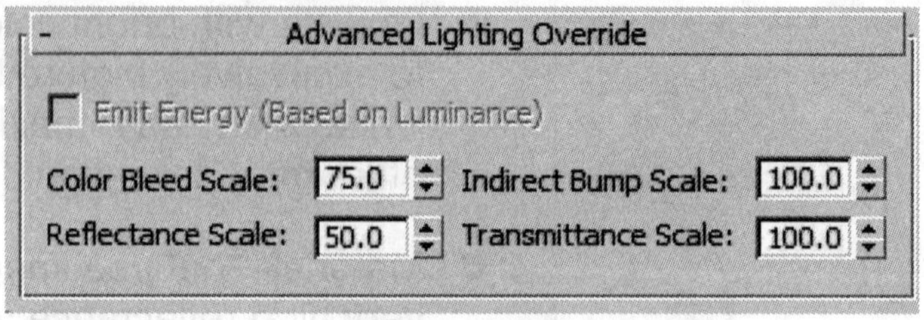

Figure A–8

- Another method to lower reflectance, when using a diffuse color map with standard materials, is to assign the diffuse color to black and enter a value less than 100% for the diffuse color map. A value such as 95%, as shown in Figure A–9, would reduce the brightness of the map by approximately 5%.

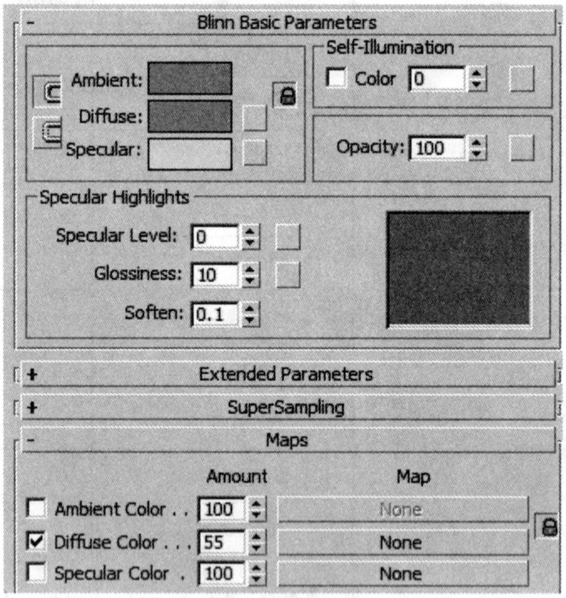

Figure A–9

> **Hint: Converting Materials**
>
> A conversion script has been developed by Zap Anderson, creator of many mental ray material types. It converts Architectural Materials to Arch & Design materials. You can also manually convert the materials by rebuilding them individually. (http://mentalraytips.blogspot.com).

A.4 Object Substitution

Learning Objective

Replace objects in a scene with AutoCAD blocks or other Autodesk 3ds Max Design objects using the Substitute modifier.

Linked or imported AutoCAD Blocks can be automatically replaced with 3D objects using the **Substitute** modifier.

- The Objects to be replaced (such as linked AutoCAD blocks) should be located with the correct 3D coordinates (including elevation) and rotation for the replacing object.
- The substituting object needs to be one object. For example, the light pole could be used if it was collapsed to a single mesh object. (To do so, right-click on the base object in the Modifier Stack and select **Convert to Editable Poly or Mesh**. Then use the object's Attach in the Command Panel to join the other parts to the mesh. Materials and mapping can be preserved during this operation).
- The substitute object can be present in the same scene as the object to be replaced or it can be XRefed in from another scene.
- Although this is commonly used for AutoCAD blocks, other Autodesk 3ds Max Design objects can be substituted as well with this modifier.

Practice A1 Substituting the Parking Lot Light Poles

Learning Objective

- Replace 2D symbol based objects with 3D photorealistic object blocks using the **Substitute** modifier.

Estimated time for completion: 10 minutes

In this practice you will substitute completed 3D light pole objects for 2D blocks in a scene.

You must set the paths to locate the External files and Xrefs used in the practice. If you have not done this already, return to the **Introduction to Autodesk 3ds Max Design** chapter and complete Task 1 to Task 3 of the **Organizing Folders and Working with the Interface** practice. You only have to set the user paths once.

If a dialog box opens prompting you about a File Load: Mismatch, click OK *to accept the default values.*

1. Open **Substitution_Start.max** from your *Class Files* folder.
2. Switch the viewport to Wireframe shading by pressing <F3>.
3. Zoom out on the area of the parking lot to display the flat, circular, and square symbols joined by a line (green), as shown in Figure A–10. These objects in the parking area are 2D light pole blocks. The parking lot surface has been hidden so that you can see the lamp symbols.

Figure A–10

4. In the Main toolbar, click . In the Select From Scene dialog box, click (Display None) and click (Display Shapes). Select only one of **Layer:LIGHTPOLE_SINGLE**, as shown in Figure A–11, and click OK.

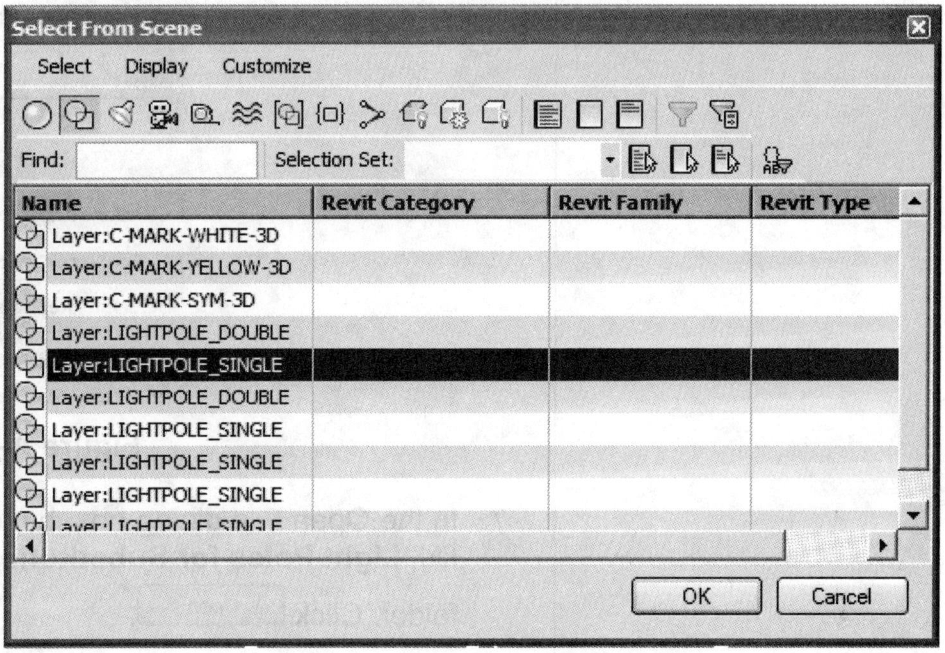

Figure A–11

5. With the layer selected, in the Command Panel, select the *Modify* panel ( ) and select **Substitute** in the Modifier List. Only one 2D object is required to be selected because AutoCAD blocks link in as instances of each other, as indicated by the bold type in the Modifier Stack, as shown in Figure A–12.

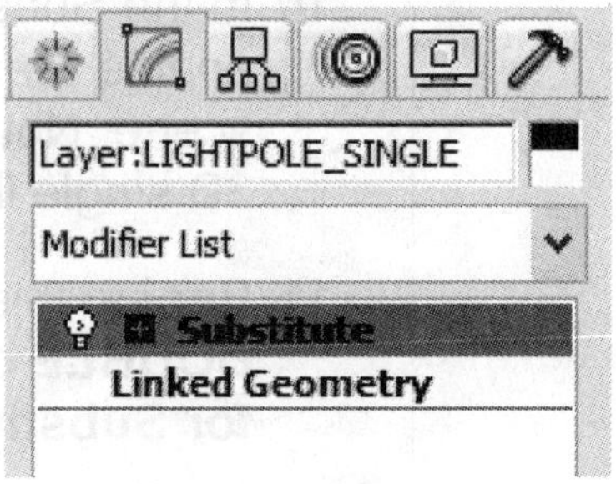

Figure A–12

6. Verify that the **Substitute** parameters match the parameters as shown in Figure A–13 (default) and click 

.

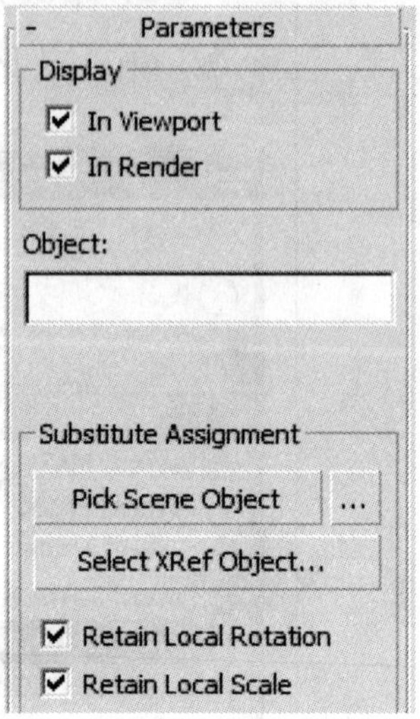

Figure A–13

7. In the Open File dialog box, browse and select the source file, **Light Poles for Substitution.max** from your *Class Files* folder. Click 

.

8. In the XRef Merge dialog box that opens, select the object named **LP_Single** and click 

.

9. A Warning message stating that an incoming material has the same name as an existing scene material is displayed. Select **Apply to All Duplicates** to keep both materials, and click 

.

10. In the Substitution Question dialog box, click 

to enable the substitute object's material to be used in this scene. Note that the 2D light pole blocks are replaced by the 3D single lightpole objects.

11. Repeat this process for one of the **Layer:LIGHTPOLE_DOUBLE** objects, substituting **LP_Double** from **Light Poles for Substitution.max**.

12. In the viewport, change to **Realistic** shading view. Both the single light poles and double light poles are displayed, as shown in Figure A–14.

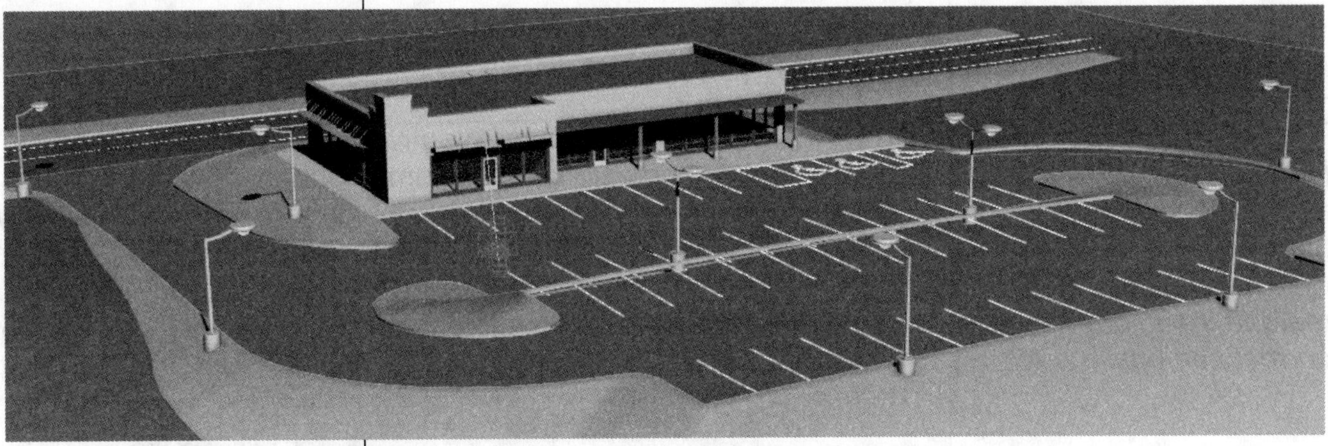

Figure A–14

- By using the **Substitute** modifier on an instanced object you have quickly taken a 2D symbol based object and replaced it with a 3D photorealistic object and it was done many times throughout the scene. This technique is a good way to save on memory when working with the files.

13. Save your work as **MyCivilBaseSubstitution.max**.

A.5 Lighting Analysis

Learning Objective

- Create a Lighting Analysis using the Lighting Analysis Assistant.

*The **NVIDIA mental ray** is required to be the active renderer for Lighting Analysis. It also requires mental ray materials with physically correct settings.*

The Autodesk 3ds Max Design software can create a lighting analysis rendering colorized by illumination or luminance values. The lighting analysis can be done using mental ray to physically correct lights and materials. Light meter objects can be placed in the scene to measure lighting. All of this is controlled using the Lighting Analysis Assistant dialog box, as shown in Figure A–15, (**Lighting Analysis>Lighting Analysis Assistant**).

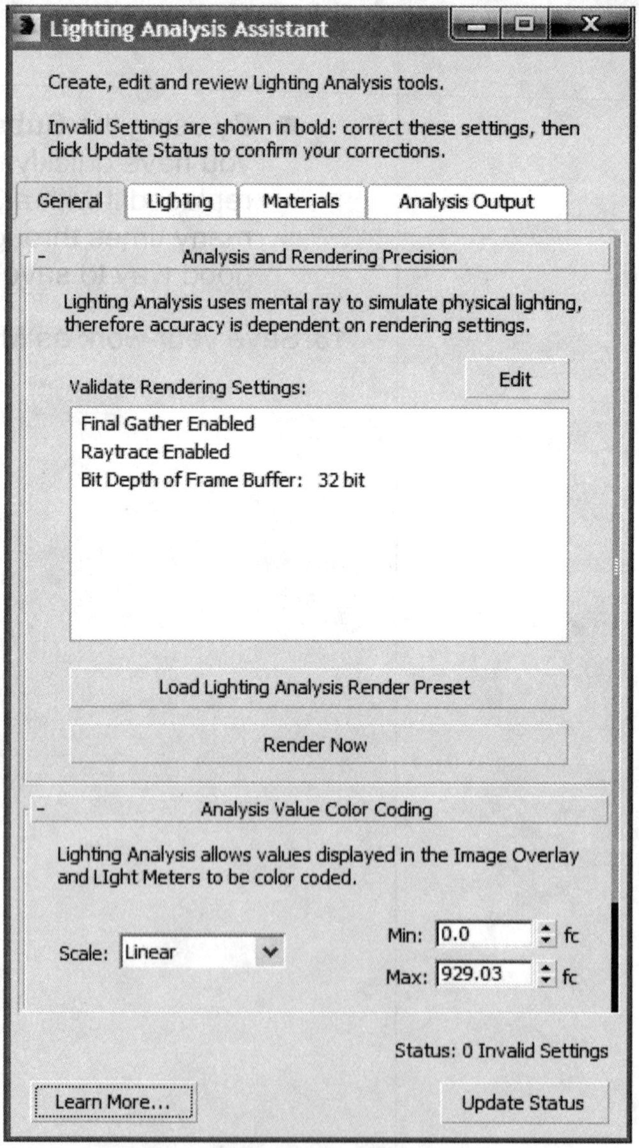

Figure A–15

There are four tabs in the Lighting Analysis Assistant dialog box: *General*, *Lighting*, *Materials*, and *Analysis Output*.

General Tab

The *General* tab validates that the rendering settings are correct. You must have Final Gather and Raytrace enabled and Bit Depth must be set to 32 bit. If any of these settings are incorrect they are flagged in the Analysis and Rendering Precision rollout. If they are flagged you must correct them and then click

to recalculate the validation/approval.

The Analysis Value Color Coding rollout enables you to adjust the color values displayed in the viewport, as shown in Figure A–16. By lowering the maximum value you can quickly find a pleasing range of colors for your output.

Figure A–16

Lighting Tab

In the *Lighting* tab, as shown in Figure A–17, you can create mr Daylight System if one does not exist. You also have quick access to the settings for the sun/sky and daylight positions. If you are doing artificial light calculations (interiors) you can also create photometric lights from here. This dialog box checks for lights that have invalid settings and enables you to select and correct them.

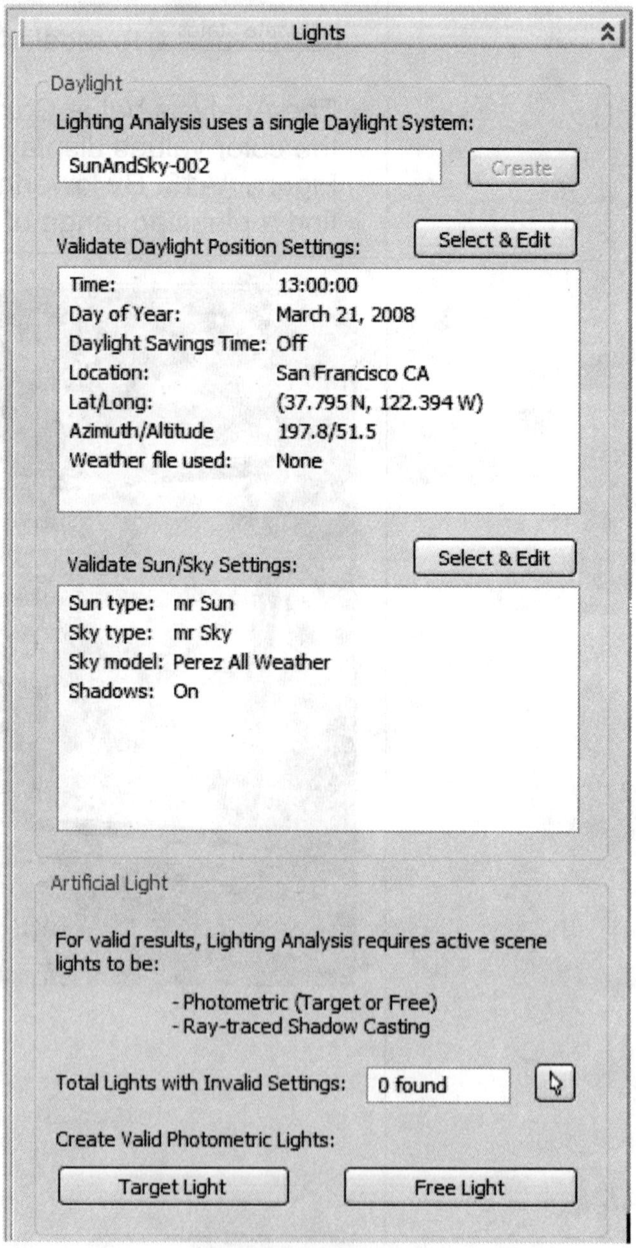

Figure A–17

Materials Tab

The *Materials* tab (shown in Figure A–18), validates the Materials in the scene.

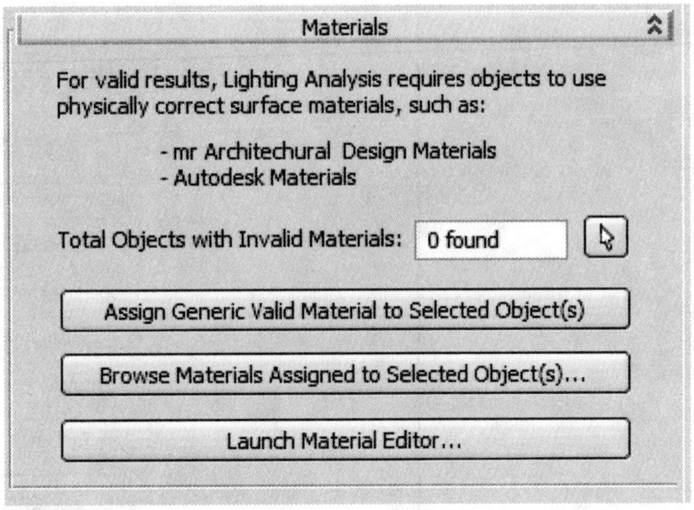

Figure A–18

The Lighting calculations require mr Arch & Design materials or Autodesk materials. If you have a scene that does not have the correct materials, they are flagged in the *Total Objects with Invalid Materials* field. Click the select arrow to select these objects in the viewport. You can then assign new materials to them yourself using the Material Editor or Material/Map Browser.

You can use Assign Generic Valid Material to Selected Object(s) if you do not care about the specific qualities of the material.

Hint: Adding Materials

Do not use Assign Generic Valid Material to Selected Object(s) on all of the selected objects in an interior. Doing so removes the glass from the windows and skylights. It is a better practice to add your own materials.

Analysis Output Tab

The *Analysis Output* tab (shown in Figure A–19), enables you create light meter objects.

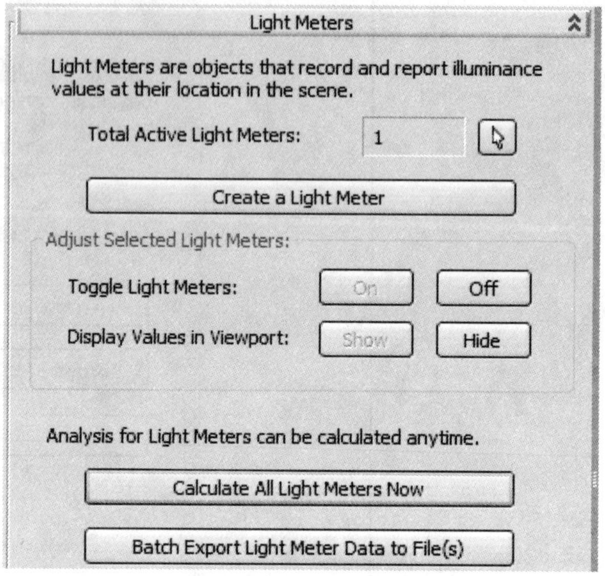

Figure A–19

To create a Light Meter object, click 

and drag a window around the objects in the viewport, as shown in Figure A–20. You can create light meters using  (Helpers) in the Command Panel in the *Create* panel, which is a shortcut to the function. Alternatively, you can select **Lighting Analysis>Create>Light Meter**. You can use **AutoGrid** to create light meters over windows or other surfaces. Once the light meter is created, ensure that it is selected and go to the *Modify* panel and adjust the parameters to create the density of the value output.

Figure A–20

You can calculate all of the Light Meters at once or batch export the light meter data to files. These files can be used for LEED 8.1 Certification for energy compliance of government standards.

You can see the values of the light meters in the viewport or you can add them to your rendering as an Image Overlay. In the Image Overlay rollout, click **Create Image Overlay Render Effect**, to create an Image Overlay. All of the Image Overlay settings and the output settings are listed, as shown in Figure A–21.

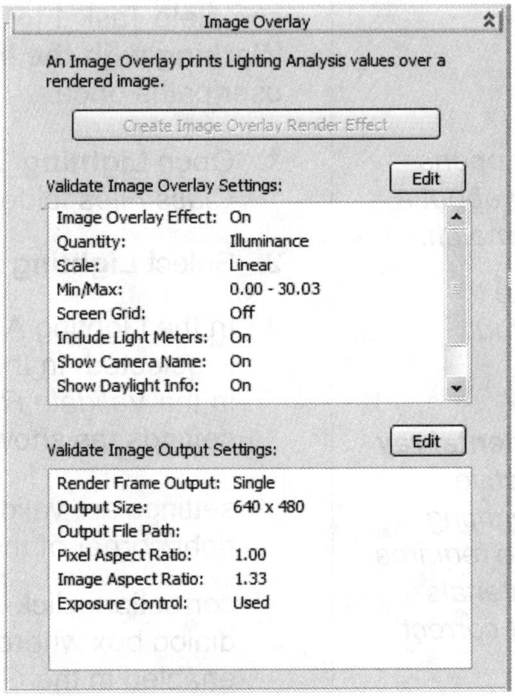

Figure A–21

The render effect that adds the printed values on top of the picture that you render, as shown in Figure A–22.

Figure A–22

Practice A2 Conduct a Lighting Analysis

Learning Objective

- Create a Lighting Analysis for a scene by creating light meter objects and then overlaying the values over the render.

Estimated time for completion: 15 minutes

You must set the paths to locate the External files and Xrefs used in the practice. If you have not done this already, return to the **Introduction to Autodesk 3ds Max Design** chapter and complete Task 1 to Task 3 of the **Organizing Folders and Working with the Interface** practice. You only have to set the user paths once.

If a dialog box opens prompting you about a File Load: Mismatch, click OK *to accept the default values.*

1. Open **Lighting_Analysis_mental_ray_start.max** from your *Class Files* folder.

2. Select **Lighting Analysis>Lighting Analysis Assistant**.

The ***NVIDIA mental ray*** *must be the active renderer for Lighting Analysis. It also requires mental ray materials with physically correct settings.*

3. In the Lighting Analysis Assistant, verify that the *General* tab is selected. In the Analysis and Rendering Precision rollout, in the *Validate Rendering Settings* area, note the rendering settings, as shown in Figure A–23. Also verify that all of the settings are valid (Displays Status: 0 Invalid Settings at the bottom right corner of the dialog box). If any of the settings need correction, click Edit, which opens the Render Setup dialog box where you can modify the settings. Final Gather is enabled in the *Global Illumination* tab, the other controls are located in the *Renderer* tab (frame buffer bit depth and enable raytrace).

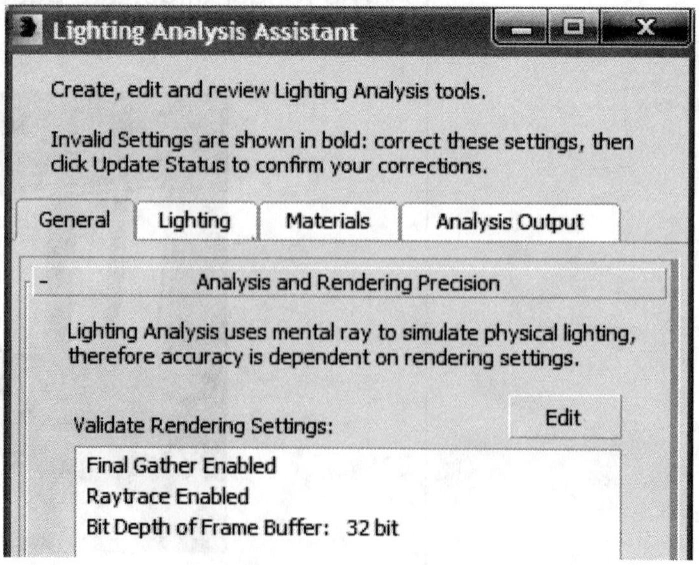

Figure A–23

Note that in the Command Panel, LightMeter *is automatically selected in*  *(Helpers).*

4. In the Lighting Analysis Assistant, select the *Analysis Output* tab. In the Light Meters rollout, click Create a Light Meter. Leave the dialog box open, but move it over the doors area in the viewport so you can work in the window.

5. In the Command Panel, toggle on **AutoGrid** at the top of the Object Type rollout.

6. In the viewport, note that the cursor displays a tripod. Hover the cursor over the lower left corner of the three large window objects and ensure that the Y-axis is pointing up vertically. Click and drag across to the diagonally opposite corner of all the three windows and release the mouse, creating a selection window., as shown in Figure A–24.

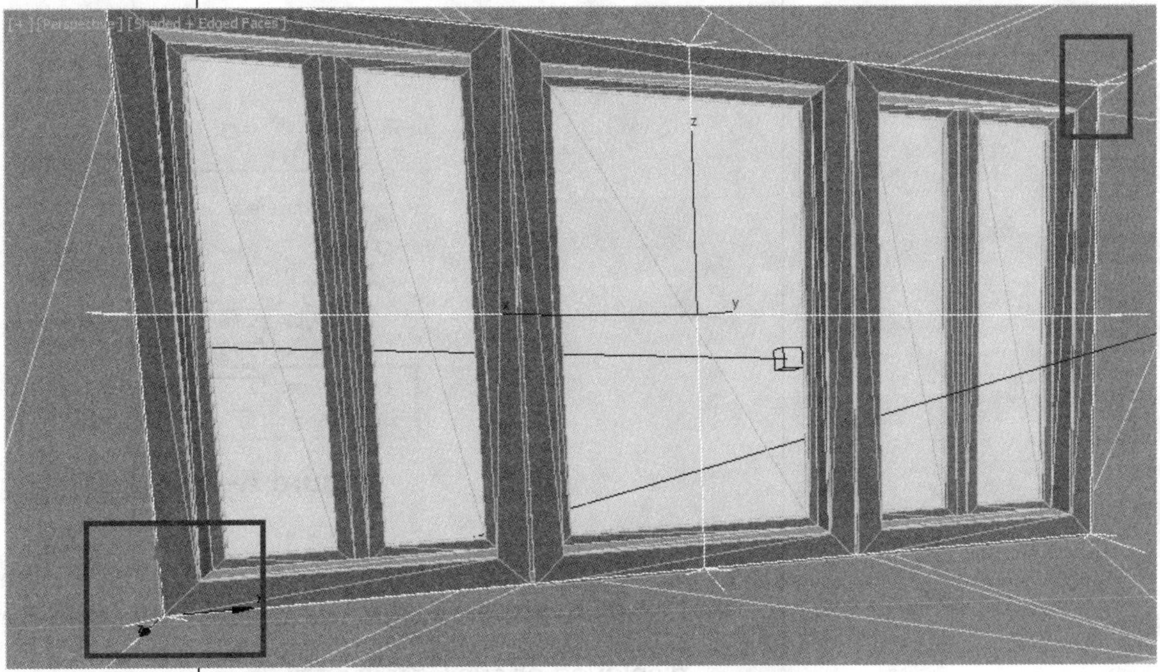

Figure A–24

7. With the selection window still selected, select the *Modify* panel (). Note that the **LightMeter Helper** is displayed in the Modifier Stack. In the Parameters rollout, set *Length Segs:* to **7** and *Width Segs:* to **10** and press <Enter>, as shown in Figure A–25. In the viewport, note that the segments are added to the helper window object. This increases the density of lighting analysis values. In the Display rollout, verify that **Show Viewport Text** is selected.

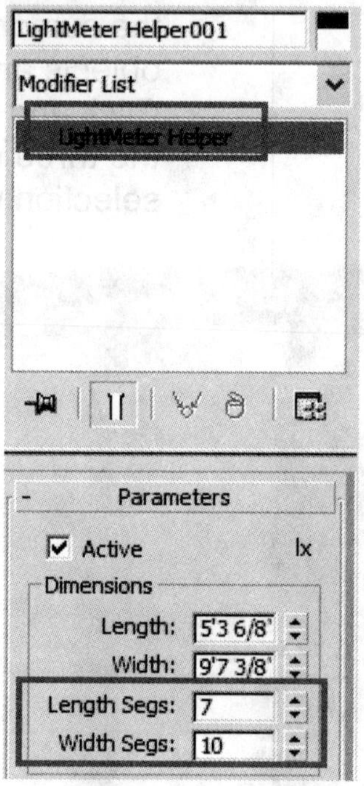

Figure A–25

8. Click  at the bottom right, as shown in Figure A–26. Verify that the **Status: 0 Invalid Settings** is still displayed above .

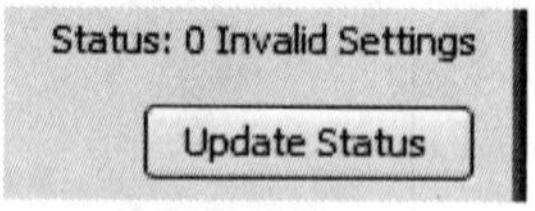

Figure A–26

9. Open the *Materials* tab and verify that **0 found** is displayed as *Total Objects with Invalid Materials*. This indicates that nothing needs to be corrected. If you did have any non-Physical materials assigned, an error would display. You can automatically assign a generic valid material to the selected objects in the scene.

- If you click **Assign Generic Valid Material to Selected Object(s)** you lose transparency in the window glass. Reassign an Arch & Design thin glass to fix this problem.

10. Select the *Analysis Output* tab, in the Light Meters rollout, click **Calculate All Light Meters Now**. A progress bar is displayed in the Status Bar in the viewport. Once the calculations are complete, the light meter values are displayed in the viewport.

The full rollout might not be displayed. Use the ***Hand*** *icon to drag it up.*

11. Select the *General* tab and expand the Analysis Value Color Coding rollout. Change the value for the *Max* spinner, as shown on right in Figure A–27, and you should see the colors change in the viewport on the light meter. Set a max value (approximately 45 fc) where the maximum portion displays as green, as shown on left in Figure A–27. Green indicates a good lighting level, red indicates overlit areas, and blue indicates underlit areas.

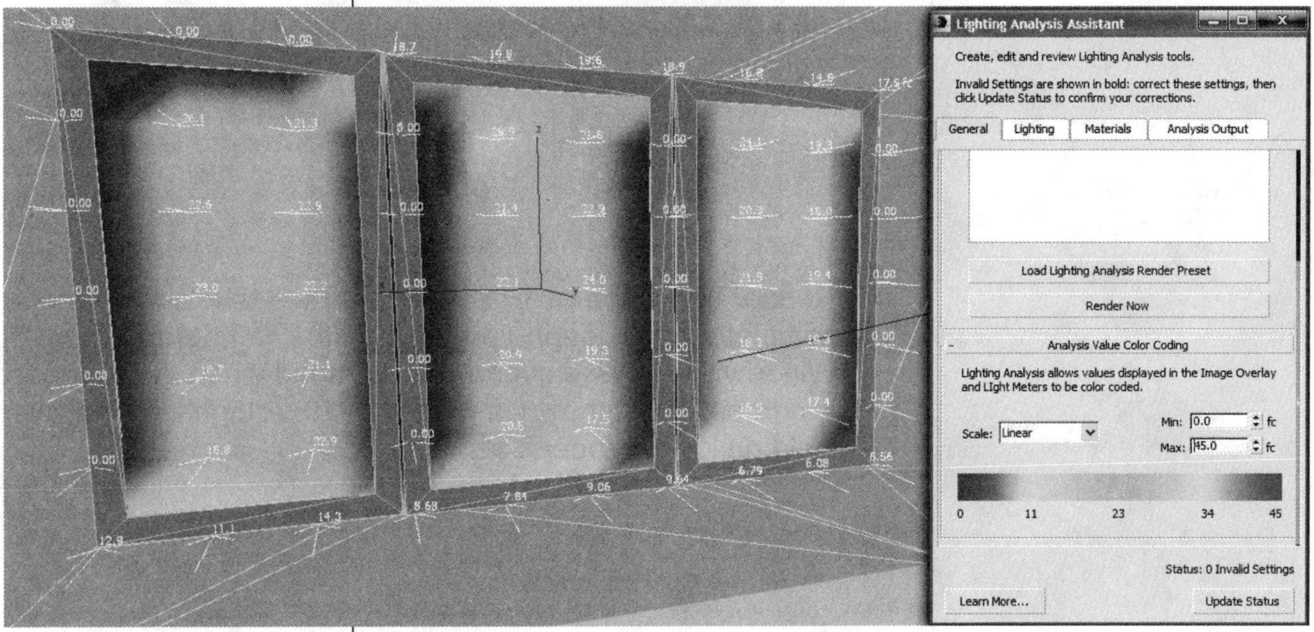

Figure A–27

12. If the status lists any invalid settings, click **Update Status** at the bottom right.

13. You can add these values to the renderer output as an overlay. Select the *Analysis Output* tab, in the Image Overlay rollout, next to *Validate Image Overlay Settings,* click **Edit**.

14. It opens the Environment and Effects dialog box in the *Effects* tab. In the Effects rollout, click Add... . In the Add Effect dialog box, select **Lighting Analysis Image Overlay** to add the effect to the overlay and click OK . In the *Parameters* area, note the Display Options settings. The first two options enable you to display the numbers over the whole image or only over the light meter object. Set the options as shown in Figure A–28.

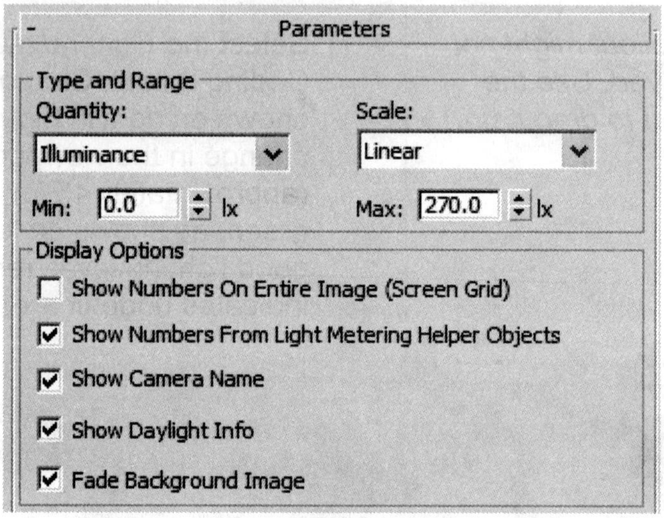

Figure A–28

15. Render the scene by clicking . It will take some time to complete the rendering process. In the Rendered Frame Window, the Image overlay is displayed when the rendering is complete, as shown in Figure A–29. A Lighting Analysis Data dialog box opens as well.

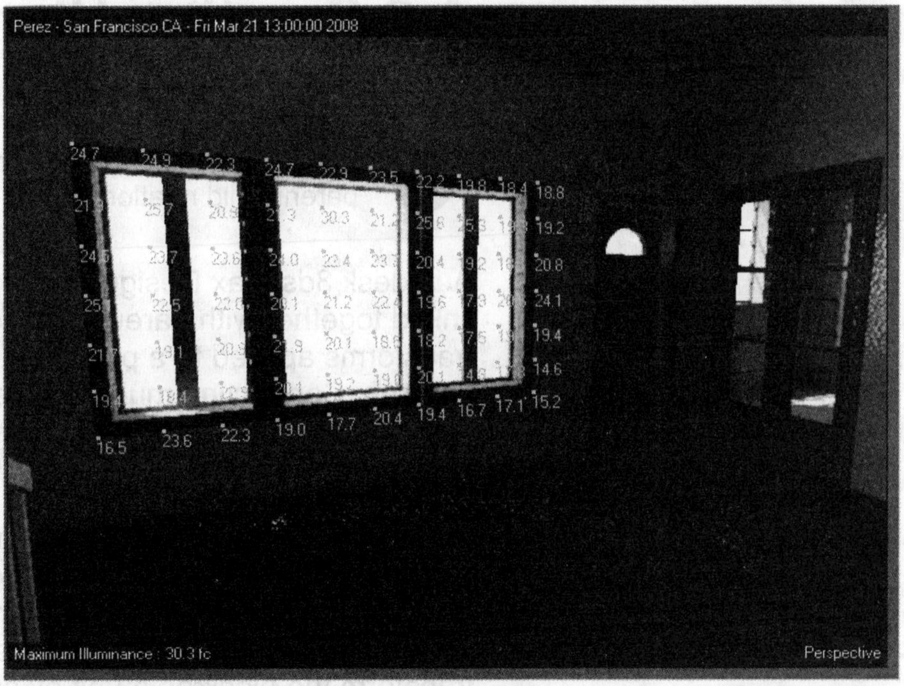

Figure A–29

16. Close the Lighting Analysis Data dialog box. In the Rendered Frame Window, save the rendered image as **LightingAnalysis.jpg**.

17. Save the scene file as **MyLightingAnalysis.max**.

A.6 Creating Hierarchies

Learning Objective

- Create hierarchies by collecting objects together with parent/child relationship.

Autodesk 3ds Max Design Hierarchies are collections of objects linked together with parent/child relationships. When used, transforms applied to a parent are automatically passed to its children. Connecting multiple objects in a hierarchical chain can enable sophisticated animations such as the motion of jointed robotic arms.

In the case of the hierarchy file link options, incoming AutoCAD blocks are brought in as multiple objects so that they can maintain multiple material assignments from AutoCAD. They display together with a Block/Style Parent object, enabling you to transform the block as a unit by selecting the parent. The parent object itself does not have any geometry and does not render. Most modifiers (such as Substitute) must be applied to the objects in the hierarchy rather than the parent.

Practice A3 Create Hierarchies

Learning Objective

- Create hierarchical relationships between objects.

Estimated time for completion: 10 minutes

In many animations you will want to create hierarchical relationships so that objects move together when moved. Once you have linkages, you can animate them using forward kinematics in which you move the parent and rotate the children.

You must set the paths to locate the External files and Xrefs used in the practice. If you have not done this already, return to the **Introduction to Autodesk 3ds Max Design** chapter and complete Task 1 to Task 3 of the **Organizing Folders and Working with the Interface** practice. You only have to set the user paths once.

If a dialog box opens prompting you about a File Load: Mismatch, click OK to accept the default values.

1. Open **Lamp Start Linking.max**. This is a model of a desk lamp, as shown in Figure A–30.

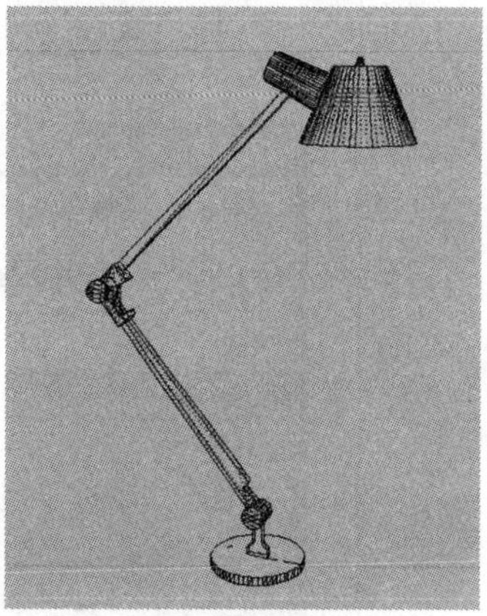

Figure A–30

2. Press <H> to open the Select From Scene dialog box. Click (Display None) and click . In the dialog box, in the Menu bar, select **Display>Display Children**. There are six geometry objects in the scene and the names are not indented, indicating that there are no linkages. Cancel the selection process by closing the dialog box.

3. In the Main toolbar, click (Select and Move) and move the Base object at the bottom of the lamp. Note that it moves by itself and the other objects are unaffected. Undo the move and clear the selection.

4. In the Main toolbar, click (Select and Link). Starting at the top, select each object and drag a dotted line to its parent. You will repeat the process five times as follows:
   - Select the **Lampshade** and link it to the **Upper Arm - Lamp**.
   - Select the **Upper Arm - Lamp** and link it to the **Lower Arm**.
   - Select the **Lower Arm** and link it to the **Lower Hub**.
   - Select the **Lower Hub** and link it to the **Stand**.
   - Select the **Stand** and link it to the **Base**.

5. In the Main toolbar, click (Select Object) to end the linking process.

6. Press <H> to open the Select From Scene dialog box. Note that only **Base** is visible. click next to Base to expand and display its dependents. Expand all of the children to display the dependencies, as shown in Figure A–31. Click Cancel.

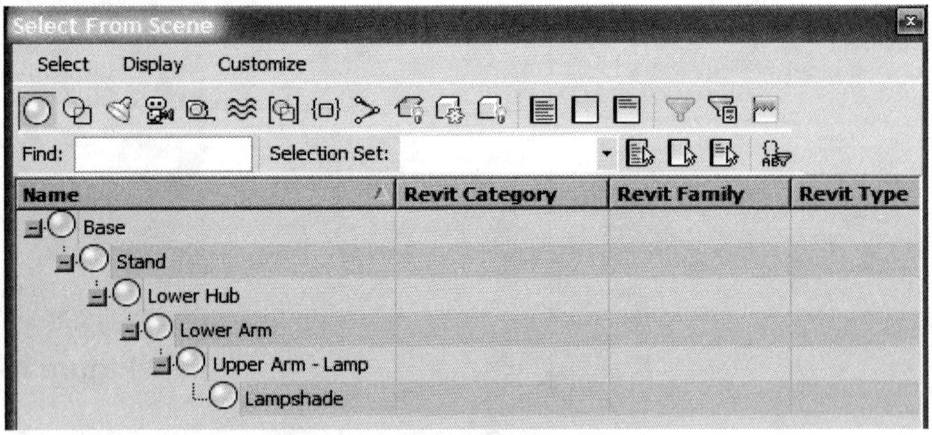

Figure A–31

7. Click (Select and Move) and move the Base. The entire lamp moves with it. The base is the parent object and other objects are children and descendants. Undo the move.

8. Click (Select and Rotate). Rotate the Lower Arm and note that the Upper Arm - Lamp and Lampshade, go along with the rotation. Undo the rotations.

9. Save your scene file as **MyLampStartLinking.max**.

Practice A4 — Create an Assembly Animation

Learning Objective

Create animation assembly to bring the different parts of an object together.

Estimated time for completion: 10 minutes

It is common to create an animation of a design that builds up over time. Here are some quick steps for creating an animation of the assembly of a lamp.

You must set the paths to locate the External files and Xrefs used in the practice. If you have not done this already, return to the **Introduction to Autodesk 3ds Max Design** chapter and complete Task 1 to Task 3 of the **Organizing Folders and Working with the Interface** practice. You only have to set the user paths once.

In this kind of animation, you will add keyframes to the end of the animation and then adjust the start and end ranges for each component.

If a dialog box opens prompting you about a File Load: Mismatch, click OK *to accept the default values.*

1. Open **Lamp Start Linking.max** from your *Class Files* folder.
2. In the Animation Controls, click (Time Configuration). In the Time Configuration dialog box, in the *Animation* area, change the *End Time* to **200**, press <Enter, and click OK.
3. Press <Ctrl>+<A> to select all objects in the viewport at once.
4. In the Time Slider, right-click on 0 / 200 to open the Create Key dialog box. Clear **Rotation** and **Scale** leaving **Position** selected and set the *Destination Time* to **160**, as shown in Figure A–32, and click OK.

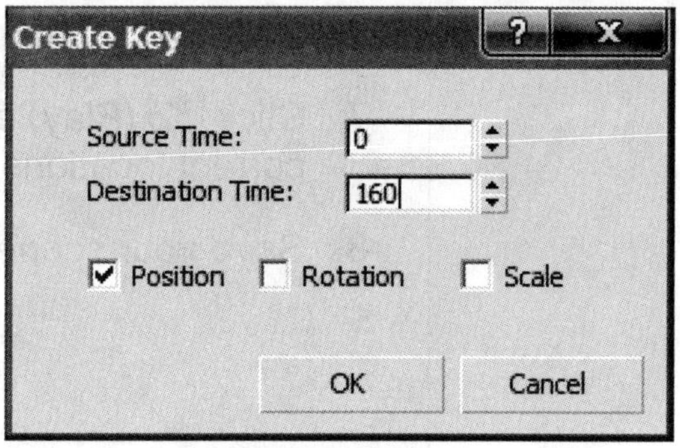

Figure A–32

- A Position key for all objects is placed at frame 160. Note that in the Track Bar, a red box is set at 160, as shown in Figure A–33.

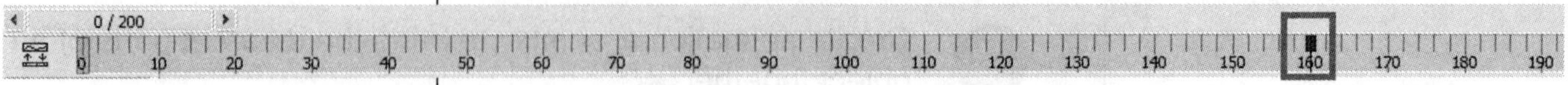

Figure A–33

5. Click Auto Key to activate it (it will display in red).

If all of the objects are selected, click in and empty area in the viewport to clear the selection and then select each object separately.

6. Verify that your slider bar is located at 0 (0/200). Clear the object selection, click (Select and Move), and move each object individually randomly on the screen, as shown in Figure A–34. (The placement of the objects can be different to that shown in Figure A–34.)

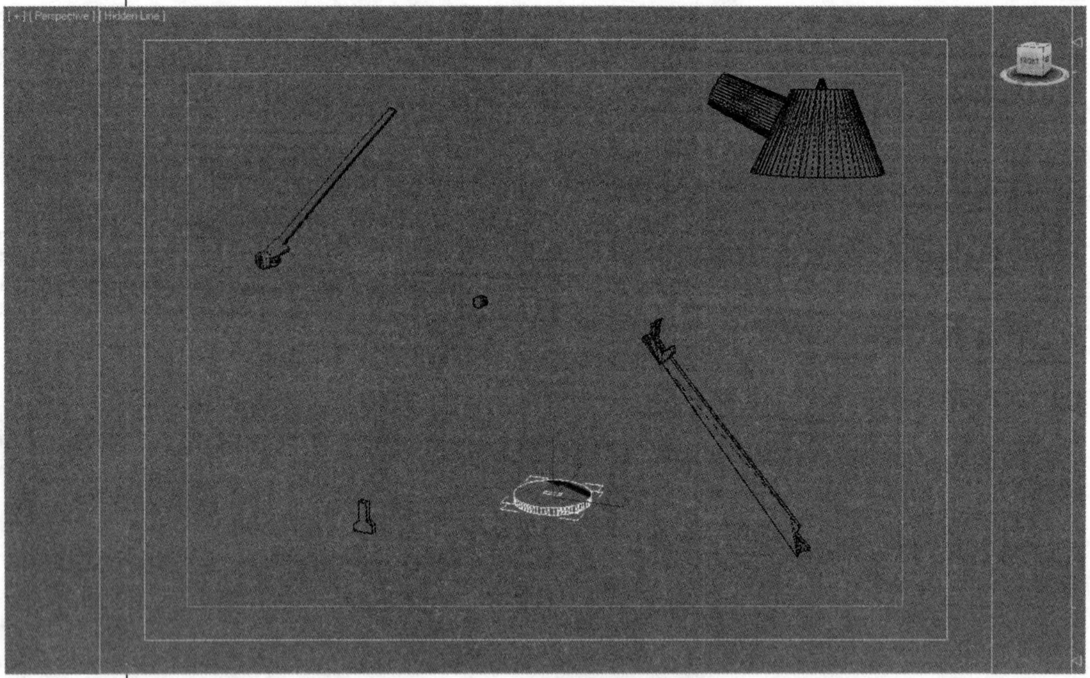

Figure A–34

7. Click (Play) and note that the components drift into their correct locations at frame 160. Stop the animation.

8. Save your scene file as **MyLampAnimation.max**.

Hint: Set the Selection Range

To have the components assemble one after another, using <Ctrl> select both the keys in the Time Slider. Right-click and select **Configure>Show Selection Range**. A bar is added below the track bar representing duration of movement for the selected component. You can now move the ends of the range to control when the object starts to move and when it finishes moving. The shorter the line, the quicker the movement of the object.

A.7 Customizing the User Interface

Learning Objective

Modify the existing settings and create new settings for the user interface elements, such as keyboard shortcuts, toolbars, menus, quad menus, mouse settings, and colors.

The Autodesk 3ds Max Design software has a flexible and highly customizable user interface that can be modified using the Customize User Interface dialog box, as shown in Figure A–35. Select **Customize>Customize User Interface**.

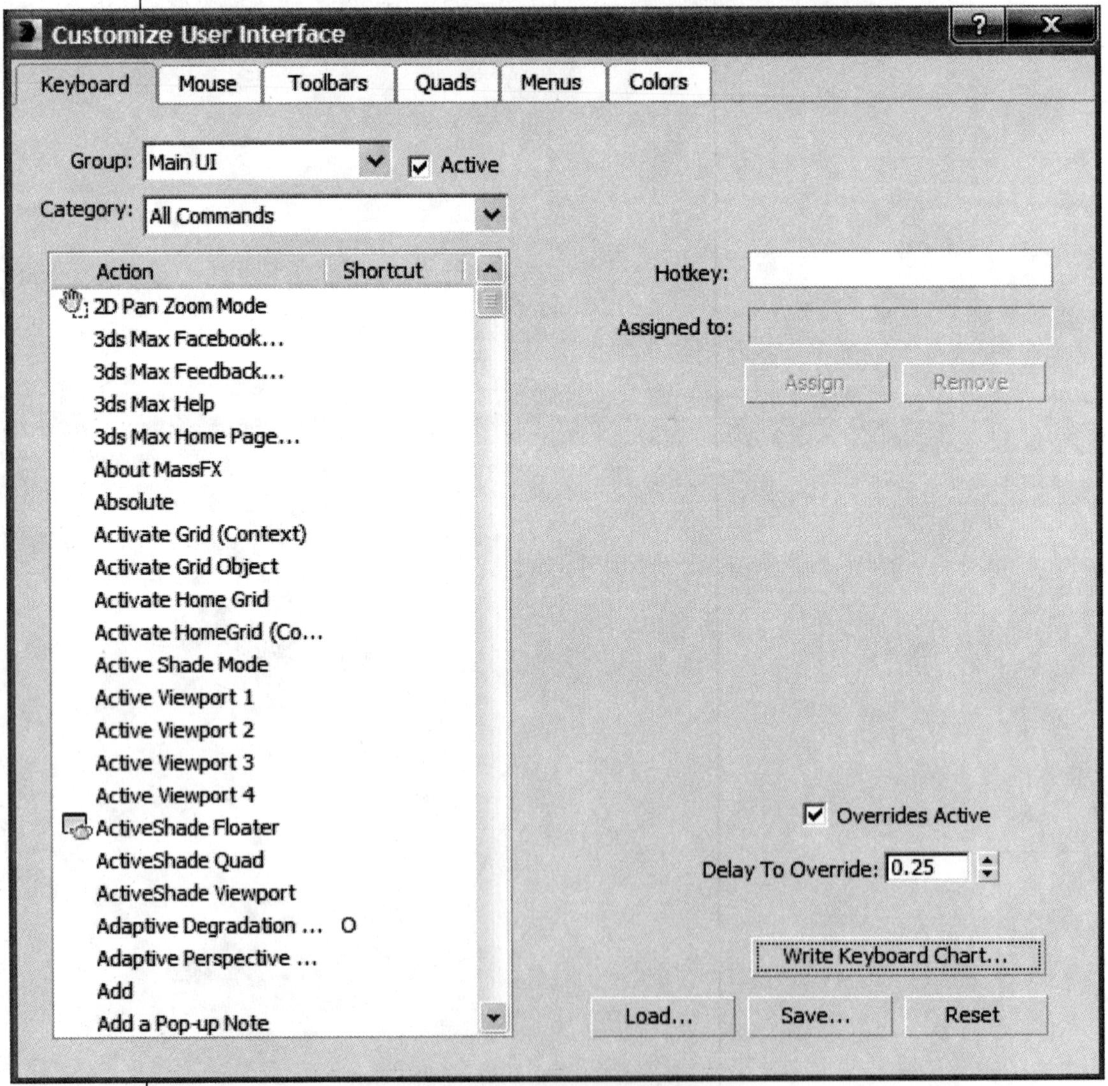

Figure A–35

- The settings located in each tab can be saved or swapped out independently with Load... and Save....

- All of the interface settings can be loaded and saved at once using **Customize>Load/Save Custom UI Scheme**.
- Using the *Keyboard* tab you can assign shortcuts or hotkeys.
- Write Keyboard Chart... in the *Keyboard* tab enables you to save a .TXT file showing all of the current hotkeys. A hotkey is a keyboard stroke or combination assigned to launch a specific option. It is good practice to develop your own set of keyboard shortcuts to improve your productivity.
- In the *Mouse* tab, you can load and save the mouse settings. The mouse settings are dependent on the interaction mode set in the Preferences dialog box in which you can set the Autodesk 3ds Max mode or Autodesk Maya mode.
- In the *Toolbars* tab, you can create custom toolbars and modify the existing one based on your requirements.
- In the *Quads* tab and *Menus* tab, you can create custom Quad sets and custom menus and modify the respective existing ones.
- The *Colors* tab has options for setting the color options for the interface elements.
- All of the keyboard shortcuts, toolbar, and menu custom settings are now saved in an upgraded file format (.KBDX for keyboard settings, .MUSX for mouse settings, .CUIX for toolbar settings, .MNUX for quad menus and pull-down menu settings, and .CLRX for color settings).

Practice A5 Customizing the User Interface

Learning Objectives

- Customize the User interface by adding commands in the Quad menu.
- Add an icon for a command to the Main toolbar

1. Reset the file, saving if necessary.
2. Select **Customize>Customize User Interface** to open the Customize User Interface dialog box.
3. Select the *Quads* tab. Click in the *Action* list and press <O>.
4. Locate Orbit View Mode. Click and drag it to the Quad list on the right, placing it just above **Clone**, as shown in Figure A–36. This enables you to select **Orbit View Mode** with a right-click quad menu.

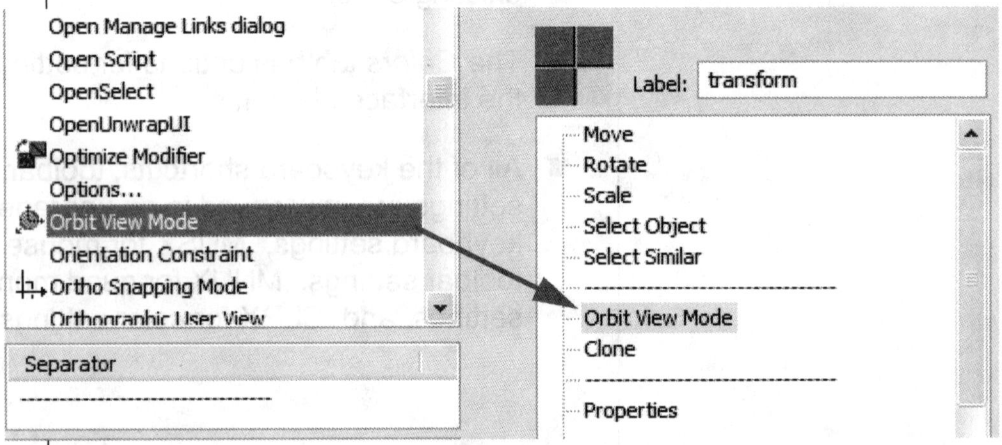

Figure A–36

5. Open the Group drop-down list and select **ViewCube** as shown in Figure A–37.

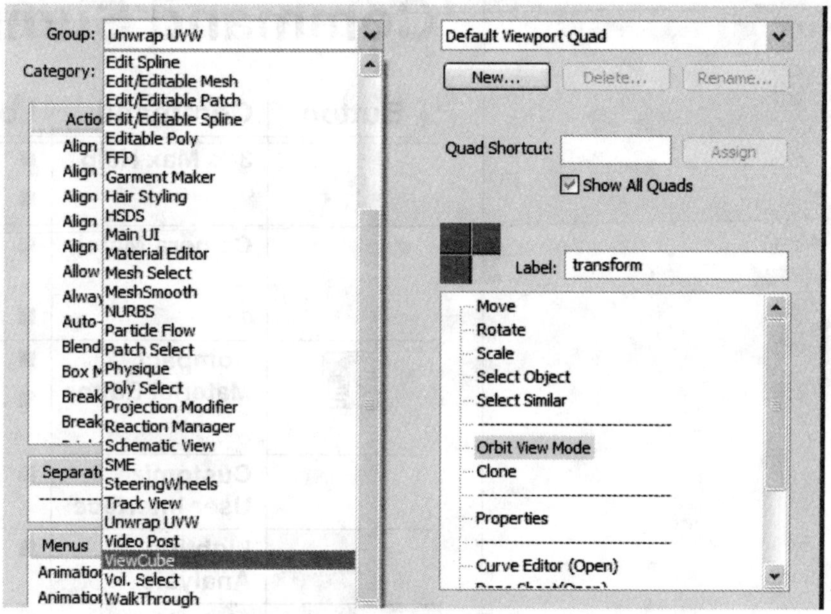

Figure A–37

*You can delete or edit the names of the listed commands by right-clicking on the command in the Action list and selecting **Delete Menu Item** or **Edit Menu item Name**.*

6. In the Action list, select **Toggle ViewCube Visibility**, drag it to the Quad list on the right, and place it just below **Orbit View Mode**, as shown in Figure A–38.

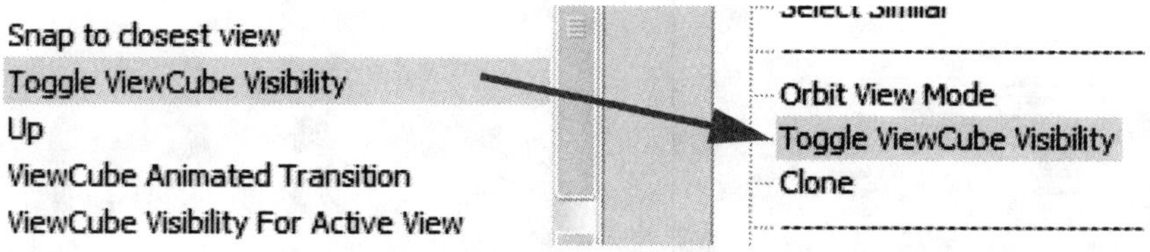

Figure A–38

7. Close the dialog box by clicking . Right-click on the viewport and select **Toggle ViewCube Visibility** to toggle it off. Note that the ViewCube is not visible anymore.

8. Select **Customize>Customize User Interface**.

*To delete a button from the Main toolbar, right-click and select **Delete Button**. Only the added buttons can be deleted.*

9. In the dialog box, select the *Toolbars* tab. In the *Action* list, click 

. Drag this entry to the Main toolbar, and drop it before the **3D Snaps** icon, as shown in Figure A–39. The **Ortho Snap** tool is now available in the Main toolbar. Close the dialog box.

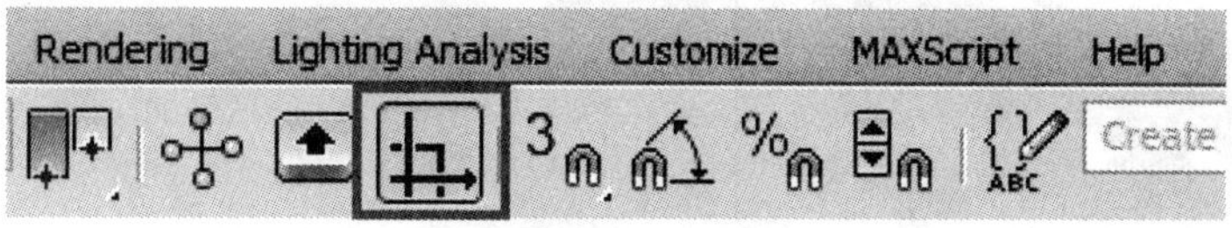

Figure A–39

Command Summary

Button	Command	Location
	**3ds Max Help**	■ **InfoCenter** ■ **Help:** Autodesk 3ds Max Design Help
	Camera Match	■ **Command Panel:** *Utilities* panel> Camera Match ■ **Tools:** Camera Match
	**Compact Material Editor**	■ **Main Toolbar:** Material Editor flyout ■ **Rendering:** Material Editor>Compact Material Editor
	Customize User Interface	■ **Customize:** Customize User Interface
	Lighting Analysis	■ **Lighting Analysis:** Lighting Analysis Assistant
	Light Meter	■ **Command Panel:** *Create* panel> *Helpers* category ■ **Lighting Analysis:** Create>Light Meter

Appendix B

Optional Practices

The appendix contains additional practices that can be worked on to provide further practice in the Autodesk® 3ds Max® Design software.

Practice B1

Create Additional Extrusions

Learning Objective

- Create 3D objects from 2D shapes using the **Extrude** modifier and its options.

You will create extrusions defining the lobby area, as shown in Figure B–1.

Estimated time for completion: 20 minutes

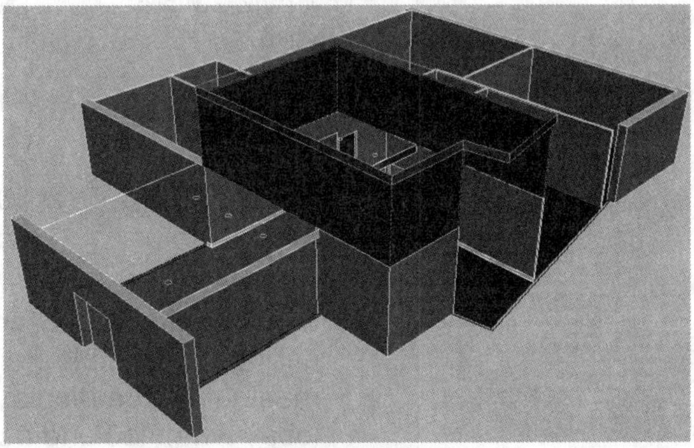

Figure B–1

1. Open **Extruded Walls with Openings.max** from your *Class Files* folder.

Press <Enter> after entering a value in the edit box.

2. Select each of the 2D shapes listed in the following table individually (use (Select by Name) and (Display Shapes)). Use the **Extrude** modifier (Modifier List>*Modify* panel ( )) on each object and extrude them as described in the table. For each object set the rest of the parameters as shown in Figure B–2. For the objects that are required to be moved up (elevation), click (Select and Move) and then, in the Status Bar, enter the *Z* value for elevation.

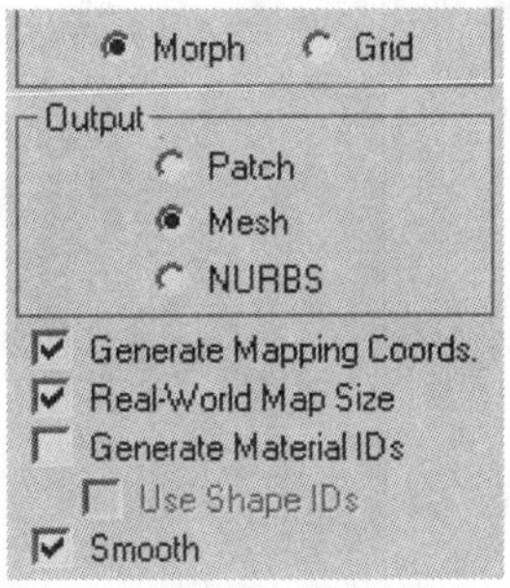

Figure B–2

Autodesk 3ds Max Design Object	Extrusion Amount	Notes
Layer:VIZ-1-Floor-Carpet	0'0"	Cap only the end (not start)
Layer:VIZ-1-Floor-Tile	0'0"	Cap only the end (not start)
Layer:VIZ-1-Ceiling	1'0"	Cap only the start (not end) Move up to elevation 10'0"
Layer:VIZ-2-Walls (Partial)	9'0"	Cap only the end (not start) Move up to elevation 11'0"
Layer:VIZ-2-Ceiling (Partial)	1'0"	Cap only the start (not end) Move up to elevation 20'0"
Layer:VIZ-1-Ceiling Lights	0'0"	Cap only the start (not end) Move up to elevation 9'11 7/8"

3. By using the **Cap Start** and **Cap End** options, note that the ceilings are visible from the top and bottom of the model. To manipulate the display so that you can still see inside the lobby when looking down at the model but see the ceilings when looking up, you can set the **Object Properties**. Select the two ceiling layers (**Layer:VIZ-1-Ceiling** and **Layer: VIZ-2-Ceiling (Partial)**) and select **Edit>Object Properties**. The Object Properties dialog box opens. In the *General* tab, in the *Display Properties* area, click [By Layer] to change it to [By Object]. Once [By Object] is enabled, select the **Backface Cull** option. This enables you to see inside the model when looking down from the top.

4. You have only included the part of the second floor that connects to the lobby area.

5. Save the file as **MyAdditional Extrude.max**.

Practice B2

Making a Chair Base by Lofting Objects

Learning Objectives

- Loft 2D shapes along a 2D path to create a 3D object with different cross-sections along its path.
- Apply deformations to the shapes using the Deformation graph.

Estimated time: 10 minutes

In this practice, you will create a loft object to represent the base of a chair. The extrude and sweep modifiers both use a single shape that sweeps along a path to create a 3D object. The Loft Compound Object modifier places multiple shapes along a spline path. It also gives you additional deformations to twist, tweeter, scale, and otherwise fit to shape on a graph

1. Open the file **airport_chair_startLoft.max** from your *Class Files* folder. The chair seat is displayed in the viewport, as shown in Figure B–3.

Figure B–3

2. In the viewport, select the straight line object directly under the chair. This shape is used at the path for the loft.

3. In the Command Panel, in the *Create* panel ( ), click (Geometry), expand the drop-down list and select **Compound Objects**.

4. In the Object Type rollout, click Loft.

As you move the cursor over a valid shape, it changes to a Get Shape cursor.

5. In the Creation Method rollout, click Get Shape. In the viewport, select the large circle object named Circle01. The circle is lofted along the selected straight line, as shown in Figure B–4.

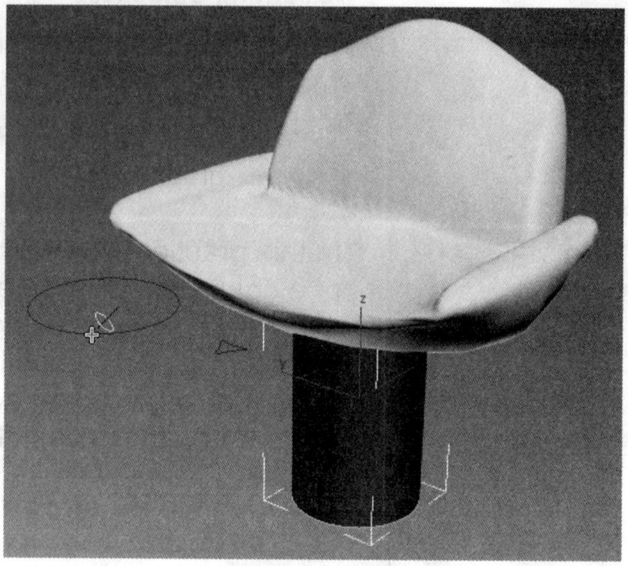

Figure B–4

6. Press <F3> to toggle to wireframe shading. In the viewport, there are three shapes: a **Circle** (that you already lofted), a **Star** with three points, and a six sided **NGon** (the NGON is inside the loft object). You will blend from shape to shape along the path.
7. With the Loft object selected, in the Command Panel, select the *Modify* panel ( ). In the Path Parameters rollout, enter **40** in the *Path* field and press <Enter>. In the viewport, a small yellow indicator moves up the path, as shown in Figure B–5.

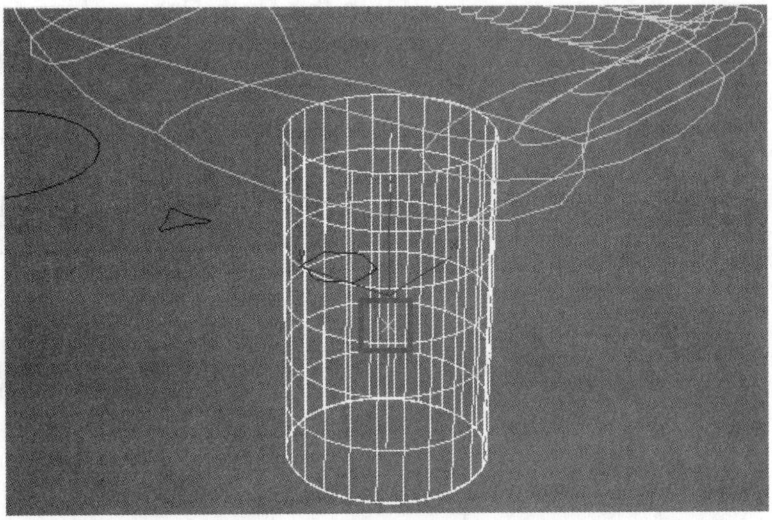

Figure B–5

8. In the Creation Method rollout, click Get Shape. In the viewport, select **NGon01** (blue Ngon inside the loft object). Change the viewport display to Shaded. The circular base shape now tapers to a post, as shown in Figure B–6. The **Orbit** command has been used to display the complete loft object.

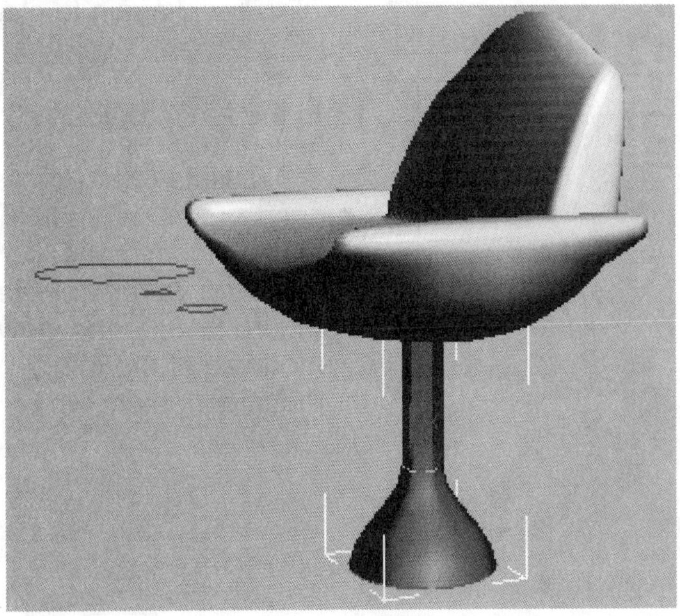

Figure B–6

9. In the Path Parameters rollout, set the *Path* value **60**.

10. Verify that Get Shape is still selected and select the NGon again. The NGON is placed at the new location, which is indicated by the cyan shape.

11. In the Path Parameters rollout, set the *Path* value to **100**. Verify that Get Shape is still selected and select the Circle. In the viewport, note that the loft flares up before touching the seat, as shown in Figure B–7.

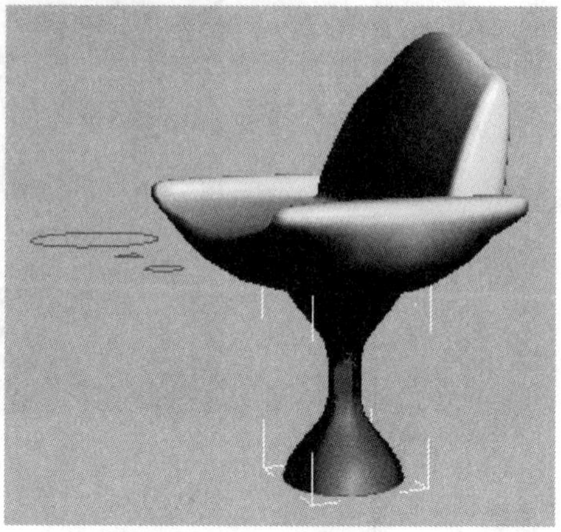

Figure B–7

12. In the Path Parameters rollout, set the *Path* value to **50**. Verify that Get Shape is still selected and select the Star. Note that in the center of the loft, the geometry does not look very good. You need to add more points to the star. Click Get Shape again to clear its selection.

13. In the Main toolbar, click (Select by Name). Using (Display Shapes), select the **Star01**, and click OK.

    In the *Modify* panel ( ), in the Parameters rollout, set the following values for the Star, as shown on the left in Figure B–8. In the viewport, note that the loft object has been modified at the middle and that the star shape has also been modified, as shown on the right in Figure B–8.

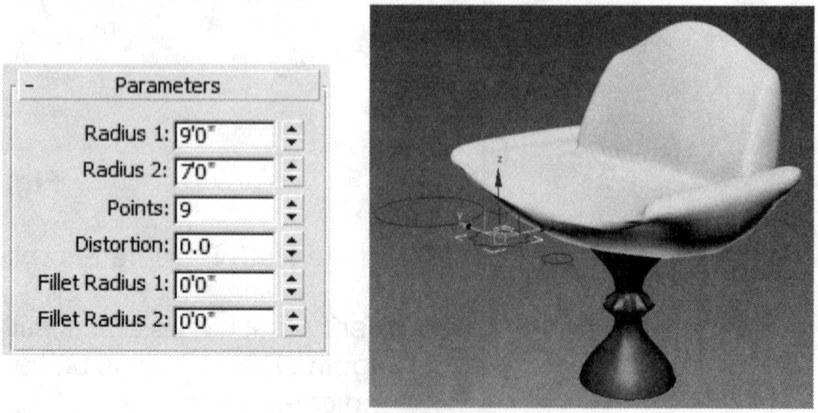

Figure B–8

14. Select the loft object and press <F4> to display in Edged Face mode, as shown in Figure B–9. Note that the mesh looks pretty dense. You can fix that by changing the interpolation on the Shapes/Path.

Figure B–9

15. With the base selected, verify that the *Modify* panel () is open in the Command Panel.

16. Expand the Skin Parameters rollout, in the *Options* area, set the *Shape Steps* and *Path Steps* to **2**. Try different values and see what they do. Increase the *Path Steps* to **4** and leave the *Shape Steps as* **2**, as shown in Figure B–10.

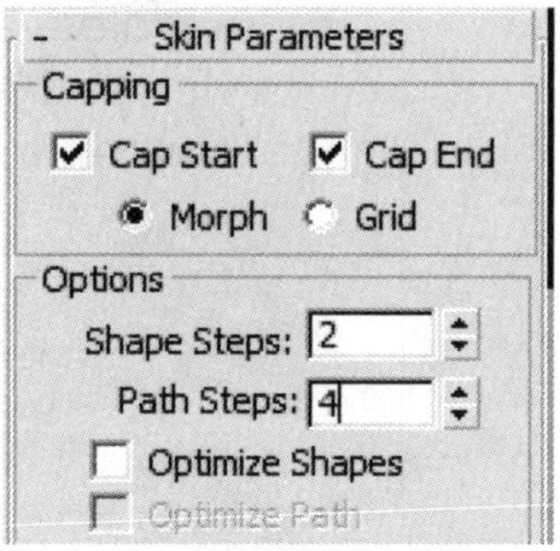

Figure B–10

17. For sculpting the final shape of the Loft object, expand the Deformations rollout and click . The Scale Deformations graph displays.

18. In the Scale Deformations toolbar, click (Insert Corner Point). When you hover the cursor over the red line, note that it displays as a plus sign. Click on the red line under 20 to set the control point at an approximate position. In the Text edit box, at the bottom of the dialog box, enter **20** and press <Enter>, as shown in Figure B–11, to move the control point to the exact position.

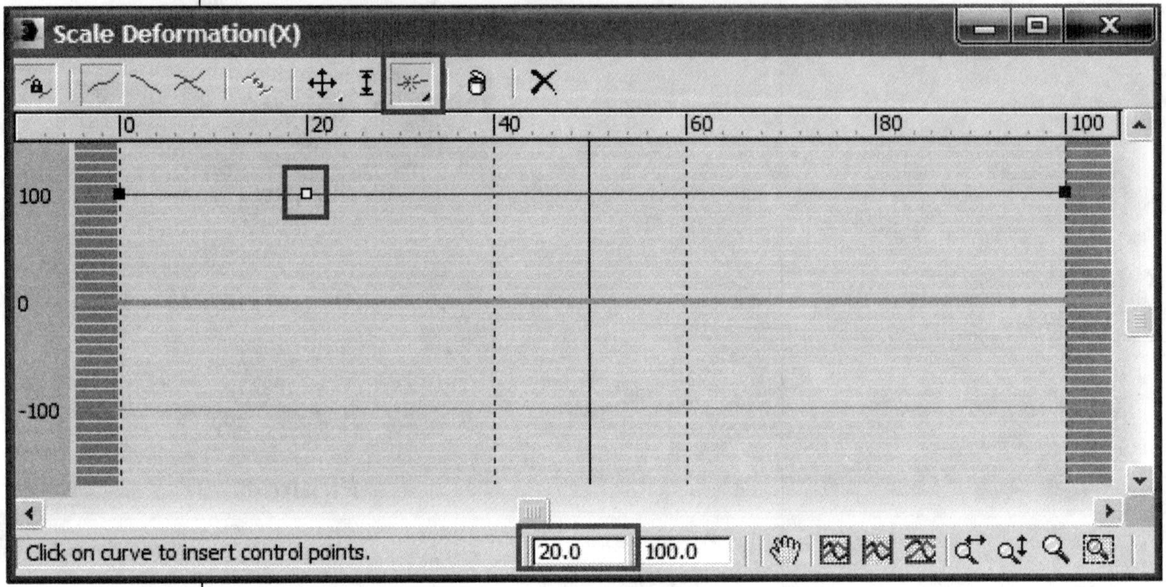

Figure B–11

19. Add new control points at **40**, **50**, and **60**.

20. In the dialog box, click (Move Control Points) to move the points on the graph. Right-click on the points and change them to **Bezier Smooth** or **Bezier Corner**, then adjust the handles, as shown in Figure B–12. Review the object in the viewport as the points are moved and modified. The changes happen interactively in the viewport.

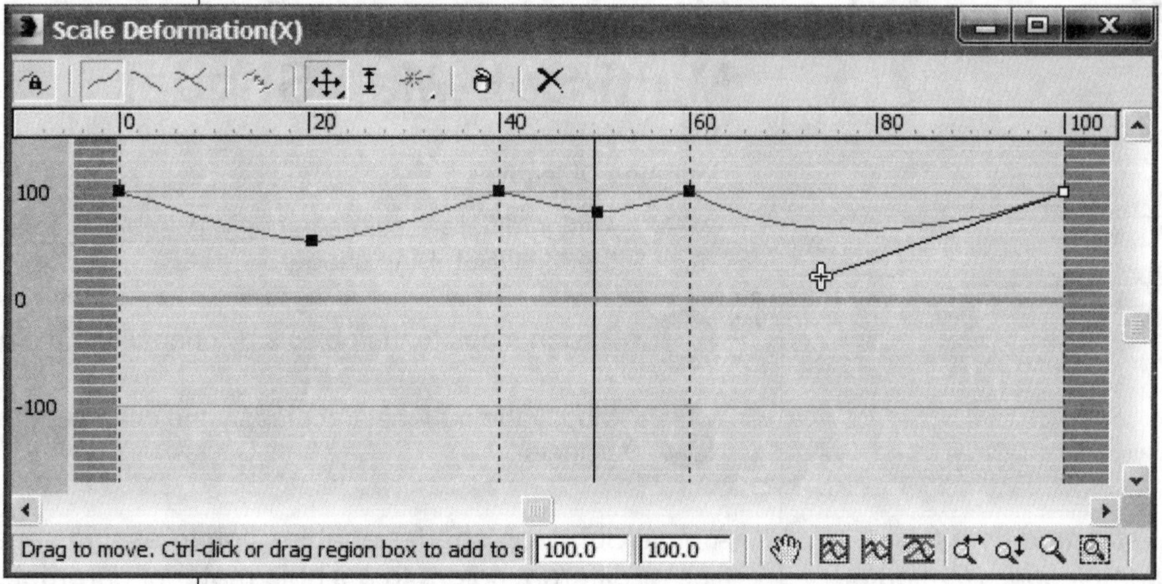

Figure B–12

21. Play with the handles and scale points while watching the interactive results in the viewport, as shown in Figure B–13.

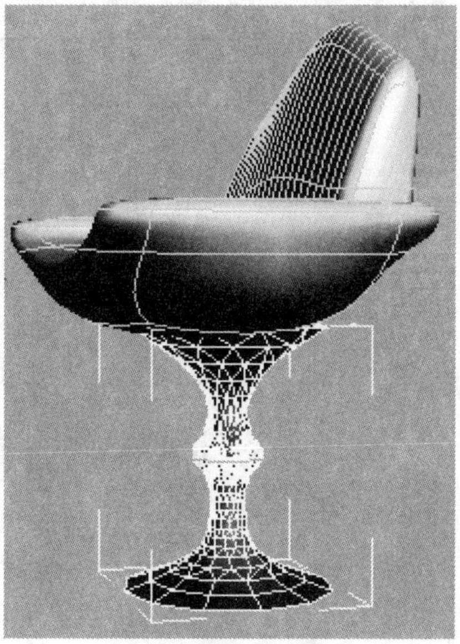

Figure B–13

22. You can use other deformation tools, such as **Twist**, **Teeter**, **Bevel**, and **Fit** and note how they effect the base of the chair.

23. Save the file as **Myarmchair_withBase.max**.

Practice B3 Using the mental ray Multi/Sub-Map Shader

Learning Objectives

- Assign different colors to copies of objects in a scene using the Multi/Sub-Map shader.
- Assign maps to the objects by changing the materials.
- Modify the materials and apply the changed material to the objects.

Estimated time for completion: 10 minutes

A Multi/Sub-Map shader enables you to assign separate map files or different colors to a single material parameter (i.e., Diffuse). In this practice you will create a mental ray shader and assign a Multi/Sub-Map that assigns multiple colors to chairs in a hall.

Task 1 - Apply and Adjust the Multi/Sub-Map shader.

1. Open **Brno_Hall_Chairs.max** from your *Class Files* folder. The scene is already set up with a stage, camera, lights and a single row of six chairs to which you will be applying the shader. The chairs are in two parts, the fabric cover and the metal frame.
2. Click  to open the Slate Material Editor.
3. In the Material/Map Browser, expand the *Materials>mental ray* categories. Double-click on mental ray to add a mental ray material to the *View1* sheet. Double-click the title bar heading for the new mental ray material to open the Parameter Editor.
4. In the Material Shaders rollout, in the *Basic Shaders* area, next to Surface, click None to open the separate Material/Map Browser.

5. Expand the *Maps>mental ray* categories. Scroll down and locate **Multi/Sub-Map** as shown on the left in Figure B–14. Double-click on **Multi/Sub-Map**. The node displays in the *View1* sheet and is linked to the mental ray *Surface Shader* channel, as shown on the right in Figure B–14.

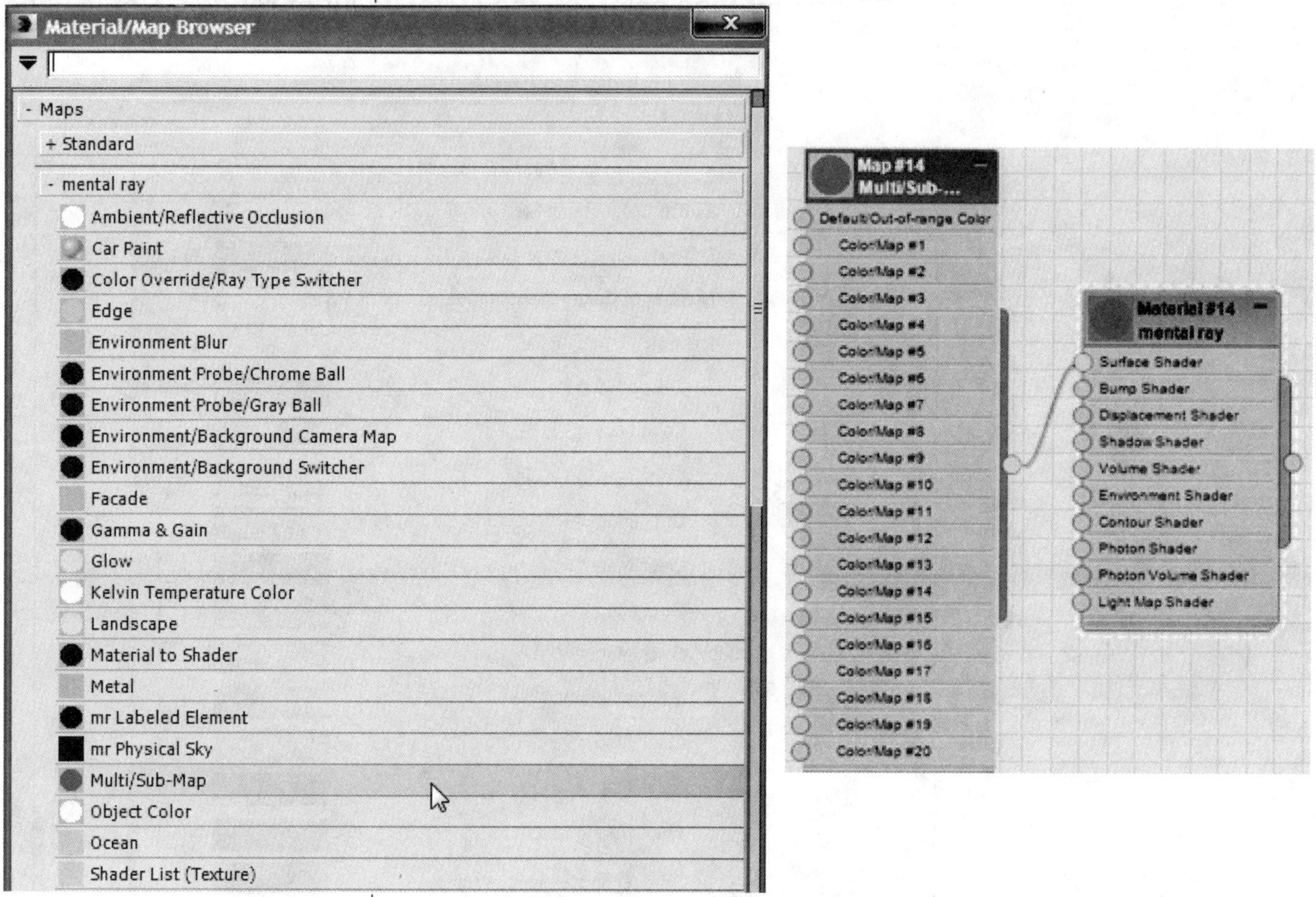

Figure B–14

6. Double-click the Map # 14 Multi/Sub-Map title bar heading to open its Parameters Editor, as shown in Figure B–15. This contains a list of 20 Color/Maps each of which is assigned to a unique channel. Maps 1 to 9 are unique colors while maps 10-20 are, by default, colored black. You will be applying these maps to objects in the scene. For any material number greater than color 20, the Default/Out-of-range Color is used.

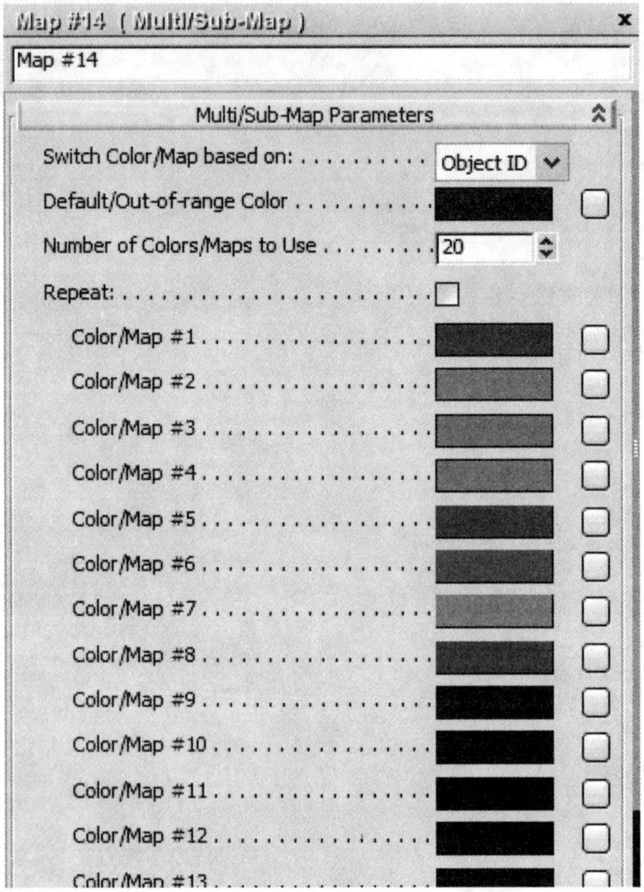

Figure B–15

7. Set *Number of Colors/Maps to Use* as **6**, as shown in Figure B–16. This identifies the first six materials as active for the shader when rendering. Each material has a unique channel assigned to it that corresponds with its position in the list, which in this case are the first six channels. Each of these channels have been assigned a default color that can be modified, as necessary. You can assign up to 100 materials using this shader.

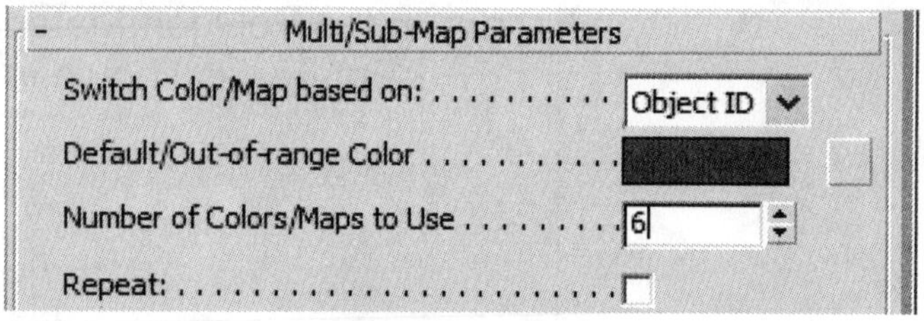

Figure B–16

Task 2 - Assign Maps to Materials.

In this task you will use another mental ray shader that has already been created and assigned. The steps in the previous task were included to describe how to create a new mental ray shader.

1. In the *View1* sheet, delete both the mental ray material and its Multi/Sub-Map node.
2. In the Material/Map Browser, in the **Scene Materials** category, double-click **Chair Fabric**. In the *View1* sheet, note that this is a mental ray material and that its Multi/Sub-Map has already been created. The first six channels in the Multi/Sub-Map have been assigned to chairs 2 through 6. You will assign the material to chair 1.
3. In the **Camera 01** viewport, select the seat back of the first chair on the left (Seat42), as shown in Figure B–17. The seat fabric and the frames are separate objects so only the seat part of the model is selected.

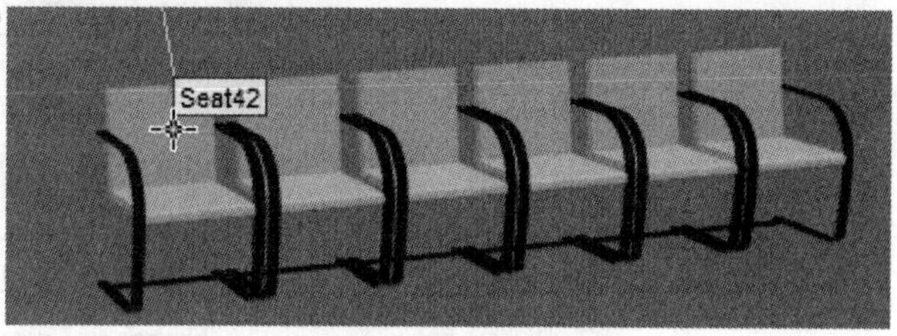

Figure B–17

4. In the Command Panel, select the *Modify* panel () and in the Modifier Stack, select **Polygon**. In the viewport, note that the complete seat (all polygons) displays in red.

5. In the Polygon:Material IDs rollout, set *Set ID* as **1** and press <Enter>, as shown in Figure B–18.

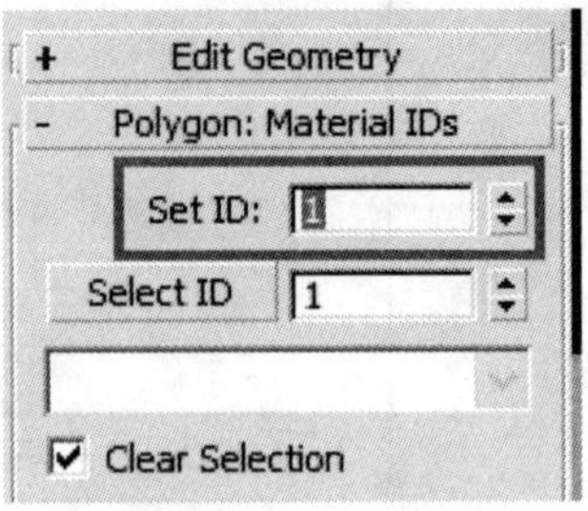

Figure B–18

6. In the *View1* sheet of Slate Material Editor, select the **Chair Fabric** mental ray node and click (Assign Material to Selection).

7. In the Command Panel, in the Modifier Stack, select **Editable Poly** to exit Sub-object mode.

8. For this scene, the remaining five channels were assigned separately to the remaining chairs and has already been completed. For example, seat 2 uses material channel *2* and seat 3 uses channel *3*. To review the materials that are assigned to the six channels, in the *View1* sheet, double-click on the Fabric Multi/Sub-Map node title bar heading to open the Parameter Editor, as shown in Figure B–19. Note that the *Number of Colors to Use* is set to **6** and are colored in six different colors, ranging from green to brown.

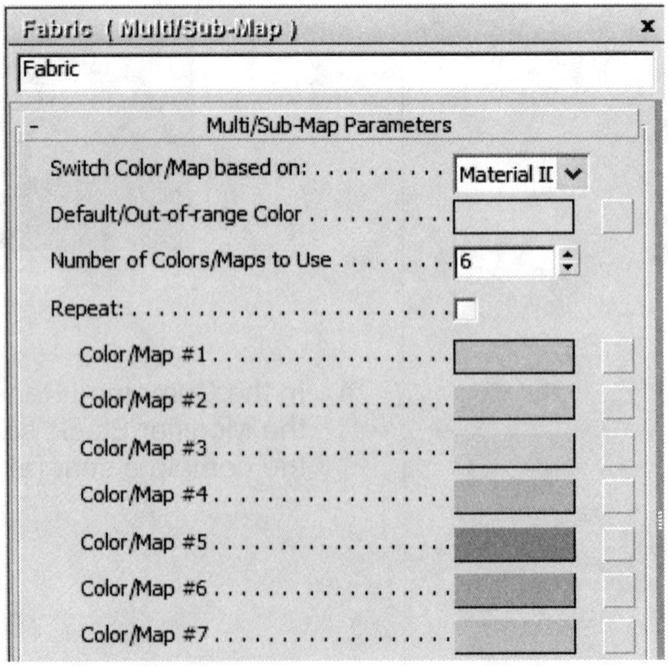

Figure B–19

9. In the viewport, select all six chair seat/backs and click (Assign material to Selection) to ensure that the materials are assigned.

10. Click to render the Camera01 view. The six seats display with their different color materials.

Task 3 - Add Additional Seats to the Scene.

You will now populate the space with additional rows and columns of seats and adjust the **Multi/Sub-Map** parameters to make it more interesting.

1. Select **Frame42** to **Frame47** (all six frames) and **Seat42** to **Seat47** (all six seats) (Use (Select by Name) with (Display None) and (Display Geometry)).

2. In the Status Bar, click (Selection Lock) to lock this selection, as shown in Figure B–20.

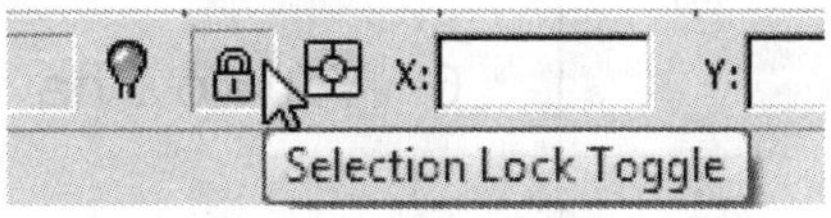

Figure B–20

3. Activate the Top viewport. Click (Zoom Extents Selected) and then click (Select and Move).

4. Hold down <Shift> and drag the chairs towards the top of the screen, as shown in Figure B–21, to create a new (cloned) row of seats. Ensure that enough space is left between the two rows and release <Shift>.

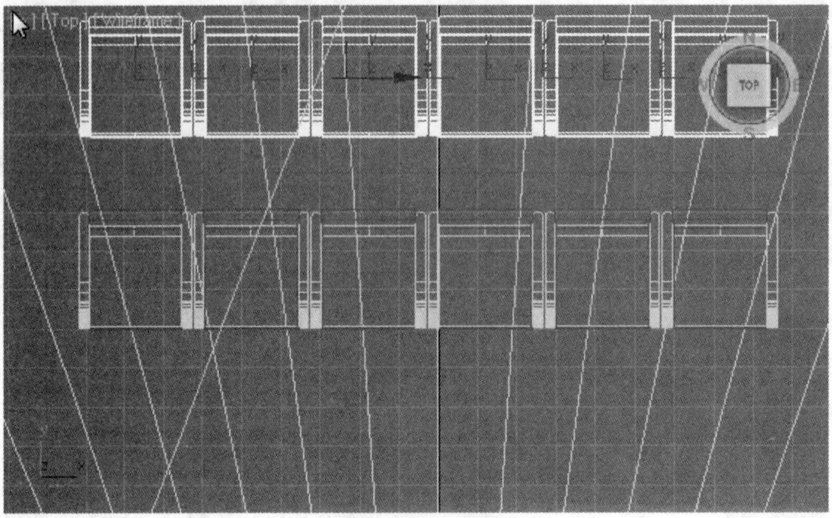

Figure B–21

5. In the Clone Options dialog box, select **Instance** and set the *Number of Copies* to **8**. Click OK.
6. You now have a total of 54 chairs in one main grouping, as shown in Figure B–22 (Camera01). Click (Select Object) to exit the Move transform.

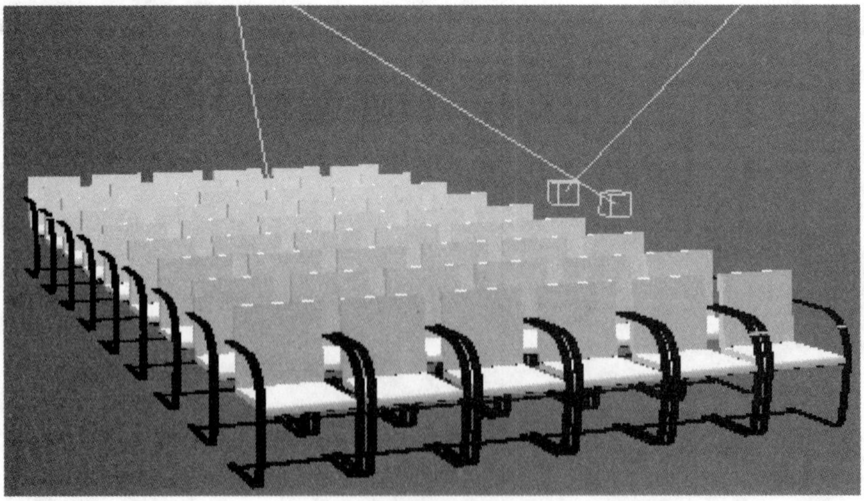

Figure B–22

7. Select all 54 chairs and their frames and lock the selection (). Zoom out in the Top viewport to see all of the chairs.

   Click and hold down <Shift>. Drag all of the chairs to the left (on the X axis) to create a second group column of 54 chairs, as shown in Figure B–23. In the Clone Options dialog box, select **Instance** and set the *Number of Copies* to **1**. Click OK.

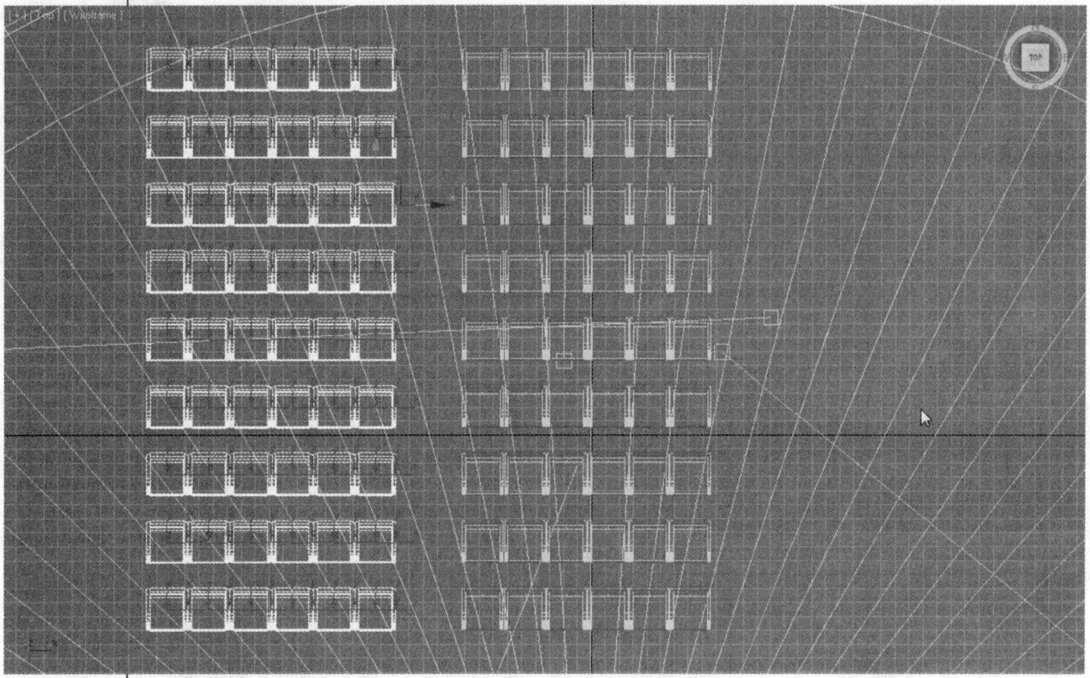

Figure B–23

8. As the group is still selected, press <Shift> and drag it to the right on the other side of the original group to create a third group column as **Instance** and set *Number of Copies* to **1**. You now have a total of 162 chairs.

9. Click  to render the Top rendering is displayed as shown in Figure B–24. Note that each group of six columns has the same regular color of chair from front to back

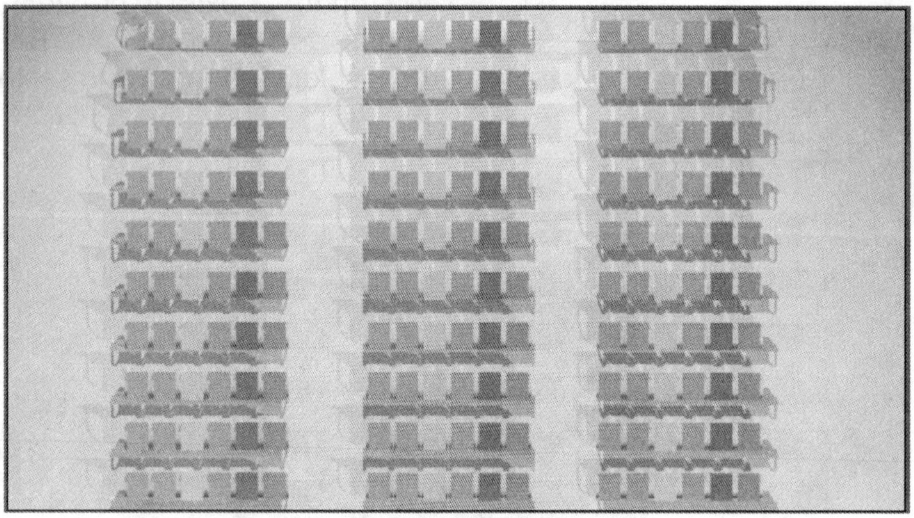

Figure B–24

You are not restricted to using solid colors with the Multi/Sub-Map shader and you can also apply maps to one or more materials. In such cases, the map replaces the color swatch.

10. To change the color scheme of the chairs, you can use the Multi/Sub-Map. Open the Slate Material Editor again if it has been closed, double-click on the Fabric Multi/Sub-Map title bar heading. In *Switch Color/Map based on* drop-down list, select **Random,** as shown in Figure B–25.

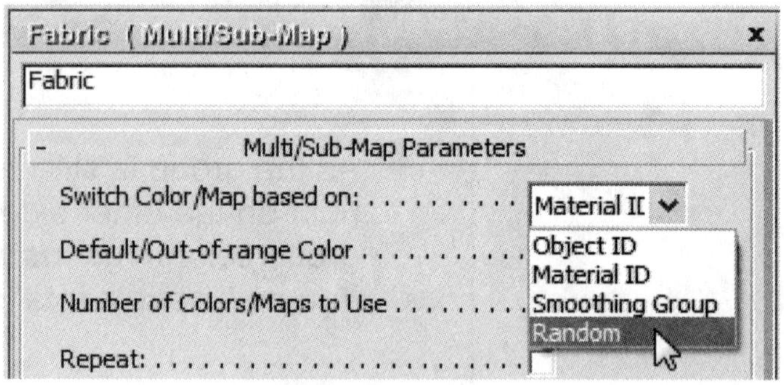

Figure B–25

11. Click  to render the Top viewport, as shown in Figure B–26. Note that the uniform color by column has been replaced with a more random layout color pattern, which is a technique used in most sports stadiums as it conveys the impression of a larger crowd.

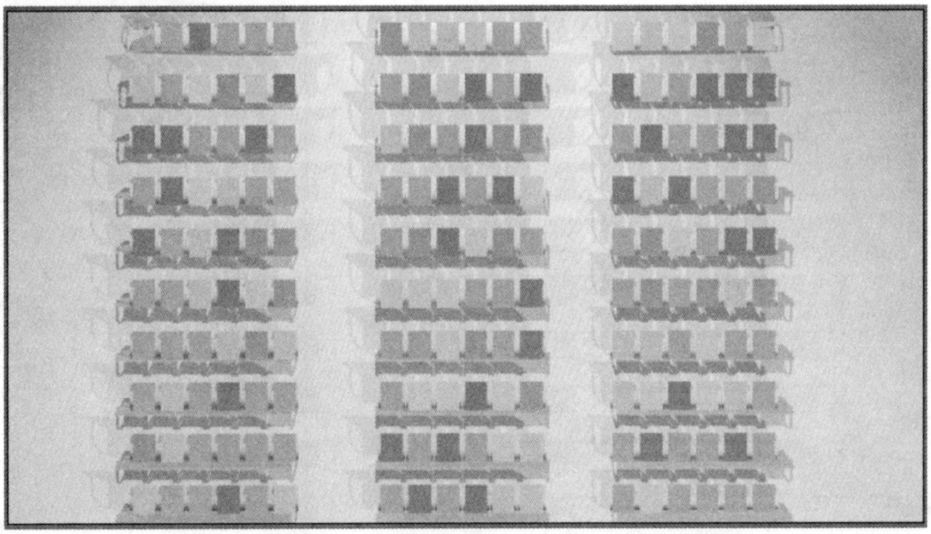

Figure B–26

Task 4 - Modify the Chair Frame Material.

The chair frames have a black glossy color applied to them but as the material is an Arch & Design type, you can change its look.

1. In the Slate Material Editor, in the Material/Map Browser, in the **Scene Materials** category, double-click on **Chair Chrome** material to add it to the View1 sheet. Double-click the title bar heading for the Chair Chrome material to display the Parameter Editor.

2. In the Templates drop-down list, select **Copper**, as shown in Figure B–27. As the material has previously been assigned to the frame and you are only modifying it, there is no need to select the frames and reapply the material.

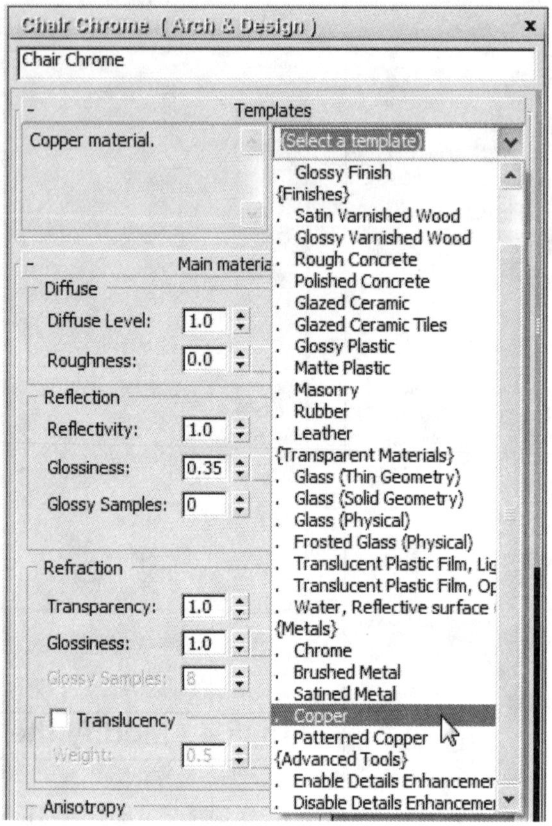

Figure B–27

3. Render the Camera01 viewport, as shown in Figure B–28. It displays a view of your chairs with random mental ray Multi/Sub-Map material applied to the chairs.

Figure B–28

4. Save the file as **Mymentalchairs.max**.

Practice B4

Shadow Study Animation

Learning Objective

Animate the movement of the daylight during a day in an exterior scene and study the movement of the shadows.

Estimated time for completion: 15 minutes

In this practice you will animate the Daylight System in the exterior scene to create an animated shadow study. This study will provide an accurate representation of how daylight will cast shadows in the scene.

1. Open **Shadow Study.max** from your *Class Files* folder.
2. Activate the Camera01 viewport if not already active. This is the non-animated camera view.
3. In the Animation controls at the bottom of the screen, click (Time Configuration). Verify that your default settings match the settings shown in Figure B–29. Click OK.

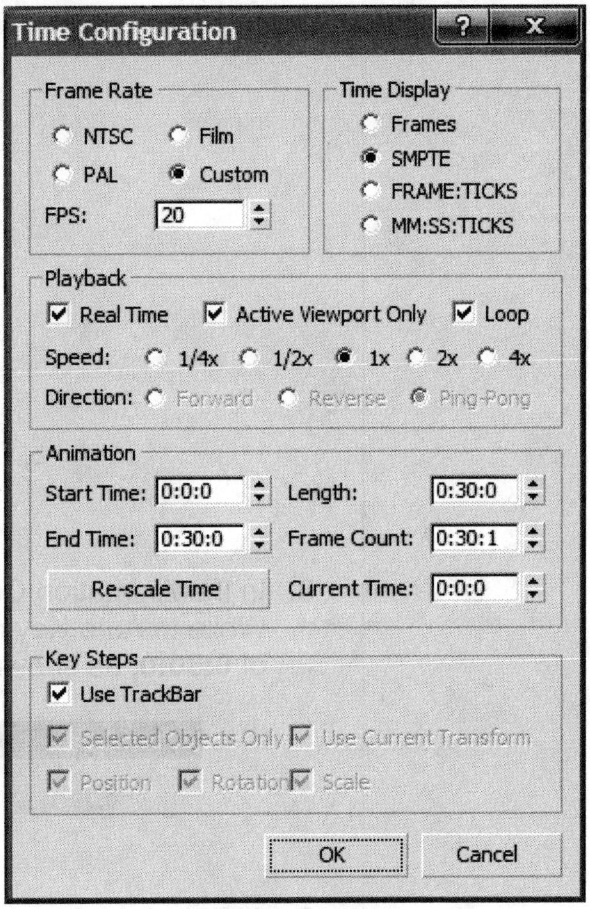

Figure B–29

4. In this shadow study you will animate the **Daylight001** object using keyframing. Select the **Daylight001** object in the **Compass001** helper object (Use (Select by Name) with (Display None) and (Display Groups)). Verify that the Time Slider is located at a time of **0:0:0** (frame 0), as shown in Figure B–30.

Figure B–30

5. In the Command Panel, select the *Motion* panel ( ). Start the shadow study animation at frame 0, representing **6:00 AM**. In the Control Parameters rollout, set the current time as shown in Figure B–31. Your *Azimuth* and *Altitude* values might be different. Accept your values.

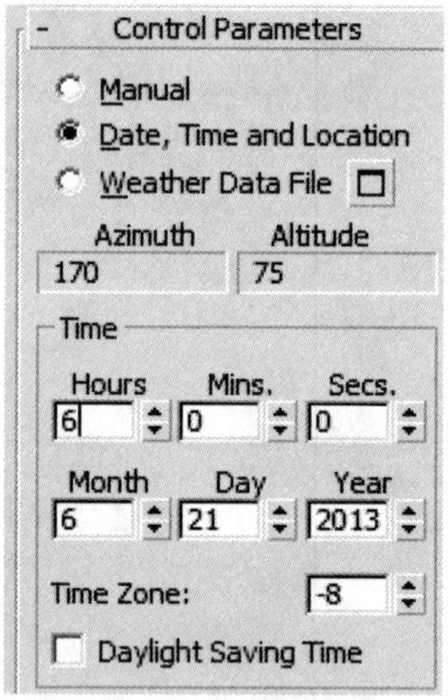

Figure B–31

6. In the Animation Controls, click Auto Key (displays in red). While in Auto Key mode, drag the time slider to the end time of **0:30:0**, as shown in Figure B–32.

Figure B–32

7. At time **0:30:0** change the sun's position to 7:00 PM by entering **19** in the *Hours* edit box in the Command Panel.

8. This is all of the animating that is required for this shadow study. Click Auto Key to end Auto Key mode.
9. Slide the Time Slider left and right (scrub) and in the viewports, watch the **Daylight001** object progress across the sky during the animation.
10. Click (Render Setup) to open the Render Setup dialog box. In the *Common* tab, in the *Output Size* area, set *Width* to **300** and press <Enter>. With your aspect ratio locked at 1.6, it should automatically calculate the *Height* of **187**, as shown in Figure B–33.

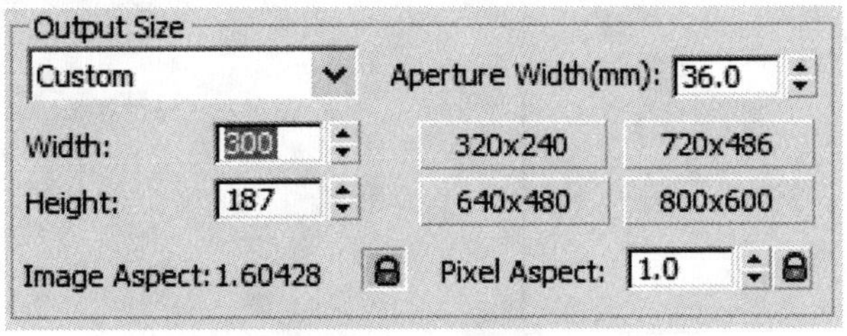

Figure B–33

11. In the *Time Output* area, set *Every Nth Frame* to **20** and verify that the **Active Time Segment** is selected, which means the entire animation.
12. At the bottom of the Render Setup dialog box, verify that the current viewport is set to **Quad 4 - Camera01** and click , as shown in Figure B–34. This enables you to always render Camera01 even if another viewport is active.

Figure B–34

13. In the *Render Output* area, click Files... . Render the animation to still frames named **shadow study.jpg** in your *Class Files* folder, *renderings* subfolder. If you are prompted to specify the JPEG quality, use the highest quality **JPEG** option.

14. Click [Render] to begin animating the individual frames of the animation through the course of a day from 6.00 a.m. to 7.00 p.m. Note the change in brightness of the daylight and the movement of the shadows from one frame to another.
15. When done, use the RAM Player (**Rendering>Compare Media in RAM Player**) to combine them into a compiled animation file called **Shadow Study.mov** or **Shadow Study.avi**.
16. Save the scene file as **My Shadow Study.max**.

Practice B5

Assigning the Renderable Spline Modifier

Learning Objective

Make the 2D lines renderable so that they are visible in the renderings.

Estimated time for completion: 10 minutes

The Renderable Spline modifier enables you to make linework renderable. This can add a significant amount of geometry to the scene, but it might look better close-up than a material map showing the same linear features. In this practice, you will assign a width to the pavement markings so that they will render appropriately.

1. Open **Renderable Spline.max** from your *Class Files* folder.
2. Click  to render the viewport and note that the parking lot does not display the corridor markings, parking lines, and handicap symbols.
3. Click  (Manage Layers) to open the Layer Manager. Expand the layer **C-MARK-YELLOW-3D**, as shown in Figure B–35. The layer contains a single object, the combined AutoCAD 3D lines that make up the yellow pavement markings.

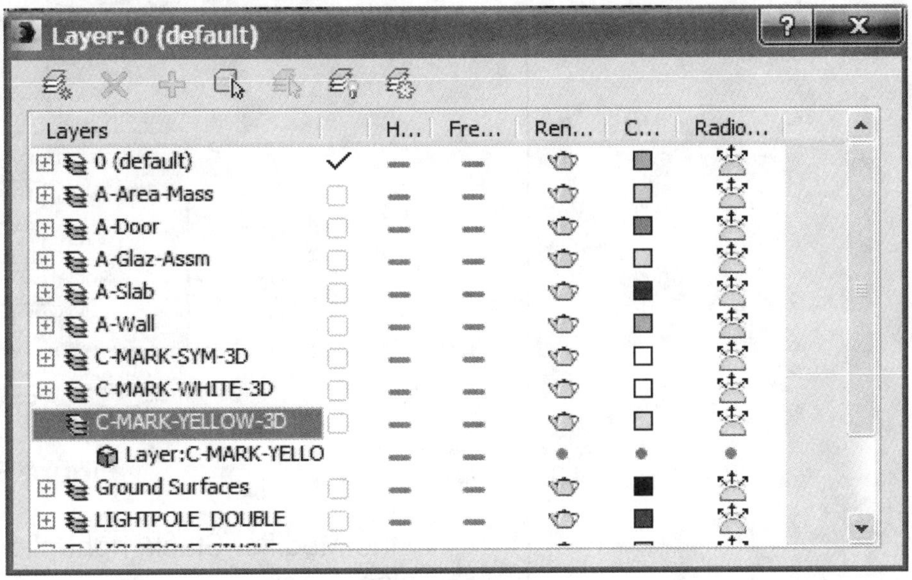

Figure B–35

4. Select **Layer:C-MARK-YELLOW-3D** object and click  (Select Highlighted Objects and Layers) to select the objects in the scene.

5. In the Command Panel, select the *Modify* tab. In the Modifier List, select **Renderable Spline**. It is displayed in the Modifier Stack, as shown in Figure B–36.

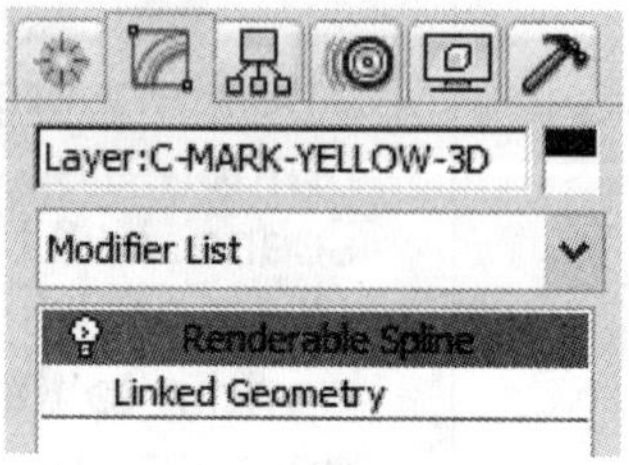

Figure B–36

6. In the Parameters rollout, select **Rectangular** and set *Width* as **0'3"** and set *Aspect* as **0.167**. The *Length* automatically sets as **0'0 4/8"**, as shown in Figure B–37. In your model, the *Length* translates into the vertical height of the pavement markings.

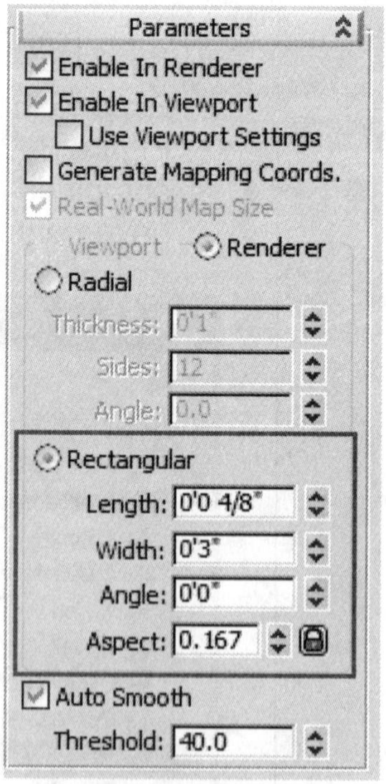

Figure B–37

7. In the Modifier Stack, right-click on **Renderable Spline** and select **Copy**.

8. In the Layer dialog box, select **Layer:C-MARK-WHITE-3D** object and click (Select Highlighted Objects and Layers). In the Modifier Stack, right-click on Linked Geometry and select **Paste** to add **Renderable Spline** with the same parameters.

9. In the Layer dialog box, select **Layer:C-MARK-SYM-3D** object and click (Select Highlighted Objects and Layers). In the Modifier Stack, right-click on Linked Geometry and select **Paste** to add **Renderable Spline** modifier. In the Parameters rollout, change the *Width* to **0'6"**.

10. In the viewport, the spline markings get some width, as shown in Figure B–38. The markings might not display entirely above the pavement due to the approximate nature of the viewport display and your computer's display driver and settings.

Figure B–38

11. Assign each of these marking layers to not cast shadows. In the Layer dialog box, right-click on one of these layers (not the object inside the layer) and select **Layer Properties**. In the Layer Properties dialog box, in the *Rendering Control* area, clear the **Cast Shadows** option. Repeat it for the other two layers.

12. Render the viewport and note the parking lines and the handicap signs are all visible in the rendering.

13. Save your work as **MyRenderable Spline.max**.

Hint: When Not to Cast Shadows

With relatively flat ground surfaces, it is recommended to not cast shadows since there is nothing to cast shadows on. This speeds up rendering time. Surfaces with abrupt elevation changes usually need to cast shadows to look realistic. This is because the raised areas of a surface often need to cast shadows on themselves or other objects to look believable. This is usually not the case for flat surfaces that do not have much relief to cast shadows with.

The pavement markings are meant to be completely flush with the pavement without any appreciable height to make shadows. Disabling the calculations save you a lot of rendering time.

It is recommended that you disable shadow casting when appropriate.

Practice B6

Using Script for Converting Materials

Certification

Topic:

✓*Scripting*

Objectives:

✓*Apply (run) scripts*

Learning Objectives

- Convert the Architectural materials to Arch & Design materials using a conversion script.
- Adjust the Exposure Control method and settings recommended for mental ray to get a realistic rendering.

Estimated time for completion: 15 minutes

A conversion script has been developed by Zap Anderson of mental images, (http://mentalraytips.blogspot.com). This script converts Architectural Materials to Arch & Design materials. In this practice you will work with this script.

1. Exit the Autodesk 3ds Max Design software.

2. Using Windows Explorer, locate the script file **Macro_mrArchMtlTools.mcr** in the *Scripts* folder of your *Class Files* folder (C:*\Autodesk 3ds Max Design Fundamentals Class Files\scripts*). Copy **Macro_mrArchMtlTools.mcr** to the *scripts* folder in the Autodesk 3ds Max Design 2014 installation directory. (Normally found under *C:\Program Files\Autodesk\3ds Max Design 2014\scripts*.)

3. Launch the Autodesk 3ds Max Design software.

4. Open **Convert_Materials_start.max**.

5. Open the Slate Material Editor and in the Material/Map Browser, locate the *Scene Materials* category. Note that the three **Finishes** materials are Architectural materials, as shown in Figure B–39.

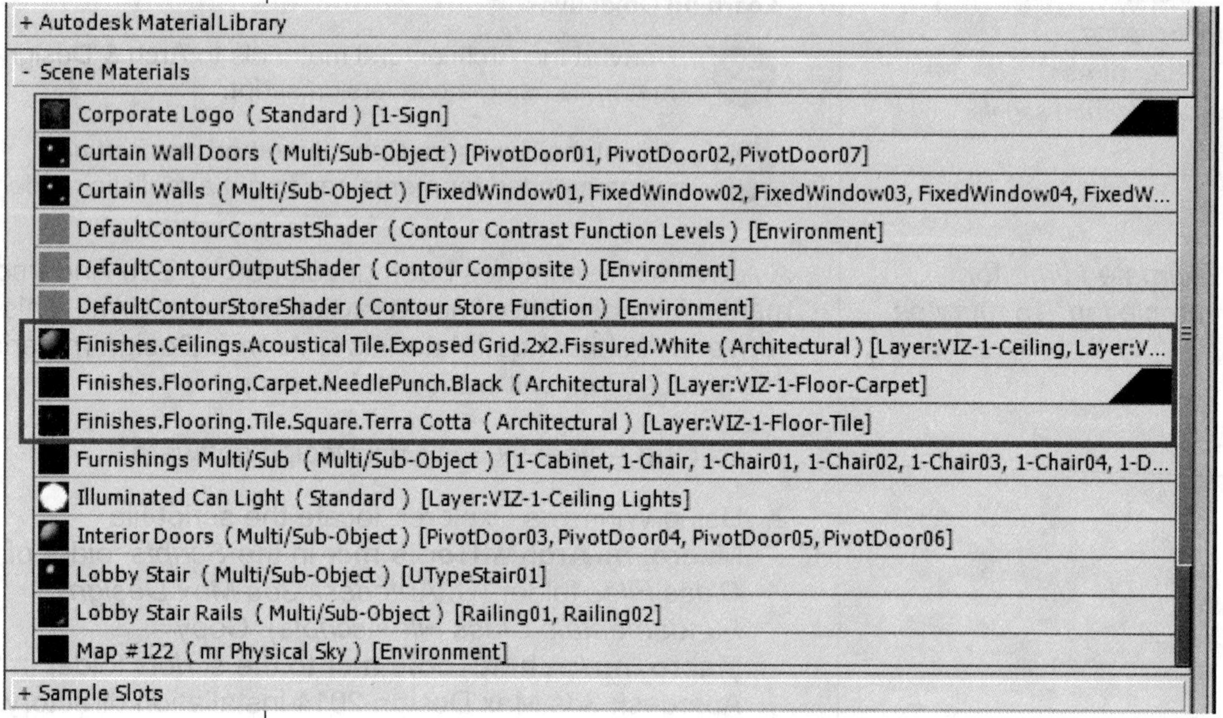

Figure B–39

6. In the Command Panel, click (Utilities) and click MAXScript.

In the MAXScript rollout, use Open Script *to open the script file.*

7. In the MAXScript rollout, click Run Script and select **Macro_mrArchMtlTools.mcr** in the Autodesk 3ds Max Design 2014 installation directory (Program Files). Click Open. By running it, you retrieve it into the Autodesk 3ds Max Design interface.

8. Select **Customize>Customize User Interface**.

9. In the Customize User Interface dialog box, select the *Menus* tab and in the Category drop-down list, select **mental ray**. In the Action list, select **mr Arch & Design Tools**, as shown in Figure B–40.

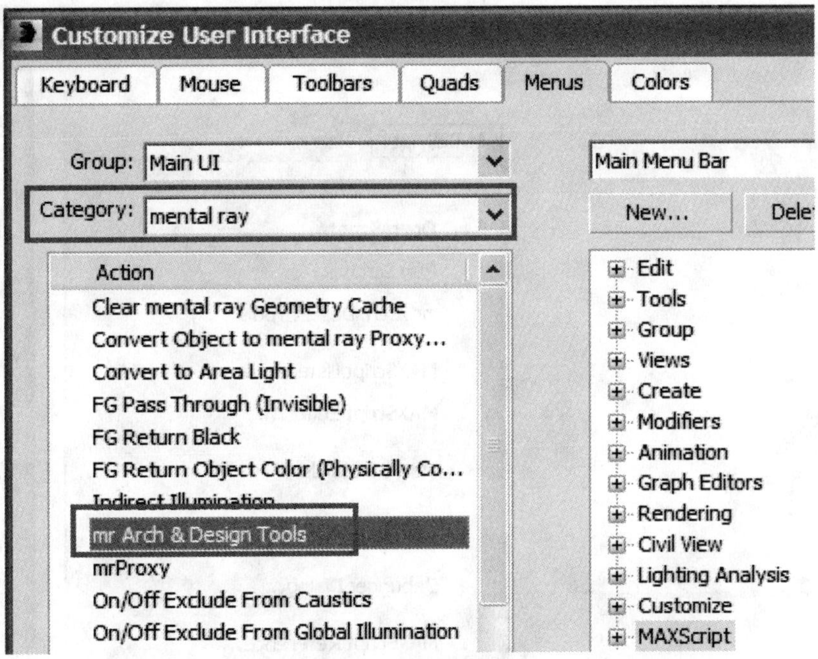

Figure B–40

10. On the right side of the dialog box, expand the **Maxscript** menu. Drag the **mr Arch & Design Tools** action onto the **Maxscript** menu, placing it wherever you want, as shown in Figure B–41. Close the dialog box.

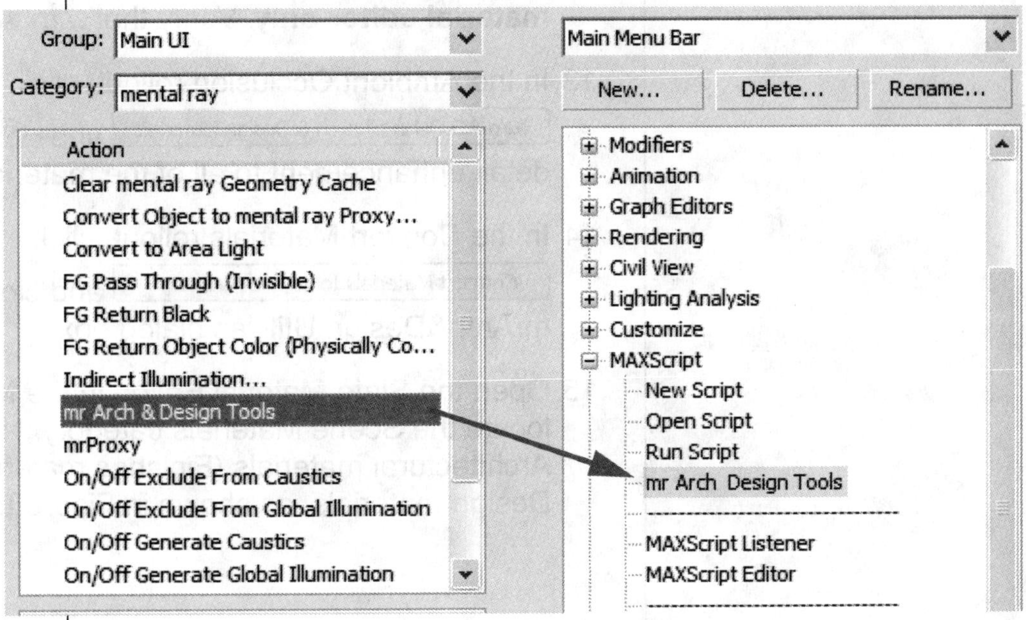

Figure B–41

11. The tool is now available from the **MAXScript** pull-down menu. Select **MAXScript>mr Arch Design Tools**, as shown on the left in Figure B–42. The mrArch&Design Utilities dialog box opens, as shown on the right in Figure B–42.

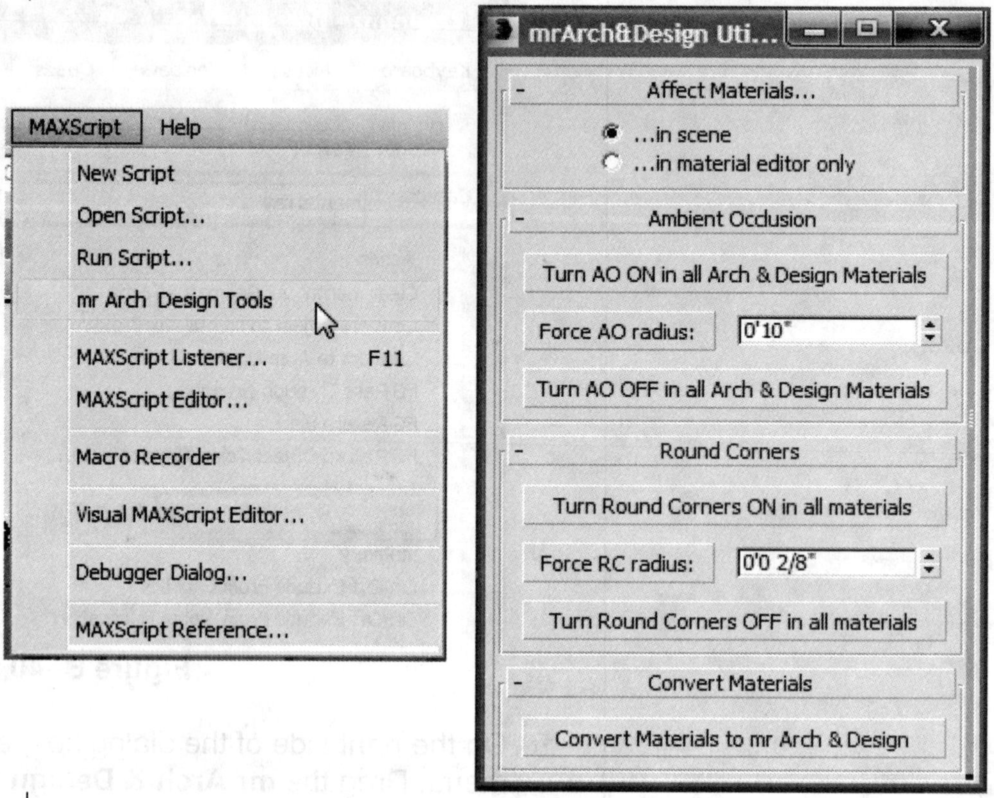

Figure B–42

12. The script enables you to select between **in scene** or **in material editor only**. Verify that **...in scene** is selected.

13. In the Ambient Occlusion rollout, click Turn AO ON in all Arch & Design Materials and Force AO radius:. This adds detail enhancement to all of the materials.

14. In the Convert Materials rollout, click Convert Materials to mr Arch & Design and close the mrArch&Design Utilities dialog box.

15. Open the Slate Material Editor, in the Material/Map Browser, locate the Scene Materials category. Note that the Architectural materials (Finishes materials) are now Arch & Design materials, as shown in Figure B–43.

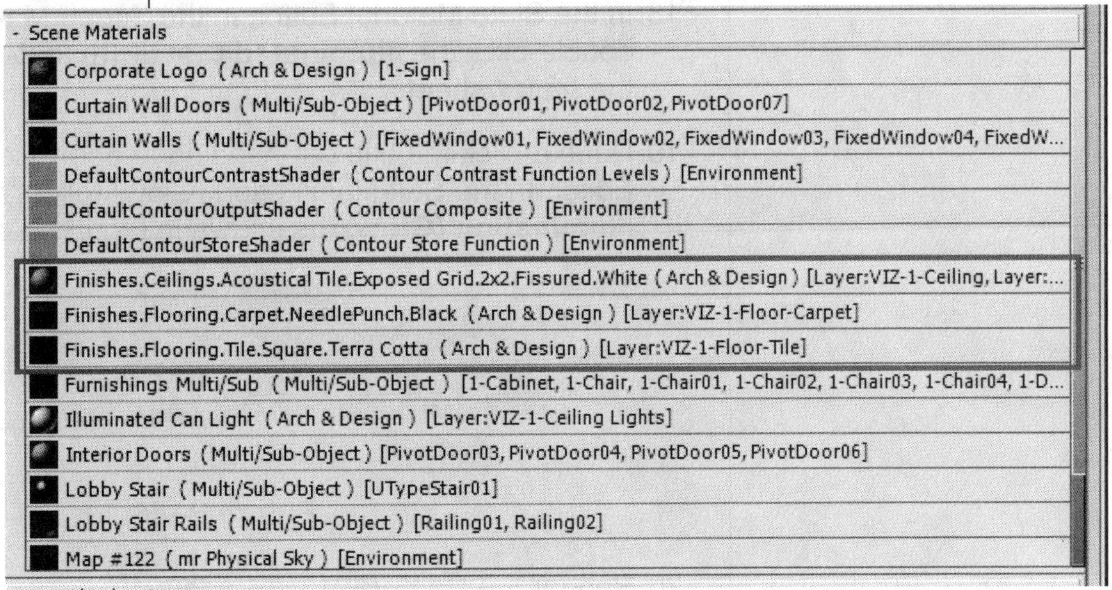

Figure B–43

Generally, adjusting the materials is required after conversion.

16. Click (Render) to render the Camera01 view, as shown in Figure B–44. Leave the Rendered Frame Window open. You will need to adjust the materials and lighting now that you have done the conversion.

Figure B–44

17. Toggle on the Self-Illumination for the materials of the overhead lights. Select the **Layer:VIZ-1-Ceiling Lights** objects. (Use (Select by Name) with (Display None) and (Display Shapes).)

18. In the Slate Material Editor, in the Scene Materials, double-click the **Illuminated Can Light** material to place it on the *View1* sheet.

19. Double-click the title bar heading to open the Parameter Editor. In the Self-Illumination (Glow) rollout, select **Self Illumination (Glow)**, as shown in Figure B–45.

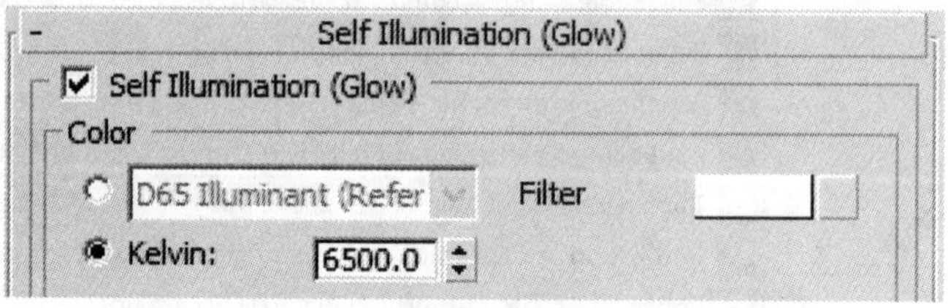

Figure B–45

20. Render the Camera01 view again.

21. In the Slate Material Editor, verify that in the *Luminance* area **Unitless** is selected. Try increasing this value and rendering until the lights in the ceiling are brighter.

22. The desk lamp material is incorrect so you will need to create a new one. In the Slate Material Editor, in the Material/Map Browser, in the *Materials>mental ray* categories, double-click on **Arch & Design** to place it on the *View1* sheet.

23. Double-click on the title bar heading of the new material to open the Parameter Editor. Rename the material **Desk Lamp**. In the Templates drop-down list, select **Glossy Finish** and change its *Diffuse* color to **Black**, as shown in Figure B–46.

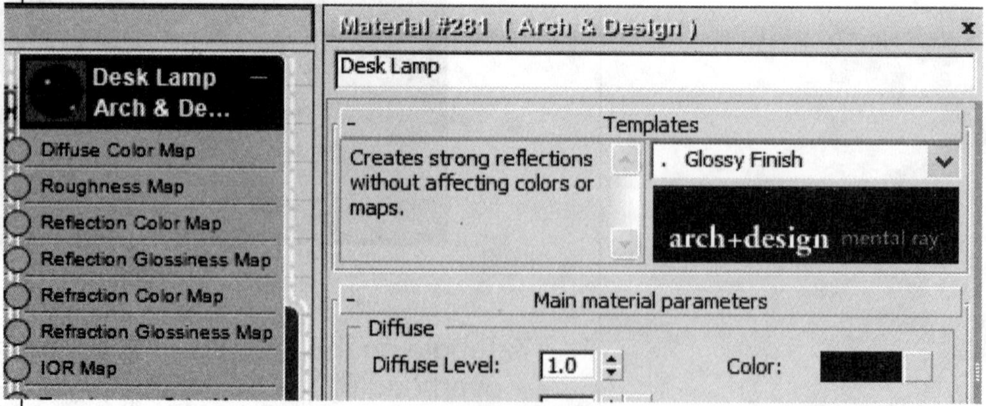

Figure B–46

24. In the viewport, select the desk lamp and in the Slate Material Editor, click  (Assign Material to Selection).

25. Render the Camera01 view again, as shown in Figure B–47.

Figure B–47

The Arch & Design materials and mrPhotographic exposure control are recommended for use with mental ray. You can get beautiful results from mental ray by combining Arch & Design materials and the mrPhotographic exposure control settings.

26. If the rendering is dark, you can adjust the Exposure Control (**Rendering>Environment** or click  (Environment and Effects) in the Rendered Frame Window). In the Exposure Control rollout, select **mr Photographic Exposure** control, and in the *Exposure* area, select **Exposure Value (EV)** and lower the *EV* value to **11.0**. In the *Image Control* area, adjust the *Highlights (Burn)*, *Midtones*, and *Shadows* values. Increase the *Whitepoint* value to **10000**. Render the Camera 01 view, as shown in Figure B–48. Note that the color is tinted and is a more yellow/sepia color, which looks warmer.

Figure B–48

27. Save your work as **MymrMaterials.max**.

Appendix C

Autodesk 3ds Max 2014 Certified Professional Exam Objectives

The following table will help you to locate the exam objectives in the *Autodesk 3ds Max Design 2014 Fundamentals* training guide to help you prepare for the Autodesk 3ds Max 2014 Certified Professional exam.

Exam Topic	Exam Objectives	Training Guide & Chapter
Animation	Analyze the animation of an object using the Curve Editor	Fundamentals - Chapter 12
	Change interpolation methods	
	Create a path animation and evaluate an object along the path	Fundamentals - Chapter 12
	Differentiate Dope Sheet from the Curve Editor	
	Explain how to edit tangents with the Curve Editor	
	Identify Controller types	Fundamentals - Chapter 12
	Identify playback settings	Fundamentals - Chapter 12
	Locate the value of keys in the Time Slider	Fundamentals - Chapter 12
Cameras	Differentiate camera types	Fundamentals - Chapter 11
	Edit FOV (Field of View)	Fundamentals - Chapter 11
	Explain Near and Far Clip Plane for your camera	
Compositing	Demonstrate how to composite multiple layers together	
	Demonstrate how to remap the color output for an image	
Data Management/ Interoperability	Create layer renders and import into Composite	
	Differentiate common file types and usages	Fundamentals - Chapter 3
	Use the import feature to import model data	Fundamentals - Chapter 3

Exam Topic	Exam Objectives	Training Guide & Chapter
Dynamics/ Simulation	Use modifiers for soft body simulation	
Effects	Identify Space Warp types	
	Identify an event	
	Identify particle systems	
	Identify Space Warp types	
Lighting	Compare Attenuation and Decay	Fundamentals - Chapter 8
	Differentiate light functions in a scene	Fundamentals - Chapter 8
	Identify parameters for modifying shadows	Fundamentals - Chapter 8 and Chapter 9
	Use the Daylight System	Fundamentals - Chapter 9
	Use the Light Lister	
Materials/Shading	Identify Shader parameters	Fundamentals - Chapter 6
	Identify standard materials	Fundamentals - Chapter 6
	Use Blending Modes	
	Use the Material Editor	Fundamentals - Chapter 6
Modeling	Differentiate reference coordinate systems	Fundamentals - Chapter 4
	Differentiate workflow	
	Identify Clone types	Fundamentals - Chapter 4
	Differentiate standard versus extended primitives	
	Identify and use line tool creation methods	Fundamentals - Chapter 5
	Identify Vertex types	Fundamentals - Chapter 5
	Use object creation and modification workflows	Fundamentals - Chapter 5
	Use polygon modeling tools	Fundamentals - Chapter 4
	Use ProBoolean	Fundamentals - Chapter 5

Exam Topic	Exam Objectives	Training Guide & Chapter
Rendering	Differentiate Renderers	Fundamentals - Chapter 10 and Chapter 11
	Identify pass types	Fundamentals - Chapter 10
	Identify rendering parameters	Fundamentals - Chapter 10 and Chapter 11
	Use Render to render an effect pass	Fundamentals - Chapter 10
Rigging/Setup	Describe common Biped features	
	Identify Bones	
	Identify Controller usage	
	Identify IK Solvers	
	Use Weight Table	
Scripting	Apply (run) scripts	Fundamentals - Appendix B
	Describe common use of scripts	
UI/Object Management	Describe and use object transformations	Fundamentals - Chapter 4
	Identify Selection Regions and methods	Fundamentals - Chapter 2
	Describe View configuration and ViewCube navigation	Fundamentals - Chapter 1 and Chapter - 2